core
JAVA™

SECOND EDITION

GARY CORNELL • CAY S. HORSTMANN

SunSoft Press
A Prentice Hall Title

The publisher offers discounts on this book when ordered in bulk quantities.
For more information, contact Corporate Sales Department, Prentice Hall PTR ,
One Lake Street, Upper Saddle River, NJ 07458. Phone: 800-382-3419; FAX: 201- 236-7141.
E-mail: corpsales@prenhall.com.

Editorial/production supervision: *Navta Associates*
Cover design director: *Jerry Votta*
Cover designer: *Anthony Gemmellaro*
Cover illustration: *Karen Strelecki*
Manufacturing manager: *Alexis R. Heydt*
Marketing manager: *Stephen Solomon*
Acquisitions editor: *Gregory G. Doench*
SunSoft Press publisher: *Rachel Borden*

10 9 8 7 6 5 4 3 2 1

ISBN 0-13-596891-7

SunSoft Press
A Prentice Hall Title

Contents

Chapter 9
Data Structures, 365

Chapter 10
Exceptions and Debugging, 423

Tables

Examples

Figures

Preface

To the Reader

In 1995, the Java language burst onto the Internet scene and gained instant celebrity status. The promise of Java is to become the *universal glue* that connects users with information, from web servers, databases, information providers, and any other imaginable source. Indeed Java is in a unique position to fulfill this promise. It is an extremely solidly engineered language that has gained wide acceptance across all vendors. Its syntax that is instantly familiar to millions of programmers. Its safety features are reassuring both for programmers and the users of those programs. Java has built-in support that makes advanced programming tasks (network programming, multithreading) straightforward and convenient. There is now a convenient mechanism for dealing with essentially any existing database and so on.

Certainly there were books galore published on Java in these early months. Ours was neither the first nor the shortest. But programmers seem to appreciate our approach, and when stock grew low of the first edition and SunSoft/Prentice Hall suggested a new edition we were happy to comply. As with the first edition of this book, we *still target serious programmers who want to put Java to work on real projects.* We still guarantee no nervous text or dancing tooth-shaped characters. We think of you, our reader, as a programmer with a solid background in a programming language such as C, C++, Visual Basic, Delphi or PowerBuilder. You probably have some experience in building graphical user interfaces in Windows, Unix or the Macintosh but this isn't necessary.

We do always assume you want to write real code for real problems and don't like books filled with toy examples of motorcycle classes and fruit trees. We assume you are willing, even eager, to learn about all the advanced features that Java puts at your disposal. For example we give detailed treatments of:

- object-oriented programming;
- graphical user interface design;
- multithreading;
- network programming.

In particular, we don't assume that you to have any special background in object-oriented techniques or in advanced topics such as network programming or multithreading. There are two full chapters on object-oriented programming, complete with hints for good design practices. The network programming chapter assumes nothing more than experience with a web browser. Our focus is on getting you up to speed quickly on the parts of Java that are important to *practical* programming.

In the second edition, in addition to dozens of small improvements, there are new sections or whole new chapters on:

- The new object serialization mechanism that has been added to Java;

- The new Java database connectivity package (usually called the JDBC);

- The new framework for distributed computing (usually called RMI because it gives a mechanism for remote method invocation);

- A survey of where we think Java is going.

We also included a section on combining Java with C (native methods) since this was probably the most requested feature that readers of the first edition wanted us to add.

We *still* don't spend much time on the fun but less serious kind of Java programs whose sole purpose is to liven up your web page. There are quite a few sources for this kind of material already—we recommend John Pew's book *Instant Java,* also published by SunSoft Press/Prentice Hall.

You will *still* find lots of (even more, in fact) sample code on the accompanying CD that demonstrates almost every language and library feature that we discuss. The sample programs are purposefully kept simple to focus on the major points, but, for the most part, they aren't fake and they don't cut corners. They should make good starting points for your own code.

When writing such a long book, some errors and inaccuracies are inevitable. We'd very much like to know about them. But frankly, we'd prefer to learn about each of them only once. We have put up a list of frequently asked questions, fixes, and workarounds in a web page at `http://www.horstmann.com`. Strategically placed at the end of the FAQ (to encourage you to read through it first) is a Java applet to report bugs and problems.

We hope that you find this book enjoyable and helpful in your Java programming.

About This Book

Chapter 1 gives an overview of the capabilities of Java that set it apart from other programming languages. We explain what the designers of the language set out to do and to what extent they succeeded. Then we give a short history how Java came into being.

In Chapter 2, we tell you how to install Java and the companion software for this book from the CD ROM onto your computer. Then we guide you through compiling and running three typical Java programs, a console application, a graphical application and an applet.

Chapter 3 starts the discussion of the Java language. In this chapter, we cover the basics: variables, loops, and simple functions. If you are a C or C++ programmer, this is smooth sailing because the syntax for these language features is essentially the same as in C. If you come from a Visual Basic or Pascal/Delphi background, you will want to read this chapter carefully.

Object-oriented programming (OOP) is now in the mainstream of programming practice, and Java is thoroughly object-oriented. Chapter 4 introduces *encapsulation,* the first of two fundamental building blocks of object-orientation, and the Java language mechanism to implement it, that is, classes and methods. In addition to the rules of the Java language, we also give advice on sound OOP design. If you are familiar with C++, then you can browse through this chapter quickly. Programmers coming from a non-object-oriented background should expect to spend some time mastering OOP concepts.

Classes and encapsulation are only one part of the OOP story, and Chapter 5 introduces the other, namely *inheritance.* Inheritance lets you take an existing class and modify it according to your needs. This is a fundamental technique for programming in Java. The inheritance mechanism in Java is quite similar to that in C++. Once again, C++ programmers can focus on the differences between the languages.

In Chapter 6, we begin application programming in earnest. We show how you can make windows, how to paint on them, and how to display images. Then we show you how to *really* display images. There are quite a few Java programming tasks that are subtle, and displaying images is one of them. The Java library is optimized to load an image piece by piece, assuming it comes in through a slow network connection. You can ignore the subtlety, but then your image flickers. In this book we make an effort to dig down into the details and show you how the pros do it. Of course, feel free to skip over this section if you don't care about images now.

Chapter 7 is the longest chapter in the book—almost 100 pages. It discusses AWT, the toolkit used in Java for building a graphical user interface. If you are used to programming a user interface by dragging controls onto a form and writing a bit of code to glue them together, then you are in for a rude surprise. Right now, Java as supplied by Sun has no user interface builder. You need to write code to place every button, text field, menu item, and so on in a window. Even the third party tools are still quite primitive, and they won't make a lot of sense to you if you don't understand the AWT fundamentals. In this chapter we cover all the techniques needed to place components in a window along with event recognition and ways to get user input.

After you finish Chapter 7 you finally have all mechanisms in place to write *applets,* those mini-programs that can live inside a web page, and so applets are the topic of Chapter 8. We show you a number of useful and fun applets, but more importantly we show you what goes on behind the scenes. One of the applets, among our favorites, crawls through the world wide web, linking itself from one web page through the next. View any Web page that it finds while the applet keeps on hunting for more pages in the background. This is possible through the power of multithreading and HTML frames.

In Chapter 9, we go back to a more mundane programming issue and show how to use the data structures in the Java library (vectors, hash tables, and so on), and how to write your own (linked lists, queues). This material is important if your Java program needs to store a large amount of data and retrieve it quickly.

Chapter 10 discusses *exception handling,* a robust mechanism to deal with the fact that bad things can happen to good programs. For example, a network connection can become unavailable in the middle of a file download, a disk can fill up, and so on. Exceptions give you an efficient way of separating the normal processing code from the error handling. Of course, even after hardening your program by handling all exceptional conditions, it still might fail to work as expected. In the second half of this chapter, we give you some debugging tips. Finally, we guide you through a sample debugging session with the JDB debugger. (That debugger is very primitive, and you would want to use it only if you are really desperate.)

The topic of Chapter 11 is another mundane but important issue—files. If your application reads or writes data, you need to know about input and output. Java has a whole zoo of classes for this purpose. We look at three different I/O scenarios in detail: binary files, random access files, and saving objects of mixed types. This chapter also contains a discussion of how to transmit, save, and restore objects using the new object *serialization mechanism* that has recently been added to Java.

Users like programs that do slow tasks in the background, leaving them in control to do other operations. In Java, this is achieved through *multithreading.* A *thread* is a flow of control within a program. Java programs can run multiple threads concurrently, switching between them to service both the user interface and slow background tasks. This is the topic of Chapter 12. We show you how to set up threads, and how to make sure none of them get stuck. We put this material to practical use by giving an implementation for a timer class that you can use in your own code. Finally, we look into the inner workings of an animation class that displays a spinning globe.

The next chapter covers one of the most exciting topics of Java programming—networking. Java makes it phenomenally easy to connect to a remote computer and to send and receive data. The chapter starts out with an introduction to sockets. We then outline a sample application—an order-taking applet that reads a price list from the server, takes the ordering information from the customer, and sends it back to the server. We then turn to the important issue of security. An applet cannot make arbitrary network connections, because it could then quietly send private data back to its server. We show how to overcome this limitation by a proxy server, opening the door to a class of very useful applets that *harvest information* from the Internet.

Chapter 14 is the first of the new chapters, it covers *JDBC*, the Java database connectivity API. This chapter is designed to show you how to write useful programs to handle realistic databases using a core subset of the JDBC API. It is not a complete treatment of everything you can do with the very rich API supplied with JDBC. (A complete treatment would certainly require a book of its own; that book would, in fact, probably be nearly as long as this book is.)

Chapter 15 covers *remote objects* and the *remote method invocation* (RMI). This API is designed to let you work with Java objects distributed over the net. As with all the chapters in this book, we try to be realistic. In particular, we show you what the rallying cry of "objects everywhere" can realistically be used for.

The last chapter is a survey of future directions. We are not employees of Sun nor are we privy to any inside information. We based this chapter on our sense of Java, together with a reading of as much of the widely scattered public information as we could find. We have tried to distill the vast quantity of information we found down to a useful form.

The appendices cover the Java keywords, the automatic Java documentation (javadoc), and some help for Macintosh users. The JDK for the Macintosh is always behind those for Solaris and Windows and is much more difficult to set up, since Java comes from the command-line school of programming. In particular, there is no version of JDBC or RMI for the Macintosh. This last appendix was contributed by Kamal Abdali, and we are very grateful for his help in coming up with a workaround for many of the problems Java users on the Mac have suffered.

Conventions

As is common in many computer books, we use `courier type` to represent computer code.

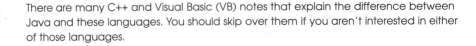

There are many C++ and Visual Basic (VB) notes that explain the difference between Java and these languages. You should skip over them if you aren't interested in either of those languages.

Notes are tagged with a "notepad" icon that looks like this.

Java comes with a large programming library or Application Programming Interface (API). When using an API call for the first time, we add a short summary description, tagged with an API icon. These descriptions are a bit more informal, but also a little more informative than those in the official on-line API documentation.

Programs whose source code is on the CD ROM are listed as examples, for instance **Example 15-8: WarehouseServer.java** refers to the corresponding code on the CD ROM.

CD ROM

The CD ROM on the back of the book contains the Sun Java Development Kit (JDK 1.02), the 1.01 version of JDBC, and the Alpha 2 release of the RMI available to us. It also contains the code for this book. These materials are available for Windows 95/NT, Solaris 2, and, except for RMI and JDBC, for the Macintosh as well.

The CD ROM also contains shareware versions of the WinEdit and WinZip programs for Windows 95/NT. We have even customized WinEdit to work very smoothly with Java. Finally, there is a 30-day trial version of Sun's web-based development environment called Java WorkShop and Café Lite, a "lite" version of Symantec's Cafe Java development environment for Windows. Please read Chapter 2 for detailed installation instructions for the Java Development Kit.

NOTE: People have often asked what the licensing requirements for using our code in a commercial situation are. You can freely use any code from this book for non-commercial use. However, if you do want to use our code as a basis for a commercial product, we simply require that every person on the development team for that project own a copy of Core Java.

Using the Core Java CD-ROM

The Core Java CD contains the Java Development Kit (Release 1.0.2) for Solaris 2.x, Windows 95, Windows NT, and Macintosh.

NOTE: If you experience any problems with the Core Java CD, check the SunSoft Press Java Series Web page for updates (http://www.prenhall.com/~java_sun).

Using the CD-ROM on Windows 95 and Windows NT

In addition to the JDK and Java applets and applications from Core Java, the Win95nt directory contains Java WorkShop (30-Day Trial), Symantec's Café Lite and shareware versions of WinEdit and WinZip. **This CD-ROM does not support Windows 3.1.**

The Win95nt directory structure is as follows:

Directory/File	Contents
Booksjdk	Contains the installation program for Core Java and the JDK (1.0.2)
Cafelite	Contains the installation program for Café Lite
Winedit	Contains the installation program for WinEdit
Winzip	Contains the installation program for WinZip
Workshop	Contains the installation program for Java WorkShop
Readme.txt	Installation notes for Windows users

To install the JDK or Java programs from Core Java:

1. Click the Start button and choose Run. (Windows NT users, Select Run from the Program Manager File menu.)
2. Type `D:\WIN95NT\BOOKSJDK\Setup.exe` and click the OK button. (If your CD-ROM drive is not drive D, substitute the appropriate letter.)
3. The installation program will prompt you to select the components you wish to install. You may install the JDK by itself or the JDK and source code from Core Java.
4. The installation program will prompt you for the drive and directory to use for the components you select.

(Please note that the Café Lite installation program also installs a copy of the JDK on your system.)

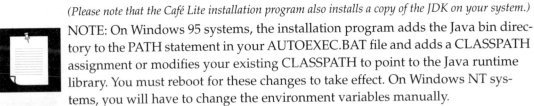

NOTE: On Windows 95 systems, the installation program adds the Java bin directory to the PATH statement in your AUTOEXEC.BAT file and adds a CLASSPATH assignment or modifies your existing CLASSPATH to point to the Java runtime library. You must reboot for these changes to take effect. On Windows NT systems, you will have to change the environment variables manually.

Please note that UNIX and Windows text files have slightly different conventions for end-of-line. UNIX expects a newline character (linefeed) and Windows expects a carriage return and a linefeed. Many Windows editors (including WinEdit) are able to cope with UNIX conventions and vice versa. Be aware, however, that some Windows editors will not display line breaks properly if you try to read text files that were created on a UNIX system. The Java compiler handles source files created under either convention.

Using the Core Java Sample Programs

When you have finished installing the Core Java files on your system, there should be sixteen subdirectories in the CoreJavaBook directory. The source code for the programs described in this book can be found in the fifteen directories named ch2, ch3...ch16. There should also be a directory named Corejava that contains java files and class files needed to run various applications.

For example, if you open up the ch10 directory, you will see 5 subdirectories:

    BuggyButtonTest
    DebugWinTest
    ExceptionalTest
    ExceptTest
    MessageCrackerTest

These directories contain the class files and java files for the programs discussed in Chapter 10.

To install Café Lite:

Café Lite is a trial version of Symantec Café, the Integrated Java Development Environment. A coupon for an upgrade to the full version of Symantec Café is included at the back of this book. Please note that the Café Lite installation program also installs a copy of the JDK (1.0) on your system.

1. Click the Start button and choose Run. (Windows NT users, Select Run from the Program Manager File menu.)

2. Type `D:\WIN95NT\CAFELITE\Cafelite.exe` and click the OK button. (If your CD-ROM drive is not drive D, substitute the appropriate letter.)

To install WinEdit:

1. Click the Start button and choose Run. (Windows NT users, Select Run from the Program Manager File menu.)

2. Type `D:\WIN95NT\WINEDIT\Setup.exe` and click the OK button. (If your CD-ROM drive is not drive D, substitute the appropriate letter.)

NOTE: The installation program adds the directory you specified for installing WinEdit to the PATH statement in your AUTOEXEC.BAT file.

To customize WinEdit for Java Programming

If you would like to customize WinEdit to make Java programming easier, Chapter 2 describes useful modifications to the standard WinEdit configuration. This CD-ROM contains a batch file named Wepatch.bat that you can run to make these modifications.

Wepatch.bat and the other files needed to modify WinEdit are on the CD-ROM in a subdirectory of Winedit named Winedita.

To run Wepatch.bat:

1. Install WinEdit as described above.

2. Change to the Winedita directory on the CD-ROM.
   `D:\WIN95NT\WINEDIT\WINEDITA`

3. Run Wepatch <WinEdit directory> <Windows directory>

For example, if you installed WinEdit in a directory on your hard drive named C:\Programs\WinEdit and your Windows directory is C:\Windows, at the system prompt you would type:

```
Wepatch C:\Programs\WinEdit C:\Windows
```

To install WinZip:

1. Click the Start button and choose Run. (Windows NT users, Select Run from the Program Manager File menu.)

2. Type `D:\WIN95NT\WINZIP\Winzip95.exe` and click the OK button. (If your CD-ROM drive is not drive D, substitute the appropriate letter.)

3. The setup program will display a dialog box asking you where to install WinZip.

4. A dialog box containing information about the WinZip license agreement will also be displayed.

To Install Java WorkShop

NOTE: Java WorkShop is compatible only with version 3.51 of Windows NT.

1. Insert the Core Java CD into your CD-ROM drive and change to the \WIN95NT\WORKSHOP directory.

2. Run the "Setupws.exe" installer—it will uncompress and copy all the necessary files to your hard drive (default directory is C:\Java-Workshop)

3. Follow the installation instructions, by clicking the appropriate buttons and entering the installation directory when, and if, needed.

4. After the installation is complete, double-click on the Java WorkShop icon to start the workshop (A program group containing all the icons will be created)

5. When Java WorkShop loads for the first time, you will be prompted to enter a serial number. Click on the "30-day trial" button and a serial number will be entered automatically.

6. To uninstall Java Workshop, double-click the uninstall icon in the Java WorkShop Program Group.

Using the CD-ROM on Solaris 2.x

Because this CD-ROM is a standard ISO-9660 disk that does not support long file names and other UNIX extensions, the Java programs and the Java Development Kit (JDK) for Solaris 2.x are stored as tar archives. Use the *more* command or *vi* to read the readme.txt file.

The solaris2 directory structure is as follows:

workshop	Java WorkShop for x86 and Sparc
corejava.tar	Programs from Core Java
jdbc.tar	Java Database Connectivity (JDBC 1.0)
jdk_sprc.tar	Java Development Kit (1.0.2) for Sparc
jdk_x86.tar	Java Development Kit (1.0.2) for x86
readme.txt	Installation notes for Solaris users
rmisparc.tar	Remote Method Invocation (RMI Alpha-2)

To install the Core Java programs:

1. Make a directory on your UNIX filesystem and change to that directory. Then copy the corejava.tar file to that directory.

2. Use the command *tar -xvf* to unarchive the file. For example:

tar -xvf corejava.tar

To install the Java Developer's Kit (Solaris 2.3 or later):

The Solaris2 directory contains the JDK (Release 1.0.2) for Sparc and x86 systems. Installation instructions are the same for Solaris 2.x for SPARC and Solaris 2.x for x86. On Intel systems, use "x86" instead of "sprc" in the filenames below. Make sure you are running an up-to-date version of Solaris 2.x, preferably Solaris 2.5.1.

1. Change directory to the location where you want to install the JDK. Let's assume you're installing it in /home/jones:

```
cd /home/jones
```

2. Untar the file:

```
tar -xvf /cdrom/corejava/solaris2/jdk_sprc.tar
```

This is a 4.7Mbyte file, so it will take a few seconds to pull off the CD.

You should see dozens of lines indicating the files being untar'd.

3. Add the JAVA_HOME environment variable to your .cshrc (or whatever initialization for the shell you use). For the cshell, add the following line:

```
setenv JAVA_HOME /home/jones/java
```

Also add $JAVA_HOME/bin to your existing search path:

```
set path=($JAVA_HOME/bin ... rest of path ...)
```

4. Logout and login again so the new variables take effect.

NOTE: The CD also contains the Alpha-2 release of Remote Method Invocation and the 1.0 release of Java Database Connectivity (JDBC). To see if a more recent release is available go to java.sun.com.

To Install Java WorkShop (Solaris 2.x):

1. Insert the Core Java CD into your CD-ROM drive.

2. If Volume Manager is running on your machine, the CD-ROM is automatically mounted to the /cdrom/corejava directory. Skip to step 3.

If the Volume Manager is NOT running on your machine, create a directory called /cdrom/corejava and mount the CD-ROM manually by becoming root and typing:

```
# mkdir -p /cdrom/corejava
# mount -rF hsfs /dev/dsk/c0t6d0s0 /cdrom/corejava
```

3. Go to the directory where you intend to install the Java WorkShop files:

```
% cd /<destination_directory>
```

4. Extract the Java WorkShop files by typing:

```
% tar -xvf
/cdrom/corejava/solaris2/workshop/jw_<platform>.tar
```

Where <platform> is either "sparc" or "intel" depending on whether you use a SPARC or Intel system.

5. If you mounted the CD-ROM manually, unmount the drive by becoming root and typing:

```
# cd /
# umount /dev/dsk/c0t6d0s0
```

Otherwise, go to Step 6.

6. Eject the CD by typing:

```
% cd /
% eject
```

You can now use Java WorkShop.

7. Start Java WorkShop by typing:

```
% /<destination_directory>/JWS/<platform>-S2/bin/jws &
```

Using the CD-ROM on Macintosh (System 7.5 or later)

The MAC_OS directory structure is as follows:

Core   Contains programs from Core Java

JDK   Contains JDK 1.0.2 installation program

To install the JDK or program files from the books:

Because this is an ISO-9660 CD-ROM, the JDK and the program files from Core Java are stored on the disc as self-extracting archives. Copy the files that you want to use to your hard drive and double-click to open.

NOTE: You should note that Macintosh, Windows, and UNIX text files have slightly different conventions for end-of-line. Macintosh expects a carriage return, Windows expects a carriage return and a linefeed, and UNIX expects a newline character (linefeed).

Most Macintosh editors are able to cope with UNIX and Windows conventions. Be aware, however, that some Macintosh editors will not display line breaks properly if you try to read text files that were created on a Windows or UNIX system. Even though some text files may not appear to be properly formatted, however, the Java compiler handles source files created under either convention.

You should also note that file names longer than 31 characters will be truncated. Therefore, some of the sample Java files on this CD will have to be renamed to execute properly on a Macintosh.

Acknowledgements

Jiaoyang Zhou was invaluable to us in tracking down bugs and testing code. We could not have completed this book on time without her help. Kamal Abdali provided the Appendix on Macintosh issues and did a careful reading of the first edition. We are very thankful for his help.

We would like to thank our editor Greg Doench of Prentice-Hall for coordinating the details of the book and CD development process with great determination and resolve under sometimes trying circumstances; Rachel Borden our publisher at SunSoft was always there to listen with a patient ear when we complained yet again about another problem—and do her best to fix it. Nikki Wise and her team at Navta Associates did a superb production job under yet another difficult schedule. Those of you who helped with the first edition, we have not forgotten you and we are still grateful. In particular, we want to thank Devang Shah and Ann Wollrath of Sun Microsystems for their help with chapter reviews. For the second edition we appreciate the reviews we received from Janet Traub and Chris Laffra.

Thanks also go to Maurie Wilson of Wilson WindowWare for allowing us to put their WinEdit editor and to Niko Mak for of Niko Mak Computing for allowing us to put his WinZip program onto the CD ROM.

Cay's thanks go to Rick Warner and Annie Chang for their help with the Solaris installation of Java, and for providing a testbed for CGI scripts. His apologies go to his coauthor and colleagues who had to suffer his testy mood when he had to find yet another workaround to a Java bug. And his love and gratitude go to his wife Hui-Chen and his son Tommy whose initial enthusiasm for this project turned into patient support as the project dragged on and on and when the second edition came all too quickly.

Gary's thanks go to all his friends who endured his stressed-out ways during these trying times—curt phone calls and no social visits were the norm. As in the first edition he wants to again thank Bruce, Caroline, and Kurt. Writing his part of the book would have been impossible without their friendship and support. The encouragement Gary received from Esther Etherington of `javaman.com` was a great help. Finally, as in the first edition, Gary still needs to thank Cay's family—perhaps even more so this time around. They were again gracious hosts on his too-frequent visits. They were remarkably patient during the seemingly endless phone calls. They were and are, in a word, extraordinary.

CHAPTER

1

- Java as a Programming Language

- Java and the Internet

- A Short History of Java

- Common Misconceptions about Java

An Introduction to Java

To open a computer magazine that does not have a feature article on Java seems impossible. Even mainstream newspapers and magazines like the *New York Times*, the *Washington Post*, and *Business Week* have run major articles on Java. It gets better (or worse, depending on your perspective): can you remember the last time National Public Radio ran a 10-minute story on a computer language? Or a $100,000,000 venture capital fund is set up solely for products produced using a specific computer language? CNN, CNBC, you name the mass medium, it seems everyone is talking about how Java will do this or Java will do that.

We decided that you bought this book because you are a serious programmer, so rather than immediately getting caught up in the Internet hype and trying to deal with the limited (if still interesting) truth behind the hype, we will write, in some detail, about Java as a programming language (including the features added for its use on the Internet). After that, we will try to separate current fact from fancy by explaining what Java can and cannot do on the Internet. In the end, we should add, a great deal of the hype *will* be justified; it is just not true *yet*. Java is still in its formative stages, but progress is occurring faster than anyone could have expected.

Java as a Programming Language

As a computer language, Java's hype is overdone: the current version of Java is a good language. It could *potentially* have been a great programming language, but it is probably too late for that. Once a language is out in the field, the ugly reality of compatibility with existing code sets in. We expect there to be some improvements over time, but, basically, the structure of the Java language tomorrow will be what it is today. So what are its advantages and disadvantages?

One obvious advantage is a run time library that provides platform independence: you can use the same code on Windows 95, Solaris, UNIX, Macintosh, and so on (although implementations on other platforms usually lag those on Windows and Solaris). This is necessary for Internet programming. Another programming advantage is that Java has a similar syntax to that of C++ which makes it economical without being absurd. Then again, Visual Basic (VB) programmers will probably find the syntax annoying and miss some of the nicer syntactic VB constructs.

NOTE: If you are coming from a language other than C++, some of the terms used in this section will be less familiar—just skip those sections. You will be comfortable with all of these terms by the end of Chapter 5.

Java is also fully object oriented—even more so than C++. Everything in Java, except for a few basic types like numbers, is an object. (Object-oriented design has replaced earlier structured techniques because it has many advantages for dealing with sophisticated projects. If you are not familiar with Object-Oriented Programming (OOP), Chapters 4 and 5 provide what you need to know.)

However, having yet another, somewhat improved, dialect of C++ would not be enough. The key points are:

- It is far easier to turn out bug-free code using Java than using C++.

  Why? The designers of Java thought hard about what makes C++ code so buggy. They added features to Java that eliminate the *possibility* of creating code with the most common kinds of bugs. (Some estimates say that roughly every 50 lines of C++ code has at least one bug.) Here are some of these new features:

- They eliminated manual memory allocation and deallocation.

  Memory in Java is automatically garbage collected. You *never* have to worry about memory leaks.

- They introduced true arrays and eliminated pointer arithmetic.

  You never have to worry about overwriting a key area of memory because of an off-by-one error when working with a pointer.

- They eliminated the possibility of confusing an assignment with a test for equality in a conditional.

  You cannot even compile if (ntries = 3) . . . . (VB programmers may not see the problem, but, trust us, this is a common source of confusion in C/C++ code.)

- They eliminated multiple inheritance, replacing it with a new notion of *interface* that they derived from Objective C.

  Interfaces give you what you want from multiple inheritance, without the complexity that comes with managing multiple inheritance hierarchies. (If inheritance is a new concept for you, Chapter 6 will explain it.)

C++ NOTE: The Java language specification is public. It may be found on the Web by going to the JavaSoft page and following the links given there. (The JavaSoft home page is at `http://java.sun.com`.)

The Java "White Paper" Buzzwords

The authors of Java have written an influential "White Paper" that explains their design goals and accomplishments. Their paper is organized along the following eleven buzzwords:

Simple

Object Oriented

Distributed

Robust

Secure

Architecture Neutral

Portable

Interpreted

High Performance

Multithreaded

Dynamic

We touched on some of these points in the last section. In this section, we will:

- summarize via excerpts from the "White Paper" what the Java designers say about each buzzword, and

- tell you what we think of that particular buzzword based on our experiences with the current version of Java.

C++ NOTE: As we write this, the "White Paper" may be found at `http://java.sun.com:80/doc/language_environment`. (If it has moved, you can find it by marching through the links at the JavaSoft home page.)

Simple

We wanted to build a system that could be programmed easily without a lot of esoteric training and which leveraged today's standard practice. ... So even though we found that C++ was unsuitable, we designed Java as closely to C++ as possible in order to make the system more comprehensible. Java omits many rarely used, poorly understood, confusing features of C++ that, in our experience, bring more grief than benefit.

The syntax for Java is, indeed, a cleaned-up version of the syntax for C++. There is no need for header files, pointer arithmetic (or even a pointer syntax), structures, unions, operator overloading, virtual base classes, and so on. (See the C++ notes interspersed throughout the text for more on the differences between Java and C++.) The designers did not, however, *improve* on some stupid features in C++, like the switch statement. If you know C++, you will find the transition to Java's syntax easy.

If you are a VB programmer, you will not find Java simple. There is much strange syntax (though it does not take long to get the hang of it). More importantly, you must do a lot more programming in Java. The beauty of VB is that the visual design environment provides a lot of the "glue" that must be programmed manually (with a fair bit of code) in Java.

At this point, the Java language is pretty simple, as object-oriented languages go. But there are many subtle points used to solve real-world problems. As time goes by, more and more of these details will be farmed off to libraries and development environments. Products like Symantec's Café and RogueWave's J Factory, for example, have a form designer that can make designing the interface of your programs much easier. They are far from perfect but they often are a step forward. (Designing forms with nothing but the JDK is tedious at best and unbearable at worst.) New third party class libraries are beginning to appear and a lot of code samples (including libraries) are available on the Net.

Another aspect of being simple is being small. One of the goals of Java is to enable the construction of software that can run stand-alone in small machines. The size of the basic interpreter and class support is about 40K bytes; adding the basic standard libraries and thread support (essentially a self-contained microkernel) adds an additional 175K.

This is a great achievement.

Object-Oriented

Simply stated, object-oriented design is a technique that focuses design on the data (= objects) and on the interfaces to it. To make an analogy with carpentry, an "object-oriented" carpenter would be mostly concerned with the chair he was building, and secondarily with the tools used to make it; a "non-object-oriented" carpenter would think primarily of his tools. … The object-oriented facilities of Java are essentially those of C++.

Object orientation has proven its worth in the last 30 years, and it is inconceivable that a modern programming language would not use it. Indeed, the object-oriented features of Java are comparable to C++. The major difference between Java and C++ lies in multiple inheritance, for which Java has found a better solution.

On the other hand, programmers coming from Smalltalk may be disappointed. Java has strong typing, which is a plus. But the metaclass model is very weak. (However, the new object serialization mechanisms make it much easier to implement persistent objects than was the case with the JDK 1.0 and the announced "reflection" mechanism of the JDK 1.1 will take this even further.)

C++ NOTE: If you do not have any experience with OOP languages you will want to carefully read Chapters 4 and 5. These chapters explain what OOP is and why it is more useful for programming sophisticated projects than traditional, procedure-oriented languages like BASIC or C.

Distributed

Java has an extensive library of routines for coping with TCP/IP protocols like HTTP and FTP. Java applications can open and access objects across the Net via URLs with the same ease as when accessing a local file system.

We have found the networking capabilities of Java to be both strong and easy to use. Anyone who has tried to do Internet programming using another language will revel in how simple Java makes onerous tasks like opening a socket connection. Java even makes common gateway interface (CGI) scripting easier. (See Chapter 13 if you do not know what a socket or a CGI script is.) The new remote method invocation mechanism enables communication between distributed objects.

Robust

Java is intended for writing programs that must be reliable in a variety of ways. Java puts a lot of emphasis on early checking for possible problems, later dynamic (run time) checking, and eliminating situations that are error

> *prone. ... The single biggest difference between Java and C/C++ is that Java has a pointer model that eliminates the possibility of overwriting memory and corrupting data.*

This is also very useful. The Java compiler (in both its original incarnation and in the various improved versions in third party implementations) detects many problems that, in other languages, would only show up at run time (or, perhaps, not even then). As for the second point, anyone who has spent hours chasing a memory leak caused by a pointer bug will be very happy with this feature of Java.

If you are coming from a language like VB that doesn't use pointers, you are probably wondering why this is so important. C programmers are not so lucky. They need pointers to access strings, arrays, objects, even files. In VB, you do not use pointers for any of these entities, nor do you need to worry about memory allocation. On the downside, in VB, you cannot easily implement some of the fancier data structures that require pointers.

Java gives you the best of both worlds. You do not need pointers for everyday constructs like strings and arrays. You have the power of pointers if you need it, for example, for linked lists. And you always have complete safety, since you can never access a bad pointer or make memory allocation errors.

Secure

> *Java is intended to be used in networked/distributed environments. Toward that end, a lot of emphasis has been placed on security. Java enables the construction of virus-free, tamper-free systems.*

In the first edition of "Core Java" we said: "Well, one should 'never say never again,'" and we turned out to be right. A group of security experts at Princeton University found the first bugs in the security features of Java 1.0—not long after the JDK 1.0 was shipped. Moreover, they and various other people have continued to find other bugs in the security mechanisms. All we can suggest is that you check:

1. The URL for the Princeton group:
    `http://www.cs.princeton.edu/~felton`

2. David Hopwood's URL
    `http://ferret.lmh.ox.ac.uk/~david/java/bugs/`

3. The comp.risks newsgroup

for opinions from outside experts on the current status of Java's security mechanisms.

The Java team has said that they will have a "zero tolerance" for security bugs and immediately work on fixing any bugs found in the Applet security mechanism (the browser companies go to work immediately as well). In particular, by making public the internal specifications of how the Java interpreter works, Sun is making it far easier for people to find any bugs in Java's security features— essentially enlisting the outside community in the ever so subtle security bug detection process. This makes one more confident that security bugs will be found as soon as possible. In any case, Java makes it extremely difficult to outwit its security mechanisms. The bugs found so far have been very subtle and (relatively) few in number.

NOTE: JavaSoft's URL for security related issues is currently at:
`http://java.sun.com:80/java.sun.com/sfaq/index.html`

Here is a sample of what Java's security features are supposed to keep a Java program from doing:

1. Overrunning the run time stack, like the famous Internet worm did.

2. Corrupting memory outside its own process space.

3. Reading or writing local files when invoked through a security-conscious class loader, like a Web browser.

Many of the bugs found to date were not trivial to find and full details are often kept secret, so all we can do is repeat what we said before with even more force attached to it:

> *"Never say never again"*

Also worth keeping in mind is that Java will soon have the notion of signed classes (see the final chapter). With a signed class, you can be sure of who wrote it. Once this signing mechanism is in place, any time you trust the author of the class (say, when it comes from behind a firewall), the class can be allowed more privileges on the host machine.

Architecture Neutral

The compiler generates an architecture neutral object file format—the compiled code is executable on many processors, given the presence of the Java run time system. ... The Java compiler does this by generating bytecode instructions which have nothing to do with a particular computer architecture. Rather, they are designed to be both easy to interpret on any machine and easily translated into native machine code on the fly.

This is not a new idea. Twenty years ago, the UCSD Pascal system did the same thing in a commercial product and, even before that, Niklaus Wirth's original implementation of Pascal used the same approach. By using byte codes, performance takes a major hit (but the new just-in-time compilers mitigate this, in many cases). The designers of Java did an excellent job developing a bytecode instruction set that works well on today's most common computer architectures. And the codes have been designed to translate easily into actual machine instructions.

Portable

Unlike C and C++, there are no "implementation-dependent" aspects of the specification. The sizes of the primitive data types are specified, as is the behavior of arithmetic on them.

For example, an `int` in Java is always a 32-bit integer. In C/C++, `int` can mean a 16-bit integer, a 32-bit integer, or any other size that the compiler vendor likes. The only restriction is that it must have at least as many bytes as a `short int` and cannot have more bytes than a `long int`. Having a fixed size of number types eliminates a major porting headache. Binary data is stored in a fixed format, eliminating the "big endian/little endian" confusion. Strings are saved in a standard Unicode format.

The libraries that are a part of the system define portable interfaces. For example, there is an abstract Window class and implementations of it for UNIX, Windows, and the Macintosh.

As anyone who has ever tried knows, it is an effort of heroic proportions to write a program that looks good on Windows, the Macintosh, and 10 flavors of UNIX. Despite the authors' claims, the designers of Java did not solve this problem. They give us a library that is good for writing programs that look equally mediocre on the different systems. (And there are often *different* bugs on the different platform graphics implementations.) But it is a start. There are many applications in which portability is more important than the nth degree of slickness.

Interpreted

The Java interpreter can execute Java bytecodes directly on any machine to which the interpreter has been ported. Since linking is a more incremental and lightweight process, the development process can be much more rapid and exploratory.

Perhaps, this is an advantage while developing an application, but it is clearly overstated.

One problem is that the JDK is fairly slow at compiling your source code to the bytecodes that will, ultimately, be interpreted in the current version. Many products such as Café and Visual J++ give you the option of using their byte code compilers—which are much faster (usually at least twice as fast). If you are used to the speed of VB's or Delphi's development cycle, you will be very disappointed unless you use a third-part byte code compiler.

High Performance

While the performance of interpreted bytecodes is usually more than adequate, there are situations where higher performance is required. The bytecodes can be translated on the fly (at run time) into machine code for the particular CPU the application is running on.

If you use the native Java interpreter, "high performance" is not the term that we would use ("middling to poor" is probably more accurate). While it is certainly true that the speed of the interpreted bytecodes can be acceptable, it isn't fast. (At best Java is only slightly faster than VB4, according to our tests.) On the other hand, you will want to run many Java programs through a compiler. For example, you will almost certainly want to do so for any program that is designed to be a stand-alone application on a specific machine. Ultimately, you will want compilers for every platform.

Native code compilers for Java are not yet generally available. Instead there are just-in-time (JIT) compilers. These work by compiling the byte codes into native code once, caching the results, and then calling them again, if needed. This speeds up loops tremendously since one has to do the interpretation only once. Although still slightly slower than a true native code compiler, just-in-time compilers can give you a 10- or even 20-fold speedup for some programs and will almost always be significantly faster than the Java interpreter.

NOTE: JITs are becoming quite common for Java. We found a page on the Web that summarizes the information about JITs for Java. The URL is:
`http://www.cen.uiuc.edu/~jjones/jit.html`

For example, Symantec has JITs for the two most popular platforms with JITs in its versions of Café for Windows and Café for the Macintosh. Microsoft and Borland have them in development for Windows as well . (Netscape uses Borland's JIT in Netscape 3.0. Microsoft uses one in Internet Explorer 3.0.) Sun has one in development for Solaris and IBM has one in development for AIX and OS/2.

Multithreaded

(Multithreading is the ability for one program to do more than one thing at once, for example, printing while getting a fax.)

> *[The] benefits of multithreading are better interactive responsiveness and real-time behavior.*

If you have ever tried to do multithreading in another language, you will be pleasantly surprised at how easy it is in Java. The threads in Java also have the capacity to take advantage of multiprocessor systems if the base operating system does so. On the downside, thread implementations on the major platforms differ widely, and Java makes no effort to be platform independent in this regard. Only the code for calling multithreading remains the same across machines; Java offloads the implementation of multithreading to the underlying operating system.

Dynamic

> *In a number of ways, Java is a more dynamic language than C or C++. It was designed to adapt to an evolving environment. ... Libraries can freely add new methods and instance variables without any effect on their clients. ... In Java, finding out run time type information is straightforward.*

This is an important feature in those situations where code needs to be added to a running program. A prime example is code that is downloaded from the Internet to run in a browser.

Java and the Internet

The idea here is simple: users will download Java bytecodes from the Internet and run them on their own machines.

Java programs that work on Web pages are called *applets*. (Actually it is the bytecodes, rather than the source file, that you download and then run.) To use an applet, you need a Java-enabled Web browser, which will interpret the bytecodes for you. Netscape 2.0 and later versions are Java enabled as is Internet Explorer 3.0, and most companies have announced (or included) Java support in their browsers. Because Sun is licensing the Java source code and insisting that there be no changes in the language and basic library structure, you can be sure that a Java applet will run on any browser that is advertised as Java enabled.

We suspect that, ultimately, most of the hype stems from the lure of making money from special-purpose software. You have a nifty "Will Writer" program. Convert it to an applet, and charge people per use—presumably, most people would be using this kind of program infrequently. Once commerce on the Net is widespread, this seems to be inevitable—and desirable. (Some people are taking this too far. They predict a time when everyone downloads software from the Net on a per-use basis. This might be great for software companies, but we think it is absurd, for example, to expect people to download and pay for a spell-checker applet each time they send an e-mail message.)

Here are some of the advantages of applets for users of the World Wide Web that we see as realistic now and in the immediate future:

1. Since Java is a true programming language, it is much easier to make an applet responsive than to do the same with a Web page. For example, we wrote a simple retirement calculator applet (see Chapter 9). Since this is a program, we could write it to allow people to see the effects of changes immediately—there is no need to go back to a Web page for updates after each change. (Without Java, making a Web page responsive involves sending data to a CGI script on the server. The CGI script then needs to process the data and send the results back in a form the browser can use. Often, this requires creating a whole new Web page on the fly—which can be painful, or even impossible, to program. It will almost always be slow.)

2. Applets can use a modern graphical user interface (GUI). This includes text boxes, buttons, list boxes, and so on. Java applets can also trap user events like keystrokes, mouse movements, and the like.

3. Processing is offloaded to the user's system, which, presumably, is going to do it much faster than some host that is dealing with a few thousand hits at that moment. Moreover, if a great deal of data needs to be computed, you do not have to worry about the speed of transmission from the host machine since the data is computed locally. By the way, this relates to one area in which Java is way overhyped: adding animation to Web pages. Sure, this is easy to do (see Chapter 9), but if the animation involves the user downloading 1 megabyte of GIF files with a 28.8K modem, you will not have a happy user. What people should do instead (if possible), is think of fast ways to compute the special effects. This lets the applet generate the data using the local processor instead of downloading it.

4. Special purpose Java applets (usually called content and protocol handlers) allow a Java-enabled Web browser to deal with new types of information dynamically. Suppose you invent a nifty fractal compression algorithm for dealing with humongous graphics files and want to let someone sample your technology before you charge them big bucks for it. Write a Java content handler that does the decompression and send it along with the compressed files. The HotJava browser by Sun Microsystems supports this feature. Netscape 2.0 and 3.0 do not.

Applets at Work

This book includes a few sample applets; ultimately, the best source for applets is the Web itself. Some applets on the Web can only be seen at work; many others include the source code. When you become more familiar with Java, these applets can be a great way to learn more about Java. A good Web site to check for Java applets is Gamelan—http://www.gamelan.com. (By the way, *gamelan* also stands for a special type of Javanese musical orchestra. Attend a gamelan performance if you have a chance—it is gorgeous music.)

To place an applet onto a Web page, you need to know or work with someone who knows hypertext markup language (HTML). The number of HTML tags needed for a Java applet are few and easy to master (see Chapter 8). Using general HTML tags to design a Web page is a design issue—it is not a programming problem.

As you can see in Figure 1-1, when the user downloads an applet, it works much like embedding an image in a Web page. (For those who know HTML, we mean one set with an IMG tag.) The applet becomes a part of the page, and the text flows around the space used for the applet. The point is, the image is *alive*. It reacts to user commands, changes its appearance, and sends data between the computer viewing the applet and the computer serving it.

Figure 1-1 shows a good example of a dynamic Web page. This is a part of the virtual laboratory at the physics department of the University of Oregon. You can see some HTML text on top and the running applet on the bottom. (The lightbulb breaks if you add power without sufficient resistors. It glows if you add the right number of resistors, thus teaching students about Ohm's law.)

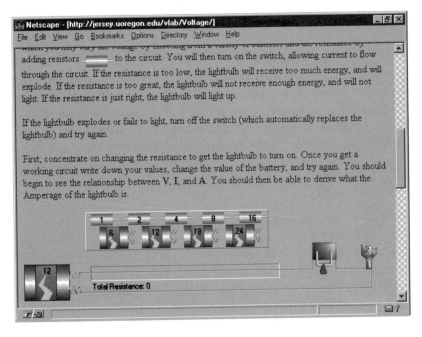

Figure 1-1: Courtesy of Sean Russell

A Short History of Java

This section gives a short history of Java's evolution. It is based on various published sources (most importantly, on an interview with Java's creators in the July 1995 issue of *SunWorld's* on-line magazine).

Java goes back to 1991, when a group of Sun engineers, led by Sun Fellow (and all-around computer wizard) James Gosling, wanted to design a small computer language that could be used for consumer devices like cable TV switchboxes. Since these devices do not have a lot of power or memory, the language had to be small and generate very tight code. Also, because different manufacturers may choose different central processing units (CPUs), it was important not to be tied down to any single architecture. The project got the code name "Green."

The requirements for small, tight code led them to resurrect the model that a language called UCSD Pascal tried in the early days of PCs and Niklaus Wirth had pioneered before that. What Wirth pioneered and UCSD Pascal did commercially, and the Green project engineers did as well, was to design a portable language that generated intermediate code for a hypothetical machine. (These are often called *virtual machines*—hence, the Java Virtual Machine or JVM.) This intermediate code could then be used on any machine that had the correct interpreter. Intermediate code generated with this model is always small, and the interpreters for intermediate code can also be quite small, so this solved their main problem.

The Sun people, however, come from a UNIX background so they based their language on C++, rather than Pascal. In particular, they made the language object oriented rather than procedure oriented. But, as Gosling says in the interview, "All along, the language was a tool, not the end." Gosling decided to call his language "Oak." (Presumably because he liked the look of an oak tree that was right outside his window at Sun.) The people at Sun later realized that Oak was the name of an existing computer language, so they changed the name to Java.

In 1992, the Green project delivered its first product, called "*7." It was an extremely intelligent remote control. (It had the power of a SparcStation in a box that was 6" by 4" by 4". Unfortunately, no one was interested in producing this at Sun, and the Green people had to find other ways to market their technology. However, none of the standard consumer electronics companies were interested. The group then bid on a project to design a cable TV box that could deal with new cable services such as video on demand. They did not get the contract. (Amusingly, the company that did was led by the same Jim Clark who started Netscape—a company that did much to make Java successful.)

The Green Project (with a new name of "First Person Inc.") spent all of 1993 and half of 1994 looking for people to buy its technology—no one was found. (Patrick Naughton, one of the founders of the group and the person who ended up doing most of the marketing, claims to have accumulated 300,000 air miles in trying to sell the technology.) First Person was dissolved in 1994.

While all of this was going on at Sun, the World Wide Web part of the Internet was growing bigger and bigger. The key to the Web is the browser that takes the hypertext page and translates it to the screen. In 1994, most people were using Mosaic, a noncommercial Web browser that came out of the supercomputing center at the University of Illinois in 1993. (Mosaic was partially written by Marc Andreessen for $6.85 an hour as an undergraduate student on a work-study project. He moved on to fame and fortune as one of the cofounders and the chief of technology at Netscape.)

In the *SunWorld* interview, Gosling says that in mid-1994, the language developers realized that "We could build a real cool browser. It was one of the few things in the client/server mainstream that needed some of the weird things we'd done: architecture neutral, real-time, reliable, secure—issues that weren't terribly important in the workstation world. So we built a browser."

The actual browser was built by Patrick Naughton and Jonathan Payne and evolved into the HotJava browser that we have today. The HotJava browser was written in Java to show off the power of Java. But the builders also had in mind the power of what are now called applets, so they made the browser capable of interpreting the intermediate bytecodes. This "proof of technology" was shown at SunWorld '95 on May 23, 1995, and inspired the Java craze that continues unabated today.

The big breakthrough for widespread Java use came in the fall of 1995, when Netscape decided to make the next release of Netscape (Netscape 2.0) Java enabled. Netscape 2.0 came out in January of 1996, and it has been (as have all subsequent releases) Java enabled. Other licensees include IBM, Symantec, Borland, and many others. Even Microsoft has licensed and supports Java. Internet Explorer 3 is Java enabled and the next version of Windows will be Java enabled.

Common Misconceptions about Java

In summary, following is a list of some common misconceptions about Java, along with commentary.

Java is an extension of HTML.

Java is a programming language; HTML is a page-description language. They have nothing in common except that there are HTML extensions for placing Java applets on a Web page.

Java is an easy programming language to learn.

No programming language as powerful as Java is easy. You always have to distinguish how easy it is to write toy programs and how hard it is to do serious work. Also, consider that only four chapters in this book discuss the Java language. The remaining chapters show how to put the language to work, using the Java *library*. The library contains over 150 classes and interfaces. You do not need to know all of them for many programming tasks, but you need to use some of them for every project.

Java is an easy environment in which to program.

The native Java development environment is *not* an easy environment to use—except for people who swear by 1970s command line tools. The main selling point of products like Café is that it begins to bring Java development into the modern era of VB-style drag-and-drop form designers combined with an integrated development platform.

Java will become a universal programming language for all platforms.

This is possible, in theory, but we wonder if you would then get a lowest-common-denominator approach to the design. Java applications do not yet look (and, perhaps, can never look) as good as, say, Windows applications developed with VB or MFC. In any case, the graphics toolkit supplied with the current version of Java is far too primitive to make the design task pleasant. Of course, we expect the libraries to get better. (There will soon be many third-party libraries that, while based on the Sun toolkits, go far beyond it.)

Java is interpreted, so it is too slow for serious applications on a specific platform.

Many programs spend most of their time on things like user-interface interactions. All programs, no matter what language they are written in, will detect a mouse click in adequate time. It is true that we would not do CPU-intensive tasks with the interpreter supplied with the Java development kit. However, on platforms where Café (or some other just in time compiler) is available all we need to do is run the byte codes using the supplied "just-in-time compiler"; most performance issues simply go away.

All Java programs run inside a Web page.

All Java *applets* run inside a Web browser. That is the definition of an applet—a Java program running inside a browser. But it is entirely possible, and quite useful, to write stand-alone Java programs that run independent of a Web browser. These programs (usually called *applications*) are completely portable. Just take the code and run them on another machine! And because Java is more convenient and less error-prone than raw C++, it is a good choice for writing programs. It will be an even more compelling choice once it is combined with database access tools like Sun's JDBC (see Chapter 14). It is certainly the obvious choice for a first language in which to learn programming.

Most of the programs in this book are stand-alone programs. Sure, applets are interesting, and right now most useful Java programs are applets. But we believe that stand-alone Java programs will become extremely important, very quickly.

Java eliminates the need for CGI scripting.

Not yet. With today's technology, CGI is still the easiest communication path between applet and server. The server will still need a CGI script to deal with the information sent by the applet. (Of course, we feel you can *write* the CGI scripts in Java much more easily than in Perl or C, but that is a separate issue.) In particular, there are technologies on the horizon that greatly reduce the need for CGI scripts. Servlets (see the final chapter) give you the same execution environment on the server that applets have on the client. JDBC (see Chapter 14) permits direct database manipulations by the client of information lying on the server.

Java will revolutionize client-server computing.

This is possible. The JDBC discussed in Chapter 14 certainly makes using Java for client-server development easier. As third party tools continue to be developed, we expect database development with Java to be as easy as the Net library makes network programming.

With Java, I can replace my computer with a $500 "Internet appliance."

Some people are betting big that this is going to happen. We believe it is pretty absurd to think that people are going to give up a powerful and convenient desktop for a limited machine with no local storage. But we can envision an Internet appliance as a portable *adjunct* to a desktop. Provided the price is right, wouldn't you rather have an Internet browsing machine to read your e-mail or the news at breakfast instead of watching television? Such an appliance could well be Java powered.

Java will allow the component-based model of computing to take off.

No two people mean the same thing when they talk about components. Regarding visual controls, like ActiveX components that can be dropped into a graphical user interface (GUI) program, Java has announced the Java Beans initiative which will certainly include this capability. (Java Beans is still in the formative stages but we will have a short discussion of it in the final chapter.) As for working with distributed computing models that use common object request broker (CORBA) compatible interfaces and OpenDoc, this is already happening through the Java IDL (interface definition language). Finally, Microsoft has given a way to use ActiveX controls directly from Java in their Internet Explorer browser.

CHAPTER

2

- Installing the Java Compiler and Tools

- Navigating the Java Directories

- Windows 95/NT as a Programming Environment

- Compiling and Running Java Programs

- Using WinEdit

- Graphical Applications

- Applets

- Troubleshooting

The Java
Programming
Environment

This chapter is about getting Java to work in various environments, concentrating on Windows 95 since that seems to be the most common platform. It is somewhat unusual for a book at this level to provide so many tips for various platforms; experienced programmers do not usually need to be told how to work with most software. However, at this point, the setup of Java is somewhat complex, and "gotchas" abound.

NOTE: A good, general source of information on Java may be found via the links on the Java frequently asked questions (FAQ) page: www.www-net.com/java/faq/.

Installing the Java Compiler and Tools

The most complete versions of Java are available for Sun's Solaris 2.x, Windows NT, or Windows 95 (Java is identical for both versions of Windows). Versions in various states of development exist for Linux, OS/2, Macintosh, Windows 3.1 and a few other platforms. In particular, if you use a PC and you want to use the Java features described in this book, you must have Windows 95 or NT to run Java. Realistically, you also need either a fast 486 or a Pentium, a minimum of 16 MB of memory, and at least 50 MB of free hard disk space.

TIP: For one of the big three—Solaris, Windows, or the Mac—you will want to periodically visit the Java home page to see if a more recent release is available for your platform. Point your browser to java.sun.com. For other platforms, you will need to cruise the Web. A good place to turn to is the comp.lang.java newsgroup.

The CD that accompanies this book contains the 1.02 version of the Java Development Kit (JDK) for Windows NT/Windows 95, together with the Alpha-2 release of Remote Method Invocation (RMI) and the 1.0 release of Java Database Connectivity (JDBC). The installation instructions in this chapter assume that you have Windows 95, and the CD-ROM comes with an installation program that unpacks the files needed for automatic installation of the Windows version. The CD-ROM also includes Solaris and Macintosh files. The Solaris files are in tar format, and the Macintosh files are self-extracting archives. You will need to unpack these archives manually and follow the installation instructions on the CD-ROM for those platforms.

NOTE: Only the installation instructions for Java are system dependent. If a full version of Java exists for your operating system, then, once you get Java up and running, everything else in this book will apply to you. System independence is a major benefit of Java.

Development Environments for Windows Users

If your programming experience comes from VB, Delphi, or a modern PC or Macintosh version of C or C++, you are used to a development environment with a built-in text editor and menus to compile and launch a program. The basic JDK contains nothing even remotely similar. *Everything* is done from the command line. We will tell you how to install and use the basic JDK, because the newest tools, in particular RMI and JDBC, are not currently available on the more convenient integrated design environments (IDEs).

We used an excellent shareware programming editor for Windows called WinEdit for developing and testing the programs in this book. WinEdit, like most good programming editors, can be configured to recognize (and color code) keywords in a language. It can also compile and execute source code. We created the necessary configuration and batch files for this and have included them on the CD. Our customized version of WinEdit became our de facto IDE for writing this book.

However, if you have a Java IDE such as Java Workshop, Microsoft J++ or Symantec Cafe, then you can continue using it, and manually add the special files and packages that are used in this book. We will give you general instructions, but of course the details depend on the particular environment that you are using. Fair warning: If you add a package to a commercial environment but the environment doesn't seem to find it, please contact the vendor, not us, for technical assistance.

In sum, you have at this time four choices for a development environment under Windows:

1. Install the JDK and our Java-enhanced version of WinEdit from the CD-ROM;

2. Install the JDK from the CD-ROM and use your favorite ASCII editor (it must support long file names);

3. Install just the Core Java code, not the JDK, and use it with the Java development environment that you already own;

4. Install one of the trial software packages on the CD-ROM, and then install just the Core Java files, not the JDK.

The disadvantage of the third approach is that your development environment may not contain or support the newest Java features, in particular, RMI and JDBC. If you want those features and your vendor cannot supply them, you must install the entire JDK from the CD-ROM or download the individual packages from http://java.sun.com and install them manually.

Unless you are very experienced with configuring Java, the last choice is probably the least attractive. The trial versions are not supported by either the vendor or the authors of this book.

If you hate choices, just pick the first option. It will work fine. You simply write the source code for your program in the editor. When you are happy with it, you can use various WinEdit menu items to compile, execute, or see the frequent syntax-error message you will encounter for the first few weeks of working with Java.

Commercial development environments such as Cafe tend to be more cumbersome to use for a simple program, since you have to set up a separate project for each program you write. These environments have the edge if you write larger Java programs, consisting of many source files.

NOTE: Keep in mind that WinEdit is shareware; you are expected to pay its author if you use the program. (We have no connection whatsoever with the author of WinEdit. We simply found it to be a capable program and easy to customize.)

Installation Tips

If you choose WinEdit, install the following components in any order:

-   The JDK;
-   Core Java files;
-   WinEdit.

If you choose to use your own ASCII text editor, such as EDIT or vi, install the following components:

- The JDK;

- Core Java files.

If you have an integrated Java environment, install Core Java files and no other components.

CD-ROM Installation

Here are more detailed instructions for the various development environments.

The JDK

On the CD-ROM, go to the `\Win95NT\BOOKSJDK` directory. Run the `SETUP` program. Select the "Java Development Kit" box, as shown in Figure 2-1. This installs version 1.02 of the JDK, RMI Alpha-2 and JDBC 1.0. Also select the "Core Java" box, since you will need the Core Java files in addition to the JDK when you run the examples in this book.

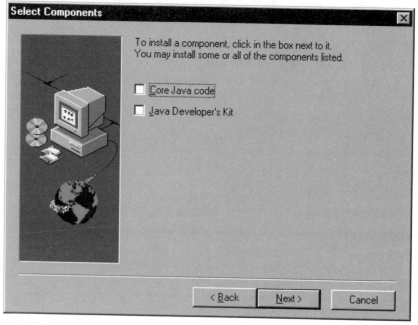

Figure 2-1: The CD-ROM installation program

When the SETUP program prompts you for the installation directories, you should accept the default c:\java. (You can change the disk drive letter if you do not have enough room on drive C and have a disk D or E. But if you tinker with the directory names, you are on your own.)

Core Java files

On the CD-ROM, go to the \Win95NT\BOOKSJDK directory. Run the SETUP program. Select the "Core Java" box. When the setup program prompts you for the installation directory, you should accept the default \CoreJavaBook.

WinEdit

Go to the \Win95NT\WINEDIT directory on the CD-ROM and run SETUP. This installs the WinEdit program. Next, run our patch file that customizes WinEdit for Java programming. Go to the \Win95NT\WINEDITA directory on the CD-ROM. Then run the WEPATCH batch file. This batch file requires two arguments:

- the name of the directory into which you installed WinEdit and
- the name of the directory that contains your Windows files.

For example,

```
WEPATCH    C:\WinEdit    C:\Windows
```

If the directory name contains spaces, enclose it in quotation marks.

```
WEPATCH    "C:\Program Files\WinEdit"    C:\Windows
```

If you use Windows NT 3.5, you need to do an additional step. You need to start WinEdit, select Project | Configure | Open, select the file Default.wpj, select Open and OK. WinEdit is now configured for use with Java.

By now, you may be feeling like the person who buys a gas grill, only to find that it is actually a gas grill assembly kit, not a ready-to-use grill. There is a reason, after all, why this is called the Java Development *Kit*. Undoubtedly, all this confusion will end once integrated development environments support the most up-to-date versions of Java.

Checking Your Configuration

When the installation is complete, check your AUTOEXEC.BAT file. There should be two modifications:

The PATH should contain the Java compiler directory (such as \java\bin or \Cafe\bin). For example,

```
SET PATH=. . .;C:\JAVA\BIN; . . .
```

There must also be an environment variable called CLASSPATH that looks like this:

```
SET CLASSPATH=C:\java\lib;.;C:\CoreJavaBook
```

The exact order of the directories in the path and class path does not matter, nor does the case. If you already have a class path, the installer should add the \java\lib and \CoreJavaBook directories to the end.

Finally, as always, you need to reboot your computer to make the changes to the path and class path effective.

TIP: On Unix, the directories of the class path are separated by colons. You must use an absolute path for each directory in the class path, for example

```
setenv CLASSPATH /java/lib:.:/home/me/CoreJavaBook
```

where /home/me is the path to your home directory. A path ~/CoreJavaBook does not work.

Adding Core Java Files to an Integrated Development Environment

If you already have another development environment such as Java Workshop, Microsoft J++ or Symantec Cafe, you should not install the JDK as it may interfere with your existing installation. You should install only the Core Java files.

Once the Core Java files are installed into the \CoreJavaBook directory, you need to add that directory to the class path of your development environment. This may be as simple as locating the CLASSPATH environment variable in your AUTOEXEC.BAT file. Or you may need to set an option in your development environment, or edit another file such as SC.INI for Symantec Cafe. Be careful—some environments have a new setting *override* all others, whereas others have the additional setting *appended* to the regular settings. Consult the documentation of your environment and contact the vendor for assistance if necessary.

Navigating the Java Directories

In your explorations of Java, you will occasionally want to peek inside the Java system files. And, of course, you will need to work extensively with our "Core Java" files. Table 2-1 shows the Java directory tree. (The layout will be different if you have an integrated development environment.)

Table 2-1: Java directory tree

```
\java
        api       library documentation in HTML format is here
                  images
        bin       the compiler and tools are here
        demo      (lots of subdirectories) look here for demos
        doc       documentation for RMI and JDBC
        include
                  win32
hotjava
        lib       (lots of subdirectories) library files
        src       look in the various subdirectories for the library source
                  java
                       lang
                       util
                       io
                       net
                       awt
                            peer
                            image
                       applet
                  sun
                       tools
                            ttydebug
```

The two most important subdirectories in this tree are \java\api and \java\src. The \java\api directory contains the Java library documentation in HTML format. You can view it with any Web browser, such as Netscape.

TIP: Set a bookmark to \java\api\tree.html in your browser like that shown in Figure 2-2. Use the File|Open File command and select the file tree.html in the \java\api directory. Then add the bookmark. You will want to refer to that page as a starting point for the library documentation. Also make a bookmark to \java\doc\rmi\tree.html and \java\doc\jdbc\tree.html for the documentations of RMI and JDBC—unfortunately they are not currently integrated into the main documentation.

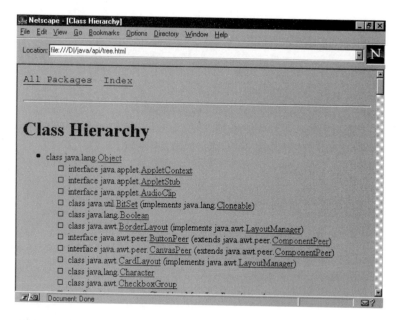

Figure 2-2: A starting point for the library doumentation

The \java\src directory contains the source code for the Java libraries. As you become more comfortable with Java, you may find yourself in situations for which this book and the on-line information do not provide what you need to know. At this point, the source code for Java is a good place to begin digging. It is occasionally reassuring to know that you can always dig into the source to find out what a library function really does. For example, if you are curious about the inner workings of the Hashtable class, you can look inside \java\src\java\util\Hashtable.java.

Here is how the program files in this book are organized:

```
\CoreJavaBook
    corejava
    ch2
        Welcome
        WelcomeApplet
        ImageViewer
    ch3
        FirstSample
        LotteryOdds
        LotteryDrawing
        Mortgage
        MortgageLoop
        Retirement
        SquareRoot
    . . .
```

> NOTE: The `corejava` directory is very important. It contains a number of useful Java routines that we wrote to supplement missing features in the standard Java library. These files are needed for a number of examples in the book. It is crucial that your CLASSPATH environment variable is set to include the `\CoreJavaBook` directory so that the programs can find our files, such as
> `\CoreJavaBook\corejava\Format.class` and
> `\CoreJavaBook\corejava\Console.class`.

There is a separate directory for each chapter of this book. Each of these directories has separate subdirectories for sample files. For example, `\CoreJavaBook\ch2\ImageViewer` contains the source code and compiled code for the imageviewer application that you will encounter later in this chapter. (There is no source code for Chapter 1.)

Windows 95/NT as a Programming Environment

If you have done all your programming in Windows, using a comfortable programming environment such as VB, Delphi or one of the C++-integrated environments, you may find the JDK primitive. ("Quaint" may be a more charitable word for it.) In this section, we give a few tips for working with Windows 95/NT. If you are a seasoned veteran, or if you do not use Windows 95/NT, just skip this section.

Long File Names

Even if you are an experienced programmer under previous versions of DOS or Windows 3.1, Windows 95 has one major new feature—*long file names*.

If you are coming from DOS or Windows 3.1, you know that a DOS file can have, at most, eight characters in the name and three characters in the extension, such as `WLCMAPPL.HTM`. These are the so-called 8.3 file names. With Windows 95 or NT, you can use as many characters as you like. For example, you can call a file `WelcomeApplet.html`. This is very welcome news, indeed.

Actually, you do not have a choice when dealing with Java; all Java source files use long file names. They *must* have the four-letter extension `java`.

Luckily, most of the new versions of the traditional DOS utility functions included in Windows NT or Windows 95 understand long file names. For example, you can type

```
del WelcomeApplet.html
```

or

```
copy *.java a:
```

Of course, if you prefer, you can delete and copy the files through the Explorer, but many programmers type faster than they mouse, and, therefore, prefer the command line.

To let you use programs that were written before long file names were invented, Microsoft gives each long file name an 8.3 file name *alias*. These aliases contain a ~ character, for example WELCOM~1.HTM. If there are two files in the same directory whose names start with WELCOM and have HTM in the extension, then their aliases are WELCOM~1.HTM and WELCOM~2.HTM.

> In the event that there are *two* names for the same file, be careful when deleting files, especially when you use wild cards. For example, the command
>
>   del *.HTM
>
> will delete all files with the extension HTM and all files whose extension *starts with* HTM. In particular, all *.html files will also be deleted.

Windows Explorer gives you access to the long file names. But if you are working with a DOS shell, how do you find the long file name?

- The DIR command shows the 8.3 alias on the left and the long file name on the right.

Figure 2-3: The DIR command with long file names

After a few weeks, you will get into the habit of looking at the right-hand side and ignoring the left-hand side.

One of the programs that has not yet been adapted to long file names is PKZIP. If you use the venerable PKZIP 2.04g to bundle and compress files, you will find that it only packs and unpacks the 8.3 file names.

You can make a real hash out of a collection of Java files by using the DOS version of PKZIP. Instead, you should use a modern zipping tool like WinZip. We include a shareware copy of WinZip on the CD-ROM. For example, you can use WinZip to peek inside the CLASSES.ZIP file in the `\java\lib` directory.

Long file names can even contain spaces. You may have noticed that some programs are installed in a directory with the name `Program Files`. As you can imagine, this can be confusing for some DOS commands that traditionally expect spaces to separate the file names and command options. You need to enclose any file or directory name that contains spaces in quotation marks, for example

```
del "The first applet in the Core Java book.java"
```

Don't worry. We will not use file names like that in our examples.

Long file names are not case sensitive *for DOS commands*. For example,

```
del WelcomeApplet.java
```

and

```
del welcomeapplet.JAVA
```

both have the same effect. But Windows 95 *retains the case* that you used when you first created the file. For example, if you named the file `WelcomeApplet.java`, then Windows will use the uppercase W and A in the directory display and all directory dialog boxes.

NOTE: Java, on the other hand, *is* case sensitive. As you will soon see, a file like `WelcomeApplet.java` contains a class with the same name, `WelcomeApplet`. If you compile this file with the command

```
java welcomeapplet.java
```

then the compiler will ask DOS to open the file. DOS has no problem opening the `welcomeApplet.java` file, but the compiler will insist that it cannot find a `welcomeapplet` class. You will get some strange error message that relates to the file not being found. The moral is that anytime you cannot compile a file that you know is there, check the case of the file name with the DIR command or with Explorer.

If you notice the problem and regret your decision, you can use the ren command to change the look of the file name.

```
ren welcomeapplet.java WelcomeApplet.java
```

Multiple Windows

When using JDK, multiple DOS windows are a way of life. You run the editor in one DOS window and the compiler in another. Graphical applications, applets, and the browser run in other windows. Windows 95 has a nifty *task bar* at the bottom of the screen that lets you easily switch between windows.

Figure 2-4: The task bar

If you use a computer with a small screen (such as a laptop computer), you may find that the task bar takes up valuable screen real estate. You can *hide* the task bar. (Click on an empty area of the task bar with the right mouse button, then select Properties and Auto Hide.) This tells Windows to display the task bar only when you move the mouse towards the bottom of the screen. (You can also drag the task bar to another corner of your screen if you like.)

Keyboard Shortcuts

As you probably know, the mouse was originally designed by researchers in the prestigious Xerox PARC lab. One of their unstated goals seems to have been to slow you down so the computer can keep up with you. Programmers do not like to be slowed down, and their programmer comrades at Microsoft have fought the mouse maniacs and kept a number of *keyboard shortcuts* in the operating system. Here are a few of these keystroke combinations that we have found helpful.

ALT+TAB: This key combination displays a small window with icons, one for each running task.

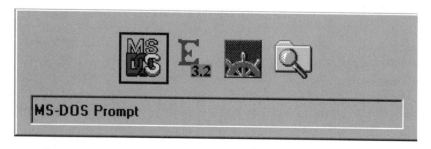

Figure 2-5: The Alt + Tab task switcher

Keep your thumb on the ALT key and hold down TAB. Different icons will be selected. Let go of both keys, and you switch to the selected window.

CTRL+ESC: This key combination pops up the start menu in the task bar. If you arrange your most-used program icons into the first level of the start menu, then you can run them with a couple of keystrokes.

TIP: Put the MS-DOS prompt, WinEdit, and Netscape into the first level of the start menu. (To edit the start menu, right-click on an empty area of the task bar, then select Properties and Start Menu Programs.)

Under Windows 95, the CTRL+ALT+DEL key combination does not reboot the computer. Instead, it pops up a window of all active applications, like this:

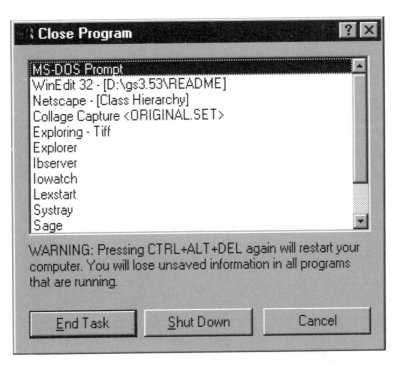

Figure 2-6: The Ctrl + Alt + Del Close Program dialog

If you have a non-responsive program

1. pop up this box,

2. select the program from the given list,

3. click on the End Task button.

> **CAUTION**
>
> Hitting Ctrl+Alt+Del *twice* does reboot the computer, so you want to have a steady hand when using this key combination.

More on DOS Shells

The humble MS-DOS shell has come a long way from that in earlier versions of Windows. In fact, the DOS shell in Windows 95 is, in many ways, a better DOS than DOS. For starters, as you have seen, you can run multiple DOS shells and toggle between them. You can also launch Windows applications directly from the DOS shell. For example, if you type

```
notepad
```

into a DOS prompt and hit ENTER, the Notepad program starts up. This is at least 10 times faster than clicking on Start Menu | Programs | Accessories | Notepad.

TIP: If you use the DOS shell, you should use the DOSKEY program. The DOSKEY utility keeps a *command history*. Type the up and down arrow keys to cycle through the previously typed commands. Use the left and right arrow keys to edit the current command. Type the beginning of a command and hit F8 to complete it. For example, if you have typed

```
appletviewer WelcomeApplet.html
```

once, then you just type

```
apF8
```

to instantly retype the command. You get a chance to edit it, in case you want to issue a slightly different command.

To install DOSKEY into your AUTOEXEC.BAT file, simply add the line

```
DOSKEY /INSERT
```

and reboot.

The EDIT Program

If you need to do a quick edit, and you do not want to wait for your regular editor to start, try the EDIT program that comes with Windows 95. You will be pleasantly surprised. This is not the QuickBasic editor that came with DOS 5 and 6, but a completely different program. In particular, this editor handles long file names, *and* it can edit up to 10 files at a time. You switch between the files by hitting ALT+1, ALT+2, and so on. You can even launch the editor with a wild card:

```
edit *.java
```

Unfortunately, EDIT is still a DOS program, which means that it is difficult to cut and paste between it and other Windows programs. (It can be done, but you need to use the Mark, Copy, and Paste icons on the top of the DOS shell window, not the usual editor commands.) Of course, you can cut and paste between different files that are loaded into the editor. (You can use Notepad if you want a more efficient way to cut and paste between Windows programs.)

Compiling and Running Java Programs

There are two methods for compiling and launching a Java program: from the command line and from an editor. Let us do it the hard way first: from the command line. Go to the \CoreJavaBook\ch2\Welcome directory. Then enter the following commands:

```
javac Welcome.java
java Welcome
```

You should see this message on the screen:

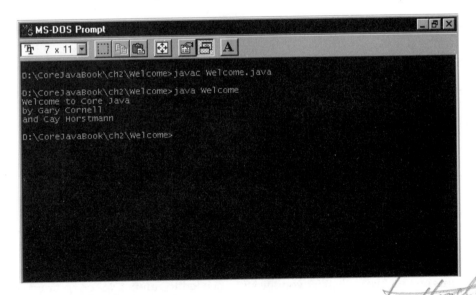

Figure 2-7: Compiling the first Java program

Congratulations! You have just compiled and run your first Java program.

What happened? The javac program is the Java compiler. It compiles the file Welcome.java into the file Welcome.class. The java program is the Java interpreter. It interprets the so-called bytecodes that the compiler placed in the class file.

The `Welcome` program is extremely simple. It simply prints a message to the console. You may enjoy looking inside the program shown in Example 2-1—we will explain how it works in the next chapter.

Example 2-1: Welcome.java

```java
public class Welcome
{  public static void main(String[] args)
    {   String greeting[] = new String[3];
        greeting[0] = "Welcome to Core Java";
        greeting[1] = "by Gary Cornell";
        greeting[2] = "and Cay Horstmann";

        int i;
        for (i = 0; i < greeting.length; i++)
            System.out.println(greeting[i]);
    }
}
```

NOTE: Every integrated environment has commands for compiling and running programs. If you do not use WinEdit, read your documentation to find out how to compile and run programs. If you want to use WinEdit, read the next section.

Using WinEdit

Compiling and Running Programs

Of course, we grew quite comfortable with our customized version of WinEdit in the course of writing this book. WinEdit defaults to using the normal editing commands that most Windows programs expect. (The keystrokes for most tasks are customizable as well.) WinEdit comes with a complete help system, so we will not go into the details of using it as an editor. (It should take an experienced programmer maybe 15 minutes to master it.)

In this section, we will show you the steps needed to run the `Welcome` program from inside the WinEdit environment. *Then* we will explain the advantages of using WinEdit when you make a typo or three.

To compile and run the `Welcome` program from our customized version of WinEdit,

1.   start up WinEdit,

2.   choose File | Open and work with the dialog box to find and then load the `Welcome.java` source code,

3. select Project | Compile from the menu. This runs the Java compiler and captures any error messages. (We hope there are none.) While Java is compiling the file, you see a screen like this:

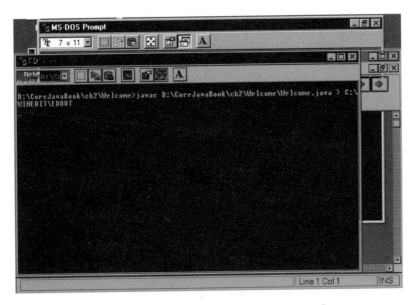

Figure 2-8: The compiler window in WinEdit

WinEdit has automatically opened a temporary DOS shell to run the Java compiler. When the compiler has finished, you will see a dialog box that looks like this:

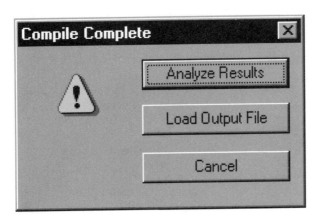

Figure 2-9: The Compile Complete notification in WinEdit

Hit the Analyze Results button. There should be a message "No errors or warnings" in the status bar. Then select Project | Execute to see the compiled code at work. This pops up another DOS window, shown here, for the output.

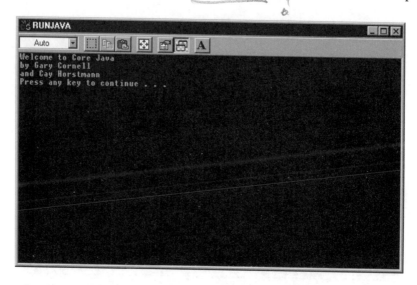

Figure 2-10: Running a Java program from WinEdit

We customized WinEdit so that this window remains open until you hit a key to continue.

Locating Compilation Errors

Presumably, our program did not have typos or bugs. (It was only a few lines of code, after all.) Let us suppose, for the sake of argument, that you occasionally have a typo (perhaps even a bug) in your code. Try it out—ruin our file, for example, by changing the capitalization in the first few lines like this:

```
Public class Welcome
{  Public Static void main(String[] args)
   {  String Greeting[] = new String[3];
      greeting[0] = "Welcome to Core Java";
      greeting[1] = "by Gary Cornell";
      greeting[2] = "and Cay Horstmann";

      int i;
      for (i = 0; i < greeting.length; i++)
         System.out.println(greeting[i]);
   }
}
```

Now run the Java compiler again by choosing Project | Compile. You will see the dialog box that contains the Analyze Results button. Click on this button. Now WinEdit will put the cursor onto the offending line and display an error message in the status bar like this:

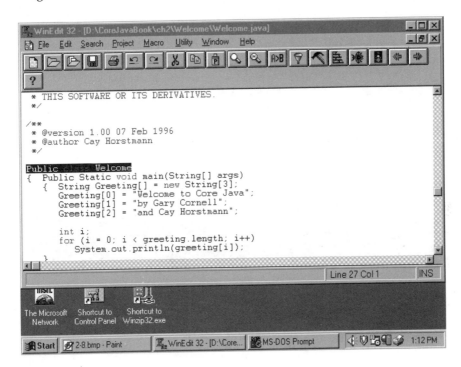

Figure 2-11: Locating compiler errors in WinEdit

Use the Search | Next error command to walk through any error messages.

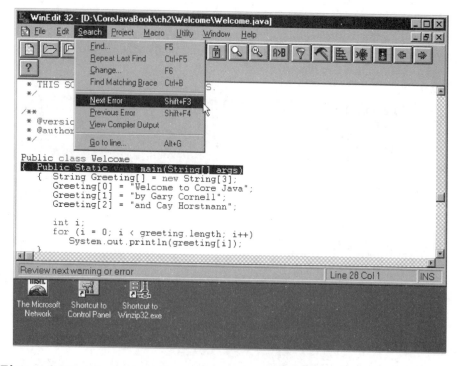

Figure 2-12: Moving to the next error in WinEdit

Again, once your program compiles without errors, you can try to run it by selecting Project I Run from the menu.

Graphical Applications

The `Welcome` program was not terribly exciting. Next, let us run a graphical application. This program is a very simple GIF file-viewer. It simply loads and displays a GIF file. Again, let us first compile and run it from the command line.

1. Open a DOS shell window.

2. Change to the directory `\CoreJavaBook\ch2\ImageViewer`.

3. Enter

   ```
   javac ImageViewer.java
   java ImageViewer
   ```

A new program window pops up with our `ImageViewer` application.

Now select File I Open and look for a GIF file to open. (We supplied a couple of sample files in the directory.)

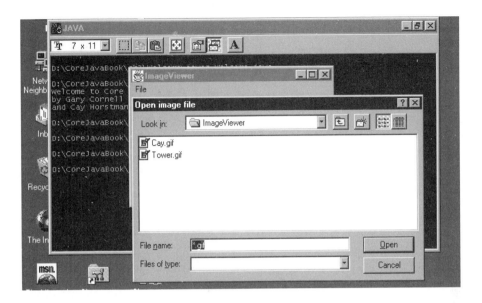

Figure 2-13: Running the ImageViewer application

To close the program, click on the Close box in the title bar or pull down the system menu and close the program. (To compile and run this program inside WinEdit or a development environment, do the same as before. For example, for WinEdit, choose Project I Compile, then choose Project I Run.)

We hope that you find this program interesting and useful. Have a quick look at the source code. The program is substantially longer than the first program, but it is not terribly complex if you consider how much code it would take in C or C++ to write a similar application. In VB, of course, it is easy to write, or, rather, drag and drop, such a program—you need only add about two lines of code to make it functional. At this time, Java does not have a visual interface builder, so you need to write code for everything, as shown in Example 2-2. We will learn how to write graphical programs like this in Chapter 6.

Example 2-2: ImageViewer.java

```
import java.awt.*;
import java.awt.image.*;
import java.io.*;

public class ImageViewer extends Frame
{  public ImageViewer()
   {  setTitle("ImageViewer");
      MenuBar mbar = new MenuBar();
      Menu m = new Menu("File");
      m.add(new MenuItem("Open"));
```

```
        m.add(new MenuItem("Exit"));
        mbar.add(m);
        setMenuBar(mbar);
    }

    public boolean handleEvent(Event evt)
    {   if (evt.id == Event.WINDOW_DESTROY) System.exit(0);
        return super.handleEvent(evt);
    }

    public boolean action(Event evt, Object arg)
    {   if (arg.equals("Open"))
        {   FileDialog d = new FileDialog(this,
                "Open image file", FileDialog.LOAD);
            d.setFile("*.gif");
            d.setDirectory(lastDir);
            d.show();
            String f = d.getFile();
            lastDir = d.getDirectory();
            if (f != null)
                image = Toolkit.getDefaultToolkit()
                    .getImage(lastDir + f);
            repaint();
        }
        else if(arg.equals("Exit")) System.exit(0);
        else return false;
        return true;
    }

    public void paint(Graphics g)
    {   if (image != null)
            g.drawImage(image, 0, 0, this);
    }

    public static void main(String args[])
    {   Frame f = new ImageViewer();
        f.resize(300, 200);
        f.show();
    }

    private Image image = null;
    private String lastDir = "";
}
```

Applets

The first two programs presented in this book are Java *applications*, stand-alone programs like any native programs. On the other hand, as we mentioned in the last chapter, most of the hype about Java comes from its ability to run *applets* inside a Web browser. We want to show you how to build and run an applet, first from the command line, then from WinEdit. Finally, we will load the applet into a Web browser (Netscape, in our case).

First, go to the directory `\CoreJavaBook\ch2\WelcomeApplet` then enter the following commands:

```
javac WelcomeApplet.java
appletviewer WelcomeApplet.html
```

Here is what you see in the applet viewer window.

Figure 2-14: The WelcomeApplet applet as viewed by the applet viewer

The first command is the now-familiar command to invoke the Java compiler. This compiles the `WelcomeApplet.java` source into the bytecode file `WelcomeApplet.class`. This time, however, we do not run the Java interpreter; we use the applet-viewer program instead. This program is a special tool included with the JDK that lets you quickly test an applet. You need to give it an HTML file, rather than the name of a `Java.class` file. The contents of the `WelcomeApplet.html` file are shown below in Example 2-3.

Example 2-3: WelcomeApplet.html

```
<HTML>
<TITLE>WelcomeApplet</TITLE>
<HR>
This applet is from the book
<A
HREF="http://www.sun.com/smi/ssoftpress/catalog/java_series.html">
Core Java</A> by Gary Cornell and
<A HREF="http://www.horstmann.com">
Cay Horstmann</A>, published by SunSoft Press/Prentice-Hall

<APPLET CODE=WelcomeApplet.class WIDTH=200 HEIGHT=200>
<PARAM NAME=greeting VALUE="Welcome to Core Java!">
</APPLET>

<HR>
<A href="WelcomeApplet.java">The source.</A>
```

If you are familiar with HTML, you will notice some standard HTML instructions and the new APPLET tag, telling the applet-viewer to load the applet whose code is stored in `WelcomeApplet.class`. The applet-viewer ignores all other codes in this file. But a Java-aware browser, such as Netscape version 2.0 or later, will display both the traditional HTML text and the applet on the same Web page. (See Chapter 8 for more on these tags.)

Try it out. You need Netscape 2.0 (or later) or another Java-enabled browser. (We do not include Netscape on the CD-ROM; you can always download a trial version from `www.netscape.com`.)

1. Start Netscape.

2. Select File | Open File.

3. Go to the `\CoreJavaBook\ch2\WelcomeApplet` directory.

You should see the `WelcomeApplet.html` file in the file dialog. Load that file. Netscape now loads the applet, including the surrounding text.

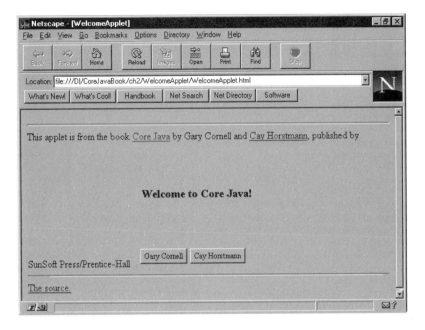

Figure 2-15: Running the WelcomeApplet applet in Netscape

You can see that this application is actually alive and willing to interact with the Internet. Click on the Gary Cornell button. The applet directs Netscape to pop up a mail window, with Gary's address already filled in. Click on the Cay Horstmann button. The applet directs Netscape to display Cay's Web page.

Notice that neither of these two buttons work in the applet viewer. The applet viewer has no capabilities to send mail or display a Web page, so it ignores your requests. The applet viewer is good for testing applets in isolation, but you need to put it inside Netscape or another Java-enabled browser to see how applets interact with the browser and the Internet.

TIP: You can also compile and run applets from inside WinEdit. As always, select Project | Compile, then Project | Run. This time, what happens is that WinEdit launches a batch file that realizes you are running an applet, not an application. It builds an HTML file on the fly and launches the applet-viewer. If you use an integrated environment such as Café, it has its own commands to launch an applet.

Finally, the code for the `Welcome` applet is shown in Example 2-4. At this point, do not give it more than a glance. We will come back to writing applets in Chapter 8.

Example 2-4: WelcomeApplet.java

```java
import java.applet.*;
import java.awt.*;
import java.net.*;

public class WelcomeApplet extends Applet
{  public void start()
   {  setLayout(new BorderLayout());
      Label l = new Label(getParameter("greeting"),
         Label.CENTER);
      l.setFont(new Font("Times", Font.BOLD, 18));
      add("Center", l);
      Panel p = new Panel();
      p.add(new Button("Gary Cornell"));
      p.add(new Button("Cay Horstmann"));
      add("South", p);
   }

   public boolean action(Event evt, Object arg)
   {  String uName;
      URL u;
      if (arg.equals("Gary Cornell"))
         uName = "mailto:75720.1524@compuserve.com";
      else if (arg.equals("Cay Horstmann"))
         uName = "http://www.horstmann.com";
      else return false;
      try
      {  u = new URL(uName);
         getAppletContext().showDocument(u);
      }
      catch(Exception e)
      {  showStatus("Error " + e);
      }
      return true;
   }
}
```

Troubleshooting

We want to end this section with a few tips whose discovery caused us some grief; we hope you can learn from our pain.

PATH, CLASSPATH, and Other Environment Variables

The single most common problem we encountered with Java is an incorrect PATH or CLASSPATH environment variable.

1. The `\java\bin` directory (or the directory containing your integrated environment's executables) must be on the *PATH*.

2. The `\java\lib` and the current directory (that is, the . directory) must be on the *CLASSPATH*.

3. The `CoreJavaBook` directory must also be on the *CLASSPATH*.

4. Some environments (like Café) also use a *JAVA_HOME* environment variable.

Double-check these settings and reboot your computer if you run into trouble.

Memory Problems

If you have only 16 MB of memory, you may get "insufficient memory" errors from the Java compiler. In that case, close memory hogs like Netscape and Microsoft Exchange. If you have less than 16 MB of memory, you will probably be unable to compile large programs.

NOTE: Only the compiler and applet viewer pig out on memory. Once you compile an application, you should have no trouble running it with the Java interpreter or Netscape, even with less than 16 MB of memory.

Case Sensitivity

Java is case sensitive. HTML is sometimes case sensitive. DOS is not case sensitive. This caused us no end of grief, especially since Java can give very bizarre error messages when it messes up because of a spelling error. Always check file names, parameter names, class names, keywords, and so on for capitalization.

About Other Platforms

Watch the Web for information on other platforms. For starters, keep track of the discussions on `comp.lang.java`. This will often be the place that first reports information on updates or on versions for new platforms. This also seems to be the place where (after you filter out some noise) you will see reports on problems with current versions.

IBM has an OS/2 site (`ncc.hursley.ibm.com/javainfo/faq.html`). The latest information about Linux can usually be found from the FAQ page (`www.www-net.com/java/faq/`), and one site that will have the current version is `ftp://java.blackdown.org/pub/Java/linux`.

Updates and Bug Fixes

The CD-ROM contains about 400 files, and some of them are bound to have minor glitches and inconsistencies. We will keep a list of frequently asked questions, bug reports, and bug fixes on the Web page `http://www.horstmann.com/corejava.html`. *Please* read the FAQ before sending in a complaint or bug report. We also welcome any suggestions for improvements.

CHAPTER

3

Fundamental Programming Structures in Java

At this point, we are assuming that you successfully installed Java and were able to run the sample programs in Chapter 2. It is time to show how to program in Java. This chapter shows you how the basic programming concepts such as data types, loops, and user-defined functions (actually, they are usually called *methods* in Java) are implemented in Java. If you are an experienced C++ programmer, you can get away with just skimming this chapter: concentrate on the C/C++ notes that are interspersed throughout the text. Programmers coming from another background, such as Visual Basic (VB), will find most of the concepts familiar and all of the syntax maddening—you will want to read this chapter very carefully.

Unfortunately, getting output from Java is cumbersome. For this reason, almost all the sample programs in this chapter will be "toy" programs, designed to illustrate a concept. In all cases they will simply send or receive information to or from the console. (For example, if you are using Windows 95, the console is an MS-DOS window.) In particular, we will be writing *applications* rather than *applets* in this chapter.

If output in Java is cumbersome, input is even worse. Since it is hard to write even toy programs without a decent method of getting input from the user, the CD contains sufficient code for doing simple (prompted) input. We suggest not worrying too much about how input works at first. We will explain some of the details later in this chapter and finish it off in the next chapter.

A Very Simple Java Program

Let's look more closely at about the simplest Java program you can have:

```
public class FirstSample
{   public static void main(String[] args)
    {   System.out.println("We will not use 'Hello world!'");
    }
}
```

After you compiled this *source code,* you obtained a byte code. After running the byte code through the Java interpreter, this code simply displays the quoted string on the console (an MS-DOS window for users of Windows 95).

It is worth spending all the time you need in order to understand the framework of this sample; the pieces will reoccur in all applications. First and foremost, *Java is case sensitive.* If you made any mistakes in capitalization (such as typing Main instead of main), the program will not compile.

Having said this, let's look at this source code from the top. The keyword public controls which code can use this code. We will have more to say about these access modifiers in Chapter 5. The keyword class is there because everything in a Java program lives inside a class. Although we will spend a lot more time on classes in the next chapter, for now think of a class as a container for the data and methods (functions) that make up part or all of an application. As mentioned in Chapter 1, classes are the building blocks with which all Java applications and applets are built. *Everything* in a Java program must be inside a class.

Following, the keyword class is the name of the class. You need to make the file name for the source code the same as the name of the class with the word *java* appended. Thus, we would store this code in a file called FirstSample.java (notice that long file names are needed). The compiled byte code is then automatically called FirstSample.class and stored in the same directory. The Java compiler looks at the name of the class and not at the name of the file where source code is stored to determine the file name for the compiled byte code.

(The CD stores the code for each sample. For example, the first sample program is stored in the \CoreJavaBook\ch3\FirstSample directory.)

NOTE: Applets have a different structure—see Chapter 8 for information on applets.

When you use

```
java NameOfClass
```

to run a compiled program, the Java interpreter always starts execution with the code in the main method in the named class. Thus you *must* have a main method (function) for your code to execute. You can, of course, add your own methods to a class and call them from the `main` function. (We cover writing your own methods later in this chapter.)

Next, notice the braces in the source code. In Java, as in C/C++ (but not in Pascal or VB), braces are used to delineate the parts (usually called *blocks*) in your program. A VB programmer can think of the outermost pair of braces as corresponding to a Sub/End Sub pair; a Pascal programmer can relate them to the first begin/end pair. In Java, the code for any method must be started by an open brace and so ended by a close brace. (We will have more to say about braces later in this chapter.)

Brace styles have inspired an inordinate amount of useless controversy. We use a style that lines up the braces that delineate each block. Since white space is irrelevant to the Java compiler, you can use whatever brace style you like. We will have more to say about the use of braces when we talk about the various kinds of loops.

If you are not a C++ programmer, don't worry about the keywords `static void`. For now, just think of them as part of the incantation needed to get a Java program to compile. By the end of Chapter 4, you will understand this incantation completely. The point to remember for now is that every Java application must have a `main` method (function) whose header is identical to the one shown here.

C++ NOTE: You know what a class is. Java classes are similar to C++ classes, but there are a few differences that can trap you. For example, in Java *all* functions are member functions of some class, and the standard terminology refers to them as *methods* rather than member functions. Thus, in Java you must have a shell class for the `main` method. You may also be familiar with the idea of *static member functions.* These are functions defined inside a class that do not operate on objects. The `main` method (function) in Java is always static. Finally, as in C/C++, the `void` keyword indicates that this method (function) does not return a value.

VB NOTE: The closest analogy in VB would be a program that uses a Sub Main rather than a startup form. Recall that if you choose to have a Sub Main, *everything* has to be explicitly called from Sub Main.

Next, turn your attention to this fragment.

```
{   System.out.println("We will not use 'Hello world!'");
}
```

Braces mark the beginning and end of the *body* of the method. This method only has one statement in it. As in most programming languages, you can think of Java statements as being the sentences of the language. In Java *every statement must end with a semicolon.* (For those coming from a Pascal background, the semicolon in Java is not the statement separator, but rather the statement terminator.)

In particular, neither white space nor carriage returns mark the end of a statement, so statements can span lines if need be. There are essentially no limits on the length of a statement. Here we are using a statement that outputs a single line of text to the console.

Here we are using the System.out object and asking it to use its println method. The println method works with a string and displays it on the standard console. It then adds a line feed. C/C++ and VB (but not Pascal), use double quotes. (See the section on strings later in this chapter for more information.)

Methods in Java, like functions in any programming languages, can use zero, one, or more *arguments* (some languages call them *parameters*). Even the main method (function) in Java accepts what the user types on the command line as its argument. You will see how to use this information later in this chapter. (Even if a method takes zero arguments, you must still use empty parentheses.)

NOTE: You also have a print method in System.out that doesn't add a carriage return/line feed combination to the string.

C++ NOTE: Although in Java, as in C/C++, the main function receives an array of command line arguments, the array syntax in Java is different. A String[] is an array of strings. The name of the program is not stored in the args array. For example, when you start up the program Bjarne.java as

```
java Bjarne Stroustrup
```

from the command line, then args[0] will be Stroustrup and not Bjarne.

Comments

Comments in Java, like comments in most programming languages, do not show up in the executable program. In fact, comments do not nest in Java. Thus, you can add as many comments as needed without fear of bloating the code. Java has three ways of showing comments. The most common method is a //, to be used for a comment that will run only the length of a line:

```
System.out.println("We will not use 'Hello world!'");
// is this too cute?
```

In the case of // comments, the end of a line is marked by a carriage return, a line feed, or both.

When larger comments are needed, you can mark each line with a //, but it is more common to use the /* and */ that let you block off a larger comment. This is shown in Example 3-1.

Example 3-1: FirstSample.java

```
/*
This is the first sample program in Core Java Chapter 3
Copyright (C) 1996 Gary Cornell and Cay Horstmann
*/
public class FirstSample
{ public static void main(String[] args)
  {  System.out.println("We will not use 'Hello world!'");
  }
}
```

The // comment style is painful to modify when you need to extend comments over multiple lines, so we suggest using it only when you are sure the comment will never grow.

Finally, there is a third kind of comment that can be used to generate documentation automatically. This comment uses a /** to start and a */ to end. For more on this type of comment and on automatic documentation generation, please see Appendix II.

Data Types

Java is an example of a *strongly typed language*. This means that every variable must have a declared type. There are eight *primitive types* in Java. Six of them are number types (four integer and two floating-point types); one is the character type char, used for characters in Unicode encoding (see the section on the char type), and one is a boolean type for truth values.

VB NOTE: Java hasn't any type analogous to the Variant data type, in which you can store all possible types. It does have a way of converting all types to strings for display purposes that you will see later in this chapter.

Integers

The integer types are for numbers without fractional parts. Negative values are allowed. Java provides four integer types shown in Table 3-1:

Table 3-1: Java integer types

Type	Storage Requirement	Range (inclusive)
int	4 bytes	–2,147,483,648 to 2,147,483,647 (just over 2 billion)
short	2 bytes	–32,768 to 32,767
long	8 bytes	–9,223,372,036,854,775,808L to 9,223,372,036,854,775,807L
byte	1 byte	–128 to 127

In most situations, the `int` type is the most practical. If you want to represent the national debt in pennies, you'll need to resort to `long`. The `byte` and `short` types are mainly intended for specialized applications such as low-level file handling, or for large arrays when storage space is at a premium. The point is that, under Java, the integer types do not depend on the machine on which you will be running the Java code. This alleviates a major pain for the programmer who wants to move software from one platform to another, or even between operating systems on the same platform. A C program that runs well on a Sparc may exhibit integer overflow under Windows 3.1. Since Java programs must run with the same results on all machines by its design, the ranges for the various types are fixed. Of course having platform-independent integer types brings a small performance penalty, but in the case of Java this is not a particular bottleneck. (There are worse bottlenecks....)

Long integer literals have a suffix L (for example, `4000000000L`). Hexadecimal numbers have a prefix `0x`, for example `0xCAFE`.

C++ NOTE: In C and C++, `int` denotes the integer type that depends on the target machine. On a 16-bit processor, like the 8086, integers are 2 bytes. On a 32-bit processor like the Sun Sparc, they are 4-byte quantities. On an Intel Pentium, the integer type depends on the operating system: for DOS and Windows 3.1, integers are 2 bytes. When using 32-bit mode for Windows 95 or Windows NT programs, integers are 4 bytes. In Java, the sizes of all numeric types are platform independent.

VB NOTE: The ranges for the integer types are quite different in Java. An integer in VB corresponds to a `short` in Java. The `int` type in Java corresponds to the `Longint` type in VB, and so on.

Floating-Point Types

The floating-point types denote numbers with fractional parts. There are two floating-point types as shown in Table 3-2:

Table 3-2: Floating-point types

Type	Storage Requirement	Range
float	4 bytes	range roughly ±3.40282347E+38F (6–7 significant decimal digits)
double	8 bytes	range roughly ±1.79769313486231570E+308 (15 significant digits)

The name `double` refers to the fact that these numbers have twice the precision of the `float` type. (Some people call these *double-precision* variables.) Here, the type of choice in most applications is `double`. The limited precision of `float` is simply not sufficient for many situations. Seven significant (decimal) digits may be enough to precisely express your annual salary in dollars and cents, but it won't be enough for your company president's salary. The only reason to use `float` is in the rare situations in which the slightly faster processing of single-precision numbers is important, or when you need to store a large number of them.

Literals of type `float` have a suffix F, for example 3.402F, doubles use a D. All the floating-point types follow the IEEE 754 specification. They will overflow on range errors and underflow on operations like a divide by zero.

The Character Type (char)

First, the `char` type, unlike the `string` type, uses single quotes to denote a `char`. Second, the `char` type denotes characters in the Unicode encoding scheme. You may not be familiar with Unicode, and, fortunately, you don't need to worry much about it if you don't program international applications. (Even if you do, you still won't have to worry about it too much because Unicode was designed to make the use of non-Roman characters easy to handle.) Because Unicode was designed to handle essentially all characters in all written languages in the world, it is a 2-byte code. This allows 65,536 characters, unlike ASCII/ANSI, which is a 1-byte code allowing only 255 characters. The familiar ASCII/ANSI code that you use in Windows programming is a subset of Unicode. More precisely, it is the first 255 characters in the Unicode coding scheme. Thus, character codes like 'a', '1', and '[' are valid Unicode characters. Unicode characters are most often expressed in terms of a hexadecimal encoding scheme that runs from '\u0000' to '\uFFFF' (with '\u0000' to '\u00FF' being the ordinary ASCII/ANSI characters). The \u prefix indicates a Unicode value.

Besides the \u escape character that denotes a Unicode character, Java allows you to use the following escape sequences for special characters

\b	backspace	\u0008
\t	tab	\u0009
\n	linefeed	\u000a
\r	carriage return	\u000d
\"	double quote	\u0022
\'	single quote	\u0027
\\	a backslash	\u005c

C++ NOTE: In C and C++, char denotes an *integral* type, namely 1-byte integers. The standard is coy about the exact range. It can be either 0...255 or –128...127. In Java, char data are not numbers. Converting from numbers to characters requires an explicit cast in Java, but chars can be considered as integers if need be without an explicit cast.

Boolean

The boolean type has two values, false and true. It is used for logical testing using the relational operators that Java, like any programming language, supports.

C++ NOTE: In C, there is no Boolean type. Instead, the convention is that any non-zero value denotes true, and zero denotes false. In C++, a Boolean type (called bool, not boolean) has recently been added to the language standard. It, too, has values false and true, but for historical reasons conversions between Boolean values and integers are allowed, and you can still use numbers or pointers in test conditions. In Java, you cannot convert between numbers and Boolean values, not even with a cast.

VB NOTE: In VB any non-zero value is regarded as true and zero is regarded as false. This simply will not work in Java—you cannot use a number where a Boolean value is needed.

Variables

Java, like C++ and Pascal-based languages, requires you to declare the type of a variable. (Of course, good programming practice in VB would require this as well.) You declare a variable by placing the type first, followed by the name of the variable. Here are some examples:

```
byte b; // for space sensitive considerations
int anIntegerVariable;
long aLongVariable; // for the national debt in pennies
char ch;
```

Notice the semicolon at the end of each declaration (and the comment in the first line). The semicolon is necessary because a declaration is a complete Java expression.

You cannot use a Java reserved word for a variable name. (See Appendix I for a list of reserved words.) The rules for a variable name are as follows:

A name must begin with a letter and be a sequence of letters or digits. A letter is defined as 'A'–'Z', 'a'–'z', '_', '$', or any Unicode character that denotes a letter in a language. For example, German users can use umlauts such as 'ä' in variable names. Digits are '0'–'9' and any Unicode characters that denote a digit in a language. Symbols like '+' or '©' cannot be used inside variable names. *All* characters in the name of a variable are significant and *case is also significant*. The length of a variable name is essentially unlimited.

You can include multiple declarations on a single line

```
int i, j; //both are integers unlike in VB!
```

but we generally comment and initialize each variable separately and so prefer declarations on separate lines.

Assignments and Initializations

After you declare a variable, you should assign it a value: explicitly initialize a variable by means of an assignment statement—you should never have uninitialized variables. (And the compiler will usually prevent you from having them anyway.) You assign to a previously declared variable using the variable name on the left, an equal sign (=), and then some Java expression that has an appropriate value on the right.

```
int foo; // this is a declaration
foo = 37; // this is an assignment
```

Here's an example of an assignment to a character variable:

```
char yesChar;
yesChar = 'Y';
```

Notice that chars (unlike strings) use single quotes to identify the character. It is also possible to use a direct hexadecimal representation of a Unicode char. To do this, you must translate the Unicode character number into a four digit hexadecimal code—and you must use the two leading zeros. For example, a capital "A" has Unicode (and ASCII/ANSI, of course) code decimal 65 = hex 41. If you wanted to use the code for the character, you could use:

```
char capitalA;
capitalA = '\u0041'; // decimal 65
```

Finally, in Java you can put declarations anywhere in your code, but you can only declare a variable once in any block in a method. (See the section on Control Flow in this chapter for more on blocks.)

> VB NOTE: One nice feature of Java that it inherited from C/C++ is the ability to both declare and initialize a variable on the same line. (This is usually called a definition of a variable and is not technically an assignment.) This is also done with an = sign. For example:
>
> ```
> int i = 10; // we will countdown with this
> ```

Conversions between Numeric Types

Java does not have any trouble multiplying, say, an integer by a double—it will treat the result as a double. More generally, any binary operations on numeric variables of different types will be acceptable and be treated in the following fashion:

- If any of the operands is of type `double`, the other one will be treated as a `double` for the scope of the operation.

- Otherwise, if any of the operands is of type `float`, the other one will be treated as a `float`.

- Otherwise, if any of the operands is of type `long`, the other one will be treated as a `long`.

This works similarly down the line of the integer types: int, short and byte.

On the other hand, there are obviously times when you want to consider a `double` as an integer. All numeric conversions are possible in Java but, of course, information may be lost. These conversions are usually done by means of *casts*. The syntax for casting is to give the target type in parentheses, followed by the variable name. For example:

```
double x = 9.997;
int nx = (int) x;
```

Then the variable nx has the value 9, as casting a floating-point value to an integer discards the fractional part.

> NOTE: Java does not complain ("throw an exception" in Java-speak—see Chapter 10) if you try to cast a number of one type to another that is out of the range for the target type. The result will be a truncated number that has a different value. It is, therefore, a good idea to explicitly test that the value is in the correct range before you perform the cast.

59

C++ NOTE: You cannot cast between Boolean values and any numeric type.

Finally, Java allows you to make certain assignment conversions by assigning the value of a variable of one type to another without an explicit cast. Those that are permitted are

byte →short →int →long →float →double

where you can always assign a variable of a type that is to the left to the type on its right in the list above.

Constants

Java has only very limited ways for defining constants. In particular, you cannot define local constants for an individual method like `main`. Instead, you can only have constants that are available to all the methods in the class. These are usually called *class constants*. The keywords used in this incantation will be explained in Chapter 4, but here is an example of using a class constant:

```
class UsesConstants
{ public static final double g = 32;
    // gravitation in feet/second squared;
  public static void main(String[] args)
  {  System.out.println(g + " feet per second squared");
  }
}
```

Note that the definition appears before the function header that defines the `main` function and must use the keywords `static final`.

C++ NOTE: `const` is a reserved Java keyword, but it is not currently used for anything. You must use `public static final` for a global constant. For a local constant, just pretend it is a variable.

Operators

The usual arithmetic operators `+ - * /` are used in Java for addition, subtraction, multiplication, and division. The `/` operator denotes integer division if both arguments are integers, and floating-point division otherwise. Integer remainder (i.e., the mod function) is denoted by `%`. For example, `15 / 4` is 3, `15 % 2` is 1, and `11.0 / 4` is 2.75. You can use the arithmetic operators in your variable initializations:

```
int n = 5;
int a = 2 * n; // a is 10
```

There is actually a shortcut for using binary arithmetic operators in an assignment. For example,

```
x += 4;
```

is equivalent to

```
x = x + 4;
```

(In general, place the operator to the left of the = sign.)

Exponentiation

Unlike languages like VB, Java has no operator for raising a quantity to a power: you must use the pow function. The pow function is part of the Math class in Java.lang that contains most of the standard math functions one would want, so one way of using it is via the incantation

```
y = Math.pow(x, a);
```

which gives you x raised to the a'th power. The pow function takes arguments that are both of type double.

Increment and Decrement Operators

Programmers, of course, know that one of the most common operations with a numeric variable is to add or subtract one. Java, following in the footsteps of C and C++, has both increment and decrement operators: x++ adds one to the current value of the variable x, and x-- subtracts one from it. For example, the code

```
int n = 12;
n++;
```

changes n to 13. Because these operators change the value of a variable, they cannot be applied to numbers themselves. For example, 4++ is not a legal statement.

There are actually two forms of these operators; you have seen the "postfix", i.e., after the variable form. There is also a prefix form, ++n. Both change the value of the variable by one. The difference between the two only appears when they are used inside expressions. The prefix form does the addition first, the postfix form evaluates to the old value of the variable.

```
int m = 7;
int n = 7;
int a = 2 * ++m; // now a is 16, m is 8
int b = 2 * n++; // now b is 14, n is 8
```

We recommend against using ++ inside other expressions as this often leads to annoying bugs that are hard to track down. Of course, while it is the ++ operator that gives the C++ language its name, it also led to the first joke made by anti-C++ programmers who have long complained about the bug-ridden code that is too often produced by sloppy C++ coding. This joke points out that even the name of the language contains a bug: "After all, it should really be called ++C, since we only want to use a language after it has been improved." Java programmers, on the other hand, really are dealing with a ++C. This is because Java really does make it easier to produce bug-free code. It does this by eliminating many of C++ more bug-prone features such as pointer arithmetic, memory allocation, and null-terminated arrays of chars. (Of course, it does retain the murky side effects of prefix and postfix ++.)

Relational and Boolean Operators

The value of a variable or expression is compared with a double equals sign, `==`. For example, the value of

```
(3==7)
```

is `false`

VB NOTE: It is important to remember that Java uses different symbols for assignment and equality.

C++ NOTE: Java eliminates the possibility of bugs resulting from the use of the `=` sign when you meant the `==`. A line that begins `if (k=0)` won't even compile since this evaluates to the integer 0, which doesn't convert to a Boolean value in Java.

Use a `!=`   for inequality
```
(3 != 7)
```
is `true`.

Finally, you have the usual `<` (less than), `>` (greater than), `<=` (less than or equal), and `>=` (greater than or equal) operators.

Java, following C++, uses `&&` for the *and* operator and `||` for the *or* operator. As you can easily remember from the `!=` operator, the exclamation point is the negation operator. The `&&` and `||` operators are evaluated in "short-circuit" fashion. This means that when you have something like:

```
A && B
```

once the truth value of the expression `A` has been determined to be false, the value for the expression `B` is *not* calculated. (See the sections on conditionals for an example of where this is useful.)

Bitwise Operators

When working with any of the integer types, you have operators that can work directly with the bits that make up the integers. This means that you can use masking techniques to get at individual bits. The bitwise operators are:

   & ("and")

   | ("or"),

   ^ ("xor"),

   ~ ("not")

VB NOTE: Remember that ^ is the xor operator and not the power operator.

These operators work on bit patterns. For example, if foo is an integer variable, then

```
int thirdBit = (foo&8)/8;
```

gives you a one if the fourth bit from the right in the binary representation of foo is on, and a zero if not. This technique lets you mask out all but a single bit when need be.

There are also >> and << operators, which shift a bit pattern to the right or left. There is no need to use these operators to divide and multiply by powers of two, though. Compilers are almost certainly smart enough to change multiplication by powers of two into the appropriate shift operators. There is even a >>> operator that fills the top bits with zero, whereas >> extends the sign bit into the top bits. There is no <<< operator.

C++ NOTE: In C/C++, there is no guarantee as to whether >> performs an arithmetic shift (extending the sign bit) or a logical shift (filling in with zeroes). Implementors are free to choose whatever is more efficient. That means, the C/C++ >> operator is really only defined for non-negative numbers. Java removes that ambiguity.

Parentheses and Operator Hierarchy

As in all programming languages, you are best off using parentheses to indicate the order in which you want operations to be carried out. However, in Java the hierarchy of operations is as follows:

[] . () (method call)	left to right
! ~ ++ -- + (unary) - (unary) () (cast) new	right to left
* / %	left to right

`+ -`	left to right
`<< >> >>>`	left to right
`< <= > >= instanceof`	left to right
`== !=`	left to right
`&`	left to right
`^`	left to right
`|`	left to right
`&&`	left to right
`||`	left to right
`?:`	left to right
`= += -= *= /= %= &= |= ^= <<= >>= >>>=`	right to left

If no parentheses are used, operations are performed in the hierarchical order indicated. Operators on the same level are processed from left to right, except for those that are right associative, as indicated in the table above.

C++ NOTE: Unlike C or C++, Java does not have a comma operator. However, you can use a *comma separated list of expressions* in the first and third slot of a `for` statement.

Strings

Strings are sequences of characters, such as `"hello"`. Java does not have a built-in string type. Instead, the standard Java library contains a predefined class called, naturally enough, `String` that contains most of what you want.

```
String e = ""; // an empty string
String greeting = "Hello";
```

Concatenation

Java, like most programming languages, allows you to use the + sign to join (concatenate) two strings together.

```
String expletive = "Expletive";
String PG13 = "deleted";
String message = expletive + PG13;
```

The above code makes the value of the string variable message `"Expletivedeleted"`. (Note the lack of a space between the words: the + sign joins two strings together in the order received, *exactly* as they are given.)

When you concatenate a string with a value that is not a string, the latter is converted to a string. (As we will see in Chapter 5, every Java object can be converted to a string.) For example:

```
String rating = "PG" + 13;
```
sets `rating` to the string `"PG13"`.

This feature is commonly used in output statements.

```
System.out.println("The answer is " + answer);
```

is perfectly acceptable and will print what one would want (and with the correct spacing because of the space after `is`).

> VB NOTE: Although Java will convert a number to a string when concatenating with another string, it does not add a space in front of a positive value.

Substrings

You extract a substring from a larger string with the `substring` method of the `String` class. For example,

```
String greeting = "Hello";
String s = greeting.substring(0, 4);
```

creates a string consisting of the characters `"Hell"`. Java counts strings in a peculiar fashion: the first character in a string has position 0, just like in C and C++. (In C, there was a technical reason for counting positions starting at 0, but that reason has long gone away, and only the nuisance remains.)

For example, the character `'H'` has position 0 in the string `"Hello"`, and the character `'o'` has position 4. The second argument of `substring` is the first position that you *do not* want to copy. In our case, we want to copy the characters in positions 0, 1, 2, and 3 (from position 0 to position 3 inclusive). As `substring` counts it, this means from position 0 inclusive to position 4 *exclusive*.

There is one advantage to the way `substring` works: It is easy to compute the length of the substring. The string `s.substring(a, b)` always has `b - a` characters. For example, the substring `"Hell"` has length 4 – 0 = 4.

String Editing

To find out the length of a string, use the `length` method. For example:

```
String greeting = "Hello";
int n = greeting.length(); // is 5.
```

Just as `char` denotes a Unicode character, `String` denotes a sequence of Unicode characters. It is possible to get at individual characters of a string. For example, `s.charAt(n)` returns the Unicode character at position n, where n is between 0 and `s.length()` – 1.

However, you can't *change* a character in the string. If you want to turn greeting into "Help!", you cannot change the third position of greeting into a 'p' and the fourth position into a '!'. If you are a C programmer, this will make you feel pretty helpless. How are you going to modify the string? In Java, it is quite easy: take the substring that you want to keep and concatenate it with the characters that you want to replace.

```
greeting = greeting.substring(0, 3) + "p!";
```

This changes the current value of the greeting variable to "Help!".

Since you cannot change the individual characters in a Java string, the documentation refers to the objects of the String class as being *immutable*. You should think of them as first-class objects just like the number 3 is always 3, and the string "Hello" will always contain the character sequence 'H', 'e', 'l', 'l', 'o'. You cannot change these values. You can, however, change the contents of the string *variable* greeting, and make it refer to a different string. (Just as you can make a numeric variable currently holding the value 3 hold the value 4.)

Isn't that a lot less efficient? It would seem simpler to change the characters than to build up a whole new string from scratch. Well, yes and no. Indeed it isn't efficient to generate a new string that holds the concatenation of "Hel" and "p!". But immutable strings have one great advantage: The compiler can arrange that strings are *shared*.

To understand how this works, think of the various strings as sitting on the heap. (For non C/C++ programmers, think of them as just being located in memory somewhere.) String variables then point to locations on the heap. For example, the substring greeting.substring(0, 3) is just a pointer to the existing "Hello" string, together with the range of characters that are used in the substring. Overall, the designers of Java decided that the efficiency of string-sharing outweighs the inefficiency of immutability.

Look at your own programs; we suspect that most of the time, you don't change strings—you just compare them. Of course, there are some cases in which direct manipulation of strings is more efficient. (One example is when assembling strings from individual characters that come from a file or the keyboard.) For these situations, Java provides a separate StringBuffer class that we describe in Chapter 11. If you are not concerned with the efficiency of string handling (which is not a bottleneck in many Java applications anyway), you can ignore StringBuffer and just use String.

66

C++ NOTE: C programmers generally are bewildered when they see Java strings for the first time, because they think of strings as arrays of characters:

```
char greeting[] = "Hello";
```

That is the wrong analogy: a Java string is roughly analogous to a `char*` pointer,

```
char* greeting = "Hello";
```

When you replace `greeting` with another string, the Java code does roughly the following:

```
char* temp = malloc(6);
strncpy(temp, greeting, 3);
strcpy(temp + 3, "p!");
greeting = temp;
```

Sure, now `greeting` points to the string `"Help!"`. And even the most hardened C programmer must admit that the Java syntax is more pleasant than a sequence of `strncpy` calls. But what if we make another assignment to `greeting`?

```
greeting = "Howdy";
```

Don't we have a memory leak? After all, the `"Help!"` string was allocated on the heap. C and C++ programmers *must* change their way of thinking because Java does automatic garbage collection. Java automatically reclaims any unused memory. If the string `"Help!"` is no longer needed, its memory will eventually be recycled.

If you are a C++ programmer and use the `string` class defined by ANSI C++, you will be much more comfortable with the Java `String` type. C++ `string` objects also perform automatic allocation and deallocation of memory. The memory management is performed explicitly by constructors, assignment operators, and destructors. However, C++ strings are mutable—you can modify individual characters in a string.

Testing Strings for Equality

To test whether or not two strings are equal, use the `equals` method,

```
s.equals(t)
```

returns `true` if the strings `s` and `t` are equal, `false` otherwise. For the `equals` method, `s` and `t` can be string variables or string constants. For example,

```
"Hello".equals(command)
```

is perfectly legal.

CAUTION: Do *not* use the == operator to find out if two strings are equal! It only determines whether or not the strings are stored in the same location.

Sure, if the strings are in the same location, they must be equal. But it is entirely possible to store multiple copies of identical strings in different places.

```
String greeting = "Hello"; //initialize greeting to a string
if (greeting == "Hello") . . . // probably true
if (greeting.substring(0, 4) == "Hell") . . . // probably false
```

If the compiler would always arrange for equal strings to be shared, then you could use == for testing equality, but it doesn't and you can't. (The trouble is that string storage is implementation dependent. The standard implementation only shares string constants, not strings that are the result of operations like + or substring.) Therefore, *never* use == to compare strings.

C++ NOTE: If you are used to the C++ string class, you have to be particularly careful about equality testing. That class does overload the == operator to test for equality of the string contents. It is pretty silly that Java goes out of its way to give strings the same "look and feel" as numeric values, but then makes strings behave like pointers for equality testing. The language designers could have redefined == for strings, just as they made a special arrangement for +. Oh well, every language has its share of inconsistencies.

C programmers never use == to compare strings, but use strcmp instead. The Java function compareTo is the exact analog to strcmp. You can use

```
    if (greeting.compareTo("Help") == 0) . . .
```

but it seems clearer to use equals instead.

To test if two strings are identical except for the upper/lowercase letter distinction, use the equalsIgnoreCase method.

Directions for Using the Console Class

Before we go on (so that we can give you some examples that are at least somewhat non-trivial!) this sidebar shows you the incantations needed in order to use the Console class to get various kinds of prompted input from the keyboard. The Console class has three methods. These methods let you:

- capture an integer by a prompted input,
- capture a floating-point number with a prompted input,
- capture a string or word by a prompted input.

The Console class may be found in the corejava subdirectory of the CoreJavaBook code that you can install from the CD. To use the Console class, it is important that you set up your CLASSPATH environment variable as described in Chapter 2.

Core Java

Directions for Using the Console Class (continued)

Be sure to add the line: `import corejava.*;` to each program that uses the Console class. Then you can use this class as in the following example:

```
import corejava.*;
public class StringPromptSample
{   public static void main(String[] args)
    {   String yourName;
        yourName = Console.readString
            ("Please enter your name.");
        System.out.println("Hello " + yourName);
    }
}
```

If you compile and run this program you will see that the `readString` method displays the string prompt and grabs the text the user enters before he or she hits the ENTER key.

More generally you will have the following methods available to you (all use a string prompt):

`readWord ()` reads the string until the first space is entered.

`readInt (String prompt)` reads an integer. If you do not enter an integer, it reprompts you to enter the integer correctly.

`readDouble (String prompt)` reads a floating-point number in the double range. If you do not enter a float it reprompts you to do so.

All these functions can be "broken out of" by hitting the CTRL+C combination, which kills any Java application under Windows or Unix.

A Mortgage Calculator

As our first semi-serious application for Java, let's write a program that calculates the cost of a mortgage. We will use our `Console` class to prompt the user to enter the principal amount, the term in years, and the interest rate. The program will then output the mortgage amount per month.

NOTE: We use the following standard formula to calculate the mortgage payment.

$$\frac{Principal \times MonthlyInterest}{(1 - (1/(1 + MonthlyInterest)^{Years \times 12}))}$$

Example 3-2 shows the code.

Example 3-2: Mortgage.java

```java
import corejava.*;
public class Mortgage
{  public static void main(String[] args)
   {  double principal;
      double yearlyInterest;
      int years;

      principal = Console.readDouble
         ("Loan amount (no commas):");
      yearlyInterest = Console.readDouble
         ("Interest rate in % (ex: use 7.5 for 7.5%):")/100;
      years = Console.readInt("The number of years:");

      double monthlyInterest = yearlyInterest / 12;
      double payment = principal * monthlyInterest
         / (1 - (Math.pow(1/(1 + monthlyInterest), years * 12)));
      System.out.println("Your payment is " + payment);
   }
}
```

Control Flow

Java, like any programming language, supports both conditional statements and loops to determine control flow. We start with the conditional statements and then move on to loops. We end with the somewhat cumbersome switch statement that can be used when you have many values of a single expression to test for. Before we get into the actual controls structures, you need to know more about *blocks*.

A block is any number of simple Java statements that are surrounded by a pair of braces. Blocks define the scope of your variables. However, it is not possible to declare identically named variables in two different blocks in the same method that exist at the same time.

NOTE: Since the scope of a variable starts at the place it was declared and goes to the end of the block in which it was declared, if you want to have a variable accessible to all the code in a method like main, you must declare it before you start a new block.

C++ NOTE: The Java control flow constructs are identical to those in C and C++, with one exception. There is no goto, but there is a "labelled" version of break that you can use to break out of a nested loop (where you perhaps would have used a goto in C).

Conditional Statements

The simplest conditional statement in Java has the form

```
if (condition) statement;
```

but in Java, as in most programming languages, you will often want to execute multiple statements when a single condition is true. In this case, the conditional takes the form:

```
if (condition) { block }
```

The condition must be surrounded by parentheses, and here the "block" is, as indicated before, any number of statements that are surrounded by a pair of braces. (See Figure 3-1). For example:

```
if (yourSales >= target)
{   performance = "Satisfactory";
    bonus = 100;
}
```

Figure 3-1: Flowchart for the if statement

Here all the statements surrounded by the braces will be executed when yourSales is greater than or equal to target.

VB NOTE: A block (sometimes called a *compound statement*) allows you to have more than one (simple) statement in any Java programming structure that might otherwise have a single (simple) statement.

The more general conditional in Java looks like this (see Figure 3-2):

> if (*condition*) statement else *statement*;

or, more likely,

> if (*condition*) {*block₁*} else {*block₂*}

For example:

```
if (yourSales >= target)
{   performance = "Satisfactory";
    bonus = 100 + 0.01 *(yourSales - target);
}
else
{   performance = "Unsatisfactory";
    bonus = 0;
}
```

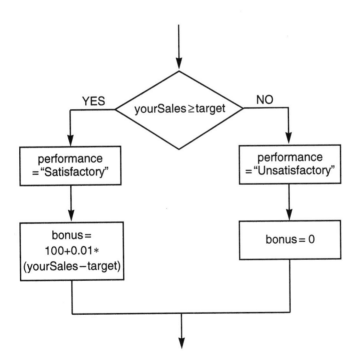

Figure 3-2: Flowchart for the if/else statement

The else part is always optional (see Figure 3-3). An else groups with the closest if. For example:

```
if {yourSales >= 2*target)
{   performance = "Excellent";
    bonus = 1000;
}
```

```
else if {yourSales >= 1.5*target)
{   performance = "Fine";
    bonus = 500;
}
else if (yourSales >= target)
{   performance = "Satisfactory";
    bonus = 100;
}
else
{   System.out.println("You're fired");
}
```

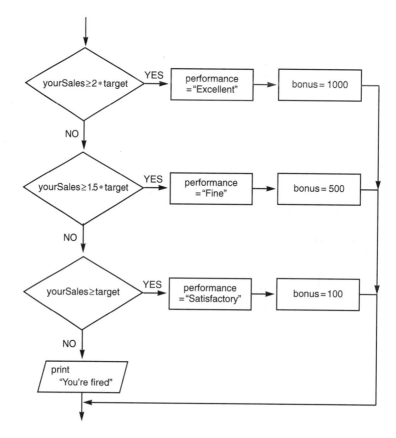

Figure 3-3: Flowchart for `if/else if` (multiple branches)

NOTE: Because of the short circuit evaluation built into Java,

```
if (x != 0 && 1 / x > 0) // no problems ever
```

does not evaluate `1 / x` if x is zero, and so cannot lead to a divide-by-zero error.

Finally, Java supports the ternary ? operator that is occassionally useful. The expression condition ? e1 : e2 evaluates to e1 if the condition is true, to e2 otherwise: For example: (x < = y) ? x : y gives the smaller of x and y (or x if x = y).

Indeterminate Loops

In Java, as in all programming languages, there are control structures that let you repeat statements. There are two forms for repeating loops that are best when you do not know how many times a loop should be processed (these are "indeterminate loops").

First, there is the *while* loop that only executes the body of the loop while a condition is true. The general form is:

```
while (condition) { block };
```

The while loop may never execute it if the condition is false at the outset (see Figure 3-4). In Example 3-3, let's use our Console class to determine how long it will take to save a specific amount of money, assuming you get a specified interest rate per year and deposit the same amount of money per year:

Example 3-3: Retirement.java

```
import corejava.*
public class Retirement
{  public static void main(String[] args)
   {   double goal;
       double interest;
       double payment;
       int years = 0;
       double balance = 0;

       goal = Console.readDouble
          ("How much money do you need to retire?");
       payment = Console.readDouble
          ("How much money will you contribute every year?");
       interest = Console.readDouble
          ("Interest rate in % (ex: use 7.5 for 7.5%):") / 100;
       while (balance < goal)
       {   balance = (balance + payment) * (1 + interest);
           years++;
       }

       System.out.println("You can retire in " + years
          + " years.");
   }
}
```

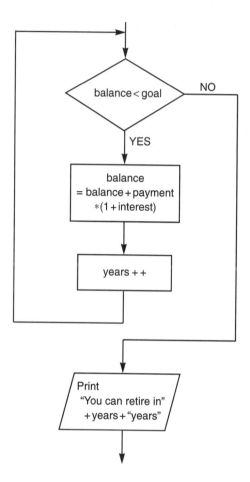

Figure 3-4: Flowchart for while statement

In this case, we are incrementing a counter and updating the amount currently accumulated in the body of the loop until the total exceeds the targeted amount. (Don't rely on this program to plan for your retirement. We left out a few niceties such as inflation and your life expectancy.)

A while loop tests at the top. Therefore, the code in the block may never be executed. If you want to make sure a block is executed at least once, you will need to move the test to the bottom. This is done with the do version of a while loop. Its syntax looks like this:

```
do { block } while (condition);
```

This executes the block and only then tests the condition. It then repeats the block and retests the condition, and so on. For instance, the code in Example 3-4 computes an approximation to the square root of any positive number, using an iterative process. Figure 3-5 illustrates this.

Example 3-4: SquareRoot.java

```java
import corejava.*
public class SquareRoot
{  public static void main(String[] args)
   {  double a = Console.readDouble("Please enter a number:");

      double xnew = a / 2;
      double xold;

      do
      {  xold = xnew;
         xnew = (xold + a / xold) / 2;
         System.out.println(xnew);
      }
      while (Math.abs(xnew - xold) > 1E-4);
   }
}
```

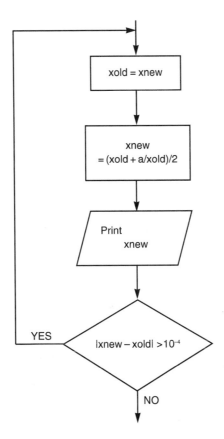

Figure 3-5: Flowchart for do/while statement

Finally, since a block may contain *any* Java statements, you can nest loops as deeply as you want.

Determinate Loops

Java, like C++, has a very general construct to support iteration. As Figure 3-6 shows, the following prints the numbers from 1 to 10 on the screen.

```
for (int i = 1; i <= 10; i++)
    System.out.println(i);
```

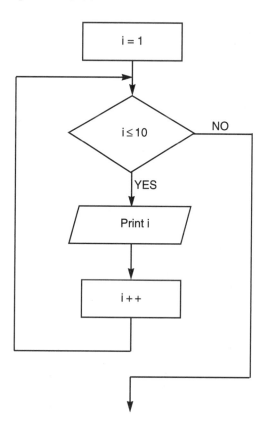

Figure 3-6: Flowchart for `for` statement

The idea is that the first slot of the `for` statement will (usually) hold the counter initialization. (The first slot is occasionally declared and initialized there as in this example). The second slot gives the condition for which to test the loop, and the third slot explains how to change the state of the counter. What follows the initialization can be a simple Java statement or a block. (Thus, nested `for` loops are possible in Java.)

Although Java, like C++, allows almost any expression in the various slots of a `for` loop, it is an unwritten rule of good taste that the three slots of a `for` statement should only initialize, test, and update a counter variable. One can write very obscure loops by disregarding this rule.

Even within the bounds of good taste, much is possible. This is because you can have variables of any type and use any method of updating them, so you can have loops that count down:

```
for (int i = 10; i > 0; i--)
    System.out.println("Counting down " + i);
System.out.println("Blastoff!");
```

Or you can have loops in which the variables and increments are of one of the floating-point types.

NOTE: Again, be careful about testing for equality of floating-point numbers. A `for` loop that looks like this

```
for (x = 0; x != 10; x += 0.01)
```

may never end.

Example 3-5 shows a reasonable use of floating-point numbers in a loop by extending the mortgage program to print out the monthly payments for a range of interest rates around the entered value that go up and down by ⅛%.

Example 3-5: MortgageLoop.java

```
import corejava.*;
public class MortgageLoop
{  public static void main(String[] args)
   {  double principal;
      double yearlyInterest;
      int years;

      principal = Console.readDouble("Loan amount (no commas):");
      yearlyInterest = Console.readDouble
         ("Interest rate in % (ex: use 7.5 for 7.5%):") / 100;
      years = Console.readInt("The number of years:");

      double y;
      for (y = yearlyInterest - 0.01; y <= yearlyInterest +
         0.01; y += 0.00125)
      {  double monthlyInterest = y / 12;
         double payment = principal * monthlyInterest
            / (1 - (Math.pow(1/(1 + monthlyInterest), years *
               12)));
```

```
      Format.print(System.out, "With rate %6.3f", 100 * y);
      Format.print(System.out, "%%, your monthly payment is
         $%10.2f\n", payment);
   }
  }
}
```

When you declare a variable in the first slot of the `for` statement, the scope of such a variable extends until the end of the body of the `for` loop. In particular, if you do this, you cannot use that value of this variable outside the loop. Therefore, if you wish to use the end value of a loop counter outside the `for` loop, be sure to declare it outside the header for the loop!

Of course, a `for` loop is equivalent to a `while` loop; choose the one that fits your picture of the situation. More precisely,

```
 for (statement₁; expression₁; expression₂) { block };
```

is completely equivalent to:

```
 {   statement₁;
     while (expression₁)
     {   block;
         expression₂;
     }
 }
```

Multiple Selections—the Switch Statement

The `if/else` construct can be cumbersome when you have to deal with multiple selections with many alternatives. Unfortunately, the only alternative available in Java is almost just as cumbersome—it is not nearly as neat as VB's Select Case statement, which allows you to test for ranges or for values in any type. Java, following the lead of C/C++, calls the device for multiple selection a `switch` statement. Unfortunately, the designers didn't improve on C/C++'s switch statement. You still can select only against all the integer types but `long` or against a `char`. You still cannot use a range of values.

For example, if you set up a menuing system with four alternatives like that in Figure 3-7, you could use code that looks like this:

```
int choice = Console.readInt
("Select an option (1 to 4)");
// reads one keypress
switch(choice)
{  case 1:
      . . .
      break;
   case 2:
      . . .
      break;
   case 3:
```

```
      . . .
    break;
case 4:
      . . .
    break;
default:
    // bad input
    break;
}
```

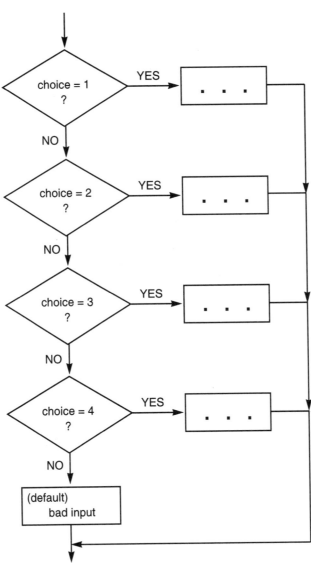

Figure 3-7: Flowchart for `switch` **statement**

Unlike in languages like VB, it is possible for multiple switches to be triggered because execution falls through to another case unless a break keyword gets you out of the whole switch statement. (It is extremely unusual to use a switch statement without a break keyword in every case. In the extremely rare situation where you want the "fall through" behavior, you ought to clearly comment it.)

In general, execution starts at the case label, matching the value on which the selection is performed, and continues until the next break, or the end of the switch. The default clause is optional.

Labeled Breaks

Although the designers of Java kept the goto as a reserved word, they decided not to include it in the language. In general, goto statements are considered poor style. Some programmers feel the anti-goto forces have gone too far (see for example the famous article of Donald Knuth called "Structured Programming with goto's"). They argue that unrestricted use of goto is error-prone, but that an occasional jump *out of a loop* is beneficial. The Java designers agreed and even added a new statement to support this programming style, the labeled break.

Let us first look at the unlabeled break statement. The same break statement that you use to exit a switch can also be used to break out of a loop. For example,

```
while (years <= 100)
{  balance = (balance + payment) * (1 + interest);
   if (balance > goal) break;
   years++;
}
```

Now the loop is exited if either years > 100 on the top of the loop or balance > goal in the middle of the loop. Of course, you could have achieved the same effect without a break. You would need an if/else inside the loop and another termination condition in the loop header.

Unlike C/C++, Java also offers a *labeled break* statement that lets you break out of multiple nested loops. The reason for this is simple: occasionally something weird happens inside a deeply nested loop. In that case, you may want to break completely out of all the nested loops. It is inconvenient to program that simply by adding extra conditions.

Here's an example that shows this at work. (Notice that the label must precede the outermost loop out of which you want to break. It also must be followed by a colon (:))

```
int n;
read_data:
```

```
while(. . .)
{  . . .
   for (. . .)
   {  n = Console.readInt(. . .);
      if (n < 0) // should never happen—can't continue
         break read_data;
      // break out of read_data loop
      . . .
   }
}
// check for sucess or failure here
if (n < 0)
{   // deal with bad situation
}
else
{  // got here normally
}
```

If there was a bad input, the labeled break moves past the end of the labeled block. As with any use of the break statement, you then need to test if the loop exited normally or as a result of a break.

Directions for Using the Format Class

Not only did we give you a console class to read characters from the screen, we also supply you with a class that can format output nicely. Java's idea of floating-point output is "no trailing zeroes, up to six digits of precision". That makes it tough to format dollars and cents like 1141.30. Rather than reinvent the wheel, we simply reimplemented the C `printf` function that has a good set of formatting options and is, for the most part, easy to use. For example, to format a floating-point number with a field width of 10 and two digits after the decimal point, you use

```
Format.print(System.out, "Your monthly payment is %10.2f\n",
   payment);
```

That sends a string like

```
"Your monthly payment is    1141.30\n"
```

to `System.out`. If you'd rather capture that string in a string variable, use

```
String s = new Format("Your monthly payment is %10.2f\n")
   .form(payment);
```

The output string contains all characters of the format string, except that the format specification (starting with a %) is replaced by the formatted value. However, a %% denotes a percent sign.

Directions for Using the Format Class (continued)

Unlike the `printf` statement in C, you can only have one formatted value at a time. If you need to print two values, use two calls.

```
Format.print(System.out, "With rate %6.3f", 100 * y);
Format.print(System.out, "%%, your monthly payment is
   %10.2f\n", payment);
```

Apart from the $\%m.nf$ format, the most common format is $\%nd$, to print an integer in a field with width n. Those two will get you a long way, and you may never need to learn more about the formatting codes.

Here are the rules for the formatting specifiers. The code starts with % and ends with one of the letters c, d, e, E, f, g, G, i, o, s, x, X. They have the following meanings:

f	floating-point number in fixed format
e, E	floating-point number in exponential notation (scientific format). The E format results in an uppercase E for the exponent (1.14130E+003), the e format in a lowercase e.
g, G	floating-point number in general format (fixed format for small numbers, exponential format for large numbers). Trailing zeroes are suppressed. The G format results in an uppercase E for the exponent (if any), the g format in a lowercase e.
d, i	integer in decimal
x	integer in hexadecimal
o	integer in octal
s	string
c	character

In between the % and the format code are the following fields. They are all optional.

+	forces display of + for positive numbers
0	show leading zeroes
–	align left in the field
space	prepend a space in front of positive numbers
#	use "alternate" format. Add 0 or 0x for octal or hexadecimal numbers. Don't suppress trailing zeroes in general floating point format.

Finally, to use our `Format` class you must also add the `import corejava.*` before any class that will use it.

Class Methods (User-Defined Functions)

Like any programming language, Java has a way of breaking down complex tasks into simpler tasks via user-defined gadgets (traditionally called *functions*). Every modern programming language takes pride in introducing a new terminology for these gadgets. As mentioned previously, in Java the terminology *method* is used instead of functions. (Well, it is used most of the time; the designers and documenters are somewhat inconsistent. They occasionally slip and use the C/C++ function terminology.) We will follow in the footsteps of the designers of Java and use the term *method* with an occasional slip when it seems appropriate. (In the next chapter, we will try to survey the ideas behind Object-Oriented Programming that lead to the multitude of possible terminologies.)

A method definition must occur inside a class. It can occur anywhere inside the class, although custom places all the other methods of a class before the `main` method. There are many types of methods, but in this chapter we will only use those that, like `main`, are `public static`. For now, don't worry about what this means—it has to do with which other methods can use a method—we will explain the terminology in the next chapter.

C++ NOTE: Java does not have "global" functions. All functions must be defined inside a class. The functions we study in this chapter don't yet operate on objects and are, therefore, defined as `static`. Except for visibility issues, there is no difference between a C function and a `static` Java method.

For example, suppose we want to write a program that computes the odds on winning any lottery that requires bettors to choose a certain number of numbers from the range 1 to n. For example, if you must match six numbers from the numbers 1 to 50, then there are $(50 \cdot 49 \cdot 48 \cdot 47 \cdot 46 \cdot 45)/(1 \cdot 2 \cdot 3 \cdot 4 \cdot 5 \cdot 6)$ possible outcomes, so your chance is 1 in 15,890,700. Good luck!

Just in case someone asks you to participate in a "pick 7 out of 38" lottery, you will want a method that computes the odds. Later we'll put it together with a `main` function that asks you for how many numbers you need to choose and then asks for the highest number from which to draw.

Here's the method:

```java
public static long lotteryOdds(int high, int number)
{   long r = 1;
    int i;
    for (i = 1; i <= number; i++)
    {   r = r * high / i;
        high--;
    }
    return r;
}
```

Notice the header for the lotteryOdds:

```
public static long lotteryOdds(int high, int number)
```

In general, the header for a method starts with keywords—in our case, `public static`—that explain the scope of the method. Next, the method header lists the type of the returned value. In our case, a `long`. Next comes the name of the method, and finally the types and names of its arguments.

After the header comes the code that implements the method. Notice the brace structure in the example above: the outermost braces (that start after the function header) mark off what is traditionally called the *body*. Variables declared inside a method (like the `int i` for the loop counter in our `lotteryOdds`) are *local* to the method. They can neither be accessed nor contaminate any similarly named variables in the other methods of the class. More precisely, when a method is called, the local variables for all function arguments are initialized as indicated in the body of the method, and the memory for them will automatically be reclaimed. Within a method, of course, the scope of a variable is determined by the block in which it is declared.

The `return` statement causes an immediate exit from the method. The expression following the `return` keyword is the method result. Methods in Java can return values of any Java type. On the other hand, methods need not return any value. In this case, the return type is `void`. (Functions that do this are commonly referred to as procedures.)

Example 3-6 is an application that actually calls the `lotteryOdds` method as needed from the `main` method.

Example 3-6: LotteryOdds.java

```java
import corejava.*;
public class LotteryOdds
{  public static long lotteryOdds(int high, int number)
   {  long r = 1;
      int i;
      for (i = 1; i <= number; i++)
      {  r = r * high / i;
         high--;
      }
      return r;
   }

   public static void main(String[] args)
   {  int numbers = Console.readInt
      ("How many numbers do you need to draw?");
      int topNumber = Console.readInt
         ("What is the highest number you can draw?");
      long oddsAre = lotteryOdds(topNumber, numbers);
```

```
        System.out.println("Your odds are 1 in " + oddsAre +
          ". Good luck!");
    }
}
```

Notice how the `lotteryOdds` method is called from the `main` method in our application:

```
    long oddsAre = lotteryOdds(topNumber, numbers);
```

As you can see, method calls for user-defined methods occur (return types permitting) in any expression for which a value is required. In our case, since the method belongs to the `lotteryOdds` class, we can call the method simply by giving its name followed by the argument. (As opposed to something like `System.out.println` for which we need to give the object on which the method operates.)

When this line of code is processed, Java uses the current values of the `topNumber` and `numbers` variables and passes this information to the `lotteryOdds` method. *All arguments to methods in Java are passed by value and not by reference.* It is, therefore, *impossible* to change variables by means of method calls. In particular, you cannot write a "swap" method in Java. See Chapter 4. (On the other hand, if you are familiar with pointers, since arrays and objects in Java are actually pointers, functions can modify the contents of arrays and objects. They just can't modify numbers.)

C++ NOTE: Methods in Java are similar but not identical to functions in C++. For example, there is no analogue to function prototypes in Java. They are not required, because functions can be defined after they are used—the compiler makes multiple passes through the code. More significantly, pointer and reference arguments do not exist in Java: you cannot pass the location of a variable. Overloading function names is always possible, just like in C++.

In general, `public` methods can be called from other classes. (An example of this is our use of the `println` method, which is a public method in `PrintStream`.)

Arguments and return values in methods can be of any type. In particular, they can be arrays (see the next section) or classes (see the next chapter).

Class Variables

Occasionally, you need to declare a variable that will be accessible by all the methods in the class. (It is possible but not recommended to declare a variable that can be seen outside its class—i.e., a true global variable.) Usually these are called *class variables* because the scope of such a variable is potentially the whole class. The syntax is similar to the *class constants* that you saw earlier, and class variables are declared above the main method using the following syntax.

```
class Employee
{
    private static double socialSecurityRate = 7.62;
    public static void main(String[] args)
    { . . .}
}
```

Class variables can be shadowed by variables of the same name declared in a block inside a method of the class. (Although this is a rather strange way to program.)

It is also possible to call a method that has a void return type simply for its side effects—for example, the change in the state of the class variables. This is done simply by giving the method's name with the appropriate arguments as a stand-alone statement.

Finally, although it completely defeats the premises behind Object-Oriented Programming, by replacing the keyword private with the keyword public one can have true global variables accessible by all methods in an application.

C++ NOTE: Except for visibility issues, there is no difference between a global variable in C/C++ and a static variable in Java.

Recursion

Recursion is a general method of solving problems by reducing them to simpler problems of a similar type. The general framework for a recursive solution to a problem looks like this:

> Solve recursively (problem)
>> If the problem is trivial, do the obvious
>> Simplify the problem
>> Solve recursively (simpler problem)
>> Turn (if possible) the solution to the simpler problem(s) into a solution to the original problem

A recursive subprogram constantly calls itself, each time in a simpler situation, until it gets to the trivial case, at which point it stops. For the experienced programmer, thinking recursively presents a unique perspective on certain problems, often leading to particularly elegant solutions and, therefore, equally elegant programs. (For example, most of the very fast sorts, such as QuickSort, are recursive.)

For a Web-oriented example of recursion, consider the problem of designing a "Web crawler" that will search *every* hyperlink that is accessible from the page that you are currently on. (We show you a simplified example of this in Chapter 8.) The pseudo-code for this kind of application is:

> Recursive URL search(link)
>
> Do
>
>> find next link
>>
>> Recursive URL search(next link)
>
> Until No more links

There are actually two types of recursion possible. The first is where the subprogram only calls itself. This is called *direct recursion*. The second type is called, naturally enough, *indirect recursion*. This occurs, for example, when a method calls another method that, in turn, calls the first one. Both types of recursion are possible in Java and (unlike Pascal, say) no special incantations are needed for the indirect situation.

Let's look at a recursive way to compute the lottery odds. If you draw one number out of 50, your chances are plainly one in 50. In general, we can write

```
public static long lotteryOdds(int high, int number)
{   if (number == 1) return high;
    . . .
}
```

That wasn't too bad. Now let's look at the number of possible ways of drawing 6 numbers out of 50. Let's just grab one number. There are 50 chances. That leaves us with 5 numbers out of 49. Aha! A simpler problem. There are `lotteryOdds(49, 5)` ways to pick those five numbers. That gives a total of `50 * lotteryOdds(49, 5)` possibilities to pick the six numbers. Actually, we have to fudge a little and divide that result by six because our process counts each combination six times, depending which number we choose first.

Replacing the 50 and 6 with the general parameters `high` and `number`, we get the recursive solution

```
public static long lotteryOdds(int high, int number)
{   if (number <= 0) return 0; // just in case
    else if (number == 1) return high;
    else return high * lotteryOdds
      (high - 1, number - 1) / number;
}
```

Note that the `number` argument gets decremented in each recursive call and, therefore, must eventually reach 1.

In this case, the recursive solution is actually somewhat less efficient than the loop that we used previously, but it clearly shows the syntax (or rather the absence of any special syntax) of the recursive call.

Arrays

In Java, arrays are first-class objects. You are better off not thinking about how arrays are implemented in Java—accept them as objects that exist in and by themselves. For example, you can assign one array of integers to another, just as you can assign one integer variable to another.

Once you create an array, you cannot change its size (although you can, of course, change an individual array element). If you need to expand the size of an array while a program is running, you need to use a different Java object called a *vector*. (See Chapter 9 for more on vectors and how to handle multi-dimensional arrays.)

You have already seen some examples of Java arrays. The `String[] args` argument in the `main` method says the only parameter in the `main` method is an array of strings. In this case, the first ("zeroth" = `args[0]`) entry is the first command line argument; `args[1]` is the second command line argument, and so on.

Arrays are the first example of objects whose creation the programmer must explicitly handle. This is done through the `new` operator. For example:

```
int[] arrayOfInt = new int[100];
```

sets up an array that can hold 100 integers. The array entries are *numbered from 0 to 99* (and not 1 to 100). Once created, the entries in an array can be filled, for example, by using a loop:

```
int[] arrayOfInt = new int[100];
for (int i = 0; i < 100; i++)
   arrayOfInt[i] = i;   // fills the array with 0 to 99
```

Entries from an array can be used anywhere a value of that type can be used. If you try to access, say, the 101st element of an array declared as having 100 elements, Java will compile and you will be able to run your program. It will, however, stop the program when this statement is encountered. If you assign one array to another, then both refer to the same set of values. Any change to one will affect the other.

Java has a shorthand to create an array object and initialize it at the same time. Here's an example of the syntax at work:

```
int[] smallPrimes = {2,3,5,7,11,13};
```

Notice that you do not use a call to new when you use this syntax.

Finally, Java has an extremely useful method in its System class for copying all or part of an array to another array. The syntax for this is:

```
System.arraycopy(sourceArray, sourcePosition,
    destinationArray, destinationPosition,
    numberOfEntriesToCopy).
```

For example, the following program sets up to arrays and then copies the last four entries of the first array to the second array. The copy starts at position 2 in the source array and copies starting at position 3 of the target. It copies 4 entries.

```
public class ArrayExample
{   public static void main(String args[])
    {    int[] smallPrimes = {2,3,5,7,11,13};
         int[] bigInts = {1001,1002,1003,1004,1005,1006,1007};
         System.arraycopy(smallPrimes, 2, bigInts, 3, 4);
         for (int i = 0; i < bigInts.length; i++)
         { System.out.println(i +
               "'th entry after copy is " + bigInts[ i]);
         }
    }
}
```

The output of this program is:

```
0'th entry after copy is 1001
1'th entry after copy is 1002
2'th entry after copy is 1003
3'th entry after copy is 5
4'th entry after copy is 7
5'th entry after copy is 11
6'th entry after copy is 13
```

C++ NOTE: You can define an array variable either as `int[] arrayOfInt` or as `int arrayOfInt[]`. Most Java programmers prefer the former style because it neatly separates the type `int[]` (integer array) from the variable name.

A Java array is quite different from a C/C++ array on the stack. It is, however, essentially the same as a pointer to an array allocated on the *heap*. The `[]` operator is predefined to perform *bounds checking*. There is no pointer arithmetic—you can't increment `arrayOfInt` to point to the second element in the array.

You can tell that arrays are pointers, because their contents can be modified when you pass an array to a function and because arrays can be assigned.

VB NOTE: There is no convenient way to use index ranges in a Java array.

Arrays can be used in a user-defined method exactly as any other type. However, since arrays in Java are actually hidden pointers, the method can change the elements. Example 3-7 is a shell sort that sorts whatever integer array is passed to it.

Example 3-7: ShellSort.java

```java
class ShellSort
{   public static void sort(int[] a)
    {   int n = a.length;
        int incr = n / 2;
        while (incr >= 1)
        {   for (int i = incr; i < n; i++)
            {   int temp = a[i];
                int j = i;
                while (j >= incr && temp < a[j - incr])
                {   a[j] = a[j - incr];
                    j -= incr;
                }
                a[j] = temp;
            }
            incr /= 2;
        }
    }

    public static void main(String[] args)
    {   // make an array of ten integers
        int[] a = new int[10];
        int i;
        // fill the array with random values
        for (i = 0; i < a.length; i++)
            a[i] = (int)(Math.random() * 100);
        // sort the array
        sort(a);
        // print the sorted array
        for (i = 0; i < a.length; i++)
            System.out.println(a[i]);
    }
}
```

The return type of a method can also be an array. This is really useful when a method computes a sequence of values. For example, let us write a method that draws a sequence of numbers in a simulated lottery and then returns the sequence. The header of the function is

```java
public static int[] drawing(int high, int number)
```

In Example 3-8, the method makes two arrays, one that holds the numbers 1, 2, 3, ..., high from which the lucky combination is drawn, and one to hold the numbers that are drawn. The first array is abandoned when the method exits and will eventually be garbage collected. The second array is returned as the computed result.

Example 3-8: LotteryDrawing.java

```java
import corejava.*;
public class LotteryDrawing
{   public static int[] drawing(int high, int number)
    {   int i;
        int numbers[] = new int[high];
        int result[] = new int[number];
        // fill an array with numbers 1 2 3 . . . high
        for (i = 0; i < high; i++) numbers[i] = i + 1;
        for (i = 0; i < number; i++)
        {   int j = (int)(Math.random() * (high - i));
            result[i] = numbers[j];
            numbers[j] = numbers[high - 1 - i];
        }
        return result;
    }

    public static void main(String[] args)
    {   int numbers = Console.readInt
        ("How many numbers do you need to draw?");
        int topNumber = Console.readInt
            ("What is the highest number you can draw?");

        int[] a = drawing(topNumber, numbers);
        ShellSort.sort(a);
        System.out.println
            ("Bet the following combination. It'll make you rich!");
        int i;
        for (i = 0; i < a.length; i++)
            System.out.println(a[i]);
    }
}
```

CHAPTER

4

- Introduction to OOP

- Using Existing Classes

- Starting to Build Your Own Classes

- Packages

- Class Design Hints

Objects
and Classes

T his chapter will:

- introduce you to Object-Oriented Programming (OOP);

- show you how Java implements OOP by going further into its notion of a *class* and how you can use existing classes supplied by Java or by third parties;

- show you how to write your own *reuseable* classes that can perform nontrivial tasks.

If you are coming from a procedure-oriented language like VB (especially versions prior to VB4), C, or COBOL, you will want to read this chapter carefully. You may also need to spend a fair amount of time on the introductory sections. OOP requires a different way of thinking than procedure-oriented languages (or even object-based languages like VB). The transition is not always easy, but you do need some familiarity with OOP to go further with Java. (We are, however, assuming you are comfortable with a procedure-oriented language.)

For experienced C++ programmers, this chapter, like the previous chapter, will present familiar information; however, there are enough differences between how OOP is implemented in Java and how it is done in C++ to warrant your reading the later sections of this chapter (concentrating on the C++ notes).

Because you need to understand a fair amount of terminology in order to make sense of OOP, we'll start with some concepts and definitions. Then, we'll show you the basics of how Java implements OOP. We should note, however, that it is possible to write endlessly about the ideas behind OOP. A quick survey of *Books in Print* shows that there are more than 150 books with "Object-Oriented Programming" in the title, and more seem to appear each week. (We do make references to the literature, if you need more information on the ideas behind OOP and object-oriented design.)

Introduction to OOP

OOP is the dominant programming paradigm these days, having replaced the "structured," procedure-based programming techniques that were developed in the early '70s. Java is totally object-oriented, and it is not possible to program it in the procedural style that you may be most comfortable with. We hope this section—especially when combined with the example code supplied in the text and on the CD—will give you enough information about OOP to become productive with Java.

Let's begin with a question that, on the surface, seems to have nothing to do with programming: How did companies like Dell, Gateway, Micron Technologies, and the other major personal computer manufacturers get so big, so fast? Most people would probably say they made generally good computers and sold them at rock-bottom prices in an era when computer demand was skyrocketing. But go further—how were they able to manufacture so many models so fast and respond to the changes that were happening so quickly?

Well, a big part of the answer is that these companies farmed out a lot of the work. They bought components from reputable vendors and then assembled them. They often didn't invest time and money in designing and building power supplies, disk drives, motherboards, and other components. This made it possible for the companies to produce a product and make changes quickly for less money than if they had done the engineering themselves.

What the personal computer manufacturers were buying was "prepackaged functionality." For example, when they bought a power supply, they were buying something with certain properties (size, shape, and so on) and a certain functionality (smooth power output, amount of power available, and so on). Compaq provides a good example of how effective this operating procedure is. When Compaq moved from engineering all of the parts in their machines to buying many of the parts, they dramatically improved their bottom line.

OOP springs from the same idea. Your program is made of objects, with certain properties and operations that the objects can perform. The current state may change over time, but you always depend on objects not interacting with each other in undocumented ways. Whether you build an object or buy it might depend on your budget or on time. But, basically, as long as objects satisfy your specifications, you don't much care how the functionality was implemented. In OOP, you only care about what the objects *expose*. So, just as clone manufacturers don't care about the internals of a power supply as long as it does what they want, most Java programmers don't care how the audio clip component in Figure 4-1 is implemented as long as it does what *they* want.

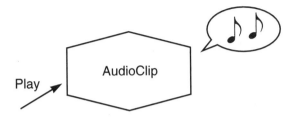

Figure 4-1: An audio clip object

Traditional structured programming consists of designing the data structures and then manipulating them with functions in specific ways that are theoretically sure to terminate. (These functions are usually called *algorithms*.) This is why the designer of the original Pascal, Niklaus Wirth, called his famous book on programming *Algorithms + Data Structures = Programs* (Prentice Hall, 1975). Notice that in Wirth's title, algorithms come first, and data structures come second. This mimics the way programmers worked at that time. First, you decided how to manipulate the data; then you decided what structure to impose on the data in order to make the manipulations easier. OOP reverses the order and puts data structures first, then looks at the algorithms that operate on the data.

The key to being most productive in OOP is to make each object responsible for carrying out a set of related tasks. If an object relies on a task that isn't its responsibility, it needs to have access to an object whose responsibilities include that task. The first object then asks the second object to carry out the task by means of a more generalized version of the function call that you are familar with in procedural programming. (Recall that in Java these function calls are usually called *method calls*.) In OOP jargon, you *have clients send messages to server objects*.

In particular, an object should never directly manipulate the internal data of another object. All communication should be via messages, that is, function calls. By designing your objects to handle all appropriate messages and manipulate their data internally, you maximize reusability and minimize debugging time.

Of course, just as with modules in a procedure-oriented language, you will not want an individual object to do *too* much. Both design and debugging are simplified when you build small objects that perform a few tasks, rather than humongous objects with internal data that are extremely complex, with hundreds of functions to manipulate the data.

The Vocabulary of OOP

You need to understand some of the terminology of OOP to go further. The most important term is *class,* which you have already seen in the code in Chapter 3. A class is usually described as the template or blueprint from which the object is actually made. This leads to the standard way of thinking about classes: as cookie cutters. Objects are the cookies themselves. The "dough," in the form of memory, will need to be allocated as well. Java is pretty good about hiding this "dough preparation" step from you. You simply use the new keyword to obtain memory, and the built-in garbage collector will eat the cookies when nobody uses them any more. (Oh well, no analogy is perfect.) When you create an object from a class, you are said to have *created an instance* of the class. When you have a line like

```
AudioClip meow = new AudioClip();
```

you are using the new operator to create a *new instance* of the AudioClip class as shown in Figure 4-2. (Actually, it turns out that you must work harder in Java to create real audio clips. We just want to show the syntax here.)

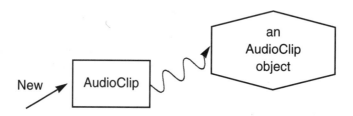

Figure 4-2: Creating a new object

As you have seen, everything you write in Java is inside a class, and Java is composed of many classes. Unfortunately, as you will see in this and the following chapters, the built-in classes in Java do not supply as rich a toolkit as languages like VB, Delphi, or Microsoft Foundation *Classes* (MFC) do. Thus, you must create your own classes for many basic tasks that, in other languages, are taken for granted.

However, when you do write your own classes, another tenet of OOP makes this easier: Classes can be (and in Java always are) built on other classes. Java, in fact, comes with a "cosmic base class," that is, a class from which all other classes are built. We say that a class that builds on another class *extends* it. In Java, all classes extend the cosmic base class called, naturally enough, Object. You will see more about the Object base class in the next chapter.

When you extend a base class, the new class initially has all the properties and functions of its parent. You can choose whether you want to modify or get rid of any function of the parent, and you can also supply new functions that apply to the child class only. The general concept of extending a base class is called *inheritance*. (See the next chapter for more on *inheritance*.)

Encapsulation is another key concept in working with objects. Formally, encapsulation is nothing more than combining data and behavior in one package and hiding the implementation of the data from the user of the object. The data in an object are usually called its *instance variables* or *fields*, and the functions and procedures in a Java class are called its *methods* (see Figure 4-3). A specific object that is an instance of a class will have specific values for its fields that define its current *state*.

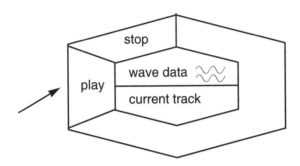

Figure 4-3: Encapsulation of data in an object

It cannot be stressed enough that the key to making encapsulation work is to have programs that *never* access instance variables (fields) in a class. Programs should interact with this data *only* through the object's methods. Encapsulation is the way to give the object its "black box" behavior, which is the key to reuse and reliability.

Objects

To work with OOP, you should be able to identify three key characteristics of objects. (For those who can remember back to high school, think of them as analogous to the "Who, What, and Where" that teachers told you characterize an event.) The three key questions are:

- What is the object's behavior?

- What is the object's state?

- What is the object's identity?

All objects that are instances of the same class share a family resemblance by supporting similar *behavior*. The behavior of an object is defined by the messages it accepts.

Next, each object stores information about what it currently looks like and how it got to be the way it currently is. This is what is usually called the object's *state.* An object's state may change over time, but not spontaneously. A change in the state of an object must be a consequence of messages sent to the object. However, the state of an object does not completely describe it.

Finally, each object has a distinct *identity.* For example, in an order-processing system, two orders are distinct even if they request identical items. Notice that the individual objects that are instances of a class *always* differ in their identity and *usually* differ in their state.

These key characteristics can influence each other. For example, the state of an object can influence its behavior. (If an order is "shipped" or "paid," it may reject a message that asks it to add or remove items. Conversely, if an order is "empty," that is, no items have yet been ordered, it should not allow itself to be shipped.)

In a traditional procedure-oriented program, you start the process at the top, with the main program. When designing an object-oriented system, there is no "top," and newcomers to OOP often wonder where to begin. The answer is: You first find classes and then you add methods to each class.

TIP: A simple rule of thumb in identifying classes is to look for nouns in the problem analysis. Methods, on the other hand, correspond to verbs.

For example, in an order-processing system, some of these nouns are:

- item
- order
- shipping address
- payment
- account

These nouns may lead to the classes `Item`, `Order`, and so on.

Next, one looks for verbs. Items are *added* to orders. Orders are *shipped* or *canceled.* Payments are *applied* to orders. With each verb, such as "add," "ship," "cancel," and "apply," you have to identify the one object that has the major responsibility for carrying it out. For example, when adding a new item to an order, the order object should be the one in charge since it knows how it stores and sorts items. That is, `add` should be a method of the `Order` class that takes an `Item` object as a parameter.

Of course, the "noun and verb" rule is only a rule of thumb, and only experience can help you decide which nouns and verbs are the important ones when building your classes.

Relationships between Classes

The most common relationships between classes are:

- *use*
- *containment* ("has–a")
- *inheritance* ("is–a")

The *use* relationship is the most obvious and also the most general. For example, the Order class uses the Account class, since Order objects need to access account objects to check for credit status. But the Item class does not use the Account class, since Item objects never need to worry about customer accounts. Thus, a class uses another class if it manipulates objects of that class.

In general, a class A uses a class B if:

- a method of A sends a message to an object of class B, or
- a method of A creates, receives, or returns objects of class B.

TIP: Try to minimize the number of classes that use each other. The point is, if a class A is unaware of the existence of a class B, it is also unconcerned about any changes to B! (And this means that revisions to B do not introduce bugs into A.)

The *containment* relationship is easy to understand because it is concrete; for example, an Order object contains Item objects. Containment means that objects of class A contain objects of class B. Of course, containment is a special case of use; if an A object contains a B object, then at least one method of the class A will make use of that object of class B.

The *inheritance* relationship denotes specialization. For example, a RushOrder class inherits from an Order class as shown in Figure 4-4. The specialized RushOrder class has special methods for priority handling and a different method for computing shipping charges, but its other methods, such as adding items and billing, are inherited from the Order class. In general, if class A extends class B, class A inherits methods from (or extends) class B, but has more capabilities. (Inheritance will be more fully described in the next chapter, in which we discuss this important notion at some length.)

NOTE: These three essential relationships between classes form the foundation of object-oriented design. *Class diagrams* show the classes (usually denoted with boxes or clouds) and their relationships (denoted with lines with various decorations that are maddeningly different from one methodologist to the next). Figure 4- 4 shows an example, using the "unified Booch/Rumbaugh notation."

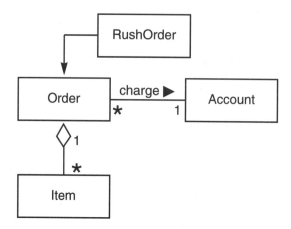

Figure 4-4: A class diagram

Contrasting OOP with Traditional Procedural Programming Techniques

We want to end this short introduction to OOP by contrasting OOP with the procedural model that you may be more familiar with. In procedure-oriented programming, you identify the tasks to be performed and then:

- by a stepwise refinement process, break the task to be performed into subtasks, and these into smaller subtasks, until the subtasks are simple enough to be implemented directly (this is the top-down approach); or

- write procedures to solve simple tasks and combine them into more sophisticated procedures, until you have the functionality you want (this is the bottom-up approach).

Most programmers, of course, use a mixture of the top-down and bottom-up strategies to solve a programming problem. The rule of thumb for discovering procedures is the same as the rule for finding methods in OOP: Look for verbs, or actions, in the problem description. The important difference is that in OOP, you *first* isolate the classes in the project. Only then do you look for the methods of the class. And there is another important difference between traditional procedures and OOP methods: Each method is associated with the class that is responsible for carrying out the operation.

For small problems, the breakdown into procedures works very well. But for larger problems, classes and methods have two advantages. Classes provide a convenient clustering mechanism for methods. A simple Web browser may require 2,000 functions for its implementation, or it may require 100 classes with an average of 20 methods per class. The latter structure is much easier to grasp by the programmer or to handle by teams of programmers. The encapsulation built into classes helps you here as well: classes hide their data representations from all code except their own methods. As Figure 4–5 shows, this means that if a programming bug messes up data, it is easier to search for the culprit among the 20 methods that had access to that data item than among 2,000 procedures.

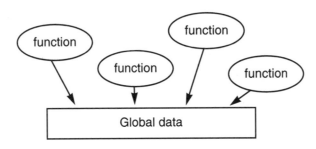

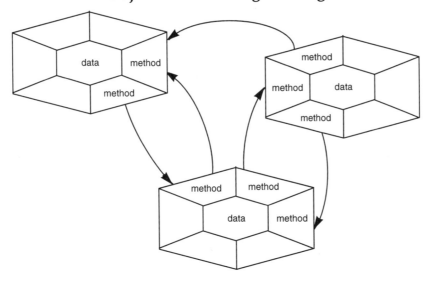

Figure 4-5: Procedural vs. OO Programming

You may say that this doesn't sound much different than *modularization*. You have certainly written programs by breaking the program up into modules that communicate with each other through procedure calls only, not by sharing data. This (if well done) goes far in accomplishing encapsulation. However, in many programming languages (such as C and VB), the slightest sloppiness in programming allows you to get at the data in another module—encapsulation is easy to defeat.

There is a more serious problem: while classes are factories for multiple objects with the same behavior, you cannot get multiple copies of a useful module. Suppose you have a module encapsulating a collection of orders, together with a spiffy balanced binary tree module to access them quickly. Now it turns out that you actually need *two* such collections, one for the pending orders and one for the completed orders. You cannot simply link the order tree module twice. And you don't really want to make a copy and rename all procedures in order for the linker to work!

Classes do not have this limitation. Once a class has been defined, it is easy to construct any number of instances of that class type (whereas a module can have only one instance).

We have only scratched a very large surface. The end of this chapter has a short section on "Class Design Hints," but for more information on understanding the OOP design process, here are some book recommendations.

C++ NOTE: The definitive book on object-oriented design with the Booch methodology is

> *Object-Oriented Analysis and Design,* 2nd Edition, by Grady Booch, (Benjamin Cummings, 1994).

You can find a lighter version of the methodology in

> *Mastering Object-Oriented Design with C++,* by Cay S. Horstmann, (John Wiley & Sons, 1995).

VB NOTE: If you are used to VB4, the best book to read to get a sense of object-oriented design is *Doing Objects in Microsoft Visual Basic 4.0,* by Deborah Kurota (Ziff-Davis Press, 1995).

Using Existing Classes

Since you can't do anything in Java without classes, we have shown you many classes at work. Unfortunately, many of these are quite anomalous in the Java scheme of things. A good example of this is our `Console` class. You have seen that you can use our `Console` class without needing to know how it is implemented—all you need to know is the syntax for its methods. That is the point of encapsulation and will certainly be true of all classes. Unfortunately, the `Console` class *only* encapsulates functionality; it neither needs nor hides data. Since there is no data, you do not need to worry about making objects and initializing their instance fields—there aren't any!

Object Variables

For most classes in Java, you create objects, specify their initial state and then work with the objects.

To access objects, you define object variables. For example, the statement

```
AudioClip meow; // meow doesn't refer to any object
```

defines an object variable, meow, that can refer to objects of type AudioClip. It is important to realize that the variable meow *is not an object*, and in fact, does not yet even refer to an object . You cannot use any methods on the variable at this time.

```
meow.play(); // not yet.
```

Use the new operator to create an object.

```
meow = new AudioClip();
    // does create an instance of AudioClip
```

Now you can start applying AudioClip methods to meow. (Actually, it is a little harder in Java to obtain a real audio clip. Here we just use audio clips to introduce the typical object notation.)

Most of the time, you will need to create multiple instances of a single class.

```
AudioClip chirp = new AudioClip();
```

Now there are two objects of type AudioClip, one attached to the object variable meow and one to the object variable chirp.

If you assign one variable to another variable using the equals sign,

```
AudioClip wakeUp = meow;
```

then both variables refer to the *same* object. This can lead to surprising behavior in your programs if you are not careful. For example, if you call

```
meow.play();
wakeUp.stop();
```

the audio clip object will play and then stop, since the *same* audio clip is referred to by the wakeUp and meow variables.

But suppose you want meow and wakeUp to refer to different objects, so you can change one of them without changing the other. As it turns out, there is no method available to change audio clips, and there isn't a method available to make a copy of one.

NOTE: Many classes do have a method called clone that makes a true copy. When you clone an existing object, you get a copy that reflects the current state of the object. Now, however (unlike when you use the equals sign), the two objects exist independently, so they can diverge over time. We will discuss the clone method further in the next chapter.

You can explicitly set an object variable to `null` to indicate that it currently refers to no objects.

```
wakeUp = null;
. . .
if (wakeUp != null) wakeUp.play();
```

If you call a method through a `null` variable like that of Figure 4-6, then a run time error occurs. Local object variables are not automatically initialized to `null`. You must initialize them, either by calling `new` or by setting them to `null`.

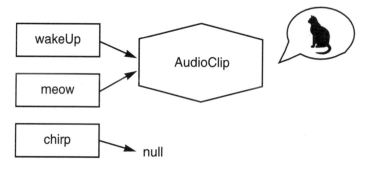

Figure 4-6: Object variables

C++ NOTE: You should think of Java object variables as analogous to *object pointers* in C++. For example,

```
AudioClip meow; // Java
```

is really the same as

```
AudioClip* meow; // C++
```

Once you make this association, everything falls into place. Of course, an `AudioClip*` pointer isn't initialized until you initialize it with a call to `new`. The syntax is almost the same in C++ and Java.

```
AudioClip* meow = new AudioClip(); // C++
```

If you copy one variable to another, then both variables refer to the same audio clip—they are pointers to the same object. The equivalent of the Java `null` object is the C++ `null` pointer.

All Java objects live on the heap. When an object contains another object variable, that variable still contains just a pointer to yet another heap object.

In C++, pointers make you nervous because they are so error-prone. It is easy to create bad pointers or to mess up memory management. In Java, these problems simply go away. If you use an uninitialized pointer, the run time system will reliably generate a run time error, instead of producing random results. You don't worry about memory management because the garbage collector takes care of it.

C++ makes quite an effort, with its support for copy constructors and assignment operators, to allow the implementation of objects that copy themselves automatically. For example, a copy of a linked list is a new linked list with the same contents but with an independent set of links. This makes it possible to design classes with the same copy behavior as the built-in types. In Java, you must use the `clone` method to get a complete copy of an object.

VB NOTE: Object variables in VB are actually quite close to object variables in Java—both have the capacity to point to objects; you even have an analogous use of `new`. The difference, of course, is that, in VB you use `set` rather than the equals sign to make one object variable point to another object and you must reclaim the memory yourself!

The Supplied `Date` Class

It is time to go further into the ways of working with Java and third-party classes that are more typical than our `Console` class. Let's start with the `Date` class that comes with Java. An instance of the `Date` class has a state, namely its current settings for its date and time. For example,

```
Date todaysDate = new Date();
```

does the following:

1. It creates a new instance of the Date class called todaysDate.
2. At the same time, it initializes the state of the todaysDate object to be the current date (as maintained by the host operating system).

You can also create an instance of the `Date` class with a specific date:

```
Date preMillenium = new Date(99,11,31);
```

This creates a `Date` instance called `preMillenium`, with the initial state of December 31, 1999.

Note that the `Date` class is actually a Date/Time class, so you can also set the time. (If you don't set it, it defaults to midnight.) For example:

```
Date preMillenium = new Date(99,11,31,23,59,59);
```

would give you a `Date` object whose instance fields are set at one second to midnight on December 31, 1999. (When you use `Date()`, you get a date instance with the time set at the one maintained in the operating system.)

Now you may be wondering: Why is `Date` a class in Java rather than (as in some languages) a built-in type, like `int`? The reason is simple: language developers are reluctant to add too many basic types. For example, suppose Java had a notation like #6/1/95#, which is used in VB to denote an example of `Date` type. Since the ordering for year, month, and day is different in different locales, the *language designers* would need to foresee all the issues of internationalization. If they do a poor job, the language becomes an unpleasant muddle, but unhappy programmers are powerless to do anything about it. By making `Date` into a class, the design task is off-loaded to a library designer. If the class is not perfect, other programmers can easily write their own `Date` class. (In fact, we will do just this in the next section.)

Unlike our `Console` class, the `Date` class must have encapsulated data (instance fields) to maintain the date to which it is set. Without looking at the source code, *it is impossible to know the representation used internally by the* `Date` *class.* But, of course, the whole point is that this doesn't matter, and this is what makes it possible to use the `Date` class in a system-independent way.

What *matters* are the methods that the `Date` class exposes. If you look at the documentation for the `Date` class, you will find that it has 25 methods.

In this book, we present a method in the following format, which is essentially the same as the on-line documentation.

`java.util.Date`←**name of class**

- `void parse(String s)`←name of method

  Given a string representing a date and time, this method parses it and converts it to a time value

  Parameters: (omitting those that are self-explanatory):

  s   the string to parse

Here are some of the most basic methods of the `Date` class. (For more of the methods of the date class, see the section that follows.)

`java.util.Date`

- `void parse(String s)`

  Given a string representing a date and time, this method parses it and converts it to a time value.

- `boolean before(Date when)`

  This method returns true if the `Date` whose method you are calling comes before the date `when`.

- ```
  boolean after(Date when)
  ```

  This method returns true if the `Date` whose method you are calling comes after the date `when`.

- ```
  String toString()
  ```

  This method (which exists in many classes) converts the date held in the `Date` object to a string representing the date (using Unix date/time conventions).

- ```
  String toLocaleString()
  ```

  This method converts the date held in the `Date` object to a string representing the date using the local ordering convention for the day, month, and year.

For example, here's all it takes in a Java application to print out the current date using the local order conventions. For example, if you configure your computer for the German "locale," then dates should be printed like 31.12.1999.

```
import java.util.*;
class WhatIstoday
{   public static void main(String arg[])
    {   Date today = new Date();
        System.out.println(today.toLocaleString());
    }
}
```

Notice that, to use the `toLocaleString` method of the `Date` class, we needed to use the dot notation in order to access a method of the `today` instance of the `Date` class.

Mutator and Accessor Methods

At this point, you are probably asking yourself: How do I change the current state of the `Date` class? Similarly, are there methods that let you get at the current day or month or year for the date encapsulated in a specific `Date` object?

Here is a list of the most important methods for getting at or changing the state of a `Date` instance:

```
java.util.Date
```

- ```
  int getDate()
  ```

  gets the day of the month of this date instance, a number between 1 and 31.

- `int getMonth()`

  returns the month of this date, an integer between 0 and 11.

- `int getYear()`

  gets the year, with 0 denoting 1900, and so on.

- `int getDay()`

  gets the weekday, an integer between 0 and 6 (with 0 being Sunday).

- `int getHours()`, `int getMinutes()`, `int getSeconds()`

  returns the hours, minutes, or seconds encapsulated in the current instance.

- `void setDate(int)`, `void setMonth(int)`, `void setYear(int)`

  In this method, `setDate` sets the current day of the month. The other functions set the month and year.

- `void setHours(int)`, `void setMinutes(int)`, `void setSeconds(int)`

  sets the hours, minutes, or seconds encapsulated in the current instance.

None of the set methods error-check the arguments you use. Some of them try to compensate for meaningless parameters. For example, `d.setDate(32)` moves into the next month. Other `set` functions produce invalid dates. This is not a good feature, as we will discuss later.

The convention is to call methods that change instance fields' *mutator methods* and those that access instance fields' *accessor methods*. As you may have suspected from looking at the above list, the convention in Java is to use the lower-case prefix `get` for accessor methods and `set` for mutator methods.

C++ NOTE: In C++, it is important to make a formal distinction between mutator operations that change an object and accessor operations that merely read its data fields. The latter need to be declared as `const` operations. This is not needed in Java.

VB NOTE: The analogous situation (in VB4) is that mutator methods correspond to a Property Let procedure, and accessor methods correspond to a Property Get procedure.

Using Our Day *Class*

Unfortunately, even if you look at *all* the methods in the Date class to see if your idea of what is important corresponds to ours, you will quickly discover that this class is missing certain types of functionality. (The lack of error-checking for the mutator methods is also annoying.) In any case, as we mentioned previously, Java's Date class is really more a Time class than a Date class.

There are instances in which you want to find the difference between two dates. For example, a retirement calculator certainly needs to compute the difference between today's date and the user's retirement date. The question then arises, What is the best way to add this functionality to the Date class? Could we build on the Date class (*i.e.*, use *inheritance*—to be described in the next chapter)?

When we tried this, we discovered that the Date class did not let us access the information we needed to do date calculations. There is a method for finding out if the current date comes before the retirement date, but that doesn't do us a lot of good—we know we aren't retired yet. The method won't tell us how many days will elapse until our well-deserved retirement. Just out of curiousity, we examined the source code for the Date class and discovered how the Date class stores its data. But that did not solve our problem because, of course, that information is encapsulated in the class and not accessible to our programs.

NOTE: The CD includes the source code for all of the publicly available parts of Java. As you become more experienced with Java, you will find the source code extremely useful for getting ideas about and (occasional) insights into Java programming.

We, therefore, decided to write our own Day class to give you a better example of a class with cleanly designed accessor and mutator functions. The source code (it's around 150 lines of code) has been installed in the corejava package inside the \CoreJavaBook directory of your hard disk during the installation described in Chapter 2. (When you finish this chapter, you may want to glance through the source code to see the basic ideas. Fair warning: some of the code is fairly obscure because of the algorithms needed to work with a year that is, in reality, slightly more than 365 days long.)

We allow two ways to create an instance of our Day class that are similar to the two methods for Java's Date class:

```
Day todaysDate = new Day();
Day preMillenium = new Day(1999, 12, 31);
```

Unlike Java's Date class, our class does not do anything with the time of day and will also prevent you from creating an illegal date.

To create an object of our Day class, you need to make sure that Java knows where the Day class is. (This can be done by setting the CLASSPATH variable appropriately to include the CoreJava directory and using import corejava.* or copying the Day class to the directory in which you are working.) What we want to stress here is that once you know how to create an instance of the Day class, then all you need to use our class is the following list that tells you how our methods affect the current state of an instance of the Day class:

   corejava.Day

- void advance(int n)

  advances the date currently set by a specified number of days. For example, d.advance(100) changes d to a date 100 days later.

- int getDay(), int getMonth(), int getYear()

  returns the day, month, or year of this day object. Days are between 1 and 31, months between 1 and 12, and years can be any year (such as 1996 or −333). The class knows about the switch from the Julian to the Gregorian calendar in 1582.

- int weekday()

  returns an integer between 0 and 6, corresponding to the day of the week (0 = Sunday).

- int daysBetween(Day b)

  This method is one of the main reasons we created the Day class. It calculates the number of days between the current instance of the Day class and instance b of the Day class.

Notice that our Day class has no method for changing the date other than to use the advance method.

The following code combines the Console class with our Day class in order to calculate how many days you have been alive.

```java
import corejava.*;
public class DaysAlive
{  public static void main(String[] args)
    {  int year;
       int month;
       int day;
```

```
month = Console.readInt
    ("Please enter the month, 1 for January and so on");
day = Console.readInt
    ("Please enter the day you were born.");

year = Console.readInt
("Please enter the year you were born (starting with 19..)");

    Day birthday = new Day(year, month, day);
    Day today = new Day();
    System.out.println("You have been alive "
        + today.daysBetween(birthday) + " days.");
    }
}
```

NOTE: If you try to enter invalid data, the program will terminate with an exception.
See Chapter 10 for more on exceptions.

A Calendar Program

As a more serious example of putting it all together, here is the code for an
application that prints out a calendar for the month and year specified in the
command line argument. For example, if you compile this class (make sure our
Day class is available of course) and then say

```
java Calendar 12 1999
```

you will see the calendar for December 1999. (December 31 is rather conveniently on a Friday that year, by the way.)

```
12    1999
Sun   Mon   Tue   Wed   Thu   Fri   Sat
                    1     2     3     4
  5     6     7     8     9    10    11
 12    13    14    15    16    17    18
 19    20    21    22    23    24    25
 26    27    28    29    30    31
```

There are two issues in writing a calendar program like this: you have to know
the weekday of the first day of the month, and you have to know how many
days the month has. We sidestep the latter problem with the following trick: we
make a Day object that starts out with the first of the month.

```
Day d = new Day(y, m, 1); // start date of the month
```

After printing each day, we advance d by one day:

```
        d.advance(1);
```

In Example 4-1 we check the month (d.month()) and see if it is still the same as m. If not, we are done.

Example 4-1: Calendar.java

```java
import corejava.*;

public class Calendar
{   public static void main(String[] args)
    {   int m;
        int y;
        if (args.length == 2)
        {   m = Format.atoi(args[0]);
            y = Format.atoi(args[1]);
        }
        else
        {   Day today = new Day(); // today's date
            m = today.getMonth();
            y = today.getYear();
        }

        Day d = new Day(y, m, 1); // start date of the month

        System.out.println(m + " " + y);
        System.out.println("Sun Mon Tue Wed Thu Fri Sat");
        for( int i = 0; i < d.weekday(); i++ )
            System.out.print("    ");
        while (d.getMonth() == m)
        {   if (d.getDay() < 10) System.out.print(" ");
            System.out.print(d.getDay());
            if (d.weekday() == 6)
                System.out.println("");
            else
                System.out.print("   ");
            d.advance(1);
        }
        if (d.weekday() != 0) System.out.println("");
    }
}
```

PITFALL: There is a tendency for programmers coming from languages that have the by value, by reference distinction for function parameters to assume that since objects are references, they are passed by reference. Unfortunately, that is wrong!

First off, consider trying to write a swap method for days. Because you got tired of writing the three lines of code that are needed you decide to write once and for all:

```
static void swap_days(Day a, Day b)
{    Day temp = b;
     b = a;
     a = temp;
}
```

Unfortunately the call `swap_days(foo, bar)` (as opposed to writing the three lines of code) still does nothing, `foo` and `bar` still refer to whatever they did before the call—*because* they were passed by value to the `swap_days` method.

As another example of this phenomenon consider the following method that *tries* to change the delivery date for a software product

```
static void changeDeliveryDay(Day d, int yearsDelayed)
// won't work
{    int month = d.getMonth();
     int day = d.getDay();
     int year = d.getYear();
     d = new Day(year + yearsDelayed, month, day);
}
```

Suppose you call this function as follows:

```
target = new Day(1996, 10, 15);
changeDeliveryDay(target, 2);
```

in order to change the delivery date to be two years later. Does target now have the correct state?

What we are doing seems natural at first glance. It *looks* like the target object is changed inside the method so that it refers to a new Day object since the parameter certainly is being changed to a new day object. However *this code will also not work*. The point is that Java never passes method parameters by reference. The variable `d` in the `changeDeliveryDay` method is a *copy* of the target variable. Now it is true that both of these variables are references and they do both point to the same `Day` object right after the method is called. It is also true that the assignment

```
d = new Day(year + yearsDelayed, month, day);
```

changes the value of the d object variable inside the method. It now refers (points) to a new day object. The original target variable however has not changed, it *still* refers to the original day object. Thus, the method call does not change what the target refers to at all. (The d object variable is abandoned when Java finishes executing the method and the memory allocated for it will eventually be garbage collected.)

To sum up: *In Java, methods can never change the values of their parameters.*

On the other hand as you have seen repeatedly, methods can change the *state* of an object used as a parameter. They can do this since they have access to the mutator methods and data of the object the parameter points to. Here's a version of a method to change the delivery day that will do the job.

```
static void changeDeliveryDay(Day d, int yearsDelayed)
// works
{    int ndays = 365 * yearsDelayed;
     d.advance(ndays);
}
```

This method changes the state of d by using the advance method of the Day class. It doesn't try to attach a different object to d, it simply uses the fact that it can access and change the data of d via its mutator methods. When you call this method with a parameter equal to target, the advance method in target is called by the line d.advance(ndays). This changes the state of the target object as one wanted to do.

Starting to Build Your Own Classes

You saw how to write simple classes in Chapter 3. In that chapter, the classes were all designed to run as stand-alone programs and depended only on the classes built into Java and our little `Console` class. When you said

```
java Mortgage
```

for example, the Java interpreter looked for the `main` method in the `Mortgage` class and ran it. The `main` method, in turn, called other methods of the class as needed. Although you will see more about methods like `main` later in this chapter, this kind of class is not what we are concerned with in this chapter. In more sophisticated Java programs, the class you choose to run from the interpreter will usually have very little functionality other than starting up the various objects that do the actual work of your program.

What we want to do in the rest of this chapter (and in the next chapter) is show you how to write the kind of "workhorse classes" that are needed for more sophisticated applications. These classes do not (and often cannot) stand alone: they are the building blocks for *constructing* stand-alone programs.

The simplest syntax for a class in Java:

```
class NameOfClass
{   // definitions of the class's features
    // includes methods and instance fields
}
```

The outermost pair of braces (block) defines the code that will make up the class. Our convention is to use initial caps for class names. Just as with the classes from Chapter 3, individual method definitions define the operations of the class. The difference is that we want to allow other classes to use our classes while still maintaining encapsulation of the data. This means that we now want to allow for (encapsulated) instance fields that will hold the private data for these classes.

NOTE: We adopt the policy that the methods for the class come first and the instance fields come at the end. (Perhaps this, in a small way, encourages the notion of leaving instance fields alone.)

An Employee *Class*

Consider the following, very simplified version of an Employee class that might be used by a business in writing a payroll system.

```
class Employee
{    public Employee(String n, double s, Day d)
     {    name = n;
          salary = s;
          hireDay = d;
     }
     public void raiseSalary(double byPercent)
     {    salary *= 1 + byPercent / 100;
     }
     public int hireYear()
     {    return hireDay.getYear();
     }
     public void print()
     {    System.out.println(name + " " + salary + " " + hireYear());
     }
      public String getName()
     { return name;
     }
     private String name;
     private double salary;
     private Day hireDay;
}
```

We will break down the code in this class in some detail in the sections that follow. First, though, example 4-2 shows some code that lets you see how to use the Employee class.

Example 4-2: EmployeeTest.java

```
import java.util.*;
import corejava.*;

public class EmployeeTest
{   public static void main(String[] args)
    {   Employee[] staff = new Employee[3];

        staff[0] = new Employee("Harry Hacker", 35000,
           new Day(1989,10,1));
        staff[1] = new Employee("Carl Cracker", 75000,
           new Day(1987,12,15));
        staff[2] = new Employee("Tony Tester", 38000,
           new Day(1990,3,15));
        int i;
        for (i = 0; i < 3; i++) staff[i].raiseSalary(5);
        for (i = 0; i < 3; i++) staff[i].print();
    }
}
```

To run the sample code, first make sure that both the `Employee` and `EmployeeTest` classes are in the same directory. Then, compile this `EmployeeTest` class and run it with the Java interpreter. This will create an instance of the `Employee` class with some sample data and then print out the state of the class in order for us to see whether or not our class appears well constructed.

C++ NOTE: In Java, all functions are defined inside the class itself. This does not automatically make them inline functions. There is no analog to the C++ syntax:

```
class Employee
{    //...
};
void Employee::raiseSalary(double byPercent) // C++, not Java
{    salary *= 1 + byPercent / 100;
}
```

Analyzing the `Employee` Class

In the sections that follow, we want to dissect the `Employee` class. Let's start with the methods in this class. As you can see by examining the source code, this class has five methods, whose headers look like this:

```
public Employee(String n, double s, Day d)
public String getName()
public void raiseSalary(double byPercent)
public int hireYear()
public void print()
```

The keyword `public` is usually called an *access modifier*. In Java, these access modifiers describe who can use the method or who can use the class if a modifier is used in the name of the class. The keyword `public` means that any method in any class that has access to an instance of the `Employee` class can call the method. (There are four possible access levels; they are covered in this and the next chapter.)

Next, notice that there are three *instance fields* that will hold the data we will manipulate inside an instance of the `Employee` class.

```
private String name;
private double salary;
private Day hireDay;
```

The `private` keyword makes sure that no outside agency can access the instance fields *except* through the methods of our class. In this book, instance fields will almost always be private. (Exceptions occur only when we have to implement very closely collaborating classes, for example a `List` and a `Link` class in a linked list data structure.)

> NOTE: It is possible to use the `public` keyword with your instance variables, but it would be a very bad idea. Having `public` data fields would allow any part of the program to read and modify the instance variables. That completely ruins encapsulation and, at the risk of repeating ourselves too often, we strongly urge against using public instance fields.

Finally, notice that we use an instance field that is itself an instance of our `Day` class. This is quite usual: classes will often contain instance fields that are themselves class instances.

For the `Employee` class to compile, either the `Day` class must be in the same directory as the `Employee` class, or your `CLASSPATH` variable must point to the `CoreJavaBook` directory.

> NOTE: Please see the section *Packages* if you want to use all of our classes in the simplest fashion, without worrying about the location of the source files and for more information on access modifiers for classes.

First Steps with Constructors

Let's look at the first method listed in our `Employee` class.

```
public Employee(String n, double s, Day d)
{    name = n;
     salary = s;
     hireDay = d;
}
```

This is an example of a *constructor method*. It is used to initialize objects of a class—giving the instance variables the initial state you want them to have. You didn't see any methods like this in Chapter 3 because we didn't initialize any objects in that chapter.

For example, when you create an instance of the `Employee` class with code like this

```
hireDate = new Day(1950, 1, 1);
Employee number007 = new Employee
    ("James Bond", 100000, hireDate);
```

you have set the instance fields as follows:

```
name = "James Bond";
salary = 100000;
hireDay = January 1, 1950 //actually a Day class with this
                          //data encapsulated
```

The new method is always used together with a constructor to create the class. This forces you to set the initial state of your objects. In Java, you cannot create an instance of a class without initializing the instance variables (either explictly or implicitly). The reason for this design decision is simple: an object created without a correct initialization is always useless and occasionally dangerous. In many languages, like Delphi, you can create uninitialized objects; the result is almost always the platform equivalent of a general protection fault (GPF) or segmentation fault, which means memory is being corrupted.

While we will have more to say about constructor methods later in this chapter, for now, always keep the following in mind:

1.   A constructor has the same name as the class.

2.   A constructor may (as in this example) take one or more (or even no) parameters.

3.   A constructor is always called with the new keyword.

Remember, too, the following important difference between constructors and other methods:

*   A constructor can only be called with new. You can't apply a constructor to an existing object to reset the instance fields. For example, d.Date(1950, 1, 1) is an error.

Of course, if resetting all fields of a class is an important and recurring operation, the designers of the class can provide a mutator method such as empty or reset for that purpose. We want to stress that only the supplied mutator methods will let you revise the state of the instance variables in an already constructed class (assuming, of course, that all data are private).

It is possible to have more than one constructor in a class. You have already seen this in both Java's Date class and our Day class. (You saw two of the three constructors available in the Date class and both of the constructors available in our Day class.)

C++ NOTE: Constructors work the same way in Java as they do in C++. But keep in mind that all Java objects are constructed on the heap and that a constructor must be combined with new. It is a common C++ programmer error to forget the new operator:

```
Employee number007("James Bond", 100000, hireDate);
    // C++, not Java
```

That works in C++, but does not work in Java.

```
public Employee(String n, double s, Day d)
{    name - n;
     hireDay = d;
     float salary = s;
}
```

The local variable `salary` *shadows* the instance field `salary`. This is a nasty error that can be hard to track down. You just have to be careful in all of your methods that you don't use variable names that equal the names of instance fields.

The Methods of the `Employee` Class

The first three methods in our `Employee` class should not pose many problems. They are much like the methods you saw in the previous chapter. Notice, however, that all of these methods can access the private instance fields by name. This is a key point: instance fields are always accessible by the methods of their own class.

For example,

```
public void raiseSalary(double byPercent)
{    salary *= 1 + byPercent / 100;
}
```

sets a new value for the `salary` instance field in the object that executes this method. (This particular method does not return a value.) For example, the call

```
number007.raiseSalary(5);
```

raises `number007`'s salary by increasing the `number007.salary` variable by 5%.

Of the remaining methods in this class, the most interesting is the one that returns the year hired. Recall that it looks like this:

```
public int hireYear()
{    return hireDay.getYear();
}
```

Notice that this method returns an integer value, and it does this by applying a method to the `hireDay` instance variable. This makes perfect sense because `hireDay` is an instance of our `Day` class, which indeed has a `getYear` method.

Finally, lets look more closely at the rather simple `getName` method.

```
public String getName()
{    return name;
}
```

This is an obvious example of an accessor method. Because it works directly with a field in the class, it is sometimes called a *field accessor method*. It simply returns the current state of the `name` field.

For the class implementor, it is obviously more trouble to write both a private field and a public accessor method than to simply write a public data field. But programmers using the class are not inconvenienced—if `number007` is the name of the instance of the `Employee` class, they simply write `number007.getName()`, rather than `number007.name`.

The point is that the `name` field has become "read-only" to the outside world. Only operations of the class can modify it. In particular, should the value ever be wrong, only the class operations need to be debugged.

By the way, the function is called `getName()` because it would be confusing to call it `name()`—that is already taken by the instance variable itself and it would be confusing to have a variable and a method with the same name. (In any case, the convention in Java is that accessor methods begin with a lowercase "get".)

Now, because secret agents come and go, one might want to modify the class at some later point to allow for a field mutator that resets the name of the current "007." But this would be done by the maintainers of the class as the need arises.

The point to keep in mind is that, in most classes, private data fields are of a technical nature and of no interest to anyone but the implementor of the operations. When the user of a class has a legitimate interest in both reading and setting a field, the class implementors need to supply *three* items:

- a private data field
- a public field accessor method
- a public field mutator method

This is a lot more tedious than supplying a single public data field, but there are considerable benefits:

1. The internal implementation can be changed without affecting any code other than the operations of the class.

Of course, the accessor and mutator methods may need to do a lot of work—especially when the data representation of the instance fields is changed. But that leads us to our second benefit.

2. Mutator methods can perform error-checking, whereas code that simply assigns to a field cannot.

Our `Day` class is a good example of a class that should *not* have mutators for each field. Suppose we had methods called `setDay`, `setMonth`, and `setYear` that do the obvious things. Suppose d was an instance of our Day class. Now consider the code:

```
d.setDay(31);
d.setMonth(3);
d.setYear(1996);
```

If the date encapsulated in d was currently at February 1, then the setDay operation described above would set it to an invalid date of February 31. What do you think setDay should do in this case? At first glance, this appears to be only a nuisance, but if you think this through carefully, you will find that there is no good answer.

Should an invalid setDay abort the program? Well, how *would* you then safely set the date from February 1 to March 31? Of course, you could set the month first:

```
d.setMonth(3);
d.setDay(31);
```

That will work. Now, how do you change it back to February 1? This time, you can't set the month first. This function would be a real hassle to use.

So perhaps setDay should just quietly adjust the date? If you set the date to February 31, then maybe the date should be adjusted to March 3 or 4, depending on whether the year is a leap year or not. The Java Date class does exactly that. We think this is a lousy idea. Consider again our effort to set the date from February 1 to March 31.

```
d.setDay(31); // now it is March 3 or 4
d.setMonth(3); // still March 3 or 4
```

Or perhaps setDay should temporarily make an invalid date and count on the fact that the programmer won't forget to adjust the month. Then we lose a major benefit of encapsulation, the guarantee that the object state is never corrupted.

We hope we have convinced you that a mutator that sets only the day field is not worth the trouble. It is obviously better to supply a single setDate(int, int, int) function that does the error-checking needed. (This also fits one's mental model better—after all, one sets a date and not a day, month, and year.)

Method Access to Private Data

You know that a method can access the private data of the object on which it is invoked. What many people find surprising is that a method can access the private data of *all objects of its class*. For example, consider a method compare that compares two dates.

```
class Day
{   . . .
    boolean equals(Day b)
    {   return year == b.year && month == b.month
            && day == b.day;
    }
}
```

A typical call is

```
if (hireday.equals(d)) . . .
```

This method accesses the private fields of `hireday`, which is not surprising. It also accesses the private fields of `d`. This is legal because `d` is an object of type `Day`, and a method of the `Day` class is permitted to access the private fields of *any* object of type `Day`.

C++ NOTE: C++ has the same rule. A member function can access the private features of any object of its class, not just the implicit argument.

Private Methods

When implementing a class, we make all data fields private, but what about the methods? While `public` data are dangerous, `private` methods occur quite frequently. These methods can be called only from other operations of the class. The reason is simple: to implement operations, you may wish to break up the code into many separate functions. Many of these functions are not particularly useful to the public. (For example, they may be too close to the current implementation or require a special protocol or calling order.) Such methods are best implemented as `private` operations.

- To implement a private method in Java, simply change the `public` keyword to `private`.

As an example, consider how our `Day` class might require a method to test whether or not a year is a leap year. By making the method private, we are under no obligation to keep it available if we change to another implementation. The method may well be *harder* to implement, or *unnecessary* if the data representation changes: this is irrelevant. The point is that as long as the operation is private, the designers of the class can be assured that it is never used outside the other class operations and can simply drop it. Had the method been public, we would be forced to reimplement it if we changed the representation, because other code might have relied on it. In sum, choose private methods:

- for those functions that are of no concern to the class user and

- for those functions that could not easily be supported if the class implementation were to change.

Static Methods

The last method modifier we want to talk about in this chapter is the `static` modifier. You saw the `static` modifier used to create class constants in Chapter 3. Classes can have both static variables and static methods. Static fields do not change from one instance of a class to another, so you should think of them as belonging to a class. Similarly, static methods belong to a class and do not operate on any instance of a class. This means that you can use them without creating an instance of a class. For example, all of the methods in the `Console` class are static methods. This is why a syntax like

```
x = Console.readDouble();
```

makes perfect sense.

The general syntax for using a static method from a class is:

```
ClassName.staticMethod(parameters);
```

NOTE: Because static methods do not work with an instance of the class they can only access static fields. In particular, if a method needs to access a non-static instance field of an object, it cannot be a static method.

C++ NOTE: Static variables and methods in Java are the same as static data members and member functions in C++. As in C++, the term "static" makes no sense. The original purpose of `static` in C/C++ was to denote local variables that don't go away when the local scope is exited. In that context, the term "static" indicates that the variable stays around and is still there when the block is entered again. Then `static` got a second meaning in C/C++, to denote functions and global variables with file scope that could not be accessed from other files. Finally, C++ reused the keyword for a third, unrelated interpretation, to denote variables and functions that belong to a class but not to any particular object of the class. That is the same meaning that the keyword has in Java.

As another example, consider the header for the `main` method:

```
public static void main(String[] args)
```

Since `main` is `static`, you don't need to create an instance of the class in order to call it—and the Java interpreter doesn't either. For example, if your `main` function is contained in the class `Mortgage` and you start the Java interpreter with

```
java Mortgage
```

then the interpreter simply starts the `main` function without creating an object of the `Mortgage` class. Because of this, `main` can only access static instance fields in the class. It is actually not uncommon for `main` to create an object of its own class!

```
class Application
{    . . .
     public static void main(String[] args)
     {    Application a = new Application();
          . . .
     }
}
```

This allows you to refer to instance variables of the class via the a object variable.

As a more serious example of a class that combines both static and public methods, the following class provides a random-number generator that is a significant improvement over the one supplied with Java. (Java uses a simple "linear congruential generator" that can be non-random in certain situations by displaying undesirable regularities. This is especially true when it is used to plot random points in space or for certain kinds of simulations.) The idea for the improvement is simple (we found it in Donald E. Knuth's *Semi-Numerical Algorithms*, which is Volume 2 of his *Art of Computer Programming* [Addison-Wesley, 1981]); instead of using the random number supplied by a call to

```
java.lang.Math.random();
```

we created a class that:

1.   adds the convenience of generating random integers in a specific range and

2.   is more "random" than the one supplied with Java (but takes about twice as long).

The class works in the following way:

1.   It fills up a small array with random numbers, using the built-in random-number generator. The size of the array and the array itself are made class constants (*i.e.*, declared with `private static final`). This way, all instances of the `randomInteger` class can share this information. (This is obviously more efficient than regenerating this information in each instance.)

2.   It has a public method, called `draw`, for drawing a random integer in the specified range. (You will need to create an instance of our `RandomIntGenerator` class in order to use this method.)

3.   The `draw` method, in turn, uses a static method called `nextRandom` that actually implements the algorithm described in Knuth's *Semi-Numerical Algorithms*, p. 32. The way this works is the method calls the built-in random number generator twice: the first time tells us which random array

element to take, and the second time, we use the resulting random number to replace the "used-up" element in the array. (It is conceptually clearer to have these operations done in a static method, since all instances of our `RandomIntGenerator` class will share these operations.)

4. We use one Java feature in this example that you haven't yet seen. It's called a *static initialization block*. Use these blocks whenever simple initialization statements for static members are either not possible or simply too clumsy. For example, the `RandomIntGenerator` class needs to initialize the buffer entries before you can call the `nextRandom` function for the first time. You need a loop to initialize the buffer array, and a loop cannot be coded with a simple initializer.

    As you can see in the RandomIntGenerator class, the syntax for a static initialization block is simply the keyword `static` followed by the braces that mark any Java code block. Java then executes the statements in the block once, before any method of that class is called. In particular, as with all static functions, you can only refer to the static data of the class in a static initialization block. You can't refer to object instance fields. Finally, you can have as many static initialization blocks as you want in a Java class. They are executed top to bottom.

5. The class constructor defines the range of integers.

The code is shown below.

```
public class RandomIntGenerator
{  public RandomIntGenerator(int l, int h)
   {  low = l;
      high = h;
   }

   public int draw()
   {  int r = low
          + (int)((high - low + 1) * nextRandom());
      if (r > high) r = high;
      return r;
   }

   public static void main(String[] args)
   {  RandomIntGenerator r1
          = new RandomIntGenerator(1, 10);
      RandomIntGenerator r2
          = new RandomIntGenerator(0, 1);
      int i;
      for (i = 1; i <= 100; i++)
         System.out.println(r1.draw() + " " + r2.draw());
   }
```

```
    private static double nextRandom()
    {   int pos =
            (int)(java.lang.Math.random() * BUFFER_SIZE);
        if (pos == BUFFER_SIZE) pos = BUFFER_SIZE - 1;
        double r = buffer[pos];
        buffer[pos] = java.lang.Math.random();
        return r;
    }

    private static final int BUFFER_SIZE = 101;
    private static double[] buffer
        = new double[BUFFER_SIZE];
    static //initialization of static data
    {   int i;
        for (i = 0; i < BUFFER_SIZE; i++)
            buffer[i] = java.lang.Math.random();
    }

    private int low;
    private int high;
}
```

Following is an example using our random integer generator. Note that the test program is simply included in the `RandomIntGenerator` class.

```
class RandomIntGenerator
{   . . .
    public static void main(String[] args)
    {   RandomIntGenerator r1
            = new RandomIntGenerator(1, 10);
        RandomIntGenerator r2
            = new RandomIntGenerator(0, 1);
        int i;
        for (i = 1; i <= 100; i++)
            System.out.println(r1.draw() + " " + r2.draw());
    }
}
```

More on Object Construction and Destruction

Overloading

Recall that both Java's `Date` class and our `Day` class had more than one constructor. We could use:

```
Day today = new Day();
```

or

```
Day preMillenium =  new Day(1999,12,31);
```

This capability is called *overloading*. Overloading occurs if several methods have the same name (in this case the Day constructor method), but different arguments. The Java interpreter must sort out which method to call. (This is usually called *overloading resolution*.) It picks the correct method by matching the argument types in the headers of the various methods with the types of the values used in the specific method call. (Even if there are no arguments, you must use the empty parentheses.) A compile-time error occurs if the compiler cannot match the arguments or if more than one match is possible.

NOTE: Java allows you to overload any method—not just constructor methods.

Overloading is something we will return to in the next chapter. Method overloading (sometimes called *ad-hoc polymorphism*) must be distinguished from true polymorphism, which Java also does support. This, too, is discussed in the next chapter.

Instance Field Initialization

Since you can overload the constructor methods in a class, you can obviously build in many ways to set the instance fields of your classes. It is always a good idea to make sure that regardless of the constructor call, every instance field is set to something meaningful. Actually, Java does set all instance fields to a default value (numbers to zero, objects to null) if you don't set them explicitly. But it is considered poor programming practice to rely on this.

NOTE: In this regard, instance variables differ from local variables in a method. Local variables must be initialized explicitly.

For example, if our Day class did not have any constructors, then the day, month, and year fields would be initialized with zero whenever you made a new Day object. (That wouldn't be a good idea. In the Julian/Gregorian calendar, there is no year 0—the year 1 B.C. is immediately followed by 1 A.D. For that reason, we supply explicit constructors.)

If all constructors of a class need to set a particular instance variable to the same value, then there is a convenient syntax for doing the initialization. You simply assign to the field in the class definition. For example, when you initialize a Customer object, you would want to set the nextOrder instance variable to 1 all the time. This can be done as in the following code:

```
class Customer
{   public Customer(String n)
    {   name = n;
        accountNumber = Account.getNewNumber();
    }
    public Customer(String n, int a)
    {   name = n;
        accountNumber = a;
    }
    . . .
    private String name;
    private int accountNumber;
    private int nextOrder = 1;
}
```

Now the `nextOrder` field is set to 1 in all `Customer` objects.

We recommend that you use this convenient syntax whenever a field is set to the same constant value by all constructors.

A *default constructor* is a constructor with no parameters. If your class has no constructors whatsoever, Java provides a default constructor for you. It sets *all* the instance variables to their default values. So all numeric data contained in the instance fields would be zeroed out and all object variables would point to `null`.

This only applies when your class has no constructors. If you design your class with a constructor, then Java insists that you provide a default constructor if you want the users of your class to have the ability to create an instance via a call to:

```
new ClassName()
```

For example, the `Customer` class defines no constructors that use no parameters, so it is illegal for the users of the class to call:

```
c = new Customer(); // ERROR--no default constructor
```

C++ NOTE: In C++, you cannot directly initialize data members of a class. All data must be set in a constructor.

Java has no analog for the C++ initializer list syntax, such as:

```
Customer::Customer(String n)
:   name(n),
    accountNumber(Account.getNewNumber())
{}
```

C++ uses this special syntax to call the constructor for member objects. In Java, there is no need for it because objects have no member objects, only pointers to other objects.

The `this` Object

Occasionally, you want to access the current object in its entirety and not a particular instance variable. Java has a convenient shortcut for this—the `this` keyword. In a method, the keyword `this` refers to the object on which the method operates.

For example, many Java classes have a method called `toString()` that prints out the object. (For example, Java's `Date` class has this method.) You can print out the current date stored in a date variable by saying `this.toString()`.

More generally, provided your class implements a `toString()` method, you can print it out simply by calling:

```
System.out.println("Customer.computeOverdue: " + this)
```

This is a useful strategy for debugging. We will later see other uses for the `this` object.

There is a second meaning for the `this` keyword. If *the first line of a constructor* has the form `this(. . .)`, then the constructor calls another constructor of the same class. Here is a typical example:

```
class Customer
{   public Customer(String n)
    {   this(n, Account.getNewNumber());
    }
    public Customer(String n, int a)
    {   name = n;
        accountNumber = a;
    }
    . . .
}
```

When you call `new Customer("James Bond")`, then the `Customer(String)` constructor calls the `Customer(String, int)` constructor.

This is a useful device to factor out (combine) common code between constructors.

In sum, as you have seen, constructors are somewhat complex in Java. Before a constructor is called, all instance fields are initialized to the value you specified in the class or to their default values (zero for numbers, `null` for objects). The first line of your constructor may call another constructor.

C++ NOTE: The `this` object in Java is identical to the `this` pointer in C++. However, in C++ it is not possible for one constructor to call another. If you want to factor out common initialization code in C++, you must write a separate member function.

Object Destruction and the finalize() Method

Many languages, such as C++ and Delphi, have explicit destructor methods for the cleanup code that may be needed. The most common activity in a destructor is reclaiming the memory set aside for objects. Since Java does automatic garbage collection, manual memory reclamation is not needed, and Java does not support destructors.

Of course, some objects utilize a resource other than memory, such as a file or a handle to another object that uses system resources. In this case, it is important that the resource be reclaimed and recycled when it is no longer needed.

Java does allow you to add a `finalize()` method to any class. The `finalize()` method will be called before the garbage collector sweeps away the object. In practice, *do not rely on the finalize method* for recycling any resources that are in short supply—you simply cannot know when this method will be called.

If a resource needs to be closed as soon as you have finished using it, you need to manage it manually. Add a `dispose` method that *you* call to clean up what needs cleaning. Just as importantly, if a class you use has a `dispose` method, you will want to call it to reclaim what the designers of the class thought was important to reclaim. In particular, if your class has an instance field that has a `dispose` method, provide a `dispose` method that invokes the field's `dispose`.

A `CardDeck` *Class*

To put together the information in this chapter, we want to show you the code needed for the simplest card game of all. The program chooses two cards at random, one for you and one for the computer. The highest card wins.

The underlying object structure in this example is this: a class called `Card` is used to build up a class called `CardDeck`. A card stores its value (a number between 1 and 13 to denote ace, 2, . . . 10, jack, queen, or king) and its suit (a number between 1 and 4 to denote clubs, diamonds, hearts, or spades). Don't worry about the `final` for the class and for some of the methods in this example. We will explain the significance of this use of the `final` keyword as applied to classes and methods in the next chapter.

```
final class Card // don't worry about the final for now
{
    public static final int ACE = 1;
    public static final int JACK = 11;
    public static final int QUEEN = 12;
    public static final int KING  = 13;
    public static final int CLUBS = 1;
    public static final int DIAMONDS = 2;
    public static final int HEARTS = 3;
    public static final int SPADES = 4;
```

. . .

```
        private int value;
        private int suit;
}
```

Here's the constructor for the Card object. As you might expect, it takes two integers, one for the value and one for the suit.

```
public Card(int v, int s)
{   value = v;
    suit = s;
}
```

The card deck stores an array of cards.

```
class CardDeck
{   . . .
    private Card[] deck;
    private int cards;
}
```

The `cards` field counts how many cards are still in the deck. At the beginning, there are 52 cards, and the count will go down as we draw cards from the deck.

Here's the constructor for the `CardDeck` class:

```
public CardDeck()
{   deck = new Card[52];
    fill();
    shuffle();
}
```

Notice that this constructor initializes the array of `Card` objects. After the array of cards is allocated, it will automatically be filled with cards and shuffled. The `fill` method fills the card deck with 52 cards.

The idea of the shuffle procedure is to choose randomly which of the cards becomes the last one. We then swap the last card with the chosen card and repeat the process with the remainder of the pile.

The full code for the `CardDeck` class is shown here in Example 4-3. Note the code for the game in the `main` function.

Example 4-3: CardDeck.java

```
import corejava.*;

public class CardDeck
{   public CardDeck()
    {   deck = new Card[52];
        fill();
        shuffle();
    }
```

```
public void fill()
{   int i;
    int j;

    for (i = 1; i <= 13; i++)
        for (j = 1; j <= 4; j++)
            deck[4 * (i - 1) + j - 1] = new Card(i, j);
    cards = 52;
}

public void shuffle()
{   int next;
    for (next = 0; next < cards - 1; next++)
    {   int r = new
            RandomIntGenerator(next, cards - 1).draw();
        Card temp = deck[next];
        deck[next] = deck[r];
        deck[r] = temp;
    }
}

public final Card draw()
{   if (cards == 0) return null;
    cards--;
    return deck[cards];
}

public static void main(String[] args)
{   CardDeck d = new CardDeck();
    int i;
    int wins = 0;
    int rounds = 10;

    for (i = 1; i <= rounds; i++)
    {   Card yours = d.draw();
        System.out.print("Your draw: " + yours + " ");
        Card mine = d.draw();
        System.out.print("My draw: " + mine + " ");
        if (yours.rank() > mine.rank())
        {   System.out.println("You win");
            wins++;
        }
        else
            System.out.println("I win");
    }
    System.out.println
("Your wins: " + wins + " My wins: " + (rounds - wins));

}
```

```
    private Card[] deck;
    private int cards;
}
```

Example 4-4 is the complete code for the Card class. Note how we encapsulate the integers that represent the card's suit and value and only return information about them. Also note that once a card object is constructed, its contents can never change.

Example 4-4: Card.java

```java
public final class Card
{   public static final int ACE = 1;
    public static final int JACK = 11;
    public static final int QUEEN = 12;
    public static final int KING  = 13;
    public static final int CLUBS = 1;
    public static final int DIAMONDS = 2;
    public static final int HEARTS = 3;
    public static final int SPADES = 4;

    public Card(int v, int s)
    {   value = v;
        suit = s;
    }

    public int getValue()
    {   return value;
    }

    public int getSuit()
    {   return suit;
    }

    public int rank()
    {   if (value == 1)
            return 4 * 13 + suit;
        else
            return 4 * (value - 1) + suit;
    }

    public String toString()
    {   String v;
        String s;
        if (value == ACE) v = "Ace";
        else if (value == JACK) v = "Jack";
        else if (value == QUEEN) v = "Queen";
        else if (value == KING) v = "King";
        else v = String.valueOf(value);
```

```
        if (suit == DIAMONDS) s = "Diamonds";
        else if (suit == HEARTS) s = "Hearts";
        else if (suit == SPADES) s = "Spades";
        else /* suit == CLUBS */ s = "Clubs";
        return v + " of " + s;
    }

    private int value;
    private int suit;
}
```

Packages

Java allows you to group classes in a collection called a *package*. Packages are convenient for organizing your work and for separating your work from code libraries provided by others.

For example, we give you a number of useful classes in a package called corejava. The standard Java library is distributed over a number of packages, including java.lang, java.util, java.net, and so on. The standard Java packages are examples of a hierarchical package. Just as you have nested subdirectories on your hard disk, you can organize packages using levels of nesting. All standard Java packages are inside the java package hierarchy.

One reason for nesting packages is to guarantee the uniqueness of package names. Suppose someone else has the bright idea of calling their package corejava. By nesting it inside a package hierarchy, such as cornell-horstmann.corejava, we could have kept our package distinct from any other corejava package. You can have as many levels of nesting as you like. In fact, to absolutely guarantee a unique package name, Sun recommends that you use your company's Internet domain name (which presumably is unique) written in reverse order as a package prefix. One of the authors of this book has the registered Internet domain name horstmann.com, so we might have called the corejava package

```
COM.horstmann.corejava
```

When you write a package, you must put the name of the package on top of your source file, *before* the code that defines the classes in the package. For example, the files in our corejava package start like this:

```
package corejava;
```

If you look into the Date.java file of the Java library, you will see the line:

```
package java.util;
```

This means that the Date.java file is part of the java.util package. The package statement must be the first statement in the file after any comments.

If your source file has no package declaration, Java adds the classes in it to its default package.

Using Packages

You can use the public classes in a package in two ways. The first is simply to give the full name of the package. For example:

```
int i = corejava.Console.readInteger();
java.util.Date today = new java.util.Date();
```

That is obviously tedious. The simpler, and more common, approach is to use the `import` keyword. You can then refer to the classes in the package without giving their full names. You can `import` a specific class or the whole package. You place the `import` statement before the source code of the class that will use it. For example:

```
import corejava.*; // imports all the clases in the
                   // corejava package
import java.util.*;
int i = Console.readInteger();
Date today = new java.util.Date();
```

You can also import a specific class inside a package. In this case, you adjust the `import` statement as in the following:

```
import corejava.Console; // imports only the Console class
```

Normally, importing all classes in a package is simpler. It has no negative effect on compile time or code size, so there is generally no reason not to do it. However, if two packages each have classes with the same name, then you can't import them both.

Finally, you can only use the * to import a single package. You cannot use `import java.*` to import all packages with the `java` prefix.

How the Compiler Locates Packages

All files of a package must be located in a subdirectory that matches the full package name. For example, all files in our `corejava` package must be in the subdirectory `corejava`. All files in the `java.util` package are in a subdirectory `java\util` (`java/util` on Unix).

These subdirectories need not branch off directly from the root directory; they can branch off from any directory named in the `CLASSPATH` variable. Suppose your `CLASSPATH` is as follows:

```
CLASSPATH=c:\java\lib;c:\corejava-book;.
```

Suppose your code contains the lines:

```
import java.util.*;
import corejava.*;
```

If you use the class `Console`, the compiler looks for the following files:

```
c:\java\lib\Console.class
c:\java\lib\corejava\Console.class
c:\java\lib\java\util\Console.class
c:\corejava-book\Console.class
c:\corejava-book\java\util\Console.class
c:\corejava-book\corejava\Console.class
.\Console.class
.\java\util\Console.class
.\corejava\Console.class
```

When it finds a matching file, it checks that the package name matches the path and that the file contains a public class named `Console` inside the package.

Actually, if you look inside `c:\java\lib`, you may not find the subdirectory `java\util`. Instead, there often is just a single ZIP file, `classes.zip`. If you look inside that ZIP file with a ZIP viewer like WinZip, you will see the paths and the class files. If you like, you can also zip up your own packages in a file named `classes.zip` that is located on the class path.

In addition, the compiler always searches the `java.lang` package. You never need to specify it, nor do you need to import it.

When you make a package, it is your responsibility to place the object files in the correct subdirectory. For example, if you compile a file that starts with the line

```
package acme.util;
```

then you must put the resulting class file into the subdirectory `acme\util`. The compiler won't do it for you.

C++ NOTE: C++ programmers usually confuse `import` with `#include`. The two have nothing in common. In C++, you must use `#include` to include the declarations of external features, because the C++ compiler does not look inside any files except the one that it is compiling and explicitly included header files. The Java compiler will happily look inside other files provided you tell it where to look.

In Java, you can entirely avoid the `import` mechanism by explicitly naming all packages, such as `java.util.Date`. In C++, you cannot avoid the `#include` directives.

The only benefit of the `import` statement is convenience. You can refer to a class by a name shorter than the full package name. For example, after an `import java.util.*` (or `import java.util.Date`) statement, you can refer to the `java.util.Date` class simply as `Date`.

The analogous construction in C++ is the *namespace* feature. Think of the `package` and `import` keywords in Java as the analogs of `namespace` and `using` in C++.

Package Scope

We have already encountered the access modifiers `public` and `private`. Features tagged as `public` can be used by any class. Private features can only be used by the class that defines them. If you don't specify either `public` or `private`, then the feature (that is, the class, method or variable) can be accessed by all methods in the same *package*.

For example, if the class `Card` is not defined as a public class, then only other classes in the same package (such as `CardDeck`) can access it. For classes, that is a very reasonable default. However, methods should generally be either explicitly public or private, and instance and static variables should be private.

NOTE: Every source file can contain, at most, one public class, which must have the same name as the file.

Class Design Hints

Without trying to be comprehensive or tedious, we want to end this chapter with some hints that may make your classes more acceptable in well-mannered OOP circles.

1. *Always keep data private.*

This is first and foremost: doing anything else violates encapsulation. You may need to write an accessor or mutator method occasionally, but you are still better off keeping the instance fields private. Bitter experience has shown that how the data are represented may change, but how they are used will change much less frequently. When data are kept private, changes in their representation do not affect the user of the class, and bugs are easier to detect.

2. *Always initialize data.*

Java won't initialize local variables for you, but it will initialize instance variables of objects. Don't rely on the defaults, but initialize the variables explicitly, either by supplying a default or by setting defaults in all constructors.

3. *Don't use too many basic types in a class.*

The idea is to replace multiple *related* uses of basic types with other classes. This keeps your classes easier to understand and to change. For example, replace the following instance fields in a `Customer` class

```java
private String street;
private String city;
private String state;
private int zip;
```

with a new class called `Address`. This way, one can easily cope with changes to addresses, such as the need to deal with international addresses.

4.   *Not all fields need individual field accessors and mutators.*

You may need to get and set a person's salary. You certainly won't need to change his or her hiring date once the object is constructed. And, quite often, objects have instance variables that you don't want others to get or set, for example, the array of cards in the card deck.

5.   *Use a standard form for class definitions.*

We always list the contents of classes in the following order:

> public features
>
> package scope features
>
> private features

Within each section, we list:

> constants
>
> constructors
>
> methods
>
> static methods
>
> instance variables
>
> static variables

After all, the users of your class are more interested in the public interface than in the details of the private implementation. And they are more interested in methods than in data.

6.   *Break up classes with too many responsibilities.*

This hint is, of course, vague: "too many" is obviously in the eye of the beholder. However, if there is an obvious way to make one complicated class into two classes that are conceptually simpler, seize the opportunity. (On the other hand, don't go overboard; 10 classes, each with only one method, is usually overkill.)

Here is an example of a bad design. In our card game, we could do without the `Card` class by having the deck store two arrays: one for the suits and one for the values. That would make it hard to draw and return a card, so we would need to fake it with functions that can look up the properties of the top card on the deck.

```
class CardDeck // bad design
{  public void CardDeck() { . . . }
   public void shuffle() { . . . }
```

```
    public int getTopValue() { . . . }
    public int getTopSuit() { . . . }
    public int topRank() { . . . }
    public void draw() { . . . }

    private int[] value;
    private int[] suit;
    private int cards;
}
```

As you can see, this is implementable, but it is clumsy. It makes sense to introduce the `Card` class because the cards are meaningful objects in this context.

7.   *Make the names of your classes and methods reflect their responsibilities.*

Just as variables should have meaningful names that reflect what they do, so should classes. (The standard library certainly contains some dubious example, such as the `Date` class that describes time and the `getDay` method that returns the weekday, not the day.)

A good convention is that a class name should be a noun (`Order`) or a noun preceded by an adjective (`RushOrder`) or a gerund (an "ing" word— `BillingAddress`). As for methods, follow the standard convention that accessor methods begin with a lowercase `get` (`getDay`), and mutator methods use a lowercase `set` (`setSalary`).

CHAPTER

5

- First Steps with Inheritance
- Casting
- Abstract Classes
- Interfaces
- More on `Object`: The Cosmic Superclass
- The Class `Class` (Run-Time Type Identification)
- Protected Access
- Design Hints for Inheritance

Going Further with OOP: Inheritance

The last chapter introduced OOP. This chapter explains most of the remaining concepts you need to know, particularly with regard to deriving new classes from existing classes. You can reuse or change the methods of existing classes, as well as add new instance fields and new methods. This concept is usually called *inheritance* and was briefly touched upon in the last chapter. It is, however, vital to Java programming. (For example, as you will see in the next chapter, you cannot even put up a window in Java without using inheritance!)

As with the previous chapter, if you are coming from a procedure-oriented language like C or COBOL, you will want to read this chapter carefully. The same holds true for *all* users of VB (even VB4 users—the crippled object model in VB4 does not allow for inheritance).

For experienced C++ programmers, or those coming from another object-oriented language like Smalltalk, this chapter will seem largely familiar, but there are *many* differences between how inheritance is implemented in Java and how it is done in C++ or in other object-oriented languages. You will probably want to read the later sections of this chapter carefully.

First Steps with Inheritance

Let's return to the `Employee` class that we discussed in the previous chapter. Suppose (alas) you work for a company at which managers are treated substantially differently than other employees. Their raises are computed differently; they have access to a secretary; and so on. This is the kind of situation that in OOP cries out for inheritance. Why? Well, you need to define a new class, `Manager`, and add functionality, but you can retain some of what you have already programmed in the `Employee` class, and *all* the instance fields of the original class can be preserved. More abstractly, there is an obvious "is–a" relationship between `Manager` and `Employee`. Every manager *is an* employee: this is the hallmark of inheritance.

Here is some code for extending the `Employee` class to be a `Manager` class.

```
class Manager extends Employee
{   public Manager(String n, double s, Day d)
    {   super(n, s, d);
        secretaryName = "";
    }

    public void raiseSalary(double byPercent)
    {   // add 1/2% bonus for every year of service
        Day today = new Day();
        double bonus = 0.5 * (today.getYear() - hireYear());
        super.raiseSalary(byPercent + bonus);
    }

    public String getSecretaryName()
    { return secretaryName;
    }

    public void setSecretaryName(String name)
    { secretaryName = name;
    }

    private String secretaryName;
}
```

Let's go over the new features of this class, line by line. First, notice that the header for this class is a little different:

```
class Manager extends Employee
```

The keyword `extends` indicates that you are making a new class that derives from an existing class. The existing class is called the *superclass, base class,* or *parent class*. The new class is called the *subclass, derived class,* or *child class*. The terms superclass and subclass are those most commonly used by Java programmers, although we prefer the parent/child analogy, which also ties in nicely with the "inheritance" theme.

The `Employee` class is a superclass, but not because it is superior to its subclass or contains more functionality. *In fact, the opposite is true:* subclasses have *more* functionality than their superclasses. For example, as you will see when we go over the rest of the `Manager` class code, it encapsulates more data and has more functionality than its superclass `Employee`. As another example, you will see in the next chapter a superclass `Window`, which we extend to many useful subclasses, such as `FileDialog`.

143

> NOTE: The prefixes *super* and *sub* come from the language of sets used in theoretical computer science and mathematics. The set of all employees *contains* the set of all managers, and this is described by saying it is a *superset* of the set of managers. Similarly, the set of all file dialog windows is *contained* by the set of all windows, so it is a *subset* of the set of all windows.

Next, notice the constructor for the `Manager` class:

```
public Manager(String n, double s, Day d)
{   super(n, s, d);
    secretaryName = "";
}:
```

The keyword `super` always refers to the superclass (in this case, `Employee`). So the line

```
super(n, s, d);
```

is shorthand for "call the constructor of the `Employee` class with n, s, and d as parameters." The reason for this line is that every constructor of a subclass is also responsible for constructing the data fields of the superclass. Unless the subclass constructor is happy with the default constructor of the superclass, it must explicitly use `super` with the appropriate parameters. The call to `super` must be the first line in the constructor for the subclass.

Next, as this example shows, subclasses can have more instance fields than the parent class. Following good programming practices, we set the `secretaryName` instance field to the empty string in order to initialize it. (By default, it would have been initialized to `null`.)

If you compare the `Manager` class with the `Employee` class, you will see that many of the methods are not repeated. This is because, unless otherwise specified, a subclass uses the methods of the superclass. In particular, when inheriting from a superclass, you need to indicate only the *differences* between the subclass and superclass. The ability to reuse methods in the superclass is automatic. Therefore, we do not need to give a new definition of, for example, a `getName` method, since the one in the superclass does what we need. However, do note that we are giving a new definition of the `raiseSalary` method:

```
public void raiseSalary(double byPercent)
{   // add 1/2% bonus for every year of service
    Day today = new Day();
    double bonus = 0.5 * (today.getYear() - hireYear());
    super.raiseSalary(byPercent + bonus);
}
```

We are also adding accessor and mutator methods to set the current name of the secretary.

The need to redefine methods is one of the main reasons to use inheritance; this is a good example. Life being the way it is, raises for managers are calculated differently than those for non-managers. In this case, suppose you give a companywide raise of three percent. For the managers, the `raiseSalary` method does the following:

1. It calculates a bonus percentage increase based on time employed.

2. Then, because of the use of `super` in the line

```
super.raiseSalary(byPercent + bonus);
```

the method looks to the `raiseSalary` method of the superclass and passes it a parameter that adds the original parameter and a bonus of half a percent for each year of service since the hire year.

The result is that when you give all employees a raise of three percent, the managers will *automatically* be given a larger raise. Here's an example of this at work: we make a new manager and set the manager's secretary's name:

```
Manager boss = new Manager("Carl Cracker", 75000,
    new Day(1987,12,15));
boss.setSecretaryName("Harry Hacker");
```

We make an array of three employees:

```
Employee[] staff = new Employee[3];
```

We populate the array with a mix of employees and managers:

```
staff[0] = boss;
staff[1] = new Employee("Harry Hacker", 35000,
    new Day(1989,10,1));
staff[2] = new Employee("Tony Tester", 38000,
    new Day(1990,3,15));
```

We raise everyone's salary by three percent:

```
for (i = 0; i < 3; i++) staff[i].raiseSalary(3);
```

Now `staff[1]` and `staff[2]` each get a raise of three percent because they are `Employee` objects. However, `staff[0]` is a `Manager` object and gets a higher raise. Finally, let's print out all employee records and the name of the secretary.

```
for (i = 0; i < 3; i++) staff[i].print();
System.out.println(boss.getName() + "'s current secretary is "
    + boss.getSecretaryName());
```

Because we didn't define a special `print` method for managers, all three objects are printed with the `Employee` print method. (We could have changed the `print` method in the `Manager` class in order to print out the current name of a manager's secretary.)

Example 5-1 is the full sample code that shows you the Manager class at work.

Example 5-1: ManagerTest.java

```java
import java.util.*;
import corejava.*;

public class ManagerTest
{   public static void main(String[] args)
    {   Employee[] staff = new Employee[3];

        staff[0] = new Employee("Harry Hacker", 35000,
            new Day(1989,10,1));
        staff[1] = new Manager("Carl Cracker", 75000,
            new Day(1987,12,15));
        staff[2] = new Employee("Tony Tester", 38000,
            new Day(1990,3,15));
        int i;
        for (i = 0; i < 3; i++) staff[i].raiseSalary(5);
        for (i = 0; i < 3; i++) staff[i].print();
    }
}

class Employee
{   public Employee(String n, double s, Day d)
    {   name = n;
        salary = s;
        hireDay = d;
    }
    public void print()
    {   System.out.println(name + " " + salary + " "
            + hireYear());
    }
    public void raiseSalary(double byPercent)
    {   salary *= 1 + byPercent / 100;
    }
    public int hireYear()
    {   return hireDay.getYear();
    }

    private String name;
    private double salary;
    private Day hireDay;
}

class Manager extends Employee
{   public Manager(String n, double s, Day d)
    {   super(n, s, d);
    }
```

```
public void raiseSalary(double byPercent)
{  // add 1/2% bonus for every year of service
   Day today = new Day();
   double bonus = 0.5 * (today.getYear() - hireYear());
   super.raiseSalary(byPercent + bonus);
}
}
```

C++ NOTE: Inheritance is similar in Java and C++. Java uses the `extends` keyword instead of the `":"` token. Java uses the keyword `super` to refer to the base class. In C++, you would use the name of the base class with the `::` operator instead. For example, the `raiseSalary` function of the `Manager` class would call `Employee::raiseSalary` instead of `super.raiseSalary`. In a C++ constructor, you do not call `super`, but you use the initializer list syntax to construct the base class. The `Manager` constructor looks like this in C++:

```
Manager::Manager(String n, double s, Day d) // C++
: Employee(n, s, d)
{
}
```

Inheritance need not stop at deriving one layer of classes. We could have an `Executive` class that derives from `Manager`, for example. The collection of all classes extending from a common parent is called an *inheritance hierarchy*. As shown in Figure 5-1, the path from a particular class to its ancestors in the inheritance hierarchy is an *inheritance chain*.

There is usually more than one chain of descent from a distant ancestor class. You could derive a `Programmer` class from `Employee` class or a `Secretary` class from `Employee`, and they would have nothing to do with the `Manager` class (or with each other). This process can continue as long as is necessary.

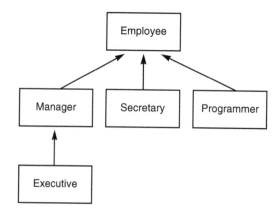

Figure 5-1: Employee inheritance hierarchy

Working with Subclasses

One way to know whether or not inheritance is right for your program is to keep in mind that any object of the subclass must be useable in place of the superclass object. If this is not true, do not use inheritance. (This is a more concrete way of thinking of the "is–a" relationship that is the hallmark of inheritance.) In particular, subclass objects are useable in any code that uses the superclass.

For example, you can assign a subclass object to a superclass variable. We did that in the sample code of the preceding section.

```
Employee[] staff = new Employee[3];
Manager boss = new Manager("Carl Cracker", 75000,
    new Day(1987,12,15));
staff[0] = boss;
```

In this case, the variables `staff[0]` and `boss` refer to the same area of memory. However, `staff[0]` is only considered to be an *Employee* object by the compiler.

Similarly, a subclass object can be passed as an argument to any method that expects a superclass parameter.

The converse is false in general: a superclass object cannot usually be assigned to a subclass object. For example, it is not legal to make the assignment:

```
boss = staff[i]; // Error
```

The reason is clear: the subclass object may have more fields than the superclass object (as it does in this case), and the subclass methods have to be able to access those fields. If the fields are not accessible, run-time errors will result. Always keep in mind that subclass objects have at least as many data items as objects from the superclass because fields can only be added, not taken away, in inheritance.

C++ NOTE: Java does not support multiple inheritance. (For ways to recover much of the functionality of multiple inheritance, see the section on Interfaces in this chapter.)

Objects Know How to Do Their Work: Polymorphism

It is important to understand what happens when a method call is applied to objects of various types in an inheritance hierarchy. Remember that in OOP, you are sending messages to objects, asking them to perform actions. When you send a message that asks a subclass to apply a method using certain parameters, here is what happens:

- The subclass checks whether or not it has a method with that name and with *exactly* the same parameters. If so, it uses it.

If not,

- Java moves to the parent class and looks there for a method with that name and those parameters. If so, it calls that method.

Since Java can continue moving up the inheritance chain, parent classes are checked until the chain of inheritance stops or until Java finds a matching method. (If Java cannot find a matching method in the whole inheritance chain, you get a compile-time error.) Notice that methods with the same name can exist on many levels of the chain. This leads to one of the fundamental rules of inheritance:

- A method defined in a subclass with the same name and parameter list as a method in one of its ancestor classes hides the method of the ancestor class from the subclass.

For example, the `raiseSalary` method of the `Manager` class is called instead of the `raiseSalary` method of the `Employee` class when you send a `raiseSalary` message to a `Manager` object.

> NOTE: The name and parameter list for a method is usually called the method's *signature.* For example, `raiseSalary(double)` and `raiseSalary(boolean)` are two methods with different signatures. In Java, having methods in a class or in a superclass and a subclass with the same signature but differing return types will give you a compile-time error. For instance, you cannot have a method `void raiseSalary(double)` in the `Employee` class and a function `int raiseSalary(double)` in the `Manager` class.

An object's ability to decide what method to apply to itself, depending on where it is in the inheritance hierarchy, is usually called *polymorphism*. The idea behind polymorphism is that while the message may be the same, objects may respond differently. Polymorphism can apply to any method that is inherited from a superclass.

The key to making polymorphism work is called *late binding*. This means that the compiler does not generate the code to call a method at compile time. Instead, every time you define a method with an object, the compiler generates code to calculate which method to call, using type information from the object. This process is usually called late binding, *dynamic binding,* or *dynamic dispatch.* The regular function call mechanism is called *static binding,* since the operation to be executed is completely determined at compile time. Static binding depends on the method alone; dynamic binding depends on the type of the object variable *and* the position of the actual object in the inheritance hierarchy.

NOTE: Many Java users follow C++ terminology and refer to *virtual functions* for functions that are dynamically bound.

C++ NOTE: In Java, you do not need to declare a method as virtual. This is the default behavior. If you do *not* want a function to be virtual, you tag it as `final`. (We discuss this in the next section.)

To sum up, inheritance and polymorphism let the application spell out the general way it wants things to proceed. The individual classes in the inheritance hierarchy are responsible for carrying out the details—using polymorphism to determine which methods to call. Polymorphism in an inheritance hierarchy is sometimes called *true polymorphism*, to distinguish it from the more limited kind of name overloading that is not resolved dynamically, but is resolved statically at compile time.

Preventing Inheritance: Final Classes and Methods

Occasionally, you want to prevent someone from deriving a class from one of your classes. Classes that cannot be parent classes are called *final* classes, and you use the `final` modifier in the definition of the class to indicate this. For example, the `Card` class from the last chapter was final, so its header began:

```
final class Card
```

You can also make a specific method in a class `final`. If you do this, then no subclass can override that method. (All methods in a `final` class are automatically `final`.) A class or method is made `final` for one of two reasons:

1. **Efficiency**

    Dynamic binding has more overhead than static binding—thus, virtual methods run slower. The dynamic dispatching mechanism is slightly less efficient than a straight procedure call. More importantly, the compiler cannot replace a trivial method with inline code because it is possible that a derived class would override that trivial code. The compiler can put final methods in line. For example, if `e.getName()` is final, the compiler can replace it with `e.name`. (So you get all the benefits of direct access to instance fields *without violating encapsulation*.)

    Microprocessors hate procedure calls because they interfere with their strategy of getting and decoding the next instructions while processing the current one. Replacing calls to trivial procedures with inline code is a big win. This is more important for a true compiler than for an interpreter like the current version of Java, but JIT's can take advantage of this, and true Java compilers are in the works.

2. **Safety**

The flexibility of the dynamic dispatch mechanism means that you have no control over what happens when you call a method. When you send a message, such as e.getName(), it is possible that e is an object of a derived class that redefined the getName method to return an entirely different string. By making the method final, you avoid this possible ambiguity.

We used final methods and final classes in the Card class of the preceding chapter. We knew that nobody would derive a new class from the Card class, so we made it final for efficiency reasons. The String class in the Java library is final for probably the same reasons.

> C++ NOTE: In C++, a member function is not virtual by default, and you can tag it as inline in order to have function calls replaced with the function source code. However, there is no mechanism that would prevent a derived class from overriding a member function. In C++, it is possible to write classes from which no other class can derive, but it requires an obscure trick, and there are few reasons to do so.

Casting

Just as you occasionally need to convert an integer to a double, you also need to convert an object from one class to another. As was the case with converting basic types, this is called *casting*. To actually make a cast, use a syntax similar to the one you used for casting between variables of the basic types. Surround the target type with parentheses and place it before the object you want to cast. For example:

```
Manager boss = (Manager)staff[0];
```

There is only one reason why you would want to make a cast—to use an object in its full capacity after its actual type has been downplayed. For example, in the Manager class, the staff array had to be an array of Employee objects since *some* of its entries were regular employees. We would need to cast the managerial elements of the array back to Manager in order to access any of its new fields. (Note that in the sample code for the first section, we made a special effort to avoid the cast. We initialized the boss variable with a Manager object before storing it in the array. We needed the correct type in order to find the secretary of the manager.)

As you know, in Java, every object variable has a type. The type describes the kind of object the variable refers to and what it can do. For example, staff[i] refers to an Employee object (so it can also refer to a Manager object).

You rely on these descriptions in your code, and the compiler checks that you do not promise too much when you describe a variable. If you assign a subclass object to a superclass variable, you are promising less, and the compiler will simply let you do it. If you assign a superclass object to a subclass variable, you are promising more, and you must confirm that you mean what you say to the compiler with the (Subclass) cast notation.

What happens if you try to cast down an inheritance chain and you are "lying" about what an object contains?

```
Manager boss = (Manager)staff[1]; // Error
```

When the program runs, Java notices the broken promise, generates an exception (see the sidebar in this chapter and Chapter 10), and the program will usually die. It is good programming practice to find out whether or not your object is an instance of another object before doing a cast. This is accomplished with the instanceof operator. For example:

```
if (staff[1] instanceof Manager)
{  boss = (Manager)staff[1];
   . . .
}
```

Finally, the compiler will not let you make a cast if there is no chance for the cast to succeed. For example, the cast

```
Window w = (Window)staff[1];
```

will not succeed because Window is not a subclass of Employee.

To sum up, you can only cast within an inheritance hierarchy. You should use instanceof to check a hierarchy before casting from a parent to a child class.

Actually, performing a cast is not usually a good idea. In our example, you do not need to cast an Employee object to Manager for most purposes. The print and raiseSalary methods will work correctly on both types, because the dynamic binding automatically locates the correct method. The only reason to perform the cast is to use a method that is unique to managers, such as getSecretaryName. If it is important to get the name of a secretary for an object of type Employee, you should redesign that class and add a getSecretaryName method, which simply returns an empty string. That makes more sense than trying to remember which array locations stored which type, or to perform tedious type inquiries. Remember, it takes only one bad cast to terminate your program.

C++ NOTE: Java uses the cast syntax from the "bad old days" of C, but it works like the safe `dynamic_cast` operation of C++. For example,

```
Manager boss = (Manager)staff[1]; // Java
```

is the same as

```
Manager* boss = dynamic_cast<Manager*>(staff[1]); // C++
```

with one important difference. If the cast fails, it does not yield a `null` object, but throws an exception. In this sense, it is like a C++ cast of *references*. This is a pain in the neck. In C++, you can take care of the type test and type conversion in one operation.

```
Manager* boss = dynamic_cast<Manager*>(staff[1]); // C++
if (boss != NULL) . . .
```

In Java, you use a combination of the `instanceof` operator and a cast.

```
if (staff[1] instanceof Manager)
{  Manager boss = (Manager)staff[1];
      . . .
}
```

Abstract Classes

As you move up the inheritance hierarchy, classes become more general and probably more abstract. At some point, the ancestor class becomes *so* general that you think of it more as a framework for other classes than as a class with specific instances you want to use. Consider, for example, an electronic messaging system that integrates your e-mail, faxes, and voice mail. It must be able to handle text messages, fax messages, and voice messages.

Following the principles of OOP, the program will need classes called `TextMessage`, `VoiceMessage`, and `FaxMessage`. Of course, a mailbox needs to store a mixture of these messages, so it will have the common parent class `Message` as well as shown in Figure 5-2.

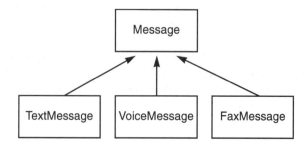

Figure 5-2: Inheritance diagram for message classes

Why bother with so high a level of abstraction? The answer is that it makes the design of your classes cleaner. (Well, it does once you are familiar with OOP.) Ultimately, one of the keys to OOP is to understand how to factor out common operations to a higher level in the inheritance hierarchy. In our case, all messages have a common method, namely `play()`. It is easy to figure out how to play a voice message—you send it to the loudspeaker. You play a text message by showing it in a text window and a fax message by showing it in a graphics window. But how do you implement `play()` in the parent class `Message`?

The answer is that you can't. In Java, you use the `abstract` keyword to indicate that a method cannot yet be specified in a class. For added clarity, a class with one or more abstract methods must itself be declared abstract.

```
public abstract class Message
{   . . .
    public abstract void play();
}
```

Abstract classes can have (some) concrete data and methods. For example, the `Message` class can store the sender of the mail message and have a concrete method that returns the sender's name.

```
abstract class Message
{   public Message(String from) { sender = from; }

    public abstract void play();
    public String getSender() { return sender; }

    private String sender;
}
```

The key point is that, in addition to the ordinary methods you have seen, an abstract class has at least one *abstract method*. An abstract method promises that all nonabstract descendants of this abstract class will implement that abstract method. Abstract methods act as placeholder methods that are implemented in the subclasses.

TIP: It is common to think that abstract classes should have only abstract methods. This is not true: it always makes sense to move as much functionality as possible into a superclass, whether or not it is abstract. In particular, move common instance fields and *nonabstract* operations to the abstract superclass. Only those operations that cannot be implemented in the superclass should be given to the subclasses.

C++ NOTE: In C++, an abstract method is called a *pure virtual function* and is tagged with a
trailing `= 0`, such as in

```
class Message // C++
{  public:
       virtual void play() = 0;
       . . .
}
```

As in Java, a C++ class is abstract if it has at least one pure virtual function. But there is no special syntax to denote abstract classes.

To see a realization of this abstract class and the `play` method, try this code for the `TextMessage` class:

```
class TextMessage extends Message
{  public TextMessage(String from, String t)
   { super(from); text = t; }

   public void play() { System.out.println(text); }

   private String text;
}
```

Notice that we only need to give a concrete definition of the abstract `play` method in the `TextMessage` class.

Here's the code for the sample messaging program. Don't worry too much about the code for playing the wave file in this example; it uses a few language features, such as streams and exceptions, that we will discuss in later chapters. It also uses an undocumented feature of Java that lets you play audio clips from within an application as opposed to an applet. This is a teaching example, so we kept the user interface simple and ugly to allow you to focus on the OOP aspects instead of being distracted by GUI code. When you run the program, you can leave a text message by typing it in or leave a voice message by typing in the name of an audio file. We supply you with two sample audio files on the CD, or you can use your own. They must be in `.au` format like Example 5-2.

Example 5-2: MailboxTest.java

```
import java.io.*;
import sun.audio.*;
import corejava.*;

public class MailboxTest
{  public static void main(String[] args)
```

```java
   {  Mailbox mbox = new Mailbox();
      while (true)
      {  System.out.println(mbox.status());
         String cmd = Console.readString
               ("play, text, voice, quit> ");
         if (cmd.equals("play"))
         {  Message m = mbox.remove();
            if (m != null)
            {  System.out.println("From: " + m.getSender());
               m.play();
            }
         }
         else if (cmd.equals("text"))
         {  String from = Console.readString("Your name: ");
            boolean more = true;
            String msg = "";
            System.out.println
               ("Enter message, 'exit' when done");

            while (more)
            {  String line = Console.readString();
               if (line.equals("exit"))
                  more = false;
               else msg = msg + line + "\n";
            }
            mbox.insert(new TextMessage(from, msg));
         }
         else if (cmd.equals("voice"))
         {  String from = Console.readString("Your name: ");
            String msg
               = Console.readString("Audio file name: ");
            mbox.insert(new VoiceMessage(from, msg));
         }
         else if (cmd.equals("quit"))
            System.exit(0);
      }
   }
}

abstract class Message
{  public Message(String from) { sender = from; }

   public abstract void play();
   public String getSender() { return sender; }

   private String sender;
}
```

```
class TextMessage extends Message
{   public TextMessage(String from, String t)
    { super(from); text = t; }

    public void play() { System.out.println(text); }

    private String text;
}

class VoiceMessage extends Message
{   public VoiceMessage(String from, String f)
    { super(from); filename = f; }

    public void play()
    {   AudioPlayer ap = AudioPlayer.player;
        try
        {   AudioStream as
               = new AudioStream(new FileInputStream(filename));
            ap.start(as);
        }
        catch(IOException e) {}
    }

    private String filename;
}

class Mailbox
{   public Message remove()
    {   if (nmsg == 0) return null;
        Message r = messages[out];
        nmsg--;
        out = (out + 1) % MAXMSG;
        return r;
    }

    public void insert(Message m)
    {   if (nmsg == MAXMSG) return;
        messages[in] = m;
        nmsg++;
        in = (in + 1) % MAXMSG;
    }

    public String status()
    {   if (nmsg == 0) return "Mailbox empty";
        else if (nmsg == 1) return "1 message";
        else if (nmsg < MAXMSG) return nmsg + " messages";
        else return "Mailbox full";
    }
```

```
private final int MAXMSG = 10;
private int in = 0;
private int out = 0;
private int nmsg = 0;
private Message[] messages = new Message[MAXMSG];
}
```

Catching Exceptions

We will cover exception handling fully in Chapter 10, but once in a while you will encounter code that involves exceptions. Here is a quick introduction on what the exceptions are and how to handle them.

When an error occurs at run time, a Java program can "throw an exception." For example, code that attempts to open a file can throw an exception if the file unexpectedly cannot be opened. Throwing an exception is less violent and less fatal than terminating the program, because it provides the option of "catching" the exception and dealing with it.

If an exception is not caught anywhere, the program will terminate, and a message will be printed to the console giving the type of the exception.

Without going into too much detail, here is the basic syntax. To run code that might throw an exception, you have to place it inside a "try" block. Then you have to provide an emergency action to deal with the exception, in the unlikely case that one actually occurs.

```
try
{   code that might
    throw exceptions
}   catch(ExceptionType e)
{   emergency action
}
```

We used that mechanism in the code that plays an audio clip.

```
    try
{   AudioStream as
        = new AudioStream(new FileInputStream(filename));
    ap.start(as);
}
    catch(IOException e) {}
```

The above says, in effect, "Do not end the program if you have an I/O (input/output) error—just ignore the error and do not play the clip."

The compiler is somewhat selective as to which exceptions *must* be handled. For example, when you access an array or perform a cast, you need not supply an exception handler, even though the array index or the cast might be invalid, causing the code to throw an exception. However, for other operations, such as input and output, you must specify what you want to happen when there is a problem.

> **Catching Exceptions (continued)**
>
> Exceptions are a complex topic, and it is not generally a good idea to ignore them when they happen. But a full discussion will have to wait until Chapter 10.

C++ NOTE: The Java and C++ exception mechanisms are similar. Chapter 10 explains the differences.

Interfaces

Suppose you wanted to write a general sorting routine that would work on many different kinds of Java objects. You now know how to organize this in an object-oriented fashion. You have the class `Sortable` with the method `compare` that determines whether or not one sortable object is less than, equal to, or greater than another.

Now you can implement a generic sorting algorithm. Here is an implementation of a shell sort, for sorting an array of `Sortable` objects.

```java
abstract class Sortable
{   public abstract int compare(Sortable b);

    public static void shell_sort(Sortable[] a)
    {   int n = a.length;
        int incr = n / 2;
        while (incr >= 1)
        {   for (int i = incr; i < n; i++)
            {   Sortable temp = a[i];
                int j = i;
                while (j >= incr
                    && temp.compare(a[j - incr]) < 0)
                {   a[j] = a[j - incr];
                    j -= incr;
                }
                a[j] = temp;
            }
            incr /= 2;
        }
    }
}
```

This seems quite elegant. You would then use polymorphism to get the sorting routine in all the subclasses of the `Sortable` abstract class (by overriding the `compare` method in the subclass).

For example, to sort an array of employees (ordering them by—what else—their salary), we

1. derive `Employee` from `Sortable`,

2. implement the `compare` method for employees,

3. call `shell_sort` on the employee array.

Here's an example of the extra code needed to do this in our `Employee` class:

```
class Employee extends Sortable
{   . . .
    public int compare(Sortable b)
    {   Employee eb = (Employee)b;
        if (salary < eb.salary) return -1;
        if (salary > eb.salary) return 1;
        return 0;
    }

    public static void main(String[] args)
    {   Employee[] staff = new Employee[3];
        . . .
        Sortable.shell_sort(staff);
        . . .
    }
}
```

There is, unfortunately, a major problem with implementing this strategy in Java. For example, we wrote a `Tile` class that models tiled windows on a screen desktop. Tiled windows are rectangles plus a "z-order." Windows with a larger z-order are displayed in front of those with a smaller z-order. To reuse code, we inherit `Tile` from `Rectangle`, a class that is already defined in the `java.awt` package.

```
class Tile extends Rectangle
{   public Tile(int x, int y, int w, int h, int zz)
    {   super(x, y, w, h);
        z = zz;
    }

    private int z;
}
```

Now we would like to sort an array of tiles by comparing z-orders. If we try to apply the procedure for making tiles sortable, we get stuck at step (1). We cannot derive `Tile` from `Sortable`—it already derives from `Rectangle`!

The point is that, in Java, a class can have only one superclass. Other programming languages, in particular C++, allow a class to have more than one superclass. This is called *multiple inheritance*.

Instead, Java introduces the notion of *interfaces* to recover much of the functionality that multiple inheritance gives you. The designers of Java chose this road because multiple inheritance makes compilers either very complex (as in C++) or very inefficient (as in Eiffel). (Interfaces also allow you to implement "callback functions" in Java—see the section on callbacks later in this chapter for more on this important topic.)

So what is an interface? Essentially, it is a promise that your class will implement certain methods with certain signatures. You even use the keyword implements to indicate that your class will keep these promises. The way in which these methods are implemented is up to the class, of course. The important point, as far as the compiler is concerned, is that the methods have the right signature.

For example, suppose you wanted to create an interface called Sortable that could be used by any class that will sort. The code for the Sortable interface might look like this:

```
public interface Sortable
{   public int compare(Sortable b);
}
```

This code promises that any class that implements the Sortable interface will have a compare method that will take a Sortable object. A Sortable object, in turn, is any instance of a class that implements Sortable (therefore, any class that has a compare method). Of course, the way in which the compare method works (or even whether or not it works as one would expect) in a specific class depends on the class that is implementing the Sortable interface. The key point is that any class can promise to implement Sortable—regardless of whether or not its superclass promises the same. All descendants of such a class would implement Sortable, since they all would have access to a compare method with the right signature.

To tell Java that your class implements Sortable, you have the class header read something like this:

```
class Tile extends Rectangle implements Sortable
```

Then all you need to do is implement a compare method inside the class.

```
class Tile extends Rectangle implements Sortable
{   public int compare(Sortable b)
    {   Tile tb = (Tile)b;
        return z - tb.z;
```

```
        }
        .  .  .

        private int z;
    }
```

Example 5-3 is the complete code for the tile example. Note that we needed to put the static `shell_sort` method in a separate class, `Sort`. You cannot put static methods into interfaces. (There is no reason for this restriction—it is merely an oversight in the language design.)

Example 5-3: TileTest.java

```java
import java.awt.*;

public class TileTest
{   public static void main(String[] args)
    {   Tile[] a = new Tile[20];

        int i;
        for (i = 0; i < a.length; i++)
            a[i] = new Tile(i, i, 10, 20,
                (int)(100 * Math.random()));

        Sort.shell_sort(a);

        for (i = 0; i < a.length; i++)
            System.out.println(a[i]);
    }
}

interface Sortable
{   public int compare(Sortable b);
}

class Sort
{   static void shell_sort(Sortable[] a)
    {   int n = a.length;
        int incr = n / 2;
        while (incr >= 1)
        {   for (int i = incr; i < n; i++)
            {   Sortable temp = a[i];
                int j = i;
                while (j >= incr
                    && temp.compare(a[j - incr]) < 0)
                {   a[j] = a[j - incr];
                    j -= incr;
                }
                a[j] = temp;
```

```
      }
        incr /= 2;
    }
  }
}

class Tile extends Rectangle implements Sortable
{  public Tile(int x, int y, int w, int h, int zz)
   {  super(x, y, w, h);
      z = zz;
   }

   public int compare(Sortable b)
   {  Tile tb = (Tile)b;
      return z - tb.z;
   }

   public String toString()
   {  return super.toString() + "[z=" + z + "]";
   }

   private int z;
}
```

C++ NOTE: C++ has multiple inheritance and all the complications that come with it, such as virtual base classes, dominance rules, and transverse pointer casts. Few C++ programmers use multiple inheritance, and some say it should never be used. Other programmers recommend using multiple inheritance only for "mix-in" style inheritance, in which a class is derived from base classes with no data and only virtual functions. These are the same as Java interfaces!

Properties of Interfaces

Although interfaces are not instantiated with new, they have certain properties similar to ordinary classes. For example, once you set up an interface you can declare that an object variable will be of that interface type with the same notation used to declare a variable to be of a specific class type:

```
Sortable x = new Tile(. . .);
Tile y = new Tile(. . .);

if (x.compare(y) < 0) . . .
```

Also, nothing prevents you from extending one interface in order to create another. This allows for multiple chains of interfaces that go from a greater degree of generality to a greater degree of specialization. For example, suppose you had an interface called Moveable.

```
public interface Moveable
{   public void move(double x, double y);
}
```

Then you could imagine an interface called `Powered` that extends it:

```
public interface Powered extends Moveable
{   public String powerSource();
}
```

> NOTE: Unfortunately, the Java documentation often refers to *classes* when it means *classes or interfaces*. You have to use contextual clues to decide whether the reference is only to classes or to both classes and interfaces.

Although you cannot put instance fields in an interface, you can supply constants. For example:

```
public interface Powered extends Moveable
{   public String powerSource(PoweredVehicle);
    public final int speedLimit = 95;
}
```

Classes can implement multiple interfaces. This gives you the maximum amount of flexibility in defining a class's behavior. For example, Java has an important interface built into it called `Cloneable`; if your class implements `Cloneable`, the `clone` method in the `Object` class will make a bitwise copy of your class's objects. If your class doesn't implement `Cloneable`, then the `clone` method causes a run-time error when any code attempts to make a clone of your object. Suppose you want clonability and sortability. Then you implement both interfaces.

```
class Tile extends Rectangle implements Cloneable, Sortable
```

Interfaces and Callbacks

Suppose you want to implement a `Timer` class in Java. You want to be able to program your class to:

- start the timer,
- have the timer measure some time interval,
- then carry out some action when the correct time has elapsed.

For this to be practical, the `Timer` class needs a way of communicating with the calling class. This is usually called a *callback function*. Interfaces are the only way to implement callback functions in Java. To see why, let's peek inside the `Timer` class.

```
class Timer extends Thread
{   . . .
    public void run()
    {  while (true)
       {   sleep(interval);
           // now what?
       }
    }
}
```

(Don't worry about the fact that this class has to extend Java's built-in `Thread` class. Threads have many uses—one of the simplest is to sleep until some time has elapsed. You will read more about threads in Chapter 12.)

The object constructing a `Timer` object must somehow tell the timer what to do when the time is up. In C++, the code creating the timer gives it a pointer to a function, and the timer calls that function at the end of every interval. Java has no function pointers. It uses interfaces instead. So the `//now what` comment in the preceding code is replaced by a method call that was declared inside an interface.

Thus, in addition to the `Timer` class, we need the interface `Timed`. It has a single method called *tick*.

```
interface Timed
{   public void tick(Timer t);
}
```

Any class wanting to be called from a timer must implement that interface.

```
class AlarmClock implements Timed
{   AlarmClock()
    {   Timer t = new Timer(this);
        t.setInterval(1000); // 1000 milliseconds
    }

    public void tick(Timer t)
    {   if(t.time() >= wakeUpTime)
           wakeUp.play();
    }
}
```

Here's the code for the `Timer` class. Notice how the constructor of the `Timer` class receives the pointer to the object that needs to be notified. It is notified through the `tick()` method, which passes the `this` reserved variable that identifies it to the `tick` method in the `Timed` interface.

```
class Timer extends Thread
{   Timer(Timed t) { owner = t; }
         . . .
    public void run()
```

```
    {  while (true)
       {  sleep(interval);
          owner.tick(this);
       }
    }
    Timed owner;
}
```

This code explains only how an interface can be used to supply a notification mechanism and, hence, callback functions; for the rest of the timer implementation, please turn to Chapter 12.

C++ NOTE: Java has no function pointers. Whenever you would like to use a function pointer, you must use polymorphism, either by deriving from a base class or by implementing an interface. You can only derive from one base class, but you can implement any number of interfaces. It is quite common in Java to have trivial interfaces for callback protocols.

More on `Object`: **The Cosmic Superclass**

The `Object` class is the ultimate ancestor—every class in Java extends `Object`. You don't have to say:

```
class Employee extends Object
```

The parent class `Object` is taken for granted if no parent is explicitly mentioned. Because *every* class in Java extends `Object`, it is important to be familiar with the services provided by the `Object` class. We will go over the basic ones in this chapter and refer you to later chapters or to the on-line documentation for what is not covered here. (Several methods of `Object` come up only when dealing with threads—see Chapter 12 for more on threads.)

The `equals` method in `Object` tests whether or not one object is equal to another. The `equals` method in the `Object` parent class determines whether or not two objects point to the same area of memory. Other classes in the Java hierarchy are free to override `equals` for a more meaningful comparison. You will often find yourself overriding `equals` in your classes.

Here are versions of the API descriptions of the basic parts of the `Object` class:

`java.lang.Object`

- `Class getClass()`

  returns a `Class` object that contains information about the object. As you will see in the next section, Java has a run-time representation for classes that is encapsulated in the Class class that you can often use to your advantage.

- `boolean equals(Object obj)`

  compares two objects for equality; returns true if the objects point to the same area of memory, and false otherwise.

- `Object clone()`

  creates a clone of the object. Java allocates memory for the new instance and copies the memory allocated for the current object.

- `String toString()`

  returns a string that represents the value of this object. Almost all classes override this method in order to give you a printed representation of the object's current state. For example, you have seen `toString` used with the Date class to give a string representation of the date.

TIP: Instead of writing `x.toString()`, you can write `" " + x`. This concatenates the empty string with the string representation of x, that is exactly `x.toString()`.

Object Wrappers

Occasionally, you need to convert a basic type like `int` to an object. All basic types have class counterparts. For example, there is a class `Integer` corresponding to the basic type `int`. These kinds of classes are usually called *object wrappers*. The wrapper classes have obvious names: `Integer`, `Long`, `Float`, `Double`, `Character`, and `Boolean`. (The first four inherit from the common parent wrapper `Number`.) The wrapper classes are `final`. (So you can't override the `toString` method in `Integer` in order to display strings in Roman numerals, sorry.) You also cannot change the values you store in the object wrapper.

The major reason for which wrappers were invented is *generic programming*. The container classes that we describe in Chapter 9 can store arbitrary objects. But they cannot store numbers unless they are turned into objects of a class.

Here is a simpler example that illustrates this concept. Suppose you want to find the index of an element in an array. This is a generic situation, and by writing the code for objects, you can reuse it for employees, dates, or whatever.

```
static int find(Object[] a, Object key)
{   int i;
    for (i = 0; i < a.length; i++)
        if (a[i].equals(key)) return i;
    return -1; // not found
}
```

For example,
```
Employee[] staff;
Employee harry;
. . .
int n = find(staff, harry);
```
But what if you want to find a number in an array of floating-point numbers? Here is where wrappers come in handy. By using `Double` objects instead of `double` variables, you can take advantage of the generic code.

You will often see the number wrappers for another reason. The designers of Java found the wrappers a convenient place to put certain basic functions, like converting strings of digits. The place is convenient, but the functionality, unfortunately, isn't.

To convert a string to an integer, you use the following:
```
int x = Integer.parseInt(s);
```
This has nothing to do with `Integer` objects—`parseInt` is a static method. But the `Integer` class was a good place to put it. Unfortunately, there is no corresponding `parseDouble` in the `Double` class. Instead, you must use the cumbersome
```
double x = new Double(s).doubleValue();
```
What this does is:

1. use a constructor in the `Double` class that accepts a string of digits in the form of a double and gives you a `Double` object,

2. use the `doubleValue` method in the `Double` class that returns an actual double.

(VB users are probably longing for a simple Val function.)

You will find this everywhere in Java code. Actually, in real life you have to contend with the possibility that the string has leading or trailing spaces, or that it may contain non-digits. So a correct version would be as follows:
```
try
{   x = new Double(s.trim()).doubleValue();
}
catch(NumberFormatException e)
{   x = 0;
}
```
We found this so cumbersome that we wrote our own string-to-number conversions in the `corejava` package. You simply use this:
```
x = Format.atof(s);
```

The API notes show some of the more important methods of the `Integer` class. The other number classes implement some (but not all) of the corresponding methods.

`java.lang.Integer`

- `int intValue()`

  returns the value of this `Integer` object as an int (overrides the `intValue` method in the `Number` class).

- `static String toString(int i)`

  returns a new `String` object representing the specified integer in base 10.

- `static String toString(int i, int radix)`

  lets you return a representation of the number `i` in the base specified by the `radix` parameter.

- `static int parseInt(String s)`

  returns the integer's value, assuming the specified `String` represents an integer in base 10.

- `static int parseInt(String s, int radix)`

  returns the integer's value, assuming the specified `String` represents an integer in the base specified by the `radix` parameter.

- `static Integer valueOf(String s)`

  returns a new `Integer` object initialized to the integer's value, assuming the specified `String` represents an integer in base 10.

- `static Integer valueOf(String s, int radix)`

  returns a new `Integer` object initialized to the integer's value, assuming the specified `String` represents an integer in the base specified by the `radix` parameter.

C++ NOTE: In C++, there is no cosmic root class. It is not needed, because templates do a better job for generic programming. But Java has no templates, so one has to make do with a common ancestor class.

C++ programmers may be surprised that the cast from `Employee[]` to `Object[]` is legal. Even if `Object` was a base class of `Employee` in C++, the equivalent cast from `Employee**` to `Object**` would not be legal. (Of course, the cast from `Employee*` to `Object*` is legal in C++.)

There is a security reason behind this restriction. If the cast `"Derived** -> Base**"` were permitted, you could corrupt the contents of an array. Consider this code:

```
Employee** a; // C++
Object** p = a; // not legal, but suppose it was
p[0] = new AudioClip();
    // legal, AudioClip also inherits from Object
for (i = 0; i < n; i++) a[i].raiseSalary(3);
    // ouch, now the audio clip gets a raise!
```

If you try the equivalent Java code, you will notice that the `Object[]` array still remembers its original type (`Employee[]` in our example). It will throw an exception if you try to insert any nonemployee object into it. This ensures that a generic array cannot be corrupted.

Reading a Page in the HTML Documents

At this point, you have seen all the basic terms that Java uses to describe its methods, classes, and interfaces. Once you are comfortable with this information, you will often consult the API documentation. Figures 5-3 through 5-5 show the pages of API documentation for the `Double` class. (We explain the documentation in the \java\api directory that is generated by the `javadoc` program. We prefer this to the more book-like format of the \java\apibook documentation.) As you can see, the API documentation pages are always organized in the same way:

1.   the name of the class (or interface);

2.   the inheritance chain for this class (starting from `java.lang.Object`);

3.   the name of the class along with the access modifiers such as public or final, the classes it extends, and the interfaces it implements (for example, as you can see in Figure 5-3, `Double` extends `Number`, which extends `Object`);

4.   a (more or less useful) discussion of the class (occasionally, this includes some sample code);

5.   a list of all the methods in the class, with the constructors given first;

6.   a more detailed discussion of the methods.

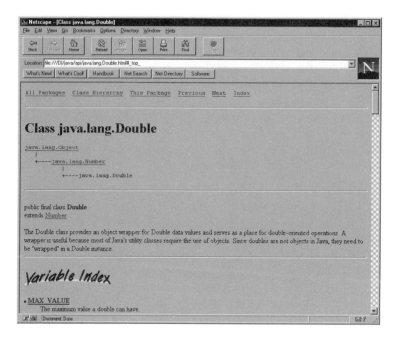

Figure 5-3: tree.html

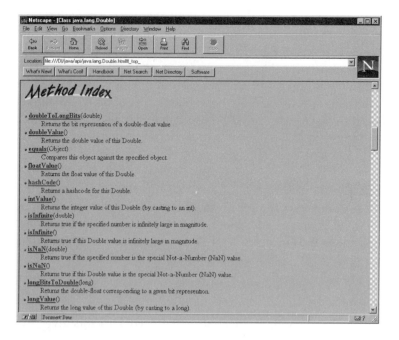

Figure 5-4: API Pages for Double class (Part 1)

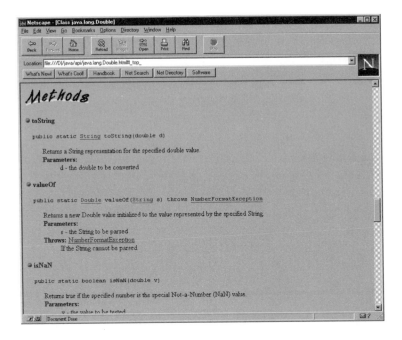

Figure 5-5: API Pages for Double class (Part 2)

The Class `Class` (Run-Time Type Identification)

While your program is running, Java always maintains what is called run-time type identification (RTTI) on all objects, which keeps track of the class to which each object belongs. This is used by Java to select the correct methods at run time. You can also access the information. The class that holds this information is called `Class`. The `getClass()` method in the `Object` class returns an instance of this class type.

Probably the most commonly used method of `getClass` is `getName`. It gets the name of the class. You can use it in a simple `println`; for example, the code

```
System.out.println(e.getClass().getName() + " "
        + e.getName());
```

prints

```
Employee Harry Hacker
```

if e is an employee, and the code prints

```
Manager Harry Hacker
```

if e is a manager.

Core Java

Aside from asking an object for the name of its corresponding class object, you can ask for a class object corresponding to a string by using the static `forName` method.

Another example of a useful method is one that lets you create an instance of a new class on the fly. This method is called, naturally enough, `newInstance()`. For example:

```
e.getClass().newInstance();
```

would create a new instance of the same class type as e, (either an employee or a manager). The `newInstance` method calls the default constructor (the one that takes no arguments) to initialize the newly created object.

The combination of `forName` and `newInstance` lets you create an object from a class name stored in a string.

```
String s = "Manager";
Manager m = (Manager) Class.forName(s).newInstance();
```

C++ NOTE: The `newInstance` method corresponds to the idiom of a *virtual constructor* in C++. The `Class` class is similar to the `type_info` class in C++, and the `getClass` method is equivalent to the `typeid` operator. The Java `Class` is quite a bit more versatile than `type_info`, though. The C++ `type_info` can only reveal a string with its name, not create new objects of that type.

java.lang.Class

- `String getName()`

  returns the name of this class.

- `Class getSuperclass()`

  returns the superclass of this class as a `Class` object.

- `Class[] getInterfaces()`

  returns an array of Class objects that give the interfaces implemented by this class; returns an array of length 0 if this class implements no interfaces. Somewhat confusingly, interface descriptions are also stored in `Class` objects.

- `boolean isInterface()`

  returns true if this class is an interface and false if not.

- `String toString()`

  returns the name of this class or this interface. The word *class* precedes the name if it is a class; the word *interface* precedes the name if it is an interface. (This method overrides the `toString` method in `Object`.)

- `static Class forName(String className)`

  returns a new instance of this class.

Protected Access

As you know, instance fields in a class are usually tagged as `private` and methods are tagged as `public`. Any features declared `private` are not visible to other classes. This is also true for subclasses. A subclass cannot access the private data members of its superclass.

For example, the `raise` method of the `Manager` class cannot access the `hireDay` field directly when computing the bonuses. It has to use the public interface like all other methods.

```
class Manager extends Employee
{   . . .
    public void raiseSalary(double byPercent)
    {   // add 1/2% bonus for every year of service
        Day today = new Day();
        double bonus = 0.5 * (today.getYear() -
            hireYear()); // can't use hireDay.year
        super.raiseSalary(byPercent + bonus);
    }
}
```

There are, however, times when you want a subclass to have access to a method or to data. In that case, you declare the feature as `protected`. For example, if the base class `Employee` declares the `hireDay` object as `protected` instead of `private`, then the `Manager` methods can access it directly.

In practice, you should use the `protected` attribute with caution. Suppose your class is used by other programmers, and it contains protected data. Unbeknownst to you, other programmers may derive classes from your class and start accessing the protected instance fields. In this case, you can no longer change the implementation of your class without upsetting the other programmers. That is against the spirit of OOP, which encourages data encapsulation.

Protected methods make more sense. A class may declare a method as `protected` if it is tricky to use. This indicates that the subclasses (which, presumably, know their ancestors well) can be trusted to use the method correctly, but other classes cannot.

A good example is the `clone` method in the class `Object`. Let us remind you why you sometimes want to clone an object. When you make a copy of a variable, the original and the copy are references to the same object. (See Figure 5-6). This means a change to either variable also affects the other.

```
Day bday = new Day(1959, 6, 16);
Day d = bday;
d.advance(100); // oops--also changed bday
```

If you would like to indicate that d should be a new object that begins as identical to bday but may later change to a different state, then you use the `clone()` method.

```
Day bday = new Day(1959, 6, 16);
Day d = (Day)bday.clone();
    // must cast--clone returns an object
d.advance(100); // ok--bday unchanged
```

copying

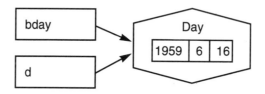

cloning

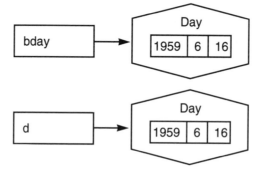

Figure 5-6: Copying and cloning

But it isn't quite so simple. The `clone` method is a `protected` method of `Object`, which means that your code cannot simply call it. Only the Day class can clone Day objects. There is a reason for this. Think about the way in which the `Object` class can implement `clone`. It knows nothing about the object at all, so it can only make a bit-by-bit copy. If all data fields in the object are numbers or other basic types, a bitwise copy is just fine. It is simply another object with the same base types and fields. But if the object contains pointers (that is, other objects), then the bitwise copy contains exact copies of the pointer fields, so the original and the cloned objects still share some information. This is shown in Figure 5-7.

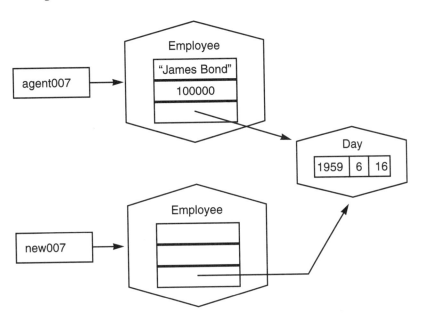

Figure 5-7: Original and cloned objects sharing information

It is up to the derived class to make a judgment whether or not

1. the default `clone` method is good enough,

2. the default `clone` method can be patched up by calling `clone` on the object instance variables,

3. the situation is hopeless and `clone` should not be attempted.

The third option is actually the default. To choose either the first or the second option, a class must

1. implement the `Cloneable` interface and

2. redefine the `clone` method with the public access privilege.

The appearance of the `Cloneable` interface is another nuisance. Objects are so paranoid about cloning that they generate a run-time exception if an object requests cloning but does not implement that interface. (There are no methods at all in the `Cloneable` interface. It serves simply as a tag.)

Here is the drudgery that the `Day` class has to do to redefine `clone`.

```
public class Day implements Cloneable
{   . . .
  public Object clone()
  {  try
     {   return super.clone();
     } catch (CloneNotSupportedException e)
     {  // this shouldn't happen, since we are Cloneable
        return null;
     }
  }
}
```

And that is the easy case. If we want to clone employees, we have to call the `Object` clone method to make a bitwise copy, then clone the `Day` object.

```
public class Employee implements Cloneable
{   . . .
  public Object clone()
  {  try
     {   Employee e = (Employee)super.clone();
         e.hireDay = hireDay.clone();
         return e;
     }  catch (CloneNotSupportedException e)
     {  // this shouldn't happen, since we are Cloneable
        return null;
     }
  }
}
```

As you can see, cloning is a subtle business, and it makes sense that it is defined as `protected` in the `Object` class. (See Chapter 11 for another method to clone objects using the new object serialization features of Java.)

C++ NOTE: As it happens, `protected` features in Java are visible to all subclasses as well as all other classes in the same package. This is slightly different from the C++ meaning of `protected`.

Here is a summary of the four access modifiers in Java that control visibility.

1.   visible to the class only (`private`)

2.   visible to the world (`public`)

3.   visible to the package and all subclasses (`protected`)

4.   visible to the package (the default—no modifier needed)

Design Hints for Inheritance

1. Common operations and fields belong in the superclass.

This is why we put the `sender` field into the `Message` class, rather than replicating it in `TextMessage` and `VoiceMessage`.

2. Use inheritance to model the "is–a" relationship.

Inheritance is a handy code saver, and sometimes people overuse it. For example, suppose we need a `Contractor` class. Contractors have names and hire dates, but they do not have salaries. Instead, they are paid by the hour, and they do not stay around long enough to get a raise. There is the temptation to derive `Contractor` from `Employee` and add an `hourlyWage` field.

```
class Contractor extends Employee
{  public Contractor(String name, double wage, Day hireDay)
   {  super(name, 0, hireDay);
      hourlyWage = wage;
   }
   private double hourlyWage;
}
```

This is *not* a good idea, however, and it will cause you no end of grief when you implement methods for printing paychecks or tax forms. You will end up writing more code than you would have by not inheriting in the first place.

The contractor/employee relationship fails the "is–a" test. A contractor is not a special case of an employee.

3. Don't use inheritance unless *all* inherited methods make sense.

Suppose we want to write a `Holiday` class . Surely every holiday is a day, so we can use inheritance.

```
class Holiday extends Day { . . . }
```

Unfortunately, this is somewhat subtle. When we say that `Holiday` extends `Day`, we have to consider that we are talking about the *class* `Day`, as specified by its public methods. One of the public methods of `Day` is `advance`. And `advance` can turn holidays into non-holidays, so it is not an appropriate operation for holidays.

```
Holiday xmas;
xmas.advance(10);
```

In that sense, a holiday is a day *but* not a Day.

4. Use polymorphism, not type information.

Whenever you find code of the form

```
if (x is of type 1)
   action1(x);
else if (x is of type 2)
   action2(x);
```

think polymorphism.

Do action1 and action2 represent a common concept? If so, make the concept a method of a common parent class or interface of both types. Then you can simply call

```
x.action();
```

and have the dynamic dispatch mechanism launch the correct action.

Code with polymorphic methods or interface implementations is much easier to maintain and extend than code with type tests.

CHAPTER

6

- The First Graphics Program
- Displaying Text in a WIndow
- More on Event-Driven Programming: Update and Paint Functions
- Text and Fonts
- Colors
- Drawing Graphical Shapes
- Filling Shapes
- Paint Mode
- Images
- Buffering
- Image Updating

Graphics
Programming
with AWT

Until now, you have only learned how to write programs that take input from the keyboard, fuss with it, and then display the results on the console screen. This type of program is old-fashioned and clearly not what users want. Modern programs don't work this way and neither do Web pages. This chapter helps you begin the process of writing Java programs that use a graphical user interface (GUI) for output. In particular, you will learn how to write programs that use windows with multiple fonts, display images, and so on. (The next chapter shows you how to add interface elements such as menus and buttons.) When you finish these two chapters, you will know what is needed to write *stand-alone* graphical applications. Chapter 8 shows how to program applets embedded in Web pages that use these features.

NOTE: Even if you are not concerned with graphics programming in the sense of displaying curves and such, you should read the first five sections of this chapter.

Java gives you a class library for basic GUI programming. It is called the Abstract Window Toolkit or AWT. At one point, it was called the "alternative" window toolkit, but you don't have another realistic alternative at this time—you must use AWT for graphical Java programming. Unfortunately, AWT is somewhat primitive, not very well documented, and not particularly powerful. On the other hand, it is platform independent. (This means that Sun Microsystems has programmed AWT to be portable to various operating systems, such as Windows 95 and Solaris. People have ported it to such platforms as Linux.)

The most obvious way in which AWT shows itself as primitive is that applications built with AWT simply do not look as nice as native Windows or

Macintosh applications. But, from the programmer's point of view there are far more serious problems: quite a few tasks that ought to be simple turn out to be quite complex in AWT. For this reason, many Java programmers believe that what AWT really stands for is "awkward window toolkit."

If you have programmed Microsoft Windows applications using VB, Delphi, or Visual C++, you are probably familiar with graphical layout tools. These tools let you design the visual appearance of your application and then generate much of the code for you. Currently, there are few such tools available for Java programming and the ones available such as Symantec's Café are often more trouble than they are worth. What this means to the programmer now is that you must usually build the user interface manually, and this often requires writing *a lot of code*.

The First Graphics Program

In this section, you will see what is probably the simplest graphical interface: a window! This is shown in Figure 6-1. As you will see, building this interface is not completely trivial. The window requires some sophisticated code to work correctly under Windows 95.

Figure 6-1: A plain window

In AWT, a top-level window (that is, a window that is not contained inside another window) is called a *frame*. Frames are Java objects, so it should not be surprising that a program that creates a frame (window) must follow the following steps:

1. Create the frame by a call to `new`.

2. Resize the frame.

3. Call the `show` method in the `Frame` class in order to display the window (frame).

Here is the program, but *please don't run this program yet:* there is one very important rule when developing programs that use AWT:

Save all of your work-in-progress before running the program.

The problem is that it is sometimes hard to kill off a program that uses AWT, as you will see below in Example 6-1.

Example 6-1: NotHelloWorld1.java

```java
import java.awt.*; //see Chapter 4 for more on import

class NotHelloWorld1
{   public static void main(String[] args)
    {   Frame f = new Frame();
        f.resize(300, 200);
        f.show();
    }
}
```

Figure 6-1 shows the result of the program: just an empty window with a border and a title. Let's go over the code, line by line. First, we have imported the AWT package. Next is the standard header for a new class. The key line

```java
Frame f = new Frame();
```

declares and makes a new `Frame` object. At this point, Java will build the data structure that contains all the necessary information for the underlying windowing system to display a frame window. This does not yet display the frame. You need to invoke the `show` method in order to display the frame. However, before you can show a frame, you need to size it. Here we make the window 300 pixels wide by 200 pixels high. If you don't explicitly size a frame, all frames will be sized at 0 by 0 pixels, and so will not be visible.

All measurements in AWT are made in pixels, and the first coordinate (*x*-coordinate) gives the width and the second (*y*-coordinate), the height. Unfortunately, you don't know the resolution of the user's screen. A program that looks nice on a laptop screen will look like a postage stamp on a high-resolution screen. For now, we will just use values that we hope work acceptably on most displays. Feel free to change the window dimensions if you have a higher-resolution or larger screen. A better approach is to measure the size of a font and derive the screen dimensions from those measurements. See the section on Text and Fonts for information on font metrics and how to work with them.

OK, suppose you do run this program. How do you (try to) close the window? If you look carefully at the window shown in Figure 6-1, you will find it has a close box in its upper, right-hand corner. Unfortunately, clicking on this close box doesn't close the window. Clicking on the upper, left-hand corner reveals a menu (see Figure 6-2), but selecting Close from the menu doesn't work either.

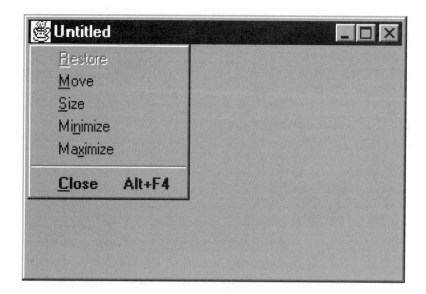

Figure 6-2: The system menu of a Java program

Guess what, nothing obvious will get this application to close. You will soon see how to write programs that can be closed properly, but right now you need a way to kill a wayward windowed Java application.

* Under Windows 95 or NT, *carefully* press CTRL+ALT+DEL. You get a dialog box similar to the one shown in Figure 6-3, which lists all running programs. Select the Java program and click on the **End Task** button. If a dialog box comes up that alerts you that the program isn't responding, confirm that you want to end it. You have to be careful when pressing CTRL+ALT+DEL. If you press the key combination twice, your computer reboots immediately, and you lose all work in all open applications.

Figure 6-3: The Windows Close Program dialog

• Under Solaris, you can select **Destroy** from the program menu or terminate
  the program with extreme prejudice with the `kill -9` command.

Obviously, you can't very well tell a user of your program that the natural way
to end your program is via something like a CTRL+ALT+DEL "three-finger
salute." Unfortunately, in Java the default behavior for a frame is to ignore all
requests for its destruction—thus necessitating drastic actions to terminate the
program.

What we need is something that is like a standard frame in most respects,
except that it destroys itself when the user asks it to. As you saw in the previous
chapter, Java has a powerful language construct to deal with just this situation:
inheritance. We need to derive a new window class from the standard `Frame`
class that somehow can respond to a request to destroy itself.

The key is that a frame can already respond to user events via what are called
event handlers. (People coming from a Windows programming background will,
of course, be familiar with event-driven programming. If you are coming from
another background, think of it this way: in an event-driven program, objects sit

around waiting for messages [events]. If they receive one, they see if they have some preprogrammed response to that message.)

In Java, each event is derived from the Event class and is assigned an *event id* for which you can test. How you handle an event is controlled by the handleEvent method in the Component class. Thus, this method is called whenever a frame receives an event it can understand. There are a number of interesting events to which frames can respond, for example: keystrokes, mouse clicks, and, of course, the destroy request. We will look at all the event types in Chapter 7. For now, we want to exit the application (i.e., use System.exit(0)) when the event ID equals the WINDOW_DESTROY constant defined in the Event class. (We do not want to change how all other events are handled so we will not override any of the other event handlers in the Frame superclass.)

The handleEvent function returns a Boolean value. You return true if you handle the event, false if you don't. Here's the code snippet that shows you how the event handler works for our class:

```
public boolean handleEvent(Event e)
{   if (e.id == Event.WINDOW_DESTROY)
        System.exit(0);
    return super.handleEvent(e);
}
```

Notice how we check to see whether or not the event id equals the WINDOW_DESTROY constant. In this case, the function calls the System.exit(0) method, which closes any Java application. Notice that this method won't return out of the call to System.exit, so it doesn't matter that we are not having the handleEvent method returning true—even though we are, in fact, handling the destroy event. Notice as well that all other events are still handled by the Frame superclass. You will see in Chapter 7 what happens to an event when a particular window refuses to handle it. You should normally return true when you handle an event in the handleEvent method. However, if the WINDOW_DESTROY event occurs, we call exit and the method does not return.

Having briefly gone through what it means to write event-handling code you can now understand the code shown in Example 6-2, which gives you a closeable window.

Example 6-2: NotHelloWorld2

```
import java.awt.*;

class NotHelloWorld2 extends Frame
{   public boolean handleEvent(Event e)
    {   if (e.id == Event.WINDOW_DESTROY)
            System.exit(0);
```

```
          return super.handleEvent(e);
    }
    public static void main(String[] args)
    {   Frame f = new NotHelloWorld2();
        f.resize(300, 200);
        f.show();
    }
}
```

This derivation process via inheritance from classes like `Frame` is the key to working with the AWT library. Every time you need a user interface component that is similar to one of the basic AWT components, you use inheritance to supply the additional functionality.

Displaying Text in a Window

Now that you can close a window without having to reboot your computer, let us try to build the first non-trivial windowed application. Rather than displaying "Not a Hello, World program" in text mode in a console window as in Chapter 3, we will display the message in a window, as in Figure 6-4.

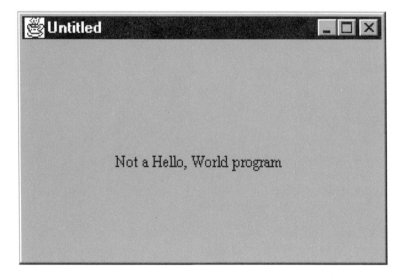

Figure 6-4: A simple graphical program

Anytime you want to put text or graphics into a window, you need to override the `paint` method from the `Component` class, so, of course, you need to write a new class for this that overrides not only the `WINDOW_DESTROY` event handler but also the `paint` method. The `paint` method has one parameter of type `Graphics`. The `Graphics` parameter is similar to a device context in Windows or a graphics context in X11 programming.

> VB NOTE: VB Programmers rarely need a device context, but it is there just the same. For now, think of a `Graphics` object as being like a Picture box (which actually encapsulates a graphics context). On a `Graphics` object, like a Picture box, you have certain methods for drawing, changing colors and pen styles, and the like.

A `Graphics` object remembers a collection of settings for drawing images and text, such as the currently selected font or the current color. All drawing in Java must go through a `Graphics` object. Displaying text (usually called *rendering text*) is considered a special kind of drawing. For example, a `Graphics` object has a `drawString` method that has the following syntax:

```
drawString(String s, int xCoord, int yCoord)
```

In our case, we want to draw the string "Not a Hello, World Program" in our original window, roughly one quarter of the way across and halfway down. Although we don't yet know how to exactly measure the size of the string, we'll start the string at (75, 100). (You will see how to draw lines and other shapes in the section on Text and Fonts.) Example 6-3 shows the code:

Example 6-3: NotHelloWorld3.java

```java
import java.awt.*;

class NotHelloWorld3 extends Frame
{   public boolean handleEvent(Event e)
    {   if (e.id == Event.WINDOW_DESTROY)
            System.exit(0);
        return super.handleEvent(e);
    }
    public void paint(Graphics g)
    {   g.drawString("Not a Hello, World program", 75, 100);
    }
    public static void main(String[] args)
    {   Frame f = new NotHelloWorld3();
        f.resize(300, 200);
        f.show();
    }
}
```

More on Event-Driven Programming: `Update` and `Paint` Functions

Just like Microsoft Windows or X Windows programming, and unlike most DOS programs, a graphical Java program is event driven. The programmer describes what needs to occur when a particular event happens. However, as with all event-driven programs, the sequence of events is beyond the control of the programmer since users may perform operations in any order.

For example, parts of an application may need to be redrawn in response to a user action or external circumstances. Perhaps the user increases the size of the window or minimizes and then restores the application. If another window has popped up and then disappeared, the covered application windows are corrupted and will need to be redrawn. (The graphics system does not usually save the pixels underneath.) And, of course, when a window is first displayed, its initial elements must be drawn.

VB NOTE: There is no way to make graphics persistent in Java; you will always need to write the code in a paint method to redraw.

Each time a window needs to be redrawn, for any reason, the event handler calls its `update` function. The default implementation for `update` (in the base class called `Component`) is to erase the background and to call `paint`. In most cases, we can leave `update` alone and just redefine `paint`. For example, in the preceding section, we defined `paint` to draw a message on the screen.

The `update`, like the `paint`, procedures take a single parameter of type `Graphics`. As with the `paint` procedure, you use the `Graphics` object to render graphics on the window and to inquire and modify the graphics state.

Text and Fonts

To display text, you must first select a font. A font is specified by its name, such as "Helvetica," the style (plain, **bold**, *italic*, or ***bold italic***), and the point size. Unfortunately, there is no way to find out what fonts have been installed on the system of the user of your program, so it seems wise to stick to the following fonts:

> Helvetica
>
> TimesRoman
>
> `Courier`
>
> `Dialog`
>
> `Symbol`

These font names are always mapped by Java to fonts that actually exist on the client machine. For example, on a Windows system, Helvetica is mapped to Arial. You are free to ask for other fonts by name, but don't be surprised if your user doesn't have Troglodyte Bold installed and your text doesn't show up right.

As you might expect, `Font` is an object in Java, so we need to create it via a call to `new` before we can use it. In this case, `Font` requires parameters that define its properties in the constructor. The syntax is

```
Font(String name, int property, int size)
```

where one uses something like `Font.BOLD` to get bold.

Here's the code in a `paint` method that would let you display "Not a Hello, World program" in Helvetica 14-point bold at the same location as before.

```
public void paint(Graphics g)
{   Font f = new Font("Helvetica", Font.BOLD, 14);
    g.setFont(f);
    g.drawString("Not a Hello, World program", 75, 100);
}
```

Actually, since we now have the freedom to choose fonts, let's display the text with a mixture of roman and italic letters, "Not a *Hello, World* program." We need two fonts, the base font, `f`, and its italicized version.

```
Font f = new Font("Helvetica", Font.BOLD, 14);
Font fi = new Font("Helvetica", Font.BOLD + Font.ITALIC, 14);
```

Now we have a problem. We need to know how long the string `Not a` is in Helvetica Bold 14 point so that we can tack the `Hello, World` string behind it. To measure a string, you need to use the `FontMetrics` class to derive properties of the font to be used with the `Graphics` object. This class reveals global size properties of the font and measures the sizes of strings rendered in the font. For example, the `stringWidth` method of `FontMetrics` takes a string and returns its current width in pixels.

VB NOTE: You cannot mix fonts in Java without carefully positioning the strings yourself. There is no notion of a last point referenced.

In Java, you need to become familiar with terminology taken from typesetting in order to handle fonts properly. Many of the properties used in typesetting correspond to methods of the `FontMetrics` class.

For example, the *ascent* is the distance from the baseline to the top of an *ascender*, which is the upper part of a letter like "b" or "k", or an uppercase character. The *descent* is the distance from the baseline to a *descender*, which is the lower portion of a letter like "p" or "g". These correspond to the `getAscent` and `getDescent` methods of the `FontMetrics` class.

You also need the `getLeading` and `getHeight` methods of the `FontMetrics` class, which correspond to what typesetters call *leading* and *height*. Leading is the space between the descent of one line and the ascent of the next line. The height of a font is the distance between successive baselines, which is the same as descent + leading + ascent.

Some characters, typically those with diacritics such as "Ã", extend above the normal ascent. (There is, in fact, a slight chance that such characters may overlap with descenders from the preceding line.) The *maximum ascent* is the largest height of such a character. Similarly, the *maximum descent* is the largest depth of a descender. You would use the ascent and descent measurements for line spacing and the maximum ascent and descent if you need to determine the maximum screen area occupied by a font.

These vertical measurements are properties of the font. In contrast, horizontal measurements are properties of the individual characters. In a proportionally spaced font such as Times or Helvetica, different characters have different sizes. For example, a "w" is much wider than an "l". In fact, the size of a word may not even equal the sum of the sizes of its characters because some fonts move certain character pairs closer together, a process called *kerning*. For example, the pair "Av" is often kerned. The `stringWidth` method of the `FontMetrics` object of a font computes the width of any string and thus takes into account any kerning that may have occurred.

The following code displays the mixed font text "Not a *Hello, World* program."

```
public void paint(Graphics g)
{   Font f = new Font("Helvetica", Font.BOLD, 14);
    Font fi = new Font("Helvetica", Font.BOLD + Font.ITALIC, 14);
    FontMetrics fm = g.getFontMetrics(f);
    FontMetrics fim = g.getFontMetrics(fi);
    String s1 = "Not a ";
    String s2 = "Hello, World";
    String s3 = " Program";
    int cx = 75;
    int cy = 100;
    g.setFont(f);
    g.drawString(s1, cx, cy);
    cx += fm.stringWidth(s1);
    g.setFont(fi);
    g.drawString(s2, cx, cy);
    cx += fim.stringWidth(s2);
    g.setFont(f);
    g.drawString(s3, cx, cy);
}
```

Actually, this code is a little unrealistic. The allocation of fonts and font metrics is time consuming, and it is usually best to allocate these items only once. We'll do that in the code below, simply by making the fonts and metrics into variables of the frame class and setting them once in a `setFonts` method. We call the `setFonts` method from `paint`. We would have preferred to set the fonts in the constructor, but the graphics context is not yet set up when the frame is constructed.

While we are at it, we want to make one final improvement: centering the string in the window. The `size` method of `Component`, a parent class of `Frame`, returns the size of the frame. Unless the user resizes the window, it will be the same 300 by 200 that we set in `main`. However, that is the size of the whole window, including borders and title bars. The `insets` method returns a structure giving the measurements of the borders around the four sides (i.e., the useable, or client, area.) We can use this information to properly center the string.

Note that this program repositions text so that the string stays centered when the user resizes the window.

VB NOTE: Think of `size` as corresponding to Height and Width and `insets` as corresponding to ScaleHeight and ScaleWidth.

Example 6-4 is the program listing. Figure 6-5 shows the screen display.

Figure 6-5: Using multiple fonts

Example 6-4: NotHelloWorld4.java

```java
import java.awt.*;

class NotHelloWorld4 extends Frame
{  public boolean handleEvent(Event evt)
   {  if (evt.id == Event.WINDOW_DESTROY) System.exit(0);
      return false;
   }

   private Font f;
   private Font fi;
   private FontMetrics fm;
   private FontMetrics fim;
   private boolean fontsSet = false;

   private void setFonts(Graphics g)
   {  if (fontsSet) return;
      f = new Font("Helvetica", Font.BOLD, 14);
      fi = new Font("Helvetica", Font.BOLD + Font.ITALIC, 14);
      fm = g.getFontMetrics(f);
      fim = g.getFontMetrics(fi);
      fontsSet = true;
   }

   public void paint(Graphics g)
   {  setFonts(g);
      String s1 = "Not a ";
      String s2 = "Hello, World";
      String s3 = " Program";
      int w1 = fm.stringWidth(s1);
      int w2 = fim.stringWidth(s2);
      int w3 = fm.stringWidth(s3);

      Dimension d = size();
      Insets in = insets();
      int client_width = d.width - in.right - in.left;
      int client_height = d.height - in.bottom - in.top;
      int cx = (client_width - w1 - w2 - w3) / 2;
      int cy = client_height / 2;
      g.drawRect(0, 0, client_width - 1, client_height - 1);

      g.setFont(f);
      g.drawString(s1, cx, cy);
      cx += w1;
      g.setFont(fi);
      g.drawString(s2, cx, cy);
      cx += w2;
      g.setFont(f);
```

```
        g.drawString(s3, cx, cy);

    }

    public static void main(String args[])
    {   Frame f = new NotHelloWorld4();
        f.resize(300, 200);
        f.show();
    }
}
```

java.awt.Font

• `Font(String name, int style, int size)`

creates a new font object.

Parameters: name the font name (e.g., "Times Roman")

       style the style (`Font.PLAIN`, `Font.BOLD`, `Font.ITALIC` or `Font.BOLD` + `Font.ITALIC`)

       size the point size (e.g., 12)

java.awt.FontMetrics

• `int getAscent()`

gets the font ascent—the distance from the baseline to the tops of uppercase characters.

• `int getDescent()`

gets the font descent—the distance from the baseline to the bottoms of descenders.

• `int getLeading()`

gets the font leading—the space between the bottom of one line of text and the top of the next line.

• `int getHeight()`

gets the total height of the font—the distance between the two baselines of text (descent + leading + ascent).

- `int getMaxAscent()`

  gets the maximum height of all characters in this font.

- `int getMaxDescent()`

  gets the maximum descent of all characters in this font.

- `int stringWidth(String str)`

  computes the width of a string.

  Parameters: `str`   the string to be measured

`java.awt.Graphics`

- `void setFont(Font font)`

  selects a font for the graphics context. That font will be used for subsequent text-drawing operations.

  Parameters: `font`   a font

- `FontMetrics getFontMetrics()`

  gets the metrics of the current font.

- `void drawString(String str, int x, int y)`

  draws a string in the current font and color.

  Parameters: `str`   the string to be drawn

                                      `x`   the *x*-coordinate of the start of the string

                                      `y`   the *y*-coordinate of the baseline of the string

Colors

The `setColor` method call selects a color that is used for all subsequent drawing operations. To draw in multiple colors, you select a color, draw, then select another color.

The `setColor` method takes a parameter of type `Color`. You can either pick one of the 13 standard colors listed in Table 6-1, or specify a color by its red, green, and blue components.

```
g.setColor(Color.pink);
g.drawString("Hello", 75, 100);
g.setColor(new Color(0, 128, 128)); // a dull blue-green
g.drawString("World", 75, 125);
```

Table 6-1: Standard Colors

black	green	red
blue	lightGray	white
cyan	magenta	yellow
darkGray	orange	
gray	pink	

To set the *background color*, you use the `setBackground` method of the `Component` class, an ancestor of `Frame`. In fact, you should set the background before displaying the frame for the first time.

```
f.resize(300, 200);
f.setBackground(Color.white);
f.show();
```

java.awt.Color

- `Color(int r, int g, int b)`

  creates a color object.

Parameters:	r	the red value (0–255)
	g	the green value (0–255)
	b	the blue value (0–255)

java.awt.Graphics

- `void setColor(Color c)`

  changes the current color. All subsequent graphics operations will use the new color.

Parameters:	c	the new color

```
java.awt.Component
```

- void setBackground(Color c)

  sets the background color.

  Parameters: c   the new background color

Drawing Graphical Shapes

The drawLine, drawArc, and drawPolygon methods in java.awt.Graphics
are used to draw straight and curved lines.

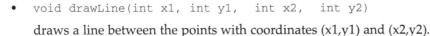

```
java.awt.Graphics
```

- void drawLine(int x1, int y1, int x2, int y2)

  draws a line between the points with coordinates (x1,y1) and (x2,y2).

  Parameters: x1   the first point's *x*-coordinate

  y1   the first point's *y*-coordinate

  x2   the second point's *x*-coordinate

  y2   the second point's *y*-coordinate

- void drawArc(int x, int y, int width, int height,
      int startAngle, int arcAngle)

  draws an arc bounded by the rectangle with the upper left corner (*x, y*) and
  the given width and height. The arc starts at startAngle and spans the
  arcAngle. (That is, the end angle is startAngle + arcAngle.) Angles are measured in degrees and follow the usual mathematical conventions: 0 degrees
  is at the three-o'clock position, and positive angles indicate counterclock-
  wise rotation. The "PacMan" figure in the example below illustrates the
  usage of the parameters.

  Parameters: x   the *x*-coordinate

  y   the *y*-coordinate

  width   the width of the rectangle

  height   the height of the rectangle

  startAngle   the beginning angle

  arcAngle   the angle of the arc (relative to *startAngle*)

In Java, a *polygon* is a sequence of line segments. (That is different from the usual definition in which a polygon is required to be closed.) The easiest way to draw a polygon in Java is to:

- create a polygon object,

- add points to the object,

- use the `drawPolygon(Polygon p)` method described here to draw the polygon.

(There is another `drawPolygon` method that takes two arrays, one for each of the *x*- and *y*-coordinates of the endpoints of the line segments, but it is less convenient.)

java.awt.Graphics

- void drawPolygon(Polygon p)

  draws a path joining the points in the `Polygon` object.

  Parameters: p   a polygon

- void drawPolygon(int[] xPoints, int[] yPoints, int nPoints)

  draws a path joining a sequence of points.

Parameters:	xPoints	an array of *x*-coordinates of the corner points
	yPoints	an array of *y*-coordinates of the corner points
	nPoints	the number of corner points

TIP: Polygons with very closely spaced points are useful to render curved shapes. (In Example 6-5, we draw a spiral made up of many vertices.)

Now let's draw these figures. In Figure 6-6 we have drawn a PacMan shape (by using an arc and two line segments), a pentagon (with one side missing because the `drawPolygon` function does not close polygons), and a spiral (actually a polygon with many closely spaced points).

Figure 6-6: Drawing arcs and polygons in Java

Example 6-5: DrawPoly.java

```
import java.awt.*;

class DrawPoly extends Frame
{   public boolean handleEvent(Event evt)
    {   if (evt.id == Event.WINDOW_DESTROY) System.exit(0);
        return false;
    }

    public void paint(Graphics g)
    {   int r = 45; // radius of circle bounding PacMan(R)
        int cx = 50; // center of that circle
        int cy = 100;
        int angle = 30; // half the opening angle of mouth

        int dx = (int)(r * Math.cos(angle * Math.PI / 180));
        int dy = (int)(r * Math.sin(angle * Math.PI / 180));

        g.drawLine(cx, cy, cx + dx, cy + dy); // lower jaw
        g.drawLine(cx, cy, cx + dx, cy - dy); // upper jaw
        g.drawArc(cx - r, cy - r, 2 * r, 2 * r, angle, 360 - 2 * angle);
        Polygon p = new Polygon();
        cx = 150;
        int i;
        for (i = 0; i < 5; i++)
```

```
        p.addPoint((int)(cx + r * Math.cos(i * 2 * Math.PI / 5)),
            (int)(cy + r * Math.sin(i * 2 * Math.PI / 5)));

    g.drawPolygon(p);

    Polygon s = new Polygon();
    cx = 250;
    for (i = 0; i < 360; i++)
    {   double t = i / 360.0;
        s.addPoint((int)(cx + r * t * Math.cos(8 * t * Math.PI)),
            (int)(cy + r * t * Math.sin(8 * t * Math.PI)));
    }
    g.drawPolygon(s);
}

public static void main(String args[])
{   Frame f = new DrawPoly();
    f.resize(300, 200);
    f.show();
}
}
```

The drawRect, drawRoundRect, draw3DRect and drawOval functions render the outlines of rectangles and ellipses (called ovals in AWT).

`java.awt.Graphics`

- `void drawRect(int x, int y, int width, int height)`

  draws the outline of the rectangle. Note that the third and fourth parameters are *not* the opposite corner points.

Parameters:	x	the *x*-coordinate of the top left corner
	y	the *y*-coordinate of the top left corner
	width	the width of the rectangle
	height	the height of the rectangle

- `void drawRoundRect(int x, int y, int width, int height,`
  `    int arcWidth, int arcHeight)`

  draws the outline of the rectangle, using curved arcs for the corners.

Parameters:	x	the *x*-coordinate of the top left corner
	y	the *y*-coordinate of the top left corner
	width	the width of the rectangle
	height	the height of the rectangle
	arcWidth	the horizontal diameter of the arcs at the corners
	arcHeight	the vertical diameter of the arcs at the corners

- `void draw3DRect(int x, int y, int width, int height, boolean raised)`

draws the outline of the rectangle. Note that the third and fourth parameters are *not* the opposite corner points.

Parameters:	x	the *x*-coordinate of the top left corner
	y	the *y*-coordinate of the top left corner
	width	the width of the rectangle
	height	the height of the rectangle
	raised	true to have the rectangle appear above the window

- `void drawOval(int x, int y, int width, int height)`

draws the outline of an ellipse. The parameters specify the bounding rectangle.

Parameters:	x	the *x*-coordinate of the top left corner of the bounding rectangle
	y	the *y*-coordinate of the top left corner of the bounding rectangle
	width	the width of the bounding rectangle
	height	the height of the bounding rectangle

Figure 6-7 and Example 6-6 show the various rectangle styles and the oval.

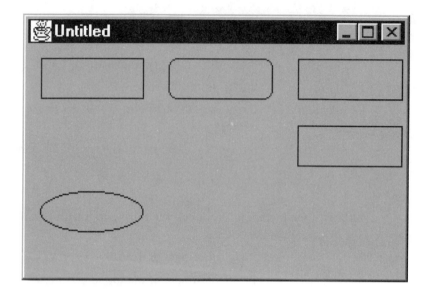

Figure 6-7: Rectangles and ovals

Example 6-6: DrawRect.java

```java
import java.awt.*;

class DrawRect extends Frame
{   public boolean handleEvent(Event evt)
    {   if (evt.id == Event.WINDOW_DESTROY) System.exit(0);
        return false;
    }

    public void paint(Graphics g)
    {   g.setColor(Color.blue);
        g.drawRect(10, 10, 80, 30);
        g.drawRoundRect(110, 10, 80, 30, 15, 15);
        g.draw3DRect(210, 10, 80, 30, true);
        g.draw3DRect(210, 60, 80, 30, false);
        g.drawOval(10, 110, 80, 30);
    }

    public static void main(String args[])
    {   Frame f = new DrawRect();
        f.resize(300, 200);
        f.show();
    }
}
```

Filling Shapes

The interiors of closed shapes (rectangles, ellipses, polygons, and pie chart segments) can be filled with a color. The method calls are similar to the `draw` calls of the preceding section, except that `draw` is replaced by `fill`.

- void fillRect(int x, int y, int width, int height)
- void fillRoundRect(int x, int y, int width, int height,
    int arcWidth, int arcHeight)
- void fill3DRect(int x, int y, int width, int height, boolean
    raised)
- void fillOval(int x, int y, int width, int height)
- void fillArc(int x, int y, int width, int height,
    int startAngle, int arcAngle)
- void fillPolygon(Polygon p)
- void fillPolygon(int[] xPoints, int[] yPoints, int nPoints)

To *fill* rectangles and ovals simply means to color the inside of the shape with the current color. There is one minor point, as Figure 6-8 illustrates: When you *fill* a rectangle, you get one pixel less on the right and on the bottom of the rectangle than when you *draw* it. When you look closely at the output of the test program (Example 6-7), you can see that the top and left line segments of the drawn rectangles are covered by the subsequent fills, but the right and bottom line segments are not. This is different from Windows API, where the end points of lines and rectangles are neither drawn nor filled.

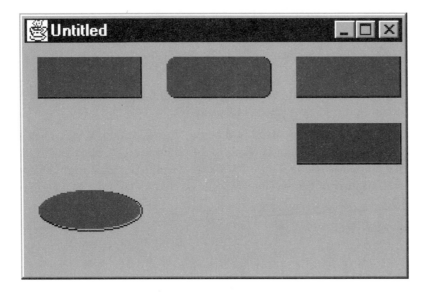

Figure 6-8: Filled rectangles and ovals

Example 6-7: FillRect.java

```java
import java.awt.*;

class FillRect extends Frame
{   public boolean handleEvent(Event evt)
    {   if (evt.id == Event.WINDOW_DESTROY) System.exit(0);
        return false;
    }

    public void paint(Graphics g)
    {   g.drawRect(10, 10, 80, 30);
        g.drawRoundRect(110, 10, 80, 30, 15, 15);
        g.draw3DRect(210, 10, 80, 30, true);
        g.draw3DRect(210, 60, 80, 30, false);
        g.drawOval(10, 110, 80, 30);
        g.setColor(Color.red);
        g.fillRect(10, 10, 80, 30);
        g.fillRoundRect(110, 10, 80, 30, 15, 15);
        g.fill3DRect(210, 10, 80, 30, true);
        g.fill3DRect(210, 60, 80, 30, false);
        g.fillOval(10, 110, 80, 30);
    }
    public static void main(String args[])
    {   Frame f = new FillRect();
        f.resize(300, 200);
        f.show();
    }
}
```

Note that filling arcs and polygons is quite different from drawing them. Arcs are filled as pie segments, by joining the center of the enclosing rectangle with the two end points of the arc and filling the interior. To see this, look at the filled PacMan in the screen picture in Figure 6-9.

Polygons, on the other hand, are closed before they are filled. If they have gaps in the interior, they are filled according to the "alternating" rule. For the alternating rule, a point is inside if an infinite ray with the point as origin crosses the path an odd number of times. The effect shows up nicely in the filled spiral in Example 6-8.

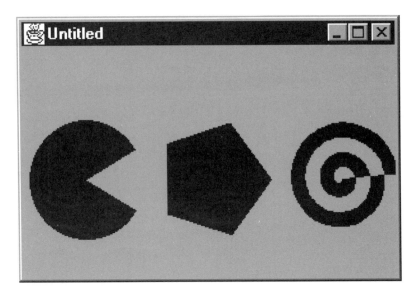

Figure 6-9: Filled shapes

Example 6-8: FillPoly.java

```
import java.awt.*;

class FillPoly extends Frame
{   public boolean handleEvent(Event evt)
    {   if (evt.id == Event.WINDOW_DESTROY) System.exit(0);
        return false;
    }

    public void paint(Graphics g)
    {   int r = 45; // radius of circle bounding PacMan(R)
        int cx = 50; // center of that circle
        int cy = 100;
        int angle = 30;; // half the opening angle of mouth

        int dx = (int)(r * Math.cos(angle * Math.PI / 180));
        int dy = (int)(r * Math.sin(angle * Math.PI / 180));

        g.fillArc(cx - r, cy - r, 2 * r, 2 * r, angle, 360 - 2 * angle);

        Polygon p = new Polygon();
        cx = 150;
        int i;
        for (i = 0; i < 5; i++)
            p.addPoint((int)(cx + r * Math.cos(i * 2 * Math.PI / 5)),
```

```
                (int)(cy + r * Math.sin(i * 2 * Math.PI / 5)));

        g.fillPolygon(p);

        Polygon s = new Polygon();
        cx = 250;
        for (i = 0; i < 360; i++)
        {   double t = i / 360.0;
            s.addPoint((int)(cx + r * t * Math.cos(8 * t * Math.PI)),
                (int)(cy + r * t * Math.sin(8 * t * Math.PI)));
        }
        g.fillPolygon(s);
    }

    public static void main(String args[])
    {   Frame f = new FillPoly();
        f.resize(300, 200);
        f.show();
    }
}
```

Paint Mode

When you paint shapes on top of one another, the shape last drawn simply writes on top of everything under it. In addition to this *overwrite* paint mode, AWT also supports a second method of combining new shapes with the old window contents; this is usually called *XOR* paint mode.

The XOR paint mode is used for highlighting a portion of the screen. Suppose you draw a filled rectangle over a part of the screen. If you draw on top of pixels that are already in the current color, then they are changed to the color specified in the setXORMode call. If you draw on top of pixels in the color of the setXORMode parameter, they are changed to the current color. Any other colors under the highlighted area are changed in some way. The key point is that XOR is a *toggle*. If you draw the same shape twice in XOR mode, the second drawing erases the first, and the screen looks just as it did at the outset. Example 6-9 provides some sample code.

Usually, you use the background (like Figure 6-10) color as the argument to setXORMode.

Example 6-9: XOR.java

```java
import java.awt.*;

class XOR extends Frame
{   public boolean handleEvent(Event evt)
    {   if (evt.id == Event.WINDOW_DESTROY) System.exit(0);
        return false;
    }

    public void paint(Graphics g)
    {   g.setColor(Color.red);
        g.fillRect(10, 10, 80, 30);
        g.setColor(Color.green);
        g.fillRect(50, 20, 80, 30);
        g.setColor(Color.blue);
        g.fillRect(130, 40, 80, 30);
        g.setXORMode(Color.green);
        g.fillRect(90, 30, 80, 30);

    }

    public static void main(String[] args)
    {   Frame f = new XOR();
        f.resize(300, 200);
        f.setBackground(Color.black);
        f.show();
    }
}
```

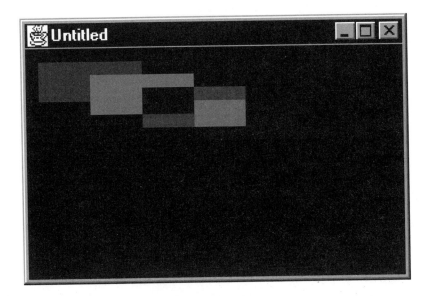

Figure 6-10: Combining colors in XOR mode

`java.awt.Graphics`

- `void setPaintMode()`

  sets the graphics context to use "paint mode," in which new pixels replace old ones.

- `void setXORMode(Color xor_color)`

  sets the graphics context to use "XOR mode." The color of a pixel is determined as `old_color ^ new_color ^ xor_color`. If you draw the same shape twice, then it is erased and the screen is restored to its original appearance.

  Parameters: `xor_color`   the color to which the current color should change during drawing

Images

We can build up simple images by drawing lines and shapes. Complex images, such as photographs, must be generated externally, for example with a scanner or special image-manipulation software, then stored in a file. Once they are in a file they can be read into a Java application. To read a graphics file into an application, you need to use a so-called `Toolkit` object. A `Toolkit` object can read most standard graphics formats, for example, GIF and JPEG files. To get a `Toolkit` object, use the static `getDefaultToolkit` method of the `Toolkit` class. Here is the code you need:

```
String name = "blue-ball.gif";
Image image = Toolkit.getDefaultToolkit().getImage(name);
```

Now the variable `image` contains the GIF file image and you can display it.

```
public void paint(Graphics g)
{   g.drawImage(image, 0, 0, this);
}
```

The `drawImage` command renders the image in the window. Example 6-10 takes this a little bit further and *tiles* the window with the graphics image looking like Figure 6-11.

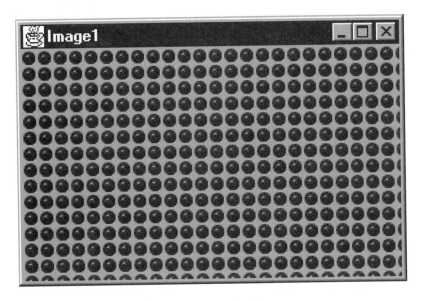

Figure 6-11: Window with tiled graphics image

Example 6-10: Image1.java

```java
import java.awt.*;
import java.awt.image.*;
import java.net.*;

class Image1 extends Frame
{   public boolean handleEvent(Event evt)
    {   if (evt.id == Event.WINDOW_DESTROY) System.exit(0);
        return false;
    }

    public Image1()
    {   setTitle("Image1");

        image = Toolkit.getDefaultToolkit()
            .getImage("blue-ball.gif");
    }

    public void paint(Graphics g)
    {   Dimension d = size();
        Insets in = insets();
        int client_width = d.width - in.right - in.left;
        int client_height = d.height - in.bottom - in.top;
```

```
      int image_width = image.getWidth(this);
      int image_height = image.getHeight(this);

      g.drawImage(image, 0, 0, this);
      for (int i = 0; i <= client_width / image_width; i++)
         for (int j = 0; j <= client_height / image_height; j++)
            if (i + j > 0) g.copyArea(0, 0, image_width,
         image_height, i * image_width, j * image_height);
   }

   Image image;

   public static void main(String args[])
   {  Frame f = new Image1();
      f.resize(300, 200);
      f.show();
   }
}
```

The tiling occurs in the paint method. We compute the sizes of the client area of
the window and of the image using insets. Then we draw one copy of the image
in the top left corner and use the `copyArea` call to copy it into the entire window.

By the way, if you look at the Image1 constructor, you will note a call to

```
   setTitle("Image1");
```

This call sets the title bar of the window.

java.awt.Toolkit

- `Toolkit getDefaultToolkit()`

  returns the default toolkit.

- `Image getImage(String filename)`

  returns an image that will read its pixel data from a file.

  Parameters: `filename` the file containing the image (e.g., a GIF or
  JPEG file)

```
java.awt.Graphics
```

- `boolean drawImage(Image img, int x, int y, int width, int height, ImageObserver observer)`

  draws an image. Note: This call may return before the image is drawn.

Parameters:	`img`	the image to be drawn
	`x`	the *x*-coordinate of the upper left corner
	`y`	the *y*-coordinate of the upper left corner
	`width`	the desired width of image
	`height`	the desired height of image
	`observer`	the object to be notified of the rendering process (may be null)

- `boolean drawImage(Image img, int x, int y, ImageObserver observer)`

  draws a scaled image. Note: This call may return before the image is drawn.

Parameters:	`img`	the image to be drawn
	`x`	the *x*-coordinate of the upper left corner
	`y`	the *y*-coordinate of the upper left corner
	`observer`	the object to be notified of the rendering process (may be null)

```
java.awt.Frame
```

- `setTitle(String title)`

  sets the title string.

Parameters:	`title`	the string to use in the title bar

Buffering

If you run the `Image1` program on a moderately slow computer, you can watch how it slowly fills the window. When something the user does requires that the window be repainted (i.e., causes a call to the `paint` method), the window again *slowly* fills with the images.

Thus, this naive image handling does not work well if you are concerned about performance or if the image arrives slowly over a network connection. In the remainder of this chapter, we explain how the professionals deal with images. If the discussion gets too technical, just skip this section and come back when you actually have to deal with images.

First, you may have noticed that the immediately preceding program sometimes flickers when it redraws the screen. That is because update, and not the paint method, is called when AWT notifies the window of the need to redraw. The default action of update is to erase the screen and then to repaint it. In our case, erasing the screen is not necessary because we completely cover it with the image. This problem is simple to solve. We just override update by calling paint directly.

```
void update(Graphics g)
{    paint(g);
}
```

To speed up the screen refresh, we first build the entire screen image in its own image buffer. We can then paint the screen by drawing just that one buffer into it. That makes the drawing much smoother and faster. The cost is the time and memory needed to fill the buffer. As an added benefit, we only need to recompute the buffer when the user makes the screen area larger.

NOTE: Windows users should think of what is occurring after the buffer is filled as corresponding to using the BitBlt API call.

VB NOTE: If you are using VB4, think of this as corresponding to a call to PaintPicture.

You create a buffer with the createImage command. To draw into that buffer, rather than directly into the window, we need to work with the graphics context that is attached *to the buffer*. (The graphics context parameter of the update and paint functions is attached to the screen window.) This is done with the getGraphics method call of the image class, which returns a Graphics object (i.e., a graphics context).

Here is the code for this:

```
Image buffered_image = createImage(client_width, client_height);
Graphics bg = buffered_image.getGraphics();
// all drawing commands that use bg fill the buffered_image
bg.drawImage(image, 0, 0, this);
for (int i = 0; i <= client_width / image_width; i++)
   for (int j = 0; j <= client_height / image_height; j++)
```

```
        if (i + j > 0) // skip the first tile
            bg.copyArea(0, 0, image_width, image_height,
                i * image_width, j * image_height);
bg.dispose();
```

NOTE: Notice the last line.

```
    bg.dispose();
```

Don't forget to dispose of a graphics context when you are done with it. Graphics contexts occupy more than just memory. They attach to finite resources in the operating systems, so you can't just rely on the garbage collection mechanism to release and then recycle them.

Finally, when the image has been built, we want to display it in the window.

```
void paint(Graphics g)
{   // if the window size has increased, recompute
    //buffered_image
    . . .
    g.drawImage(buffered_image, 0, 0, null);
}
```

java.awt.Component

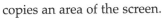

- `void update(Graphics g)`

  updates the component; unless overridden, it erases the screen area and calls the paint method.

  Parameters: g   the graphics context to use for the drawing

- `Image createImage(int width, int height)`

  creates an off-screen image buffer to be used for double buffering.

  Parameters: `width`   the width of the image

                  `height`   the height of the image

java.awt.Graphics

- `void copyArea(int x, int y, int width, int height, int dx, int dy)`

  copies an area of the screen.

Parameters:	x	the *x*-coordinate of the upper left corner of the source area
	y	the *y*-coordinate of the upper left corner of the source area
	`width`	the width of the source area
	`height`	the height of the source area
	dx	the horizontal distance from the source area to the target area
	dy	the vertical distance from the source area to the target area

- `void dispose()`

  disposes of this graphics context and releases operating system resources. You should always dispose of the graphics contexts that you allocate, but not the ones handed to you by `paint` or `update`.

`java.awt.Image`

- `Graphics getGraphics()`

  gets a graphics context to draw into this image buffer.

Image Updating

The buffering technique you saw works well if you draw lines or text into the buffer. However, *it does not work for images.* If you try out the code that we have described so far, the paint procedure will probably paint a blank rectangle! The reason for that is subtle, but important.

AWT was written with the assumption that an image may arrive slowly over a network connection. The *first* call to the `drawImage` function recognizes that the GIF file has not yet been loaded. Instead of loading the file and returning to the caller when the image is actually loaded, Java spawns a new thread of execution to load the image, *and then returns to the caller without actually having completed that task.*

This is—to say the least—surprising to anyone who expects that a function won't return until it has done its job. But here the multi-threaded aspect of Java works against your assumptions. What will happen is that Java will run the code in your program in parallel with the code to load the image. Eventually, the image will be loaded and available. Of course, in the meantime, our code has tiled the entire buffer with copies of a blank array.

The solution of course is to find out when the GIF image is completely loaded and *then* tile the buffer. When we were trying to figure out how this is accomplished (and this is a technique you should be prepared to use yourself), we needed to look at the Java on-line documentation and then study the ancestors of the Frame class. As Figure 6-12 shows, Frame extends Window, which extends Container, which extends Component, which extends Object *and implements* ImageObserver.

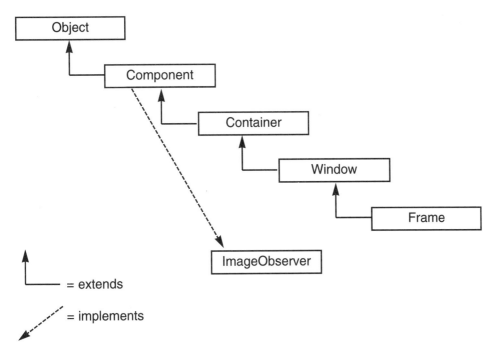

Figure 6-12: Inheritance hierarchy for the Frame class

ImageObserver is an interface with a single method, imageUpdate. This is a *callback* function. That is, the thread that loads the image periodically calls the imageUpdate function of the object that was passed as the last argument of the drawImage call

```
bg.drawImage(image, 0, 0, this);
```

That parameter must be of type ImageObserver. Now you know why we passed this as the last parameter. The this object is our application object derived from Frame. Since Frame (indirectly) implements ImageObserver, this is a legal argument. (By the way, you pass null if you don't want to be notified of the image acquisition process.)

The default implementation of `imageUpdate` simply calls `update`. Now you know why the first program worked, and why it flickered more than it should have. During the first call to `paint`, the first call to `drawImage` returned immediately, and the first attempt at tiling didn't actually work. But as soon as the image was acquired, the `paint` procedure was called again and the screen was rendered correctly.

However, this mechanism fails if we use buffering. The sole reason for using buffering was not to render the screen again with every call to `paint`. Instead, we must let the initial image acquisition take its course and only build up the buffer when it is finished. To find out when the image is complete, we override the `imageUpdate` function in `ImageObserver`.

The `imageUpdate` function has six parameters (see API). The second parameter indicates the kind of notification used in a particular call. The image acquisition mechanism notifies the observer many times during the acquisition process. The `imageUpdate` function is called when the image size is known, each time that a chunk of the image is ready, and, finally, when the entire image is complete. When you use an Internet browser and look at a Web page that contains an image, you know how these notifications are translated into actions. An Internet browser lays out a Web page as soon as it knows the sizes of the images in the page. Then it gradually fills in the images, as more detailed information becomes available.

We are not interested in incremental rendering. Our code just needs to wait for the image to be complete, copy the image into the buffer, start the tiling, and finally, paint the window. Timing is everything—if any one of these events happens out of order, then the image is not correctly rendered. In Chapter 12, you will learn an elegant way of controlling the timing by synchronizing different threads. Right now, we'll do it by brute force. In the first call to `paint`, we render the GIF file in a buffer of size 1 by 1, simply to force the loading of the GIF file. In Example 6-11, when the `imageUpdate` function finds that the image is complete, it calls `repaint`, which notices that the buffer needs to be filled, fills the buffer, and then displays it in the window.

Example 6-11: Image2.java

```
import java.awt.*;
import java.awt.image.*;
import java.net.*;
import java.io.*;

class Image2 extends Frame
{  public boolean handleEvent(Event evt)
   {  if (evt.id == Event.WINDOW_DESTROY) System.exit(0);
      return false;
   }
```

```
public Image2()
{  setTitle("Image2");
   image = Toolkit.getDefaultToolkit().getImage
      ("blue-ball.gif");
}

public void update(Graphics g)
{  paint(g);
}

public void paint(Graphics g)
{  if (image_width <= 0 || image_height <= 0)
   {  buffered_image = createImage(1,1);
      Graphics bg = buffered_image.getGraphics();
      bg.drawImage(image, 0, 0, this);
      bg.dispose();
      return;
   }

   Dimension d = size();
   Insets in = insets();

   int client_width = d.width - in.right - in.left;
   int client_height = d.height - in.bottom - in.top;

   if (client_width > buffer_width || client_height >
      buffer_height)
   // size has increased
   {  buffer_width = client_width;
      buffer_height = client_height;

      buffered_image = createImage
         (buffer_width, buffer_height);
      Graphics bg = buffered_image.getGraphics();
      bg.drawImage(image, 0, 0, null);
      for (int i = 0; i <= buffer_width / image_width; i++)
         for (int j = 0; j <= buffer_height / image_height; j++)
            if (i + j > 0) bg.copyArea
               (0, 0, image_width, image_height, i
                  * image_width, j * image_height);
      bg.dispose();
   }
   g.drawImage(buffered_image, 0, 0, this);
}

public boolean imageUpdate(Image img, int infoflags,
   int x, int y, int width, int height)
{  if ((infoflags & ImageObserver.ALLBITS) != 0)
```

```
    {  // image is complete
       image_width = image.getWidth(null);
       image_height = image.getHeight(null);
       repaint();
       return false;
    }
    return true; // want more info
  }

  int buffer_width = 0;
  int buffer_height = 0;
  int image_width = 0;
  int image_height = 0;
  Image image;
  Image buffered_image;

  public static void main(String args[])
  {  Frame f = new Image2();
     f.resize(300, 200);
     f.show();
  }
}
```

java.awt.image.ImageObserver

- boolean imageUpdate(Image img, int infoflags, int x, int y, int width, int height)

  this function is called to notify the observer of progress in the rendering process.

Parameters:	img	the image that is being acquired
	infoflags	a combination of the following flags:

  - ABORT   the image acquisition was aborted
  - ALLBITS   all bits of the image are now available
  - ERROR   an error was encountered in the acquisition process
  - FRAMEBITS   a complete frame of a multi-frame image is now available for drawing
  - HEIGHT   the height of the image is now known (and passed in the height argument of this call)
  - PROPERTIES   the properties of the image are now available

- SOMEBITS   some (but not all) bits of the image are available. The x, y, width, and height arguments of this call give the bounding box of the new pixels

- WIDTH   the width of the image is now known (and passed in the width argument of this call)

x, y, width, height   further information about the image, dependent on infoflags

`java.awt.Component`

- `void repaint()`

  causes a repaint of the component by calling update "as soon as possible."

- `public void repaint(int x, int y, int width, int height)`

  causes a repaint of a part of the component by calling `update` "as soon as possible."

  Parameters: x   the *x*-coordinate of the top left corner of the area to be repainted

             y   the *y*-coordinate of the top left corner of the area to be repainted

             width   the width of the area to be repainted

             height   the height of the area to be repainted

CHAPTER

7

- Panels
- Canvases
- Text Input
- Text Areas
- Making Choices
- Flow Layouts Revisited
- Border Layout
- Card Layout
- Grid Layout
- Grid Bag Layout
- Using No Layout Manager
- Custom Layout Managers
- Dialog Boxes
- Data Exchange
- Menus
- Keyboard Events
- Mouse Events
- Scroll Bars

Designing User Interfaces with AWT

his chapter shows you how to design a graphical user interface (GUI) in Java applications. In Java, the various GUI building blocks are usually called *components*. The idea is that you construct the user interface with various building blocks such as buttons, input areas for text (text fields), and scroll bars. You can then program the interface to respond to various events. (After all, what good is a button if you can't tell when it is clicked, or a text field box if you can't detect keystrokes in it.)

Components, in turn, are placed inside a Java object called a *container*. For example, a dialog box in Java would be made up of the surrounding container and, inside of it, the components needed to make the dialog box useable, such as a text field and at least one button.

(This way of working should be familiar to Windows or X-Windows programmers. These building blocks are called *controls* in Windows programming and *widgets* in X-Windows programming. The best analogy to a container is probably the Windows notion of a *parent window*. In X-Windows there actually is a notion of a *container widget*, which is [probably] where the Java designers got the idea for a container.) (A VB *form* is also a good analogy for the Java notion of a container.)

NOTE: The same user interface components are used to build both stand-alone programs and applets. (For GUI-based browser *applets* please see Chapter 8.)

To build a user interface you obviously need to decide how your interface should look. In particular, what components are needed and how should they appear? This is often easiest with old-fashioned paper and pencil since Java has no form designer like those in VB or Delphi. When you are satisfied with the design, you need to convert the design to Java code. Unfortunately, because of the lack of a form designer to generate code templates, you need to write code for *everything*. In particular, code (often lots of it) is needed to:

1.   make the components in the user interface look the way you want them to,

2.   position (lay out) the user interface components where you want them to be inside a window,

3.   Handle user input, in particular, program the components to recognize the events to which you want them to respond.

We start this chapter with an example that demonstrates how things work in a simple situation. The rest of this chapter shows you how to use all the user interface components and layout mechanisms that AWT has to offer.

A Simple Example

Our first example is a window populated with *lots* of buttons—see Figure 7-1. When you click on one of the buttons, the background color of the window changes. Although this is not a terribly useful program, it will show you the basic methods for building an AWT-based user interface. For example, we need to position and size the buttons as well as make them respond to a mouse click. (Even this simple application requires 30 lines of code. This gives you an idea of how complex a sophisticated GUI application, with many different components responding to multiple events, will be!)

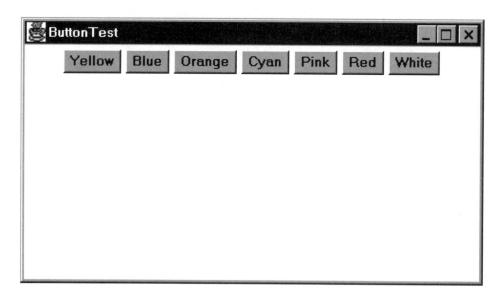

Figure 7-1: Button Test

Let us go through the elements of this program one by one. First, as you learned in the last chapter, *every* graphics application uses a class derived from Frame to describe the top-level window. For a GUI-based program, you add the code to create the user interface elements in the class constructor of the derived class.

We begin by using the setTitle method that you saw in the last chapter to give a title to the window. Thus, the constructor begins:

```
public class ButtonTest extends Frame
{   public ButtonTest()
    {   setTitle("Button Test");
        . . .
    }
    . . .
}
```

Actually adding the buttons to the frame occurs through a call to a method named (quite mnemonically) add. For our example, the appropriate piece of the constructor is shown below. (The blank line is for a statement that lays out the buttons—we will cover this statement shortly.)

```
public class ButtonTest extends Frame
{   public ButtonTest()
    {   setTitle("Button Test:");
        // important line for the layout is missing next
        add(new Button("Yellow"));
        add(new Button("Blue"));
        . . .
    }
    . . .
}
```

The idea is that the add method takes as a parameter the specific component to be added to the frame. Since a component is a Java object, it is usually convenient to create it when you add it to the frame—hence the call to new in the above example. Of course, we always use new with a constructor for the object concerned. Notice that, in this case, the Button constructor for the Button class actually lets us specify the string that we want to appear on the button.

If you want to set the color of the button, you must:

1. first give a name to the button instance,

2. invoke the setBackground method on it,

3. then add the button.

Here's an example of a fragment that would do this:

```
Button yellowButton = new Button("Yellow");
yellowButton.setBackground(Color.yellow);
add(yellowButton);
```

Layout

Notice that, in the code above, we did not specify the positions of the buttons. This is true of AWT in general. You do not specify absolute positions for interface elements. This is very different from Windows programming, for example, for which you would specify the exact position of each button in a dialog box. (You may not have paid attention to this if you use a "resource editor" that lets you drag and drop buttons onto the dialog box or if you use VB or Delphi. But, if you look carefully into the resource description—the .RC file or the property sheet of the button—you will find the *x* and *y* positions of every button listed.)

There is a reason why AWT works this way: it is designed to be platform independent. In particular, you have no idea what fonts are installed on your user's computer, or how thick the buttons are in the user interface in his or her system. For example, Motif buttons have a different shape than Windows buttons.

(To some degree, Windows programmers have the same problem—they usually just don't bother compensating. For example, the user of a Windows program may have a high-resolution graphics adapter with large fonts or a simple VGA with small fonts. Similarly, buttons look different in the various versions of Windows. To partially compensate for this, button coordinates in Windows are not measured in pixels, but in "dialog units." These dialog units are derived from the size of the system font. This is a bit of a hack that actually works pretty well most of the time. Of course, users who install Troglodyte Bold as their system font probably get some overlapping buttons on their dialog boxes—the feeling in Redmond is, of course, if you choose to do this, you don't deserve better results.)

AWT has a much more general and elegant mechanism. When you add buttons in the container, you specify a general rule for the layout. The buttons are then laid out automatically, regardless of the size of the Window. In our program, the one line that was missing in the fragments above was for the statement that constructed a new *flow layout* for the class. Usually it is important that the layout be done *before* we add the interface elements. (Although in the case of flow layouts, strictly speaking, it isn't necessary.) The actual constructor thus begins like this:

```
public class ButtonTest extends Frame
{  public ButtonTest()
   {  setTitle("Button Test:");
      setLayout(new FlowLayout());
      add(new Button("Yellow"));
      add(new Button("Blue"));
      . . .
   }
   . . .
}
```

A flow layout object simply adds buttons until the current row is full, then starts a new row of buttons. Moreover, the flow layout object keeps each set of buttons centered in an individual row. You can see the flow layout in action when you resize the test application (see Figure 7-2). If you make the window narrower, the buttons are rearranged. That is a neat feature of Java and a great savings in programming time. Regardless of how the user resizes the window, you can be sure the buttons always stay neatly centered.

NOTE: The add method belongs to the panel, not the layout manager. But the layout manager needs to know about the added items, and, more importantly, the layout directives (such as "North"). It needs that information so it can do the layout. Thus, whenever you add an item to a container, the container passes on the item and any layout directives to the layout manager."

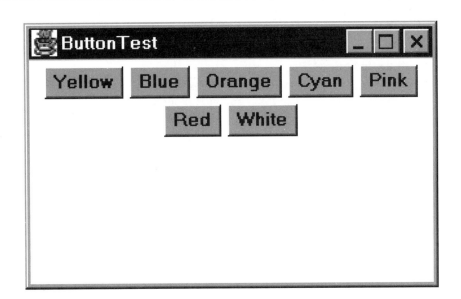

Figure 7-2: Changing the window size will rearrange the buttons

Making the Buttons Responsive

Finally, you must learn how to make the program respond when a user clicks on one of the buttons. As you saw in the previous chapter, AWT programs can be event driven. The operating system sends event notifications to the running Java program when various events occur. Then, as an AWT programmer, you need to know:

- what events to expect and

- how to trap them (that is, which methods get called when the event occurs).

Then, all you need to do is:

- override those methods in your class and

- insert the desired actions into the methods that are called by the event handler.

When a button is clicked, the `action` method is the one that is triggered (called). It has two arguments: a description of the event (which we will analyze in greater detail later) and a generic argument that varies with different event types. For button events, the second argument is simply the string on the face of the button. In this program (as well as in most—if not all—applets), the strings of all the buttons are distinct, so we can use them to determine what happened. (If there were two buttons, both labeled "OK," we would need to work much harder to differentiate between the two—but, of course, having two OK buttons in the same window is rather poor GUI design.) Here's the framework code for the `action` method:

```
public boolean action(Event evt, Object arg)
{   if (arg.equals("Yellow")) setBackground(Color.yellow);
    else if (arg.equals("Blue")) setBackground(Color.blue);
    else if . . .
    else return super.action(evt,arg); // action not handled
    repaint(); // force color change
    return true; // action handled
}
```

VB NOTE: If you declare an object instance in Java with code like this

```
Button yesButton = new Button("Yes");
```

your instinct would be to regard `yesButton` as the name of the button: unfortunately, this can lead you astray. A better analogy is to think of this as an alias for the button, much like the one you would get by using the `Set` command. There is no real notion of a name property of objects in Java.

The Complete Code for the Button Test Example

Since you now have seen at least one way to accomplish the three essential tasks of AWT user interface programs, you might want to see the whole code for the Button Test application. (The only significant addition is the `main` method to size the window and make sure the window will die if the user tries to close it!) You saw this kind of code in the last chapter. Example 7-1 shows the entire code:

Example 7-1: ButtonTest.java

```java
import java.awt.*;

public class ButtonTest extends Frame
{   public ButtonTest()
    {   setTitle("ButtonTest");
        setLayout(new FlowLayout());
        add(new Button("Yellow"));
        add(new Button("Blue"));
        add(new Button("Orange"));
        add(new Button("Cyan"));
        add(new Button("Pink"));
        add(new Button("Red"));
        add(new Button("White"));
    }

    public boolean handleEvent(Event evt)
    {   if (evt.id == Event.WINDOW_DESTROY) System.exit(0);
        return super.handleEvent(evt);
    }

    public boolean action(Event evt, Object arg)
    {   if (arg.equals("Yellow")) setBackground(Color.yellow);
        else if (arg.equals("Blue")) setBackground(Color.blue);
        else if (arg.equals("Orange")) setBackground(Color.orange);
        else if (arg.equals("Cyan"))
            setBackground(Color.cyan);
        else if (arg.equals("Pink"))
            setBackground(Color.pink);
        else if (arg.equals("Red"))
            setBackground(Color.red);
        else if (arg.equals("White"))
            setBackground(Color.white);
        else return super.action(evt,arg);
        repaint();
        return true;
    }

    public static void main(String[] args)
    {   Frame f = new ButtonTest();
        f.resize(320, 200);
        f.show();
    }
}
```

API Syntax Elements

`java.awt.Button`

- `Button(String s)`

  constructs a button.

  Parameters: s   the label that will appear on the face of the button

`java.awt.Container`

- `setLayout(LayoutManager m)`

  sets the layout manager for this container.

- `add(Component c)`

  adds a component to this container.

Panels

In our first example, we dumped all the buttons into a window and let the flow layout manager worry about arranging them. In practice, that would result in a very messy and unstructured dialog box in most situations. You obviously need a more precise method of locating components. In Java, you can think of dividing a top-level window into *panels*. Panels act as (smaller) containers for interface elements and can themselves be arranged inside the window. For example, you can have one panel for the buttons and another for the text fields. The result can be a precise positioning of components. What you do in Java is:

- build up a panel the way you want it to look,

- then add the panel to the window.

VB NOTE: Think of a panel as corresponding to a picture box without a boundary—it is invisible to the user but still functions as a container.

For example, look at Figure 7-3. The three buttons at the bottom of the screen are all contained in a panel. The panel is put into the "south" end of the window.

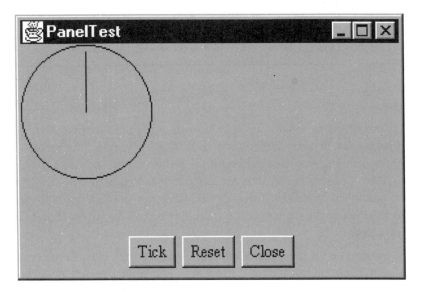

Figure 7-3: A panel placed at the south end of the window

So suppose you want to add a panel with three buttons as in Figure 7-3. As you might expect, you first create a new instance of a `Panel` object, before you add the individual buttons to it. You then use the `setLayout` method of the `Panel` class to tell the panel that you will be using a `FlowLayout` manager in it. Finally you add the individual buttons, using the `add` method you have seen before. (And you add buttons under the control of the `FlowLayout` manager, so they have all the good properties you have seen before.)

Here's a code fragment that (after you import `java.awt.*` and add the other necessary code) adds a panel in the south end of a container.

```
public class PanelTest extends Frame
{   public PanelTest()
    {   setTitle("Panel test");
        Panel p = new Panel();
        p.setLayout(new FlowLayout());
        p.add(new Button("Tick"));
        p.add(new Button("Reset"));
        p.add(new Button("Close"));
        add("South", p);
    }
    //rest of the code goes here

}
```

NOTE: When Java displays a window, the panel boundaries are not visible to the user. Panels are just an organizing mechanism for the user interface designer.

Canvases

Once you start filling up a window with lots of interface elements and multiple panels, it is best not to draw directly onto the window surface any more. This is because your drawing may interfere with the buttons. Instead, you add a *canvas* to the window. A canvas is simply a rectangular area in which you can draw. (In contrast, a panel is a rectangular area into which you can place user interface components.) We use the canvas in the sample program for this section to draw the face of a clock.

Making a canvas is a bit more complex than using a panel, because you need to specify how to draw on the canvas. This means you must derive a new class from `Canvas` and then override (redefine) the `paint` procedure in your derived class. Here is an outline of the `ClockCanvas` class:

```
class ClockCanvas extends Canvas
{   public void paint(Graphics g)
    {   g.drawOval(0, 0, 100, 100);
        // draw hour and minute hand
        . . .
    }
    public void tick() { minutes++; repaint(); }
    public void reset() { minutes = 0; }
    private int minutes = 0;
}
```

Just as we derived classes from `Frame` in the previous chapter to draw on the entire frame, we now derive a new class from `Canvas` to draw on a specific area of the window. We also add methods to communicate with the canvas. (In our case, the `tick` and `reset` functions.)

Our sample program is getting a bit more complicated; it has two classes:

*   The first class is derived from `Frame`. It describes how the main window is different from the default window. (In our case, the difference is simply that it has buttons and a canvas.)

*   The second class is derived from `Canvas`. It describes how our canvas is different from the default. (It draws a clock face!)

Notice that we didn't need to extend the `Panel` class because the standard class already does everything necessary to manage the buttons we want to place on the window.

Example 7-2 is the complete program.

Example 7-2: PanelTest.java

```java
import java.awt.*;
public class PanelTest extends Frame
{  public PanelTest()
   {  setTitle("PanelTest");
      Panel p = new Panel();
      p.setLayout(new FlowLayout());
      p.add(new Button("Tick"));
      p.add(new Button("Reset"));
      p.add(new Button("Close"));
      add("South", p);
      clock = new ClockCanvas();
      add("Center", clock);
   }

   public boolean handleEvent(Event evt)
   {  if (evt.id == Event.WINDOW_DESTROY) System.exit(0);
      return super.handleEvent(evt);
   }

   public boolean action(Event evt, Object arg)
   {  if (arg.equals("Tick")) clock.tick();
      else if (arg.equals("Reset")) clock.reset();
      else if (arg.equals("Close")) System.exit(0);
      else return super.action(evt,arg);
      return true;
   }

   public static void main(String[] args)
   {  Frame f = new PanelTest();
      f.resize(300, 200);
      f.show();
   }

   private ClockCanvas clock;

}

class ClockCanvas extends Canvas
{  public void paint(Graphics g)
   {  g.drawOval(0, 0, 100, 100);
      double hourAngle = 2 * Math.PI * (minutes - 3 * 60)
         / (12 * 60);
      double minuteAngle = 2 * Math.PI * (minutes - 15)
         / 60;
      g.drawLine(50, 50,
```

```
            50 + (int)(30 * Math.cos(hourAngle)),
            50 + (int)(30 * Math.sin(hourAngle)));
        g.drawLine(50, 50,
            50 + (int)(45 * Math.cos(minuteAngle)),
            50 + (int)(45 * Math.sin(minuteAngle)));
    }

    public void reset()
    {   minutes = 0;
        repaint();
    }

    public void tick()
    {   minutes++;
        repaint();
    }

    private int minutes = 0;
}
```

API Definitions Used

`java.awt.Container`

• `Component add(String name, Component c)`

adds a component to this container.

Parameters:	name	a string that has a meaning for the layout manager. For example, "South" directs the `BorderLayout` manager (the default manager for frames) to add the component to the bottom of the container.
	c	the component to be added

Text Input

Obviously, Java programs would have little use if they could only draw pretty pictures. You need to have a way to accept input from a user. In Java, the areas used to input text are called *text fields*.

The usual way to add a text field to a window is to actually add it to a panel—just as you would a button:

```
Panel p = new Panel();
TextField tf = new TextField("New text field", 20);
p.add(tf);
```

This code adds a text field and initializes the text field by placing the string `"New text field"` inside of it. The second parameter of this constructor sets the width. In this case the width is 20 "columns." Unfortunately, a column is a rather imprecise measurement. One column is the expected width of one character in the font you are using for the text. The idea is that if you expect the inputs to be n characters or less, you are supposed to specify n as the column width. In practice, this measurement doesn't work out too well, and you should add 1 or 2 to the maximum input length to be on the safe side.

The column width that you set in the `TextField` constructor is not an upper limit on the number of characters the user can enter. The user can still type in longer strings, but the input scrolls when the text exceeds the length of the field, which is irritating.

In general, of course, you want to let the user add text (or edit the existing text) in a text field. Of course, quite often text fields start out blank. For this, just use the empty string as the first parameter for the `TextField` constructor:

```
TextField tf = new TextField("", 20);
```

You can change the contents of the text field at any time with the `setText` method. For example:

```
hourField.setText("12");
```

And you can find out what the user typed by calling the `getText` method. For example, if you want to trim any extraneous spaces from the data in a text field, use something like:

```
String hour = hourField.getText().trim();
```

To change the font in which the user text appears, use the `setFont` method in `java.awt.Component` (see the previous chapter for more on this method).

`java.awt.TextField`

- `TextField(String text, int cols)`

  constructs a new `TextField`.

  Parameters: `text`   the text to be displayed

                    `cols`   the number of columns

`java.awt.TextComponent`

* `void setText(String t)`

    changes the text of a text component.

    Parameters: t   the new text

`java.awt.TextComponent`

* `String getText()`

    returns the text contained in this text component.

A Text Box Example

Let us put a few text boxes to work in the clock program that we mentioned a moment ago. Figure 7-4 shows the running application. Instead of a reset button, there are now two text fields for entering the hours and minutes. When you click on the "Set time" button, the clock changes.

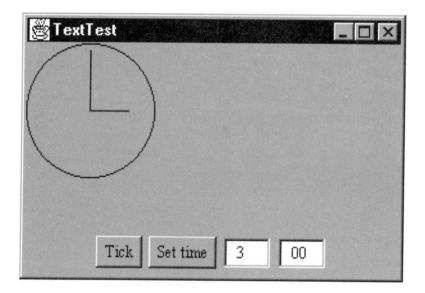

Figure 7-4: Text box example

The program is essentially a straightforward extension of what you have seen before—except for two important points. The first is that you add text fields to a panel in a different fashion than the way in which you added buttons. Notice the contrast in the following code:

```
    p.add(new Button("Set time"));
    hourField = new TextField("12", 3);
    p.add(hourField);
```

Why did we not just use `p.add(new TextField("12", 3))`? If we did this, we would have no handle for the text field component, so there would be no way to refer to it for future code. And we *do* need to remember the text fields in order to track them (in particular, to get text into them and to get the data out). (We don't need to have handles for buttons because they can be identified by their title strings.)

When the user clicks on the "Set time" button, we use the `getText` method to obtain the user input string. Unfortunately, that is what we get: a string. We need to convert the string to an integer. Java would like us to use the unbelievably complex incantation

```
    int hours = Integer.parseInt(hourField.getText().trim());
```

But this code won't work right when the user types a non-integer string, such as `"two"`, into the text field, or even leaves the field blank. Try it out: the terminal window will display an ugly error message complaining about a `java.lang.NumberFormatException`.

We use our `atoi` helper function in the `corejava` package in Example 7-3, but it does no error-checking at all, which isn't good for user interface design. We will tackle the issue of validating input in the next section.

Example 7-3: TextTest.java

```
import java.awt.*;
import corejava.*;

public class TextTest extends Frame
{   public TextTest()
    {   setTitle("TextTest");
        Panel p = new Panel();
        p.setLayout(new FlowLayout());
        p.add(new Button("Tick"));
        p.add(new Button("Set time"));
        hourField = new TextField("12", 3);
        p.add(hourField);
        minuteField = new TextField("00", 3);
        p.add(minuteField);

        add("South", p);
        clock = new ClockCanvas();
        add("Center", clock);
    }
```

```
        public boolean handleEvent(Event evt)
        {   if (evt.id == Event.WINDOW_DESTROY) System.exit(0);
            return super.handleEvent(evt);
        }

        public boolean action(Event evt, Object arg)
        {   if (arg.equals("Tick")) clock.tick();
            else if (arg.equals("Set time"))
            {   int hours = Format.atoi(hourField.getText());
                int minutes = Format.atoi(minuteField.getText());
                clock.setTime(hours, minutes);
            }
            else return super.action(evt,arg);
            return true;
        }

        private TextField hourField;
        private TextField minuteField;
        private ClockCanvas clock;

        public static void main(String[] args)
        {   Frame f = new TextTest();
            f.resize(300, 200);
            f.show();
        }
    }

    class ClockCanvas extends Canvas
    {   public void paint(Graphics g)
        {   g.drawOval(0, 0, 100, 100);
            double hourAngle = 2 * Math.PI * (minutes - 3 * 60) / (12 * 60);
            double minuteAngle = 2 * Math.PI * (minutes - 15) / 60;
            g.drawLine(50, 50, 50 + (int)(30 * Math.cos(hourAngle)),
                50 + (int)(30 * Math.sin(hourAngle)));
            g.drawLine(50, 50, 50 + (int)(45 * Math.cos(minuteAngle)),
                50 + (int)(45 * Math.sin(minuteAngle)));
        }

        public void setTime(int h, int m)
        {   minutes = h * 60 + m;
            repaint();
        }

        public void tick()
        {   minutes++;
            repaint();
        }

        private int minutes = 0;
    }
```

Input Validation

The problems mentioned in the last section are commonplace—if you have a place to enter text, you will need to check that the input makes sense before you work with it. For most text fields you need to test whether or not:

- the input value is legal (that is, not blank and a number) and

- the number is within the correct range (*e.g.*, 0–59 for minutes).

In either case, if there are problems, then it is usually best to move the cursor back into the edit field with the faulty entry so that the user can correct the problem.

Because this is such a common task, we will develop a class for it as shown in code of Example 7-4. (We hope you find this class—or a version of your own that you build on it—useful in your own coding.)

The class `IntTextBox` that we will design next is a text box especially for integer input. It would, of course, be nice if we could simply block all keystrokes except `'0' ... '9'`, but unfortunately, that is not possible. The native user interface component (that is, the actual Windows or X-Windows text box) handles the keystrokes and puts the characters on the screen before telling AWT what has happened. At any rate, we do have to allow a minus sign and then must check that the user has typed no more than one minus sign in the first position.

A good time to check for valid inputs would be when the user moves the mouse out of the current field. The natural way to do this is in some sort of "lost focus" event. There is supposed to be a "lost focus" event generated whenever the text box loses the focus, but, at least for Windows 95, the current version of Java doesn't support one. Instead, our class requires the programmer to manually determine when to check the input. In our case, the best point at which to check is when the user clicks on the "Set time" button. The code is as follows:

```
if (hourField.isValid() && minuteField.isValid())
    clock.setTime(hourField.getValue(), minuteField.getValue());
```

The `isValid()` method has the side effect of moving the cursor back to the field if the content is not valid. For example, if the user entered 27 for the hour, then the first call to `hourField.isValid()` fails, and the clock won't be set. Furthermore, the code moves the cursor back into the `hourField` field.

See page 239 for the code of the `IntTextField` class. Don't worry about the exception and the `try` block—we will get to that in Chapter 10. Note how we use the `requestFocus` method call to shift the focus back into the text component if its content is not valid.

Example 7-4: ValidationTest.java

```java
import java.awt.*;
import corejava.*;

public class ValidationTest extends Frame
{  public ValidationTest()
   {  setTitle("ValidationTest");
      Panel p = new Panel();
      p.setLayout(new FlowLayout());
      p.add(new Button("Tick"));
      p.add(new Button("Set time"));
      hourField = new IntTextField(12, 0, 23, 3);
      p.add(hourField);
      minuteField = new IntTextField(0, 0, 59, 3);
      p.add(minuteField);

      add("South", p);
      clock = new ClockCanvas();
      add("Center", clock);
   }

   public boolean handleEvent(Event evt)
   {  if (evt.id == Event.WINDOW_DESTROY) System.exit(0);
      return super.handleEvent(evt);
   }

   public boolean action(Event evt, Object arg)
   {  if (arg.equals("Tick")) clock.tick();
      else if (arg.equals("Set time"))
      {  if (hourField.isValid() && minuteField.isValid())
            clock.setTime(hourField.getValue(),
               minuteField.getValue());
      }
      else return super.action(evt, arg);
      return true;
   }

   public static void main(String[] args)
   {  Frame f = new ValidationTest();
      f.resize(300, 200);
      f.show();
   }

   private IntTextField hourField;
   private IntTextField minuteField;
   private ClockCanvas clock;

}
```

```
class ClockCanvas extends Canvas
{  public void paint(Graphics g)
    {  g.drawOval(0, 0, 100, 100);
       double hourAngle = 2 * Math.PI * (minutes - 3 * 60) / (12 * 60);
       double minuteAngle = 2 * Math.PI * (minutes - 15) / 60;
       g.drawLine(50, 50, 50 + (int)(30 * Math.cos(hourAngle)),
           50 + (int)(30 * Math.sin(hourAngle)));
       g.drawLine(50, 50, 50 + (int)(45 * Math.cos(minuteAngle)),
           50 + (int)(45 * Math.sin(minuteAngle)));
    }

    public void setTime(int h, int m)
    {  minutes = h * 60 + m;
       repaint();
    }

    public void tick()
    {  minutes++;
       repaint();
    }

    private int minutes = 0;
}

package corejava;

import java.awt.*;

public class IntTextField extends TextField
{  public IntTextField(int def, int min, int max,
       int size)
    {  super("" + def, size);
       low = min;
       high = max;
    }

    public boolean isValid()
    {  int value;
       try
       {  value = Integer.valueOf(getText().trim()).intValue();
          if (value < low || value > high)
              throw new NumberFormatException();
       }
       catch (NumberFormatException e)
       {  requestFocus();
          return false;
       }
       return true;
    }
```

```
public int getValue()
{  int value;
   try
   {    value = Integer.valueOf(getText().trim()).intValue();
   }
   catch(NumberFormatException e)
   {    value=0;
   }
   return value;
}
private int low;
private int high;
}
```

java.awt.Component

• void requestFocus()

requests that this component gets the input focus.

Text Areas

Sometimes you need to collect user input that is more than one line long. Use the TextArea component for this. When you place a text area in your program, a user can enter any number of lines of text; each line ends with '\n'. Figure 7-5 shows a text area.

Figure 7-5: A text area

In the `TextArea` constructor, you specify the number of rows and columns for the component. For example:

```
Comments = new TextArea(8, 40); // 8 lines of 40 columns each
```

(where the columns parameter works as before—add a few more columns for safety's sake). And, as before, the user is not restricted to the number of rows and columns; the text simply scrolls when the user inputs too much.

Example 7-5 is the complete code for the text area demo.

Example 7-5: TextAreaText.java

```java
import java.awt.*;

public class TextAreaTest extends Frame
{  public TextAreaTest()
    {  setTitle("TextAreaTest");
       Panel p = new Panel();
       p.setLayout(new FlowLayout());
       p.add(new Button("Print"));
       p.add(new Button("Close"));

       add("South", p);
       ta = new TextArea(8, 40);
       add("Center", ta);
    }

    public boolean handleEvent(Event evt)
    {  if (evt.id == Event.WINDOW_DESTROY) System.exit(0);
       return super.handleEvent(evt);
    }

    public boolean action(Event evt, Object arg)
    {  if (arg.equals("Print"))
           System.out.println(ta.getText());
       else if (arg.equals("Close"))
           System.exit(0);
       else return super.action(evt, arg);
       return true;
    }

    public static void main(String[] args)
    {  Frame f = new TextAreaTest();
       f.resize(300, 200);
       f.show();
    }

    private TextArea ta;
}
```

java.awt.TextArea

• TextArea(int rows, int cols)

constructs a new text area.

Parameters: rows   the number of rows

cols   the number of columns

Selecting Text

The text field and text area classes have methods to select (highlight) the text contained in the component. They can also check which text is currently selected.

First, there is the selectAll() method, which highlights all the text in the field. You would use this method when presenting the user with an input that they either will want to use exactly as provided, or that they won't want to use at all. In the latter case, they can just type their own input and the first keystroke replaces the selection.

The select method selects a part of the text. The arguments of select are the same as for substring: the first index is the start of the substring, the last is one more than the end. For example, t.select(10, 15) selects the tenth to fourteenth character in the text control. End-of-line markers count as one character.

The getSelectionStart and getSelectionEnd methods return the current selection, and getSelectedText returns the highlighted text. How users highlight text is system-dependent. In Windows, you can use the mouse or the standard SHIFT + arrow keys.

java.awt.TextComponent

• void selectAll()

selects all text in the component.

• void select(int selStart,int selEnd)

selects a range of text in the component.

Parameters: selStart   the first position to select

selEnd   one past the last position to select

• int getSelectionStart()

returns the first position of the selected text.

- `int getSelectionEnd()`

  returns one past the last position of the selected text.

- `String getSelectedText()`

  returns the selected text.

Text Editing

You can write code that modifies the contents of a text area (but not a text field). You can append text at the end, insert text in the middle, and replace text. To delete text, simply replace the text to be deleted with an empty string.

Example 7-6 shows how to implement a simple "find-and-replace" feature. In Figure 7-6, each time you click on the Replace button, the first match of the text in the first field is replaced by the text in the second field.

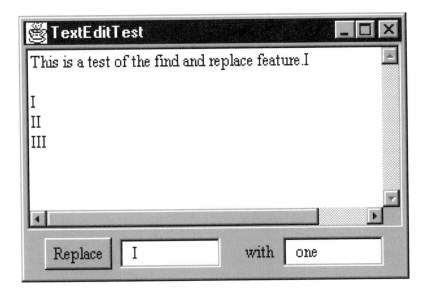

Figure 7-6: Testing text editing

Example 7-6: TextEditText.java

```java
import java.awt.*;

public class TextEditTest extends Frame
{  public TextEditTest()
   {  setTitle("TextEditTest");
      Panel p = new Panel();
```

```
        p.setLayout(new FlowLayout());
        p.add(new Button("Replace"));
        from = new TextField(10);
        p.add(from);
        p.add(new Label("with"));
        to = new TextField(10);
        p.add(to);
        add("South", p);
        ta = new TextArea(8, 40);
        add("Center", ta);
    }

    public boolean handleEvent(Event evt)
    {   if (evt.id == Event.WINDOW_DESTROY) System.exit(0);
        return super.handleEvent(evt);
    }

    public boolean action(Event evt, Object arg)
    {   if (arg.equals("Replace"))
        {   String f = from.getText();
            int n = ta.getText().indexOf(f);
            if (n >= 0 && f.length() > 0)
                ta.replaceText(to.getText(), n, n + f.length());
        }
        else return super.action(evt, arg);
        return true;
    }

    public static void main(String[] args)
    {   Frame f = new TextEditTest();
        f.resize(300, 200);
        f.show();
    }

    private TextArea ta;
    private TextField from, to;
}
```

This is not a very realistic application, but you could use this feature to correct spelling or typing errors in URLs.

`java.awt.TextArea`

- `void insertText(String str, int pos)`

  inserts a string into the text area.

Parameters:	`str`	the text to insert
	`pos`	the position at which to insert (0 = first position. Newlines count as one character)

- `void appendText(String str)`

  appends the given text to the end of the text already in the text area.

Parameters:	`str`	the text to insert

- `void replaceText(String str, int start, int end)`

  replaces a range of text with another string.

Parameters:	`str`	the new text
	`start`	the start position of the text to be replaced
	`end`	one past the end position of the text to be replaced

Labeling Fields

Unlike buttons, text fields have no label. If you want to label a field, you need to construct a `Label` object and place it before the field. If you look at the previous program, you will see how one of the text fields is preceded by a label with the text `"with"`. Labels are simple plain-text strings. They have no decorations (for example, no boundaries). They also do not react to user input. However, labels can be positioned inside a container like any other component, using the techniques you have seen before. This lets you place them where you need them.

For example, in the code for the search-and-replace example,

```
p.add(new Label("with"));
```

used the flow layout object to position the label.

`java.awt.Label`

- `Label(String s)`

Parameters:	`s`	the label text

- `public Label(String s, int align)`

   Parameters: `s`   the label text

   `align`   one of `LEFT`, `CENTER`, or `RIGHT`

Making Choices

You now know how to collect text input from users, but there are many occasions where you would rather give a user a finite set of choices, rather than have them enter the data in a text field. Using something like a set of check boxes tells the user what choices he or she has. (It also saves you from the trouble of error-checking.) In this section, you will learn how to program check boxes and what Java calls choice lists (which are a special type of list box).

Check Boxes

If you just want to collect a "yes" or "no" input, use a check box component. The user checks the box by clicking inside it and turns off the check mark by clicking inside the box again. Figure 7-7 shows a simple program with two check boxes, one to turn on or off the "italic" attributes of a font and the other for boldface. Each time the user clicks one of the check boxes, we refresh the screen, using the new font attributes.

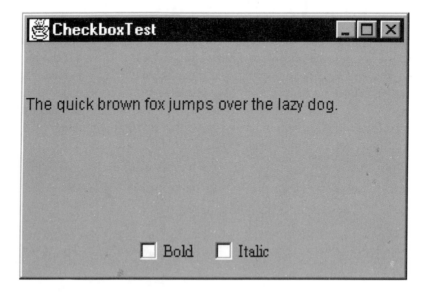

Figure 7-7: Check boxes

When creating a check box, you need to be able to identify the check box object, since you need this information to identify the sender of a check box event. Check boxes will need text next to them to identify them. You give the text that identifies the check box in the constructor. (The text will always appear to the right of the check box.)

```
class MyFrame extends Frame
{   public MyFrame()
    {   Panel p = new Panel();
        p.setLayout(new FlowLayout());
        bold = new Checkbox("Bold");
        p.add(bold);
        . . .
    }
    . . .
    private Checkbox bold;
}
```

When the user clicks on a check box, this triggers an action event. The `target` field of the event structure is the originating check box. "Target" is really a misnomer. The check box is the source of the event.

The `getState` method then retrieves the current state of the check box. It is `false` if unchecked, `true` if checked.

Here is the event handler for the font application. When the state of either check box changes, the code retrieves the current states of both check boxes and then notifies the canvas of the new font attributes to use.

```
public boolean action(Event evt, Object arg)
{   if (evt.target.equals(bold) || evt.target.equals(italic))
    {   int m = 0;
        if (bold.getState()) m += Font.BOLD;
        if (italic.getState()) m += Font.ITALIC;
        fox.setFont(m);
    }
    . . .
}
```

Example 7-7 is the complete program listing for the check box example.

Example 7-7: CheckboxTest.java

```
import java.awt.*;

public class CheckboxTest extends Frame
{   public CheckboxTest()
    {   setTitle("CheckboxTest");
        Panel p = new Panel();
        p.setLayout(new FlowLayout());
```

```
          p.add(bold = new Checkbox("Bold"));
          p.add(italic = new Checkbox("Italic"));
          add("South", p);
          fox = new FoxCanvas();
          add("Center", fox);
       }

       public boolean handleEvent(Event evt)
       {  if (evt.id == Event.WINDOW_DESTROY) System.exit(0);
          return super.handleEvent(evt);
       }

       public boolean action(Event evt, Object arg)
       {  if (evt.target.equals(bold)
             || evt.target.equals(italic))
          {  int m = (bold.getState() ? Font.BOLD : 0)
             + (italic.getState() ?
                Font.ITALIC : 0);
             fox.setFont(m);
          }
          else return super.action(evt, arg);
          return true;
       }
       public static void main(String[] args)
       {  Frame f = new CheckboxTest();
          f.resize(300, 200);
          f.show();
       }
       private FoxCanvas fox;
       private Checkbox bold;
       private Checkbox italic;
    }

class FoxCanvas extends Canvas
{   public FoxCanvas()
    {  setFont(Font.PLAIN);
    }

    public void setFont(int m)
    {   setFont(new Font("Helvetica", m, 12));
       repaint();
    }
    public void paint(Graphics g)
    {   g.drawString
       ("The quick brown fox jumps over the lazy dog.", 0, 50);
    }
}
```

`java.awt.Checkbox`

- `Checkbox(String label)`

  Parameters: `label`   the label on the check box

- `boolean getState()`

  returns the state of the check box.

- `void setState(boolean state)`

  sets the check box to a new state.

Check Box Groups

In the previous example, the user could check either, both, or none of the two check boxes. In many cases, we want to require the user to check only one of several boxes. When another box is checked, the current one is automatically unchecked. Such a group of boxes is often called a *radio button group* because the buttons work like the station selector buttons on a radio. When you push in one button, the previously depressed button pops out. Figure 7-8 shows a typical example. We allow the user to select a font size among the choices "small", "medium", "large" and "extra large", but of course only one size can be selected at a time.

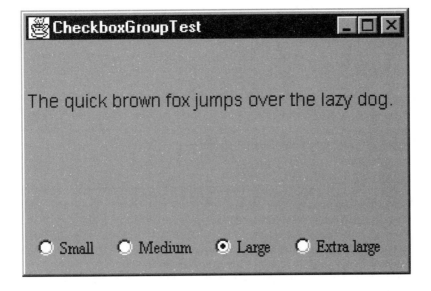

Figure 7-8: A check box group

Implementing radio button groups is easy in AWT. You construct one object of type CheckboxGroup for every group of buttons. The object has no data; it simply serves as the common identifier of the group. You pass the group object into the constructors of the individual buttons.

```
CheckboxGroup g = new CheckboxGroup();
small = new Checkbox("Small", g, false);
medium = new Checkbox("Medium", g, true);
large = new Checkbox("Large", g, false);
extraLarge = new Checkbox("Extra large", g, false);
```

The third argument of the constructor is true for the box that should be checked initially, false for all others.

If you look again at Figures 7-7 and 7-8, you will note that the appearance of the selection indicators is different. Individual check boxes without a group are square and use a check mark. Grouped check boxes are round and use a dot.

The event notification mechanism is simple for a check box group. When the user checks a box that is part of a group, Java generates an action event whose "target" is the checked box. You override action to test for these events. (Note that the unchecked box does not generate an action.)

```
public boolean action(Event evt, Object arg)
{   if (evt.target.equals(small))
        fox.setSize(8);
    else if (evt.target.equals(medium))
        fox.setSize(10);
    else if (evt.target.equals(large))
        fox.setSize(14);
    else if (evt.target.equals(extraLarge))
        fox.setSize(18);
    else return super.action(evt, arg);
    return true;
}
```

Example 7-8 is the complete program.

Example 7-8: CheckboxGroupTest.java

```
import java.awt.*;

public class CheckboxGroupTest extends Frame
{   public CheckboxGroupTest()
    {   setTitle("CheckboxGroupTest");
        Panel p = new Panel();
        p.setLayout(new FlowLayout());
        CheckboxGroup g = new CheckboxGroup();
        p.add(small = new Checkbox("Small", g, false));
        p.add(medium = new Checkbox("Medium", g, true));
```

```java
      p.add(large = new Checkbox("Large", g, false));
      p.add(extraLarge =
          new Checkbox("Extra large", g, false));
      add("South", p);
      fox = new FoxCanvas();
      add("Center", fox);
   }

   public boolean handleEvent(Event evt)
   {  if (evt.id == Event.WINDOW_DESTROY) System.exit(0);
      return super.handleEvent(evt);
   }

   public boolean action(Event evt, Object arg)
   {  if (evt.target.equals(small))
         fox.setSize(8);
      else if (evt.target.equals(medium))
         fox.setSize(10);
      else if (evt.target.equals(large))
         fox.setSize(14);
      else if (evt.target.equals(extraLarge))
         fox.setSize(18);
      else return super.action(evt, arg);
      return true;
   }
   public static void main(String[] args)
   {  Frame f = new CheckboxGroupTest();
      f.resize(300, 200);
      f.show();
   }

   private FoxCanvas fox;
   private Checkbox small;
   private Checkbox medium;
   private Checkbox large;
   private Checkbox extraLarge;
}

class FoxCanvas extends Canvas
{  public FoxCanvas()
   {  setSize(10);
   }

   public void setSize(int p)
   {  setFont(new Font("Helvetica", Font.PLAIN, p));
      repaint();
   }
```

```
public void paint(Graphics g)
{  g.drawString
  ("The quick brown fox jumps over the lazy dog.", 0, 50);
}
}
```

`java.awt.Checkbox`

- `Checkbox(String label, CheckboxGroup group, boolean state)`

Parameters:	`label`	the label on the check box
	`group`	the group to which this check box belongs
	`state`	the initial state of the check box

Choice Boxes (Drop-Down Lists)

If you have more than a handful of alternatives, radio buttons are not a good choice, because they take up too much screen space. Instead, you should probably use a choice box which is a drop-down list box. When the user clicks on the field, this drops down a list of choices, and the user can then select one of them (see Figure 7-9).

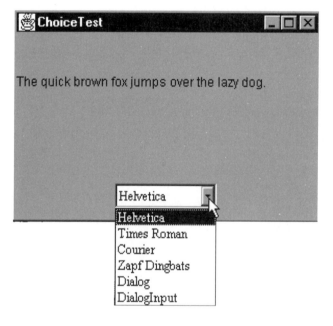

Figure 7-9: A choice box

The `Choice` class implements these lists. In the example program, the user can choose a font style from a list of styles (Times Roman, Helvetica, Courier, etc.). You add the choice items with the `addItem` method. In our program, `addItem` is only called in the constructor, but you can call it any time.

```
style = new Choice();
style.addItem("Times Roman");
style.addItem("Helvetica");
 . . .
```

NOTE: Once added, items cannot be removed from a choice box.

When the user selects an item from a choice box, this generates an action event. The target of the action event is the component chosen, and the second argument of the call to `action` is the selected string.

```
public boolean action(Event evt, Object arg)
{    if (evt.target.equals(style))
     fox.setStyle((String)arg);
     . . .
}
```

NOTE: AWT has no "combo box" control. (A combo box is a combination of a text box and a choice list, in which you can pick one of the choices or type in another input.)

`java.awt.Choice`

• `void addItem(String item)`

adds an item to this choice component.

Parameters: `item`   the item to add

The `List` *Component*

The `List` component is similar to the `Choice` component except that the user will always see the items. `List` components take up more screen space, but also make it obvious to the user what can be chosen from a list.

One other difference is that for a `List` component, but not a `Choice` component, you can allow the user to make multiple selections. If you permit multiple selection for a list box, the user can select any combination of the strings in the box, using whatever techniques are appropriate in the target operating system (SHIFT + Click or CTRL + Click for Windows, for example).

Figure 7-10 shows an admittedly silly example. The user can select the attributes for the fox, such as `"quick"`, `"brown"`, `"hungry"`, `"wild"`, and, because we ran out of attributes, `"static"`, `"private"`, and `"final"`. You can, thus, have the *static, final* fox jump over the lazy dog.

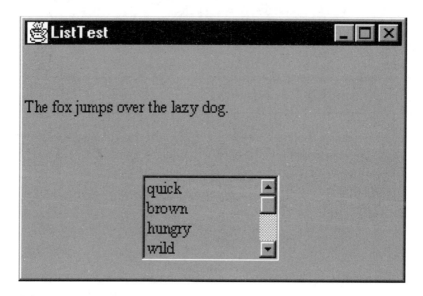

Figure 7-10: A List box

Here is a more realistic application: you are going to design an order-taking system; you will use a list box to give users a choice of items to order. Why a list box rather than a choice box? Well, your employer hopes that the customer will order most or all of the items, so you want to make it easy for him or her to select more than one.

The constructor of the list box has

- a parameter that takes the number of items you want to display at one time (if you add more items, they scroll) and

- a flag to indicate whether or not you want to allow multiple selection.

You initialize a list box just as you would a choice component (drop-down list): use the `addItem` method. If you want to activate an initial set of selections, use the select method.

```
words = new List(4, true); //4 items allow multiple selections
words.addItem("quick");
words.addItem("brown");
   . . .
words.addItem("final");
words.select(0);
words.select(1);
```

The method with which Java notifies a list box of relevant events is not quite as easy as that for the other components. Java triggers the `action` function *only* when the user double-clicks on an item in the list box. The problem is that this is not very intuitive for most users.

Instead, the most user-friendly solution is to track all changes in what the user is selecting. Every time the user selects an item, Java generates an event with the ID `LIST_SELECT`. Every time the user removes an item from the selection, an event with the ID `LIST_DESELECT` is generated. These events can be trapped in the `handleEvent` function.

> NOTE: As a general observation, we could have handled other events in `handleEvent` instead of `action`, but it is easier to override `action`, since it deals with fewer events. We will discuss this in detail in the section on event handling.

Once you are notified that an event has happened, you will want to find out what items are currently selected. This is phenomenally convenient in Java. The `getSelectedItems` method returns an *array of strings* containing all selected items. (If you have ever done this in C, you probably suffered through a lookup loop, a callback procedure, a memory allocation headache, or all of the above.)

Here is the event handler for our toy program.

```
public boolean handleEvent(Event evt)
{   if (evt.target.equals(words) && (evt.id == Event.LIST_SELECT
        || evt.id == Event.LIST_DESELECT))
      fox.setAttributes(words.getSelectedItems());
}
```

Example 7-9 is the program listing. Notice how the `setAttributes` function builds up the message string from the selected items.

Example 7-9: ListTest.java

```
import java.awt.*;

public class ListTest extends Frame
{   public ListTest()
    {   setTitle("ListTest");

        words = new List(4, true);
        words.addItem("quick");
        words.addItem("brown");
        words.addItem("hungry");
        words.addItem("wild");
        words.addItem("silent");
```

```
        words.addItem("huge");
        words.addItem("private");
        words.addItem("abstract");
        words.addItem("static");
        words.addItem("final");

        Panel p = new Panel();
        p.add(words);
        add("South", p);
        fox = new FoxCanvas();
        add("Center", fox);
    }

    public boolean handleEvent(Event evt)
    {   if (evt.id == Event.LIST_SELECT
            || evt.id == Event.LIST_DESELECT)
        {   if (evt.target.equals(words))
                fox.setAttributes(words.getSelectedItems());
        }
        else if (evt.id == Event.WINDOW_DESTROY)
            System.exit(0);
        else return super.handleEvent(evt);
        return true;
    }

    private FoxCanvas fox;
    private List words;

    public static void main(String[] args)
    {   Frame f = new ListTest();
        f.resize(300, 200);
        f.show();
    }
}

class FoxCanvas extends Canvas
{   public FoxCanvas()
    {   setAttributes(new String[0]);
    }

    public void setAttributes(String[] w)
    {   text = "The ";
        for (int i = 0; i < w.length; i++)
            text += w[i] + " ";
        text += "fox jumps over the lazy dog.";
        repaint();
    }

    public void paint(Graphics g)
```

```
{  g.drawString(text, 0, 50);
}

private String text;
}
```

`java.awt.List`

- `List(int rows, boolean multipleSelections)`

  Parameters: `rows`   the number of items to show

                       `multipleSelections`   true when multiple selections are allowed

- `String getItem(int index)`

  gets an item from a list component.

  Parameters: `index`   the position of the item to get

- `void select(int index)`

  selects an item in a list component.

  Parameters: `index`   the position of the item to select

- `String[] getSelectedItems()`

  returns an array containing all selected items.

Sophisticated Layout Management

We have managed to lay out the user interface components of our toy applications by using a couple of panels and canvases, but for more complex tasks, that method is not going to be sufficient. In this section, we discuss all the layout managers that AWT provides to organize components.

TIP: If none of the layout schemes fit your needs, break the surface of your window into separate panels, and lay out each panel separately. Then use another layout manager to organize the panels.

In AWT, *components* are laid out inside *containers*. A component is either a button, a text field or other user interface element, or another container. For example, as we have seen before, a window can contain a canvas (a basic component) and a panel (a component that is itself a container).

Because every container is itself a possible component, the class `Container` derives from `Component`. Figure 7-11 shows the inheritance hierarchy.

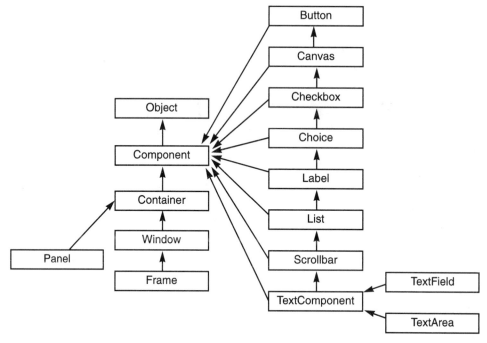

Figure 7-11: Class container inheritance hierarchy

As usual, the complexities of real life muddy this issue somewhat. Indeed, panels are containers that can themselves be components, but frames are not. You would not want to stick several frames inside another container. Nevertheless, it is helpful to understand the roles of containers and components when browsing the AWT on-line documentation.

To organize the components in a container, you first specify a layout manager. For example,

```
panel.setLayout(new CardLayout());
```

will use the CardLayout class to lay out the panels. After you set the layout manager, you add components to the container. The details of doing this depend on the specific layout manager, but in all cases the information will be obtained from the add method of the underlying panel. With the flow layout manager that you have already seen, you can insert the components in random order.

```
panel.add(new Button("Ok"), 4);
```

With the border layout manager, you give a string to indicate component placement.

```
panel.add("South", new TextField());
```

With the grid bag layout, you need to add components sequentially.

```
panel.add(new Checkbox("italic"));
panel.add(new Checkbox("bold"));
```

Flow Layouts Revisited

The simplest layout manager is the one you have already seen: the flow layout. We have used the flow layout for laying out panels in quite a few test programs in this chapter. Components are lined up horizontally until there is no more room, and then a new line of components is started.

You can choose how you want to arrange the components in each line. The default is to center them in the container. The other choices are to align them to the left or to the right of the container. To select that alignment, you specify LEFT or RIGHT in the constructor of the FlowLayout object.

```
toolbar.setLayout(new FlowLayout(FlowLayout.LEFT));
```

When the container is resized, Java automatically reflows the components to fill the available space.

`java.awt.FlowLayout`

- `FlowLayout(int align)`

  constructs a new FlowLayout with the specified alignment.

  Parameters:　　align　　one of LEFT, CENTER, or RIGHT

Border Layout

The border layout divides the area to be laid out into five areas, called north, south, east, west, and center (see Figure 7-12).

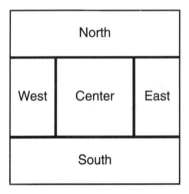

Figure 7-12: Border Layouts

The borders are laid out first, and the remaining available space is occupied by the center. When the container is resized, the thickness of the borders is unchanged, but the center area changes its size.

You add components by specifying a string that says in what area the object should be placed. You can specify `"North"`, `"South"`, `"East"`, `"West"`, or `"Center"`. Not all of the positions need to be occupied. Here's an example of using a border layout manager:

```
panel.add("East", new Scrollbar());
```

Border layout is the default for frames and other windows. You need not specify a layout manager for those containers if the border layout works for you.

It is not common to use all four border areas simultaneously. Figure 7-13 and Example 7-10 show a typical case, with scroll bars to the right and bottom, and a tool bar on the top. If you look closely, you will notice that the horizontal scroll bar extends below the vertical scroll bar. If you really want to achieve a more symmetrical and pleasant layout of the scroll bars, you need to use the grid bag layout.

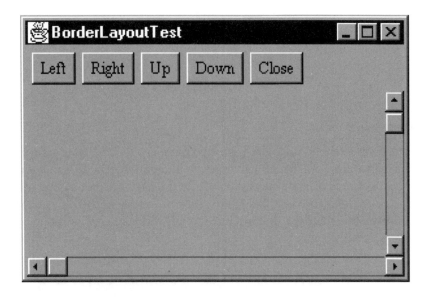

Figure 7-13: Border layout example

Example 7-10: BorderLayoutTest.java

```java
import java.awt.*;

public class BorderLayoutTest extends Frame
{   public BorderLayoutTest()
    {   setTitle("BorderLayoutTest");
        Panel p = new Panel();
        p.setLayout(new FlowLayout(FlowLayout.LEFT));
        p.add(new Button("Left"));
        p.add(new Button("Right"));
        p.add(new Button("Up"));
        p.add(new Button("Down"));
        p.add(new Button("Close"));
        add("North", p);
        add("East", new Scrollbar(Scrollbar.VERTICAL));
        add("South", new Scrollbar(Scrollbar.HORIZONTAL));
    }

    public boolean handleEvent(Event evt)
    {   if (evt.id == Event.WINDOW_DESTROY) System.exit(0);
        return super.handleEvent(evt);
    }
```

```
public static void main(String[] args)
{  Frame f = new BorderLayoutTest();
   f.resize(300, 200);
   f.show();
}
}
```

Card Layout

Windows 95 uses tabbed dialog boxes when there is a lot of related information to set that can still be organized conveniently into panels. The reason is simple: if you need to gather a lot of information from the user, it is not a good idea to cram dozens of fields into one dialog box. As an example of this, consider the "tabbed dialog" in Netscape that organizes a multitude of configuration options (Figure 7-14).

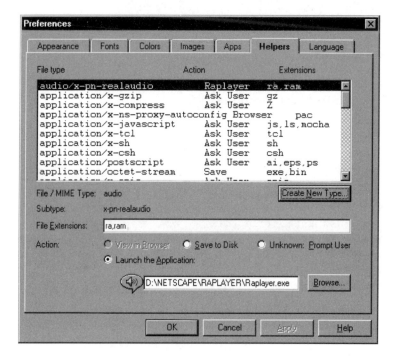

Figure 7-14: A tabbed dialog

The settings are grouped onto individual "index cards," and you flip through them by clicking on one of the tabs.

Java does not have such an elegant looking dialog layout, but the `CardLayout` manager provides the bare rudiments of this functionality. (It gives you only a bit more functionality than using multiple panels would give—although it is more convenient to use.) Unlike the other layouts, which place the objects to be laid out *next to each other*, the card layout places them *behind each other*.

The Figure 7-15 window consists of two areas. The top area is a panel containing a row of buttons that make the different cards show up in the top area. These are analogous to the "tabs" in the tabbed dialogs. For example, if you click on the "Options" button, the "Options" card will show up. Unlike tabbed dialog boxes, we also provided buttons to cycle through the cards and to go to the first and last card in the stack. That probably isn't terribly useful, and we only did it to show how it can be done. The second area holds cards managed by the `CardLayout` manager.

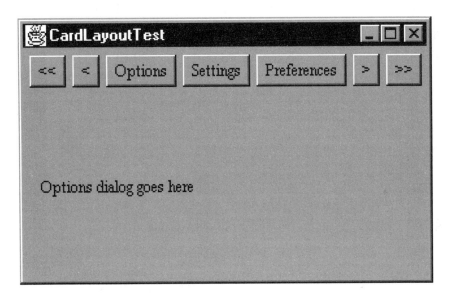

Figure 7-15: Card layout

Here is the procedure to set up a card layout.

1. Make a panel of buttons, one for each card.

```
tabs = new Panel(new FlowLayout());
tabs.add(new Button("Options"));
tabs.add(new Button("Settings"));
. . .
```

2. Below it, place another panel. This one will be managed by the
    CardLayout object.

    ```
    cards = new Panel();
    layout = new CardLayout();
    cards.setLayout(layout);
    ```

3. Then add the individual labels that identify the cards with the panel.

    ```
    cards.add("Options", new SimpleDialog("Options"));
    cards.add("Settings", new SimpleDialog("Settings"));
    cards.add("Preferences", new SimpleDialog("Preferences"));
    ```

(Java internally keeps track of the fact that there are now three "cards" *i.e.*,
labels that are filling up the cards. You do not add three different panels when
using a card layout manager; instead you add individual cards via a call to add.
In our case, the individual cards are identified by the strings "Options",
"Settings", and "Preferences". Window's users might want to think of
what is going on as analogous to using an MDI interface—with the panel being
the parent window and the various cards being child windows. The analogy is,
of course, not precise, since one cannot "tile" the cards being managed by a card
layout manager.)

Finally, write an action procedure that makes the tab buttons switch the cards.
You use the show method of the card layout manager in order to show a particular card. The next and previous methods show another card in the card
sequence. The first and last methods show the first and last cards.

```
public boolean action(Event evt, Object arg)
{ if (evt.target instanceof Component &&
      ((Component)evt.target).getParent().equals(tabs))
   // it was one of the tab keys
   {  if (arg.equals("<"))
         layout.previous(cards));
      else if (arg.equals(">"))
         layout.next(cards));
      else
         layout.show(cards, (String)arg);
   }
   . . .
}
```

(To keep this example simple, we didn't actually put any data-entry fields on
any of the cards. There's just a label that says, for example, "Options dialog
goes here". In an actual program, of course, you would have a full-fledged
container that is populated by the necessary components.)

Example 7-11 is the code listing for the sample program.

Example 7-11: CardLayoutTest.java

```java
import java.awt.*;

public class CardLayoutTest extends Frame
{  public CardLayoutTest()
   {  setTitle("CardLayoutTest");

      tabs = new Panel();
      tabs.add(new Button("<<"));
      tabs.add(new Button("<"));
      tabs.add(new Button("Options"));
      tabs.add(new Button("Settings"));
      tabs.add(new Button("Preferences"));
      tabs.add(new Button(">"));
      tabs.add(new Button(">>"));
      add("North", tabs);

      cards = new Panel();
      layout = new CardLayout();
      cards.setLayout(layout);

      cards.add("Options", new SimpleDialog("Options"));
      cards.add("Settings", new SimpleDialog("Settings"));
      cards.add("Preferences",
         new SimpleDialog("Preferences"));

      add("Center", cards);
   }

   public boolean handleEvent(Event evt)
   {  if (evt.id == Event.WINDOW_DESTROY) System.exit(0);
      return super.handleEvent(evt);
   }

   public boolean action(Event evt, Object arg)
   {  if (evt.target instanceof Component &&
         ((Component)evt.target).getParent().equals(tabs))
      {  if (arg.equals("<<")) layout.first(cards);
         else if (arg.equals("<")) layout.previous(cards);
         else if (arg.equals(">")) layout.next(cards);
         else if (arg.equals(">>")) layout.last(cards);
         else layout.show(cards, (String)arg);
      }
      else return super.action(evt, arg);
      return true;
   }

   public static void main(String[] args)
```

```
    {   Frame f = new CardLayoutTest();
        f.resize(320, 200);
        f.show();
    }
    private Panel cards;
    private Panel tabs;
    private CardLayout layout;
}

class SimpleDialog extends Panel
{   SimpleDialog(String name)
    {   setLayout(new BorderLayout());
        add("Center", new Label(name + " dialog goes here"));
    }
}
```

java.awt.CardLayout

- void show(Container parent, String name)

  flips to a card of the card layout.

Parameters:	parent	the container with the card layout
	name	the name of the card

- void first(Container parent)

  flips to the first card.

Parameters:	parent	the container with the card layout

- void next(Container parent)

  flips to the next card.

Parameters:	parent	the container with the card layout

- void previous(Container parent)

  flips to the previous card.

Parameters:	parent	the container with the card layout

- void last(Container parent)

  flips to the last card.

Parameters:	parent	the container with the card layout

Grid Layout

The grid layout arranges all components in rows and columns. The calculator program in Figure 7-16 uses a grid to arrange the calculator buttons. When you resize the window, the buttons grow and shrink.

Calculator			
0			
0	1	2	3
4	5	6	7
8	9	+	-
*	/	%	=

Figure 7-16: A calculator

In the constructor of the grid layout object, you specify how many rows and columns you need.

```
panel.setLayout(new GridLayout(5, 4));
```

You add the components, starting with the first entry in the first row, then the second entry in the first row, and so on.

```
panel.add(new Button("1"));
panel.add(new Button("2"));
```

Example 7-12 is the source listing for the calculator program. This is a regular calculator, not the "reverse Polish" variety that is so oddly popular with Java fans.

Example 7-12: Calculator.java

```java
import java.awt.*;
import corejava.*;

public class Calculator extends Frame
{  public Calculator()
   {  setTitle("Calculator");

      display = new TextField("0");
      display.setEditable(false);
      add("North", display);

      Panel p = new Panel();
      p.setLayout(new GridLayout(4, 4));
      for (int i = 0; i <= 9; i++)
      p.add(new Button("" + (char)('0' + i)));
      p.add(new Button("+"));
      p.add(new Button("-"));
      p.add(new Button("*"));
      p.add(new Button("/"));
      p.add(new Button("%"));
      p.add(new Button("="));
      add("Center", p);
   }

   public boolean handleEvent(Event evt)
   {  if (evt.id == Event.WINDOW_DESTROY) System.exit(0);
      return super.handleEvent(evt);
   }

   public boolean action(Event evt, Object arg)
   {  if (arg instanceof String)
      {  String s = (String) arg;
         if ('0' <= s.charAt(0) && s.charAt(0) <= '9')
         {  if (start) display.setText(s);
            else display.setText(display.getText() + s);
            start = false;
         }
         else
         {  if (start)
            {  if (s.equals("-"))
               { display.setText(s); start = false; }
               else op = s;
            }
            else
            {  calculate(Format.atoi(display.getText()));
               op = s;
               start = true;
            }
```

```
            }
        }
        else return super.action(evt, arg);
        return true;
    }

    public void calculate(int n)
    {   if(op.equals("+")) arg += n;
        else if (op.equals("-")) arg -= n;
        else if (op.equals("*")) arg *= n;
        else if (op.equals("/")) arg /= n;
        else if (op.equals("%")) arg %= n;
        else if (op.equals("=")) arg = n;
        display.setText("" + arg);
    }

    public static void main(String[] args)
    {   Frame f = new Calculator();
        f.resize(300, 200);
        f.show();
    }

    private TextField display;
    private int arg = 0;
    private String op = "=";
    private boolean start = true;
}
```

Of course, few applications have as rigid a layout as the face of a calculator. In practice, small grids (usually with just one or two columns) are useful to organize partial areas of a window.

Grid Bag Layout

This is the mother of all layout managers. You can think of a grid bag layout as a piece of graph paper—each component will be told to occupy one or more of the little boxes on the paper. The idea is that this layout manager lets you align components without requiring that they all be the same size—since you are only concerned with which cells they will occupy. (Many word processors have the same capability when editing tables: you start out with a grid, and then can merge adjacent cells if need be.)

Fair warning: using grid bag layouts can be incredibly complex. (The payoff is that they have the most flexibility and will work in the widest variety of situations.) Keep in mind that the purpose of layout managers is to keep the arrangement of the components reasonable under different font sizes and operating systems, so it is not surprising that you need to work somewhat harder than when you design a layout just for one environment.

Consider the font selection dialog of Figure 7-17. It consists of the following components:

- a list box to specify the font style
- two check boxes to select bold and italic
- a text field for the font size
- a label for that text box
- a text field at the bottom for the sample string.

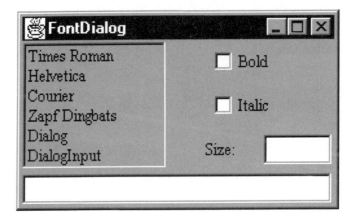

Figure 7-17: Font dialog

Now chop up the dialog box into a four-by-three grid of cells, as shown in Figure 7-18. As you can see, the list box spans three rows; each check box spans two columns; and the text field at the bottom spans three columns.

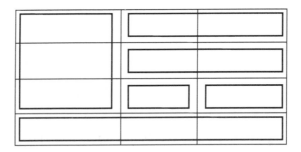

Figure 7-18: Dialog box grid used in design

To describe the layout to the grid bag manager, you must go through the following convoluted procedure.

- Create an object of type `GridBagLayout`. (You don't tell it how many rows and columns the underlying grid has. Instead, Java will try to guess it from the information you give it later.)

- Set this `GridBagLayout` object to be the layout manager for the component.

- Create an object of type `GridBagConstraints`. (The `GridBagConstraints` object will specify how the components are laid out within the grid bag.)

- For *each component*, fill in the `GridBagConstraints` object and call the `setConstraints` object to pass this information to the `GridBagLayout`. Then (finally) add the component.

Here's an example of the code needed (we will go over the various constraints in more detail in the sections that follow—so don't worry if you don't know what some of the constraints do).

```
GridBagLayout layout = new GridBagLayout();
panel.setLayout(layout);
GridBagConstraints constraints = new GridBagConstraints();
constraints.weightx = 100;
constraints.weighty = 100;
constraints.gridx = 0;
constraints.gridy = 0;
constraints.gridwidth = 1;
constraints.gridheight = 3;
List style = new List(4);
layout.setConstraints(style, constraints);
panel.add(style);
```

(It is obviously best to write a small helper function for this kind of repetitive code—see the listing below for an example of one.)

The trick is knowing how to set the state of the `GridBagConstraints` object; this can be incredibly convoluted. We will go over the most important constraints for using this object in the sections that follow.

The `gridx`, `gridy`, `gridwidth`, *and* `gridheight` *Parameters*

These constraints define where the component is located in the grid. The `gridx` and `gridy` values specify the column and row positions of the upper left corner of the component to be added. The `gridwidth` and `gridheight` values determine how many columns and rows it occupies.

Weight Fields

You always need to set the *weight* fields (`weightx` and `weighty`) for each area in a grid bag layout. If you set the weight to 0, then the area never grows or shrinks beyond its initial size in that direction. In the grid bag layout for the figure given on page 270, we set the `weighty` field of the text field at the bottom to be 0. This allows the bottom field to remain a constant height when you resize the window. On the other hand, if you set the weights for all areas to 0, the container will huddle in the center of its allotted area, rather than stretching to fill it.

Note that the weights don't actually give the relative sizes of the columns. They tell what proportion of the "slack" space Java should allocate to each area. This isn't particularly intuitive. We recommend that you set the weights at 100. Then run the program and see how the layout looks. If you want to tweak the sizes of the columns or rows, adjust the weights. In our example, we set the weight of the first column to 20, to compress it somewhat relative to the rest of the dialog box.

The `fill` and `anchor` *Parameters*

If you don't want a component to stretch out and fill the entire area, you need to set the `fill` field for the layout manager. You have four possibilities for this parameter: the valid values are used in the forms `GridBagConstraints.NONE`, `GridBagConstraints.HORIZONTAL`, `GridBagConstraints.VERTICAL`, and `GridBagConstraints.BOTH`.

If the component does not fill the entire area, you can specify where in the area you want it by setting the `anchor` field. The valid values are: `GridBagConstraints.CENTER` (the default), `GridBagConstraints.NORTH`, `GridBagConstraints.NORTHEAST`, `GridBagConstraints.EAST`, and so on.

An Alternative Method to Specify the `gridx`, `gridy`, `gridwidth`, and `gridheight` *Parameters*

The AWT documentation recommends that, instead of setting the `gridx` and `gridy` values to absolute positions, you set them to the constant `GridBagConstraints.RELATIVE`. Then add the components to the grid bag layout in a standardized order, going from left to right in the first row, then moving along the next row, and so on.

You still specify the number of columns and rows spanned in the `gridwidth` and `gridheight` fields. Except, if the component extends to the *last* row or column, you aren't supposed to specify the actual number, but the constant `GridBagConstraints.REMAINDER`. This tells the layout manager that the component is the last one in its row. And if it is the *next-to-last* component in the current row or column, you are supposed to specify the constant `RELATIVE`.

This scheme does seem to work. But it sounds really goofy to hide the actual placement information from the layout manager and hope that it will rediscover it.

Example 7-13 is the complete code to implement the font dialog example.

Example 7-13: FontDialog.java

```java
import java.awt.*;
import corejava.*;

public class FontDialog extends Frame
{  private void add(Component c, GridBagLayout gbl,
      GridBagConstraints gbc,
      int x, int y, int w, int h)
   {  gbc.gridx = x;
      gbc.gridy = y;
      gbc.gridwidth = w;
      gbc.gridheight = h;
      gbl.setConstraints(c, gbc);
      add(c);
   }
   public FontDialog()
   {  setTitle("FontDialog");
      GridBagLayout gbl = new GridBagLayout();
      setLayout(gbl);

      style = new List(4, false);
      style.addItem("Times Roman");
      style.addItem("Helvetica");
      style.addItem("Courier");
      style.addItem("Zapf Dingbats");
      style.addItem("Dialog");
      style.addItem("DialogInput");
      style.select(0);

      bold = new Checkbox("Bold");
      italic = new Checkbox("Italic");
      Label label = new Label("Size: ");
      size = new IntTextField(10,1,100,4);
      sample = new TextField();

      GridBagConstraints gbc = new GridBagConstraints();
      gbc.fill = GridBagConstraints.BOTH;
      gbc.weightx = 20;
      gbc.weighty = 100;
      add(style, gbl, gbc, 0, 0, 1, 3);
      gbc.weightx = 100;
      gbc.fill = GridBagConstraints.NONE;
      gbc.anchor = GridBagConstraints.CENTER;
      add(bold, gbl, gbc, 1, 0, 2, 1);
      add(italic, gbl, gbc, 1, 1, 2, 1);
```

```
        add(label, gbl, gbc, 1, 2, 1, 1);
        gbc.fill = GridBagConstraints.HORIZONTAL;
        add(size, gbl, gbc, 2, 2, 1, 1);
        gbc.anchor = GridBagConstraints.SOUTH;
        gbc.weighty = 0;
        add(sample, gbl, gbc, 0, 3, 3, 1);
        sample.setText("The quick brown fox");
    }

    public boolean handleEvent(Event evt)
    {   if ((evt.target.equals(bold) || evt.target.equals(italic) ||
            evt.target.equals(style) || evt.target.equals(size))
              && size.isValid())
        {   int m = (bold.getState() ? Font.BOLD : 0)
            + (italic.getState() ?
              Font.ITALIC : 0);
            sample.setFont(new Font(style.getSelectedItem(), m,
              size.getValue()));
            sample.show();
        }
        else if (evt.id == Event.WINDOW_DESTROY) System.exit(0);
        return super.handleEvent(evt);
    }

    public static void main(String[] args)
    {   Frame f = new FontDialog();
        f.resize(250, 150);
        f.show();
    }

    private List style;
    private Checkbox bold;
    private Checkbox italic;
    private IntTextField size;
    private TextField sample;
}
```

java.awt.GridBagConstraints

- `int gridx, gridy`

  indicates starting column and row of cell

- `int gridwidth, gridheight`

  indicates column and row extent of cell

- `double weightx, weighty`

  indicates capacity of cell to grow

- `int anchor`

  indicates alignment of component inside cell, one of CENTER, NORTH, NORTHEAST, EAST, SOUTHEAST, SOUTH, SOUTHWEST, WEST, and NORTHWEST

- `int fill`

  indicates the fill behavior of component inside cell, one of NONE, BOTH, HORIZONTAL, and VERTICAL

- `int ipadx, ipady`

  indicates the "internal" padding around the component

- `Insets insets`

  indicates the "external" padding along the cell boundaries

`java.awt.GridBagLayout`

- `void setConstraints(Component comp, GridBagConstraints constraints)`

  sets the constraints for a component.

Parameters:	comp	the component for which constraint information is to be supplied
	constraints	the constraints to be applied

Using No Layout Manager

There will be times when you don't want to bother with layout managers, but just want to drop a component at a fixed location. This is not a great idea for platform-independent applications, but there is nothing wrong with it for a quick prototype.

Here is what you do to place a component at a fixed location:

- Don't select a layout manager at all.

- Add the component you want to the container.

- Then specify the position and size that you want.
  ```
  panel.setLayout(null);
  Button ok = new Button("Ok");
  panel.add(OK);
  ok.reshape(10, 10, 30, 15);
  ```

`java.awt.Component`

- `void reshape(int x, int y, int width, int height)`

    moves and resizes a component.

Parameters:	x, y	the new top left corner of the component
	width, height	the new size of the component

Custom Layout Managers

In principle, it is possible to design your own `LayoutManager` class that manages components in a special way. For example, you could arrange all components in a container to form a circle (see Figure 7-19). This will almost always be a major effort and a real time sink, but as Figure 7-19 shows, the results can be quite dramatic.

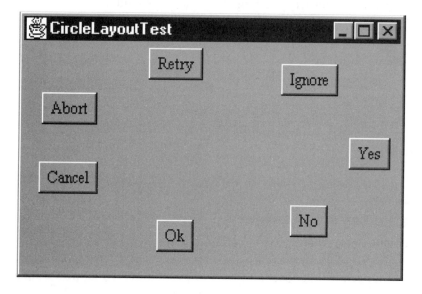

Figure 7-19: Circle layout

If you do feel you can't live without your own layout manager, here is what you do. Your own layout manager must implement the `LayoutManager` interface. You need to override the following five functions.

```
void addLayoutComponent(String s, Component c);
void removeLayoutComponent(Component c);
```

```
        Dimension preferredLayoutSize(Container parent);
        Dimension minimumLayoutSize(Container parent);
        void layoutContainer(Container parent);
```

The first two functions are called when a component is added or removed. If you don't keep any additional information about the components, you can make them do nothing. The next two functions compute the space required for the minimum and the preferred layout of the components. These are usually the same quantity. The fifth function does the actual work and invokes reshape on all components.

Example 7-14 is a simple implementation of the CircleLayout manager, which, amazingly and uselessly enough, lays out the components along an ellipse inside the parent.

Example 7-14: CircleLayoutTest.java

```java
import java.awt.*;

public class CircleLayoutTest extends Frame
{  public CircleLayoutTest()
   {  setTitle("CircleLayoutTest");
      setLayout(new CircleLayout());
      add(new Button("Yes"));
      add(new Button("No"));
      add(new Button("Ok"));
      add(new Button("Cancel"));
      add(new Button("Abort"));
      add(new Button("Retry"));
      add(new Button("Ignore"));
   }

   public boolean handleEvent(Event evt)
   {  if (evt.id == Event.WINDOW_DESTROY) System.exit(0);
      return super.handleEvent(evt);
   }

   public static void main(String args[])
   {  Frame f = new CircleLayoutTest();
      f.resize(300, 200);
      f.show();
   }
}

class CircleLayout implements LayoutManager
{  public void addLayoutComponent(String name,
      Component comp)
   {}
```

```java
public void removeLayoutComponent(Component comp)
{}

public void setSizes(Container parent)
{  if (sizesSet) return;
   int n = parent.countComponents();

   preferredWidth = 0;
   preferredHeight = 0;
   minWidth = 0;
   minHeight = 0;
   maxComponentWidth = 0;
   maxComponentHeight = 0;

   for (int i = 0; i < n; i++)
   {  Component c = parent.getComponent(i);
      if (c.isVisible()) {
      Dimension d = c.preferredSize();
      maxComponentWidth = Math.max(maxComponentWidth,
         d.width);
      maxComponentHeight = Math.max(maxComponentWidth,
         d.height);
      preferredHeight += d.height;
      }
   }
   preferredHeight += maxComponentHeight;
   preferredWidth = 2 * maxComponentWidth;
   minHeight = preferredHeight;
   minWidth = preferredWidth;
   sizesSet = true;
}

public Dimension preferredLayoutSize(Container parent)
{  Dimension dim = new Dimension(0, 0);
   setSizes(parent);
   Insets insets = parent.insets();
   dim.width = preferredWidth + insets.left
      + insets.right;
   dim.height = preferredHeight + insets.top
      + insets.bottom;
   return dim;
}

public Dimension minimumLayoutSize(Container parent)
{  Dimension dim = new Dimension(0, 0);
   setSizes(parent);
   Insets insets = parent.insets();
   dim.width = minWidth + insets.left + insets.right;
   dim.height = minHeight + insets.top + insets.bottom;
```

```
            return dim;
    }

    public void layoutContainer(Container parent)
    {   Insets insets = parent.insets();
        int containerWidth = parent.size().width
            - insets.left - insets.right;
        int containerHeight = parent.size().height
            - insets.top - insets.bottom;
        int xradius = (containerWidth - maxComponentWidth)
            / 2;
        int yradius = (containerHeight - maxComponentHeight)
            / 2;

        setSizes(parent);
        int xcenter = insets.left + containerWidth / 2;
        int ycenter = insets.top + containerHeight / 2;

        int n = parent.countComponents();
        for (int i = 0 ; i < n ; i++)
        {   Component c = parent.getComponent(i);
            if (c.isVisible())
            {   Dimension d = c.preferredSize();
                double angle = 2 * Math.PI * i / n;
                int x = xcenter
                    + (int)(Math.cos(angle) * xradius);
                int y = ycenter
                    + (int)(Math.sin(angle) * yradius);

                c.reshape(x - d.width / 2, y - d.width / 2,
                    d.width, d.height);
            }
        }

    }

    private int minWidth = 0;
    private int minHeight = 0;
    private int preferredWidth = 0, preferredHeight = 0;
    private boolean sizesSet = false;
    private int maxComponentWidth = 0;
    private int maxComponentHeight = 0;
}
```

- void addLayoutComponent(String name, Component comp)

  adds a component to the layout.

Parameters:	name	an identifier for the component placement
	comp	the component to be added

- void removeLayoutComponent(Component comp)

  removes a component from the layout.

Parameters:	comp	the component to be removed

- Dimension preferredLayoutSize(Container parent)

  returns the preferred size dimensions for the container under this layout.

Parameters:	parent	the container whose components are being laid out

- Dimension minimumLayoutSize(Container parent)

  returns the minimum size dimensions for the container under this layout.

Parameters:	parent	the container whose components are being laid out

- void layoutContainer(Container parent)

  lays out the components in a container.

Parameters:	parent	the container whose components are being laid out

Dialog Boxes

So far, all of our user interface components have appeared inside a frame window that was created in the application. This is the most common situation if you write *applets* that run inside a Web browser. But if you write applications, you usually want separate dialogs to pop up to get information from the user.

Just as with most windowing systems, AWT distinguishes between *modal* and *modeless* dialogs. A modal dialog won't let the user interact with the remaining windows of the application until he or she deals with it. You use a modal dialog when you need information from the user before you can proceed with execution. For example, when the user wants to read a file, a modal file dialog is the one to pop up. The user must specify a file name before beginning to the read operation. Only when the modal dialog is closed can the application proceed.

A modeless dialog lets the user enter information in both the dialog and the remainder of the application. One example of a modeless dialog is for a tool bar. The tool bar can stay in place as long as needed, and the user can interact with both the application window and the tool bar.

Figure 7-20 shows a typical modal dialog, a program information box that is displayed when the user selects the About button.

To implement a dialog box, you derive a class from `Dialog`. This is essentially the same process as deriving the main window for the application from `Frame`.

More precisely:

1. In the constructor of your dialog box, call the constructor of the base class `Dialog`. You will need to tell it the name of the parent window, the title of the window, and a boolean flag to indicate if the dialog is modal or modeless.

2. Add the controls of the dialog box.

3. Set the size for the dialog box.

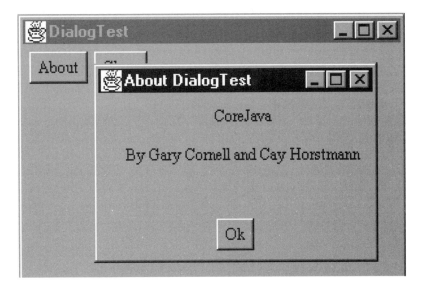

Figure 7-20: An about dialog

Here's an example of how the code will start:

```
class AboutDialog extends Dialog
{   public AboutDialog(Frame parent)
    {   super(parent, "About this program", true /* modal */);
        . . .
```

```
        Panel p = new Panel();
        p.add(new Button("Ok"));
        add("South", p);
        resize(220, 150);
    }
}
```

To display the dialog box, you create a new dialog object and invoke the show method.

```
Dialog d = new AboutDialog(this);
d.show();
```

When the user clicks on the OK button, the dialog should close. This is handled in the action procedure.

```
public boolean action(Event evt, Object arg)
{   if (arg.equals("Ok")) dispose();
    else return false;
    return true;
}
```

Notice the call to dispose() here. This removes the dialog from the screen and reclaims the operating system resources that the dialog box was allocated.

If you want your user to be able to cancel a dialog by closing it (for example, by a click on the Exit button in Windows 95), you need to provide a handler for the WINDOW_DESTROY event.

```
public boolean handleEvent(Event evt)
{   if (evt.id == WINDOW_DESTROY) dispose();
    else return super.handleEvent(evt);
    return true;
}
```

If you don't supply this handler, the user can only close the dialog by clicking on the OK button. If your application spawns child windows (such as dialogs), you must be careful about the WINDOW_DESTROY handler of the frame window. Suppose you use the following event handler for the frame component:

```
class MyFrame extends Frame
{   . . .
    public boolean handleEvent(Event evt)
    {   if (evt.id == WINDOW_DESTROY) System.exit(0);
        else . . .
        else return super.handleEvent(evt);
        return true;
    }
    . . .
}
```

Suppose you don't override the event handler in the dialog box to handle the WINDOW_DESTROY event for the dialog box. Since no event handler was provided for the derived class, that event will be transmitted to the parent—the frame window of the application. Closing the dialog box would then have the unfortunate side effect of closing the entire application!

To remedy this, find out where the WINDOW_DESTROY event originated. In particular, did it originate from the frame or the dialog box?

```
class MyFrame extends Frame
{   . . .
    public boolean handleEvent(Event evt)
    {   if (evt.id == WINDOW_DESTROY && evt.target == this)
            System.exit(0);
        else . . .
        else return super.handleEvent(evt);
        return true;
    }
    . . .
}
```

Similarly, one would have a handle-event procedure in the Dialog class.

Example 7-15 is the code for the "About" dialog box test program.

Example 7-15: DialogTest.java

```
import java.awt.*;

public class DialogTest extends Frame
{   public DialogTest()
    {   setTitle("DialogTest");

        Panel p = new Panel();
        p.setLayout(new FlowLayout(FlowLayout.LEFT));
        p.add(new Button("About"));
        p.add(new Button("Close"));
        add("North", p);
    }

    public boolean action(Event evt, Object arg)
    {   if(arg.equals("About"))
        {   AboutDialog ab = new AboutDialog(this);
            ab.show();
        }
        else if(arg.equals("Close"))
        {   System.exit(0);
        }
        else return super.action(evt, arg);
        return true;
    }
```

```
    public boolean handleEvent(Event evt)
    {   if (evt.id == Event.WINDOW_DESTROY
            && evt.target == this)
            dispose();
        return super.handleEvent(evt);
    }

    public static void main(String args[])
    {   Frame f = new DialogTest();
        f.resize(300, 200);
        f.show();
    }
}

class AboutDialog extends Dialog
{   public AboutDialog(Frame parent)
    {   super(parent, "About DialogTest", true);
        Panel p1 = new Panel();
        p1.add(new Label("CoreJava"));
        p1.add(new Label("By Gary Cornell and Cay Horstmann"));
        add("Center", p1);

        Panel p2 = new Panel();
        p2.add(new Button("Ok"));
        add("South", p2);
        resize(220, 150);
    }

    public boolean action(Event evt, Object arg)
    {   if(arg.equals("Ok"))
        {   dispose();
            return true;
        }
        return false;
    }

    public boolean handleEvent(Event evt)
    {   if (evt.id == Event.WINDOW_DESTROY
            && evt.target == this)
            dispose();
            else return super.handleEvent(evt);
            return true;
    }
}
```

```
java.awt.Dialog
```

- `public Dialog(Frame parent, String title, boolean modal)`

  constructs a dialog. The dialog is not visible until it is explicitly shown.

Parameters:	`parent`	the owner of the dialog
	`title`	the title of the dialog
	`modal`	true for modal dialogs (a modal dialog blocks input to other windows)

Data Exchange

The most common reason to put up a dialog box is to get information from the user. You have already seen how easy it is to make a dialog box object: give it initial data and then call `show()` in order to have Java display the dialog box on the screen. Unfortunately, in AWT it is hard to get the user-supplied data out of a dialog box.

Consider the dialog box in Figure 7-21 that could be used to obtain a user name and a password to connect to some on-line service.

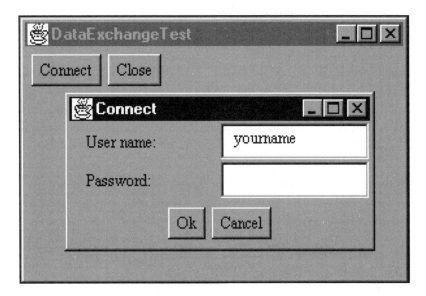

Figure 7-21: Password dialog

```
ConnectInfo defaults = new ConnectInfo(defaultName, "");
ConnectDialog d = new ConnectDialog(this, defaults);
d.show();
```

Unfortunately, the call to `show()` returns immediately, *even though the dialog is modal*. That means the following code will not work.

```
d.show();
name = d.getName();
ConnectInfo result = d.getResult(); // NO
```

This is—to say the least—annoying. There are two methods for getting results back from the dialog box. The first is to have the `"OK"` handler call a procedure of the frame class to tell it that the answer is ready. For example, the following code uses a `ConnectInfo` object to gather this information. The `ConnectInfo` object has instance fields for the needed information. Then you must provide a method called `processConnect()` in your frame class to deal with the information. Here's one way to write the event handler for a dialog box to reclaim the information.

```
public boolean action(Event evt, Object arg)
{   if (arg.equals("Ok")
    {   dispose();//clear resources
        ConnectInfo result = new ConnectInfo(username.getText(),
            password.getText());
        ((MyFrame)getParent()).processConnect(result);
    }
    else return false;
    return true;
}
```

This method has a major drawback—it tightly couples the dialog box code with the code in your frame class. In particular, this affects reusability: if you want to reuse the dialog box code in another program, you have to rename the `(MyFrame)` cast appropriately.

A better approach is to provide a generic interface:

```
interface ResultProcessor
{   public void processResult(Dialog source, Object obj);
}
```

Then have the dialog box call its implementation of `processResult` upon completion by casting to the interface.

```
public boolean action(Event evt, Object arg)
{   if (arg.equals("Ok"))
    {   dispose();
        ConnectInfo result = new ConnectInfo(username.getText(),
            password.getText());
```

```
        ((ResultProcessor)getParent()).processResult
            (this, result);
    }
    else return false;
    return true;
}
```

For this to work, the frame you create in the application must implement the `ResultProcessor` interface. It can then get all the data stored in the dialog box in the `processResults` method.

```
class MyFrame extends Frame implements ResultProcessor
{   . . .
    public void processResult(Dialog source, Object obj)
    {   if (source instanceof ConnectDialog)
        {   ConnectInfo result = (ConnectInfo)obj;
            // process connect information
        }
    }
    . . .
}
```

Both methods have another major drawback: the handling of an action is chopped up into two pieces of code—from the pre-dialog phase and the post-dialog phase—but this is inevitable in Java.

Example 7-16 is the complete code that illustrates the data flow into and out of a dialog box.

Example 7-16: DataExchangeTest.java

```
import java.awt.*;

public class DataExchangeTest extends Frame
    implements ResultProcessor
{   public DataExchangeTest()
    {   setTitle("DataExchangeTest");

        Panel p = new Panel();
        p.setLayout(new FlowLayout(FlowLayout.LEFT));
        p.add(new Button("Connect"));
        p.add(new Button("Close"));
        add("North", p);
    }

    public boolean action(Event evt, Object arg)
    {   if (arg.equals("Connect"))
        {   ConnectInfo in = new ConnectInfo("yourname", "");
            ConnectDialog pd = new ConnectDialog(this, in);
            pd.show();
        }
        else if(arg.equals("Close"))
```

```
            System.exit(0);
        else return super.action(evt, arg);
        return true;
    }

    public boolean handleEvent(Event evt)
    {   if (evt.id == Event.WINDOW_DESTROY
            && evt.target == this)
            System.exit(0);
        else
            return super.handleEvent(evt);
        return true;
    }

    public void processResult(Dialog source, Object result)
    {   if (source instanceof ConnectDialog)
        {   ConnectInfo info = (ConnectInfo)result;
            System.out.println(info.username + " "
                + info.password);
        }
    }

    public static void main(String args[])
    {   Frame f = new DataExchangeTest();
        f.resize(300, 200);
        f.show();
    }
}

interface ResultProcessor
{   public void processResult(Dialog source, Object obj);
}

class ConnectInfo
{   String username;
    String password;
    ConnectInfo(String u, String p)
        { username = u; password = p; }
}

class ConnectDialog extends Dialog
{   public ConnectDialog(DataExchangeTest parent,
        ConnectInfo u)
    {   super(parent, "Connect", true);
        Panel p1 = new Panel();
        p1.setLayout(new GridLayout(2, 2));
        p1.add(new Label("User name:"));
        p1.add(username = new TextField(u.username, 8));
        p1.add(new Label("Password:"));
```

```
      p1.add(password = new TextField(u.password, 8));
      add("Center", p1);

      Panel p2 = new Panel();
      p2.add(new Button("Ok"));
      p2.add(new Button("Cancel"));
      add("South", p2);
      resize(240, 120);
   }

   public boolean action(Event evt, Object arg)
   {  if(arg.equals("Ok"))
      {  dispose();
         ((ResultProcessor)getParent()).processResult(this,
            new ConnectInfo(username.getText(),
               password.getText()));
      }
      else if (arg.equals("Cancel"))
         dispose();
      else return super.action(evt, arg);
      return true;
   }

   public boolean handleEvent(Event evt)
   {  if (evt.id == Event.WINDOW_DESTROY)
         dispose();
      else return super.handleEvent(evt);
      return true;
   }

   private TextField username;
   private TextField password;
}
```

File Dialogs

When you write an applet, you cannot access files on the remote user's machine, so this topic won't be of great interest to you. However, when you write an application, you usually want to be able to open and save files. A good file dialog that shows files and directories and lets the user navigate the file system is hard to write, and you definitely don't want to reinvent that wheel. Fortunately, AWT provides a file dialog class that displays the same file dialog that most native applications use. Figures 7-22 and 7-23 show examples of file dialog boxes under Windows 95 and Solaris.

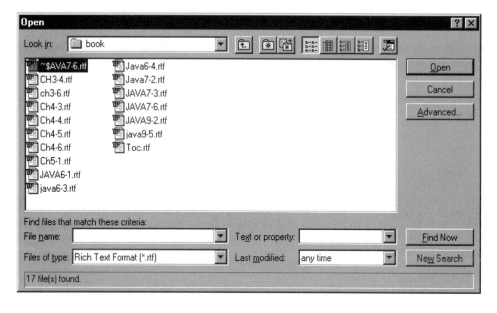

Figure 7-22: File dialog under Windows 95

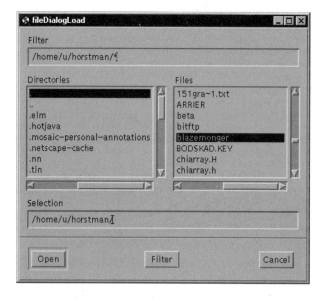

Figure 7-23: File dialog under Solaris

Here are the steps needed to put up a file dialog box and get what the user chooses from the box:

1.   Make a file dialog object.

```
FileDialog d = new FileDialog(parent, "Save note file",
   FileDialog.SAVE);
```

The third argument is either LOAD or SAVE. Set the directory.

```
d.setDirectory(".");
```

If you have a default file name that you expect the user to choose, supply it here.

```
d.setFile(filename);
```

2. Then show the dialog box.

```
d.show();
```

Unlike the show() call for a regular dialog box, this call does not return until the user has filled in the file dialog box. You get the selected file back with the getFile() method. If the user cancels the dialog, getFile() returns null.

```
filename = d.getFile();
if (filename != null). . .
```

java.awt.FileDialog

*   FileDialog(Frame parent, String title, int mode)

    creates a file dialog for loading or saving a file.

Parameters:	parent	the owner of the dialog
	title	the title of the dialog
	mode	the mode of the dialog, one of LOAD or SAVE

*   setFilenameFilter(FilenameFilter filter)

    sets the initial file mask for the file dialog. (This feature does not currently work.)

*   setDirectory(String dir)

    sets the initial directory for the file dialog.

*   setFile(String file)

    sets the default file choice for the file dialog.

*   String getFile()

    gets the file that the user selected (or returns null if the user didn't select any file).

More on Event-Handling

In AWT, events can come from the following sources:

- the keyboard
- the mouse
- window creation, destruction, and movement
- scroll bar activities
- list box item selection and deselection
- change of input focus
- component and menu actions

> NOTE: Windows has a more sophisticated event structure than AWT. There are hundreds of Windows events, compared to fewer than two dozen events in AWT. For example, Windows routes all paint notifications through the event queue. That is smart since it lets the queue sort and aggregate the paint events. In AWT, a window is instructed to paint itself by a method call to update, not by receiving an event. AWT does not have timer events either. We will discuss how to implement timers in Chapter 12.

Each event is described by an object of the Event class. The class has the following fields (all of which are public—you don't need to use accessor functions).

id   an identifier for this event (one of ACTION_EVENT, GOT_FOCUS, KEY_ACTION, KEY_ACTION_RELEASE, KEY_PRESS, KEY_RELEASE, LIST_DESELECT, LIST_SELECT, LOAD_FILE, LOST_FOCUS, MOUSE_DOWN, MOUSE_DRAG, MOUSE_ENTER, MOUSE_EXIT, MOUSE_MOVE, MOUSE_UP, SAVE_FILE, SCROLL_ABSOLUTE, SCROLL_LINE_DOWN, SCROLL_LINE_UP, SCROLL_PAGE_DOWN, SCROLL_PAGE_UP, WINDOW_DEICONIFY, WINDOW_DESTROY, WINDOW_EXPOSE, WINDOW_ICONIFY, and WINDOW_MOVED)

target   the component originating the event

when   a time stamp (not present with action events, and not usually interesting)

x, y   the x and y coordinates of mouse events

clickCount   the number of clicks in a MOUSE_DOWN event. Used to detect double clicks

key   the character or function key in a keyboard event. This is either a byte representing a printable character (> 32), space (32), or control character (between 0 and 32), or one of LEFT, RIGHT, UP, DOWN, HOME, END, PGUP, PGDN, F1, ... and F12 `modifier`   this is a set of four bits describing the states of the SHIFT, CTRL, ALT and meta keys. (The meta key is present on some workstation keyboards. It has a purpose similar to the ALT key on a PC keyboard.) You use bitwise masking techniques to analyze the state of the modifier. For example, if the bitwise AND of the modifier field and the flag `SHIFT_MASK`, `CTRL_MASK`, `ALT_MASK`, or `META_MASK` are non-zero, then the corresponding key was depressed. This is useful to detect SHIFT + a function key or CTRL + a mouse click, for example.

NOTE: AWT does not distinguish between the mouse buttons because it is intended to be useable on platforms for which mice have only one button, such as the Macintosh.

Event-Handler Procedures

Every time an event is generated, it is passed to a `handleEvent` procedure. The object whose `handleEvent` procedure is initially called is the one that is "closest" to the event. For example, when the user types a keystroke into a component, the component that processes the keystroke gets first crack at it. If that component does not process the event, it is passed to the parent component.

NOTE: *Parent* here refers to the parent in the *window* hierarchy, not in the inheritance hierarchy. For example, the parent of a text field is the panel that contains the text field. Its parent is the frame containing the panel.

If you put only standard components into your window, you don't care about this part of the event-routing. You just wait for the event to reach the frame window. However, if you design your own components, you can achieve special effects by grabbing events in the event-handler for your component. For example, consider the `IntTextField` that we introduced earlier in this chapter. We could trap keyboard events in that class and erase any character text that the user entered when the user hit a key other than a number.

When you write your own `handleEvent` procedure, remember that there are *three* possible exits from the procedure:

> `return true:` the event is handled—don't propagate

> `return false:` the event is not handled—propagate to parent in the *window* hierarchy (don't do it)

> `return super.handleEvent(evt):` the event is not handled—propagate to the parent in the *inheritance* hierarchy

You should never use the second option, returning `false`. *Always* handle an event or pass it to its parent *class*, not its parent *window*, if you won't handle it in the current class. The predefined handler in the AWT base class will eventually route the message to the parent window, but if you skip a base class, then some actions that you may be relying on may be skipped as well.

If an action, mouse, keyboard, or focus event was not handled in a `handleEvent` procedure, then Java calls a *convenience function* to give the window a second chance to process the event. The convenience functions are `action`, `mouseEnter`, `mouseExit`, `mouseMove`, `mouseUp`, `mouseDown`, `mouseDrag`, `keyDown`, `keyUp`, `lostFocus`, and `gotFocus`, and the names are self-explanatory.

Strictly speaking, these convenience events are not needed, but using them can make your code clearer. For example, we have used the `action` function in many examples in the previous sections. There is actually no need to process action events in the `action` function. You can process them in the `handleEvent` function when `evt.id` equals `Event.ACTION_EVENT`. But processing them separately makes the code a little less cluttered.

What is wrong with the following handler?

```
class MyFrame extends Frame
{   . . .
    public boolean handleEvent(Event evt) // won't work
    {   if (evt.id == Event.WINDOW_DESTROY) System.exit(0);
        return false; // all other events handled in action
                      // method
    }

    public boolean action(Event evt, Object arg)
    {    if (arg.equals("Ok") . . .
    }
}
```

The answer is that `action` is never called. Here is why. The `handleEvent` function returns `false`. When an action event occurs, it is first passed to `MyFrame.handleEvent`, which returns `false`. It is then passed to the parent of `MyFrame` in the *window* hierarchy. But the `MyFrame` object is a top-level window, so it has no parent. The `Frame.handleEvent` function is never executed, and it is that function that calls `action`. The remedy is simple and is worth repeating: don't return `false`, return `super.handleEvent(evt)`.

java.awt.Component

- boolean action(Event evt, Object obj)

  is called if a user interface action (button click, menu select,...) occurs.

  Parameters: evt the event

  obj additional information on the event (usually the label of the originating component)

Menus

AWT supports the same kind of pull-down menus with which you are familiar from all Windows and Motif applications. A *menu bar* on top of the window contains the names of the pull-down menus. Clicking on a name opens up the menu containing *menu items* and *submenus*. When the user clicks on a menu item, all menus are closed and a message is sent to the program. Figure 7-24 shows a typical menu with a submenu.

Adding menus is straightforward. You create a menu bar.

```
MenuBar mb = new MenuBar();
```

For each menu, you create a menu object.

```
Menu editMenu = new Menu("Edit");
```

You add menu items, separators, and submenus to the menu object.

```
editMenu.add(new MenuItem("Paste"));
editMenu.addSeparator();
editMenu.add(optionsMenu);
...
```

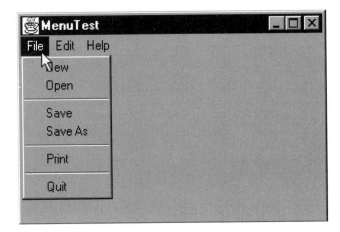

Figure 7-24: A menu

When the user selects a menu, Java triggers an action event. You catch the event in the `action` procedure. Menu events are distinguished by the fact that the event target is a menu item. The `arg` string contains the menu item name.

```
public boolean action(Event evt, Object arg)
{   if (evt.target instanceof MenuItem)
    {   if (arg.equals("Open")) . . .
        else if (arg.equals("Save")) . . .
        . . .
    }
}
```

A check box menu item is one that can display a check box next to the name (see Figure 7-25). When the user selects the menu, the state of the item automatically toggles between checked and unchecked. Use the `getState` method of the `CheckboxMenuItem` class to test the current state and the `setState` method to set the state.

In Windows programs, menus are generally defined in an external resource file and tied to the application with resource identifiers. It is possible to build menus in the menu bar used by Java, but it is not commonly done. In Java, menus must be built inside the program, because Java applications have no external resources. It is a common Windows programming error to have a mismatch of the resource numbers. In Java, you must, likewise, make sure that the string of the menu name matches the string in the action procedure.

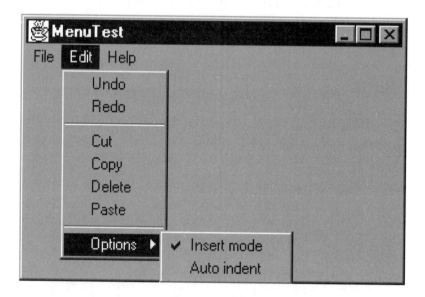

Figure 7-25: A checked menu item

Example 7-17 is a sample program that generates a set of menus.

Example 7-17: MenuTest.java

```java
import java.awt.*;

public class MenuTest extends Frame
{  public MenuTest()
   {  setTitle("MenuTest");

      MenuBar mbar = new MenuBar();
      Menu m = new Menu("File");
      m.add(new MenuItem("New"));
      m.add(new MenuItem("Open"));
      m.addSeparator();
      m.add(new MenuItem("Save"));
      m.add(new MenuItem("Save As"));
      m.addSeparator();
      m.add(new MenuItem("Print"));
      m.addSeparator();
      m.add(new MenuItem("Quit"));
      mbar.add(m);

      m = new Menu("Edit");
      m.add(new MenuItem("Undo"));
      m.add(new MenuItem("Redo"));
      m.addSeparator();
      m.add(new MenuItem("Cut"));
      m.add(new MenuItem("Copy"));
      m.add(new MenuItem("Delete"));
      m.add(new MenuItem("Paste"));
      m.addSeparator();

      Menu f = new Menu("Options");
      f.add(new CheckboxMenuItem("Insert mode"));
      f.add(new CheckboxMenuItem("Auto indent"));
      m.add(f);

      mbar.add(m);

      m = new Menu("Help");
      m.add(new MenuItem("Index"));
      m.add(new MenuItem("About"));
      mbar.add(m);

      setMenuBar(mbar);
   }
```

```java
public boolean action(Event evt, Object arg)
{  if (evt.target instanceof MenuItem)
   {  if(arg.equals("Quit"))
         System.exit(0);
   }
   else return false;
   return true;
}

public boolean handleEvent(Event evt)
{  if (evt.id == Event.WINDOW_DESTROY
      && evt.target == this)
      System.exit(0);
   return super.handleEvent(evt);
}

public static void main(String args[])
{  Frame f = new MenuTest();
   f.resize(300, 200);
   f.show();
}
}
```

 java.awt.Menu

- Menu(String label)

  Parameters: label   the menu description in the menu bar or parent menu

- void add(MenuItem item)

  adds a menu item (or a menu).

  Parameters: item   the item or menu to add

- void addSeparator()

  adds a separator line to the menu.

 java.awt.MenuItem

- MenuItem(String label)

  Parameters: label   the label for this menu item (the label " - " is reserved for a separator between menu items)

`java.awt.CheckboxMenuItem`

- `CheckboxMenuItem(String label)`

  Parameters: `label`   the label for this menu item

- `boolean getState()`

  returns the check state of this item.

- `void setState(boolean t)`

  sets the check state of this item.

  Parameters: `t`   the new check state

Keyboard Events

When a key is pressed, a "key down" event is generated. When the key is released, there is a corresponding "key up" event. The most convenient place to trap these events are in the `keyDown` and `keyUp` procedures.

The key code is either the ASCII code of the key or a special code for a function key (`LEFT`, `RIGHT`, `UP`, `DOWN`, `HOME`, `END`, `PGUP`, `PGDN`, `F1`, ... `F12`). You get the state of the SHIFT, CONTROL, ALT, and meta keys by bit masking using the AND operator. For example, the following code tests whether or not the user hits SHIFT + RIGHT ARROW:

```
public boolean keyDown(Event evt, int key)
{   if (key == Event.RIGHT &&
        (evt.modifiers & Event.SHIFT_MASK) != 0)
    {  . . .
    }
}
```

In general, you use one of the following flags: `Event.SHIFT_MASK`, `Event.CTRL_MASK`, `Event.ALT_MASK`, and `Event.META_MASK`.

Example 7-18 shows how to handle keystrokes. The program is a simple implementation of the Etch-A-Sketch toy shown in Figure 7-26. You move a pen up, down, left, and right with the cursor keys. If you hold down the SHIFT key, the pen moves by a larger increment.

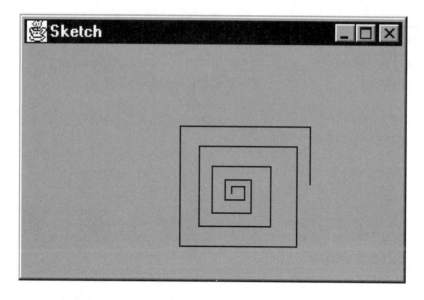

Figure 7-26: A sketch program

Example 7-18: Sketch.java

```java
import java.awt.*;

public class Sketch extends Frame
{  public Sketch()
   {  setTitle("Sketch");
   }

   public boolean handleEvent(Event evt)
   {  if (evt.id == Event.WINDOW_DESTROY) System.exit(0);
      return super.handleEvent(evt);
   }

   public boolean keyDown(Event evt, int key)
   {  int d = ((evt.modifiers & Event.SHIFT_MASK) == 0) ?
      1 : 5;
      if (key == Event.LEFT) add(-d, 0);
      else if (key == Event.RIGHT) add(d, 0);
      else if (key == Event.UP) add(0, -d);
      else if (key == Event.DOWN) add(0, d);
      else return false;
      return true;
   }
```

```
public void update(Graphics g)
{  paint(g);
   requestFocus();
}

public void paint(Graphics g)
{  g.drawLine(start.x, start.y, end.x, end.y);
   start.x = end.x;
   start.y = end.y;
}

public void add(int dx, int dy)
{  end.x += dx;
   end.y += dy;
   repaint();
}

public static void main(String[] args)
{  Frame f = new Sketch();
   f.resize(300, 200);
   f.show();
}

private Point start = new Point(0, 0);
private Point end = new Point(0, 0);
```

}

java.awt.Component

- `boolean keyDown(Event evt, int key)`

  is called when a key is pressed.

Parameters:	evt	the event
	key	the key that is pressed

- `boolean keyUp(Event evt, int key)`

  is called when a key is released.

Parameters:	evt	the event
	key	the key that is released

Mouse Events

Users can use a mouse for three separate purposes: for selection, for navigation between components of a frame, and for drawing. The AWT mechanism recognizes when the user selects menu items or clicks on a button. It then notifies you of what happened in the appropriate action event.

If you want to enable the user to draw with the mouse, you will need to trap the `mouseMove`, `mouseUp`, `mouseDown`, and `mouseDrag` functions. (How often a `mouseMove` event is checked for and then reported is operating system dependent. It will be checked frequently but you cannot rely on it to be continuous.)

Java is also supposed to trigger an event in an application when the mouse has entered or exited a subwindow, or when a subwindow has gained or lost the keyboard focus. You trap these events with the `mouseEnter`, `mouseExit`, `gotFocus`, and `lostFocus` methods. At the time of this writing, these events are generated inconsistently on different platforms, and we cannot yet recommend that you rely on them. Nonetheless, at some point, these events should be more consistently generated, so it is worth learning how to handle them in preparation for that happy moment.

In this section, we will consider a simple graphics editor application that allows the user to place, move and erase squares on a canvas (see Figure 7-27).

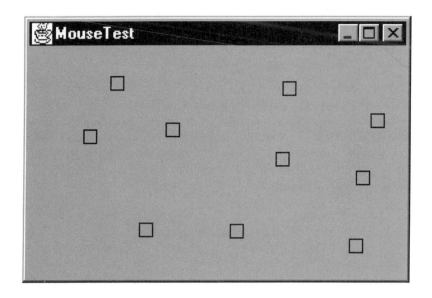

Figure 7-27: A mouse test program

When the user clicks a mouse button, Java calls the `mouseDown` function of the active window. Its arguments include the event and the *x*- and *y*-coordinates of the pointer when the mouse was clicked. If you want to distinguish between single and double clicks, look at the `clickCount` field of the event structure. (You can even get triple clicks, but your users will hate you if you force them to exercise their fingers too much.) You *cannot*, however, distinguish between the mouse buttons, assuming the user has more than one.

Here is the `mouseDown` function for our sample program. When you click onto a pixel that is not inside any of the squares that have been drawn, a new square is added. When you double-click inside an existing square, it is erased.

```
public boolean mouseDown(Event evt, int x, int y)
{  current = find(x, y);
   if (current < 0) // no square under the cursor
      add(x, y);
   else if (evt.clickCount >= 2)
      remove(current);
   return true;
}
```

As the mouse moves over a window, the window receives a steady stream of `mouseMove` calls. These are ignored by most applications. However, our test application traps the events to change the cursor to a different shape when it is under a square.

```
public boolean mouseMove(Event evt, int x, int y)
{  if (find(x, y)) setCursor(Frame.CROSSHAIR_CURSOR);
   else setCursor(Frame.DEFAULT_CURSOR);
}
```

If a mouse button is depressed while the mouse is in motion, `mouseDrag` calls are generated instead. Our test application lets you drag the square under the cursor. Before the square is moved, we erase the old location by drawing it over itself in XOR mode. (A bug under Windows 95 seems to leave the four pixels at the corners of the square intact.) Then we set the new location for the square and draw it again.

```
public boolean mouseDrag(Event evt, int x, int y)
{  if (current >= 0)
   {  Graphics g = getGraphics();
      g.setXORMode(getBackground());
      draw(current);
      squares[current].x = x;
      squares[current].y = y;
      draw(current);
      g.dispose();
   }
}
```

Example 7-19 is the program listing.

Example 7-19: MouseTest.java

```java
import java.awt.*;

public class MouseTest extends Frame
{   public MouseTest()
    {   setTitle("MouseTest");
    }

    public boolean handleEvent(Event evt)
    {   if (evt.id == Event.WINDOW_DESTROY) System.exit(0);
        return super.handleEvent(evt);
    }

    public void paint(Graphics g)
    {   for (int i = 0; i < nsquares; i++)
            draw(g, i);
    }

    public int find(int x, int y)
    {   for (int i = 0; i < nsquares; i++)
            if (squares[i].x <= x && x <= squares[i].x
                + SQUARELENGTH && squares[i].y <= y
                && y <= squares[i].y + SQUARELENGTH)
                return i;
        return -1;
    }

    public void draw(Graphics g, int i)
    {   g.drawRect(squares[i].x, squares[i].y, SQUARELENGTH,
        SQUARELENGTH);
    }

    public void add(int x, int y)
    {   if (nsquares < MAXNSQUARES)
        {   squares[nsquares] = new Point(x, y);
            nsquares++;
            repaint();
        }
    }

    public void remove(int n)
    {   nsquares--;
        squares[n] = squares[nsquares];
        if (current == n) current = -1;
        repaint();
    }
```

```java
public boolean mouseDown(Event evt, int x, int y)
{   current = find(x, y);
    if (current < 0) // not inside a square
    {   add(x, y);
    }
    else if (evt.clickCount >= 2)
    {   remove(current);
    }
    return true;
}

public boolean mouseMove(Event evt, int x, int y)
{   if (find(x, y) >= 0)
        setCursor(Frame.CROSSHAIR_CURSOR);
    else
        setCursor(Frame.DEFAULT_CURSOR);
    return true;
}

public boolean mouseDrag(Event evt, int x, int y)
{   if (current >= 0)
    {   Graphics g = getGraphics();
        g.setXORMode(getBackground());
        draw(g, current);
        squares[current].x = x;
        squares[current].y = y;
        draw(g, current);
        g.dispose();
    }
    return true;
}

public static void main(String args[])
{   Frame f = new MouseTest();
    f.resize(300, 200);
    f.show();
}
private static final int SQUARELENGTH = 10;
private static final int MAXNSQUARES = 100;
private Point[] squares = new Point[MAXNSQUARES];
private int nsquares = 0;
private int current = -1;
}
```

`java.awt.Component`

- `boolean mouseMove(Event evt, int x, int y)`

  is called when the mouse moves with no mouse button depressed.

Parameters:	evt	the event
	x, y	the mouse location

- `boolean mouseUp(Event evt, int x, int y)`

  is called when a mouse button is released.

Parameters:	evt	the event
	x, y	the mouse location

- `boolean mouseDown(Event evt, int x, int y)`

  is called when a mouse button is clicked.

Parameters:	evt	the event
	x, y	the mouse location

- `boolean mouseDrag(Event evt, int x, int y)`

  is called when the mouse moves with a mouse button depressed.

Parameters:	evt	the event
	x, y	the mouse location

- `boolean mouseEnter(Event evt, int x, int y)`

  is called when the mouse enters this component.

Parameters:	evt	the event
	x, y	the mouse location

- `boolean mouseExit(Event evt, int x, int y)`

  is called when the mouse exits the component.

Parameters:	evt	the event
	x, y	the mouse location

- `boolean lostFocus(Event evt, Object other)`

  is called when this component has lost the input focus.

Parameters:	evt	the event
	other	the object that gained the input focus

- `boolean gotFocus(Event evt, Object other)`

  is called when this component has gained the input focus.

Parameters:	`evt`	the event
	`other`	the object that lost the input focus

Scroll Bars

The two most common uses for scroll bars in a Java application are as follows:

- You can use a scroll bar in a control as a slider.

- You can place scroll bars at the right and at the bottom of a window, to scroll through its contents.

We will look briefly at both of these uses in this section.

You create a scroll bar by specifying its direction (`HORIZONTAL` or `VERTICAL`). The default range of the scroll bar is 0–100. If you want to change the range, use the `setValues` method. It takes four arguments: the value of the scroll position, the size of the "visible area," and the minimum and maximum values of the scroll bar positions. If you use scroll bars to scroll the contents of a window, the visible area is the size of the window. A positive visible area value limits scrolling so that the *right* (or bottom) edge of the window scrolls up to the right (or bottom) edge of the logical area. If you just use a scroll bar as a slider control, set the visible area to zero.

When the user clicks on a scroll bar, the scroll bar value changes. The scroll bar sends messages to the parent window. When the user clicks on the arrow on either end of the scroll bar, Java changes the value by the *line increment*. When the user clicks on the area between the arrow and the slider, the value is changed by the *page increment*. The default values for these quantities are 1 and 10. You can change these quantities with the `setLineIncrement` and `setPageIncrement` methods.

In our first example, we use scroll bars to pick red, green, and blue values to mix and display a color value. (See Figure 7-28.) Each scroll bar is initialized like this.

```
red = new Scrollbar(Scrollbar.HORIZONTAL);
red.setValues(0, 0, 0, 255);
red.setPageIncrement(16);
```

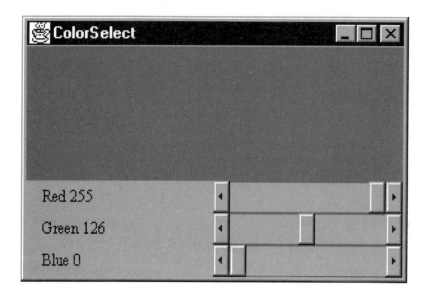

Figure 7-28: Scroll bars

When the user clicks on a scroll bar or moves the scroll bar slider to a new position, the scroll bar sends messages to the parent window. When the user clicks on the arrow on either end of the scroll bar, SCROLL_LINE_DOWN and SCROLL_LINE_UP events are generated. When the user clicks between the arrow and the slider, SCROLL_PAGE_DOWN and SCROLL_PAGE_UP events are generated. When the slider is moved and dropped to a new position, a SCROLL_ABSOLUTE event is generated.

AWT does not support continuous tracking of the slider.

There are no convenience functions to trap scroll bar events. You need to catch them in the handleEvent procedure for the class you derive from Frame. When processing a scroll bar event, you use the getValue() method to obtain the current position of the scroll bar. As an example of this, here is the event-handler for the color mixer application.

```
public boolean handleEvent(Event evt)
{   if (evt.id == Event.SCROLL_ABSOLUTE
       || evt.id == Event.SCROLL_LINE_DOWN
       || evt.id == Event.SCROLL_LINE_UP
       || evt.id == Event.SCROLL_PAGE_DOWN
       || evt.id == Event.SCROLL_PAGE_UP)
    {   Color nc = new Color(red.getValue(), green.getValue(),
           blue.getValue());
       . . .
    }
    . . .
}
```

Example 7-20 is the complete source code for the color selection application.

Example 7-20: ColorSelect.java

```java
import java.awt.*;

public class ColorSelect extends Frame
{   public ColorSelect()
    {   setTitle("ColorSelect");
        Panel p = new Panel();
        p.setLayout(new GridLayout(3, 2));
        p.add(redLabel = new Label("Red 0"));
        p.add(red = new Scrollbar(Scrollbar.HORIZONTAL, 0, 0,
            0, 255));
        red.setPageIncrement(16);
        p.add(greenLabel = new Label("Green 0"));
        p.add(green = new Scrollbar(Scrollbar.HORIZONTAL, 0,
            0, 0, 255));
        green.setPageIncrement(16);
        p.add(blueLabel = new Label("Blue 0"));
        p.add(blue = new Scrollbar(Scrollbar.HORIZONTAL, 0, 0,
            0, 255));
        blue.setPageIncrement(16);
        add("South", p);

        c = new Canvas();
        c.setBackground(new Color(0, 0, 0));
        add("Center", c);
    }

    public boolean handleEvent(Event evt)
    {   if (evt.id == Event.WINDOW_DESTROY) System.exit(0);
        else if (evt.id == Event.SCROLL_ABSOLUTE
            || evt.id == Event.SCROLL_LINE_DOWN
            || evt.id == Event.SCROLL_LINE_UP
            || evt.id == Event.SCROLL_PAGE_DOWN
            || evt.id == Event.SCROLL_PAGE_UP)
        {   redLabel.setText("Red " + red.getValue());
            greenLabel.setText("Green " + green.getValue());
            blueLabel.setText("Blue " + blue.getValue());
            c.setBackground(new Color(red.getValue(),
                green.getValue(), blue.getValue()));

            c.repaint();
            return true;
        }
        return super.handleEvent(evt);
    }

    public static void main(String[] args)
```

```
{   Frame f = new ColorSelect();
    f.resize(300, 200);
    f.show();
}

private Label redLabel;
private Label greenLabel;
private Label blueLabel;

private Scrollbar red;
private Scrollbar green;
private Scrollbar blue;

private Canvas c;
}
```

java.awt.Scrollbar

- Scrollbar(int orientation)

  Parameters: orientation   either HORIZONTAL or VERTICAL

- void setValue(int value)

  Parameters: value   the new scroll position. Set to the current minimum or maximum if it is outside the scroll range

- void setPageIncrement(int l)

  sets the page increment, the amount by which the scroll position changes when the user clicks between the arrows and the slider. This method does not currently work correctly on all platforms.

- void setLineIncrement(int l)

  sets the line increment, the amount by which the scroll position changes when the user clicks on the arrows at the ends of the scroll bar.

- int getValue()

  returns the current scroll position.

- void setValues(int value, int visible, int minimum, int maximum)

Parameters:	value	the scroll position
	visible	the visible area of the window, or 0 for a slider control
	minimum	the minimum position value of the scroll bar
	maximum	the maximum position value of the scroll bar

Scrolling a Window

In this section, we add scroll bars to the drawing application in the section on mouse events. Suppose we want to allow an area of 600 by 400 pixels to be filled with squares. Our window has an area of only 300 by 200 pixels, so we want the user to be able to scroll over the total area.

The basic idea is simple. Whenever we draw the window, we translate the graphics coordinates by the negatives of the scroll values. For example, if the values of the horizontal and vertical scroll bars are 200 and 100, then we want to draw the area starting at (200, 100). We move the origin to (–200, –100) and repaint the entire 600-by-400-pixel image. Much of the image is clipped, but the part of the underlying image that we want to see is then shown in the window (see Figure 7-29).

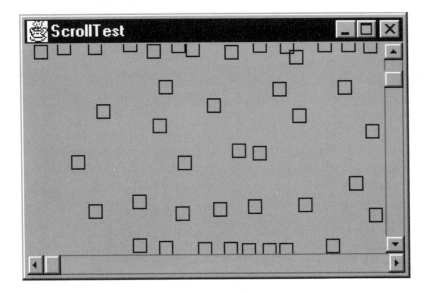

Figure 7-29: A scroll bar test program

Thus what we need to do is:

- trap all scroll events and

- force a redraw when an event occurs.

Here's an example of the code to do this:

```
public boolean handleEvent(Event evt)
{   if (evt.id == Event.SCROLL_ABSOLUTE
        || evt.id == Event.SCROLL_LINE_DOWN
        || evt.id == Event.SCROLL_LINE_UP
        || evt.id == Event.SCROLL_PAGE_DOWN
        || evt.id == Event.SCROLL_PAGE_UP)
    {   canvas.translate(horiz.getValue(), vert.getValue());
    }
    . . .
}
```

The `translate` method of our canvas class stores the scroll offset and calls `repaint`.

```
public void translate(int x, int y)
{   dx = x;
    dy = y;
    repaint();
}
```

The data structure that stores the list of rectangles keeps them in *absolute coordinates*. That is not a problem in the `paint` procedure because we can translate the origin of the graphics context.

```
public void paint(Graphics g)
{   g.translate(-dx, -dy);
    for (int i = 0; i < nsquares; i++) draw(g, i);
}
```

But the mouse functions report the mouse locations in window coordinates. To test that a mouse click falls inside a square, we must add the scroll offset to all mouse coordinates.

```
public boolean mouseDown(Event evt, int x, int y)
{   x += dx;
    y += dy;
    current = find(x, y);
    . . .
}
```

The exact dimensioning of the scroll bars is a bit tricky. The visible area of the window is somewhat less than 300 by 200, because the scroll bars take some amount of space. We override the `show` procedure of the frame class as a convenient spot to initialize the scroll bars.

```
public void show()
{   super.show();
    Dimension d = canvas.size();
    horiz.setValues(0, d.width, 0, 600);
    vert.setValue(0, d.height, 0, 400);
}
```

If the window is resized, we have to redo the entire computation. Resizing the window results in a WINDOW_MOVED (!) event. We trap it in the handleEvent function.

```
public boolean handleEvent(Event evt)
{   if (evt.id == Event.WINDOW_MOVED)
    {   Dimension d = canvas.size();
        horiz.setValues(horiz.getValue(), d.width, 0, 600);
        vert.setValue(vert.getValue(), d.height, 0, 400);
    }
    else . . .
}
```

Example 7-21 is the listing of the program.

Example 7-21: ScrollTest.java

```
import java.awt.*;

public class ScrollTest extends Frame
{   public ScrollTest()
    {   setTitle("ScrollTest");
        add("East", vert = new Scrollbar(Scrollbar.VERTICAL));
        add("South", horiz =
            new Scrollbar(Scrollbar.HORIZONTAL));
        add("Center", canvas = new SquareCanvas());
    }

    public boolean handleEvent(Event evt)
    {   if (evt.id == Event.WINDOW_DESTROY) System.exit(0);
        else if (evt.id == Event.WINDOW_MOVED)
        {   Dimension d = canvas.size();
            horiz.setValues(horiz.getValue(), d.width, 0, 600);
            vert.setValues(vert.getValue(), d.height, 0, 400);
        }
        else if (evt.id == Event.SCROLL_ABSOLUTE
            || evt.id == Event.SCROLL_LINE_DOWN
            || evt.id == Event.SCROLL_LINE_UP
            || evt.id == Event.SCROLL_PAGE_DOWN
            || evt.id == Event.SCROLL_PAGE_UP)
        {   canvas.translate(horiz.getValue(), vert.getValue());
            return true;
        }
        return super.handleEvent(evt);
    }
```

```java
    public void show()
    {   super.show();
        Dimension d = canvas.size();
        horiz.setValues(0, d.width, 0, 600);
        vert.setValues(0, d.height, 0, 400);
    }

    public static void main(String args[])
    {   Frame f = new ScrollTest();
        f.resize(300, 200);
        f.show();
    }

    private Scrollbar horiz;
    private Scrollbar vert;
    private SquareCanvas canvas;
}

class SquareCanvas extends Canvas
{   public void translate(int x, int y)
    {   dx = x;
        dy = y;
        repaint();
    }

    public void paint(Graphics g)
    {   g.translate(-dx, -dy);
        for (int i = 0; i < nsquares; i++)
            draw(g, i);
    }

    public int find(int x, int y)
    {   for (int i = 0; i < nsquares; i++)
            if (squares[i].x <= x
                    && x <= squares[i].x + SQUARELENGTH
                    && squares[i].y <= y
                    && y <= squares[i].y + SQUARELENGTH)
                return i;
        return -1;
    }

    public void draw(Graphics g, int i)
    {   g.drawRect(squares[i].x, squares[i].y, SQUARELENGTH,
        SQUARELENGTH);
    }

    public void add(int x, int y)
    {   if (nsquares < MAXNSQUARES)
```

```
       {    squares[nsquares] = new Point(x, y);
            nsquares++;
            repaint();
       }
   }

   public void remove(int n)
   {   nsquares--;
       squares[n] = squares[nsquares];
       if (current == n) current = -1;
       repaint();
   }

   public boolean mouseDown(Event evt, int x, int y)
   {   x += dx; y += dy;
       current = find(x, y);
       if (current < 0) // not inside a square
       {   add(x, y);
       }
       else if (evt.clickCount >= 2)
       {   remove(current);
       }
       return true;
   }

   public boolean mouseDrag(Event evt, int x, int y)
   {   x += dx; y += dy;
       if (current >= 0)
       {   Graphics g = getGraphics();
           g.translate(-dx, -dy);
           g.setXORMode(getBackground());
           draw(g, current);
           squares[current].x = x;
           squares[current].y = y;
           draw(g, current);
           g.dispose();
       }
       return true;
   }

   private static final int SQUARELENGTH = 10;

   private static final int MAXNSQUARES = 100;
   private Point[] squares = new Point[MAXNSQUARES];
   private int nsquares = 0;
   private int current = -1;
   private int dx = 0;
   private int dy = 0;
}
```

`java.awt.Graphics`

- `void translate(int x, int y)`

  changes the origin of the coordinate system used for drawing. All subsequent drawing operations are shifted left and up by the translation amount.

  Parameters: `x, y`   the coordinates of the top left corner of the screen

CHAPTER
8

- Applet Basics

- Converting Applications to Applets

- The Applet HTML Tags

- Passing Information to Applets

- Dialog Boxes in Applets

- Multimedia

- The Applet Context

- The Life Cycle of an Applet

- It's an Applet. It's an Application. It's Both!

Applets

A t this point, you should be comfortable with most of Java's language elements. We hope that you agree that Java is a nice (if not perfect), general purpose OOP language. The class libraries need improvements—but that will certainly come with time. Of course, being a simplified dialect of C++ is not enough to justify the hype surrounding Java. The unbelievable hype (as was mentioned in Chapters 1 and 2) stems from Java's ability to create programs ("applets") that can be downloaded from the Net and run in any Java-enabled WWW browser. Since you know the basics of the Java language, it is now time to learn the few extra details needed to write applets.

NOTE: Applets work best when combined with Java's networking abilities and its ability to handle multiple threads. Please see Chapter 12 for information about threads and Chapter 13 for more on networking than we cover here.

Applet Basics

Java Applets and HTML Files

You run Java applications from the command line by having the Java interpreter interpret the bytecode contained in a class file. Applets, on the other hand, usually run within a Web page via a Java-enabled browser such as Netscape 2.0 or above or Internet Explorer 3.0. The JDK does come with a stand-alone applet viewer program that allows you to test your applets more easily—see the section "Viewing Applets" for more on the applet viewer. (For Solaris and Windows 95, this program is called `appletviewer.exe` and may be found in the `bin` directory below the `java` directory if you use the normal installation defaults.)

To load applets into your Web browser, you must create a separate file that contains HTML tags to tell the browser which applets to load and where to put each applet on the Web page. Before the development of Java, HTML was simply a vehicle to indicate elements of a hypertext page. For example, <TITLE> indicates the title of the page, and any text that follows this tag becomes the title of the page. You indicate the end of the title with the </TITLE> tag. (This is one of the general rules for tags: a slash followed by the name of the element indicates the end of the element.)

The Java extensions to HTML tell any Java-enabled browser the following:

1.   the name of the class file,

2.   the location of the class file,

3.   how the applet sits on the Web page.

The browser then retrieves the class file from the Net (or from a directory on the user's machine) and automatically runs the applet.

In addition to the applet itself, the Web page can contain all the other HTML elements you have seen in use on Web pages: multiple fonts, bulleted lists, graphics, links, and so on. Applets are just one part of the hypertext page. It is always worth keeping in mind that Java is *not* a tool for designing HTML pages; it is a tool for *bringing them to life*. This is not to say that the GUI design elements in a Java applet are not important, but they must work with (and, in fact, are subservient to) the underlying HTML design of the Web page.

NOTE: We do not cover general HTML tags at all; we assume that you know—or are working with someone who knows—the basics of HTML. There are only a few special HTML tags needed for Java applets. We do, of course, cover those later in this chapter. As for learning HTML, there are probably dozens of HTML books at your local bookstore. One that covers what you need and will not insult your intelligence (in spite of the title) is Mary Morris's *HTML Authoring for Fun and Profit* (SunSoft Press, 1995).

A Simple Applet

From a programmer's point of view, an applet is simply a Java class that extends the Applet class. Applet is part of the java.applet package. The Applet class is closely related to the AWT classes that you saw in the previous two chapters. For example, the event-handling and the buffering techniques you learned in Chapter 6 to avoid a flicker when loading images are useful for building applets as well.

Here is an example of one of the simplest Java applets:

```
import java.awt.*;
import java.applet.*;

public class NotHelloAgain extends Applet
{
    public void paint(Graphics g)
        Font f = new Font("System", Font.BOLD, 18);
    {   g.setFont(f);
        g.drawString("We won't use 'hello world.'", 25, 50);
    }
}
```

Notice, as usual, that we are overriding the `paint` method in order to actually display something.

In addition to this Java file, which needs to be compiled into a class file, we need, at the minimum, a trivial HTML file. It is customary (but not necessary) to give it the same name as that of the major applet inside. Let us call it `NotHelloAgain.html`. Here is what you need in this file:

```
<APPLET CODE="NotHelloAgain.class" WIDTH=100 HEIGHT=100>
</APPLET>
```

We will explain the options for the APPLET tag later in this chapter.

TIP: If you are using our customized version of WinEdit, then you can get a first glimpse at your applet by compiling the program from within WinEdit and choosing Execute from the Project menu.

This invokes a (rather weird) batch file that:

1. creates a file and puts in the minimum number of HTML tags needed to be able to run your code as an applet (the size of the applet is fixed at 300 by 200 pixels),

2. saves the file with an HTM extension (so it will not overwrite any of your `.html` files),

3. invokes Sun's applet viewer on this file.

Close the applet viewer when you have finished testing your applet.

This method gives you a quick and dirty way to test your applets without creating a full-blown HTML page.

Viewing Applets

More generally, there are three ways for you to see your applet at work.

1. You can use Sun's applet viewer directly.

    Enter

    ```
    appletviewer NotHelloAgain.html
    ```

The command line for the applet viewer program is the name of the HTML file, not the class file.

2. In Netscape, you can load a local file by choosing File | Open File from the File menu and entering the file name or by selecting the file name from the dialog box. This tells Netscape to load the HTML file.

3. You can give Netscape the URL for the HTML page that contains the applet and tell it to open this URL. Do this by selecting File | Open Location (or click the Open button, of course) and typing in a file URL. For example, something like:

    ```
    file:///C|/CoreJavaBook/ch8/NotHelloAgain/NotHelloAgain.html
    ```

    or, you can open the file through a bookmark that you previously saved.

Netscape saves bookmarks to local files as file URLs and not as file names. For security purposes, Netscape considers a local file location saved as a bookmark just as alien as a Net URL. (See below for more on security restrictions on applets.)

Instead of Netscape, you can use another Java-enabled browser such as Hot Java or Internet Assistant.

There are pros and cons to all three approaches.

*   The applet viewer program is simple and it starts up quickly. However, it only shows you the applet, not the surrounding HTML text. (If an HTML file contains multiple applets, the applet viewer pops up multiple windows.)

*   Netscape shows you the text and graphics of the Web page together with the applet, exactly as the user of your page would see it. Also, if you load the file as a URL (either directly or via a bookmark), Netscape enforces its security restrictions for downloaded applets. This is the most realistic test you can give your applets: your applet will behave exactly as it would on your users' Web pages. The applet viewer does not enforce security restrictions, and Netscape does not enforce them on applets opened inside a local file.

*   For debugging applets, you will find Netscape maddening. If you load your applet into Netscape, do not like the result, fix up the applet, and reload the Web page containing it, Netscape will continue to use your old applet code. You need to quit and restart Netscape to reload the new version of the applet. (Another possibility is to set both disk and memory cache size to 0, but then performance will suffer.) When you are still debugging the applet code, the applet viewer is a better choice than Netscape. Use Netscape to test the look of the final Web page and to test the security aspects.

The key point is that when you run the applet inside the applet viewer, all of the text in the HTML file is ignored. The applet viewer only shows the applet. But when you view the applet with Netscape, it sits inside a Web page filled with text. You should use the surrounding text to your advantage. Explain what the applet is good for, and make clear how to use it. We have seen far too many applets that require double-clicking to activate them, or users must type in unadvertised keystrokes. You have plenty of space on the Web page to explain every aspect of the applet.

Getting Your Computer Ready for Java Networking

Several of the applets in this chapter require Internet access so that the applets can retrieve Web pages from the Internet. There are many ways to connect to the Net; unfortunately, not all of them are compatible with Java. For example, a connection through CompuServe or America Online does not yet work. Merely being connected to the Net is not enough; Java expects that your network supports the TCP/IP protocol. (TCP/IP stands for Transmission Control Protocol/Internet Protocol.)

If your computer has a network card and is currently connected to a network running the TCP/IP protocol, then you are all set. That is certainly the case when you are running Unix or Linux and are connected to a local network that, in turn, is connected to the Internet. If you have a PC running Windows 95 or NT and are using an Internet browser such as Netscape through a network connection, then you are also almost certainly ready.

The problems arise if you are browsing the Net through a telephone connection. This is done through the intermediary of a program, usually called a "stack." The stack program implements the TCP/IP protocol for communicating with the Internet. (Some services, such as CompuServe, do not use a standard stack at all.) Unfortunately, there are various possible stacks that you can use for your Internet connection. Many third-party Internet providers have their own version of a TCP/IP stack (or WinSock driver, as it is often called in the Windows world). On Windows-based machines, the applet viewer in Java 1.0 *requires* that you use the Microsoft TCP/IP stack.

This means that if you are using a dialup connection with a third-party WinSock driver such as Trumpet WinSock, you will need to replace that driver with the Windows Dial-up Networking package that uses the Microsoft TCP/IP stack. This software comes free with both Windows 95 and Windows NT. Of course, actually removing your old stack and telling the operating system that you are using a new stack may require pulling out a manual—we will leave those details to you.

Security Basics

Because applets are designed to be loaded from a remote site and then executed locally, security becomes important. For this reason, applets (unlike applications) are restricted in what they can do. In particular, at the present time

1. applets can *never* run any local executable program;

2. applets cannot communicate with any host other than the server from which they were downloaded (that server is called the *originating host*);

3. applets cannot read or write to the local computer's file system (this is true only of Netscape. It is possible that other browsers will implement less stringent security restrictions because Sun has not made this part of the Java specification);

4. applets cannot find any information about the local computer, except for the Java version used; the name and version of the operating system; and the characters used to separate files (for instance, / or \), paths (such as : or ;), and lines (such as \n or \r\n). In particular, applets cannot find out the user's name, e-mail address, and so on.

NOTE: At some point signed applets will be possible. It is likely that if you trust the signer of the applet, you can tell the browser to give it more privileges.

Table 8-1 shows what Java programs can do in the following four scenarios:

Table 8-1: Java program capabilities

	NL	NF	AV	JA
read local file	no	no	yes	yes
write local file	no	no	yes	yes
get file information	no	no	yes	yes
delete file	no	no	no	yes
run another program	no	no	yes	yes
read the `user.name` property	no	yes	yes	yes
connect to network port on server	yes	yes	yes	yes
connect to network port on other host	no	yes	yes	yes
load Java library	no	yes	yes	yes
call `exit`	no	no	yes	yes
create a pop-up window	with warning	yes	yes	yes

NL = Netscape loading a URL

NF = Netscape loading a local file

AV = Applet viewer

JA = Java running an application (not an applet)

Converting Applications to Applets

It is easy to convert a graphical Java application (that is, one you can start with the `java` command line interpreter) into an applet that you can embed in a Web page. Essentially, all of the user-interface code is completely unchanged. To understand why, look at Figure 8-1.

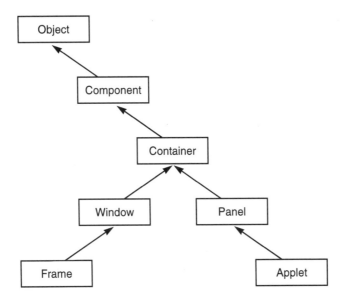

Figure 8-1: Inheritance diagram

Notice that the `Applet` and the `Frame` class both descend from `Container`. Therefore, you can continue to use the same methods to add user-interface components. For example, you add a button to an applet with a call to

```
add(new Button("Start"));
```

or a canvas with a call to

```
add(new Canvas());
```

On the other hand, there are a few subtle points that can trip you up. Probably the most common is that the default layout managers are different. Recall that, for frames (used in applications), the default layout manager is `BorderLayout`. For panels (and, hence, applets), it is the `FlowLayout` manager. This means that, if you have not set a specific layout manager for your application, you will have implicitly used the `BorderLayout` manager. In that case, you will need to change the layout manager in the applet to `BorderLayout`.

Here are the specific steps for converting an application to an applet.

1. Make an HTML page with an APPLET tag.

2. Eliminate the `main` method in the application. Usually `main` contains code to make a new frame object. With applets, that is automatically taken care of by the browser, since it makes an object of the class specified in the APPLET tag. Also, `main` usually sets the frame size. For applets, this is done with the WIDTH and HEIGHT fields of the APPLET tag in the actual HTML file.

3. Derive the class from `Applet`, not from `Frame`.

4. Replace the constructor with a method called `init`. When the browser creates an object of the applet class, it calls the `init()` method.

5. If the application's frame implicitly uses a border layout, you must set the layout manager for the applet in the `init` function. For example, compare the following code with the constructor for the calculator program in Chapter 7:

```
public class CalculatorApplet extends Applet
{  public void init()
   {  setLayout(new BorderLayout());

      // required in applet, not in frame
      display = new TextField("0");
      display.setEditable(false);
      add("North", display);
      . . .
   }

}
```

6. If the application calls `setTitle`, eliminate the call to the method. Applets do not have title bars. (You can, of course, title the Web page itself, using the <TITLE> HTML tag.) If the application uses menus, eliminate them and replace them with buttons or some other user-interface component. Applets cannot have menu bars.

As an example of this transformation, we will change the calculator application from Chapter 7 into an applet. In Figure 8-2, you can see how it looks, sitting inside a Web page:

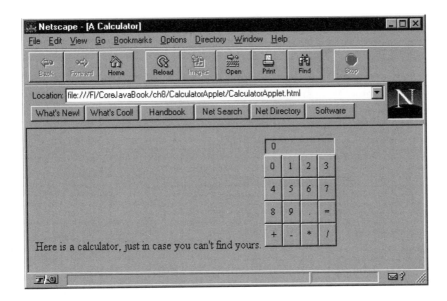

Figure 8-2: A calculator applet

Here is the HTML page:

```
<HTML>
<TITLE>A Calculator</TITLE>
<BODY>
Here is a calculator, just in case you can't find yours.
<APPLET CODE="CalculatorApplet.class" WIDTH=100 HEIGHT=150>
</APPLET>
</BODY>
</HTML>
```

Example 8-1 is the code for the applet.

Example 8-1: CalculatorApplet.java

```
public class CalculatorApplet extends Applet
{  public void init()
   {  setLayout(new BorderLayout());

      display = new TextField("0");
      display.setEditable(false);
      add("North", display);

      Panel p = new Panel();
      p.setLayout(new GridLayout(4, 4));
      for (int i = 0; i <= 9; i++)
```

```
        p.add(new Button("" + (char)('0' + i)));
        p.add(new Button("."));
        p.add(new Button("="));
        p.add(new Button("+"));
        p.add(new Button("-"));
        p.add(new Button("*"));
        p.add(new Button("/"));
        add("Center", p);
    }

    public boolean handleEvent(Event evt)
    {   if (evt.id == Event.WINDOW_DESTROY) System.exit(0);
        return super.handleEvent(evt);
    }

    public boolean action(Event evt, Object arg)
    {   if (arg instanceof String)
        {   String s = (String) arg;
            char ch = s.charAt(0);
            if ('0' <= ch && ch <= '9' || ch == '.')
            {   if (start) display.setText(s);
                else display.setText(display.getText() + s);
                start = false;
            }
            else
            {   if (start)
                {   if (s.equals("-"))
                    { display.setText(s); start = false; }
                    else op = s;
                }
                else
                {   calculate(Format.atof(display.getText()));
                    op = s;
                    start = true;
                }
            }
        }
        else return super.action(evt, arg);
        return true;
    }

    public void calculate(double n)
    {   if (op.equals("+")) arg +=n;
        else if (op.equals("-")) arg -=n;
        else if (op.equals("*")) arg *=n;
        else if (op.equals("/")) arg /=n;
        else if (op.equals("%")) arg %=n;
        else if (op.equals("=")) arg =n;
        display.setText("" + arg);
    }
```

```
    private TextField display;
    private double arg = 0;
    private String op = "=";
    private boolean start = true;
}
```

`java.applet.Applet`

- `void init()`

  This method is called when the applet is first loaded. You must override this method and place all intialization code here.

- `void resize(int width, int height)`

  This method requests that the applet be resized. This would be a great method if it worked on Web pages; unfortunately, it does not usually work in browsers because it interferes with their page-layout mechanisms. This method does nothing in Netscape 2.0, but it does work in the applet viewer.

The Applet HTML Tags

The Required Tags

We have already seen the APPLET tag in action. In its most basic form, it looks like this:

```
<APPLET CODE="NotHelloAgain.class" WIDTH=100 HEIGHT=100>
```

As you have seen, the CODE tag gives the name of the class file and must include the .class extension; the WIDTH and HEIGHT tags size the window that will hold the applet. Both are measured in pixels. You also need a matching </APPLET> tag that marks the end of the HTML tagging needed for an applet. These tags are required. If any are missing, the browser cannot load your applet.

All of this would usually be embedded in an HTML page that, at the very least, might look like this:

```
<HTML>
<HEAD>
<TITLE>NotHelloAgain</TITLE>
</HEAD>
<BODY>
The next line of text is displayed through
the auspices of Java:
<APPLET CODE= "NotHelloAgain.class" WIDTH=100 HEIGHT= 100>
```

```
Any text here appears in non-Java enabled browsers only.
</APPLET>
</BODY>
</HTML>
```

> NOTE: Whether or not case is relevant in the various applet tags such as `<APPLET>` depends on your system. Windows 95 and Solaris ignore case in HTML tags. The beta version of the applet viewer on the Macintosh only likes lowercase for all applet related HTML tags. (Case is relevant in identifying the name of the applet class.)

What follows are short discussions of the various attributes you can (or must) use following the `<APPLET>` tag in order to position your applet. (For those familiar with HTML, these tags are similar to those used with the <IMG> tag for image placement on a Web page.)

Applet Tags for Positioning

WIDTH, HEIGHT

These attributes are required and give the width and height of the applet, as measured in pixels. In the applet viewer, this is the initial size of the applet. You can resize any window that the applet viewer creates. In Netscape, you *cannot* resize the applet. You will need to make a good guess about how much space your applet requires to show up well for all users.

ALIGN

This attribute specifies the alignment of the applet. There are two basic choices. The applet can be a block, with text flowing around it. Or the applet can be *inline*, floating inside a line of text as if it were an oversized text character. The first two values (LEFT and RIGHT) make the text flow around the applet. The others make the applet flow with the text.

The choices are described as follows, and can be seen in Figure 8-3.

Attribute	What It does
LEFT	Places the applet at the left margin of the page. Text that follows on the page goes in the space to the right of the applet.
RIGHT	Places the applet at the right margin of the page. Text that follows on the page goes in the space to the left of the applet.
BOTTOM	Places the bottom of the applet at the bottom of the text in the current line.
TOP	Places the top of the applet with the top of the current line.

TEXTTOP	Places the top of the applet with the top of the text in the current line.
MIDDLE	Places the middle of the applet with the baseline of the current line.
ABSMIDDLE	Places the middle of the applet with the middle of the current line.
BASELINE	Places the bottom of the applet with the baseline of the current line.
ABSBOTTOM	Places the bottom of the applet with the bottom of the current line.

VSPACE, HSPACE

These optional attributes specify the number of pixels above and below the applet (VSPACE) and on each side of the applet (HSPACE).

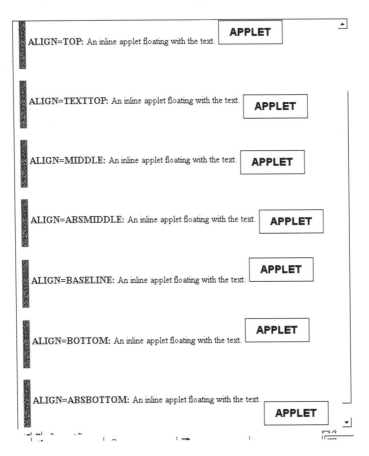

Figure 8-3: Applet alignment

The Applet Tags for Coding

There are four applet tags that work directly with the code you write; here are short descriptions of the first three. (The last one is for passing parameters to your applets; we take that up in the next section.)

CODE

This required tag gives the name of the applet's class (or compiled) file. This name is taken relative to where the current page was located. This could be either a local directory or a Net URL. You cannot use absolute path names here. For example, if you are reading a page in a directory called `C:\applets`, you can only use class files in this directory. (See the `CODEBASE` tag that we discuss next for how to get at the subdirectories of this directory.)

CODEBASE

This optional attribute tells Java that your class files are found below the directory where the current page is located. For example, if an applet called `FirstApplet.class` is in the directory `MyApplets`, and the `MyApplets` directory is *below* the current location, you would use:

```
<APPLET CODE="FirstApplet.class" CODEBASE="MyApplets" WIDTH=100
    HEIGHT=100>
```

NAME

This is a rare tag, but it is essential when you want two applets on the same page to communicate with each other. It specifies a name for the current applet instance. You would pass this string to the `getApplet` method of the `AppletContext` class if your browser permits inter-applet communication.

Embedding an Applet into a Web Page

Here is a fun and useful applet that calculates whether or not you are saving enough money for your retirement. You enter your age, how much money you save every month, and so on, as seen in Figure 8-4.

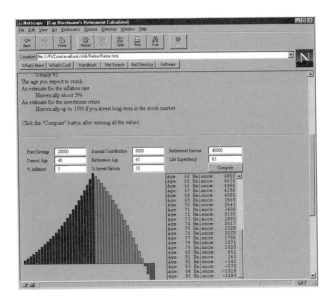

Figure 8-4: A retirement calculator

The text box and the graph show the balance of the retirement account for every year. If the numbers turn negative towards the later part of your life, and the bars in the graph turn red, you need to do something, for example, save more money or postpone your retirement. The surrounding Web page tells how to enter the information and how to interpret the outcome.

When you look at the code for the applet in Example 8-2, you will find that it is almost identical to the code for the graphical applications that we discussed in the last two chapters. There are two differences. We derive from `Applet`, not `Frame`. And we move the code from the `main` function and the constructor into the `init` method.

Example 8-2: Retire.java

```java
import java.awt.*;
import java.applet.*;
import java.io.*;
import corejava.*;

public class Retire extends Applet
{  public void init()
   {  GridBagLayout gbl = new GridBagLayout();
      setLayout(gbl);

      GridBagConstraints gbc = new GridBagConstraints();
      gbc.fill = GridBagConstraints.BOTH;
```

```
        gbc.weightx = 100;
        gbc.weighty = 100;
        add(new Label("Prior Savings"), gbl, gbc, 0, 0, 1, 1);
        add(savingsField, gbl, gbc, 1, 0, 1, 1);
        add(new Label("Annual Contribution"),
            gbl, gbc, 2, 0, 1, 1);
        add(contribField, gbl, gbc, 3, 0, 1, 1);
        add(new Label("Retirement Income"),
            gbl, gbc, 4, 0, 1, 1);
        add(incomeField, gbl, gbc, 5, 0, 1, 1);
        add(new Label("Current Age"), gbl, gbc, 0, 1, 1, 1);
        add(currentAgeField, gbl, gbc, 1, 1, 1, 1);
        add(new Label("Retirement Age"), gbl, gbc, 2, 1, 1, 1);
        add(retireAgeField, gbl, gbc, 3, 1, 1, 1);
        add(new Label("Life Expectancy"), gbl, gbc, 4, 1, 1, 1);
        add(deathAgeField, gbl, gbc, 5, 1, 1, 1);
        add(new Label("% Inflation"), gbl, gbc, 0, 2, 1, 1);
        add(inflationPercentField, gbl, gbc, 1, 2, 1, 1);
        add(new Label("% Invest Return"), gbl, gbc, 2, 2, 1, 1);
        add(investPercentField, gbl, gbc, 3, 2, 1, 1);
        add(new Button("Compute"), gbl, gbc, 5, 2, 1, 1);
        add(retireCanvas, gbl, gbc, 0, 3, 4, 1);
        add(retireText, gbl, gbc, 4, 3, 2, 1);
        retireText.setEditable(false);
        retireText.setFont(new Font("Courier", Font.PLAIN, 10));
    }

    private void add(Component c, GridBagLayout gbl,
        GridBagConstraints gbc, int x, int y, int w, int h)
    {   gbc.gridx = x;
        gbc.gridy = y;
        gbc.gridwidth = w;
        gbc.gridheight = h;
        gbl.setConstraints(c, gbc);
        add(c);
    }

    public boolean action(Event evt, Object arg)
    {   if (arg.equals("Compute"))
        {   if (savingsField.isValid()
                && contribField.isValid()
                && incomeField.isValid()
                && currentAgeField.isValid()
                && retireAgeField.isValid()
                && deathAgeField.isValid()
                && inflationPercentField.isValid()
                && investPercentField.isValid())
            {   RetireInfo info = new RetireInfo();
                info.savings = savingsField.getValue();
```

```
                  info.contrib = contribField.getValue();
                  info.income = incomeField.getValue();
                  info.currentAge = currentAgeField.getValue();
                  info.retireAge = retireAgeField.getValue();
                  info.deathAge = deathAgeField.getValue();
                  info.inflationPercent
                     = inflationPercentField.getValue();
                  info.investPercent
                     = investPercentField.getValue();
                  retireCanvas.redraw(info);
                  int i;
                  retireText.setText("");
                  for (i = info.currentAge; i <= info.deathAge; i++)
                  {  retireText.appendText(
                        new Format("Age: %3d").form(i)
                           + new Format(" Balance: %8d\n")
                           .form(info.getBalance(i)));
                  }
               }
            }
         }
         else return super.action(evt, arg);
         return true;
      }

   private IntTextField savingsField
      = new IntTextField(0, 0, 10000000, 10);
   private IntTextField contribField
      = new IntTextField(9000, 0, 1000000, 10);
   private IntTextField incomeField
      = new IntTextField(0, 0, 1000000, 10);
   private IntTextField currentAgeField
      = new IntTextField(0, 0, 150, 4);
   private IntTextField retireAgeField
      = new IntTextField(65, 0, 150, 4);
   private IntTextField deathAgeField
      = new IntTextField(85, 0, 150, 4);
   private IntTextField inflationPercentField
      = new IntTextField(5, 0, 1000, 4);
   private IntTextField investPercentField
      = new IntTextField(10, 0, 1000, 4);
   private RetireCanvas retireCanvas = new RetireCanvas();
   private TextArea retireText = new TextArea(10, 25);
}

class RetireInfo
{  int getBalance(int year)
   {  if (year < currentAge) return 0;
      else if (year == currentAge)
      {  age = year;
```

```
            balance = savings;
            return balance;
         }
         else if (year == age)
            return balance;
         if (year != age + 1)
            getBalance(year - 1);
         age = year;
         if (age < retireAge)
            balance += contrib;
         else
            balance -= income;
         balance = (int)(balance
            * (1 + (investPercent - inflationPercent) / 100.0));
         return balance;
      }

      int savings;
      int contrib;
      int income;
      int currentAge;
      int retireAge;
      int deathAge;
      int inflationPercent;
      int investPercent;

      private int age;
      private int balance;
}

class RetireCanvas extends Canvas
{   RetireCanvas()
    {   resize(400, 200);
    }
    void redraw(RetireInfo newInfo)
    {   info = newInfo;
        repaint();
    }

    public void paint(Graphics g)
    {   if (info == null) return;

        int minValue = 0;
        int maxValue = 0;
        int i;
        for (i = info.currentAge; i <= info.deathAge; i++)
        {   int v = info.getBalance(i);
            if (minValue > v) minValue = v;
            if (maxValue < v) maxValue = v;
        }
```

```
        if (maxValue == minValue) return;

        Dimension d = size();
        int barWidth = d.width / (info.deathAge
            - info.currentAge + 1);
        double scale = (double)d.height
            / (maxValue - minValue);

        for (i = info.currentAge; i <= info.deathAge; i++)
        {   int x1 = (i - info.currentAge) * barWidth + 1;
            int y1;
            int v = info.getBalance(i);
            int height;
            int yOrigin = (int)(maxValue * scale);

            if (v >= 0)
            {   y1 = (int)((maxValue - v) * scale);
                height = yOrigin - y1;
            }
            else
            {   y1 = yOrigin;
                height = (int)(-v * scale);
            }

            if (i < info.retireAge)
                g.setColor(Color.blue);
            else if (v >= 0)
                g.setColor(Color.green);
            else
                g.setColor(Color.red);
            g.fillRect(x1, y1, barWidth - 2, height);
            g.setColor(Color.black);
            g.drawRect(x1, y1, barWidth - 2, height);
        }
    }

    private RetireInfo info = null;
}
```

Passing Information to Applets

Just as applications have the ability to use command line information, applets
have the ability to use parameters that are embedded in the HTML file. This is
done via the HTML tag PARAM. For example, suppose you want to let the Web
page determine the size of the font to use in your applet. You could use the following HTML tags:

```
<APPLET CODE="FontTestApplet.class" WIDTH = 200, HEIGHT = 200>
<PARAM NAME=font VALUE="Helvetica">
</APPLET>
```

You then pick up the value of the parameter using the `getParameter` method of the `Applet` class, as in the following example of a `paint` procedure:

```
import java.applet.*;
import java.awt.*;

public class FontTestApplet extends Applet
{  public void paint(Graphics g)
    { String fontName = getParameter("font");
      Font f = new Font(fontName, Font.BOLD, 18);
      g.setFont(f);
      g.drawString("We won't use 'hello world.'", 25, 50);
    }
}
```

Parameters are always returned as strings. You need to convert the string to a numeric type if that is what is called for. You do this in the standard ways: either by using the appropriate method, such as `parseInt` of the `Integer` class, or by using methods such as `atof` in our `Format` class.

For example, if we wanted to add a size parameter for the font, then the HTML code might look like this:

```
<APPLET CODE="FontTestApplet.class" WIDTH = 200 HEIGHT = 200>
<PARAM NAME=font VALUE="Helvetica">
<PARAM NAME=size VALUE="24">
</APPLET>
```

The following source code shows how to read the integer parameter.

```
import java.awt.*;
import java.applet.*;

 public class FontTestApplet extends Applet
{  public void paint(Graphics g)
    {  String fontName = getParameter("font");
       int fontSize = Integer.parseInt(getParameter("size"));
       Font f = new Font(fontName, Font.BOLD, fontSize);
       g.setFont(f);
       g.drawString("We won't use 'hello world.'", 25, 50);
    }
}
```

NOTE: The strings used when you define the parameters via the PARAM tag and those used in the `getParameter` method must match exactly. In particular, both are case sensitive.

In addition to assuring that the parameters match in your code, you should find out whether or not the `sizeString` parameter was left out. You do this with a simple test for `null`. For example:

```
int fontsize;
String sizeString = getParameter("size");
if (sizeString ==null) fontSize = 12;
else fontSize = Integer.parseInt(sizeString);
```

Here is a useful applet that uses parameters extensively. The applet draws a bar chart, shown in Figure 8-5.

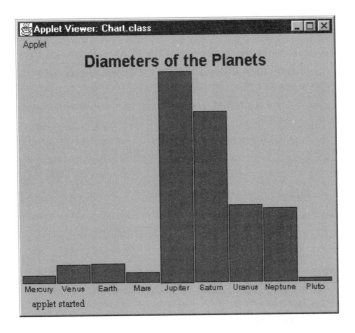

Figure 8-5: A chart applet

The applet takes the labels and the heights of the bars from the PARAM values in the HTML file. Here is what the HTML file for Figure 8-4 looks like:

```
<APPLET CODE="Chart.class" WIDTH=400 HEIGHT=300>
<PARAM NAME="title" VALUE="Diameters of the Planets">
<PARAM NAME="values" VALUE="9">
<PARAM NAME="name_1" VALUE="Mercury">
```

```
<PARAM NAME="name_2"  VALUE="Venus">
<PARAM NAME="name_3"  VALUE="Earth">
<PARAM NAME="name_4"  VALUE="Mars">
<PARAM NAME="name_5"  VALUE="Jupiter">
<PARAM NAME="name_6"  VALUE="Saturn">
<PARAM NAME="name_7"  VALUE="Uranus">
<PARAM NAME="name_8"  VALUE="Neptune">
<PARAM NAME="name_9"  VALUE="Pluto">
<PARAM NAME="value_1"  VALUE="3100">
<PARAM NAME="value_2"  VALUE="7500">
<PARAM NAME="value_3"  VALUE="8000">
<PARAM NAME="value_4"  VALUE="4200">
<PARAM NAME="value_5"  VALUE="88000">
<PARAM NAME="value_6"  VALUE="71000">
<PARAM NAME="value_7"  VALUE="32000">
<PARAM NAME="value_8"  VALUE="30600">
<PARAM NAME="value_9"  VALUE="1430">
</APPLET>
```

You could have set up an array of strings and an array of numbers in the applet. But there are two advantages to using the PARAM mechanism instead. You can have multiple copies of the same applet on your Web page, showing different graphs: just put two APPLET tags with different sets of parameters on the page. And you can change the data that you want to chart. Admittedly, the diameters of the planets will stay the same for quite some time, but suppose your Web page contains a chart of weekly sales data. It is easy to update the Web page, because it is plain text. Editing and recompiling a Java file on a weekly basis is more tedious.

In fact, someone has probably figured out how to do fancier graphs than the one in our chart applet. If you find one, you can drop it into your Web page and feed it parameters without ever needing to know how the applet renders the graphs.

Example 8-3 is the source code of our chart applet. Note that the `init` method reads the parameters, and the `paint` method draws the chart.

Example 8-3: Chart.java

```
import java.awt.*;
import java.applet.*;
import java.io.*;
import corejava.*;

public class Chart extends Applet
{

    public void init()
```

```
{   int n = Format.atoi(getParameter("values"));
    values = new double[n];
    names = new String[n];
    title = getParameter("title");
    int i;
    for (i = 0; i < n; i++)
    {   values[i]
            = Format.atof(getParameter("value_" + (i + 1)));
        names[i] = getParameter("name_" + (i + 1));
    }
}

public void paint(Graphics g)
{   int i;
    int n = Format.atoi(getParameter("values"));
    double minValue = 0;
    double maxValue = 0;
    for (i = 0; i < values.length; i++)
    {   if (minValue > values[i]) minValue = values[i];
        if (maxValue < values[i]) maxValue = values[i];
    }

    Dimension d = size();
    Insets in = insets();
    int clientWidth = d.width - in.right - in.left;
    int clientHeight = d.height - in.bottom - in.top;
    int barWidth = clientWidth / n;

    Font titleFont = new Font("Helvetica", Font.BOLD, 20);
    FontMetrics titleFontMetrics
        = g.getFontMetrics(titleFont);
    Font labelFont = new Font("Helvetica", Font.PLAIN, 10);
    FontMetrics labelFontMetrics
        = g.getFontMetrics(labelFont);

    int titleWidth = titleFontMetrics.stringWidth(title);
    int y = titleFontMetrics.getAscent();
    int x = (clientWidth - titleWidth) / 2;
    g.setFont(titleFont);
    g.drawString(title, x, y);

    int top = titleFontMetrics.getHeight();
    int bottom = labelFontMetrics.getHeight();
    if (maxValue == minValue) return;
    double scale = (clientHeight - top - bottom)
        / (maxValue - minValue);
    y = clientHeight - labelFontMetrics.getDescent();
    g.setFont(labelFont);

    for (i = 0; i < n; i++)
```

```
      {   int x1 = i * barWidth + 1;
          int y1 = top;
          int height = (int)(values[i] * scale);
          if (values[i] >= 0)
              y1 += (int)((maxValue - values[i]) * scale);
          else
          {   y1 += (int)(maxValue * scale);
              height = -height;
          }

          g.setColor(Color.red);
          g.fillRect(x1, y1, barWidth - 2, height);
          g.setColor(Color.black);
          g.drawRect(x1, y1, barWidth - 2, height);
          int labelWidth
              = labelFontMetrics.stringWidth(names[i]);
          x = i * barWidth + (barWidth - labelWidth) / 2;
          g.drawString(names[i], x, y);
      }
   }
   private double [] values;
   private string [] names;
   private string title;
}
```

`java.applet.Applet`

- `public String getParameter(String name)`

  This gets a parameter defined with a PARAM directive in the Web page loading the applet. The string is case sensitive.

- `public String getAppletInfo()`

  This is a method that many applet authors override to return a string that contains information about the author, version, and copyright of the current applet. You need to create this information by overriding this method in your applet class.

- `public String[][] getParameterInfo()`

  This is a method that many applet authors override to return an array of PARAM tag options that this applet supports. Each row contains three entries: the name, the type, and a description of the parameter. Here is an example:

```
"fps", "1-10", "frames per second"
"repeat", "boolean", "repeat image loop?"
"images", "url", "directory containing images"
```

Dialog Boxes in Applets

An applet sits embedded in a Web page, in a frame of a size that is fixed by the WIDTH and HEIGHT values in the APPLET tag of the HTML page. This can be quite limiting. Many programmers wonder whether or not they can have a pop-up dialog box or menus to make better use of the available space. It is, indeed, possible to create a pop-up dialog box. Here is a simple applet with a single button labeled "Calculator." When you click on the button, a calculator pops up in a separate window.

This is easy to do. We simply use the `Calculator` class from Chapter 7. Recall that it is derived from `Frame`, so we add the necessary code to create a new calculator object as indicated by the bold line of the following code.

```
class PopupCalculatorApplet extends Applet
{  public void init()
    {  add(new Button("Calculator"));
    }

    public boolean action(Event evt, Object arg)
    {  if (arg.equals("Calculator"))
        {  if (calc.isShowing()) calc.hide();
          else calc.show();
        }
       else return super.action(evt, arg);
       return true;
    }

    Frame calc = new Calculator();
}
```

When you click on the calculator button, the dialog box pops up and floats over the Web page. When you click on the button again, the calculator goes away.

There is, however, a catch that you need to know about before you put this applet on your Web page. To see how the calculator looks to a potential user, load the Web page from a file URL (for example, by making a bookmark to it, exiting and restarting Netscape, and then opening the bookmark). The calculator will be surrounded by a border with an ominous warning message (see Figure 8-6).

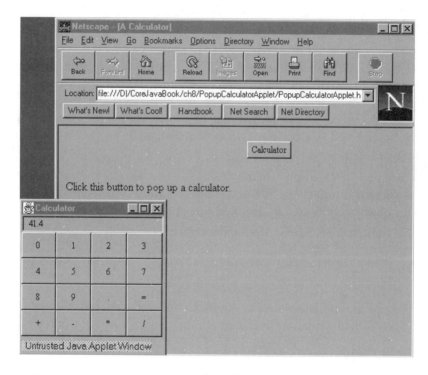

Figure 8-6: A popup window inside a browser

This is a security feature of Netscape. Netscape wants to make sure that your applet does not launch a window that the user might mistake for a local application. It does this regardless of the fact that it would take a super-human effort to write AWT code that even remotely resembles a professional Windows program. The fear is that if such a feat could be done, an unsuspecting user could visit a Web page, which automatically launches the applets on it, and mistakenly type in a password or credit card number, which the applet would send back to its host.

To avoid any possibility of shenanigans like this, all pop-up windows launched by an applet bear the "Untrusted Java Applet" label. (Netscape 3 uses "Unauthenticated Java Applet" instead.) That label is likely to be so scary to most users that you may want to avoid launching any external frames from your applet.

By the way, an applet inside a Web page cannot have menus. But a frame spawned by the Web page can have a menu bar. Of course, such a frame still has a warning border.

> NOTE: The warning label is applied only if the Web page is loaded through a URL, not if you load it through the File | Open File dialog.

Multimedia

URLs

A URL is really nothing more than a description of a resource on the Internet. For example, `"http://java.sun.com"` tells the browser to use the hypertext transfer protocol on the file located at `java.sun.com`. Java has the class `URL` that encapsulates URLs. The simplest way to make a URL is to give a string to the URL constructor:

```
URL u = new URL("http://java.sun.com");
```

This is called an *absolute* URL because we specify the entire resource name. Another useful URL constructor is a *relative* URL.

```
URL data = new URL(u, "data/planets.dat");
```

This specifies the file `planets.dat`, located in the data subdirectory of the URL `u`.

Both constructors make sure that you have used the correct syntax for a URL. If you haven't, they cause a run time error, a so-called `MalformedURLException`. Up to now, you have been able to ignore most run time errors, but this error is one the compiler will not let you ignore. You must tell the compiler that you are prepared for the error condition. The relevant code is as follows:

```
try
{   String s = "http://java.sun.com";
    URL u = new URL(s);
      . . .
}
catch(MalformedURLException e)
{   // deal with error
    System.out.println("Error " + e);
}
```

We will discuss this syntax for dealing with exceptions in detail in Chapter 10. For now, if you see code like this in one of our code samples, just gloss over the `try` and `catch` keywords.

A common way of obtaining a URL is to ask an applet where it came from, in particular,

*   What is the URL of the page that is calling it?

*   What is the URL of the applet itself?

To find the former, use the `getDocumentBase` method; to find the latter, use `getCodeBase`. You do not need to place these calls in a `try` block.

Obtaining Multimedia Files

You can retrieve images and audio files with the `getImage` and `getAudioClip` methods.

```
Image cat = getImage(getDocumentBase(), "images/cat.gif");
AudioClip meow = getAudioClip(getDocumentBase(),
    "audio/meow.au");
```

Here we use the `getDocumentBase` method that returns the URL from which your applet is loaded. The second argument to the URL constructor specifies where the image or audio clip is located, relative to the base document.

Once you have the images and audio clips, what can you do with them? You saw in Chapter 6 how to display a single image. In Chapter 12, you will see how to play an animation sequence composed of multiple images. To play an audio clip, simply invoke its `play` method.

You can also call `play` without first loading the audio clip.

```
play(getDocumentBase(), "audio/meow.au");
```

But, to show an image, you must first load it.

java.net.URL

- `URL(String name)`

  creates a URL object from a string describing an absolute URL.

- `URL(URL base, String name)`

  creates a relative URL object. If the string `name` describes an absolute URL, then the `base` URL is ignored. Otherwise, it is interpreted as a relative directory from the base URL.

java.applet.Applet

- `public URL getDocumentBase()`

  gets the URL for the page that contains the applet.

- `public URL getCodeBase()`

  gets the URL of the applet code itself.

- void play(URL url)
- void play(URL url, String name)

The first form plays an audio file specified by the URL. The second form uses the string to provide a path relative to the URL in the first argument. Nothing happens if the audio clip cannot be found.

- AudioClip getAudioClip(URL url)
- AudioClip getAudioClip(URL url, String name)

gets an audio clip, given a URL. The second form uses the string to provide a path relative to the URL in the first argument. The function returns null if the audio clip cannot be found.

- Image getImage(URL url)
- Image getImage(URL url, String name)

gets an image, given a URL. This method always returns an image object immediately, even if the image does not exist. The actual image data are loaded when the image is first displayed. See Chapter 6 for details on image acquisition.

The Applet Context

Locating the Ambient Browser

An applet runs inside a browser such as Netscape or the applet viewer. An applet can ask the browser to do things for it, for example, to fetch an audio clip, show a short message in the status line, or show a different Web page. The ambient browser can carry out these requests, or it can ignore them. For example, if an applet running inside the applet viewer asks the applet viewer program to show a Web page, nothing happens.

To communicate with the browser, an applet calls the getAppletContext method. That method returns an object of type AppletContext.

Inter-Applet Communication

A Web page can contain more than one applet. If a Web page contains multiple applets, they can communicate with each other. Naturally, this is an advanced technique that you probably will not need very often. Furthermore, since a security hole was discovered in the implementation of the Java virtual machine when it services multiple applets, Netscape 3.0 has deactivated this feature.

If you give NAME tags to each applet in the HTML file, you can use the getApplet(String) method of the AppletContext class to get a reference to the applet. For example, if your HTML file contains the tag

```
<APPLET CODE="Chart.class" WIDTH=100 HEIGHT=100 NAME="Chart1">
```

then the call

```
Applet chart1 = getAppletContext().getApplet("Chart1");
```

gives you a reference to the applet. What can you do with the reference? Provided you give the `Chart` class a method to accept new data and redraw the chart, you can call it by making the appropriate cast.

```
((Chart)chart1).setData(3, "Earth", 9000);
```

You can also list all applets on a Web page, whether or not they have a NAME tag. The `getApplets` method returns a so-called *enumeration object*. (You will learn more about enumeration objects in Chapter 9.) Here is a loop that prints the class names of all applets on the current page.

```
Enumeration e = getAppletContext().getApplets();
while (e.hasMoreElements())
{  Object a = e.nextElement();
   System.out.println(a.getClass().getName());
}
```

An applet cannot communicate with an applet on a different Web page.

Displaying Items in the Browser

You have access to two areas of the ambient browsers: the status line and the Web page display area. Both use methods of the `AppletContext` class.

You can display a string in the status line at the bottom of the browser with the `showStatus` message, for example

```
getAppletContext().showStatus("Loading data . . . please wait");
```

TIP: In our experience, `showStatus` is of limited use. The browser is also using the status line, and more often than not it will overwrite your precious message with chatter like `"Applet running"`. Use the status line for fluff messages like `"loading data . . . please wait"`, but not for something that the user cannot afford to miss.

You can tell the browser to show a different Web page with the `showDocument` method. There are several ways to do this. The simplest is with a call to `showDocument` with one argument, the URL you want to show.

```
URL u = new URL("http://java.sun.com");
getAppletContext().showDocument(u);
```

The problem with this call is that it opens the new Web page in the same window as your current page, thereby displacing your applet. To return to your applet, the user must select Back.

You can tell the browser to show the applet in another window by giving a second parameter in the call to showDocument. The second argument is a string. If it is the special string "_blank", the browser opens a new window with the document, instead of displacing the current document. More importantly, if you take advantage of the Netscape frame feature, you can split a browser window into multiple frames, each of which has a name. You can put your applet into one frame and have it show documents in other frames. We will discuss this in detail in the next section.

Table 8-2 shows all possible arguments to showDocument.

Table 8-2: ShowDocument arguments

Second Parameter to showDocument	Location
"_self" or none	Show the document in the current frame.
"_parent"	Show the document in the parent container.
"_top"	Show the document in the topmost frame.
"_blank"	Show in new, unnamed top-level window.
any other string	Show in the frame with that name.

A Bookmark Applet

This applet takes advantage of the frames feature in Netscape. The screen is tiled into two frames. The left frame contains a Java applet that shows a list of bookmarks. When you double-click on any of the bookmarks in the list, the corresponding Web page, like that shown in Figure 8-7 is displayed in the frame on the right.

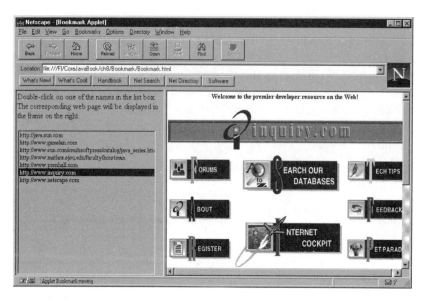

Figure 8-7: A bookmark applet

Frames are a new HTML feature, and you may not have seen the relevant tags. Here is the HTML file (on the CD as well) that defines the frames.

```
<HTML>
<HEAD>
<TITLE>Bookmark Applet</TITLE>
</HEAD>
<FRAMESET COLS="320,*">
<FRAME NAME="left" SRC="Left.html" MARGINHEIGHT=2 MARGINWIDTH=2
    SCROLLING = "no" NORESIZE>
<FRAME NAME="right" SRC="Right.html" MARGINHEIGHT=2 MARGINWIDTH=2
    SCROLLING = "yes" NORESIZE>
</FRAMESET>
</HTML>
```

We will not go over the exact syntax elements. What is important is that each frame has two essential features: a name (given by the NAME tag) and a URL (given by the SRC tag). We could not think of any good names for the frames, so we simply named them "left" and "right".

The left frame loads a file that we called Left.html, which loads the applet into the left frame. It simply specifies the applets and the bookmarks. You can customize this file for your own Web page by changing the bookmarks.

```
<HTML>
<TITLE>A Bookmark Applet</TITLE>
<BODY>
Double-click on one of the names in the list box. The correspond-
ing web page will be displayed in the frame on the right.
<P>
<APPLET CODE="Bookmark.class" WIDTH=290 HEIGHT=300>
<PARAM NAME=link_1 VALUE="http://java.sun.com">
<PARAM NAME=link_2 VALUE="http://www.gamelan.com">
<PARAM NAME=link_3 VALUE
    ="http://www.sun.com/smi/ssoftpress/catalog/java_series.html">
<PARAM NAME=link_4
VALUE="http://www.mathcs.sjsu.edu/faculty/horstman">
<PARAM NAME=link_5 VALUE="http://www.prenhall.com">
<PARAM NAME=link_6 VALUE="http://www.inquiry.com">
<PARAM NAME=link_7 VALUE="http://www.netscape.com">
</APPLET>
</BODY>
</HTML>
```

The right frame loads a dummy file that we called Right.html. (Netscape did not approve when we left the right frame blank, so we gave it a dummy file for starters.)

```
<HTML>
<TITLE>
Web pages will be displayed here.
</TITLE>
<BODY>
Double-click on one of the names in the list box to the left. The
web page will be displayed here.
</BODY>
</HTML>
```

The bookmark applet in Example 8-4 is extremely simple. It reads the values of the parameters link_1, link_2, and so on into the list box. When you double-click on one of the items in the list box, the showDocument method displays it in the right frame.

Example 8-4: Bookmark.java

```java
import java.awt.*;
import java.applet.*;
import java.net.*;
import java.io.*;

public class Bookmark extends Applet
{   public void init()
    {   setLayout(new BorderLayout());
        add("Center", links);
        int i = 1;
        String s;
        while ((s = getParameter("link_" + i)) != null)
        {   links.addItem(s);
            i++;
        }
    }

    public boolean action(Event evt, Object arg)
    {   if (evt.target == links)
        {   try
            {   AppletContext context = getAppletContext();
                URL u = new URL((String)arg);
                context.showDocument(u, "right");
            } catch(Exception e)
            {   showStatus("Error " + e);
            }
        }
        else return super.action(evt, arg);
        return true;
    }

    private List links = new List(10, false);
}
```

 `java.applet.Applet`

- `public AppletContext getAppletContext()`

  This gives you a handle on the applet's browser environment. On most browsers, you can use this information to control the browser in which the applet is running.

java.applet.AppletContext

- void showStatus(String msg)

    shows the string specified in the status line of the browser.

- Enumeration getApplets()

    returns an enumeration (see Chapter 9) of all the applets in the same context, that is, the same Web page.

- Applet getApplet(String name)

    returns the applet in the current context with the given name; returns null if none exists. Only the current Web page is searched.

- void showDocument(URL url)
- void showDocument(URL url, String target)

    These calls show a new Web page in a frame in the browser. In the first form, the new page displaces the current page. The second form uses the string to identify the target frame. The target string can be one of the following: "_self" (show in current frame, equivalent to the first form of the method), "_parent" (show in parent frame), "_top" (show in topmost frame), and "_blank" (show in new, unnamed top-level window). Or it can be the name of a frame.

NOTE: Not every browser will accept these commands. For example, Sun's applet viewer does not show Web pages. The second form of the method requires that the browser support Netscape 2.0-style frames.

- Image getImage(URL url)

    returns an image object that encapsulates the image specified by the URL. If the image does not exist, this immediately returns null. Otherwise, a separate thread is launched to load the image. See Chapter 6 for details on image acquisition.

- AudioClip getAudioClip(URL url)

    returns an AudioClip object, which stores the sound file specified by the URL. Use the play method to actually play the file.

The Life Cycle of an Applet

There are four methods in the `Applet` class that give you the framework on which you build any serious applet: `init()`, `start()`, `stop()`, `destroy()`. We want to show you when these methods are called and what code you should place into them.

init

This method is used for whatever initializations are needed for your applet. This works much like a constructor—it is automatically called by the system when Java launches the applet for the first time. Common actions in an applet include processing PARAM values and adding user-interface components.

Applets can have a default constructor, but it is customary to perform all initialization in the `init` method, instead of the default constructor.

start

This method is automatically called *after* Java calls the `init` method. It is also called whenever the user returns to the page containing the applet after having gone off to other pages. This means that the `start` method can be called repeatedly, unlike the `init` method. For this reason, put the code that you want executed only once in the `init` method, rather than in the `start` method. For example, the `start` method is where you usually restart a thread for your applet, for example, to resume an animation. We will look at an example of this later in this section.

If your applet does nothing that needs to be suspended when the user leaves the current Web page, you do not need to implement this method (or the `stop` method described next).

stop

This method is automatically called when the user moves off the page on which the applet sits. It can, therefore, be called repeatedly in the same applet. The purpose is to give you a chance to stop a time-consuming activity from slowing down the system when the user is not paying attention to the applet. You should not call this method directly. If your applet does not perform animation, play audio files, or perform calculations in a thread, you do not usually need to use this method.

destroy

Unlike the `finalize` method for objects, Java is guaranteed to call this method when the browser shuts down normally. Since applets are meant to live on an HTML page, you do not need to worry about destroying the panel. This will happen automatically when the browser shuts down. What you *do* need to put in the `destroy` method is the code for reclaiming any non-memory dependent resources such as window handles that you may have consumed. (Of course, Java calls the `stop` method before calling the `destroy` method if the applet is still active.)

A Web-Crawler Applet

You do not yet know how to write a program that works with threads, but because threads are so common in sophisticated applets, we want to give you one example in this chapter. We will simply explain the general mechanism here, and you should turn to Chapter 12 for the details.

This example is similar to the bookmark example, except that the applet does something useful while you are admiring the Web page in Figure 8-8.

1. It opens the Web pages whose URLs are in the list box in the left-hand side, one by one, without displaying them.

2. It then searches through the HTML tags for links to other Web pages.

3. Whenever it finds a link, it adds it to the list box.

   (Such a program is usually called a *Web crawler.*)

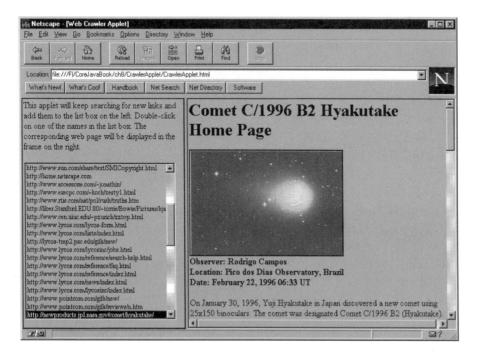

Figure 8-8: A web crawler applet

The Web crawler relentlessly fills the list box with more and more URLs until you go to another Web page; then it temporarily stops. That is as it should be—the applet should not occupy machine and network resources if you are not using it. When you return to the Web page containing the applet, it resumes its crawling activity.

As we said, we do not want to get into the details about threads and the Runnable interface here (see Chapter 12 for more details). Suffice to say:

1.   A thread represents a separate task that your computer can be asked to do.

2.   A thread can be suspended and restarted.

This is exactly what happens in our Web-crawler applet's start and stop methods, as shown here.

```
class CrawlerApplet extends Applet implements Runnable
{   . . .


    public void start()
    {   if (runner != null && runner.isAlive())
            runner.resume();
        else if (runner == null)
        {   runner = new Thread (this);
            runner.start();

        }
    }

    public void stop()
    {   if (runner != null && runner.isAlive())
            runner.suspend();
    }

    Thread runner;
}
```

Example 8-5 is the complete program. The file-search code is not difficult. We get an input stream from a URL with the openStream method. The read method of the input stream yields the contents of the HTML page a character at a time. The Searcher class looks for HTML tags of the form
<A HREF="http://. . .">.

Example 8-5: CrawlerApplet.java

```
import java.awt.*;
import java.applet.*;
import java.net.*;
import java.io.*;
import java.util.*;
```

```java
public class CrawlerApplet extends Applet implements Runnable
{  public void init()
   {  setLayout(new BorderLayout());
      add("Center", links);
       int i = 1;
      String s;
      while ((s = getParameter("link_" + i)) != null)
      {  links.addItem(s);
         i++;
      }
   }

   public boolean action(Event evt, Object arg)
   {  if (evt.target == links)
      {  try
         {  AppletContext context = getAppletContext();
            URL u = new URL((String)arg);
            context.showDocument(u, "right");
         } catch(Exception e)
         {  showStatus("Error " + e);
         }
      }
      else return super.action(evt, arg);
      return true;
   }

   private void add(String s)
   {  int i;
      for (i = 0; i < links.countItems(); i++)
          if (links.getItem(i).equals(s)) return;
      links.addItem(s);
      repaint();
   }

   public void search(String s)
   {  if (s == null) return;
      try
      {  AppletContext context = getAppletContext();
         URL u = new URL(s);
         showStatus("Opening " + s);
         InputStream input = u.openStream();
         showStatus("Opened " + s);
         Searcher search = new Searcher(input);
         String name;
         while ((name = search.nextURL()) != null)
             add(name);
         input.close();
         showStatus("Done");
      } catch(Exception e)
```

```
          {   showStatus("Error " + e);
          }
      }

      public void run()
      {   while (current < links.countItems())
          {   String s = links.getItem(current);
              current++;
              search(s);
              runner.yield();
          }
      }

      public void stop()
      {   if (runner != null && runner.isAlive())
              runner.suspend();
      }

      public void start()
      {   if (runner == null)
          {   runner = new Thread(this);
              runner.setPriority(Thread.MIN_PRIORITY);
              runner.start();
          }
          else if (runner.isAlive())
              runner.resume();
      }

      private Thread runner = null;
      private List links = new List(10, false);
      private int current = 0;
  }

class Searcher
{   public Searcher(InputStream input) { is = input; }

    public String nextURL()
    {   while (true)
        {   boolean ok = skipUntil('<');
            if (!ok) return null;
            String s = getUntil('>');
            if (s.length() == 0) return null;
            if (s.length() >= 6 &&
                s.substring(0, 6).toLowerCase().equals("a href"))
            {   int from = s.indexOf("\"");
                if (from >= 0)
                {   int to = s.indexOf("\"", from + 1);
                    if (to > 0)
```

```
            {  s = s.substring(from + 1, to);
               if (s.startsWith("http://"))
               {  return s;
               }
            }
         }
      }
   }
}

private boolean skipUntil(char ch)
{  try
   {  while (true)
      {  int nextch = is.read();
         if (nextch == -1) return false;
         if ((char)nextch == ch) return true;
      }
   } catch(IOException e)
   {  return false;
   }
}

private String getUntil(char ch)
{  String s = "";
   try
   {  while (true)
      {  int nextch = is.read();
         if (nextch == -1 || (char)nextch == ch) return s;
         else s = s + (char)nextch;
      }

   } catch(IOException e)
   {  return s;
   }
}

private InputStream is;
}
```

`java.applet.Applet`

- `void start()`

   Override this method for code that needs to be executed *every time* the user visits the browser page containing this applet. A typical action is to reactivate a thread.

- void stop()

    Override this method for code that needs to be executed *every time* the user leaves the browser page containing this applet. A typical action is to suspend a thread.

- void destroy()

    Override this method for code that needs to be executed when the user exits the browser. A typical action is to call destroy on system objects.

`java.net.URL`

- InputStream openStream()

    opens an input stream from which the raw data in the URL can be read. Normally, we pass URLs on to showDocument, getAudioClip, or getImage. But, in the case of the Web crawler, we actually look inside the text of the Web pages.

It's an Applet. It's an Application. It's Both!

Quite a few years ago, a "Saturday Night Live" skit poking fun at a television commercial showed a couple arguing about a white, gelatinous substance. The husband said, "It's a dessert topping." The wife said, "It's a floor wax." And the announcer concluded triumphantly, "It's both!"

Well, in this section we will show you how to write a Java program that is *both* an applet and an application. That is, you can load the program with the applet viewer or Netscape, or you can start it from the command line with the java interpreter. We are not sure how often this comes up—we found it interesting that this could be done at all and thought you would, too.

The screen shots in Figure 8-9 show the *same* program, launched from the command line as an application and viewed inside the applet viewer as an applet.

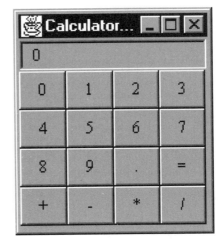

Figure 8-9: The calculator as an applet and an application

Let us see how this can be done. Every class file has exactly one public class. In order for the applet viewer to launch it, that class must derive from `Applet`. In order for `java` to start the application, it must have a static `main` method. So far, we have

```
class AppletApplication extends Applet
{  public void init() { . . . }
     . . .
     static public void main(String[] args) { . . . }
}
```

What can we put into `main`? Normally, we make an object of the class and invoke `show` on it. But this case is not so simple. You cannot show a naked applet. The applet must be placed inside a frame. And once it is inside the frame, its `init` method needs to be called.

To provide a frame, we create the class `AppletFrame`, like this:

```
public class AppletFrame extends Frame
{  AppletFrame(Applet a, int x, int y)
   {  setTitle(a.getClass().getName());
      resize(x, y);
      add("Center", a);
      a.init();
      show();
      a.start();
   }
```

```
public boolean handleEvent(Event evt)
{  if (evt.id == Event.WINDOW_DESTROY)
   {  System.exit(0);
   }
   return super.handleEvent(evt);
}
}
```

The constructor of the frame puts the applet (which derives from `Panel`) inside the frame, calls the `init` function, calls `show` (to show the frame) and then starts the applet. The frame also supplies a handler to close the program when the user closes the window.

In the `main` method of the applet/application, we make a new frame of this kind. In this example, we just reuse the calculator.

```
class AppletApplication extends Applet
{  . . .
   public static void main(String args[])
   {  new AppletFrame(new AppletApplication(), 620, 400);
   }
}
```

There is one catch. If the program is started with the `java` interpreter and not the applet viewer, and it calls `getAppletContext`, it gets a `null` pointer because it has not been launched inside a browser. This causes a run time crash whenever we have code like

```
getAppletContext().showStatus(message);
```

While we do not want to write a full-fledged browser, we do need to supply the bare minimum to make calls like this work. The call displays no message, but at least it will not crash the program. It turns out that all we need to do is implement two interfaces, `AppletStub` and `AppletContext`.

You have seen applet contexts in action already. They are responsible for fetching images and audio files, and for displaying Web pages. They can, however, politely refuse, and this is what our applet context will do. The major purpose of the `AppletStub` interface is to locate the applet context. Every applet has an applet stub (set with the `setStub` method of the `Applet` class).

In our case, `AppletFrame` implements both `AppletStub` and `AppletContext`. We supply the bare minimum functionality.

```
public class AppletFrame extends Frame
implements AppletStub, AppletContext
{  . . .

   // AppletStub methods
   public boolean isActive() { return true; }
```

```
    public URL getDocumentBase() { return null; }
    public URL getCodeBase() { return null; }
    public String getParameter(String name) { return ""; }
    public AppletContext getAppletContext() { return this; }
    public void appletResize(int width, int height) {}

    // AppletContext methods
    public AudioClip getAudioClip(URL url) { return null; }
    public Image getImage(URL url) { return null; }
    public Applet getApplet(String name) { return null; }
    public Enumeration getApplets() { return null; }
    public void showDocument(URL url) {}
    public void showDocument(URL url, String target) {}
    public void showStatus(String status) {}
}
```

Next, the constructor of the frame class calls setStub on the applet to make itself its stub.

```
class AppletFrame extends Frame
implements AppletStub, AppletContext
{   AppletFrame(Applet a, int x, int y)
    {   setTitle(a.getClass().getName());
        resize(x, y);
        add("Center", a);
        a.setStub(this);
        a.init();
        show();
        a.start();
    }
    . . .
}
```

There is one final twist. Suppose we want to use the calculator as an applet and application simultaneously. Rather than moving the methods of the CalculatorApplet class into the AppletApplication class, we will just use inheritance. Here is the entire class.

```
public class CalculatorAppletApplication extends
CalculatorApplet
{   public static void main(String args[])
    {   new AppletFrame(new CalculatorApplet(), 150, 100);
    }
}
```

You can do this with any applet. If you like, you can make a RetireAppletApplication in exactly the same way. You simply pass a new Retire() object to the AppletFrame instead.

CHAPTER

9

- Vectors

- Bit Sets

- Hash Tables

- Linked Lists

- Stacks

- Multi-Dimensional Arrays

Data Structures

OP encapsulates the data inside classes, but this doesn't make how you organize the data inside the classes any less important than in traditional programming languages. Of course, how you choose to structure the data depends on the problem you are trying to solve. Does your class need a way to easily search through thousands (or even millions) of items quickly? Does it need an ordered sequence of elements *and* the ability to rapidly insert and remove elements in the middle of the sequence? Does it need an array-like structure with random-access ability that can grow at run time? The way you structure your data inside your classes can make these problems easy—or almost impossible—to solve.

The purpose of this chapter is to show how Java can help you accomplish the traditional data-structuring needed for serious programming. Equally traditionally, there is a course called *Data Structures* that takes at least a semester to complete at most schools, so there are many, many books completely devoted to this important topic. Exhaustively covering all the data structures that may be useful is not our goal in this chapter; instead, we cover the fundamental ones such as dynamic, array-like objects (vectors), hash tables, and linked lists. We hope that, after you finish this chapter, you will find it easy to translate any of your data structures to your Java programming.

Vectors

In many programming languages—in particular, C and C++—you have to fix the sizes of all arrays at compile time. Programmers hate this because it forces them into uncomfortable trade-offs. How many items will the customer order? Surely no more than 10. What if one customer needs 15 items? Do we want to waste 14 entries if the majority of customers wants only one item?

In Java, the situation is quite a bit better. You can set the size of an array at run time.

```
int n;
. . .
Item[] itemsOrdered = new Item[n + 1];
```

This code does not solve the problem completely. Once you set the array size, you cannot change it. (Java has no command analogous to `realloc` in C or to Redim Preserve in VB that lets you enlarge an existing array at run time.) Unfortunately, you don't know how many items the customer will order before taking the order information. If you ask, then set the array size accordingly, your boss might be furious that you cannot give the customer the opportunity of adding items to the order. Of course, you can read the order into an array that is surely sufficient (say 1,000 items), then determine how many items the customer really ordered, then make an array of just the right size, and then copy all items from the temporary array into the item array of the invoice object. That works fine, provided the customer doesn't call up later to add more items to the same order—something your boss would surely like you to implement.

What the Java world needs is an array that can grow on demand after it has been allocated. And, while we are at it, wouldn't it be nice if we could also shrink the array if it has grown too much?

In Java, a *vector* is the answer: vectors are array-like objects that can grow and shrink. There is one important difference to keep in mind between Java vectors and Java arrays:

• Arrays in Java hold any type, including number types and all class types.

• Vectors in Java must hold instances of `Object`.

For example, for a vector of integers, you will need to cast the integers to the `Integer` object wrapper.

NOTE: The name "vector" is a bit of a misnomer. Vectors in Java have nothing to do with the vectors used in mathematics and physics. (There, vectors are arrays of floating-point numbers, but their dimensions are fixed.)

You make a new vector by specifying its initial *capacity* in the `Vector` constructor.

```
Vector itemsOrdered = new Vector(3);
    // start out with space for 1 order item,
    // plus two items for tax and shipping charges
```

There is an important distinction between the capacity of a vector and the size of an array. If you allocate an array with three entries, then the array has three slots, ready for use. A vector with a capacity of three elements has the potential of holding three elements (and, in fact, more than three), but at the beginning, even after its initial construction, a vector holds no elements at all.

You use the `addElement` method to add new elements. For example, suppose you have a class called `Item` and use the following code to create three item objects.

```
Item nextItem = new Item();
Item stateTax = new Item();
Item shipping = new Item();
```

Then you use the following code to add these items to a vector called `itemsOrdered` (that started out with a capacity of three objects, as indicated in the above code):

```
itemsOrdered.addElement(nextItem);
itemsOrdered.addElement(stateTax);
itemsOrdered.addElement(shipping);
```

Let's suppose you created the vector so that it had an original capacity of three items. If you insert another item, then you have exceeded the capacity of the vector in our example. This is where vectors work their magic: the vector *relocates and resizes itself*. The vector finds a bigger home and automatically copies all the objects it is currently storing to its new home.

How much bigger is the relocation? By default, the allocation doubles each time the vector relocates. Because of the problem of exponential growth, you may not want to rely on this for potentially massive memory reallocation for enormous vectors. Instead, specify a *capacity increment* as the second constructor argument when you create the vector. For example:

```
Vector itemsOrdered = new Vector(3, 10);
```

Now the vector grows in increments of 10 at each relocation.

On the other hand, if Java has to reallocate the space for the vector often, it slows down your program, so it pays to set reasonable estimates for the initial capacity and the capacity increment.

NOTE: For simple programs, you may not want to worry about the capacity and capacity increment for your vectors at all. If you use the default constructor

```
Vector itemsOrdered = new Vector();
```

the vector has an initial capacity of 10 and doubles in size every time the capacity is exceeded. This works fine for situations in which the items to be handled are few, and it frees you from micromanaging the vector allocations.

C++ NOTE: The Java `Vector` class differs in a number of important ways from the C++ `vector` template. Most noticeably, since `vector` is a template, only elements of the correct type can be inserted, and no casting is required to retrieve elements from the vector. For example, the compiler will simply refuse to insert a `Rectangle` object into a `vector<Employee>`.

The C++ `vector` template overloads the `[]` operator for convenient element access. Since Java does not have operator-overloading, it must use explicit method calls instead.

C++ vectors are copied by value. If `a` and `b` are two vectors, then the assignment `a = b;` makes `a` into a new vector with the same length as `b`, and all elements are copied from `b` to `a`. The same assignment in Java makes both `a` and `b` refer to the same vector.

VB NOTE: If you don't mind the extra syntax and occasionally casting a basic type to its wrapper class (and casting the retrieved objects), vectors in Java give you all the convenience of Redim Preserve (and quite a bit more).

Working with an Existing Vector

The `size` method returns the current number of elements in the vector. Thus,

```
v.size()
```

is the vector equivalent of

```
a.length
```

for an array `a`. Of course, the size of a vector is always less than or equal to its capacity.

Once you are reasonably sure that the vector is at its permanent size, you can call the `trimToSize` method. This method adjusts the size of the memory block to use exactly as much storage space as is required to hold the current number of elements. Any excess memory will be recycled by the memory manager.

NOTE: Once you trim a vector's size, adding new elements will move the block again, which takes time. You should only `trimToSize` when you are sure you won't add any more elements to the vector.

Example 9-1 lets the user add new order entries to a purchase order. A vector holds the entries. When the user clicks on Done, the tax and shipping charge are added, and the vector is trimmed to size.

Figure 9-1: Purchase order test application

Example 9-1: PurchaseOrderTest.java

```java
import java.awt.*;
import java.util.*;
import corejava.*;

public class PurchaseOrderTest extends Frame
{  public PurchaseOrderTest()
   {  Panel p = new Panel();
      p.setLayout(new FlowLayout());
      name = new Choice();
      name.addItem("Toaster");
      name.addItem("Blender");
      name.addItem("Microwave oven");
      name.addItem("Citrus press");
      name.addItem("Espresso maker");
      name.addItem("Rice cooker");
      name.addItem("Waffle iron");
      name.addItem("Bread machine");
      quantity = new IntTextField(1, 0, 100, 4);
      p.add(name);
      p.add(quantity);
      p.add(new Button("Add"));
      p.add(new Button("Done"));
      add("South", p);
      add("Center", canvas = new PurchaseOrderCanvas());
      canvas.redraw(a);
   }
```

```java
    public boolean handleEvent(Event evt)
    {   if (evt.id == Event.WINDOW_DESTROY) System.exit(0);
        return super.handleEvent(evt);
    }

    public boolean action(Event evt, Object arg)
    {   if (arg.equals("Add"))
        {   if (quantity.isValid())
                a.addElement(new Item(name.getSelectedItem(),
                    quantity.getValue(), 0.00));
        }
        else if (arg.equals("Done"))
        {   a.addElement(new Item("State Tax", 1, 0.00));
            a.addElement(new Item("Shipping", 1, 5.00));
            a.trimToSize();
        }
        else return super.action(evt, arg);
        canvas.redraw(a);
        return true;
    }

    public static void main(String args[])
    {   Frame f = new PurchaseOrderTest();
        f.resize(300, 200);
        f.show();
    }

    private Vector a = new Vector();
    private Choice name;
    private IntTextField quantity;
    private PurchaseOrderCanvas canvas;
    private int m = 1;

}

class Item
{   public Item(String n, int q, double u)
    {   name = n;
        quantity = q;
        unitPrice = u;
    }

    public String toString()
    {   return new Format("%-20s").form(name)
            + new Format("%6d").form(quantity)
            + new Format("%8.2f").form(unitPrice);
    }

    private String name;
    private int quantity;
    private double unitPrice;
}
```

```
class PurchaseOrderCanvas extends Canvas
{  public void redraw(Vector new_a)
   {  a = new_a;
      repaint();
   }

   public void paint(Graphics g)
   {  Font f = new Font("Courier", Font.PLAIN, 12);
      g.setFont(f);
      FontMetrics fm = g.getFontMetrics(f);
      int height = fm.getHeight();
      int x = 0;
      int y = 0;
      int i = 0;
      for (i = 0; i < a.size(); i++)
      {  y += height;
         g.drawString(a.elementAt(i).toString(), x, y);
      }
   }

   private Vector a;
}
```

`java.util.Vector`

- `Vector()`

  constructs an empty vector (initial capacity is 10, and the capacity doubles whenever current capacity is exceeded).

- `Vector(int initialCapacity)`

  constructs an empty vector with the specified capacity.

Parameters:	`initialCapacity`	the initial storage capacity of the vector

- `Vector(int initialCapacity, int capacityIncrement)`

  constructs an empty vector with the specified capacity and the specified increment.

Parameters:	`initialCapacity`	the initial storage capacity of the vector
	`capacityIncrement`	the amount by which the capacity is increased when the vector outgrows its current capacity

- `void addElement(Object obj)`

  appends an element at the end of the vector so that it becomes the last element of the vector.

  Parameters: `obj`   the element to be added

- `int size()`

  returns the number of elements currently stored in the vector. (This is different from, and of course never larger than, the vector's capacity.)

- `void trimToSize()`

  reduces the capacity of the vector to its current size.

Vector Element Access

Unfortunately, nothing comes for free; the extra convenience that vectors give requires a more complicated syntax for accessing the elements of the vector. Also, the `Vector` class is not a part of the Java language; it is just a utility class programmed by someone and supplied in the standard library.

NOTE: Vectors, like arrays, are zero-based.

The two most important differences in working with vectors, as opposed to arrays, are as follows:

1. Instead of using the pleasant `[]` syntax to access or change the element of an array, you must use the `elementAt` and `setElementAt` methods.

Array	Vector
`x = a[i];`	`x = v.elementAt(i);`
`a[i] = x;`	`v.setElementAt(x, i);`

    This is not so wonderful. It would have been nice if the author of the vector class could have called these methods `get` and `set`.

TIP: You can sometimes get the best of both worlds, flexible growth and convenient element access, with the following trick. First, make a vector and add all the elements.
```
Vector v = new Vector();
while (. . .)
{   String s = . . .
    v.addElement(s);
}
```
When you are done, make an array and copy the elements into it. There is even a special method `copyInto` for this purpose.
```
String[] a = new String[v.size()];
v.copyInto(a);
```

---

2. There is a single `Vector` class that holds elements of any type: a vector stores a sequence of *objects*.

That is not a problem when inserting an element into a vector—all classes implicitly inherit from `Object`. (Actually, there is a problem if you want to build a vector of numbers. Then you must use a wrapper class like `Integer` or `Double`.)

Consider the code:

```
Item nextItem = new Item();
itemsOrdered.setElementAt(nextItem, n);
```

The variable `nextItem` is automatically cast from the type `Item` to the type `Object` and then inserted into the vector.

But when you read an item from the vector, you get an `Object`, and you must cast it back to the type that will work with it.

```
Item currentItem = (Item)itemsOrdered.elementAt(n);
```

If you forget the `(Item)` cast, the compiler generates an error message.

Vectors are inherently somewhat *unsafe*. It is possible to accidentally add an element of the wrong type to a vector.

```
Rectangle r = new Rectangle();
itemsOrdered.setElementAt(r, n);
```

The compiler won't complain. It is perfectly willing to convert a `Rectangle` to an `Object`.

But when the accidental rectangle is later retrieved out of the vector container, it will probably be cast into an `Item`. This is an invalid cast that causes the program to abort. That *is* a problem! And it is unique to vectors. Had `itemsOrdered` been an array of `Item` values, then the compiler would not have allowed a rectangle inside it.

```
Rectangle r = new Rectangle();
itemsOrdered[n] = r; // ERROR
```

How serious is this problem? It depends. In practice, you can often guarantee that the elements inserted into a vector are of the correct type, simply because there are only one or two locations in the code where the insertion into the vector takes place. You can then write code that checks the type before you store it in the vector.

Consider the example of a `PurchaseOrder` class.

```
class PurchaseOrder
{   . . .
    public void add(Item i)
    {   itemsOrdered.addElement(i);
    }

    . . .
    private Vector itemsOrdered;
}
```

The `itemsOrdered` vector is a private field of the `PurchaseOrder` class. The only function that adds objects into that vector is `add`. Plainly, since the argument of `add` is an `Item`, only items can be added into the vector. The compiler can check the type at that level—a call to `order.add(new Rectangle())` will give an error message. Thus, we can safely remove elements from that vector and cast them as `Item` objects.

There is another way to achieve the same effect. Create the class `ItemVector` (derive it from `Vector`), in which you check that the inserted items are of the correct type. We give an example of this below. (As an added convenience, we also provide a retrieval function that casts the objects into items.)

```
class ItemVector extends Vector
{   public void set(Item i, int n)
    {   setElementAt(i, n);
    }
    public void append(Item i)
    {   addElement(i);
    }
    public Item get(int n)
    {   return (Item)elementAt(n);
    }
}
```

This gives the user completely safe `set`, `append`, and `get` vector access methods. Unfortunately, there is no way to hide the unsafe `setElementAt` in the derived class. All we can do is hope that the programmer will be seduced into using the safer functions `set` and `get` because they are easier to type. After all, we are not concerned about stopping malicious programmers, only about enlisting the compiler's help to prevent accidental errors!

On very rare occasions, vectors are useful for *heterogeneous collections*. Objects of completely unrelated classes are inserted into the vector on purpose. When retrieving a vector entry, the type of every retrieved object must be tested, as in the following code:

```
Vector purchaseOrder;
purchaseOrder.addElement(new Name(. . .));
purchaseOrder.addElement(new Address(. . .));
purchaseOrder.addElement(new Item(. . .));
. . .
```

```
Object obj = purchaseOrder.elementAt(n);
if (obj instanceof Item)
{   Item i = (Item)obj;
    sum += i.price();
}
```

Actually, this is a crummy way to write code. It is not a good idea to throw away type information and laboriously try to retrieve it later. (Of course, there are exceptions. One exception will occur if Java can eventually handle OLE. OLE automation information is difficult to type ahead of time.)

VB NOTE: You may be wondering about arrays of variants. Well, we think using variants, except for OLE automation, is also a crummy way to write code (even though copying arrays is easier if you turn them into variants).

Finally, this is a good time to explain the use of the *wrapper classes*, like `Integer` and `Double` for vectors.

Suppose we want a vector of `Double`. As mentioned previously, simply adding numbers won't work.

```
Vector v = new Vector();
v.addElement(3.14); // ERROR
```

The floating-point number 3.14 is not an `Object`. Here the `Double` wrapper class comes in. An instance of `Double` is an object that wraps the `double` type.

```
v.addElement(new Double(3.14));
```

Of course, to retrieve a number from a vector of `Double` objects, we need to extract the actual value from the wrapper.

```
double x = ((Double)v.elementAt(n)).doubleValue();
```

Ugh. Here it really pays off to derive the class `DoubleVector`, with methods `get` and `set` that hide all this ugliness.

java.util.Vector

- `void setElementAt(Object obj, int index)`

  puts a value in the vector at the specified index, overwriting the previous contents.

  Parameters: obj   the new value

                  index   the position (must be between 0 and size() - 1)

- `Object elementAt(int index)`

  gets the value stored at a specified index.

  Parameters: index   the index of the element to get (must be between 0 and size() - 1)

Inserting and Removing Elements in the Middle of a Vector

Instead of appending elements at the end of a vector, you can also insert them in the middle.

```
int n = itemsOrdered.size() - 2;
itemsOrdered.insertElementAt(nextItem, n);
```

The elements at locations n and above are shifted up to make room for the new entry. After the insertion if the new size of the vector after the insertion exceeds the vector's current capacity, then Java reallocates its storage.

Similarly, you can remove an element from the middle of a vector.

```
Item i = (Item)itemsOrdered.removeElementAt(n);
```

The elements located above it are copied down, and the size of the array is reduced by one.

Inserting and removing elements is not terribly efficient. It is probably not worth worrying about for small vectors. But if you store many elements and frequently insert and remove in the middle of the sequence, consider using a linked list instead. We will talk about linked lists later in this chapter.

`java.util.Vector`

- `void insertElementAt(Object obj, int index)`

  shifts up elements in order to insert an element.

  Parameters: `obj`   the new element

                `index`   the insertion position (must be between 0 and `size()`)

- `void removeElementAt(int index)`

  removes an element and shifts down all elements above it.

  Parameters: `index`   the position of the element to be removed (must be between 0 and `size() - 1`)

Bit Sets

The Java `BitSet` class stores a sequence of bits. (It is not a *set* in the mathematical sense—bit *vector* or bit *array* would have been more appropriate terms.) Use a bit set if you need to store a sequence of bits (for example, flags) efficiently. Because a bit set packs the bits into bytes, it is far more efficient than using a vector of `Boolean` objects. The `BitSet` class gives you a convenient interface for reading, setting, or resetting individual bits. This avoids the masking and other bit-fiddling operations.

For example, if you have a `BitSet` named `bucketOfBits`:

    bucketOfBits.get(i)

returns true if the `i`'th bit is on, and false otherwise. Similarly,

    bucketOfBits.set(i)

turns the `i`'th bit on. Finally,

    bucketOfBits.clear(i)

turns the `i`'th bit off.

C++ NOTE: The C++ vector template has the specialization `vector<bool>`, which has the same functionality as the Java `BitSet`.

`java.util.BitSet`

- `BitSet(int nbits)`

  Parameters: `nbits`   the initial number of bits

- `boolean get(int bit)`

  gets a bit.

  Parameters: `bit`   the position of the requested bit

- `void set(int bit)`

  sets a bit.

  Parameters: `bit`   the position of the bit to be set

- `void clear(int bit)`

  clears a bit.

  Parameters: `bit`   the position of the bit to be cleared

- `void and(BitSet set)`

  logically ANDs this bit set with another.

  Parameters: `set`   the bit set to be combined with this bit set

- `void or(BitSet set)`

  logically ORs this bit set with another.

  Parameters: `set`   the bit set to be combined with this bit set

- `void xor(BitSet set)`

    logically XORs this bit set with another.

    Parameters:　　`set`　　the bit set to be combined with this bit set

The Sieve of Eratosthenes Benchmark

As an example of using bit sets, we want to show you an implementation of the "sieve of Eratosthenes" algorithm for finding prime numbers. (A prime number is a number like 2, 3, or 5 that is divisible only by itself and 1, and the sieve of Eratosthenes was one of the first methods discovered to enumerate these fundamental building blocks.) This isn't a terribly good algorithm for finding the number of primes, but for some reason it has become a popular benchmark for compiler performance. (It isn't a good benchmark either, since it mainly tests bit operations.)

Oh well, we bow to tradition and include an implementation. This program counts all prime numbers between 2 and 1,000,000. (There are 78,498 primes, so you probably don't want to print them all out.) You will find that the program takes a little while to get going, but eventually it picks up speed.

Without going into too many details of this program, the key is to march through a bit set with one million bits. We first turn on all the bits. After that, we turn off the bits that are multiples of numbers known to be prime. The positions of the bits that remain on after this process are, themselves, the prime numbers. Example 9-2 illustrates this program in Java and Example 9-3 is the C++ code.

Example 9-2: Sieve.java

```
import java.util.*;

public class Sieve
{  public static final boolean PRINT = false;

   public static void main(String[] s)
   {  int n = 1000000;
      BitSet b = new BitSet(n);
      int count = 0;
      int i;
      for (i = 2; i <= n; i++)
         b.set(i);
      i = 2;
      while (i * i <= n)
      {  if (b.get(i))
         {  if (PRINT) System.out.println(i);
            count++;
            int k = 2 * i;
            while (k <= n)
```

```
                { b.clear(k);
                  k += i;
                }
            }
            i++;
        }
        while (i <= n)
        {   if (b.get(i))
            {   if (PRINT) System.out.println(i);
                count++;
            }
            i++;
        }
        System.out.println(count + " primes");
    }
}
```

NOTE: Even though the sieve isn't a good benchmark, we couldn't resist timing the process as implemented in different languages. The CD contains implementations in C++ and one for the 32-bit version of VB4. We used C++ and VB4 implementations that are as close as possible to the one used in Java. In VB4 we used class modules. We also used an array of bytes rather than an array of Boolean values in both cases. In the VB version, we also wrote the appropriate property procedures for manipulating bits in order to make the code as similar as possible to that used in the C++ and Java versions.

Here are the timing results on a Pentium-90 with 32 megabytes of RAM, running Windows 95.

C++	1.53 seconds
Java (JDK, no JIT)	59.93 seconds
Java (Café, JIT)	5.97 seconds
VB4	65.69 seconds

TIP: The easiest way to do timings in Java is with the `CurrentTimeMillis` method in `java.lang.System`.

Example 9-3: Sieve.cpp

```cpp
#include <iostream.h>
//C++
class BitSet
{
public:
    BitSet(int n) : bits(new char[(n - 1) / 8 + 1]), size(n) {}
    bool get(int n)
    {   if (0 <= n && n < size)
            return (bits[n >> 3] & (1 << (n & 7))) != 0;
        else return false;
    }
```

```
      void set(int n)
      {   if (0 <= n && n < size)
              bits[n >> 3] |= 1 << (n & 7);
      }
      void clear(int n)
      {   if (0 <= n && n < size)
              bits[n >> 3] &= ~(1 << (n & 7));
      }

private:
   char* bits;
   int size;
};

void main()
{   int n = 1000000;
    BitSet b(n);
    int count = 0;
    int i;
    for (i = 2; i <= n; i++)
       b.set(i);
    i = 2;
    while (i * i <= n)
    {   if (b.get(i))
        {   count++;
            int k = 2 * i;
            while (k <= n)
            {   b.clear(k);
                k += i;
            }
        }
        i++;
    }
    while (i <= n)
    {   if (b.get(i))
            count++;
        i++;
    }
    cout << count << " primes\n";
}
```

Hash Tables

Suppose you want to keep a list of employees. Every employee has an ID number (possibly their social security number). You want to be able to find the records of an individual employee quickly, *given* the employee ID number. If the ID number is a small integer, that is, if your employee numbers are 1, 2, 3, and so forth, you can use a vector. But if you use social security numbers, they will be too long for an array index.

The `Hashtable` class in Java offers a solution to this kind of problem. Data items that are Java objects (like employee records) are identified by a *key* (like the ID number). The hash table then computes a small integer out of the key, called a *hash code*. The computation does not matter much, provided it is quick and the resulting integers are evenly distributed. Then the hash table stores the key and the data item in an array, at the location given by the hash code. All this is invisible to the user of Java's `Hashtable` class.

Here is how we set up a hash table for storing employees.

```
Hashtable staff = new Hashtable();
Employee harry = new Employee("Harry Hacker");
staff.put("987-98-9996", harry);
. . .
```

NOTE: The name of the class is `Hashtable`, with a lowercase `t`. Under Windows, you'll get strange error messages if you use `HashTable`, because the Windows file system is not case sensitive, but the Java compiler is.

Whenever you add an object to a hash table, you must supply a key as well. In our case, the key is a string, and the corresponding value is an `employee` object. Neither the key nor the value stored in a hash table can be `null`.

To retrieve an object, you must use (and, therefore, remember) the key.

```
String s = "149-16-2536";
e = staff.get(s); // gets harry
```

If no information is stored in the hash table with the particular key specified, then `get` returns `null`.

NOTE: As with vectors, hash tables store everything as an object. This means you *must* cast the return value of `get` to the correct type, as was done in the example code above.

Keys must be unique. You cannot store two values with the same key. If you call the `put` method twice with the same key, then the second value replaces the first one. In fact, `put` returns the previous value stored with the key parameter. (This is useful; if `put` returns a non-`null` value, then you know you replaced a previous entry.)

The `remove()` method removes an element from the hash table. The `size()` method returns the number of entries in the hash table. In the section on enumerations, we will see how to iterate through all entries in a hash table.

You can think of a hash table as implementing a number of "buckets." Ideally, every bucket contains, at most, one object, but so-called *collisions* (keys with the same hash value) are inevitable. These are then placed in the same bucket by the hash table implementation. Thus, some buckets will contain lists with multiple values. The `Hashtable` class then has to implement special code in order to take care of buckets with more than one item in them. (But, again, you don't need to worry about what is going on under the hood to resolve these collisions.)

If you want more control over the performance of the hash table, you can specify the initial bucket count. The bucket count gives the number of buckets that are used to collect objects with identical hash values. If too many elements are inserted into a hash table, the number of collisions increases, and retrieval performance suffers. Then the hash table should be reallocated with a larger number of buckets.

If you know approximately how many elements will eventually be in the table, then you should set the initial bucket size to about 150% of the expected element count. It is actually a good idea to make the size of the hash table a prime number because this prevents a clustering of keys. For example, if you need to store about 100 entries, set the initial bucket size to 151.

```
Hashtable staff = new Hashtable(151);
```

You can also set the *load factor* in the constructor. The load factor gives a percentage threshold before Java moves the hash table to a new location. For example, if the load factor is 0.75 (which is the default), and the hash table becomes more than 75% full, then Java automatically allocates a larger table, with twice as many entries. Java reorganizes all the entries into the bigger table. This is a good strategy because hash tables that are nearly full perform poorly. For most applications, it is reasonable to leave the load factor at 0.75. (In the current implementation, the size of the larger table is not a prime number.)

Example 9-4 illustrates the hash table interface at work. We use a hash table to store prices for products.

Example 9-4: HashtableTest.java

```
import java.awt.*;
import java.util.*;
import corejava.*;

public class HashtableTest extends Frame
{  public HashtableTest()
   {  Panel p = new Panel();
      p.setLayout(new FlowLayout());
      name = new Choice();
      add("Toaster", 19.95);
      add("Blender", 59.95);
```

```
      add("Microwave oven", 179.95);
      add("Citrus press", 19.95);
      add("Espresso maker", 199.95);
      add("Rice cooker", 29.95);
      add("Waffle iron", 39.95);
      add("Bread machine", 119.95);
      quantity = new IntTextField(1, 0, 100, 4);
      p.add(name);
      p.add(quantity);
      p.add(new Button("Add"));
      add("South", p);
      add("Center", canvas = new PurchaseOrderCanvas());
      canvas.redraw(a);
   }

   public void add(String n, double price)
   {  name.addItem(n); // add to choice field
      prices.put(n, new Double(price));
   }

   public boolean handleEvent(Event evt)
   {  if (evt.id == Event.WINDOW_DESTROY) System.exit(0);
      return super.handleEvent(evt);
   }

   public boolean action(Event evt, Object arg)
   {  if (arg.equals("Add"))
      {  if (quantity.isValid())
         {  String n = name.getSelectedItem();
            double price =
               ((Double)prices.get(n)).doubleValue();
            a.addElement(new Item(n, quantity.getValue(),
               price));
         }
      }
      else return super.action(evt, arg);
      canvas.redraw(a);
      return true;
   }


   public static void main(String args[])
   {  Frame f = new HashtableTest();
      f.resize(300, 200);
      f.show();
   }

   private Vector a = new Vector();
   private Choice name;
```

```
        private IntTextField quantity;
        private PurchaseOrderCanvas canvas;
        private Hashtable prices = new Hashtable();
        private int m = 1;

}


class Item
{   public Item(String n, int q, double u)
    {   name = n;
        quantity = q;
        unitPrice = u;
    }

    public String toString()
    {   return new Format("%-20s").form(name)
            + new Format("%6d").form(quantity)
            + new Format("%8.2f").form(unitPrice);
    }

    private String name;
    private int quantity;
    private double unitPrice;
}


class PurchaseOrderCanvas extends Canvas
{   public void redraw(Vector new_a)
    {   a = new_a;
        repaint();
    }

    public void paint(Graphics g)
    {   Font f = new Font("Courier", Font.PLAIN, 12);
        g.setFont(f);
        FontMetrics fm = g.getFontMetrics(f);
        int height = fm.getHeight();
        int x = 0;
        int y = 0;
        int i = 0;
        for (i = 0; i < a.size(); i++)
        {   y += height;
            g.drawString(a.elementAt(i).toString(), x, y);
        }
    }

    private Vector a;

}
```

`java.util.Hashtable`

- `Hashtable()`

  constructs an empty hash table.

- `Hashtable(int initialCapacity)`

  constructs an empty hash table with the specified capacity.

  Parameters: `initialCapacity`   the initial number of buckets

- `Hashtable(int initialCapacity, float loadFactor)`

  constructs an empty hash table with the specified capacity and load factor.

  Parameters: initialCapacity   the initial number of buckets

  loadFactor   a number between 0.0 and 1.0 that determines at what percentage of fullness the hash table will be rehashed into a larger one

- `Object get(Object key)`

  gets the object associated with the key; returns the object associated with the key, or `null` if the key is not found in the hash table.

- `Object put(Object key, Object value)`

  puts the association of a key and an object into the hash table. If the key is already present, the new object replaces the old one previously associated with the key. This method returns the old value of the key, or `null` if the key was not previously present.

  Parameters: `key`   the key to use for retrieval (may not be `null`)

  `value`   the associated object (may not be `null`)

- `Object remove(Object key)`

  removes the key and the element associated with it. Does nothing if the key is not present. This method returns the value of the key, or `null` if the key was not found.

  Parameters: `key`   the key whose association you want to remove

- `int size()`

  returns the number of elements contained in the hash table.

Keys and Hash Functions

We were able to use strings as keys because the `String` class has a `hashCode` method that computes a *hash code* for a string. A hash code is an integer that is somehow derived from the characters in the string. Table 9-1 lists a few examples of hash codes that result from the `hashCode` function.

Table 9-1: Hash codes resulting from the `hashCode` function.

String	Hash code
Hello	140207504
Harry	140013338
Hacker	884756206

In fact, every object has a default hash code that is derived from the object's memory address. In general, this is not a good hash code to use because objects with identical contents may yield different hash codes. Consider this example.

```
String s = "Ok";
Button bs = new Button(s);
System.out.println(s.hashCode() + " " + bs.hashCode());
String t = "Ok";
Button bt = new Button(t);
System.out.println(t.hashCode() + " " + bt.hashCode());
```

Table 9-2 shows the result:

Table 9-2: Hash codes of objects with identical contents.

"Ok" String hash code	"Ok" Button hash code
3030	20526976
3030	20527144

Note that the strings s and t have the same hash value because, for strings, the hash values are derived from their *contents*. The buttons bs and bt have different hash values because no special hash function has been defined for the Button class, and the default hash code function in the Object class derives the hash code from the object's memory address.

Creating Your Own Hashable Classes

In the Java library, all classes that define their own hashCode method form the hash code according to the contents of their objects. If your hash table keys are objects of a class that you defined yourself, you should define the hashValue method of the key class. This method should return an integer (which can be negative). The hash table code will later reduce the integer by dividing by the bucket count and taking the remainder. Just scramble up the hash codes of the data fields in some way that will give the hash codes for different objects a good chance of being widely scattered.

For example, suppose we have the class PartNumber for inventory part numbers. A part number consists of a description string and a release number.

```
pn = new PartNumber("WDGT", 4);
```

If we want to use part numbers as keys in a hash table, we need to define a hash code.

```
class PartNumber
{   . . .
    public int hashCode()
    {   return 13 * description.hashCode() + 17 * version;
    }
    . . .
    private String description;
    private int version;
}
```

There is another important function that we need to define for user-defined key classes, namely equals. The Object class defines equals, but the function only tests whether or not two objects are *identical*. We need to redefine equals to check for equal contents.

```
class PartNumber()
{   . . .
    public boolean equals(Object b)
    {   if (b instanceof PartNumber)
        {   PartNumber p = (PartNumber)b;
            return description.equals(p.description)
                && version == p.version;
        }
        else
```

```
            return false;
    }
    . . .
    private String description;
    private int version;
}
```

If we don't redefine `equals`, then a lookup like the one below will always fail—a new part number is never identical to one in the hash table.

```
Hashtable parts;
. . .
PartNumber pn = new PartNumber("WDGT", 4);
p = (Part)parts.get(pn);
```

java.lang.Object

- `boolean equals (Object obj)`

  compares two objects for equality; returns true if both objects are equal; false otherwise.

  Parameters: obj   the object to compare with the first object

- `int hashCode()`

  returns a hash code for this object. A hash code can be any integer, positive or negative. Equal objects need to return identical hash codes.

Enumerations

Suppose we want to print all employees in a `staff` hash table. If we have a separate list of all ID numbers, then, of course, we can call `get` for every ID number, and retrieve the employee records, one by one. But suppose we don't actually have the ID numbers handy. We can't very well try all keys in turn—if we use social security numbers as keys, then there are a billion possible keys.

Instead, we call the `elements()` method of the `Hashtable` class. It returns an object of a type that implements the `Enumeration` interface.

```
Enumeration e = staff.elements();
```

The `Enumeration` interface has two methods, `hasMoreElements` and `nextElement`. The following loop uses these methods to iterate through all values in the hash table.

```
while (e.hasMoreElements())
{   String id = (String)e.nextElement();
    . . .
}
```

Why does the hash table return an object of a new type, instead of just having methods called `getFirstElement` and `getNextElement`? There are a number of advantages, and this is why many Java classes return objects that implement the `Enumeration` interface. (These are often called enumeration objects.) For example, if you have a vector `v` of items, then `v.elements()` returns an enumeration object that can be used to traverse all elements of the vector. Once you have an enumeration object, you can pass it to a method that retrieves the data. The big advantage is that this method does not need to know to which data structure the enumeration is attached.

For example, here is code that adds a sequence of items to a purchase order. It does not matter from where the items came. Their source might have been a vector, a hash table, or another container that reveals an enumeration of its elements.

```
class PurchaseOrder
{   . . .
    void addItems(Enumeration e)
    {   while (e.hasMoreElements())
        {   Object i = e.nextElement();
            if (i instanceof Item)
                itemsOrdered.addElement(i);
        }
    }
    . . .
}
```

NOTE: If you want to enumerate just the keys of a hash table, not the elements, use the `keys` method to get an enumeration object for the keys.

C++ NOTE: The Java enumeration roughly corresponds to the iterators in the C++ standard template library, or, more precisely, to a `forward_iterator`. The `elements` method is the same as the call `p = a.begin()`, which yields an iterator pointing to the beginning of the container. The `nextElement` method is the same as the `*p++` operation on an iterator. The `hasMoreElements` test is the same as the test `p != a.end()`.

`java.util.Enumeration`

• `boolean hasMoreElements()`

returns true if there are more elements yet to be inspected.

- `Object nextElement()`

  returns the next element to be inspected. Do not call this method if `hasMoreElements()` returned false.

`java.util.Hashtable`

- `Enumeration keys()`

  returns an enumeration object that traverses the keys of the hash table.

- `Enumeration elements()`

  returns an enumeration object that traverses the elements of the hash table.

`java.util.Vector`

- `Enumeration elements()`

  returns an enumeration object that traverses the elements of the vector.

Property Sets

A *property set* is a tabular structure that is essentially a hash table of a very special type. It has three particular characteristics.

- The keys and values are strings.
- The table can be saved to a file and loaded from a file.
- There is a secondary table for defaults.

The Java class that implements a property set is called `Properties`.

Property sets are useful in specifying configuration options for programs. The environment variables in Unix and DOS are good examples. On a PC, your AUTOEXEC.BAT file might contain the settings:

```
SET PROMPT=$p$g
SET TEMP=C:\Windows\Temp
SET CLASSPATH=c:\java\lib;c:\CoreJavaBook;.
```

Here is how you would model that as a property set in Java.

```
Properties settings = new Properties();
settings.put("PROMPT", "$p$g");
settings.put("TEMP", "C:\\Windows\\Temp");
settings.put("CLASSPATH", "c:\\java\\lib;c:\\CoreJavaBook;.");
```

Use the `save` method to save this list of properties to a file. Here we just print the property set to the standard output. The second argument is a comment that is included in the file.

```
settings.save(System.out, "Environment settings");
```

The sample table gives the following output.

```
#Environment settings
#Sun Jan 21 07:22:52  1996
CLASSPATH=.;c:\\java\\lib
TEMP=C:\\Windows\\Temp
PROMPT=$p$g
```

System Information

Here's another example of the ubiquity of the `Properties` set: Java stores information about your system in a `Properties` object that is part of the `System` class. Applications would normally have complete access to this information but Applets have only restricted access to this information. The level of access is controlled by the `checkPropertyAccess` method in the `Security Manager` class. With most browsers, however, applets would not be able to find information such as the user name or user's home directory and would only be able to find out things like the file separator character and the information about the version of Java on the client machine.

The following code gives one standard way of printing out the key value pair in a `Properties` object. In this program, keep in mind that the `nextElement` method in the `Enumeration` interface returns an `Object` so we need to do an explicit cast to a string in order to retrieve the key value via a call to `getProperty`.

```
import java.util.*;

public class SystemInfo
{  public static void main(String args[])
    {    Properties systemStuff = System.getProperties();
        Enumeration enum = systemStuff.propertyNames();
        while (enum.hasMoreElements())
        {   String key = (String)enum.nextElement();
            // nextElement gives objects, keys must
            // be strings, so cast
            System.out.println(key + " value is " +
                systemStuff.getProperty(key));
        }
    }
}
```

Here is what you would see when you run the program as an application. You can see all the values stored in this Properties object. (What you would get will, of course, reflect your machine's settings):

```
java.home value is  C:\JAVA
awt.toolkit value is  sun.awt.win32.MToolkit
java.version value is  internal_build
file.separator value is  \
line.separator value is
java.vendor value is  Sun Microsystems Inc.
user.name value is  unknown
os.arch value is  x86
os.name value is  Windows 95
java.vendor.url value is  http://www.sun.com/
user.dir value is  c:\CoreJavaBook\ch9\SystemInfo
java.class.path value is
.;C:\CAFE\JAVA\BIN\..\..\bin\..\JAVA\LIB\CLASSES.ZIP;
C:\CAFE\JAVA\BIN\..\..\bin\..\JAVA\LIB\SYMCLASS.ZIP
java.class.version value is  45.3
os.version value is  4.0
path.separator value is  ;
user.home value is  C:\JAVA
```

Figure 9-2 shows you an example of what you will see if you modify this program to be an Applet running under Netscape 3.0 loaded as a local file.

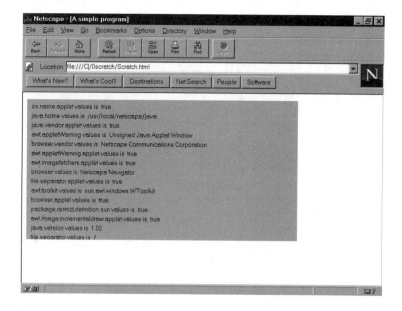

Figure 9-2: The output of the System Info program in Netscape 3.0

NOTE: You may be wondering why we don't show you this applet running as a URL. The answer is that Netscape doesn't let an applet running this way get at the system properties object as a whole because of security concerns.

Property Defaults

A property set is also a useful gadget whenever you want to allow the user to customize an application. Here is how your users can customize the `NotHelloWorld` program to their hearts' content. We'll allow them to specify the following in the configuration file `CustomWorld.ini`:

- window size
- font
- point size
- background color
- message string

If the user doesn't specify some of the settings, we will provide defaults.

The `Properties` class has two mechanisms for providing defaults. First, whenever you look up the value of a string, you can specify a default that should be used automatically when the key is not present.

```
String font = settings.getProperty("FONT", "Courier");
```

If there is a `"FONT"` property in the property table, then `font` is set to that string. Otherwise `font` is set to `"Courier"`.

If you find it too tedious to specify the default in every call to `getProperty`, then you can pack all the defaults into a secondary property set and supply that in the constructor of your lookup table.

```
Properties defaultSettings = new Properties();
defaultSettings.put("FONT", "Courier");
defaultSettings.put("SIZE", "10");
defaultSettings.put("MESSAGE", "Hello, World");
   . . .
Properties settings = new Properties(defaultSettings);
FileInputStream sf = new FileInputStream("CustomWorld.ini");
settings.load(sf);
   . . .
```

(Yes, you can even specify defaults to defaults if you give another property set parameter to the `defaultSettings` constructor, but it is not something one would normally do.)

Example 9-5 is the customizable `"Hello, World"` program. Just edit the `.ini` file to change the program's appearance to the way *you* want.

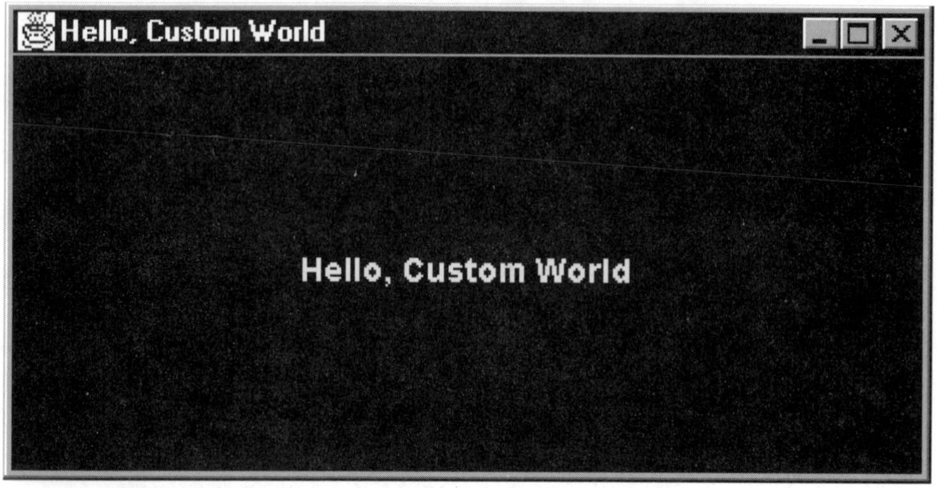

Figure 9-3: The customized Hello World program

Example 9-5: CustomWorld.java

```
import java.awt.*;
import java.util.*;
import java.io.*;
import corejava.*;

public class CustomWorld extends Frame
{  public CustomWorld()
   {  Properties defaultSettings = new Properties();
      defaultSettings.put("FONT", "Courier");
      defaultSettings.put("SIZE", "300 200");
      defaultSettings.put("MESSAGE", "Hello, World");
      defaultSettings.put("COLOR", "0 50 50");
      defaultSettings.put("PTSIZE", "12");

      Properties settings = new Properties(defaultSettings);
      try
      {  FileInputStream sf = new FileInputStream
            ("CustomWorld.ini");
         settings.load(sf);
      }
      catch (FileNotFoundException e) {}
      catch (IOException e) {}

      StringTokenizer st = new StringTokenizer
         (settings.getProperty("COLOR"));
      int red = Format.atoi(st.nextToken());
      int green = Format.atoi(st.nextToken());
      int blue = Format.atoi(st.nextToken());

      setBackground(new Color(red, green, blue));
```

```java
        foreground = new Color(255 - red, 255 - green,
            255 - blue);

        String name = settings.getProperty("FONT");
        int size = Format.atoi(settings.getProperty("PTSIZE"));
        f = new Font(name, Font.BOLD, size);

        st = new StringTokenizer
            (settings.getProperty("SIZE"));
        int hsize = Format.atoi(st.nextToken());
        int vsize = Format.atoi(st.nextToken());
        resize(hsize, vsize);
        setTitle(settings.getProperty("MESSAGE"));
    }

    public boolean handleEvent(Event evt)
    {   if (evt.id == Event.WINDOW_DESTROY) System.exit(0);
        return false;
    }

    public void paint(Graphics g)
    {   g.setColor(foreground);
        g.setFont(f);

        String s = getTitle();
        FontMetrics fm = g.getFontMetrics(f);
        int w = fm.stringWidth(s);

        Dimension d = size();
        Insets in = insets();
        int client_width = d.width - in.right - in.left;
        int client_height = d.height - in.bottom - in.top;
        int cx = (client_width - w) / 2;
        int cy = (client_height + fm.getHeight()) / 2;

        g.drawString(s, cx, cy);
    }

    public static void main(String args[])
    {   Frame f = new CustomWorld();
        f.show();
    }

    private Color foreground;
    private Font f;

}
```

Here are the current property settings.

```
#Environment settings
#Sun Jan 21 07:22:52  1996
FONT=Times New Roman
SIZE=400 200
MESSAGE=Hello, Custom World
COLOR=0 25 50
PTSIZE=14
```

NOTE: The `Properties` class *extends* the `Hashtable` class. That means, all methods of `Hashtable` are available to `Properties` objects. Some functions are useful. For example, `size` returns the number of possible properties (well, it isn't *that* nice—it doesn't count the defaults). Similarly, `keys` returns an enumeration of all keys, except for the defaults. There is also a second function, called `propertyNames`, that returns all keys. The `put` function is downright dangerous. It doesn't check that you put strings into the table.

Does the *is–a* rule for using inheritance apply here? Is every property set a hash table? Not really. That these are true is really just an implementation detail. Maybe it is better to think of a property set as having a hash table. But then the hash table should be a private data field. Actually, in this case, a property set has two hash tables, one for the defaults and one for the non-default values.

We think a better design would be the following:

```
class Properties
{   public String getProperty(String) { . . . }
    public void put(String, String) { . . . }
    . . .
    private Hashtable nonDefaults;
    private Hashtable defaults;
}
```

We don't want to tell you to avoid the `Properties` class in the Java library. Provided you are careful to put nothing but strings in it, it works just fine. But think twice before using "quick-and-dirty" inheritance in your own programs.

java.util.Properties

- `Properties()`

  creates an empty property list.

- `Properties(Properties defaults)`

  creates an empty property list with a set of defaults.

  Parameters: defaults   the defaults to use for lookups

- `String getProperty(String key)`

  gets a property association; returns the string associated with the key, or the string associated with the key in the default table if it wasn't present in the table.

  Parameters: key   the key whose associated string to get

- `String getProperty(String key, String defaultValue)`

  gets a property with a default value if the key is not found; returns the string associated with the key, or the default string if it wasn't present in the table.

  Parameters: key   the key whose associated string to get

                    defaultValue   the string to return if the key is not present

- `void load(InputStream in) throws IOException`

  loads a property set from an `InputStream`.

  Parameters: in   the input stream

- `void save(OutputStream out, String header)`

  saves properties to an `OutputStream`.

  Parameters: out   the output stream

                    header   the header comment string

Hash Sets

Sometimes you just want to collect a bunch of objects, but no obvious key comes to mind. Suppose you need a collection of fonts. What can you use as a key? The face name? No, keys must be unique. Helvetica 10-point and Helvetica 14-point bold both have the same face name, "Helvetica", but they are not the same font. If you need to use the face name, point size, and style of a font, then you might as well use the font object itself as the key.

We just want to collect the fonts, test whether or not a particular font is in our set, and, perhaps, iterate through the ones we collected. A data structure that supports these operations is called a *set*. Of course, we can implement a set as a vector, but it isn't very efficient. Testing whether or not a particular object is already in the set (so we don't insert it twice) requires that we test all elements. A hash table is a much more attractive solution since it only tests elements with the same hash code.

We will use the standard `Hashtable` class in Java as the basis for our set implementation. Because we are only interested in the keys, we could use any (non-`null`) object for the value field. The simplest method is to use the same entry for the key and the value.

Here is a `HashSet` class that implements this idea:

```
class HashSet extends Hashtable
{   public void put(Object o) { super.put(o, o); }
    public boolean contains(Object o)
    {   return super.containsKey(o);
    }
    public Enumeration elements()
    {   return super.keys();
    }
}
```

(In this case, we don't mind inheriting from `Hashtable` because it turns out that none of the base class methods do anything dangerous.)

Example 9-6 shows how to put a hash set to work.

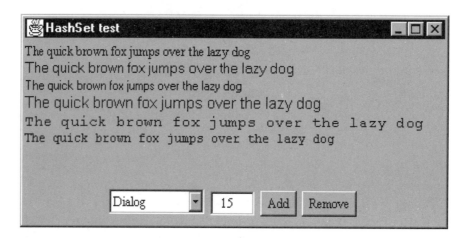

Figure 9-4: Hash set demo

Example 9-6: HashSetTest.java

```
import java.awt.*;
import java.util.*;
import corejava.*;

public class HashSetTest extends Frame
{   HashSetTest()
```

```
{   Panel p = new Panel();
    p.setLayout(new FlowLayout());
    name = new Choice();
    String[] f = Toolkit.getDefaultToolkit().getFontList();
    int i;
    for (i = 0; i < f.length; i++)
        name.addItem(f[i]);
    ptsize = new IntTextField(12, 1, 100, 4);
    p.add(name);
    p.add(ptsize);
    p.add(new Button("Add"));
    p.add(new Button("Remove"));
    add("South", p);
    add("Center", canvas = new FontCanvas());
    canvas.redraw(fonts);
}

public boolean handleEvent(Event evt)
{   if (evt.id == Event.WINDOW_DESTROY) System.exit(0);
    return super.handleEvent(evt);
}

public boolean action(Event evt, Object arg)
{   if (arg.equals("Add"))
    {   if (ptsize.isValid())
        {   String n = name.getSelectedItem();
            fonts.put(new Font(n, Font.PLAIN,
                ptsize.getValue()));
        }
    }
    else if (arg.equals("Remove"))
    {   if (ptsize.isValid())
        {   String n = name.getSelectedItem();
            fonts.remove(new Font(n, Font.PLAIN,
                ptsize.getValue()));
        }
    }
    else return super.action(evt, arg);
    canvas.redraw(fonts);
    return true;
}
public static void main(String args[])
{   Frame f = new HashSetTest();
    f.resize(300, 200);
    f.show();
}

private Choice name;
private IntTextField ptsize;
```

```
    private FontCanvas canvas;
    private HashSet fonts = new HashSet();

}

class HashSet extends Hashtable
{   public void put(Object o) { super.put(o, o); }
    public boolean contains(Object o)
    {   return super.containsKey(o);
    }
    public Enumeration elements()
    {   return super.keys();
    }
}

class FontCanvas extends Canvas
{   public void redraw(HashSet new_a)
    {   a = new_a;
        repaint();
    }

    public void paint(Graphics g)
    {   Enumeration e = a.elements();
        int x = 0;
        int y = 0;
        while (e.hasMoreElements())
        {   Font f = (Font)e.nextElement();
            g.setFont(f);
            FontMetrics fm = g.getFontMetrics(f);
            y += fm.getHeight();
            g.drawString(
            "The quick brown fox jumps over the lazy dog", x, y);
        }
    }

    private HashSet a;
}
```

Linked Lists

So far, we have seen two data structures for collecting elements, vectors and hash sets. Hash sets perform well when all that you are interested in doing is adding and removing elements from the structure. The drawback is that the elements are scattered all over the hash table. In particular, the order in which the elements were inserted is completely lost when we enumerate the elements.

If you want an ordered sequence of elements *and* the ability to rapidly insert and remove elements in the middle of the sequence, then you need a linked list. Figure 9-5 shows a diagram for a linked list data structure. The *list header* contains a pointer to the first *link*, which stores a data item and a pointer to the next link. That link, likewise, stores a data item and a pointer to the next link, and so on. The last link has a `null` pointer to denote the end of the list.

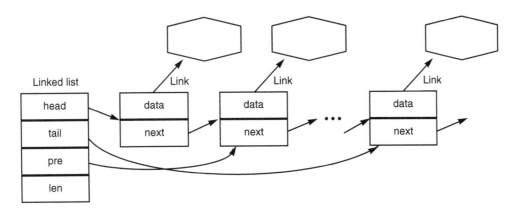

Figure 9-5: Linked lists

Some people think that you cannot program a linked list in Java, because linked lists need pointers, and Java doesn't have them. Nothing could be further from the truth. Lists are actually easier to program in Java than in just about any other programming language. Every object reference in Java is already a pointer. This makes a basic `Link` class particularly simple.

```
class Link
{   Object data;
    Link next; //pointer to another object of the class
}
```

In addition, we need a `List` class. It holds a pointer to the head link, and (in order to make rapid insertion at the tail end of the list easier) we include a pointer to the tail as well. We also keep a field for the list size, so we don't need to traverse the entire list every time the caller wants to have an element count.

Furthermore, there must be some way of inserting in the middle of the list. We do this by storing a *cursor* with the list object. The cursor marks a specific element in the linked list. The `reset` method resets the cursor to the beginning of the list. The `nextElement` method advances it to the next element. This permits positioning of the cursor anywhere in the linked list. The `remove` method removes the element under the cursor, and the `put` method inserts a new object before the cursor. (The cursor functions just like the cursor on a terminal. Characters are inserted before the cursor and deleted from under the cursor.)

The advantage of using a cursor is that the individual links are completely hidden from the list user, so the list user can't mess them up.

There is a technical difficulty with storing the cursor position. When implementing the `remove` operation, we must relink the *predecessor* of the cursor link. But in a singly linked list, we cannot easily locate a link's predecessor. For that reason, we actually save the cursor's predecessor—not the actual cursor position—in the `List` data structure.

Before looking at the implementation code, here is an example of how you use the list. We first insert all employees in a list and then remove those whose salary is less than $50,000.

```
LinkedList a = new LinkedList();
for (i = 0; i < staff.length; i++) a.append(staff[i]);
a.reset();
while (a.hasMoreElements())
{  Employee e = (Employee)a.currentElement();
   if (e.salary() < 50000) a.remove();
   else a.nextElement();
}
```

The Code for Our Linked List Class

Unless you are a list enthusiast, you probably don't want to look at the details of the linking and unlinking. Note, however, that there is one significant difference between the Java code and its equivalent C++ code: because of garbage collection, you *never* need to worry about recycling links. Example 9-7 gives you the code for the LinkedList class. It may be found in the corejava directory.

Example 9-7: LinkedList.java

```
public class LinkedList
{  public void reset()
   /**
    * reset the cursor
    */
   {  pre = null;
   }


   public boolean hasMoreElements()
   /**
    * @return true iff the cursor is not at the end of the
    * list
    */
   {  return cursor() != null;
   }
```

```java
public Object nextElement()
/**
 * move the cursor to the next position
 * @return the current element (before advancing the
 * position)
 * @exception NoSuchElementException if already at the
 * end of the list
 */
{   if (pre == null) pre = head; else pre = pre.next;
    if (pre == null)
        throw new java.util.NoSuchElementException();
    return pre.data;
}


public Object currentElement()
/**
 * @return the current element under the cursor
 * @exception NoSuchElementException if already at the
 * end of the list
 */
{   Link cur = cursor();
    if (cur == null)
        throw new java.util.NoSuchElementException();
    return cur.data;
}


public void insert(Object n)
/**
 * insert before the iterator position
 * @param n the object to insert
 */
{   Link p = new Link(n, cursor());

    if (pre != null)
    {   pre.next = p;
        if (pre == tail) tail = p;
    }
    else
    {   if (head == null) tail = p;
        head = p;
    }

    pre = p;
    len++;
}
```

```java
public void append(Object n)
/**
  * insert after the tail of the list
  * @param n - the value to insert
  */
{   Link p = new Link(n, null);
    if (head == null) head = tail = p;
    else
    {   tail.next = p;
        tail = p;
    }
    len++;
}


public Object remove()
/**
  * remove the element under the cursor
  * @return the removed element
  * @exception NoSuchElementException if already at the
  * end of the list
  */
{   Link cur = cursor();
    if (cur == null)
        throw new java.util.NoSuchElementException();
    if (tail == cur) tail = pre;
    if (pre != null)
        pre.next = cur.next;
    else
        head = cur.next;
    len--;
    return cur.data;
}


 int size()
/**
  * @return the number of elements in the list
  */
{   return len;
}

public java.util.Enumeration elements()
/**
  * @return an enumeration to iterate through all elements
  * in the list
  */
{   return new ListEnumeration(head);
}
```

```
    public static void main(String[] args)
    {   LinkedList a = new LinkedList();
        for (int i = 1; i <= 10; i++)
            a.insert(new Integer(i));
        java.util.Enumeration e = a.elements();
        while (e.hasMoreElements())
            System.out.println(e.nextElement());

        a.reset();
        while (a.hasMoreElements())
        {   a.remove();
            a.nextElement();
        }
        a.reset();
        while (a.hasMoreElements())
            System.out.println(a.nextElement());
    }

    private Link cursor()
    {   if (pre == null) return head; else return pre.next;
    }

    private Link head;
    private Link tail;
    private Link pre; // predecessor of cursor
    private int len;

}

class Link
{   Object data;
    Link next;
    Link(Object d, Link n) { data = d; next = n; }
}

class ListEnumeration implements java.util.Enumeration
{   public ListEnumeration( Link l)
    {   cursor = l;
    }

    public boolean hasMoreElements()
    /**
     * @return true iff the iterator is not at the end of the
     * list
     */
    {   return cursor != null;
    }
```

```
    public Object nextElement()
    /**
      * move the iterator to the next position
      * @return the current element (before advancing the
      * position)
      * @exception NoSuchElementException if already at the
      * end of the list
      */
    {   if (cursor == null)
          throw new java.util.NoSuchElementException();
        Object r = cursor.data;
        cursor = cursor.next;
        return r;
    }

    private Link cursor;
}
```

A Linked List Demonstration

Finally, Example 9-8 is a graphical program that shows how the lists really work (shown in Figure 9-6). Click on the buttons to simulate the list operations, and see the list change before your very eyes!

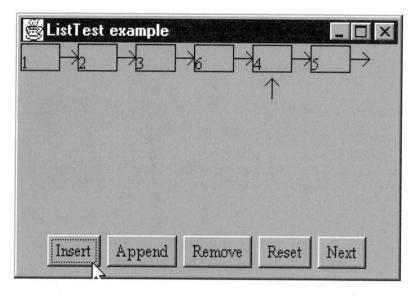

Figure 9-6: Linked list demo at work

Example 9-8: ListTest.java

```java
import java.awt.*;
import java.util.*;

public class ListTest extends Frame
{   public ListTest()
    {   Panel p = new Panel();
        p.setLayout(new FlowLayout());
        p.add(new Button("Insert"));
        p.add(new Button("Append"));
        p.add(new Button("Remove"));
        p.add(new Button("Reset"));
        p.add(new Button("Next"));
        add("South", p);
        add("Center", canvas = new ListCanvas());
        canvas.redraw(a);
    }

    public boolean handleEvent(Event evt)
    {   if (evt.id == Event.WINDOW_DESTROY) System.exit(0);
        return super.handleEvent(evt);
    }

    public boolean action(Event evt, Object arg)
    {   if (arg.equals("Insert"))
        {   a.insert(new Integer(m));
            m++;
        }
        else if (arg.equals("Append"))
        {   a.append(new Integer(m));
            m++;
        }
        else if (arg.equals("Remove"))
            a.remove();
        else if (arg.equals("Next"))
            a.nextElement();
        else if (arg.equals("Reset"))
            a.reset();
        else return super.action(evt, arg);
        canvas.redraw(a);
        return true;
    }

    public static void main(String args[])
    {   Frame f = new ListTest();
        f.resize(300, 200);
        f.show();
    }
```

```
      private LinkedList a = new LinkedList();
      private ListCanvas canvas;
      private int m = 1;

}

class ListCanvas extends Canvas
{   public void redraw(LinkedList new_a)
    {   a = new_a;
        repaint();
    }


    public void paint(Graphics g)
    {   Enumeration e = a.elements();
        int x = 0;
        int y = 0;
        int cx = 0;
        while (e.hasMoreElements())
        {   g.drawRect(x, y, 30, 20);
            Integer i = (Integer)e.nextElement();
            if (a.hasMoreElements()
                && i.equals(a.currentElement()))
                cx = x;

            g.drawString(i.toString(), x + 1, y + 19);
            g.drawLine(x + 30, y + 10, x + 45, y + 10);
            g.drawLine(x + 45, y + 10, x + 40, y + 5);
            g.drawLine(x + 45, y + 10, x + 40, y + 15);
            x += 45;
        }
        if (!a.hasMoreElements()) cx = x;
        g.drawLine(cx + 15, 25, cx + 15, 40);
        g.drawLine(cx + 15, 25, cx + 10, 30);
        g.drawLine(cx + 15, 25, cx + 20, 30);
    }

    private LinkedList a;

}
```

Linked List Enumeration

If you need to inspect all elements in a list, you can use the following traversal
code:

```
a.reset();
while (a.hasMoreElements())
{         Object o = a.nextElement();
          do something with o;
}
```

But that messes up the list cursor. This can be a problem: maybe the cursor was at an important position before the traversal, but after the traversal the old cursor position is lost—it is now at the end of the list. For that reason, and also as a general token of support for the Enumeration interface, we also supply an elements method that returns an Enumeration object. You can use it just like you use any other object that implements the enumeration interface.

```
Enumeration e = a.elements();
while (e.hasMoreElements())
{   Object o = e.nextElement();
    //do something with o;
}
```

So far, we have been consumers of enumeration objects, and the List class is the producer of such an object. This is a good place to learn how to create such an entity. Enumeration is an interface, not a class, so we cannot simply call new Enumeration() to get a new enumeration object.

Even if Enumeration were a class, it couldn't possibly know about the structure of our List class, since it is not a part of standard Java. Instead, we need to design a new class that implements the Enumeration interface.

```
class ListEnumeration implements Enumeration
{   public boolean hasMoreElements()
    {   return current != null;
    }
    public Object nextElement()
    {   Object r = current.data;
        current = current.next;
        return r;
    }
    ListEnumeration(Link first) { current = first; }
    private Link current;
}
```

The elements method of the LinkedList class generates a new enumeration object.

```
class LinkedList
{   . . .
    Enumeration elements()
    {   return new ListEnumeration(head);
    }
}
```

Access to Links

Note that the data fields of the `Link` structure are defined without either
`public` or `private` access specified in the list module. Of course, we didn't
want them to be public, but we couldn't make them private either. The
`LinkedList` class needs access to the data fields of the links. Making the data
items private and supplying public access methods wouldn't have done us any
good. We don't want any class but the `LinkedList` class to call those methods.

The Java protection mechanism is not exact enough to express this concept. In
Java, you can set the protection to the class (`private`), the world (`public`), the
package and all subclasses (`protected`), or the package (the default). The first
four options are not appropriate in this case, so we settled for the last one. That
does mean that any other code in the same package has the potential to mess
with the links. If we put the `LinkedList` class in a separate package, like
`corejava`, then it is unlikely that other programmers will smuggle their code
to the package just to invade the list. But if the `List` class is part of the default
package, then Java offers no good method for protecting the linked data.

Queues

In many programs, data are generated faster than can be processed. Then you
want to put the incoming data into a queue and remove it later, so that the first
item inserted also becomes the first one removed. This is often called FIFO (first
in, first out).

For example, in Chapter 8 we implemented a very simple Web crawler, a program that reads through a Web page, looks up all links to other Web pages, and
then follows each link that it finds. That program inserted URLs at the end of a
queue. When it was done, it took out the first element of the queue and visited
that Web page. At the time, we used a list box, hardly a robust data structure.

Linked lists are ideally suited for this purpose. We simply append elements at
the end of the list and remove them from the head. Here is a queue class that
implements this idea.

```
class Queue
{   public void append(Object o) { data.append(o); }
    public Object remove() { return data.remove(); }
    public int size() { data.size(); }
    public Enumeration elements() { data.elements(); }
    private LinkedList data;
}
```

The following example program uses a queue to produce a *breadth-first* listing of
a directory tree. We start at the root directory. Whenever we visit a new directory, we get all subdirectories and add them to the tail of the queue. Then we

remove the head of the queue and repeat the process. Because the first directories in the queue are the children of the root directory, we first visit all subdirectories in level 1. Then their subdirectories are added to the queue, and we visit the level 2 subdirectories. The process is repeated until all subdirectories have been visited. Try it out—you will find the order of the subdirectories somewhat unconventional. It is just the opposite of the *depth-first* listing that you get from the DOS DIR/S or TREE commands. Here's what you see:

```
\.
\.\CoreJavaBook
\.\CoreJavaBook\ch8
\.\CoreJavaBook\WinEdit
\.\CoreJavaBook\corejava
\.\CoreJavaBook\ch2
\.\CoreJavaBook\ch3
\.\CoreJavaBook\ch4
\.\CoreJavaBook\ch5
\.\CoreJavaBook\ch6
\.\CoreJavaBook\ch7
\.\CoreJavaBook\ch9
\.\CoreJavaBook\ch12
\.\CoreJavaBook\ch10
\.\CoreJavaBook\ch11
\.\CoreJavaBook\ch13
\.\CoreJavaBook\ch8\Chart
\.\CoreJavaBook\ch8\Retire
\.\CoreJavaBook\ch8\AppletApplication
\.\CoreJavaBook\ch8\CrawlerApplet
```

Example 9-9 shows the program.

Example 9-9: DirQueue.java

```java
import java.io.*;
import java.util.*;

public class DirQueue
{  public static void main(String[] args)
   {  Queue dirs = new Queue();
      dirs.append(new File(File.separator + "."));
      while (dirs.size() > 0)
      {  File f = (File)dirs.remove();
         System.out.println(f);
```

```
        String[] s = f.list();
        if (s != null)
        {   for (int i = 0; i < s.length; i++)
            {   File d = new File(f.getAbsolutePath()
                + File.separator + s[i]);
                if (d.isDirectory())
                    dirs.append(d);
            }
        }
    }
}

class Queue
{   public void append(Object o) { data.append(o); }
    public Object remove() { return data.remove(); }
    public int size() { return data.size(); }
    public Enumeration elements() { return data.elements(); }
    private LinkedList data = new LinkedList();
}
```

Stacks

In the last section, we saw how to implement a FIFO data structure. Occasionally, a "last in, first out" structure is required. The Java library supplies such a data structure, called Stack. The push method in the Stack class adds an element to the top of the stack; the pop method removes the top element from the stack.

The Stack class derives from Vector. Conceptually, this is dubious because you can use the Vector methods to change the stack contents in the middle. On the other hand, you can also use the elements method to inspect the elements of the vector, which is occasionally useful.

We traverse all directories on a disk, pushing newly found directories onto the top of the stack. Since we always pop the most recently found directory for further investigation, we get a *depth-first* traversal of the directory tree. Here's what you will see:

```
\.
\.\CoreJavaBook
\.\CoreJavaBook\ch13
\.\CoreJavaBook\ch13\MailOrderTest
\.\CoreJavaBook\ch13\EchoServer
\.\CoreJavaBook\ch13\ProxySvr
\.\CoreJavaBook\ch13\PriceListTest
\.\CoreJavaBook\ch13\MailTo
```

```
\.\CoreJavaBook\ch13\ThreadedEchoServer
\.\CoreJavaBook\ch13\WeatherApplet
\.\CoreJavaBook\ch13\SocketTest
\.\CoreJavaBook\ch11
\.\CoreJavaBook\ch11\DataFileTest
\.\CoreJavaBook\ch11\PolyDataTest
\.\CoreJavaBook\ch11\PersistentTest
\.\CoreJavaBook\ch11\RandomFileTest
```

Example 9-10 shows the program.

Example 9-10: DirStack.java

```java
import java.io.*;
import java.util.*;

public class DirStack
{  public static void main(String[] args)
   {  Stack dirs = new Stack();
      dirs.push(new File(File.separator + "."));
      while (dirs.size() > 0)
      {  File f = (File)dirs.pop();
         System.out.println(f);
         String[] s = f.list();
         if (s != null)
         {  for (int i = 0; i < s.length; i++)
            {  File d = new File(f.getAbsolutePath()
               + File.separator + s[i]);
               if (d.isDirectory())
                  dirs.push(d);
            }
         }
      }
   }
}
```

`java.util.Stack`

*   `void push(Object item)`

    pushes an item onto the stack.

    Parameters: `item`   the item to be added

*   `Object pop()`

    pops and returns the top item of the stack. Don't call this method if the stack is empty.

- `Object peek()`

  returns the top of the stack without popping it. Don't call this method if the stack is empty.

Multi-Dimensional Arrays

Suppose you want to make a table of numbers that shows how much an investment of $10,000 will grow after a number of years under different interest rate scenarios in which interest is paid monthly and reinvested. Table 9-3 illustrates this scenario.

Table 9-3: Interest rates for different investment time periods

Years	Interest rate					
	5.00%	5.50%	6.00%	6.50%	7.00%	7.50%
10	16453.09	17293.07	18175.94	19103.88	20079.20	21104.31
20	26959.70	29770.53	32874.42	36301.92	40086.77	44266.24
30	43997.90	51024.07	59172.28	68621.70	79580.14	92288.56
40	71519.81	87070.09	106001.40	129048.88	157107.49	191266.77
50	115804.66	147944.43	189004.10	241459.24	308472.48	394084.20

The obvious way to store this information is in a two-dimensional array (or matrix) which we will call `balance`.

The definition of a matrix in Java is simple enough. For example:

```
double[][] balance;
```

As always in Java, you cannot use an array until you initialize it with a call to new. In this case, the initialization is as follows:

```
balance = new double[5][6];
```

Once the array is initialized, you can access individual elements:

```
balance[i][j] = futureValue(10000, 10 + 10 * i, 5 + 0.5 * j);
```

Example 9-11 shows the full program that computes the table.

Example 9-11: CompoundInterest.java

```
import corejava.*;

public class CompoundInterest
{  public static double futureValue(double initialBalance,
```

```
      double p, double nyear)
    {   return initialBalance * Math.pow(1 + p / 12 / 100,
        12 * nyear);
    }

    public static void main(String[] args)
    {   double[][] balance;
        balance = new double[5][6];
        int i;
        int j;
        for (i = 0; i < 5; i++)
            for (j = 0; j < 6; j++)
                balance[i][j] = futureValue(10000, 10 + 10 * i,
                    5 + 0.5 * j);
        System.out.print("     ");
        for (j = 0; j < 6; j++)
            Format.print(System.out, "%9.2f%", 5 + 0.5 * j);
        System.out.println("");
        for (i = 0; i < 5; i++)
        {   Format.print(System.out, "%3d", 10 + 10 * i);
            for (j = 0; j < 6; j++)
                Format.print(System.out, "%10.2f",
                    balance[i][j]);
            System.out.println("");
        }
    }
}
```

Under the Hood of Multi-Dimensional Arrays

So far, what you have seen is not too different from other programming languages. But there is actually something subtle going on behind the scenes that you can sometimes turn to your advantage: Java has *no* multi-dimensional arrays at all, only one-dimensional arrays. Multi-dimensional arrays are faked as "arrays of arrays."

For example, the balance array in the preceding example is actually an array that contains five elements, each of which is an array of six floating-point numbers.

The expression balance[i] refers to the i'th subarray, that is, the i'th row of the table. It is, itself, an array, and balance[i][j] refers to the j'th entry of that array.

Because rows of arrays are individually accessible, you can actually swap them!

```
    double[] temp = balance[i];
    balance[i] = balance[i + 1];
    balance[i + 1] = temp;
```

It is easy to make "ragged" arrays, that is, arrays in which different rows have different lengths. Here is the standard example. Let us make an array to store "Pascal's triangle." Pascal's triangle is the following arrangement:

```
            1
         1     1
       1    2    1
     1    3    3    1
   1    4    6    4    1
  1    5   10   10    5    1
 1   6   15   20   15    6    1
```

You put a 1 at the corners of the triangle, and then fill each element with the sum of the two numbers above it diagonally. To store the triangle as a matrix, simply visualize the rows pushed to the left, like this:

```
1
1    1
1    2    1
1    3    3    1
1    4    6    4    1
1    5   10   10    5    1
1    6   15   20   15    6    1
```

Actually, there is no need to store the right half of a row, because it is identical to the left half read backwards. So we will simply store the following:

```
1
1
1    2
1    3
1    4    6
1    5   10
1    6   15   20
```

That is, the i'th row has (i / 2) + 1 elements. (Recall that the top row corresponds to i = 0.) To build this ragged array, first allocate the array holding the rows.

```
int[][] binom = new int[n + 1][];
```

Next, allocate the rows.

```
for (i = 0; i <= n; i++)
   binom[i] = new int[i / 2 + 1];
```

Now that the array is allocated, we can access the elements in the normal way, provided we do not overstep the bounds.

```
for (i = 0; i <= n; i++)
   for (j = 0; j <= i / 2; j++)
      if (j == 0)
         binom[i][j] = 1;
      else if (2 * j < i)
         binom[i][j] = binom[i - 1][j - 1] + binom[i - 1][j];
      else
         binom[i][j] = 2 * binom[i - 1][j - 1];
```

C++ NOTE: Recall that a one-dimensional array in Java really corresponds to a C++ pointer to a heap array. That is,

```
int[] numbers = new int[50]; // Java
```

is not the same as

```
int numbers[50]; // C++
```

but rather

```
int* numbers = new int[50]; // C++
```

Similarly,

```
double[][] balance = new double[5][6]; // Java
```

is not the same as

```
double balance[5][6]; // C++
```

or even

```
double (*balance)[6] = new double[5][6]; // C++
```

Instead, an array of five pointers is allocated:

```
double** balance = new double*[5];
```

Then each element in the pointer array is filled with an array of 6 numbers:

```
for (i = 0; i < 5; i++) balance[i] = new double[6];
```

Mercifully, this loop is automatic when you ask for a `new double[5][6]`. When you want ragged arrays, you allocate the row arrays separately.

Just for fun, we give a nice application of the Pascal triangle. We compute the remainders of the numbers in the triangle and color them with different colors. For example, if you choose the quotient 5 in the text field, all values in the Pascal triangle that are divisible by 5 show up as one color, all that leave a remainder of 1 as another color, and so on, as shown in Figure 9-7 and Example 9-12.

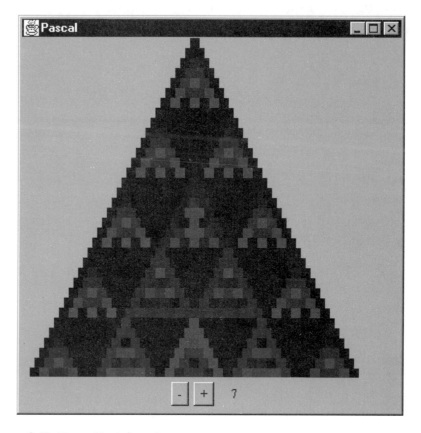

Figure 9-7: Pascal's triangle

Example 9-12: Pascal.java

```
import java.awt.*;

public class Pascal extends Frame
{  public Pascal()
   {  Panel p = new Panel();
      p.setLayout(new FlowLayout());
      p.add(new Button("-"));
```

```
        p.add(new Button("+"));
        label = new Label("2    ");
        p.add(label);
        add("South", p);
        canvas = new PascalCanvas();
        add("Center", canvas);
    }

    public boolean handleEvent(Event evt)
    {   if (evt.id == Event.WINDOW_DESTROY) System.exit(0);
        return super.handleEvent(evt);
    }

    public boolean action(Event evt, Object arg)
    {   if (arg.equals("-"))
        {   if (m > 1) m--;
            label.setText(m + "    ");
            canvas.redraw(m);
        }
        if (arg.equals("+"))
        {   m++;
            label.setText(m + "    ");
            canvas.redraw(m);
        }
        else return super.action(evt, arg);
        return true;
    }

    public static void main(String args[])
    {   Frame f = new Pascal();
        f.resize(400, 400);
        f.show();
    }

    private Label label;
    private PascalCanvas canvas;
    private int m = 2;
}

class PascalCanvas extends Canvas
{   public PascalCanvas()
    {   binom = new int[n + 1][];
        int i;
        int j;
        for (i = 0; i <= n; i++)
            binom[i] = new int[i / 2 + 1];
        for (i = 0; i <= n; i++)
            for (j = 0; j <= i / 2; j++)
```

```java
          if (j == 0)
              binom[i][j] = 1;
          else if (2 * j < i)
              binom[i][j] = binom[i - 1][j - 1]
                  + binom[i - 1][j];
          else
              binom[i][j] = 2 * binom[i - 1][j - 1];
   }
   public void redraw(int new_m)
   {   m = new_m;
       repaint();
   }

   public void paint(Graphics g)
   {   int i;
       int j;

       int nmax = 1 + size().height / 10;
       if (nmax > n) nmax = n;
       for (i = 0; i <= nmax; i++)
       {   for (j = 0; j <= i; j++)
           {   int k = 2 * j <= i ? j : i - j;
               int b = binom[i][k] % m;
               g.setColor(new Color((255 * b) / (m - 1), 0, 0));
               g.fillRect(5 * (nmax + 1 - i + 2 * j), 10 * i,
                   10, 10);
           }
       }
   }

   private int[][] binom;
   private int m = 7;
   private final int n = 100;


}
```

CHAPTER
10

- Dealing with Errors

- Throwing Exceptions

- Catching Exceptions

- Some Tips on Using Exceptions

- Debugging Techniques

- Using the JDB Debugger

Exceptions and Debugging

In a perfect world, users would never enter data in the wrong form, files they choose to open would always exist, and code would never have bugs. So far, we have mostly presented code as though we lived in this kind of perfect world. It is now time to turn to the mechanisms Java has for dealing with the real world of bad data and buggy code.

Encountering errors is unpleasant. If a user loses all the work he or she did during a program session due to a programming mistake or some external circumstance, that user may forever turn away from your program. At the very least, you must:

- notify the user of an error
- save all work
- allow users to gracefully exit the program.

For exceptional situations such as bad input data with the potential to bomb the program, Java uses a form of error-trapping called, naturally enough, *exception-handling*. Exception-handling in Java is similar to that in C++ or Delphi. It is far more flexible than the `On Error GoTo` syntax used in VB. The first part of this chapter covers Java's exceptions.

The second part of this chapter concerns finding bugs in your code before they cause exceptions at run time. Unfortunately, at the time of this writing, Java's native bug detection is back in the dark ages. We give you some tips and a few tools to ease the pain. Then we explain how to use the command line debugger as a tool of last resort. Third party products such as Sun's Java Workshop (a 30 day trial is included on the CD), Symantec's Café and Microsoft's Visual J++ have quite useful debuggers that are well worth the cost of the product for the serious Java developer.

Dealing with Errors

Suppose an error occurs in a Java program. The error might be caused by a file containing wrong information, a flaky network connection, or (we hate to mention it) an invalid array or null reference access in your code. Users expect that programs will act sensibly under error conditions. If an operation cannot be completed because of an error, the program ought to either:

- return to a safe state and enable the user to execute other commands, or

- save all work and terminate the program gracefully.

This is not an easy task. The code that detects (or even causes) the error condition is usually far removed from the code that can roll back data to a safe state, or save the user's work and exit cheerfully. The central mission of exception-handling is to transfer control from where the error occurred to an error-handler that can deal with the situation.

To handle exceptional situations in your program, you must take into account the errors and problems that may occur. What sorts of problems do you need to consider?

User input errors. In addition to the inevitable typos, some users like to blaze their own trail instead of following directions. Suppose, for example, that a user asks to connect to a URL that is syntactically wrong. Your code should check the syntax, but suppose it does not. Then the network package will complain. Similarly, a user may enter a syntactically correct URL to a Web page that no longer exists or is too busy.

Device errors. Hardware does not always do what you want it to. The printer may be off. Serial ports may be unavailable. Devices will often fail in the middle of a task. For example, a printer may run out of paper in the middle of a print-out.

Physical limitations. Disks can fill up; you run out of available memory.

Code errors. A method may not perform correctly. For example, it could deliver wrong answers or use other methods incorrectly. Computing an invalid array index, trying to find a nonexistent entry in a hash table, and trying to pop an empty stack are all examples of a method's responding to code errors.

The traditional reaction to an error in a function is to return a special error code that the calling function analyzes. For example, functions that read information back from files return a –1 end-of-file value marker rather than a standard character. This is still an efficient method for dealing with many exceptional conditions. Unfortunately, it is not always possible to return an error code. There may be no obvious way of distinguishing valid and invalid data. A function returning an integer cannot simply return –1 to denote the error. The value –1 might be perfectly valid.

Instead, as we mentioned back in Chapter 5, Java allows every method an alternate exit path if it is unable to complete its task in the normal way. In that case, the method does not return a value. Instead, it *throws* an object that encapsulates the error information. The method exits immediately; it does not return a value. The code calling the method is not activated. Instead, the exception-handling mechanism begins its search for a *handler* that can deal with that particular error condition.

Exceptions have their own syntax and are part of a special inheritance hierarchy. We take up the syntax first and then give a few hints on how to use this language feature effectively.

Throwing Exceptions

The Classification of Error Types

In Java, an exception is always an instance of a class derived from `Throwable`. In particular, as you will soon see, you can create your own exception classes by inheritance if the ones built into Java do not suit your needs.

Figure 10-1 is a simplified diagram of the exception hierarchy in Java:

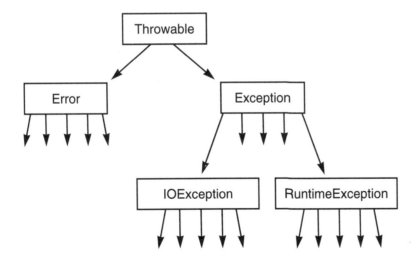

Figure 10-1: Exception hierarchy in Java

Notice that all exceptions descend from `Throwable`, but immediately split into two branches: `Error` and `Exception`.

The `Error` hierarchy describes internal errors and resource exhaustion inside the Java run time system. You should not throw an object of such a type. Furthermore, there is little you can do if such an internal error occurs, beyond notifying the user and trying to terminate the program gracefully. These error conditions are quite rare.

In your programming, you will focus on the `Exception` hierarchy. The exception hierarchy is also split into two branches: exceptions that derive from `RuntimeException` and those that do not. The general rule is this: A `RuntimeException` happens because you made a programming error. Any other exception occurs because a bad thing, such as an I/O error, happened to your otherwise good program.

Exceptions that inherit from `RuntimeException` include such problems as:

- a bad cast,

- an out-of-bounds array access,

- a null pointer access.

Exceptions that do not inherit from `RuntimeException` include:

- trying to read past the end of a file,

- trying to open a malformed URL,

- trying to find a `Class` object for a string that does not denote an existing class.

The rule "If it is a `RuntimeException`, it was your fault" works pretty well. You could have avoided that `ArrayIndexOutOfBoundsException` by testing the array index against the array bounds. The `NullPointerException` would not have happened had you checked whether or not the variable was `null` before using it.

How about a malformed URL? Isn't it also possible to find out whether or not it is "malformed" before using it? Well, different browsers can handle different kinds of URLs. For example, Netscape can deal with a `mailto:` URL, whereas the applet viewer cannot. Thus, the notion of "malformed" depends on the environment, not just on your code.

NOTE: The name `RuntimeException` is somewhat confusing. Of course, all of the errors we are discussing occur at run time.

Let us have a final look at the classes that inherit from `Exception`. Outside of the `RuntimeException` branch, there are six subclasses used in the JDK 1.02. There are more exception classes for JDBC and for RMI. We deal with them in Chapters 14 (JDBC) and 15 (RMI). For a listing of the exception subclasses, see Table 10-1. The first two are important for input/output and for multithreading. The remaining four subclasses are specialized. It is best to handle them right away if you call a method that throws them.

Table 10-1: Exception subclasses used in the JDK 1.02.

`IOException`	used for input/output (see Chapters 11 and 13)
`InterruptedException`	used for multithreading (see Chapter 12)
`ClassNotFoundException`	thrown by `Class.forName`
`CloneNotSupportedException`	thrown by `Object.clone` (see Chapter 5)
`IllegalAccessException`	thrown by `Class.newInstance` if the class has no default constructor
`InstantiationException`	thrown by `Class.newInstance` if the class is abstract or an interface

C++ NOTE: If you are familiar with the (much more limited) exception hierarchy of the ANSI C++ library, you will be really confused at this point. C++ has two fundamental exception classes, `runtime_error` and `logic_error`. The `logic_error` class is the equivalent of Java's `RuntimeException` and also denotes logical errors in the program. The `runtime_error` class is the base class for exceptions caused by unpredictable problems. It is equivalent to exceptions in Java that are *not* of type `RuntimeException`.

Advertising the Exceptions That a Method Throws

A Java method can throw an exception if it encounters a situation it cannot handle. The idea is simple: a function is not only going to tell the Java compiler what values it can return, *it is also going to tell the compiler what can go wrong.*

For example, code that attempts to read from a file knows the file might not exist or might be empty. The code should be able to throw some sort of `IOException`. The idea is that the header of a method changes to reflect the exceptions it can throw. For example, here is the header for a method in the

`DataInputStream` class to read a line of text from a stream, such as a file or network connection. (See Chapter 12 for more on files.)

```
public String readLine() throws IOException
```

This method returns a string but also has the capacity to go wrong, in which case the method will not return a string, but instead will throw a special object of the `IOException` class. If it does, then Java will begin to search for a handler that can deal with `IOException` objects.

Exceptions are thrown for one of four possible scenarios:

- you call a method that throws an exception, for example, the `readLine` method of the `DataInputStream`;

- you detect an error and throw an exception with the `throw` statement (we will cover the `throw` statement in the next section);

- you make a programming error, such as `a[-1] = 0;`

- an internal error occurs in Java.

If either of the first two scenarios occurs, you must tell the public that your method may throw an exception. Why? Any method that throws an exception is a potential death trap. If no handler catches the exception, the program terminates. You declare the possibility that your method may throw an exception with an *exception specification* in the method header.

```
class Animation
{   . . .
    public Image loadImage(String s) throws IOException
    {   . . .
    }
}
```

If a method must deal with more than one exception, you must indicate all exceptions in the header:

```
class Animation
{   . . .
    public Image loadImage(String s)
        throws EOFException, MalformedURLException
    {   . . .
    }
}
```

However, you do not need to advertise internal Java errors, that is, exceptions inheriting from `Error`. Any code could potentially throw those exceptions, and they are entirely beyond your control.

Similarly, you should not advertise exceptions inheriting from `RuntimeException`.

```
class Animation
{   . . .
    void drawImage(int i)
        throws ArrayIndexOutOfBoundsException // NO!!!
    {   . . .
    }
}
```

These run time errors are completely under your control. If you are so concerned about array index errors, you should spend the time needed to fix them, instead of advertising the possibility that they can happen.

Some people call any exception that derives from the class `Error` or the class `RuntimeException` an *implicit* exception. All other exceptions are called *explicit* exceptions. This is useful terminology that we will adopt. The explicit exceptions are those you must deal with. Implicit exceptions are either beyond your control (`Error`) or result from conditions that you should not have allowed in the first place (`RuntimeException`).

The Java rule for exception specifications is simple:

A method must declare all the explicit exceptions it throws.

When a class declares that it throws an exception of a particular class, then it may throw an exception of that class or its child classes. For example, the `readLine` method of the `DataInputStream` says that it throws an `IOException`. We do not know what kind of `IOException`. It could be a plain `IOException` or an object of one of the various child classes, such as `EOFException`.

If you override a method from a parent class, the child class method cannot throw more explicit exceptions than the parent class method. (It can throw fewer, if it likes.) In particular, if the parent class method throws no explicit exception at all, neither can the child class.

C++ NOTE: The `throws` specifier is the same as the `throw` specifier in C++, with one important difference. In C++, `throw` specifiers are enforced at *run time,* not at compile time. That is, the C++ compiler pays no attention to exception specifications. But if an exception is thrown in a function that is not part of the `throw` list, then the `unexpected` function is called, and, by default, the program terminates.

Also, in C++ a function may throw any exception if no `throw` specification is given. In Java, a method without a `throws` specifier may not throw any exception at all.

How to Throw an Exception

Let us suppose something terrible has happened in your code. You are reading in a file whose header promised

```
Content-length: 1024
```

But you get an end of file after 733 characters. You decide this situation is so abnormal that you want to throw an exception.

You need to decide what exception type to throw. Some kind of IOException would be a good choice. Perusing the tree.html file in the Java API documentation, you find an EOFException with the description "Signals that an EOF has been reached unexpectedly during input". Perfect. Here is how you throw it:

```
throw new EOFException();
```

or, if you prefer,

```
EOFException e = new EOFException();
throw e;
```

The EOFException has a second constructor that takes a string argument. You can put this to good use by describing the exceptional condition more carefully.

```
String gripe = "Content-length: " + len + " Received: " + n;
throw new EOFException(gripe);
```

Here is how it all fits together:

```
String readData(DataInput in) throws EOFException
{   . . .
    while (. . .)
    {   if (ch == -1) // EOF encountered
        {   if (n < len)
                throw new EOFException();
        }
        . . .
    }
    return s;
}
```

As you can see, throwing an exception is easy:

1.   Find an appropriate exception class.

2.   Make an object of that class.

3.   Throw it.

Once Java throws an exception, the method does not return to its caller. This means that you do not have to worry about cooking up a default return value or an error code.

C++ NOTE: Throwing an exception is the same in C++ and in Java, with one small exception. In Java, you can throw only objects of child classes of `Throwable`. In C++, you can throw values of any type.

Creating Exception Classes

Your code may run into a problem that is not adequately described by any of the standard exception classes. In this event, you can create your own exception class. Just derive it from `Exception` or from a child class such as `IOException`. It is customary to give both a default constructor and a constructor that contains a detailed message. (The `toString` method of the `Throwable` base class prints out that detailed message, which is handy for debugging.)

```java
class FileFormatException extends IOException
{  public FileFormatException() {}
   public FileFormatException(String gripe)
   {  super(gripe);
   }
}
```

Now you are ready to throw your very own exception type.

```java
String readData(DataInput in) throws FileFormatException
{   . . .
    while (. . .)
    {  if (ch == -1) // EOF encountered
       {  if (n < len)
              throw new FileFormatException();
       }
       . . .
    }
    return s;
}
```

`java.lang.Throwable`

* `Throwable()`

   constructs a new `Throwable` object with no detailed message.

* `Throwable(String message)`

   constructs a new `Throwable` object with the specified detailed message. By convention, all derived exception classes support both a default constructor and a constructor with a detailed message.

- ```
  String getMessage()
  ```
  gets the detailed message of the `Throwable` object.

Catching Exceptions

What Do You Do When an Exception Occurs?

You now know how to throw an exception. It is pretty easy. You throw it and you forget it. Of course, some code has to catch the exception. Catching exceptions requires more planning.

If an exception occurs that is not caught anywhere in a nongraphical application, Java will terminate the program and print a message to the console giving the type of the exception and a stack trace. In a graphics program (both an applet and an application), Java prints the same error message, but the program goes back to its user-interface processing loop.

To catch an exception, you have to set up a `try`/`catch` block. The simplest form of the `try` block is as follows:

```
try
{   code
    more code
    more code
}
catch(ExceptionType e)
{   handler for this type
}
```

If any of the code inside the `try` block throws an exception of the class given in the `catch` clause, then

1. Java skips the remainder of the code in the `try` block, and

2. it executes the handler code inside the `catch` clause.

If none of the code inside the `try` block throws an exception, then Java skips the `catch` clause.

If any of the code in a method throws an exception of a type other than the one named in the catch clause, Java exits this method immediately. (Hopefully, one of its callers has already coded a catch clause for that type.)

Here is some code in our `Console` class.

```
public static String readString()
{   int ch;
    String r = "";
```
```

```
      boolean done = false;
      while (!done)
      {  try
         {  ch = System.in.read();
            if (ch < 0 || (char)ch == '\n')
               done = true;
            else
               r = r + (char) ch;
         }
         catch(IOException e)
         {  done = true;
         }
      }
      return r;
   }
```

Notice that most of the code in the `try` clause is straightforward: it accumulates characters until we encounter the end of the line or the end of the file. As you can see by looking at the Java API, there is the possibility that the `read` method will throw an `IOException`. In that case, the `if` statement is skipped and we set `done` to `true`. We figure that if there is a problem with the input, the caller does not want to know about it and only wants to use the characters that we have accumulated so far.

For the `Console` class, that seems like a reasonable way to deal with this exception. What other choice do we have?

Often, the best choice is to do nothing at all. If an error occurs in the `read` method, let the caller of the `readString` method worry about it! If we take that approach, then we have to advertise the fact that the method may throw an `IOException`.

```
      public static String readString()
         throws IOException
      {  int ch;
         String r = "";
         boolean done = false;
         while (!done)
         {  ch = System.in.read();
            if (ch < 0 || (char)ch == '\n')
               done = true;
            else
               r = r + (char) ch;
         }
         return r;
      }
```

The compiler strictly enforces the `throws` specifiers. If you call a method that throws an explicit exception, you must either handle it or propagate it.

Which of the two is better? As a general rule, you should catch those exceptions that you know how to handle and propagate those that you do not know how to handle. When you propagate an exception, you must add a `throws` modifier to alert the caller that an exception may be thrown.

Look at the Java API documentation to see what methods throw which exceptions. Then decide whether you should handle them or add them to the `throws` list. There is nothing embarrassing about the latter. It is better to direct an exception to a competent handler than to squelch it.

There is one exception to this rule. If you are writing a method that overrides a parent class method that throws no exceptions (such as `start` in `Applet`), then you *must* catch each explicit exception in the method's code. You are not allowed to add more `throws` specifiers to a child class method than are present in the parent class method.

TIP: Your fellow programmers will hate you if you write methods that throw exceptions left and right, that they must handle or propagate. If you can do something intelligent about an exception, then you should catch it.

C++ NOTE: Catching exceptions is almost the same in Java and in C++. Strictly speaking, the analog of

```
catch(Exception e) // Java
```

is

```
catch(Exception& e) // C++
```

There is no analog to the C++ `catch(...)`. This is not needed in Java because all exceptions derive from a common base class.

Catching Multiple Exceptions

You can catch multiple exception types in a `try` block and handle each type differently.

```
try
{   code that might
    throw exceptions
}
catch(MalformedURLException e1)
{    // emergency action for malformed URLs
}
```

```
catch(UnknownHostException e2)
{    // emergency action for unknown hosts
}
catch(IOException e3)
{    // emergency action for all other I/O problems
}
```

The exception object (e1, e2, e3) may contain information about the nature of the exception. To find out more about the object, try

```
e3.getMessage()
```

to get the detailed error message (if there is one), or

```
e3.getClass().getName()
```

to get the actual type of the exception object.

Rethrowing Exceptions

Occasionally, you need to catch an exception without addressing the root cause of it in order to do some local cleanup. In this case, you want to take your emergency action and again call `throw` to send the exception back up the calling chain.

```
Graphics g = image.getGraphics();
try
{   code that might
    throw exceptions
}   catch(MalformedURLException e)
{   g.dispose();
    throw e;
}
```

The above code shows one of the most common reasons for having to rethrow an exception that you have caught. If you do not dispose of the graphics context object in the `catch` clause, it will never be disposed of, since it is a local object of this method. (Of course, its `finalize` method might dispose of it, but that can take a long time.)

On the other hand, the underlying cause, the malformed URL exception, *has not disappeared*. You still want to report it to the authorities, who presumably know how to deal with such an exception. (See the next section for a more elegant way to achieve the same result.)

You can also throw a different exception than the one you catch.

```
try
{   acme.util.Widget a = new acme.util.Widget();
    a.load(s);
    a.paint(g);
}
```

```
catch(RuntimeException e)
{   // sheesh--another ACME error
    throw new Exception("ACME error");
}
```

The finally *Clause*

When Java throws an error, it stops processing all code in your method. This is a problem if the local method has acquired some resource that only it knows about and if that resource must be cleaned up. One solution is to catch and rethrow exceptions. But this is tedious because you need to clean in two places, in the normal code and in the exception code.

Java has a better solution, the finally clause:

```
Graphics g = image.getGraphics();
try
{   code that might
    throw exceptions
}
catch(IOException e)
{   done = true;
}
finally
{   g.dispose();
}
```

The code in the finally clause is executed whether or not an exception is caught. For instance, in the example above Java will dispose of the graphics context *under all circumstances.*

Let us look at the three possible scenarios in which the finally clause is executed.

1. The code throws no exceptions. In this event, Java first executes all the code in the try block. Then it executes the code in the finally clause and executes the first line after the try block.

2. The code throws an exception that is caught in a catch clause, in our case, an IOException. For this, Java executes all code in the try block, up to the point at which the exception is thrown. The remaining code in the try block is skipped. Then Java executes the code in the matching catch clause, and the code in the finally clause.

   If the catch clause does not throw an exception, then the first line after the try block is executed. If it does, then the exception is thrown back to the caller of this method.

3.   The code throws an exception that is not caught in any `catch` clause. For this, Java executes all code in the `try` block, until the exception is thrown. The remaining code in the `try` block is skipped. Then Java executes the code in the `finally` clause, and the exception is thrown back to the caller of this method.

> C++ NOTE: There is one fundamental difference between C++ and Java with regard to exception handling. Java has no destructors; thus, there is no stack unwinding as in C++. This means that the Java programmer must manually place code to reclaim resources in `finally` blocks. Of course, since Java does garbage collection, there are far fewer resources that require manual deallocation.

A Final Look at Java Error-Handling

The following sample program deliberately generates a number of different errors and catches various exceptions (see Figure 10-2).

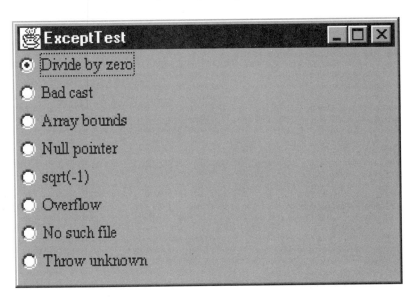

Figure 10-2: A program that generates errors

Try it out. Click on the buttons and see what exceptions are thrown.

As you know, a programmer error such as a bad array index throws a `RuntimeException`. An attempt to open a nonexistent file triggers an `IOException`. The program catches `RuntimeException` objects, then general `Exception` objects.

```
try
{   // various bad things
}
catch(RuntimeException e)
{   System.out.println("Caught RuntimeException: " + e);
}
catch(Exception e)
{   System.out.println("Caught Exception: " + e);
}
```

You can see which exception you caused in the Console window. If you click on the Throw Unknown button, an `UnknownError` object is thrown. This is not a child class of `Exception`, so our program does not catch it. Instead, the user-interface code prints an error message and a stack trace to the console.

NOTE: As you can see from this program in Example 10-1, not all the bad things you can do in Java throw exceptions. Divides by zero, overflows, and math errors do not throw any exceptions at all.

Example 10-1: ExceptTest.java

```
import java.awt.*;
import java.io.*;

class ExceptTest extends Frame
{   ExceptTest()
    {   setTitle("ExceptTest");
        setLayout(new GridLayout(8, 1));
        CheckboxGroup g = new CheckboxGroup();
        add(new Checkbox("Divide by zero", g, false));
        add(new Checkbox("Bad cast", g, false));
        add(new Checkbox("Array bounds", g, false));
        add(new Checkbox("Null pointer", g, false));
        add(new Checkbox("sqrt(-1)", g, false));
        add(new Checkbox("Overflow", g, false));
        add(new Checkbox("No such file", g, false));
        add(new Checkbox("Throw unknown", g, false));
    }

    public boolean handleEvent(Event evt)
    {   if (evt.id == Event.WINDOW_DESTROY) System.exit(0);
        return super.handleEvent(evt);
    }

    public boolean action(Event evt, Object arg)
    {   try
```

```
    {   if (evt.target instanceof Checkbox)
        {   String name = ((Checkbox)evt.target).getLabel();
            if (name.equals("Divide by zero"))
            {   a[1] = a[2] / (a[3] - a[3]);
            }
            else if (name.equals("Bad cast"))
            {   f = (Frame)arg;
            }
            else if (name.equals("Array bounds"))
            {   a[1] = a[10];
            }
            else if (name.equals("Null pointer"))
            {   f = null;
                f.resize(200, 200);
            }
            else if (name.equals("sqrt(-1)"))
            {   a[1] = Math.sqrt(-1);
            }
            else if (name.equals("Overflow"))
            {   a[1] = 1000 * 1000 * 1000 * 1000;
                int n = (int)a[1];
            }
            else if (name.equals("No such file"))
            {   FileInputStream is = new FileInputStream(name);
            }
            else if (name.equals("Throw unknown"))
            {   throw new UnknownError();
            }
        }
        else return super.action(evt, arg);
    }
    catch(RuntimeException e)
    {   System.out.println("Caught RuntimeException: " + e);
    }
    catch(Exception e)
    {   System.out.println("Caught Exception: " + e);
    }
    return true;
}
public static void main(String[] args)
{   Frame f = new ExceptTest();
    f.resize(300, 200);
    f.show();
}

private double[] a = new double[10];
private Frame f = null;
}
```

Some Tips on Using Exceptions

There is a tendency to overuse exceptions. After all, who wants to go to the trouble to write methods that parse input before using it when exception-handling makes it so easy? Instead of parsing a URL when the user enters it, just send it off to a method that catches a `MalformedURLException`. Saves time, saves trouble. Wrong! Exception handling will almost always cost time. Misusing exceptions can slow your code down dramatically. Here are three tips on using exceptions.

1. *Exception handling is not supposed to replace a simple test.*

As an example of this, we wrote some code that uses the built-in `Stack` class (see Chapter 9). The following code tries 1,000,000 times to pop an empty stack. It first does this by finding out whether or not the stack is empty.

```
if (!s.empty()) s.pop();
```

Next, we tell it to pop the stack no matter what. Then we catch the `EmptyStackException` that tells us that we should not have done that.

```
try()
{   s.pop();
}
catch(EmptyStackException e)
{
}
```

On our test machine, we got the timing data in Table 10-2.

Table 10-2: Timing Data

Test	Throw/Catch
6 sec.	64 sec.

As you can see, it takes roughly 10 times longer to catch an exception as it does to perform a simple test. The moral is: Use exceptions for exceptional circumstances only.

2. *Do not micromanage exceptions.*

Many people wrap every statement in a separate `try` block.

```
istream is;
Stack s;

for (i = 0; i < 100; i++)
{   try
```

```
{     n = s.pop();
}
catch (EmptyStackException s)
{     // stack was empty
}
try
{     out.writeInt(n);
}
catch (IOException e)
{     // problem reading file
}
}
```

This blows up your code dramatically. Think about the task that you want the code to accomplish. Here we want to pop 100 numbers off a stack and save them to a file. (Never mind why—it is just a toy example.) There is nothing we can do if a problem rears its ugly head. If the stack is empty, it will not become occupied. If there is an error in the file, this will not magically go away. It, therefore, makes sense to wrap the *entire task* in a `try` block. If any one operation fails, you can then abandon the task.

```
try
{   for (i = 0; i < 100; i++)
    {   n = s.pop();
        out.writeInt(n);
    }
}
catch (IOException e)
{ // problem reading file
}
catch (EmptyStackException s)
{ // stack was empty
}
```

This looks much cleaner. It fulfills one of the promises of exception-handling, to *separate* normal processing from error-handling.

3.   *Do not squelch exceptions.*

In Java, there is the tremendous temptation to shut up exceptions. You write a method that calls a method that might throw an exception once a century. The compiler whines because you have not declared the exception in the `throws` list of your method. You do not want to put it in the `throws` list because then the compiler will whine about all the methods that call your method. So you just shut it up:

```
Image loadImage(String s)
{   try
    {   lots of code
    }
    catch(Exception e)
    {} // so there
}
```

Now your code will compile without a hitch. It will run fine, except when an exception occurs. Then the exception will be silently ignored. If you believe that exceptions are at all important, you need to make some effort to handle them right.

Debugging Techniques

Useful Tricks

Suppose you wrote your program and made it bulletproof by catching and properly handling all exceptions. Then you run it, and it does not work right. Now what? (If you never have this problem, you can skip the remainder of this chapter.)

Of course, it is best if you have a convenient and powerful debugger. You can purchase excellent debuggers on most platforms. If you are on a budget or work on an unusual platform, you may still need to do a great deal of debugging by the time-honored method of inserting print statements into your code.

Here are some tips for efficient debugging:

1. You can print the value of any variable with code like this:

    ```
    System.out.println("x = " + x);
    ```

    If x is a number, it is converted to its string equivalent. If x is an object, then Java calls its toString method. Most of the classes in the Java library are very conscientious about overriding the toString method to give you useful information about the class. This is a real boon for debugging. You should make the same effort in your classes.

2. To get the state of the current object, print this.

    ```
    System.out.println("Entering loadImage. this = " + this);
    ```

    This calls the toString method of the current class, and you get a printout of all instance fields. (Provided, of course, that the toString method in this class does a conscientious job.)

3. You can get a stack trace from any exception object with the printStackTrace method in the Throwable class. The following code catches any exception, prints the exception object and the stack trace, and rethrows the exception so it can find its intended handler.

```
try
{   . . .
}
catch(Throwable t)
{   t.printStackTrace();
    throw t;
}
```

4. One seemingly little-known but very useful trick is that you can put a separate `main` function in each public class. Inside it, you can put a unit test stub that tests the class in isolation. Make a few objects, call all methods, and check that each of them does the right thing. You can leave all these `main` functions in place and call the Java interpreter separately on each of the files to run the tests. When you run an applet, none of these `main` functions are ever called. When you run an application, only the `main` function of the start-up class is called. All others are ignored. (For example, look at our `Format.java` file in the corejava directory. It has a `main` function that tests the formatting extensively.)

`java.lang.Throwable`

*   void printStackTrace()

    prints the `Throwable` and the stack trace.

Trapping AWT Events

When you write a fancy user-interface in Java, you need to know what events AWT sends to what components. Unfortunately, the AWT documentation is somewhat sketchy in this regard. For example, suppose you want to show hints in the status line when the user moves the mouse over different parts of the screen. AWT does generate MOUSE_ENTER, MOUSE_EXIT, GOT_FOCUS, and LOST_FOCUS events that you may be able to trap.

We give you a useful `MessageCracker` class to spy on these events. It prints out a text description of the event, cracking the event codes and printing only those fields of the `Event` structure that are relevant to a particular event. See Figure 10-3 for a display of the cracked messages. (Look in the terminal window.)

Figure 10-3: The MessageCracker class at work

To spy on messages, you need only to add one line of code to your event-handler.

```
boolean handleEvent(Evt event)
{  MessageCracker.print(event);
    . . .
}
```

This prints out a textual description of all events, except for MOUSE_MOVE events. (You would not want to see a flood of mouse move events every time you move the mouse.)

Example 10-2 shows the code for the MessageCrackerTest class.

Example 10-2: MessageCrackerTest.java

```
import java.awt.*;

public class MessageCrackerTest extends Frame
{  public MessageCrackerTest()
    {  super("MessageCrackerTest");
        Panel p = new Panel();
        p.setLayout(new FlowLayout());
```

```
        p.add(new Button("Tick"));
        p.add(new Label("Set time:"));
        p.add(new TextField(4));
        p.add(new Checkbox("Daylight Savings"));
        CheckboxGroup g = new CheckboxGroup();
        p.add(new Checkbox("GMT", g, true));
        p.add(new Checkbox("Local", g, false));
        add("South", p);
        add("East", new Scrollbar(Scrollbar.VERTICAL));
        add("Center", new TextArea(12, 40));

        initializeMenus();
    }


    private void initializeMenus()
    {   MenuBar mbar = new MenuBar();
        Menu m = new Menu("File");
        m.add(new MenuItem("New"));
        m.add(new MenuItem("Open"));
        m.add(new MenuItem("Save"));
        m.add(new MenuItem("Save As"));
        m.add(new MenuItem("Print"));
        m.addSeparator();
        m.add(new MenuItem("Quit"));
        mbar.add(m);
        setMenuBar(mbar);
    }

    public boolean handleEvent(Event evt)
    {   MessageCracker.print(evt);
        if (evt.id == Event.WINDOW_DESTROY) System.exit(0);
        return super.handleEvent(evt);
    }


    public static void main(String[] args)
    {   Frame f = new MessageCrackerTest();
        f.resize(400, 200);
        f.show();
    }
}
```

Displaying Debug Messages in Graphics Programs

If you run an applet inside a browser, you may not be able to see any messages that are sent to `System.out`. Actually, with Netscape, you are in luck. As shown in Figure 10-4, Netscape has a nice "Java console" (available in the

5

Options menu) that displays all the strings sent to `System.out`. That window has a set of scroll bars, so you can retrieve messages that have scrolled off the window, a definite advantage over the DOS shell window in which the `System.out` output normally appears.

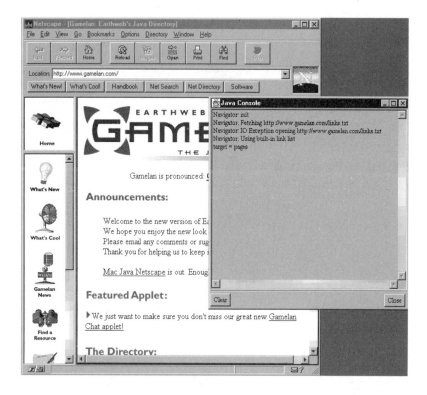

Figure 10-4: Netscape's "Java Console"

This is a nice feature, and we give you a similar window class, so you can enjoy the same benefit of seeing your debugging messages in a window when not running Netscape. Figure 10-5 shows our `DebugWinTest` class in action.

The class is easy to use. You need to make a variable of type `DebugWin` in your `Frame` or `Applet` class and use the `print` method to print an object in the window. Here is an example of debugging code to spy on all action events.

```
class DebugWinTest
{  . . .
   public boolean action(Event evt, Object arg)
   {  dw.print("Event = " + evt);
      dw.print("Object = " + arg);
      . . .
```

```
      }
      . . .
      DebugWin dw = new DebugWin();
  }
```

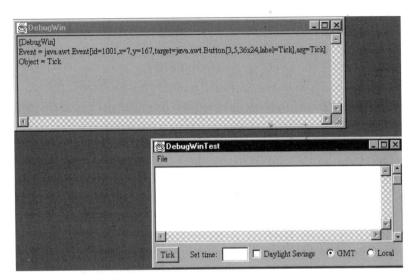

Figure 10-5: The debug window

Example 10-3 lists the code for the DebugWinTest class.

Example 10-3: DebugWinTest.java

```
import java.awt.*;

public class DebugWinTest extends Frame
{   public DebugWinTest()
    {   setTitle("DebugWinTest");
        Panel p = new Panel();
        p.setLayout(new FlowLayout());
        p.add(new Button("Tick"));
        p.add(new Label("Set time:"));
        p.add(new TextField(4));
        p.add(new Checkbox("Daylight Savings"));
        CheckboxGroup g = new CheckboxGroup();
        p.add(new Checkbox("GMT", g, true));
        p.add(new Checkbox("Local", g, false));
        add("South", p);
        add("East", new Scrollbar(Scrollbar.VERTICAL));
        add("Center", new TextArea(12, 40));

        initializeMenus();
    }
```

```
private void initializeMenus()
{   MenuBar mbar = new MenuBar();
    Menu m = new Menu("File");
    m.add(new MenuItem("New"));
    m.add(new MenuItem("Open"));
    m.add(new MenuItem("Save"));
    m.add(new MenuItem("Save As"));
    m.add(new MenuItem("Print"));
    m.addSeparator();
    m.add(new MenuItem("Quit"));
    mbar.add(m);
    setMenuBar(mbar);
}

public boolean handleEvent(Event evt)
{   if (evt.id == Event.WINDOW_DESTROY) System.exit(0);
    return super.handleEvent(evt);
}

public boolean action(Event evt, Object arg)
{   dw.print("Event = " + evt);
    dw.print("Object = " + arg);
    return super.action(evt, arg);
}

public static void main(String[] args)
{   Frame f = new DebugWinTest();
    f.resize(400, 200);
    f.show();
}

DebugWin dw = new DebugWin();
}
```

(The Chapter 10 directory contains the code for DebugWin.java.)

Using the JDB Debugger

Debugging with print statements is not one of life's more joyful experiences. You constantly find yourself adding and removing the statements, then recompiling the program. Using a debugger is better because a debugger runs your program in full motion until it reaches a break-point, and then you can look at everything that interests you.

The JDK includes JDB, an extremely rudimentary command-line debugger. Its user interface is so minimal that you will not want to use it, except as a last resort. It really is more a proof of concept than a useable tool. We, nevertheless, give a brief introduction because there are situations in which it is better than no debugger at all.

Have a look at a deliberately corrupted version of the ButtonTest (Figure 10-6) program from Chapter 7.

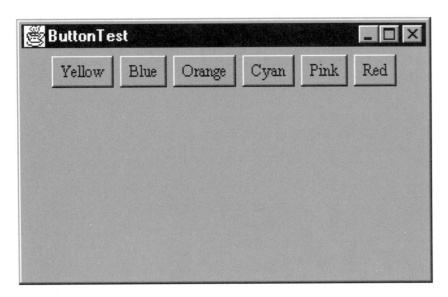

Figure 10-6: The buggy button application

When you click on any of the buttons, nothing happens. Look at the source code—it is supposed to set the background color to the color specified by the button name.

Example 10-4: ButtonTest.java

```java
import java.awt.*;

public class ButtonTest extends Frame
{   public ButtonTest()
    {   setTitle("ButtonTest");
        setLayout(new FlowLayout());
        add(new Button("Yellow"));
        add(new Button("Blue"));
        add(new Button("Orange"));
        add(new Button("Cyan"));
        add(new Button("Pink"));
        add(new Button("Red"));
    }

    public boolean handleEvent(Event evt)
```

```
    {   if (evt.id == Event.WINDOW_DESTROY) System.exit(0);
        return super.handleEvent(evt);
    }

    public boolean action(Event evt, Object arg)
    {   if (arg.equals("yellow")) setBackground(Color.yellow);
        else if (arg.equals("blue")) setBackground(Color.blue);
        else if (arg.equals("orange")) setBackground(Color.orange);
        else if (arg.equals("cyan"))
            setBackground(Color.cyan);
        else if (arg.equals("pink"))
            setBackground(Color.pink);
        else if (arg.equals("red"))
            setBackground(Color.red);
        else return super.action(evt,arg);
        repaint();
        return true;
    }

    public static void main(String[] args)
    {   Frame f = new ButtonTest();
        f.resize(320, 200);
        f.show();
    }
}
```

In this short a program, you may be able to find the bug just by reading the source code. Let us pretend that this was so complicated a program that reading the source code is not practical. Here is how you can run the debugger to locate the error.

To use JDB, you must first compile your program with the -g option, for example:

```
javac -g ButtonTest.java
```

Then you launch the debugger:

```
jdb ButtonTest
```

> NOTE: JDB *requires* that you have TCP/IP networking services running, even if you are not debugging a network application. If you are not connected to a local area network but occasionally use a dialup connection, you can activate that connection, and JDB will work. If not, you need to enable TCP/IP services in order to use JDB.

Once you launch the debugger, you will see a display like this:

```
Initializing jdb...
0x139f3c8:class(ButtonTest)
>
```

Now you must type a debugger command. Table 10-3 shows all the debugger commands. Items enclosed in [...] are optional. The suffix (s) means that you can supply more than one argument.

Table 10-3: Debugging Commands

threads [*threadgroup*]	lists threads
thread *thread_id*	sets default thread
suspend [*thread_id(s)*]	suspends threads (default: all)
resume [*thread_id(s)*]	resumes threads (default: all)
where [*thread_id*] or all	dumps a thread's stack
threadgroups	lists threadgroups
threadgroup *name*	sets current threadgroup
print *name(s)*	prints object or field
dump *name(s)*	prints all object information
locals	prints all current local variables
classes	lists currently known classes
methods *class*	lists a class's methods
stop in *class.method*	sets a break-point in a method
stop at *class:line*	sets a break-point at a line
up [*n*]	moves up a thread's stack
down [*n*]	moves down a thread's stack
clear *class:line*	clears a break-point
step	executes the current line
cont	continues execution from break-point
catch *class*	breaks for the specified exception
ignore *class*	ignores the specified exception
list [*line*]	prints source code
use [*path*]	displays or changes the source path
memory	reports memory usage
gc	frees unused objects
load *class*	loads Java class to be debugged
run [*class* [*args*]]	starts execution of a loaded Java class
!!	repeats last command
help (or ?)	lists commands
exit (or quit)	exits debugger

We will cover only the most useful commands here.

The basic idea is that you set one or more break-points, then run the program. When the program reaches a break-point, it stops, and you can inspect the values of the local variables.

To set a breakpoint, you use the

```
stop in class.method
```

or

```
stop at class:line
```

command.

Let us set a break-point in the `action` method. To do this, enter:

```
stop in ButtonTest.action
```

Then we want to run the program.

```
run
```

Now click on the **Yellow** button . The debugger breaks at the start of the `action` procedure.

```
Breakpoint hit: ButtonTest.action (ButtonTest:49)
```

Because the debugger does not give you a window with the current source line, it is easy to lose track of where you are. At any time, you can type `list` to see the current line and a couple of lines above and below. You also see the line numbers.

```
45              return super.handleEvent(evt);
46          }
47
48          public boolean action(Event evt, Object arg)
49  =>      {   if (arg.equals("yellow")) setBackground(Color.yellow);
50              else if (arg.equals("blue")) setBackground(Color.blue);
51              else if (arg.equals("orange")) setBackground(Color.orange);
52              else if (arg.equals("cyan"))
53                  setBackground(Color.cyan);
```

Type `locals` to see all local variables.

```
Local variables and arguments:
  this = ButtonTest[0,0,320x200,layout=java.awt.FlowLayout,
resizable, title=ButtonTest]
  evt = java.awt.Event[id=1001,x=27,y=28,target=
java.awt.Button[27,28,48x24,label=Yellow],arg=Yellow]
  arg = Yellow
```

For more detail, use:

```
dump variable
```

For example,

```
dump evt
```

displays all instance variables of the `evt` variable.

```
evt = (java.awt.Event)0x13a1988 {
    private int data = 0
    public Object target = (java.awt.Button)0x13a13e0
    public long when = 0
    public int id = 1001
    public int x = 27
    public int y = 28
    public int key = 0
    public int modifiers = 0
    public int clickCount = 0
    public Object arg = Yellow
    public Event evt = null
```

Unfortunately, there is no good way to single-step through the program. The `step` command steps into every call and easily becomes confused between threads.

Now let us set a break-point in the next line and one at the end of the `if` statement.

```
stop at ButtonTest:50
stop at ButtonTest:59
```

To continue the program until it encounters the next breakpoint, type:

```
cont
```

The program stops in line 50. Type `list` one more time to see where you are.

```
46          }
47
48          public boolean action(Event evt, Object arg)
49          {  if (arg.equals("yellow")) setBackground(Color.yellow);
50  =>       else if (arg.equals("blue")) setBackground(Color.blue);
51          else if (arg.equals("orange")) setBackground(Color.orange);
52          else if (arg.equals("cyan"))
53              setBackground(Color.cyan);
54          else if (arg.equals("pink"))
```

That is not what should have happened. It was supposed to set the background color to yellow and then go to the `repaint` command.

Now we can see what happened. The argument was `"Yellow"`, with an upper-case Y, but the comparison tested

```
if (arg.equals("yellow"))
```

with a lowercase y. Mystery solved.

To quit the debugger, type:

```
quit
```

As you can see from this example, the debugger can be used to find an error, but only barely. Setting breakpoints in an `action` method works pretty well. Use `list` and `locals` whenever you are confused about where you are. Get a better debugger as soon as you run into a more serious bug.

CHAPTER
11

- Streams

- The Stream Zoo

- Putting Streams to Use

- Writing Delimited Output

- Random-Access Streams

- Object Streams

Input and
Output

Streams

The Concept of Streams

Input/output techniques are not particularly exciting, but without the ability to
read and write data, your applications and applets are severely limited. This
chapter concerns how to use Java to work with files. Generalizing from this, you
could say the chapter is also about how to get input from any source of data
that can send a sequence of bytes and how to send output to any destination
that can receive a sequence of bytes. These sources and destinations of byte
sequences can be—and often are—files, but they can also be network connections
and even blocks of memory. There is a nice payback to keeping this generality
in mind: information stored in files and information retrieved from a network
connection is handled in *essentially the same way.* (See Chapter 13 for information
on how to work with networks.)

In Java, an object from which we can read a sequence of bytes is called an *input
stream.* An object to which we can write a sequence of bytes is called an *output
stream.* These are implemented in the abstract classes `InputStream` and
`OutputStream`.

You saw abstract classes in Chapter 5. Recall that the point of an abstract class is
to provide a mechanism for factoring out the common behavior of classes to a
higher level. This leads to cleaner code and makes the inheritance tree easier to
understand. The same game is at work with input and output in Java.

As you will soon see, Java derives from these two abstract classes a zoo of
concrete classes: you can visit almost any conceivable input/output creature in
this zoo.

Finally, this chapter shows you the new *object serialization* mechanism that is
being added to Java. This lets you store objects as easily as the JDK 1.02 let you
store text or numeric data.

Reading and Writing Bytes

The `InputStream` class has an abstract method:

```
public abstract int read() throws IOException
```

It reads one byte and returns the byte read, or –1 if it encounters the end of the input source. The designer of a concrete input stream class reimplements this function. For example, the `FileInputStream` class defines this method to read one byte from a file.

Out of this single input method, the `InputStream` class constructs a function to read an array of bytes or 1 to skip a number of bytes.

Similarly, the `OutputStream` class defines the abstract method

```
public abstract void write(int b) throws IOException
```

which writes one byte to an output file.

Both `read` and `write` can *block* a thread until the byte is actually read or written. In other words, if the byte cannot immediately be read or written (usually because of a busy network connection), the thread in which the call happens is suspended, and other threads are given the chance to do useful work while the method is waiting for the stream to again become available. (We discuss threads in Chapter 12.)

When you have finished reading and writing a stream, you should close it by calling the `close` method. Streams occupy operating system resources, and if an application opens many streams without closing them, the system resources may become depleted. Closing an output stream also *flushes* the output stream: any characters that have been temporarily placed in a buffer so that they could be delivered as a larger packet are sent. If you do not close a file, the last partial packet of bytes will never be delivered. You can also manually flush the output with the `flush` method, but this is rarely necessary.

Java programmers seldom work with these raw `read` and `write` functions because there are few occasions to read and write streams of bytes. The data probably contain numbers, strings, and objects. There are many stream classes that are derived from the basic `InputStream` and `OutputStream` classes that help you with those tasks.

`java.io.InputStream`

- `abstract int read() throws IOException`

  reads a byte of data and returns the byte read. The `read` method returns a –1 at the end of the stream.

- `int read(byte b[]) throws IOException`

  reads into an array of bytes and returns the number of bytes read. As before, the `read` method returns a –1 at the end of the stream.

- `int read(byte b[], int off, int len) throws IOException`

  reads into an array of bytes. The `read` method returns the actual number of bytes read, or –1 at the end of the stream.

Parameters:	`b`	the array into which the data is read
	`off`	the offset into `b` where the first bytes should be placed
	`len`	the maximum number of bytes to read

- `long skip(long n) throws IOException`

  skips n bytes in the input stream. It returns the actual number of bytes skipped (which may be less than n if the end of the stream was encountered).

- `int available() throws IOException`

  returns the number of bytes available without blocking. (Recall that blocking means that the current thread loses its turn.)

- `void close() throws IOException`

  closes the input stream.

- `void mark(int readlimit)`

  The `mark` method puts a marker at the current position in the input stream. (Not all streams support this feature.) If more than `readlimit` bytes have been read from the input stream, then the stream is allowed to forget the marker.

- `void reset() throws IOException`

  returns to the last marker. Subsequent calls to `read` reread the bytes.

- `boolean markSupported()`

  returns `true` if the stream supports marking.

java.io.OutputStream

- `public abstract void write(int b) throws IOException`

  writes a byte of data.

- `public void write(byte b[]) throws IOException`

  writes all bytes in the array b.

- `public void write(byte b[], int off, int len) throws IOException`

Parameters:	b	the array from which to write the data
	`off`	the offset into b to the first byte that will be written
	`len`	the number of bytes to write

- `public void close() throws IOException`

  closes the output stream.

- `public void flush() throws IOException`

  flushes the output stream, that is, sends any buffered data to its destination.

The Stream Zoo

Unlike C, which gets by just fine with a single type `FILE*`, or VB, which has three file types, Java has a whole zoo of 26 (!) different stream types (see Figure 11-1). Library designers claim that there is a good reason to give users a wide choice of stream types: it is supposed to reduce programming errors. For example, in C, some people think it is a common mistake to send output to a file that was open only for reading. (Well, it is not that common, actually.) Naturally, the output is ignored at run time. In Java and C++, the compiler catches that kind of mistake because an `InputStream` (Java) or `istream` (C++) has no methods for output.

(We would argue that, in C++ and even more so in Java, the main tool that the stream interface designers have against programming errors is intimidation. The sheer complexity of the stream libraries keeps programmers on their toes.)

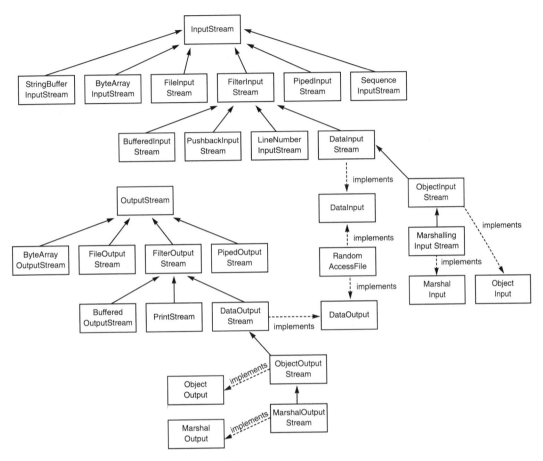

Figure 11-1: Java's family of different stream types

C++ NOTE: C++ gives us more stream types than we want, such as `istream`, `ostream`, `iostream`, `ifstream`, `ofstream`, `fstream`, `istream_with_assign`, `istrstream`, and so on. The ANSI library takes away some of them and gives back others, such as `wistream`, to deal with wide characters, and `istringstream`, to handle string objects. But Java really goes overboard with streams and gives you the choice (or forces you to specify, depending on your outlook) of having buffering, lookahead, random access, text formatting, or binary data.

Let us divide the stream class zoo by usage. You have already seen the two abstract classes that are at the base of the zoo: `InputStream` and `OutputStream`. You do not make objects of these types, but other functions can return them. For example, as you saw in Chapter 8, the URL class has the method `openStream` that returns an `InputStream`. You then use this `InputStream` object to read from the URL.

The `InputStream` and `OutputStream` classes let you read and write only individual bytes and arrays of bytes. In particular, please note that they *cannot* handle strings—strings in Java are sequences of Unicode characters, not bytes. Nor can they read or write numbers. You need a more capable child stream class to read and write strings and numbers!

File Streams

`FileInputStream` and `FileOutputStream` give you input and output streams attached to a disk file. You give the name of the file in the constructor.

```
FileInputStream in = new FileInputStream("employee.dat");
```

Like the abstract `InputStream` and `OutputStream` classes, these classes only support reading and writing on the byte level.

Print Streams

For text output, you want to use `PrintStream`. A print stream can print strings and numbers in text format. To make a print stream, take any output stream object and use it as the argument of the `PrintStream` constructor.

```
FileOutputStream fout = new FileOutputStream("employee.dat");
PrintStream pout = new PrintStream(fout);
```

The print stream is not a new stream. It is an alias to the output file, but one with a more capable interface.

You already know how to print strings and numbers to a print stream because the `System.out` stream object is actually of type `PrintStream`. As you have seen with `System.out`, you can use the `print` method to print numbers (`int`, `short`, `long`, `float`, `double`), characters, Boolean values, strings, and objects to the stream.

For example, consider this code.

```
String name = "Harry Hacker";
double salary = 75000;
pout.print(name);
pout.print(' ');
pout.println(salary);
```

This prints the ASCII characters

```
Harry Hacker 75000\n
```

to the stream `pout`, that is, to the file `employee.dat`. Note that it prints ASCII characters, not Unicode characters! Java truncates the top byte of each character.

`java.io.PrintStream`

- `void print(Object obj)`

  prints an object by printing the string resulting from `toString`.

  Parameters: `obj`   the object to be printed

- `void print(String s)`

  prints a string in ASCII (not Unicode).

- `void println(String s)`

  prints a string followed by a new line.

- `void print(char s[])`

  prints an array of characters in ASCII (not Unicode).

- `void print(char c)`

  prints a character in ASCII (not Unicode).

- `void print(int i)`

  prints an integer in text format.

- `void print(long l)`

  prints a long integer in text format.

- `void print(float f)`

  prints a floating-point number in text format.

- `void print(double d)`

  prints a double-precision floating-point number in text format.

- `void print(boolean b)`

  prints a Boolean value in text format.

Data Streams

You often need to write the result of a computation or read one back. The data streams support methods for reading back all of the basic types and also objects (see the end of this chapter). To write a number, character, Boolean value, or string, use one of the following methods:

```
writeChars
writeInt
writeShort
writeLong
writeFloat
writeDouble
writeChar
writeBoolean
writeUTF
```

For example, `writeInt` writes an integer as a 4-byte binary quantity, as does `writeFloat`.

> NOTE: There are two different methods of storing integers and floating-point numbers in memory, depending on the platform you are using. Suppose, for example, you are working with a 4-byte quantity, like an `int` or a `float`. This can be stored in such a way that the first of the 4 bytes in memory holds the most significant byte (MSB) of the value, the so-called "big-endian" method, or it can hold the least significant byte (LSB) first, which is called, naturally enough, the "little-endian" method. For example, the Sparc uses big-endian; the Pentium, little-endian. This can lead to problems. For example, when saving a file using C or C++, the data are saved *exactly* as the processor stores them. That makes it challenging to move even the simplest data files from one platform to another. In Java, all values are written in the big-endian fashion, regardless of the processor. That makes Java data files platform independent.

The `writeUTF` method writes string data using Unicode Text Format (UTF). UTF format is as follows. A 7-bit ASCII value (that is, a 16-bit Unicode character with the top 9 bits zero) is written as one byte:

$$0a_6a_5a_4a_3a_2a_1a_0$$

A 16-bit Unicode character with the top 5 bits zero is written as a 2-byte sequence:

$$110a_{10}a_9a_8a_7a_6 \qquad 10a_5a_4a_3a_2a_1a_0$$

(The `writeUTF` method actually writes only the 11 lowest bits.)

All other Unicode characters are written as 3-byte sequences:

$$1110a_{15}a_{14}a_{13}a_{12} \qquad 10a_{11}a_{10}a_9a_8a_7a_6 \qquad 10a_5a_4a_3a_2a_1a_0$$

This is a useful format for text consisting mostly of ASCII characters, because ASCII characters still take only a single byte. On the other hand, it is not a good format for Asiatic languages, for which you are better off writing sequences of double-byte Unicode characters directly. Use the `writeChars` method for that purpose.

Note that the top bits of a UTF byte determine the nature of the byte in the encoding scheme.

```
0xxxxxxx  :  ASCII
10xxxxxx  :  Second or third byte
110xxxxx  :  First byte of 2-byte sequence
1110xxxx  :  First byte of 3-byte sequence
```

To read the data back in, use the following methods:

```
readInt
readShort
readLong
readFloat
readDouble
readChar
readBoolean
readUTF
```

NOTE: The binary data format is compact and platform independent. Except for the UTF strings, it is also suited to random access. The major drawback is that binary files are not readable by humans.

`java.io.DataInput`

- `boolean readBoolean() throws IOException`

  reads in a Boolean value.

- `byte readByte() throws IOException`

  reads an 8-bit byte.

- `char readChar() throws IOException`

  reads a 16-bit Unicode character.

- `double readDouble() throws IOException`

  reads a 64-bit double.

- `float readFloat() throws IOException`

  reads a 32-bit float.

- `void readFully(byte b[]) throws IOException`

  reads bytes, blocking until all bytes are read.

  Parameters: b   the buffer into which the data is read

- `void readFully(byte b[], int off, int len) throws IOException`
  reads bytes, blocking until all bytes are read.

Parameters:	b	the buffer into which the data is read
	off	the start offset of the data
	len	the maximum number of bytes read

- `int readInt() throws IOException`
  reads a 32-bit integer.

- `String readLine() throws IOException`
  reads in a line that has been terminated by a \n, \r, \r\n, or EOF. Returns a string containing all bytes in the line converted to Unicode characters.

- `long readLong() throws IOException`
  reads a 64-bit long integer.

- `short readShort() throws IOException`
  reads a 16-bit short integer.

- `String readUTF() throws IOException`
  reads a string of characters in UTF format.

- `int skipBytes(int n) throws IOException`
  skips bytes, blocking until all bytes are skipped.

Parameters:	n	the number of bytes to be skipped

java.io.DataOutput

- `void writeBoolean(boolean b)`
  writes a Boolean value.

- `void writeByte(byte b)`
  writes an 8-bit byte.

  `void writeChar(char c)`
  writes a 16-bit Unicode character.

- `void writeChars(string s)`
  writes a string as a sequence of characters.

- `void writeDouble(double d)`

  writes a 64-bit double.

- `void writeFloat(float f)`

  writes a 32-bit float.

- `void writeInt(int i)`

  writes a 32-bit integer.

- `void writeLong(long l)`

  writes a 64-bit long integer.

- `void writeShort(short s)`

  writes a 16-bit short integer.

- `void writeUTF(String s)`

  writes a string of characters in UTF format.

Random-Access File Streams

The `RandomAccessFile` stream class lets you find or write data anywhere in a file. Disk files are random access, but streams of data from a network are not.

You open a random-access file either for reading only or for both reading and writing. You specify the option by using the string `"r"` (for read access) or `"rw"` (for read/write access) as the second argument in the constructor.

```
RandomAccessFile in = new RandomAccessFile("employee.dat", "r");
RandomAccessFile inOut
    = new RandomAccessFile("employee.dat", "rw");
```

A random-access file also has a *file pointer* setting that comes with it. The file pointer always indicates the position of the next record that will be read or written. The `seek` method sets the file pointer to an arbitrary byte position within the file. The argument to `seek` is a `long` integer between zero and the length of the file in bytes.

Finally, the `getFilePointer` method returns the current position of the file pointer.

To read from a random-access file, you use the same methods—such as `readInt` and `readUTF`—as for `DataInputStream` objects. That is no accident. These methods are actually defined in the `DataInput` interface that both `DataInputStream` and `RandomAccessFile` implement.

Similarly, to write a random-access file, you use the same `writeInt` and `writeUTF` methods as in the `DataOutputStream` class. These methods are defined in the `DataOutput` interface that is common to both classes.

The advantage of this setup is that you can write methods whose argument types are the `DataInput` and `DataOutput` *interfaces*.

```
class Employee
{   . . .
    read(DataInput in) { . . . }
    write(DataOutput out) { . . . }
}
```

Note that the `read` method can handle either a `DataInputStream` or a `RandomAccessFile` object because both of these classes implement the `DataInput` interface. The same is true for the `write` method.

java.io.RandomAccessFile

- `RandomAccessFile(String name, String mode)`

    Parameters: name   system-dependent file name

    mode   `"r"` for reading only, or `"rw"` for reading and writing

- `long getFilePointer() throws IOException`

    returns the current location of the file pointer.

- `void seek(long pos) throws IOException`

    sets the file pointer to `pos` bytes from the beginning of the file.

- `public long length() throws IOException`

    returns the length of the file in bytes.

Mixing and Matching Stream Filters

If you look again at Figure 11-1, you will find the classes `FilterInputStream` and `FilterOutputStream`. You can mix and match the child classes to construct the streams you want. For example, if you want buffering *and* text output, you can make the following streams:

```
PrintStream ps = new PrintStream
    (new BufferedOutputStream
        (new FileOutputStream("employee.dat")));
```

Apart from the rather monstrous constructors, this is a useful feature. We put the `PrintStream` *last* in the chain of constructors because we want to use the `PrintStream` methods, and we want *them* to use the buffered `write` method.

`java.io.BufferedInputStream`

- `BufferedInputStream(InputStream in)`

  creates a new buffered stream with a default buffer size. A buffered input stream reads characters from a stream without causing a device access every time. When the buffer is empty, a new block of data is read into the buffer.

- `BufferedInputStream(InputStream in, int n)`

  creates a new buffered stream with a user-defined buffer size.

`java.io.LineNumberInputStream`

- `LineNumberInputStream(InputStream in)`

  constructs an input stream that keeps track of line numbers.

- `void setLineNumber(int lineNumber)`

  sets the current line number.

- `int getLineNumber()`

  returns the current line number.

`java.io.PushbackInputStream`

- `PushbackInputStream(InputStream in)`

  constructs a stream with one-character lookahead.

- `void unread(int ch) throws IOException`

  pushes back a character, which is retrieved again by the next call to `read`. You can push back only one character at a time.

  Parameters: `ch`   the character to be read again

`java.io.BufferedOutputStream`

- `BufferedOutputStream(OutputStream out)`

  creates a new buffered stream with a default buffer size. A buffered output stream collects characters to be written without causing a device access every time. When the buffer fills up, the data is written.

- `BufferedOutputStream(OutputStream out, int n)`

  creates a new buffered stream with a user-defined buffer size.

Putting Streams to Use

In the next four sections, we will show you how to put some of the creatures in the stream zoo to good use. For these examples we will assume you are working with the `Employee` class and some of its derived classes, such as `Manager`. (See Chapters 4 and 5 for more on these example classes.) We will consider four separate scenarios for saving an array of employee records to a file and then reading them back into memory.

1. Saving data of the same type (`Employee`) in text format

2. Saving data of the same type in binary format

3. Saving and restoring polymorphic data (a mixture of `Employee` and `Manager` objects)

4. Saving and restoring data containing embedded references (managers with pointers to other employees)

Writing Delimited Output

In this section, you will learn how to store an array of `Employee` records in the time-honored "delimited" format. This means that each record is stored in a separate line. Instance fields are separated from each other by delimiters. We use a vertical bar (|) as our delimiter. (A colon : is another popular choice. Part of the fun is that everyone uses a different delimiter.) Naturally, we punt on the issue of what might happen if a | actually occurred in one of the strings we save.

NOTE: Especially on Unix systems, an amazing number of files are stored in exactly this format. We have seen entire employee databases with thousands of records in this format, queried with nothing more than the Unix `awk`, `sort`, and `join` utilities. (In the PC world, where excellent database programs are available at low cost, this kind of ad-hoc storage is much less common.)

Here is a sample set of records:

```
Harry Hacker|35500|1989|10|1
Carl Cracker|75000|1987|12|15
Tony Tester|38000|1990|3|15
```

Writing records is simple. Since we write to a text file, we use the `PrintStream` class. We simply write all fields, followed by either a | or, for the last field, a \n. (One problem is what to do with floating-point numbers. The `print` method only prints up to six significant digits. Our solution is simple: we ignore the limited `print` method supplied with Java and use the `print` function of our `Format` class, instead.) Finally, in keeping with the idea that we want the *class* to be responsible for responding to messages, we add a method, `writeData`, to our `Employee` class.

```
public void writeData(PrintStream os) throws IOException
{   os.print(name); os.print("|");
    Format.print(os, "%.14g|", salary);
    os.print(hireDay.getYear()); os.print("|");
    os.print(hireDay.getMonth()); os.print("|");
    os.println(hireDay.getDay());
}
```

To read records, we read in a line at a time and separate the fields. This is the topic of the next section, in which we use a utility class supplied with Java to make our job easier.

String Tokenizers and Delimited Text

When reading a line of input, we get a single long string. We want to split it into individual strings. This means finding the | delimiters and then separating out the individual pieces, that is, the sequence of characters up to the next delimiter. (These are usually called *tokens*.) The `StringTokenizer` class in `java.util` is designed for exactly this purpose. It gives you an easy way to break up a large string that contains delimited text.

A string tokenizer object attaches to a string. When you construct the tokenizer object, you specify which characters are the delimiters. For example, we need to use

```
StringTokenizer t = new StringTokenizer(line, "|");
```

You can specify multiple delimiters in the string. For example, to set up a string tokenizer that would let you search for any delimiter in the set

```
" \t\n\r"
```

use the following:

```
StringTokenizer t = new StringTokenizer(line, " \t\n\r");
```

(Notice that this means that any white space marks off the tokens.)

NOTE: These four delimiters are used as the defaults if you construct a string tokenizer like this:

```
StringTokenizer t = new StringTokenizer(line);
```

Once you have constructed a string tokenizer, you can use its methods to quickly extract the tokens from the string. The `nextToken` method returns the next unread token. The `hasMoreTokens` method returns `true` if more tokens are available.

NOTE: In our case, we know how many tokens we have in every line of input. In general, you have to be a bit more careful: call `hasMoreTokens` before calling `nextToken`. This is because the `nextToken` method throws an exception when no more tokens are available.

`java.util.StringTokenizer`

- `StringTokenizer(String str, String delim)`

  Parameters: `str`   the input string from which tokens are read

                   `delim`   a string containing delimiter characters (any character in this string is a delimiter)

- `StringTokenizer(String str)`

  constructs a string tokenizer with the default delimiter set `" \t\n\r"`.

- `boolean hasMoreTokens()`

  returns true if more tokens exist.

- `String nextToken()`

  returns the next token. Throws a `NoSuchElementException` if there are no more tokens.

- `String nextToken(String delim)`

  returns the next token, after switching to the new delimiter set. The new delimiter set is subsequently used.

- `int countTokens()`

  returns the number of tokens still in the string.

Reading Delimited Input

Reading in an `Employee` record is simple. We simply read in a line of input with the `readLine` method of the `DataInputStream` class. This is a convenient method that is not available in any other input stream class. The `readLine` method reads in a line of ASCII text and converts it to a Unicode string. (Each character from the input is padded with a 0 byte in the process.) Notice that, in our case, we are not at all interested in the methods of the `DataInputStream` class for dealing with binary data; we just want to use `readLine`. Here is the code needed to read one record in a string.

```
DataInputStream in
    = new DataInputStream(new FileInputStream("employee.dat"));
    . . .
String line = in.readLine();
```

Next, we need to extract the individual tokens. When we do this, we end up with *strings*, so we need to convert them into numbers when appropriate. To do this, we turn to the `atoi` and `atof` methods from the `Format` class in our `corejava` package.

Just as with the `writeData` method, we add a `readData` method of the `Employee` class. When you call

```
e.readData(in);
```

this method overwrites the previous contents of `e`. Note that the method may throw an `IOException` if the `getLine` function throws that exception. There is nothing this method can do if an `IOException` occurs, so we just let it propagate up the chain.

NOTE: The `readData` method actually takes an argument of type `DataInput`, not `DataInputStream`. `DataInput` is an interface that defines the `readLine`, `readInt`, `readUTF`, and other read methods. It was broken out as an interface by the designers of Java so that it could be shared between the `DataInputStream` class and the `RandomAccessFile` class. A `RandomAccessFile` implements both `DataInput` and `DataOutput`.

Here is the code for this method:

```
public void readData(DataInputStream in) throws IOException
{   String line = in.readLine();
    if (line == null) return;
    StringTokenizer t = new StringTokenizer(line, "|");
    name = t.nextToken();
    salary = Format.atof(t.nextToken());
    int y = Format.atoi(t.nextToken());
    int m = Format.atoi(t.nextToken());
    int d = Format.atoi(t.nextToken());
    hireDay = new Day(y, m, d);
}
```

Finally, in the code for a program that tests these methods, the static method

```
void writeData(Employee[] e, PrintStream out)
```

first writes the length of the array, then writes each record. The static method

```
readData(Employee[] DataInputStream in)
```

first reads in the length of the array, then reads in each record, as illustrated in Example 11-1 that follows.

Example 11-1: DataFileTest.java

```java
import java.io.*;
import java.util.*;
import corejava.*;

class DataFileTest
{   static void writeData(Employee[] e, PrintStream os) throws
        IOException
    {   Format.print(os, "%d\n", e.length);
        int i;
        for (i = 0; i < e.length; i++)
            e[i].writeData(os);
    }

    static Employee[] readData(DataInputStream is) throws
        IOException
    {   int n = Format.atoi(is.readLine());
        Employee[] e = new Employee[n];
        int i;
        for (i = 0; i < n; i++)
        {   e[i] = new Employee();
            e[i].readData(is);
        }
        return e;
    }

    public static void main(String[] args)
    {   Employee[] staff = new Employee[3];

        staff[0] = new Employee
            ("Harry Hacker", 35500, new Day(1989,10,1));
        staff[1] = new Employee
            ("Carl Cracker", 75000, new Day(1987,12,15));
        staff[2] = new Employee
            ("Tony Tester", 38000, new Day(1990,3,15));
        int i;
        for (i = 0; i < staff.length; i++)
            staff[i].raiseSalary(5.25);

        try
        {   PrintStream os
            = new PrintStream(new
            FileOutputStream("employee.dat"));
            writeData(staff, os);
            os.close();
        }
        catch(IOException e)
        {   System.out.print("Error: " + e);
            System.exit(1);
        }
```

```
      try
      {   DataInputStream is = new DataInputStream
          (new FileInputStream("employee.dat"));
          Employee[] in = readData(is);
          for (i = 0; i < in.length; i++) in[i].print();
          is.close();
      }
      catch(IOException e)
      {   System.out.print("Error: " + e);
          System.exit(1);
      }


   }
}


class Employee
{   public Employee(String n, double s, Day d)
    {   name = n;
        salary = s;
        hireDay = d;
    }
    public Employee(){}
    public void print()
    {   System.out.println
        (name + " " + salary + " " + hireYear());
    }
    public void raiseSalary(double byPercent)
    {   salary *= 1 + byPercent / 100;
    }
    public int hireYear()
    {   return hireDay.getYear();
    }
    public void writeData(PrintStream os) throws IOException
    {   Format.print(os, "%s|", name);
        Format.print(os, "%.14g|", salary);
        Format.print(os, "%d|", hireDay.getYear());
        Format.print(os, "%d|", hireDay.getMonth());
        Format.print(os, "%d\n", hireDay.getDay());
    }

    public void readData(DataInput is) throws IOException
    {   String s = is.readLine();
        StringTokenizer t = new StringTokenizer(s, "|");
        name = t.nextToken();
        salary = Format.atof(t.nextToken());
        int y = Format.atoi(t.nextToken());
        int m = Format.atoi(t.nextToken());
        int d = Format.atoi(t.nextToken());
        hireDay = new Day(y, m, d);
    }
```

```
    private String name;
    private double salary;
    private Day hireDay;
}
```

Random-Access Streams

If you have a large number of employees, the storage technique used in the preceding section suffers from one limitation. It is not possible to read a record in the middle of the file without first reading all records that come before it. In this section, we will make all records the same length. This lets us implement a random-access method of reading back the information—we can get at any record in the same amount of time.

We will store the numbers in the instance fields in our classes in a binary format. This is done using the writeInt and writeDouble methods of the DataOutput interface. (This is the common interface of the DataOutputStream and the RandomAccessFile classes.)

However, since the size of each record must remain constant, we need to make all the strings the same size when we save them. The variable-size UTF format does not do this, and the rest of the Java library provides no convenient means for accomplishing this. We need to write a bit of code to implement two helper methods. We will call them writeFixedString and readFixedString. These methods read and write Unicode strings that always have the same length.

The writeFixedString function takes the parameter size. Then it writes the specified number of characters, starting at the beginning of the string. (If there are too few characters, it pads the string using characters whose ASCII/Unicode values are zero.) Here is the code for the writeFixedString method:

```
static void writeFixedString
    (String s, int size, DataOutput out)
    throws IOException
{   int i;
    for (i = 0; i < size; i++)
    {   char ch = 0;
        if (i < s.length()) ch = s.charAt(i);
        out.writeChar(ch);
    }
}
```

The readFixedString method reads characters from the input stream until it has consumed size characters, or until it encounters a character with ASCII/Unicode 0. Then it should skip past the remaining zero characters in the input field.

For added efficiency, this function uses the `StringBuffer` class to read in a string. A `StringBuffer` is an auxiliary class that lets you preallocate a memory block of a given length. In our case, we know that the string is, at most, `size` bytes long. We make a string buffer in which we reserve `size` characters. Then we append the characters as we read them in.

NOTE: This is more efficient than reading in characters and appending them to an existing string. Every time you append characters to a string, Java needs to find new memory to hold the larger string: this is time consuming. Appending even more characters means the string needs to be relocated again and again. Using the `StringBuffer` class allows you to avoid this problem.

Once the string buffer holds the desired string, we need to convert it to an actual `String` object. This is done with the `String(StringBuffer b)` constructor. This constructor does not copy the characters in the string buffer. Instead, it freezes the buffer contents. If you later call a method that makes a modification to the `StringBuffer` object, the buffer object first gets a new copy of the characters and then modifies those.

```
static String readFixedString(int size, DataInput in)
   throws IOException
{  StringBuffer b = new StringBuffer(size);
   int i = 0;
   boolean more = true;
   while (more && i < size)
   {  char ch = in.readChar();
      i++;
      if (ch == 0) more = false;
      else b.append(ch);
   }
   in.skipBytes(2 * (size - i));
   return b.toString();
}
```

NOTE: These two functions are packaged inside the `DataIO` helper class.

To write a fixed-size record, we simply write all fields in binary.

```
public void writeData(DataOutput out) throws IOException
{  DataIO.writeFixedString(name, NAME_SIZE, out);
   out.writeDouble(salary);
   out.writeInt(hireDay.getYear());
   out.writeInt(hireDay.getMonth());
   out.writeInt(hireDay.getDay());
}
```

Reading the data back is just as simple.

```
public void readData(DataInput in) throws IOException
{   name = DataIO.readFixedString(NAME_SIZE, in);
    salary = in.readDouble();
    int y = in.readInt();
    int m = in.readInt();
    int d = in.readInt();
    hireDay = new Day(y, m, d);
}
```

In our example, each employee record is 100 bytes long because we specified that the name field would always be written using 40 characters. This gives us a breakdown as indicated in the following:

40 characters = 80 bytes for the name

1 `double` = 8 bytes

3 `int` = 12 bytes

As an example, suppose we want to position the file pointer to the third record. We can use the following version of the `seek` method:

```
long int n = 3;
int RECORD_SIZE = 100;
in.seek((n - 1) * RECORD_SIZE);
```

To determine the total number of bytes in a file, use the `length` method. The total number of records is the length divided by the size of each record.

```
long int nbytes = in.length(); // length in bytes
int nrecords = (int)(nbytes / RECORD_SIZE);
```

The test program shown in Example 11-2 writes three records into a data file and then reads them from the file in reverse order. To do this efficiently requires random access—we need to get at the third record first.

Example 11-2: RandomFileTest.java

```
import java.io.*;
import corejava.*;

class RandomFileTest
{   public static void main(String[] args)
    {   Employee[] staff = new Employee[3];

        staff[0] = new Employee
            ("Harry Hacker", 35000, new Day(1989,10,1));
        staff[1] = new Employee
            ("Carl Cracker", 75000, new Day(1987,12,15));
        staff[2] = new Employee
            ("Tony Tester", 38000, new Day(1990,3,15));
```

```
      int i;
      try
      {  DataOutputStream out = new DataOutputStream
         (new FileOutputStream("employee.dat"));
         for (i = 0; i < staff.length; i++)
            staff[i].writeData(out);
         out.close();
      }
      catch(IOException e)
      {  System.out.print("Error: " + e);
         System.exit(1);
      }

      try
      {  RandomAccessFile in
            = new RandomAccessFile("employee.dat", "r");
         int n = (int)(in.length() / Employee.RECORD_SIZE);
         Employee[] newStaff = new Employee[n];

         for (i = n - 1; i >= 0; i--)
         {  newStaff[i] = new Employee();
            in.seek(i * Employee.RECORD_SIZE);
            newStaff[i].readData(in);
         }
         for (i = 0; i < newStaff.length; i++)
            newStaff[i].print();
      }
      catch(IOException e)
      {  System.out.print("Error: " + e);
         System.exit(1);
      }

   }
}

class Employee
{  public Employee(String n, double s, Day d)
   {  name = n;
      salary = s;
      hireDay = d;
   }
   public Employee() {}
   public void print()
   {  System.out.println
      (name + " " + salary + " " + hireYear());
   }
   public void raiseSalary(double byPercent)
   {  salary *= 1 + byPercent / 100;
   }
```

```java
      public int hireYear()
      {  return hireDay.getYear();
      }
      public void writeData(DataOutput out) throws IOException
      {  DataIO.writeFixedString(name, NAME_SIZE, out);
         out.writeDouble(salary);
         out.writeInt(hireDay.getYear());
         out.writeInt(hireDay.getMonth());
         out.writeInt(hireDay.getDay());
      }

      public void readData(DataInput in) throws IOException
      {  name = DataIO.readFixedString(NAME_SIZE, in);
         salary = in.readDouble();
         int y = in.readInt();
         int m = in.readInt();
         int d = in.readInt();
         hireDay = new Day(y, m, d);
      }

      public static final int NAME_SIZE = 40;
      public static final int RECORD_SIZE
         = 2 * NAME_SIZE + 8 + 4 + 4 + 4;

      private String name;
      private double salary;
      private Day hireDay;
}

class DataIO
{  static String readFixedString(int size, DataInput in)
         throws IOException
      {  StringBuffer b = new StringBuffer(size);
         int i = 0;
         boolean more = true;
         while (more && i < size)
         {  char ch = in.readChar();
            i++;
            if (ch == 0) more = false;
            else b.append(ch);
         }
         in.skipBytes(2 * (size - i));
         return b.toString();
      }

   static void writeFixedString(String s, int size,
      DataOutput out) throws IOException
      {  int i;
         for (i = 0; i < size; i++)
```

```
    {   char ch = 0;
        if (i < s.length()) ch = s.charAt(i);
        out.writeChar(ch);
    }
  }
}
```

java.lang.StringBuffer

- `StringBuffer()`

  constructs an empty string buffer.

- `StringBuffer(int length)`

  constructs an empty string buffer with the initial capacity `length`.

- `StringBuffer(String str)`

  constructs a string buffer with the initial contents `str`.

- `int length()`

  returns the number of characters of the buffer.

- `int capacity()`

  returns the current capacity, that is, the number of characters that can be contained in the buffer before it must be relocated.

- `void ensureCapacity(int m)`

  enlarges the buffer if the capacity is fewer than `m` characters.

- `void setLength(int n)`

  If n is less than the current length, characters at the end of the string are discarded. If n is larger than the current length, the buffer is padded with `'\0'` characters.

- `char charAt(int i)`

  returns the i'th character (i is between 0 and `length()-1`); throws a `StringIndexOutOfBoundsException` if the index is invalid.

- `void getChars(int from, int to, char a[], int offset)`

  copies characters from the string buffer into an array.

Parameters:	from	the first character to copy
	to	the first character not to copy
	a	the array to copy into
	offset	the first position in a to copy into

- `void setCharAt(int i, char ch)`

  sets the i'th character to `ch`.

- `StringBuffer append(String str)`

  appends a string to the end of this buffer (the buffer may be relocated as a result); returns `this`.

- `StringBuffer append(char c)`

  appends a character to the end of this buffer (the buffer may be relocated as a result); returns `this`.

- `StringBuffer insert(int offset, String str)`

  inserts a string at position `offset` into this buffer (the buffer may be relocated as a result); returns `this`.

- `StringBuffer insert(int offset, char c)`

  inserts a character at position `offset` into this buffer (the buffer may be relocated as a result); returns `this`.

- `String toString()`

  returns a string pointing to the same data as the buffer contents. (No copy is made.)

 `java.lang.String`

- `String(StringBuffer buffer)`

  makes a string pointing to the same data as the buffer contents. (No copy is made.)

Object Streams

Using a fixed-length record format is a good choice if you need to store data of the same type. However, objects that you create in an object oriented program are rarely all of the same type. For example, you may have an array called `staff` that is nominally an array of `Employee` records, but contains objects that are actually instances of a child class such as `Manager`.

If we want to save files that contain this kind of information, we must first save the type of each object and then the data that defines the current state of the object. When we read this information back from a file, we must

- first read the object type,
- then create a blank object of that type,
- then fill it with the data that we stored in the file.

It is entirely possible to do this by hand, and the first edition of this book did exactly this. However, JavaSoft has released the part of Java 1.1 that allows this to be done with much less effort. As you will soon see, this mechanism, called *object serialization,* almost completely automates what was previously a very tedious process. (You will see later in this chapter where the term "serialization" comes from.)

NOTE: In this chapter, we use the Alpha 2 interface of object serialization. That is the version of the library on the CD-ROM. Sun has announced several small changes to the interface for the final version. These changes are summarized in a note at the end of this chapter.

Storing Objects of Variable Type

To save object data, you first need to open an `ObjectOutputStream` object:

```
ObjectOutputStream out = new ObjectOutputStream(new
    FileOutputStream("employee.dat"));
```

Now, to save an object you simply use the `writeObject` method of the `ObjectOutputStream` class as in the following fragment.

```
Employee harry = new Employee("Harry Hacker",
    35000, new Day(1989, 10, 1));
Manager carl = new Manager("Carl Cracker",
    75000, new Day(1987, 12, 15));
out.writeObject(harry);
out.writeObject(carl);
```

To read the objects back in, first get an `ObjectInputStream` object:

```
ObjectInputStream in = new ObjectInputStream(new
    FileInputStream("employee.dat"));
```

Then retrieve the objects in the same order in which they were written using the `readObject` method.

```
Employee e1 = (Employee)in.readObject();
Employee e2 = (Employee)in.readObject();
```

When reading objects back, you must carefully keep track of the number of objects that were saved, their order and their types. Each call to `readObject` reads in another object of the type `Object`. You will then need to cast it to its correct type.

If you don't need the exact type, or you don't remember it, then you can cast it to any superclass or even leave it as type `Object`. For example, e2 is an `Employee` object variable even though it actually refers to a `Manager` object. If you need to query the type of the object dynamically, you can use the `getClass` method that we described in Chapter 5.

You can only write and read *objects*, not numbers. To write and read numbers, you use methods such as `writeInt`/`readInt` or `writeDouble`/`readDouble` that the object stream classes inherit from their data stream superclasses. Of course, numbers inside objects (such as the salary field of an `Employee` object) are saved and restored automatically. (Recall that in Java, strings and arrays are objects and can, therefore, be restored with the `writeObject`/`readObject` methods.)

Example 11-3 is a test program that writes an array containing two employees and one manager to disk and then restores it. Once the information is restored, we give each employee a 100% raise, not because we are feeling generous, but because you can then easily distinguish employee and manager objects by their different `raiseSalary` actions. This should convince you that we did restore the correct type.

Example 11-3: ObjectFileTest.java

```java
import java.io.*;
import corejava.*;

class ObjectFileTest
{  public static void main(String[] args)
   {  try
      {  Employee[] staff = new Employee[3];

         staff[0] = new Employee("Harry Hacker", 35000,
            new Day(1989,10,1));
         staff[1] = new Manager("Carl Cracker", 75000,
            new Day(1987,12,15));
         staff[2] = new Employee("Tony Tester", 38000,
            new Day(1990,3,15));

         ObjectOutputStream out = new
            ObjectOutputStream(new FileOutputStream("test1.dat"));
         out.writeObject(staff);
         out.close();

         ObjectInputStream in =  new
            ObjectInputStream(new FileInputStream("test1.dat"));
         Employee[] newStaff = (Employee[])in.readObject();
```

```
            int i;
            for (i = 0; i < newStaff.length; i++)
               newStaff[i].raiseSalary(100);
            for (i = 0; i < newStaff.length; i++)
               newStaff[i].print();
         }
         catch(Exception e)
         {  System.out.print("Error: " + e);
            System.exit(1);
         }
      }
   }
}

class Employee
{  public Employee(String n, double s, Day d)
   {  name = n;
      salary = s;
      hireDay = d;
   }

   public Employee() {}

   public void print()
   {  System.out.println(name + " " + salary + " " + hireYear());
   }

   public void raiseSalary(double byPercent)
   {  salary *= 1 + byPercent / 100;
   }

   public int hireYear()
   {  return hireDay.getYear();
   }

   private String name;
   private double salary;
   private Day hireDay;
}

class Manager extends Employee
{  public Manager(String n, double s, Day d)
   {  super(n, s, d);
      secretaryName = "";
   }

   public Manager() {}
```

```
public void raiseSalary(double byPercent)
{   // add 1/2% bonus for every year of service
    Day today = new Day();
    double bonus = 0.5 * (today.getYear() - hireYear());
    super.raiseSalary(byPercent + bonus);
}

public void setSecretaryName(String n)
{   secretaryName = n;
}

public String getSecretaryName()
{   return secretaryName;
}

private String secretaryName;
}
```

java.io.ObjectOutputStream

- `ObjectOutputStream(OutputStream out) throws IOException`

  creates an `ObjectOutputStream` so that you can write to the specified `OutputStream`.

- `final void writeObject(Object obj) throws ClassMismatchException, MethodMissingException, IOException`

  writes the specified object to the `ObjectOutputStream`. The class of the object, the signature of the class, and the values of any field not marked as `transient` are written as well as the non-static fields of the class and all of its supertypes.

- `ObjectInputStream(InputStream is) throws IOException, StreamCorruptedException`

  this creates an `ObjectInputStream` to read back object information from the specified `InputStream`.

- `final Object readObject() throws MethodMissingException, ClassMismatchException, StreamCorruptedException, ClassNotFoundException, IOException`

  reads an object from the `ObjectInputStream`. In particular, this reads back the class of the object, the signature of the class, and the values of the non-transient and non-static fields of the class and all of its superclasses. It does deserializing to allow multiple object references to be recovered.

The Format Currently Used for Serialization

The format used by object streams is not currently documented and may change. Nonetheless, we found studying the data format to be extremely helpful for gaining insight into the object streaming process. We did this by looking at hex dumps of various saved object files. However, the details are somewhat technical, so feel free to skip this section if you are not interested in the implementation. (The `writeObject`/`readObject` can be used without knowing the current serialization format.)

Every file begins with the 4-byte sequence

```
0A CE 00 03
```

(We will be using hexadecimal numbers throughout this section to denote bytes.) Then it contains a sequence of objects, in the order that they were saved.

String objects are saved as

```
7D 04     2-byte length     characters
```

For example, the string `"Harry"` is saved as

```
7D 04 00 05 H a r r y
```

When saving an object, the class of that object must be saved as well. The class description contains the name of the class, and a 20-byte hash code of the data field types and method signatures. Java gets the hash code by:

- First ordering the field types and method signatures in a canonical way.

- Then applying the so-called Secure Hash Algorithm (SHA) to that data.

SHA is a very fast algorithm that gives a "fingerprint" to a larger block of information. This fingerprint is always a 20-byte data packet, regardless of the size of the original data. It is created by a clever sequence of bit operations on the data that makes it essentially 100% certain that the fingerprint will change if the information is altered in any way. SHA is a U.S. standard, recommended by the National Institute for Science and Technology (NIST). (For more details on SHA, see for example, William Stallings, Network and Internetwork Security, Prentice-Hall.)

In our situation, using SHA means that the class fingerprint will change if the data fields or methods change in any way. We can then check the class fingerprint in order to protect us from the following scenario: An object is saved to a disk file. Later, the designer of the class makes a change, for example, by adding or removing a data field. Then the old disk file is read in again. Now the data layout on the disk no longer matches the data layout in memory. If the data were read back in its old form, it could corrupt memory. Java takes great care to make such memory corruption close to impossible. Hence, it checks using the

SHA fingerprint that the class definition has not changed when restoring an object. It does this by comparing the fingerprint on disk with the fingerprint of the current class.

NOTE: Technically, as long as the data layout of a class has not changed, it ought to be safe to read objects back in. But Java is conservative and checks that the methods have not changed either. (After all, the methods describe the meaning of the stored data.)

Here is how a class identifier is stored:

    7D 02   2-byte length of classname   class name   20-byte hash code
    2-byte end marker

The end markers are numbers starting with 7F 01, and increasing by 1. For example, the descriptor of the Day class is

    7D 02 00 0C c o r e j a v a . D a y C3 CC . . . 7F 01

These descriptors are fairly long. If the *same* class descriptor is needed again in the file, then an abbreviated form is used:

    7D 01 00 7E   2-byte serial number

(The serial number refers to the previous explicit class descriptor. We will discuss the numbering scheme later.)

An object is stored as

    7D 03   class descriptor   object data   2-byte end marker

For example, here is how a Day object is stored:

7D 03	new object
7D 02	new class
00 0C	length
c o r e j a v a . D a y	class name
20-byte hash code	
7F 01	end marker
00 00 00 01	integer 1
00 00 00 0A	integer 10
00 00 07 C5	integer 1989
7F 02	end marker

As you can see, the data file contains enough information to restore the Day object.

Arrays are saved in the following format:

   7D 05   2-byte length of classname   class name

       4-byte number of entries   entries   2-byte end marker

The class name is in the same format as that used by native methods (which is slightly different from the class name used by class descriptors—see Chapter 14).

For example, here is an array of two Day objects.

7D 05	array
00 0F	length
[L c o r e j a v a . D a y ;	class name
00 00 00 02	number of entries
7D 03	new object
7D 02	new class
00 0C	length
c o r e j a v a . D a y	class name
20-byte hash code	
7F 01	end marker
00 00 00 01	integer 1
00 00 00 0A	integer 10
00 00 07 C5	integer 1989
7F 02	end marker
7D 03	new object
7D 01	existing class
00 7E 00 01	descriptor has serial #1
00 00 00 0F	integer 15
00 00 00 0C	integer 12
00 00 07 C3	integer 1987
7F 03	end marker
7F 04	end marker

Of course, studying these codes can be about as exciting as reading the average phone book. But it is still instructive to know that the object stream contains a detailed description of all the objects that it contains, with sufficient detail to be able to reconstruct both objects and arrays of objects.

The Problem of Saving Object References

We now know how to save objects that contain numbers, strings, or other simple objects (like the Day object in the Employee class). However, there is one important situation that we still need to consider. What happens when one object is shared by several objects as part of its state?

To illustrate the problem, let us make a slight modification to the Manager class. Rather than storing the name of the secretary, save a reference to a secretary object, which is an object of type Employee. (It would make sense to derive a class Secretary from Employee for this purpose, but we will not do that here.)

```
class Manager extends Employee
{  // previous code remains the same
   private Employee secretary;
}
```

This is a better approach to designing a realistic Manager class than simply using the name of the secretary—the Employee record for the secretary can now be accessed without having to search the staff array.

Having done this, you must keep in mind that the Manager object now contains a *reference* to the Employee object that describes the secretary, *not* a separate copy of the object.

In particular, two managers can share the same secretary, as is the case in Figure 11-2 and the following code:

```
harry = new Employee("Harry Hacker", . . .);
Manager carl = new Manager("Carl Cracker", . . .);
carl.setSecretary(harry);
Manager tony = new Manager("Tony Tester, . . .);
tony.setSecretary(harry);
```

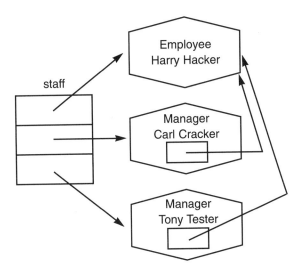

Figure 11-2: Two managers can share a mutual employee

Now suppose we write the employee data to disk. What we *don't* want is that the Manager saves its information according to the following logic:

- save employee data

- save secretary data

Then the data for `harry` would be saved *three times*. When reloaded, the objects would have the configuration shown in Figure 11-3.

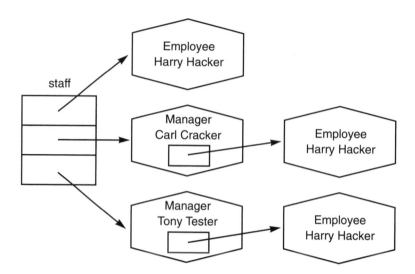

Figure 11-3: Here, Harry is saved three times

This is not what we want. Suppose the secretary gets a raise. We would not want to hunt for all other copies of that object and apply the raise as well. We want to save and restore *only one* copy of the secretary. To do this, we must copy and restore the original references to the objects. In other words, we want the object layout on disk to be exactly like the object layout in memory. This is called *persistence* in object-oriented circles.

Of course, we cannot save and restore the memory addresses for the secretary objects. When an object is reloaded, it will likely occupy a completely different memory address than it originally did.

Instead, Java uses a *serialization* approach. Hence, the name *object serialization* for this new mechanism. Remember:

- All objects that are saved to disk are given a serial number (1, 2, 3, and so on as shown in Figure 11-4).

- When saving an object to disk, find out if the same object has already been stored.

- If it has been stored previously, just write "same as previously saved object with serial number x". If not, store all its data.

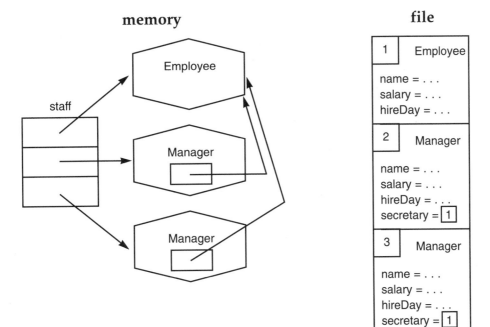

Figure 11-4: An example of object serialization

When reading back the objects, we simply reverse the procedure. For each object that we load, we note its sequence number and remember where we put it in memory. When we encounter the tag "same as previously saved object with serial number x", we look up where we put the object with serial number x and set the object reference to that memory address.

Note that the objects need not be saved in any particular order. Figure 11-5 shows what happens when a manager occurs first in the staff array.

memory   file

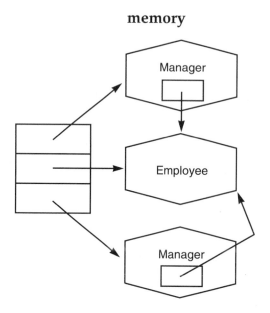

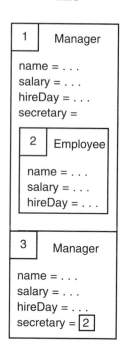

Figure 11-5: Objects saved in random order

All of this sounds confusing, and it is. Fortunately, when using object streams, it is also *completely automatic*. Object streams assign the serial numbers and keep track of duplicate objects. The exact numbering scheme is slightly different from that used in the figures—see the next section.

NOTE: In this chapter, we use serialization to save a collection of objects to a disk file and retrieve it exactly as we stored it. Another very important application is the transmittal of a collection of objects across a network connection to another computer. Just as raw memory addresses are meaningless in a file, they are also meaningless when communicating with a different processor. Since serialization replaces memory address with serial numbers, it permits the transport of object collections from one machine to another. We will study that use of serialization in chapter 16.

Example 11-4 is a program that saves and reloads a network of employee and manager objects (some of which share the same employee as a secretary). Note that the secretary object is unique after reloading—when `staff[0]` gets a raise, that is reflected in the secretary fields of the managers.

Example 11-4: ObjectRefTest.java

```
import java.io.*;
import java.util.*;
import corejava.*;

class ObjectRefTest
{  public static void main(String[] args)
   {  try
      {
          Employee[] staff = new Employee[3];

          Employee harry = new Employee("Harry Hacker", 35000,
             new Day(1989,10,1));
          staff[0] = harry;
          staff[1] = new Manager("Carl Cracker", 75000,
             new Day(1987,12,15), harry);
          staff[2] = new Manager("Tony Tester", 38000,
             new Day(1990,3,15), harry);

          ObjectOutputStream out = new
             ObjectOutputStream(new
                FileOutputStream("test2.dat"));
          out.writeObject(staff);
          out.close();

          ObjectInputStream in =  new
             ObjectInputStream(new
                FileInputStream("test2.dat"));
          Employee[] newStaff = (Employee[])in.readObject();

          for (int i = 0; i < newStaff.length; i++)
             newStaff[i].raiseSalary(100);
          for (int i = 0; i < newStaff.length; i++)
             newStaff[i].print();
      }
      catch(Exception e)
      {  e.printStackTrace();
         System.exit(1);
      }
   }
}

class Employee
{  public Employee(String n, double s, Day d)
   {  name = n;
      salary = s;
      hireDay = d;
   }
```

```
      public Employee() {}

      public void raiseSalary(double byPercent)
      {  salary *= 1 + byPercent / 100;
      }

      public int hireYear()
      {  return hireDay.getYear();
      }

      public void print()
      {  System.out.println(name + " " + salary + " " +
            hireYear());
      }

      private String name;
      private double salary;
      private Day hireDay;
   }

class Manager extends Employee
{  public Manager(String n, double s, Day d, Employee e)
   {  super(n, s, d);
      secretary = e;
   }

   public Manager() {}

   public void raiseSalary(double byPercent)
   {  // add 1/2% bonus for every year of service
      Day today = new Day();
      double bonus = 0.5 * (today.getYear() - hireYear());
      super.raiseSalary(byPercent + bonus);
   }

   public void print()
   {  super.print();
      System.out.print("Secretary: ");
      if (secretary != null) secretary.print();
   }

   private Employee secretary;
}
```

The Output Format for Object References

This section continues the discussion of the output format of object streams. If you skipped the discussion before, you should skip this section as well.

All objects (including arrays and strings) and all class descriptors are given serial numbers as they are saved in the output file. The count starts at 0. This process is referred to as *serialization* since every saved object is assigned a serial number.

We already saw that a full class descriptor for any given class only occurs once. Subsequent descriptors refer to it:

```
7D 01 00 7E   2-byte serial number
```

The same mechanism is used for objects. If a reference to a previously saved object is written, it is saved in exactly the same way. It is always clear from the context whether the particular serial reference denotes a class descriptor or an object.

Finally, a null reference is stored as

```
7D 00
```

Here is the commented output of the `ObjectRefTest` program of the preceding section. If you like, run the program, look at a hex dump of its data file test2.dat and compare it with the commented listing. The important lines (in bold) show the reference to a previously saved object.

`0A CE 00 03`	header
`7D 05`	array (serial #0)
`00 0B`	length
`[ L E m p l o y e e ;`	class name
`00 00 00 03`	number of entries
`7D 03`	new object (serial #2)
`7D 02`	new class (serial #1)
`00 08`	length
`E m p l o y e e`	class name
20-byte hash code	
`7F 01`	end marker
8-byte `double`	salary
`7D 03`	new object (serial #4)
`7D 02`	new class (serial #3)
`00 0C`	length
`c o r e j a v a . D a y`	
20-byte hash code	
`7F 02`	end marker
12 bytes	3 integers
`7F 03`	end marker

7D 04	string (serial #5)
00 0C	length
H a r r y H a c k e r	
7F 04	end marker
7D 03	new object (serial #7)
7D 04	new class (serial #6)
00 07	length
M a n a g e r	class name
20-byte hash code	
7F 05	end marker
8-byte double	salary
7D 03	new object (serial #8)
7D 01	**existing class**
00 7E 00 03	**use serial #3**
12 bytes	3 integers
7F 06	end marker
7D 04	string (serial #9)
00 0C	length
C a r l C r a c k e r	
7D 01	**existing object**
00 7E 00 02	**use serial #2**
7F 07	end marker
7D 03	new object (serial #10)
7D 01	**existing class**
00 7E 00 06	**use serial #6**
8-byte double	salary
7D 03	new object (serial #11)
7D 01	**existing class**
00 7E 00 03	**use serial #3**
12 bytes	3 integers
7F 08	end marker
7D 04	string (serial #9)
00 0B	length
T o n y T e s t e r	
7D 01	**existing object**

00 7E 00 02	use serial #2
7F 09	end marker
7F 0A	end marker

It is usually not important to know the exact file format (unless you are trying to create an evil effect by modifying the data—see the next section). What you should remember is that:

- The object stream output contains the types and data fields of all objects.

- Each object is assigned a serial number.

- Repeated occurrences of the same object are stored as references to that serial number.

Security

Even if you only glanced at the file format description of the preceding section, it should become obvious that a trained hacker can exploit that knowledge and modify an object file so that invalid objects are read in when the file is reloaded.

Consider, for example, the `Day` class in the `corejava` package. That class has been carefully designed so that all of its constructors check that the day, month and year fields never represent an invalid date. For example, if you try to build a `new Day(1996, 2, 31)`, no object is created and an `IllegalArgumentException` is thrown instead.

However, this safety guarantee can be subverted through serialization. When a `Day` object is read in from an object stream, it is possible—either through a device error or through malice—that the stream contains an invalid date. There is nothing that the serialization mechanism can do in this case—it has no understanding of the constraints that define a legal date.

For that reason, the serialization mechanism provides a means for individual classes to add validation or any other desired action. The class must define methods with the signature

```
private void readObject(ObjectInputStream in)
    throws IOException, ClassNotFoundException;
private void writeObject(ObjectOutputStream out)
    throws IOException;
```

Then the data fields are no longer automatically serialized, and these methods are called instead. For example, the Day class can and should be enhanced as follows:

```
class Day
{  . . .
    private void readObject(ObjectInputStream in)
        throws IOException, ClassNotFoundException
```

```
{   day = in.readInt();
    month = in.readInt();
    year = in.readInt();
    if (!isValid()) throw new IOException();
}
private void writeObject(ObjectOutputStream out)
    throws IOException
{   out.writeInt(day);
    out.writeInt(month);
    out.writeInt(year);
}
}
```

Notice that these special `readObject` and `writeObject` methods only need to save and load their data fields. They should not concern themselves with superclass data or any other class information.

If a class doesn't want to allow serialization of its objects, for example, to avoid the leakage of confidential information, then it can redefine `writeObject` to throw a `NoAccessException`. Any attempt to serialize an object of that class will then fail with this exception.

Finally, there are certain data members that should never be serialized, for example, integer values that store file handles or handles of windows that are only meaningful to native methods. Such information is guaranteed to be useless when an object is reloaded at a later time or transported to a different machine. In fact, improper values for such fields can actually cause native methods to crash. Java has an easy mechanism to prevent such fields from ever being serialized. Mark them with the keyword `transient`. Transient fields are always skipped when objects are serialized.

NOTE: Another way of protecting serialized data from tampering is encryption and authentication. This is best achieved by using a different stream abstraction that provides the encryption. For example, if `CryptoOutputStream` encrypts its output, you would use a stream obtained through

```
new ObjectOutputStream(new CryptoOutputStream(...));
```

for serialization.

NOTE: The security mechanism for serialization will change in the final version of object serialization. In particular, only classes that implement the `serializable` interface will be serialized by Java, and only classes that implement the `Externalizable` interface will be serialized with their own `writeExternal` and `readExternal` methods.

Using serialization for cloning

There is one other amusing (and, occasionally, very useful) use for the new serialization mechanism: it gives you an easy way to clone an object *provided* all its data fields are serializable. (Recall from Chapter 5 that you need to do a bit of work in order to allow an object to be cloned.) As the following example program shows, to get `clone` for free when its instance data is serializable, simply derive from the `SerialCloneable` class, and you are done.

```java
import java.io.*;
import corejava.*;

public class SerialCloneTest
{  public static void main(String[] args)
    {  Employee harry = new Employee("Harry Hacker", 35000,
            new Day(1989,10,1));
        Employee harry2 = (Employee)harry.clone();
        harry.raiseSalary(100);
        harry.print();
        harry2.print();
    }
}

class SerialCloneable implements Cloneable
{  public Object clone()
    {  try
        {  ByteArrayOutputStream bout = new ByteArrayOutputStream();
            ObjectOutputStream out = new ObjectOutputStream(bout);
            out.writeObject(this);
            out.close();
            ByteArrayInputStream bin = new
                ByteArrayInputStream(bout.toByteArray());
            ObjectInputStream in = new ObjectInputStream(bin);
            Object ret = in.readObject();
            in.close();
            return ret;
        } catch(Exception e)
        {  return null;
        }
    }
}

class Employee extends SerialCloneable
{  public Employee(String n, double s, Day d)
    {  name = n;
        salary = s;
        hireDay = d;
    }
    public Employee() {}
```

Using serialization for cloning (continued)

```java
public void print()
{   System.out.println(name + " " + salary + " " +
        hireYear());
}

public void raiseSalary(double byPercent)
{   salary *= 1 + byPercent / 100;
}

public int hireYear()
{   return hireDay.getYear();
}

private String name;
private double salary;
private Day hireDay;
}
```

NOTE: This chapter discusses the alpha2 version of object serialization. That is the version of the library on the CD-ROM. However, a few details of the interface will change in the final version that will be a part of Java 1.1. This note summarizes the most important changes.

1. Classes will no longer be serializable by default. They must implement the
   `Serializable` interface to allow the default Java mechanism for serialization.
2. Classes can choose to use their own serialization protocol by implementing the
   `Externalizable` protocol. Those classes need to define the methods
      `void writeExternal(ObjectOutput out) throws IOException;`
      `void readExternal(ObjectInput in) throws IOException;`
These methods are responsible for saving and restoring the entire state of the object.
3. Classes that implement neither of these interfaces cannot be serialized.
4. Classes can supply a *version number*, and there will be support by object streams to read an older or newer version of a class, trying to set default values for those fields that are not available in the streamed object.
5. The `OutputObjectStream` class will extend `OutputStream` and implement `DataOutput`, instead of extending `DataOutputStream`. Similarly, the `InputObjectStream` class will extend `InputStream` and implement `DataInput`, instead of extending `DataInputStream`.
The file format for serialization will change as well. In particular, class versioning will require additional information in the streams.

CHAPTER
12

Multithreading

You are probably familiar with *multitasking:* the ability to have more than one program working at what seems like the same time. For example, you could print while editing or sending a fax. Of course, unless you have a multiple-processor machine, what is really going on is that the operating system is doling out resources to each program. This is practical because, although the user may think he or she is keeping the computer busy by, for example, entering data, most of the CPU's time will be idle. Multitasking can be done in two ways, depending on whether the operating system insists that a program let go or the program must cooperate in letting go. The former is called *preemptive multitasking*; the latter is called *cooperative* (or, simply, nonpreemptive multitasking). Windows 3.1 is a cooperative multitasking system, and Windows NT (and Windows 95 for 32-bit programs) is preemptive. (Although harder to implement, preemptive multitasking is much more effective. With cooperative multitasking, a badly behaved program can hog everything.)

Multithreaded programs extend the idea of multitasking by taking it one level lower: individual programs have the ability to run multiple computations at the same time. (Each computational unit is usually called a *thread*. Programs that run more than one computation at once are said to be *multithreaded*.) Think of each thread as running in a separate *context*: contexts make it seem as though each thread has its own CPU—with registers, memory, and its own code.

There is one essential difference between multiple *processes* and multiple *threads*. Each process has a complete set of its own variables. But threads share data in the program in which they live. This sounds somewhat risky, and indeed it can be, as we will see in this chapter. But it takes much less overhead to create and destroy individual threads than it does to launch new processes, which is why all modern operating systems support multithreading.

Multithreading is extremely useful in practice: for example, a browser should have the ability to deal with multiple hosts or to open an e-mail window while downloading more data. Java itself uses a thread to do garbage collection in the background—thus saving you the trouble of managing memory! The purpose of this chapter is to show you how to add multithreading capability to your Java applications and applets.

NOTE: In many programming languages, you have to use an external thread package to do multithreaded programming. Java has multithreading built into the language, which makes your job much easier.

What Are Threads?

Let us start by looking at a Java program that does not use multiple threads and that, as a consequence, makes it difficult for the user to perform several tasks with that program. After we dissect it, we will then show you how easy it is to have this program run separate threads. This program animates a bouncing ball by continually moving the ball, finding out if it bounces against a wall, and then redrawing it. (See Figure 12-1.)

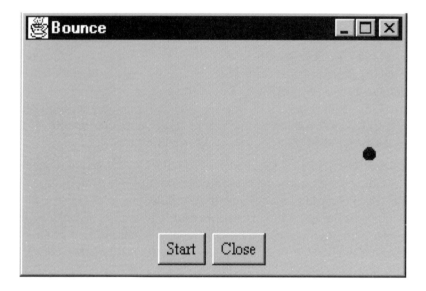

Figure 12-1: Using a thread to animate a bouncing ball

As soon as you hit the Start button, the program launches a ball from the upper left corner of the screen, and it begins bouncing. The handler of the Start button calls the method bounce() of the Ball class, which contains a loop running through 1,000 moves. After each move, we call the static `sleep` method of the `Thread` class to pause the ball for 5 milliseconds.

```
class Ball
{   . . .
    public void bounce()
    {   draw();
        for (int i = 1; i <= 1000; i++)
        {   move();
            try { Thread.sleep(5); }
            catch(InterruptedException e) {}
        }
    }
}
```

When you run the program, you will find that the ball bounces well, but it completely takes over the application. If you become tired of the bouncing ball before it has finished with its 1,000 iterations and click on the Close button, the ball continues bouncing anyway. You can not interact with the program until the ball has finished bouncing.

This is not a good situation in practice. Especially with software that reads data over a network connection, it is all too common to be stuck in time-consuming tasks that you would like to interrupt. For example, suppose you download a large image and decide, after seeing a fraction of it, that you do not need to see the rest; you would like to be able to click on a Stop or Back button to interrupt the loading process. In the next section, we will see how to keep the user in control by running part of the code in a separate *thread*.

Example 12-1 presents the entire code for the program.

Example 12-1: Bounce.java

```
import java.awt.*;

public class Bounce extends Frame
{   public Bounce()
    {   setTitle("Bounce");
        canvas = new Canvas();
        add("Center", canvas);
        Panel p = new Panel();
        p.add(new Button("Start"));
        p.add(new Button("Close"));
        add("South", p);
    }

    public boolean handleEvent(Event evt)
    {   if (evt.id == Event.WINDOW_DESTROY) System.exit(0);
        return super.handleEvent(evt);
    }
```

```java
    public boolean action(Event evt, Object arg)
    {   if (arg.equals("Start"))
        {   Ball b = new Ball(canvas);
            b.bounce();
        }
        else if (arg.equals("Close"))
            System.exit(0);
        else return super.action(evt, arg);
        return true;
    }

    public static void main(String[] args)
    {   Frame f = new Bounce();
        f.resize(300, 200);
        f.show();
    }

    private Canvas canvas;
}

class Ball
{   public Ball(Canvas c) { box = c; }

    public void draw()
    {   Graphics g = box.getGraphics();
        g.fillOval(x, y, XSIZE, YSIZE);
        g.dispose();
    }

    public void move()
    {   Graphics g = box.getGraphics();
        g.setXORMode(box.getBackground());
        g.fillOval(x, y, XSIZE, YSIZE);
        x += dx;
        y += dy;
        Dimension d = box.size();
        if (x < 0) { x = 0; dx = -dx; }
        if (x + XSIZE >= d.width) { x = d.width - XSIZE; dx = -dx; }
        if (y < 0) { y = 0; dy = -dy; }
        if (y + YSIZE >= d.height) { y = d.height - YSIZE; dy = -dy; }
        g.fillOval(x, y, XSIZE, YSIZE);
        g.dispose();
    }

    public void bounce()
    {   draw();
        for (int i = 1; i <= 1000; i++)
        {   move();
            try { Thread.sleep(5); } catch(InterruptedException e) {}
```

```
      }
   }

   private Canvas box;
   private static final int XSIZE = 10;
   private static final int YSIZE = 10;
   private int x = 0;
   private int y = 0;
   private int dx = 2;
   private int dy = 2;
}
```

Using Threads to Give Other Tasks a Chance

We will make our bouncing-ball program more responsive by running the code that moves the ball in a separate thread. Recall that a thread is a separate flow of control within a program. Because Java implements multithreading, multiple threads can run at the same time.

NOTE: Since most computers do not have multiple processors, Java uses a mechanism in which each thread gets a chance to run for a little while, and then it activates another thread.

In our next program, we use *two* threads: one for the bouncing ball and another for the *main thread* that takes care of the user interface. Because each thread gets a chance to run, the main thread has the opportunity to notice when you click on the Close button while the ball is bouncing. It can then process the "close" action.

There is a simple process for running code in a separate thread in Java: place the code into the run method of a class derived from Thread.

To make our bouncing-ball program into a separate thread, we only need to derive Ball from Thread and rename the bounce method run, as in the following code:

```
class Ball extends Thread
{   . . .
   public void run()
   {  draw();
      for (int i = 1; i <= 1000; i++)
      {  move();
         try { sleep(5); }
         catch(InterruptedException e) {}
      }
   }
}
```

You may have noticed that we are catching an exception called `InterruptedException`. Methods like `sleep` and `wait` throw this exception when your thread is interrupted because another thread has called `interrupt`. Interrupting a thread is a very drastic way of getting the thread's attention. In our programs, we never call `interrupt`, so we supply no exception handler for it.

Running and Starting Threads

When you construct an object derived from `Thread`, Java does not automatically call the `run` method.

```
Ball b = new Ball(. . .); // won't run yet
```

You should call the `start` method in your object to actually start a thread.

```
b.start();
```

> NOTE: Do *not* call the `run` method directly— `start` will call it when the thread is set up and ready to go.

In Java, a thread needs to tell the other threads when it is idle, so the other threads can grab the chance to execute the code in their `run` procedures. (See Figure 12-2.) The usual way to do this is through the `sleep` method (`sleep` is a static method in `Thread`). The `run` method of the `Ball` class uses the call to `sleep(5)` to indicate that it will be idle for the next 5 milliseconds. After 5 milliseconds, it will start up again, but in the meantime, other threads have a chance to get work done.

From a design point of view, it seems strange to have the class `Ball` extend the class `Thread`. A ball is an object that moves on the screen and bounces off the corners. Does the is–a rule for inheritance apply here? Is a ball a thread? Not really. Here we are using inheritance strictly for technical reasons. To get a thread you can control, you need a thread object with a `run` method. We might as well add that

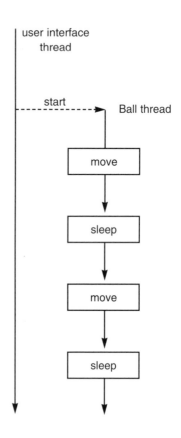

Figure 12-2: The UI and ball threads

run method to the class whose methods and instance fields the run method uses. Therefore, we make Ball a child class of Thread.

The complete code is shown here in Example 12-2.

Example 12-2: BounceThread.java

```
import java.awt.*;

public class BounceThread extends Frame
{   public BounceThread()
    {   setTitle("BounceThread");
        canvas = new Canvas();
        add("Center", canvas);
        Panel p = new Panel();
        p.add(new Button("Start"));
        p.add(new Button("Close"));
        add("South", p);
    }

    public boolean handleEvent(Event evt)
    {   if (evt.id == Event.WINDOW_DESTROY) System.exit(0);
        return super.handleEvent(evt);
    }

    public boolean action(Event evt, Object arg)
    {   if (arg.equals("Start"))
        {   Ball b = new Ball(canvas);
            b.start();
        }
        else if (arg.equals("Close"))
            System.exit(0);
        else return super.action(evt, arg);
        return true;
    }

    public static void main(String[] args)
    {   Frame f = new BounceThread();
        f.resize(300, 200);
        f.show();
    }

    private Canvas canvas;
}

class Ball extends Thread
{   public Ball(Canvas c) { box = c; }
```

```
public void draw()
{   Graphics g = box.getGraphics();
    g.fillOval(x, y, XSIZE, YSIZE);
    g.dispose();
}

public void move()
{   Graphics g = box.getGraphics();
    g.setXORMode(box.getBackground());
    g.fillOval(x, y, XSIZE, YSIZE);
    x += dx;
    y += dy;
    Dimension d = box.size();
    if (x < 0) { x = 0; dx = -dx; }
    if (x + XSIZE >= d.width) { x = d.width - XSIZE; dx = -dx; }
    if (y < 0) { y = 0; dy = -dy; }
    if (y + YSIZE >= d.height) { y = d.height - YSIZE; dy = -dy; }
    g.fillOval(x, y, XSIZE, YSIZE);
    g.dispose();
}

public void run()
{   draw();
    for (int i = 1; i <= 1000; i++)
    {   move();
        try { sleep(5); } catch(InterruptedException e) {}
    }
}

private Canvas box;
private static final int XSIZE = 10;
private static final int YSIZE = 10;
private int x = 0;
private int y = 0;
private int dx = 2;
private int dy = 2;
}
```

`java.lang.Thread`

- `Thread()`

  constructs a new thread. The thread must have a `run` method. You must
  `start` the thread to activate its `run` function.

- `void run()`

  You must override this function and add the code that you want to have executed in the thread.

- `void start()`

  starts this thread. This will cause the `run()` method to be called. This method will return immediately. The new thread runs concurrently.

- `static void sleep(long millis)`

  puts the currently executing thread to sleep for the specified number of milliseconds. Note that this is a static method.

- `void interrupt()`

  sends an interrupt request to a thread.

- `static boolean interrupted()`

  asks whether or not the current thread has been interrupted. Note that this is a static method.

Running Multiple Threads

Run the program in the preceding section. Now click on the Start button again while a ball is running. Click on it a few more times. You will see a whole bunch of balls bouncing away like in Figure 12-3. Each of them will move 1,000 times until it comes to its final resting place.

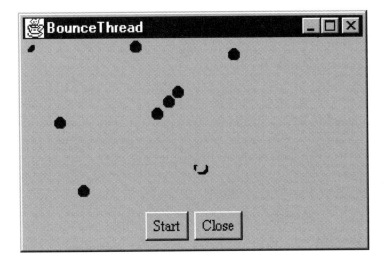

Figure 12-3: Multiple threads

This is a great advantage of the Java thread architecture. It is very easy to create any number of autonomous objects that appear to run in parallel.

You can enumerate the currently running threads—see the API note in the "Thread Groups" section.

Thread Properties

Thread States

Threads can be in one of four states:

- new
- runnable
- blocked
- dead

Each of these states is explained as follows:

New

When you create a thread with the `new` operator—for example, `new Ball()`—it is not yet running. This means that it is in the *new* state. When a thread is in the new state no code inside of it is being executed. A certain amount of book-keeping needs to be done before a thread can run. Doing the bookkeeping and determining the memory allocation needed are the tasks of the `start` method.

Runnable

Once you invoke the `start` method, the thread is *runnable*. A runnable thread may not yet be running. It is up to the operating system to give it time to do so. When the code inside the thread begins executing, the thread is *running*. (The Java documentation does not call this a separate state, though. A running thread is still in the runnable state.)

How this happens is up to the operating system. The thread package in Java needs to work with the underlying operating system. Only the operating system can provide the CPU cycles. The so-called "green threads" package that is used by Java 1.0 on Solaris, for example, keeps a running thread active until a higher-priority thread awakes and takes control. Other thread systems (such as Windows 95 and Windows NT) give each runnable thread a slice of time to per-form its task. When that slice of time is exhausted, the operating system gives another thread an opportunity to work. This is more sophisticated and makes better use of the multithreading capabilities of Java. The next release of Java on Solaris is expected to allow use of the native Solaris threads, which also perform time slicing.

Always keep in mind that a runnable thread may or may not be running at any given time. See Figure 12-4. (This is why the state is called "runnable" and not "running.")

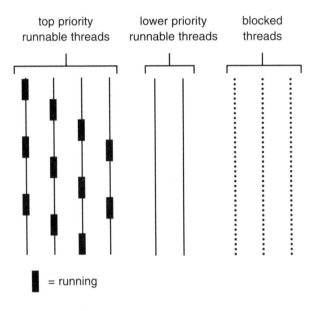

Figure 12-4: Time slicing on a single CPU

Blocked

A thread enters the *blocked* state when one of the four following actions occur:

1. Someone calls the `sleep()` method of the thread.

2. Someone calls the `suspend()` method of the thread.

3. The thread calls the `wait()` method.

4. The thread calls an operation that is *blocking on input/output*, that is, an operation that will not return to its caller until input and output operations are complete.

Figure 12-5 shows the states that a thread can have and the possible transitions from one state to the other. When a thread is blocked (or, of course, when it dies), another thread is scheduled to run. When a blocked thread is reactivated (for example, because it has slept the required number of milliseconds or because the I/O it waited for is complete), the scheduler checks to see if it has a higher priority than currently running thread. If so, it *preempts* the current thread and starts running the blocked thread again. (On a machine with multiple processors, each processor runs a separate thread.)

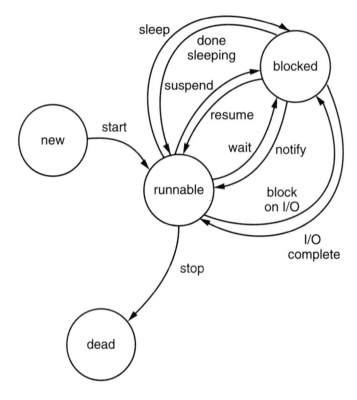

Figure 12-5: Thread states

For example, the `run` method of the `Ball` thread puts itself to sleep for 5 milliseconds after it has completed a move.

```
class Ball extends Thread
{   . . .
    public void run()
    {   draw();
        for (int i = 1; i <= 1000; i++)
        {   move();
            try { sleep(5); }
            catch(InterruptedException e) {}
        }
    }
}
```

This gives other threads (in our case, other balls and the main thread) the chance to run. If the computer has multiple processors, then more than one thread has a chance to run at the same time.

Moving Out of a Blocked State

The thread must move out of the blocked state and back into the runnable state using the opposite of the route that put it into the blocked state.

1. If a thread has been put to sleep, the specified number of milliseconds must expire.

2. If a thread has been suspended, then someone must call its `resume` method.

3. If a thread called `wait`, then the owner of the monitor on whose availability the thread is waiting must call `notify` or `notifyAll`. (We will cover monitors later in this chapter.)

4. If a thread is waiting for the completion of an input or output operation, then the operation must have finished.

If you try to activate a blocked thread in a way that does not match the route that blocked it in the first place, the activation attempt will not work. For example, if a thread is blocked on input and you call its `resume` method, it stays blocked.

If you invoke a method on a thread that is incompatible with its state, then the `IllegalThreadStateException` is thrown. For example, this happens when you call `suspend` on a thread that is not currently runnable.

Dead Threads

A thread is dead for one of two reasons.

*   It dies a natural death because the `run` method exits.

*   It is killed because someone invoked its `stop` method.

If you stop a thread, it does not immediately die. Technically, the `stop` method throws an object of type `ThreadDeath` to the thread object. Once the thread passes a `ThreadDeath` object to its `Thread` base class, the thread dies. `ThreadDeath` is a child class of `Error`, not `Exception`, so you do not have to catch it. In most circumstances, you would not want to catch this exception, but you would in the rare situation in which you must clean up prior to the thread's demise. You must then be sure to rethrow the exception in order to make the thread actually die.

Finding Out the State of a Thread

To find out whether a thread is currently runnable or blocked, use the `isAlive` method. It returns false if the thread is still new and not yet runnable or if the thread is dead.

NOTE: You cannot find out if a thread is actually running, nor can you differentiate between a thread that has not yet become runnable and one that has already died.

`java.lang.Thread`

- `boolean isAlive()`

  returns true if the thread has started and has not been stopped.

- `static void yield()`

  causes the currently executing thread to yield. If there are other runnable threads, they will be scheduled next. Note that this is a static method.

- `void suspend()`

  suspends this thread's execution.

- `void resume()`

  resumes this thread. This method is only valid after `suspend()` has been invoked.

- `void stop()`

  kills the thread.

- `void join()`

  waits until the thread dies.

Thread Priorities

Every thread in Java has a *priority*. By default, a thread inherits the priority of its parent thread. You can increase or decrease the priority of any thread with the `setPriority` method. You can set the priority to any value between `MIN_PRIORITY` (defined as 1 in the `Thread` class) and `MAX_PRIORTY` (defined as 10). `NORM_PRIORITY` is defined as 5.

Whenever the thread-scheduler has a chance to pick a new thread, it picks the *highest priority thread that is currently runnable*. The highest-priority runnable thread keeps running until it either:

- yields by calling the `yield` method,

- ceases to be runnable (either by dying or by entering the blocked state), or

- is replaced by a higher-priority thread that has become runnable (because it has slept long enough, because its I/O operation is complete, or because someone called `resume` or `notify`).

Then the scheduler selects a new thread to run. The highest-priority remaining thread is picked among those that are runnable.

What happens if there is more than one thread with the same priority? Each thread at that priority gets a turn in round-robin fashion. In other words, a thread is not scheduled again for execution until all other threads with the same priority have been scheduled at least once.

Consider the following test program, which modifies the previous program to allow the thread of one ball (the red one) to run with a higher priority than the other threads. If you click on the Express button, then you launch a red ball whose thread runs at a higher priority than the regular balls.

```
class BounceExpress
{   . . .
    public boolean action(Event evt, Object arg)
    {   if (arg.equals("Start"))
        {   Ball b = new Ball(canvas, Color.black);
            b.setPriority(Thread.NORM_PRIORITY);
            b.start();
        }
        else if (arg.equals("Express"))
        {   Ball b = new Ball(canvas, Color.red);
            b.setPriority(Thread.NORM_PRIORITY + 2);
            b.start();
        }
        else . . .
    }
}
```

Try it out. Launch a few regular balls and an express ball. You will notice that the express balls seem to run faster. This is solely a result of their higher priority. The code to move the express balls is the same as that of the regular balls.

Here is why this works. 5 milliseconds after an express thread is put to sleep, it is awoken. Then the scheduler again evaluates the priorities of all threads and finds that the express thread has the highest priority. So it gets another turn right away. If you launch two express balls, (as in Figure 12-6) they take turns, and only if both are asleep do the lower-priority threads get a chance to run. See the code in Example 12-3.

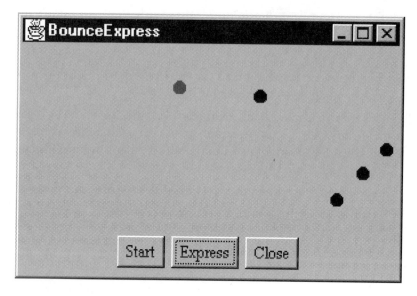

Figure 12-6: Threads with different priorities

Example 12-3: BounceExpress.java

```java
import java.awt.*;

public class BounceExpress extends Frame
{   public BounceExpress()
    {   setTitle("BounceExpress");
        canvas = new Canvas();
        add("Center", canvas);
        Panel p = new Panel();
        p.add(new Button("Start"));
        p.add(new Button("Express"));
        p.add(new Button("Close"));
        add("South", p);
    }

    public boolean handleEvent(Event evt)
    {   if (evt.id == Event.WINDOW_DESTROY) System.exit(0);
        return super.handleEvent(evt);
    }

    public boolean action(Event evt, Object arg)
    {   if (arg.equals("Start"))
        {   Ball b = new Ball(canvas, Color.black);
            b.setPriority(Thread.NORM_PRIORITY);
            b.start();
        }
```

```
            else if (arg.equals("Express"))
            {   Ball b = new Ball(canvas, Color.red);
                b.setPriority(Thread.NORM_PRIORITY + 2);
                b.start();
            }
            else if (arg.equals("Close"))
                System.exit(0);
            else return super.action(evt, arg);
            return true;
        }


    Canvas canvas;

    public static void main(String[] args)
    {   Frame f = new BounceExpress();
        f.resize(300, 200);
        f.show();
    }
}

class Ball extends Thread
{   Ball(Canvas c, Color co) { box = c; color = co; }

    public void draw()
    {   Graphics g = box.getGraphics();
        g.setColor(color);
        g.fillOval(x, y, XSIZE, YSIZE);
        g.dispose();
    }

    public void move()
    {   Graphics g = box.getGraphics();
        g.setColor(color);
        g.setXORMode(box.getBackground());
        g.fillOval(x, y, XSIZE, YSIZE);
        x += dx;
        y += dy;
        Dimension d = box.size();
        if (x < 0) { x = 0; dx = -dx; }
        if (x + XSIZE >= d.width) { x = d.width - XSIZE; dx = -dx; }
        if (y < 0) { y = 0; dy = -dy; }
        if (y + YSIZE >= d.height) { y = d.height - YSIZE; dy = -dy; }
        g.fillOval(x, y, XSIZE, YSIZE);
        g.dispose();
    }
```

```
public void run()
{   draw();
    for (int i = 1; i <= 1000; i++)
    {   move();
        try { sleep(5); } catch(InterruptedException e) {}
    }
}

Canvas box;
private static final int XSIZE = 10;
private static final int YSIZE = 10;
private int x = 0;
private int y = 0;
private int dx = 2;
private int dy = 2;
Color color;
}
```

`java.lang.Thread`

- `void setPriority(int newPriority)`

  Sets the priority of this thread. Must be between `Thread.MIN_PRIORITY` and `Thread.MAX_PRIORITY`. Use `Thread.NORM_PRIORITY` for normal priority.

- `static int MIN_PRIORITY`

  the minimum priority that a `Thread` can have. The minimum priority value is 1.

- `static int NORM_PRIORITY`

  the default priority to a `Thread`. The default priority is equal to 5.

- `static int MAX_PRIORITY`

  the maximum priority that a `Thread` can have. The maximum priority value is 10.

Cooperating and Selfish Threads

Our ball threads were well behaved and cooperated with each other. They did this by using the `sleep` function to wait their turns. The `sleep` function blocks the thread and gives others a chance to be scheduled.

Even if a thread does not want to put itself to sleep for any amount of time, it can call `yield()` whenever it does not mind being interrupted.

A thread should always call `yield` or `sleep` when it is executing a long loop, to ensure that it is not monopolizing the system. A thread that does not follow this rule is called *selfish*.

The following program shows what happens when a thread contains a *tight loop*, a loop in which it carries out a lot of work without giving other threads a chance. When you click on the Selfish button, a blue ball is launched whose `run` method contains a tight loop.

```
class SelfishBall extends Ball
{   . . .
    public void run()
    {   draw();
        for (int i = 1; i <= 1000; i++)
        {   move();
            long t = new Date().getTime();
            while (new Date().getTime() < t + 5)
                ;
        }
    }
}
```

The `run` procedure will last about 5 seconds before it returns, ending the thread. In the meantime it never calls `yield` or `sleep`.

What actually happens when you run this program depends on your operating system. For example, when you run this program under Solaris, you will find that the selfish ball indeed hogs the whole application. Try closing the program or launching another ball; you will have a hard time getting even a mouse click into the application. However, when you run the same program under Windows 95 or NT, nothing untoward happens. The blue ball can run in parallel with other balls.

The reason is that the underlying thread package in Windows performs *time-slicing*. It periodically interrupts threads in midstream, even if they are not cooperating. When one thread is interrupted, another thread (of the top priority level among the runnable threads) is activated. The "green threads" implementation used by Java 1.0 on Solaris does not perform time-slicing, but future versions will. If you *know* that your program will execute on a machine whose operating system performs time-slicing, then you do not need to worry about making your threads polite. But the point of Internet computing is that you generally *do not know* the environments of the people who will use your program. You should, therefore, plan for the worst and put calls to `yield` or `sleep` in every loop. See Example 12-4.

Example 12-4: BounceSelfish.java

```java
import java.awt.*;
import java.util.*;

public class BounceSelfish extends Frame
{  public BounceSelfish()
   {  setTitle("BounceSelfish");
      canvas = new Canvas();
      add("Center", canvas);
      Panel p = new Panel();
      p.add(new Button("Start"));
      p.add(new Button("Express"));
      p.add(new Button("Selfish"));
      p.add(new Button("Close"));
      add("South", p);
   }

   public boolean handleEvent(Event evt)
   {  if (evt.id == Event.WINDOW_DESTROY) System.exit(0);
      return super.handleEvent(evt);
   }

   public boolean action(Event evt, Object arg)
   {  if (arg.equals("Start"))
      {  Ball b = new Ball(canvas, Color.black);
         b.setPriority(Thread.NORM_PRIORITY);
         b.start();
      }
      else if (arg.equals("Express"))
      {  Ball b = new Ball(canvas, Color.red);
         b.setPriority(Thread.NORM_PRIORITY + 2);
         b.start();
      }
      else if (arg.equals("Selfish"))
      {  Ball b = new SelfishBall(canvas, Color.blue);
         b.setPriority(Thread.NORM_PRIORITY + 2);
         b.start();
      }
      else if (arg.equals("Close"))
         System.exit(0);
      else return super.action(evt, arg);
      return true;
   }

   public static void main(String[] args)
   {  Frame f = new BounceSelfish();
      f.resize(300, 200);
      f.show();
```

```
   }

   private Canvas canvas;
}

class Ball extends Thread
{  public Ball(Canvas c, Color co) { box = c; color = co; }

   public void draw()
   {  Graphics g = box.getGraphics();
      g.setColor(color);
      g.fillOval(x, y, XSIZE, YSIZE);
      g.dispose();
   }

   public void move()
   {  Graphics g = box.getGraphics();
      g.setColor(color);
      g.setXORMode(box.getBackground());
      g.fillOval(x, y, XSIZE, YSIZE);
      x += dx;
      y += dy;
      Dimension d = box.size();
      if (x < 0) { x = 0; dx = -dx; }
      if (x + XSIZE >= d.width) { x = d.width - XSIZE; dx = -dx; }
      if (y < 0) { y = 0; dy = -dy; }
      if (y + YSIZE >= d.height) { y = d.height - YSIZE; dy = -dy; }
      g.fillOval(x, y, XSIZE, YSIZE);
      g.dispose();
   }

   public void run()
   {  draw();
      for (int i = 1; i <= 1000; i++)
      {  move();
         try { sleep(5); } catch(InterruptedException e) {}
      }
   }

   private Canvas box;
   private static final int XSIZE = 10;
   private static final int YSIZE = 10;
   private int x = 0;
   private int y = 0;
   private int dx = 2;
   private int dy = 2;
   private Color color;
}
```

```
class SelfishBall extends Ball
{   public SelfishBall(Canvas c, Color co) { super(c, co); }

    public void run()
    {   draw();
        for (int i = 1; i <= 1000; i++)
        {   move();
            long t = new Date().getTime();
            while (new Date().getTime() < t + 5)
                ;
        }
    }
}
```

Thread Groups

Some programs contain quite a few threads. It then becomes useful to categorize them by functionality. For example, consider an Internet browser. If many threads are trying to acquire images from a server, and the user clicks on a Stop button to interrupt loading the current page, then it is handy to have a way of killing all of these threads simultaneously.

You construct a thread group with the constructor:

```
ThreadGroup g = new ThreadGroup(string)
```

The string identifies the group and must be unique. For example:

```
class ImageLoader extends ThreadGroup
{   public ImageLoader(String name, ThreadGroup g)
    {   super(g, "Loading " + name);
        . . .
    }
}
```

To find out whether or not any threads of a particular group are still runnable, use the `activeCount` method.

```
if (g.activeCount() == 0)
{   // all threads in the group g have stopped
}
```

To kill all threads in a thread group, simply call `stop` on the group object.

```
g.stop(); // stops all threads in g
```

Thread groups can have child subgroups. By default, a newly created thread group becomes a child of the current thread group. But you can also explicitly name the parent group in the constructor (see the API notes). Methods such as `activeCount` and `stop` refer to all threads in their group and all child groups.

java.lang.ThreadGroup

- ThreadGroup(String name)

  creates a new ThreadGroup. Its parent will be the thread group of the current thread.

  Parameters: name   the name of the new thread group

- ThreadGroup(ThreadGroup parent, String name)

  creates a new ThreadGroup.

  Parameters: parent   the parent thread group of the new thread group

                    name   the name of the new thread group

- int activeCount()

  returns an upper bound for the number of active threads in the thread group.

- int enumerate(Thread list[])

  gets references to every active thread in this thread group. You can use the activeCount() method to get an upper bound for the array; this returns the number of threads put into the array.

  Parameters: list   an array to be filled with the thread references

- ThreadGroup getParent()

  gets the parent of this Thread group.

- void resume()

  resumes all threads in this thread group and all of its child groups.

- void stop()

  stops all threads in this thread group and all of its child groups .

- void suspend()

  suspends all threads in this thread group and all of its child groups.

`java.lang.Thread`

- `ThreadGroup getThreadGroup()`

  returns the thread group of this thread.

Synchronization

Thread Communication without Synchronization

A running thread can access any object to which it has a reference. What happens if two threads have access to the same object, and each calls a method that modifies the state of the object? As you might imagine, the threads can step on each other's toes, leading to corrupted objects. To solve this problem, we must learn how to *synchronize* access to shared objects. In this section, we see what happens if you do not deal with synchronization. In the next section, we will learn how to synchronize object access in Java.

In the next test program, we will simulate a bank with 10 accounts. We will randomly generate transactions that move money between these accounts. There will be 10 threads, one for each account. Each transaction will move a random amount of money from the account serviced by the thread to another random account.

The simulation code is straightforward. We have the class `Bank` with the method `transfer`. This method transfers some amount of money from one account to another. If the source account does not have enough money in it, then the thread calling the `transfer` method is put to sleep for a short time so that other threads have a chance to transfer some money into this account.

Here is the code for the `transfer` method of the `Bank` class.

```
public void transfer(int from, int to, int amount)
{  while (accounts[from] < amount)
     // wait for another thread to add more money
   {  try {  Thread.sleep(5); }
      catch(InterruptedException e) {}
   }

   accounts[from] -= amount;
   accounts[to] += amount;
   ntransacts++;
   if (ntransacts % 5000 == 0) test();
}
```

Each thread generates a random transaction, calls `transfer` on the bank object, and then puts itself to sleep. Here is the code for the `run` method of the thread class.

```
public void run()
{  while (true)
   {  int to = (int)((Bank.NACCOUNTS - 1) * Math.random());
      if (to >= from) to++;
      int amount = 1 +
          (int)(Bank.INITIAL_BALANCE * Math.random()) / 2;
      bank.transfer(from, to, amount);
      try { sleep(1); } catch(InterruptedException e) {}
   }
}
```

When this simulation runs, we do not know how much money is in any one bank account at any time. But we do know that the total amount of money in all the accounts should remain unchanged since all we do is move money from one account to another.

Every 5,000 transactions, the `transfer` method calls a `test` method that recomputes the total and prints it out.

This program never finishes. Just hit CTRL+C to kill the program.

Here is a typical printout.

```
Transactions:0 Sum: 100000
Transactions:5000 Sum: 100000
Transactions:10000 Sum: 100000
Transactions:15000 Sum: 99840
Transactions:20000 Sum: 98079
Transactions:25000 Sum: 98079
Transactions:30000 Sum: 98079
Transactions:35000 Sum: 98079
Transactions:40000 Sum: 98079
Transactions:45000 Sum: 98079
Transactions:50000 Sum: 98079
Transactions:55000 Sum: 98079
Transactions:60000 Sum: 98079
Transactions:65000 Sum: 95925
Transactions:70000 Sum: 95925
Transactions:75000 Sum: 95925
```

As you can see, something is very wrong. For several thousand transactions, the bank balance remains at $100,000, which is the correct total for 10 accounts of $10,000 each. But after some time, the balance changes slightly. This does not inspire confidence, and we would probably not want to deposit our hard-earned money into this bank.

Example 12-5 provides the complete source code. Have a look at it to see if you can spot the problem with the code. We will unravel the mystery in the next section.

Example 12-5: UnsynchBankTest.java

```java
class UnsynchBankTest
{  public static void main(String[] args)
   {  Bank b = new Bank();
      int i;
      for (i = 1; i <= Bank.NACCOUNTS; i++)
         new TransactionSource(b, i).start();
   }
}

class Bank
{  public Bank()
   {  accounts = new long[NACCOUNTS];
      int i;
      for (i = 0; i < NACCOUNTS; i++)
         accounts[i] = INITIAL_BALANCE;
      ntransacts = 0;
      test();
   }

   public void transfer(int from, int to, int amount)
   {  while (accounts[from] < amount)
      {  try {  Thread.sleep(5); } catch(InterruptedException e) {}
      }

      accounts[from] -= amount;
      accounts[to] += amount;
      ntransacts++;
      if (ntransacts % 5000 == 0) test();
   }

   public void test()
   {  int i;
      long sum = 0;

      for (i = 0; i < NACCOUNTS; i++) sum += accounts[i];
      System.out.println("Transactions:" + ntransacts + " Sum: "
         + sum);
   }

   public static final int INITIAL_BALANCE = 10000;
   public static final int NACCOUNTS = 10;
   private long[] accounts;
   private int ntransacts;
}
```

```
class TransactionSource extends Thread
{  public TransactionSource(Bank b, int i)
   {  from = i - 1;
      bank = b;
   }

   public void run()
   {  while (true)
      {  int to = (int)((Bank.NACCOUNTS - 1) * Math.random());
         if (to == from) to = (to + 1)% Bank.NACCOUNTS;
         int amount = 1 + (int)(Bank.INITIAL_BALANCE
            * Math.random()) / 2;
         bank.transfer(from, to, amount);
         try { sleep(1); } catch(InterruptedException e) {}
      }
   }

   private Bank bank;
   private int from;
}
```

Synchronizing Access to Shared Resources

In the previous section, we ran a program in which several threads updated bank account balances. After a few thousand transactions, errors crept in and some amount of money was either lost or spontaneously created. This problem occurs when two threads are simultaneously trying to update an account. Suppose two threads simultaneously carry out the instruction:

```
accounts[to] += amount;
```

The problem is that these are not *atomic* operations. The instruction might be processed as follows:

1. load `accounts[to]` into a register,

2. add `amount`,

3. move the result back to `accounts[to]`.

Now, suppose the first thread executes steps 1 and 2, and then it is interrupted. Suppose the second thread awakens and updates the same entry in the `account` array. Then the first thread awakens and completes its step 3.

That wipes out the modification of the other thread. As a result, the total is no longer correct. (See Figure 12-7.)

Our test program detects this corruption. (Of course, there is a slight chance of false alarms if the thread is interrupted as it is performing the tests!)

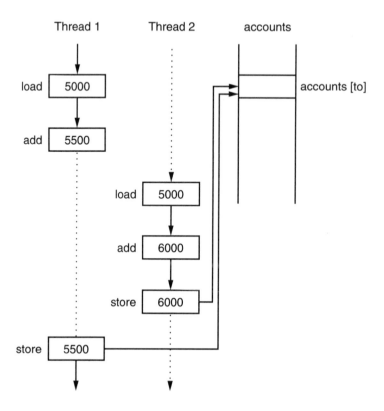

Figure 12-7: Simultaneous access by two threads

 NOTE: You can actually peek at the Java bytecodes that execute each statement in our class. Run the command

```
javap -c -v Bank
```

to decompile the `Bank.class` file. (You need to unzip `\java\lib\classes.zip` for this to work.) For example, the line

```
accounts[to] += amount;
```

is translated into the following bytecodes.

```
aload_0
getfield #16 <Field Bank.accounts [J>
iload_1
dup2
laload
iload_3
i21
lsub
lastore
```

> What these codes mean does not matter. The point is that the increment command is made up of several instructions, and the thread executing them can be interrupted at the point of any instruction.

What is the chance of this happening? It is fairly common when the operating system performs time-slicing on threads. Our test program shows a corruption of the buffer every few thousand entries under Windows 95. When a thread system, such as the "green threads" on Solaris, does not perform time-slicing on threads, corruption is less frequent. (To simulate the behavior on Solaris, run another higher-priority thread that occasionally wakes up. When it goes to sleep, another transaction thread is scheduled.)

Of course, as Java programmers, we must cope with the worst possible scenario and must assume that threads will be frequently interrupted.

We must have some way of ensuring that once a thread has begun inserting an element into the buffer, it can complete the operation without being interrupted. Most programming environments force the programmer to fuss with so-called semaphores and critical sections to gain uninterrupted access to a resource, which is painful and the process is error prone. Java has a nicer mechanism, inspired by the *monitors* invented by Tony Hoare.

You simply tag any operation shared by multiple threads as synchronized, like this:

```
public synchronized void transfer(int from, int to,
    int amount)
{   . . .
    accounts[from] -= amount;
    accounts[to] += amount;
    ntransacts++;
    if (ntransacts % 5000 == 0) test();
    . . .
}
```

When one thread enters a synchronized method, Java guarantees that it can finish it before another thread can execute any synchronized method on the same object. When one thread calls transfer and then another thread also calls transfer, the second thread cannot continue. Instead, it is deactivated and must wait for the first thread to finish executing the transfer method.

When you create an object with one or more synchronized methods, Java sets up a queue of all the threads waiting to be "let inside" the object. This is shown in Figure 12-8. Whenever one thread has completed its work with the object, the highest-priority thread in the waiting queue gets the next turn.

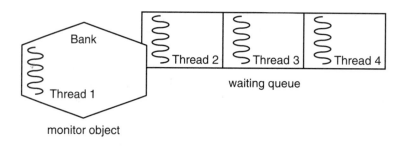

monitor object

Figure 12-8: A monitor

An object that can block threads and notify them when it becomes available is called a *monitor*. In Java, any object with one or more synchronized methods is a monitor.

In our simulation of the bank, we do not want to transfer money out of an account that does not have the funds to cover it. Note that we cannot use code like:

```
if (bank.getBalance(from) >= amount)
    bank.transfer(from, to, amount);
```

It is entirely possible that the current thread will be interrupted between the successful outcome of the test and the call to `transfer`. By the time the thread is running again, the account balance may have fallen below `amount`. We must make sure that the thread cannot be interrupted between the test and the insertion. You can do this by putting the test inside a synchronized version of the `transfer` method.

```
public synchronized void transfer(int from, int to,
    int amount)
{   while (accounts[from] < amount)
    {   // wait
    }
    // transfer funds
}
```

Now what do we do when there is not enough money in the account? We wait until some other thread has added funds. But this thread has just gained exclusive access to the bank object, so no other thread has a chance to make a deposit. A second feature of synchronized methods takes care of this situation. You use the `wait` method in the thread class.

When a thread calls `wait` inside a synchronized method, it is deactivated, and Java puts it in the waiting queue for that object. This lets in another thread that can, hopefully, change the account balance. Java awakens the original thread again when another method calls the `notify` method. This is the signal that the state of the bank object has changed and that waiting threads should be given another chance to inspect the object state. In our buffer example, we will call notify when we have finished with the funds transfer.

This gives the waiting threads the chance to run again. A thread that was waiting for a higher balance then gets a chance to check the balance again. If the balance is sufficient, it performs the transfer. If not, it calls wait again.

It is important that the notify function is called by some thread—otherwise, the threads that called wait, will wait forever. The waiting threads are *not* automatically reactivated when no other thread is working on the object.

TIP: If your multithreaded program gets stuck, double-check that every wait is matched by a notify.

Here is the code for the transfer method that uses synchronized methods. Notice the calls to wait and notify.

```
public synchronized void transfer(int from, int to, int
    amount)
{   while (accounts[from] < amount)
    {   try { wait(); } catch(InterruptedException e) {}
    }
    accounts[from] -= amount;
    accounts[to] += amount;
    ntransacts++;
    if (ntransacts % 5000 == 0) test();
    notify();
}
```

If you run the sample program with the synchronized version of the transfer method, you will notice that nothing goes wrong. The total balance stays at $100,000 forever. (Again, you need to hit CTRL+C to terminate the program.)

You will also notice that the program in Example 12-6 runs quite a bit slower—this is the price you pay for the added bookkeeping involved in the synchronization mechanism.

Example 12-6: SynchBankTest.java

```
class SynchBankTest
{   public static void main(String[] args)
    {   Bank b = new Bank();
        int i;
        for (i = 1; i <= Bank.NACCOUNTS; i++)
            new TransactionSource(b, i).start();
    }
}
```

```java
class Bank
{   public Bank()
    {   accounts = new long[NACCOUNTS];
        int i;
        for (i = 0; i < NACCOUNTS; i++)
            accounts[i] = INITIAL_BALANCE;
        ntransacts = 0;
        test();
    }

    public synchronized void transfer(int from, int to, int
        amount)
    {   while (accounts[from] < amount)
        {   try { wait(); } catch(InterruptedException e) {}
        }
        accounts[from] -= amount;
        accounts[to] += amount;
        ntransacts++;
        if (ntransacts % 5000 == 0) test();
        notify();
    }

    public void test()
    {   int i;
        long sum = 0;

        for (i = 0; i < NACCOUNTS; i++) sum += accounts[i];
        System.out.println("Transactions:" + ntransacts + " Sum: "
            + sum);
    }

    public static final int INITIAL_BALANCE = 10000;
    public static final int NACCOUNTS = 10;

    private long[] accounts;
    private int ntransacts;
}

class TransactionSource extends Thread
{   public TransactionSource(Bank b, int i)
    {   from = i - 1;
        bank = b;
    }

    public void run()
    {   while (true)
        {   int to = (int)((Bank.NACCOUNTS - 1) * Math.random());
            if (to == from) to = (to + 1) % Bank.NACCOUNTS;
```

```
            int amount = 1 + (int)(Bank.INITIAL_BALANCE
               * Math.random()) / 2;
            bank.transfer(from, to, amount);
            try { sleep(1); } catch(InterruptedException e) {}
         }
      }
   }

   private Bank bank;
   private int from;
}
```

Here is a summary of how the synchronization mechanism works.

1. If a class has one or more synchronized methods, each object of the class gets a queue that holds all threads waiting to execute one of the synchronized methods.

2. There are two ways for a thread to get onto this queue, either by calling the method while another thread is using the object or by calling `wait` while using the object.

3. When a synchronized method call returns, or when a method calls `wait`, another thread gets access to the object.

4. As always, the scheduler chooses the highest-priority thread among those in the queue.

5. If a thread was put in the queue by a call to `wait`, it must be "unfrozen" by a call to `notify` before it can be scheduled for execution again.

The scheduling rules are undeniably complex, but it is actually quite simple to put them into practice. Just follow these three rules.

1. If two or more threads modify an object, declare the methods that carry out the modifications as `synchronized`.

2. If a thread must wait for the state of an object to change, it should wait inside the object, not outside, by entering a synchronized method and calling `wait`.

3. Whenever a method changes the state of an object, it should call `notify`. That gives the waiting threads a chance to see if circumstances have changed.

`java.lang.Object`

- `void notify()`

  notifies the threads waiting on this monitor object that the state of the object has changed. This method can only be called from within a synchronized method. The method throws an `IllegalMonitorStateException` if the current thread is not the owner of the object's monitor.

- `void wait()`

  causes a thread to wait until it is notified. This method can only be called from within a synchronized method. It throws an `IllegalMonitorStateException` if the current thread is not the owner of the object's monitor.

Deadlocks

The synchronization feature in Java is convenient and powerful, but it cannot solve all problems that might arise in multithreading. Consider the following situation:

> Account 1: $2000
>
> Account 2: $3000
>
> Thread 1: Transfer $3000 from Account 1 to Account 2
>
> Thread 2: Transfer $4000 from Account 2 to Account 1.

As Figure 12-9 indicates, Threads 1 and 2 are clearly blocked. Neither can proceed since the balances in Accounts 1 and 2 are insufficient.

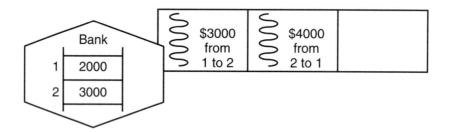

Figure 12-9: A deadlock situation

Is it possible that all 10 threads are blocked because each is waiting for more money? Such a situation is called a *deadlock*.

In our program, a deadlock could not occur for a simple reason. Each transfer amount is for, at most, $10,000. Since there are 10 accounts and a total of $100,000 in them, at least one of the accounts must have more than $10,000 at any time. The thread moving money out of that account can, therefore, proceed.

But if you change the `run` method of the threads to remove the $10,000 transaction limit, deadlocks can occur quickly. (Another way to create a deadlock is to make the `i`th thread responsible for putting money into the `i`th account, rather than for taking it out of the `i`th account. In this case, there is a small chance that all threads will gang up on one account, each trying to remove more money from it than it contains.)

There is nothing that Java can do to avoid or break these deadlocks. You must design your threads to ensure that a deadlock situation cannot occur. Analyze your program and ensure that every thread awaiting an object will eventually be activated.

Thread synchronization and deadlock avoidance are difficult subjects, and we refer the interested reader to the book *Programming with Threads,* by Steve Kleiman, Devang Shah, and Bart Smaalders (Sunsoft Press/Prentice-Hall, 1996).

Timers

In many programming environments, you can set up timers. A timer alerts your program elements at regular intervals. For example, to display a clock in a window, the clock object must be notified once every second.

Java does not have a built-in timer class, but it is easy enough to build one using threads. In this section, we describe how to do that. You can use this timer class in your own code.

Our timer runs in its own thread, so it must extend `Thread`. In its `run` method, it goes to sleep for the specified interval, then notifies its target.

```
class Timer extends Thread
{   . . .
    public void run()
    {   while (true)
        {   try { sleep(interval); }
            catch(InterruptedException e) {}
            // notify target
        }
    }

    private int interval;
}
```

There is a slight problem with writing a general purpose timer class. The timer holds an object reference to the target, and it is supposed to notify the object whenever the time interval has elapsed. In C or C++ programming, the timer object would hold a pointer to a function, and it would call that function periodically. For safety reasons, Java does not have function pointers.

We showed you in Chapter 5 how to overcome this problem by making a special interface for the callback. In our case, the interface is called `Timed` and the callback is called `tick`. Thus, an object that wants to receive timer ticks must implement the `Timed` interface. The action to be repeated in regular intervals must be put into the `tick` method.

Figure 12-10 shows six different clocks:

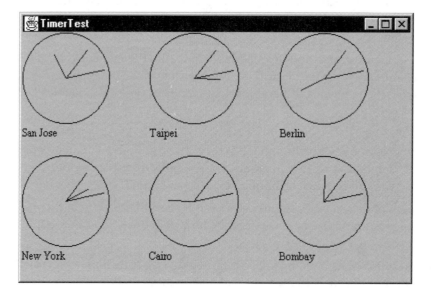

Figure 12-10: Clock threads

Each clock is an instance of the `ClockCanvas` class, which implements `Timed`. The `tick` method of the `Clock` class redraws the clock.

```
class ClockCanvas extends Canvas implements Timed
{   . . .
    public void tick(Timer t)
    {   Date d = new Date();
        seconds = (d.getHours() - LOCAL + offset)* 60 * 60
            + d.getMinutes() * 60 + d.getSeconds();
        repaint();
    }
}
```

Note that the `tick` method does not actually get the time from the timer object `t`. The timer ticks only come *approximately* once a second. For an accurate clock display, we still need to get the system time.

Example 12-7 is the complete code:

Example 12-7: TimerTest.java

```
import java.awt.*;
import java.util.*;


public class TimerTest extends Frame
{  public TimerTest()
   {  setTitle("TimerTest");
      setLayout(new GridLayout(2, 3));
      add(new ClockCanvas("San Jose", 16));
      add(new ClockCanvas("Taipei", 8));
      add(new ClockCanvas("Berlin", 1));
      add(new ClockCanvas("New York", 19));
      add(new ClockCanvas("Cairo", 2));
      add(new ClockCanvas("Bombay", 5));
   }


   public boolean handleEvent(Event evt)
   {  if (evt.id == Event.WINDOW_DESTROY) System.exit(0);
      return super.handleEvent(evt);
   }

   public static void main(String[] args)
   {  Frame f = new TimerTest();
      f.resize(450, 300);
      f.show();
   }
}

interface Timed
{  public void tick(Timer t);
}

class Timer extends Thread
{  public Timer(Timed t, int i)
   {  target  = t; interval = i;
      setDaemon(true);
   }

   public void run()
   {  while (true)
      {  try { sleep(interval); }
```

```
                catch(InterruptedException e) {}
                target.tick(this);
            }
        }

    private Timed target;
    private int interval;
}

class ClockCanvas extends Canvas implements Timed
{   public ClockCanvas(String c, int off)
    {   city = c; offset = off;
        new Timer(this, 1000).start();
        resize(125, 125);
    }

    public void paint(Graphics g)
    {   g.drawOval(0, 0, 100, 100);
        double hourAngle = 2 * Math.PI * (seconds - 3 * 60 * 60)
            / (12 * 60 * 60);
        double minuteAngle = 2 * Math.PI * (seconds - 15 * 60)
            / (60 * 60);
        double secondAngle = 2 * Math.PI * (seconds - 15) / 60;
        g.drawLine(50, 50, 50 + (int)(30 * Math.cos(hourAngle)),
            50 + (int)(30 * Math.sin(hourAngle)));
        g.drawLine(50, 50, 50 + (int)(40 * Math.cos(minuteAngle)),
            50 + (int)(40 * Math.sin(minuteAngle)));
        g.drawLine(50, 50, 50 + (int)(45 * Math.cos(secondAngle)),
            50 + (int)(45 * Math.sin(secondAngle)));
        g.drawString(city, 0, 115);
    }

    public void tick(Timer t)
    {   Date d = new Date();
        seconds = (d.getHours() - LOCAL + offset)* 60 * 60
            + d.getMinutes() * 60
            + d.getSeconds();
        repaint();
    }

    private int seconds = 0;
    private String city;
    private int offset;
    private final int LOCAL = 16;
}
```

Daemon Threads

If you look carefully into the constructor of the timer class above, you will note the method call that looks like this:

```
setDaemon(true);
```

This makes the timer thread a *daemon thread*. There is nothing demonic about it. A daemon is simply a thread that has no other role in life than to serve others. When only daemon threads remain, then the program exits. There is no point in keeping the program running if all remaining threads are daemons.

In a graphical application, the timer class threads do not affect the end of the program. It stays alive until the user closes the application. (The user-interface thread is not a daemon thread.) But when you use the timer class in a text application, you need not worry about stopping the timer threads. When the non-timer threads have finished their `run` methods, the application will automatically terminate.

`java.lang.Thread`

• `void setDaemon(boolean on)`

marks this `Thread` as a daemon thread or a user thread. When there are only daemon threads left running in the system, Java exits. This method must be called before the thread is started.

Animation

In the previous sections, you learned what is required to split a program into multiple concurrent tasks. Each task needs to be placed into a `run` method of a class that extends `Thread`. But what if we want to add the `run` method to a class that already extends another class? This occurs most often when we want to add multithreading to an applet. An applet class already inherits from `Applet`, and in Java, we cannot inherit from two parent classes, so we need to use an Interface. The necessary interface is built into Java. It is called `Runnable`. We take this important interface up next.

The Runnable Interface

Whenever you need to use multithreading in a class that is already derived from a class other than `Thread`, make the class implement the `Runnable` interface. As though you had derived from `Thread`, put the code that needs to run in the `run` method. For example,

```
class Animation extends Applet implements Runnable
{   . . .
    public void run()
    {   // thread action goes here
    }
}
```

You still need to make a thread object to launch the thread. Give that thread a reference to the Runnable object in its constructor. It then calls the run method of that object.

This is most commonly done in the start method of an applet, as in the following example:

```
class Animation extends Applet implements Runnable
{   . . .
    public void start()
    {   if (runner == null)
        {   runner = new Thread(this);
            runner.start();
        }
    }
    . . .
    private Thread runner;
}
```

In this case, the this argument to the Thread constructor specifies that the object whose run function should be called when the thread executes is an instance of the Animation object.

Wouldn't it be easier if we just defined another class from Thread and launched it in the applet?

```
class AnimationThread extends Thread
{   public void run()
    {   // thread action goes here
    }
}

class Animation extends Applet
{   . . .
    public void start()
    {   if (runner == null)
        {   runner = new AnimationThread();
            runner.start();
        }
    }
    . . .
    private Thread runner;
}
```

Indeed, this would be clean and simple. However, if the `run` method must have access to an applet's private data, then it makes a a great deal of sense to keep the `run` method with the applet and use the `Runnable` interface instead.

`java.lang.Thread`

- `Thread(Runnable target)`

  constructs a new thread that calls the `run()` method of the specified target.

`java.lang.Runnable`

- `void run()`

  You must override this method and place the code that you want to have executed in the thread.

Loading and Displaying Frames

In this section, we will dissect one of the most common uses for threads in Java applets: animation. An animation sequence displays images, giving the viewer the illusion of motion. Each of the images in the sequence is called a *frame*. Of course, the frames must be rendered ahead of time—today's personal computers do not have the horse-power to compute the drawing fast enough for real-time animation.

You can put each frame in a separate file or put them all into one file. We do the latter. It makes the process of loading the image much easier. In our example, we use a file with 36 images of a rotating globe, as shown in Figure 12-11, courtesy of Silviu Marghescu of the University of Maryland. Here are the first few frames.

The animation applet must first acquire all the frames. Then it shows each of them, in turn, for a fixed time. You know from Chapter 6 how to load an image file. When you call `getImage`, the image is not actually loaded. Instead, the first time you access the image data with `drawImage`, a separate thread is spawned to start the loading process. Loading an image can be very slow, especially if it has

Figure 12-11: This file has 36 images of a globe

many frames or is located across the network. The thread acquiring the image periodically calls the `imageUpdate` method of the applet. Eventually, the ALL-BITS flag of the `infoflags` parameter is set, and the image is complete.

Once the image is loaded, we render a frame at a time. To draw the ith frame, we make a method call as follows:

```
g.drawImage(image, 0, - i * imageHeight, imageCount, null);
```

In Figure 12-12 the *negative* offset of the y-coordinate. This causes the first frame to be well above the origin of the canvas. The top of the ith frame becomes the top of the canvas.

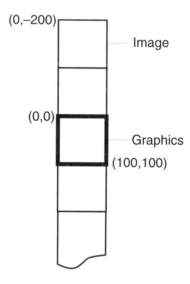

Figure 12-12: Picking a frame from a strip of frames

After a delay, we increment i and draw the next frame.

Using a Thread to Control the Animation

Our applet will have a single thread.

```
class Animation extends Runnable
{   . . .
    Thread runner = null;
}
```

You will see such a thread variable in many Java applets. Often it is called `kicker`, and we once saw `killer` as the variable name. We think `runner` makes more sense, though.

First and foremost, we will use this thread to:

- start the animation when the user is watching the applet, and

- stop it when the user has switched to a different page in the browser.

We do this by creating the thread in the `start` method of the applet and by destroying it in the `stop` method. You can do this with the following code, which you will find in many applets.

```
class Animation implements Runnable
{   public void start()
    {   if (runner == null)
        {   runner = new Thread(this);
            runner.start();
        }
    }
    public void stop()
    {   if (runner != null && runner.isAlive())
            runner.stop();
        runner = null;
    }

    . . .

}
```

Note the method call:

```
runner = new Thread(this);
```

This creates a thread that calls the `run` function of this applet.

Here is the `run` method. If the image is not yet loaded, the `loadImage` function is called to load it. Otherwise, the `run` function loops, painting the screen and sleeping when it can.

```
class Animation implements Runnable
{   public void run()
    {   if (!loaded) loadImage();
        while (runner != null)
        {   repaint();
            try { Thread.sleep(200); }
            catch (InterruptedException e) {}
        }
    }

    . . .

}
```

The `loadImage` procedure of the `Animation` class (in the listing at the end of this section) is interesting. It is a synchronized method (that is, it is capable of *blocking* the current thread). When the thread enters the `loadImage` procedure, it creates the `image` object and then checks whether or not the image is already loaded. It does this by looking at the `loaded` instance variable of the `Animation` class. The first time around, that flag is certainly false, and the runner thread is suspended.

Independently, the user interface thread calls `paint`. The `paint` method finds that `loaded` is false and starts the loading process by rendering the `image` in a 1 x 1 off-screen bitmap. (You saw in Chapter 6 that this is a way of kick-starting the image-loading process.)

Whenever the image-loading thread has acquired another scan line of the image, it calls the `imageUpdate` method. (See Figure 12-13). Once the image is complete, it sets the `loaded` flag to `true` *and calls* `notify()`! This awakens the runner thread that was pending in the `loadImage` method.

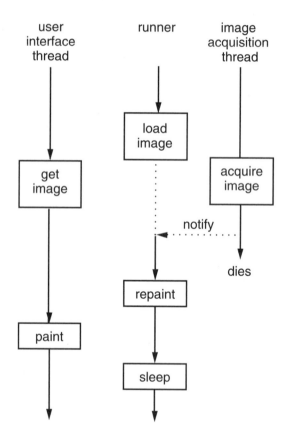

Figure 12-13: Threads in the image loading process

This explains how the applet suppresses animation while image-loading is still in progress. If you do not implement this interlocking mechanism, partially loaded frames will be drawn, which looks quite unsightly.

TIP: If you load multiple images and audio files, it becomes tedious to monitor their loading progress. The `MediaTracker` class does this for you automatically. In this example, we chose to do it by hand to show you what goes on behind the scenes.

Finally, we implement another method of stopping and restarting the animation. When you click with the mouse on the applet window, the animation stops. When you click again, it restarts. This is implemented in the `handleEvent` procedure.

```
public boolean handleEvent(Event evt)
{  if (evt.id == Event.MOUSE_DOWN && loaded)
   {  if (runner != null && runner.isAlive())
      {  if (stopped)
            runner.resume();
         else
         {  showStatus("Click to restart");
            runner.suspend();
         }
         stopped = !stopped;
      }
      else
      {  stopped = false;
         current = 0;
         runner = new Thread(this);
         runner.start();
      }
   }
   else return super.handleEvent(evt);
   return true;
}
```

Figure 12-14 shows the state-transition diagram of the runner thread.

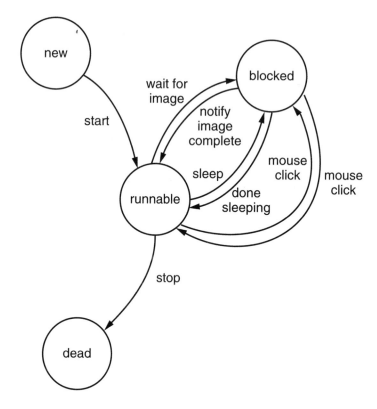

Figure 12-14: State diagram for runner thread

The applet reads the name of the image and the number of frames in the strip from the PARAM section in the HTML file (on the CD-ROM as well).

```html
<html>
<title>Animation Applet</title>
<body>
<applet code=Animation.class width=100 height=100>
<param name=imagename value="globe.gif">
<param name=imagecount value="36">
</applet>
</body>
</html>
```

Example 12-8 is the code of the applet. Have a close look at the interplay between the run, loadImage, paint, and imageUpdate methods.

Example 12-8: Animation.java

```
import java.awt.*;
import java.awt.image.*;
import java.applet.*;
import java.net.*;
public class Animation extends Applet implements Runnable
{  public void start()
   {  if (runner == null)
      {  runner = new Thread(this);
         runner.start();
      }
   }

   public void stop()
   {  if (runner != null && runner.isAlive())
         runner.stop();
      runner = null;
   }

   public void init()
   {  try
      {  imageName = getParameter("imagename");
         if (imageName == null) imageName = "";

         imageCount = 1;
         String param = getParameter("imagecount");
         if (param != null)
            imageCount = Integer.parseInt(param);
      }
      catch (Exception e)
         showStatus("Error: " + e);
   }

   public synchronized void loadImage()
   {  if (loaded) return;
      try
         {  URL url = new URL(getDocumentBase(), imageName);
            showStatus("Loading " + imageName);
            image = getImage(url);
         }
         catch(Exception e)
            showStatus("Error: " + e);

      while (!loaded)
         try { wait(); } catch (InterruptedException e) {}
      resize(imageWidth, imageHeight / imageCount);
   }

   public void run()
```

```
{   if (!loaded) loadImage();
    while (runner != null)
    {   repaint();
        try { Thread.sleep(200); } catch
            (InterruptedException e) {}
        current = (current + 1) % imageCount;
    }
}

public void paint(Graphics g)
{   if (!loaded)
    {   Image bufferedImage = createImage(1,1);
        Graphics bg = bufferedImage.getGraphics();
        bg.drawImage(image, 0, 0, this);
        bg.dispose();
        return;
    }

    g.drawImage
        (image, 0, - (imageHeight / imageCount) * current, null);
}

public void update(Graphics g)
{   paint(g);
}

public boolean handleEvent(Event evt)
{   if (evt.id == Event.MOUSE_DOWN && loaded)
    {   if (runner != null && runner.isAlive())
        {   if (stopped)
            {   showStatus("Click to stop");
                runner.resume();
            }
            else
            {   showStatus("Click to restart");
                runner.suspend();
            }
            stopped = !stopped;
        }
        else
        {   stopped = false;
            current = 0;
            runner = new Thread(this);
            runner.start();
        }
    }
    else return super.handleEvent(evt);
    return true;
}
```

```
public synchronized boolean imageUpdate
    (Image img, int infoflags,
    int x, int y, int width, int height)
{   if ((infoflags & ImageObserver.ALLBITS) != 0)
    {   // image is complete
        imageWidth = image.getWidth(null);
        imageHeight = image.getHeight(null);
        showStatus("Click to stop");
        loaded = true;
        notify();
        return false;
    }
    return true; // want more info
}

private Image image;
private int imageCount;
private int imageWidth = 0;
private int imageHeight = 0;
private String imageName;
private Thread runner = null;
private int current = 0;
private boolean loaded = false;
private boolean stopped = false;
}
```

This animation applet is simple in order to show you what goes on behind the scenes. If you are only interested in how to put a moving image on your Web page, look instead at the `Animator` applet in the demo section of the JDK. That applet has many more options than ours, and it lets you add sound.

CHAPTER
13

- Connecting to a Server

- Implementing Servers

- Retrieving Information from a Remote Site

- Sending Information to the Server

- Harvesting Information from the Web

Networking

Java is supposed to become the premier tool for connecting computers over the Internet. In this realm, Java mostly lives up to the hype. If you are used to programming network connections in C or C++, you will be pleasantly surprised at how easy it is in Java. For example, as you saw in Chapter 8, it is easy to open a URL (uniform resource locator) on the Net: simply pass the URL to the showDocument method in the AppletContext class.

We begin this chapter by talking a little bit about basic networking. Then we move on to reviewing and extending the information that was briefly presented in Chapter 8. The rest of the chapter moves on to the intricacies of doing sophisticated work on the Net with Java. For example, we show you how to do common gateway interface (CGI) programming on the server using a Java application. In particular, we show you how to use a combination of a Java applet and a Java CGI application to harvest information on the Internet.

In the first part of this chapter, we assume that you have no networking programming experience. If you have written TCP/IP programs before, and ports and sockets are no mystery to you, you should breeze through the sample code. Towards the end of this chapter, the code becomes complex and is geared more toward those with some experience in network programming.

Connecting to a Server

Before writing our first network program, let's learn about a great debugging tool for networking programming that you already have, namely telnet. (Windows 95 and NT come with a simple telnet program. However, it is optional and you may not have installed it when you installed the operating system. Just look for TELNET.EXE in the \Windows directory. If you don't find it, run Setup again.)

You may have used telnet to connect to a remote computer and to check your e-mail, but you can use it to communicate with other services provided by Net hosts as well. Here is an example of what you can do:

1. Start telnet.

2. Give any host name that you are familiar with. (If in doubt, use `java.sun.com`, MIS host should respond.)

3. In the port field, type `13`. (It doesn' t matter what terminal type you choose.)

If you have a command line version of telnet, type

`telnet java.sun.com 13` as shown in Figure 13-1.

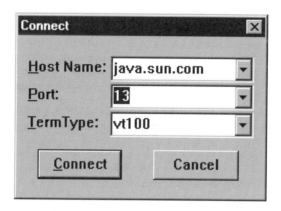

Figure 13-1: The Telnet Connect dialog

As Figure 13-2 shows, you should get back a line like this:

`Tue Feb 20 11:21:31 1996`

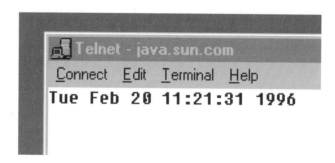

Figure 13-2: Output of the "Time of day" service

What is going on? You have connected to the "time of day" service that virtually every Unix machine constantly runs. By convention, the service is always attached to "port" number 13.

NOTE: In network parlance, a port is not a physical device, but an abstraction to facilitate communication between a server and a client.

What is happening is that the server software is continuously running on the remote machine, waiting for any network traffic that wants to chat with port 13. When the operating system on the remote computer gets a network package that contains a request to connect to port number 13, it wakes up the listening process and establishes the connection.

The connection stays up until it is terminated by one of the parties.

When you began the telnet session with `java.sun.com` at port 13, an unrelated piece of network software knew enough to convert the string `java.sun.com` to its correct Internet address, 206.26.48.100. The software then sent a connection request to that computer, asking for a connection to port 13. Once the connection was established, the remote program sent back a line of data and then closed the connection. In general, of course, clients and servers engage in a more extensive dialog before one or the other closes the connection.

Here is another experiment, along the same lines, that is a bit more interesting. First, turn the local key echo on. (In Windows 95, this is done from the Terminal | Preferences dialog box in the Windows telnet program.) Then do the following:

1. Connect to `java.sun.com` on port 80.

2. Type the following, *exactly as it appears, without hitting backspace.*

    ```
    GET / HTTP/1.0
    ```

3. Now hit the ENTER key *two times.*

Figure 13-3 shows the response. It should look eerily familiar—you got a page of HTML formatted text, namely the `new.html` Web page.

This is *exactly* the same process that your Web browser goes through to get a Web page.

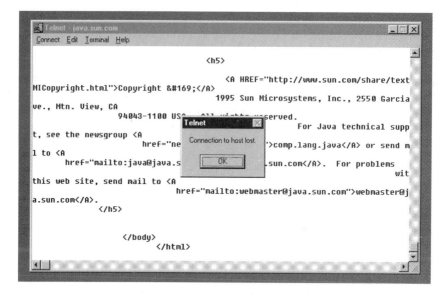

Figure 13-3: Using Telnet to access an HTTP port

Our first network program in Example 13-1 will do the same thing we did using telnet—connect to a port and print out what it finds.

Example 13-1: SocketTest.java

```java
import java.io.*;
import java.net.*;

class SocketTest
{  public static void main(String[] args)
   {  try
      {  Socket t = new Socket("java.sun.com", 13);

         DataInputStream is
            = new DataInputStream(t.getInputStream());
         boolean more = true;
         while (more)
         {  String str = is.readLine();
            if (str == null) more = false;
            else
               System.out.println(str);
         }

      }
      catch(IOException e) { System.out.println("Error" + e); }
   }

}
```

This program is extremely simple, but before we analyze the two key lines, note that we are importing the `java.net` class (most of Java's networking capability may be found in this package) and catching any input/output errors because the code is encased in a `try/catch` block. (Since there are many things that can go wrong with a network connection, most of the network-related methods threaten to throw I/O errors. You must catch them for the code to compile.)

As for the code itself, the key lines are as follows:

```
Socket t = new Socket("java.sun.com", 13);
DataInputStream is = new
    DataInputStream(t.getInputStream());
```

The first line opens a *socket*, which is an abstraction for the network software that enables communication out of and into this program. We pass the remote address and the port number to the socket constructor. If the connection fails, an `UnknownHostException` is thrown. If there is another problem, an `IOException` occurs. Since `UnknownHostException` is derived from IOException, and this is a sample program, we just catch the base class.

Once the socket is open, the `getInputStream` method in `java.net.Socket` returns an `InputStream` object that you can use just like any other file. (See Chapter 11.) Once you have grabbed the stream, this program simply:

1. reads all characters sent by the server using `readLine` and

2. prints each line out to standard output.

This process continues until the stream is finished and the server disconnects. You know this happens when the `readLine` method returns a null string.

Plainly, the `Socket` class is pleasant and easy to use in Java. Java hides the complexities of establishing a networking connection and sending data across and, essentially, gives you the same programming interface you would use to work with a file.

`java.net.Socket`

*   `Socket(String host, int port) throws UnknownHostException, IOException`

    creates a socket and connects it to a port on a remote host.

    Parameters: `host`   the host name

                          `port`   the port number

- `synchronized void close() throws IOException`

  closes the socket.

- `InputStream getInputStream() throws IOException`

  gets the input stream to read from the socket.

- `OutputStream getOutputStream() throws IOException`

  gets an output stream to write to this socket.

Implementing Servers

Now that we have implemented a basic network client that receives data from the Net, let's implement a simple server that can send information out to the Net. Once you start the server program, it waits for some client to attach to its port. We chose port number 8189, which is not used by any of the standard services. The `ServerSocket` class is used to establish a socket. In our case the command

```
ServerSocket s = new ServerSocket(8189);
```

establishes a server that monitors port 8189. The command

```
Socket incoming = s.accept();
```

tells Java to wait indefinitely until a client connects to that port. Once someone connects to this port by sending the correct request over the Net, this method returns a `Socket` object that represents the connection that was made. You can use this object to get an input stream and an output stream from that socket, as is done in the following code:

```
DataInputStream in = new
    DataInputStream(incoming.getInputStream());
PrintStream out = new
    PrintStream(incoming.getOutputStream());
```

Everything that the server sends to the output stream becomes the input of the client program, and all the output from the client program ends up in our input stream.

We turned the streams into data input and print streams because we need the `readLine` method (defined in `DataInputStream`, but not in `InputStream`) and the `println` method (defined in `PrintStream`, but not in `OutputStream`).

Let's send the client a greeting.

```
out.println("Hello! Enter BYE to exit.");
```

When you use telnet to connect to this server program at port 8189, you will see the above message on the terminal screen.

In this simple server, we just read the client input, a line at a time, and echo it. This demonstrates that the program gets the client's input. An actual server would obviously compute and return an answer that depended on the input.

```
String str = in.readLine();
if (str != null)
{   out.print("Echo: " + str + "\r\n");
    if (str.trim().equals("BYE")) done = true;
}
else done = true;
```

In the end, we close the incoming socket.

```
incoming.close();
```

That is all that there is to it. Every server program, such as an http Web server, continues performing this loop:

1. It gets a command from the client ("get me this information") through an incoming data stream.

2. It fetches the information somehow.

3. It sends the information to the client through the outgoing data stream.

Example 13-2 is the complete program.

Example 13-2: EchoServer.java

```
import java.io.*;
import java.net.*;

class EchoServer
{   public static void main(String[] args )
    {   try
        {   ServerSocket s = new ServerSocket(8189);
            Socket incoming = s.accept( );
            DataInputStream in
                = new DataInputStream(incoming.getInputStream());
            PrintStream out
                = new PrintStream(incoming.getOutputStream());

            out.println( "Hello! Enter BYE to exit.\r" );

            boolean done = false;
            while (!done)
            {   String str = in.readLine();
                if (str == null) done = true;
```

```
            else
            {   out.println("Echo: " + str + "\r");

                if (str.trim().equals("BYE"))
                    done = true;
            }
        }
        incoming.close();
    }
    catch (Exception e)
    {   System.out.println(e);
    }
  }
}
```

To try it out, you need to compile and run the program. Then use telnet to connect to the following server and port:

Server: 127.0.0.1

Port: 8189

The IP address 127.0.0.1 is a special address, called the *local loopback address*, that denotes the local machine. Since you are running the echo server locally, that is where you want to connect.

NOTE: If you are using a dial-up connection, you need to have it running for this experiment. Even though you are only talking to your local machine, the network software must be loaded.

Actually, anyone in the world can access your echo server, provided it is running and they know your IP address and the magic port number.

When you connect to the port, you will get the message shown in Figure 13-4:

```
Hello! Enter BYE to exit.
```

Type anything and watch the input echo on your screen. Type BYE (all uppercase letters) to disconnect. The server program will terminate as well.

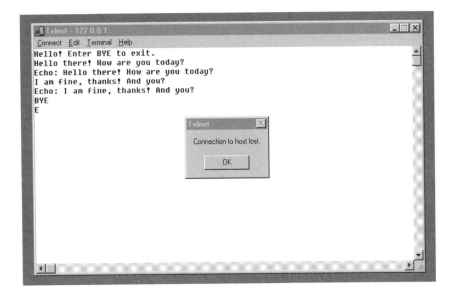

Figure 13-4: Accessing an echo server

Serving Multiple Clients

There is one problem with the simple server in the preceding example. Suppose we want to allow multiple clients to connect to our server at the same time. This is quite common. Typically, a server runs constantly on a server computer, and clients from all over the Internet may want to use the server at the same time. Rejecting multiple connections allows any one client to monopolize the service by connecting to it for a long time. We can do much better through the magic of threads.

Every time we know Java has established a new socket connection, that is, when the call to `accept` was successful, we will launch a new thread to take care of the connection between the server and *that* client. The main program will just go back and wait for the next connection. In order for this to happen, the main loop of the server should look like this:

```
while (true)
{  Socket incoming = s.accept();
   Thread t = new ThreadedEchoHandler(incoming);
   t.start();
}
```

The `ThreadedEchoHandler` class derives from `Thread` and contains the communication loop with the client in its `run` method.

```
class ThreadedEchoHandler extends Thread
{  . . .
   public void run()
```

```
{  try
   {  DataInputStream in = new
          DataInputStream(incoming.getInputStream());
      PrintStream out = new
          PrintStream(incoming.getOutputStream());
      out.println("Hello! Enter BYE to exit.");
      boolean done = false;
      while (!done)
      {  String str = in.readLine();
         if (str != null)
         {  out.print("Echo: " + str + "\r\n");
            if (str.trim().equals("BYE")) done = true;
         }
         else done = true;
      }
      incoming.close();
   }
   catch(Exception e)
   {  System.out.println(e);
   }
}
}
```

Because each connection starts a new thread, multiple clients can connect to the server at the same time. You can easily check this out. Compile and run the server program (Example 13-3). Open several telnet windows like we have in Figure 13-5. You can communicate through all of them simultaneously. The server program never dies. Use CTRL+C to kill it.

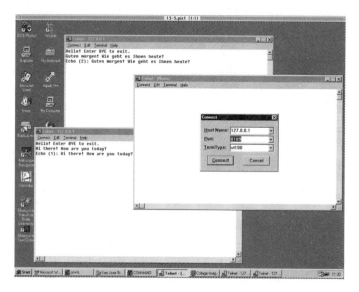

Figure 13-5: Simultaneous access to the threaded Echo server

Example 13-3: ThreadedEchoServer.java

```java
import java.io.*;
import java.net.*;

public class ThreadedEchoServer
{   public static void main(String[] args )
    {   int i = 1;
        try
        {   ServerSocket s = new ServerSocket(8189);

            for (;;)
            {   Socket incoming = s.accept( );
                System.out.println("Spawning " + i);
                new ThreadedEchoHandler(incoming, i).start();
                i++;
            }
        }
        catch (Exception e)
        {   System.out.println(e);
        }
    }
private Socket incoming:
private int counter;
}

public class ThreadedEchoHandler extends Thread
{
    public ThreadedEchoHandler(Socket i, int c)
        { incoming = i; counter = c; }
    public void run()
    {   try
        {   DataInputStream in
                = new DataInputStream(incoming.getInputStream());
            PrintStream out
                = new PrintStream(incoming.getOutputStream());

            out.println( "Hello! Enter BYE to exit.\r" );

            boolean done = false;
            while (!done)
            {   String str = in.readLine();
                if (str == null) done = true;
                else
                {   out.println
                    ("Echo (" + counter + "): " + str + "\r");

                    if (str.trim().equals("BYE"))
                        done = true;
                }
```

```
        }
        incoming.close();
    }
    catch (Exception e)
    {  System.out.println(e);
    }
}
private Socket incoming;
private int counter;
}
```

java.net.ServerSocket

- `ServerSocket(int port) throws IOException`
  creates a server socket that monitors a port.
  Parameters: `port`   the port number

- `Socket accept() throws IOException`
  waits for a connection. This method will block (that is, idle) the current thread until the connection is made. The method returns a `Socket` object through which the program can communicate with the connecting client.

- `void close() throws IOException`
  closes the server socket.

Retrieving Information from a Remote Site

In this section, we want to use as an example an applet that takes orders from visitors to a Web page. Since this is meant as an illustration, this applet is a simplified form of what would be used in a commercial setting. It is certainly not enough to convince any actual customers to fork over their money.

The key point is that you will always want to make applets flexible. For example, you will want to be able to change the prices or the goods offered at a moment's notice—without having to reprogram the applet. The obvious (and probably easiest) way to do this is to store the data in a file. Whenever you want to change the goods and prices, just update that file. The applet and the HTML code for the Web page can stay the same.

When the client visits your Web page, the browser downloads the HTML page and the applet code from your server. The applet then runs on the client's computer. First, the applet downloads the data file containing the price list. Let's suppose that the data are stored in a file called `prices.dat`, in the same directory as the HTML page. The applet then needs to open the URL, which is accomplished in the following code:

```
URL url = new URL(getDocumentBase(), "prices.dat");
```

This constructor creates a URL for the file `prices.dat`, relative to the URL returned by `getDocumentBase`. As you saw in Chapter 8, this method returns the URL of the Web page that contained the applet—it is the one given by the `APPLET` tag in the HTML file.

TIP: It is a good idea to use relative URLs. Then, if you move your files, you do not need to recompile the Java code.

The other important method you need is `showDocument`, which we also discussed in Chapter 8. This method yields an `InputStream` object. Using this stream object, we can easily read the contents of the file.

```
InputStream in = url.openStream();
```

In our case, the price list is formatted in the `Properties` data format, like this:

```
#Price list
#Wed Feb 07 21:04:53  1996
Toaster=19.95;
Blender=59.95;
Microwave+oven=179.95;
Citrus+press=19.95;
Espresso+maker=199.95;
Rice+cooker=29.95;
Waffle+iron=39.95;
Bread+machine=119.95;
```

See Chapter 9 for more information on the `Properties` class. For now, recall that it is simply a dictionary that can load and save its contents to a disk file. Note that we use + signs instead of spaces in the data file. The `load` method of the `Properties` class does not like spaces. We later replace the + signs with spaces using code like this:

```
prices.get(itemName).replace('+', ' ');
```

As long as none of the product names contain a +, we can get away with this.

You would probably find this format limiting in a real-life applet, but it is handy for this toy example since we can now read the data into the `Properties` object with a single statement.

```
prices.load(in);
```

This example shows one method with which your applet can get information from the server, by reading in a file. There is no limit on the structure of the file—it can be a text or binary file of any convenient format. Obviously, using a file for data storage is better than building the data right into the applet. It keeps the applet small and flexible.

The information flow in the price list applet is shown in Figure 13-6.

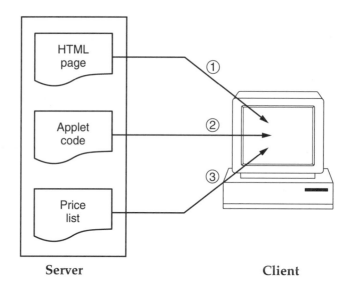

Figure 13-6: Information flow in the price list applet

If the data set is large, it may not make sense to send the entire file to the client site. Instead, the applet should find out what information the client needs, and ask for just that information as in Figure 13-7. You will see later in this chapter how to implement such a query. This code is presented in Example 13-4.

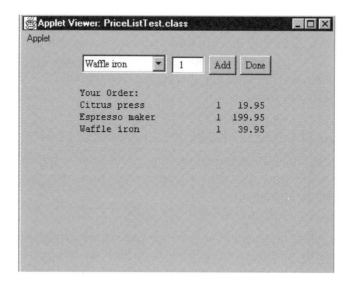

Figure 13-7: Price list test applet

Example 13-4: PriceListTest.java

```java
import java.awt.*;
import java.applet.*;
import java.util.*;
import java.net.*;
import corejava.*;

public class PriceListTest extends Applet
{  public void init()
   {  setLayout(new BorderLayout());
      Panel p = new Panel();
      p.setLayout(new FlowLayout());
      name = new Choice();

      try
      {  URL url = new URL(getDocumentBase(), "prices.dat");
         prices.load(url.openStream());
      } catch(Exception e) {}

      Enumeration e = prices.propertyNames();
      while (e.hasMoreElements())
         name.addItem(((String)e.nextElement())
            .replace('+', ' '));
      quantity = new IntTextField(1, 0, 100, 4);
      p.add(name);
      p.add(quantity);
      p.add(new Button("Add"));
      p.add(new Button("Done"));
      add("North", p);
      add("Center", canvas = new PurchaseOrderCanvas());
      canvas.resize(250, 150);
      canvas.redraw(a);
   }

   public boolean action(Event evt, Object arg)
   {  if (arg.equals("Add"))
      {  if (quantity.isValid())
         {  String itemName = name.getSelectedItem();
            a.addElement(new Item(itemName,
               quantity.getValue(),
               Format.atof((String)prices.get(itemName
               .replace(' ', '+')))));
         }
      }
      else if (arg.equals("Done"))
      {  a.addElement(new Item("State Tax", 1, 0.00));
         a.addElement(new Item("Shipping", 1, 5.00));
         a.trimToSize();
      }
```

```
            else return super.action(evt, arg);
            canvas.redraw(a);
            return true;
        }

      private Vector a = new Vector();
      private Choice name;
      private IntTextField quantity;
      private PurchaseOrderCanvas canvas;
      private int m = 1;
      private Properties prices = new Properties();
}

class Item
{   Item(String n, int q, double u)
    {   name = n;
        quantity = q;
        unitPrice = u;
    }

    public String toString()
    {   return new Format("%-20s").form(name)
           + new Format("%6d").form(quantity)
           + new Format("%8.2f").form(unitPrice);
    }

    private String name;
    private int quantity;
    private double unitPrice;
}

class PurchaseOrderCanvas extends Canvas
{   public void redraw(Vector new_a)
    {   a = new_a;
        repaint();
    }

    public void paint(Graphics g)
    {   Font f = new Font("Courier", Font.PLAIN, 12);
        g.setFont(f);
        FontMetrics fm = g.getFontMetrics(f);
        int height = fm.getHeight();
        int x = 80;
        int y = 0;
        int i = 0;
        y += height;
        g.drawString("Your Order: ", x, y);
```

```
        for (i = 0; i < a.size(); i++)
        {   y += height;
            g.drawString(a.elementAt(i).toString(), x, y);
        }
    }

    private Vector a;
}
```

Sending Information to the Server

Let us now complete the order-taking applet. Once the customer has specified the order, the information must be returned to the server. To do this, we need to enhance the applet to give it the ability to get the name and address of the customer. In a realistic application, we would also concern ourselves with billing information (such as a credit card number), but we will ignore that for now. Figure 13-8 shows the complete order screen.

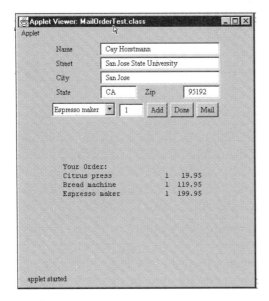

Figure 13-8: Mail order test applet

When the user clicks the Mail button, the ordering information (name, address, and items ordered) must be sent off to the server. The applet makes contact with the server, opens a stream, and sends the information through that stream.

To make contact with the server, a special server process can continually monitor an agreed-upon port, such as port 8189 in the preceding example. The applet then connects to that port and sends the ordering information. The server program on the host computer must connect to a database and enter the order.

Another alternative is for the applet to connect to a service that already runs on the server. For example, the applet can make a socket connection to port 25, the sendmail daemon. Then it sends a mail header (in the format expected by the sendmail daemon, which is easy to generate), followed by the ordering information. The order arrives by e-mail. This looks like an attractive idea for a simple ordering application that processes only a couple of orders every day. And it is easy to do; here's how:

1. Open a socket to your host.

   ```
   Socket s = new Socket("www.corejava.com", 25); // 25 is SMTP
   PrintStream out = new PrintStream(s.getOutputStream());
   ```

2. Send the following information to the print stream:

   ```
   HELO sending host
   MAIL FROM: sender
   RCPT TO: recipient
   DATA
   mail message
   (any number of lines)
   .
   QUIT
   ```

Since the applet cannot determine the sending host and the sender name, you need placeholders for this information. The sendmail program does not check this information. (Keep this in mind the next time you get an e-mail message from president@whitehouse.gov inviting you to a black-tie affair on the front lawn. Anyone can telnet into any sendmail host and create a fake message.)

We will not pursue this route in our program because if you get more than a handful of orders, you probably do not want them to clutter up a mailbox. More importantly, many system administrators disable the sendmail port on Web servers because it serves no useful function and is potentially a security risk. As we will see later in this chapter, an applet can only establish a socket connection to the server on which it resides. If that server does not monitor the sendmail port, you cannot use this port to send data from the applet to the server.

The third route from your applet to the server is the CGI. It is the topic of the next section.

CGI Scripts

Before Java came along, there existed a mechanism to send information from a Web browser to the host. A person would fill out a *form*, like the one in Figure 13-9.

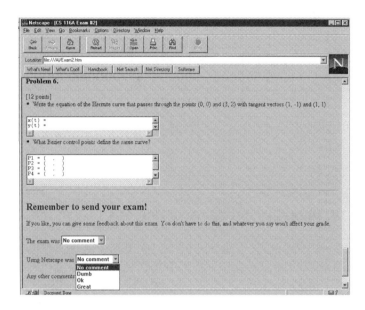

Figure 13-9: An HTML form

When the user clicks on the Submit button, the text in the text fields and the settings of the check boxes and radio buttons are sent back to the server, to a so-called CGI script.

The CGI script is a program that resides on the server computer. There are usually many CGI scripts on a server. The HTML tag of the Submit button specifies the script to use to process that particular form. The http daemon on the server launches the CGI script and feeds it the form data. The CGI script processes the form data and sends another HTML page back to the browser. This is illustrated in FIgure 13-10. That page can contain new information (for example, in an information-search program) or just an acknowledgment. The Web browser then displays the response page.

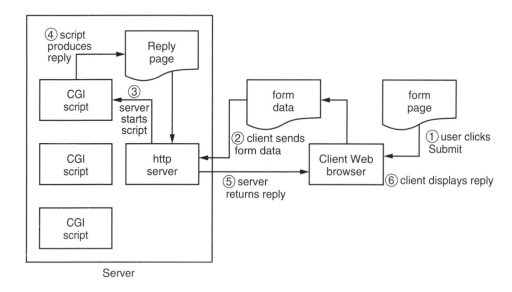

Figure 13-10: Data flow during execution of a CGI script

CGI programs are commonly written in Perl, but they can be written in any language that can read from standard input and write to standard output. In particular, they can be written in Java. (Of course, a CGI script written in Java is not an applet. It is an *application* running on the http server. This application will need to be launched by the http server whenever a client submits a query naming that script as the processing agent.)

NOTE: We will not discuss how to design HTML forms that interact with CGI. A good reference for that topic is Mary Morris' s *HTML for Fun and Profit* (SunSoft Press/Prentice-Hall, 1995). Our interest lies in the interface between CGI and Java applets, not HTML forms.

CGI is a good mechanism to use because it is well established, and system administrators are familiar with it. If you are like most of us, you do not have your own, personal http server, and you need to work with a system administrator or service provider to run programs on a server.

Obviously, there would be some advantages if there were a way for an applet to use the CGI mechanism that is already present in the browser. Unfortunately, the standard Java library does not provide such a communication path. We need to invoke a CGI script manually, in the same way that a Web browser would. We connect to the http port (port 80) of the server.

```
Socket s = new Socket("www.corejava.com", 80);
```

(The last time we checked, there was no `corejava.com` domain. You will need to change these names in your programs.)

As always, we get streams for input and output.

```
DataInputStream in
   = new DataInputStream(s.getInputStream());
DataOutputStream out
   = new DataOutputStream(s.getOutputStream());
```

There are two methods with which to send information to the CGI program. They are called the GET method and the POST method. In the GET method, we send the following string through the `out` stream in order to ask the http daemon to process a specific script.

```
GET scriptname?parameters
```

The string must be followed by a blank line.

For example, suppose we wanted to ask the script `priceinfo`, located in the `cgi-bin` subdirectory (which is the customary directory for CGI scripts), about the price of an item. Then we would print the following command to the `out` stream:

```
os.writeBytes("GET /cgi-bin/priceinfo?Toaster\n\n");
```

The `priceinfo` script would receive the information following the `?` as a command line parameter (`args[0]` in Java). You can send more than one argument to the command line, but you must separate the arguments by + signs, not spaces. For example, when you send the query

```
os.writeBytes("GET /cgi-bin/priceinfo?Toaster+oven\n\n");
```

the script receives two command line arguments, `args[0]` as `"Toaster"` and `args[1]` as `"oven"`. You are supposed to encode all non-alphanumeric characters, except `"+"` and `"&"` using a `"%"`, followed by a two-digit hexadecimal number. For example, to transmit the book title *Mastering C++*, you use `Mastering+C%2b%2b`, since the hexadecimal number 2b (or decimal 43) is the ASCII code of the "+" character. This keeps any intermediate programs from messing with spaces and interpreting other special characters. This encoding scheme is called *URL encoding*.

With the GET method, the CGI script gets no further input.

The POST method works the other way around. The CGI script gets no command line arguments, but it gets all its input from standard input. The applet must send the information for the CGI script through the `out` stream. The applet first sends a header, then the data. The first line of the header must be

```
Content-type: type
```

where *type* is usually one of the following:

```
text/plain
text/html
application/octet-stream
application/x-www-form-urlencoded
```

The `application` types must be followed by the line

```
Content-length: length
```

for example,

```
Content-length: 1024
```

The end of the header is indicated by a blank line. Then the data portion follows. The http daemon strips off the header and routes the data portion to the server script.

Here is how you might ask about the price of the toaster oven if your script uses the POST method:

```
String sdata = "Toaster oven"
os.writeBytes("POST /cgi-bin/priceinfo\n");
os.writeBytes("Content-type: plain/text\n");
os.writeBytes("Content-length: " + sdata.length() + "\n\n");
os.writeBytes(sdata);
```

As a response to either a GET or a POST query, the script on the server sends a reply to standard output. The first part of the reply is, again, a header. The http daemon strips off the header and routes the data portion to the client socket. Your program captures it by reading from the in stream. If the information arrives in text format, it can be captured with the following code:

```
String rdata = "";
String line;
while ((line = in.readLine()) != null)
   rdata += line + "\n";
```

The format of the data is completely up to you and the server. Unless you need to use an existing script designed to interact with Web pages, there is no requirement to use the rather complex form used for encoding input to the script, or even to use HTML for the reply. In fact, using ASCII text or binary data is usually more convenient. In the case of the price-information script, the price information can be sent back either in ASCII or as binary data that can be read with the readDouble method.

Completing the Mail-Order Applet

In a realistic situation, the order-taking applet would send the order information to a CGI script that routes it to a database. The major database vendors have CGI-to-database interfaces, but they are, at this point, neither standardized nor freely available (that is, they cost big bucks). For this reason, our sample applet simply mails the received data to orders@corejava.com.

Example 13-5 is the CGI script in Java.

Example 13-5: MailTo.java

```
import java.io.*;

class MailTo
{  public static void main(String[] args)
    {  try
        {  Runtime rt = Runtime.getRuntime();
            Process p = rt.exec
                ("/usr/lib/sendmail orders@corejava.com");
            PrintStream os
                = new PrintStream(p.getOutputStream());
            os.println("Subject: order");
            String line;
            DataInputStream is = new DataInputStream(System.in);
            while ((line = is.readLine()) != null)
                os.println(line);
            os.close();
        }
        catch (Exception e)
        {  System.out.println("Error " + e);
        }
    }
}
```

Example 13-6 is the CGI script in Perl, in case your system administrator will not let you run a Java program on the server.

Example 13-6: mailto.pl

```
#!/usr/bin/perl

# This should match the mail program on your system.
$mailprog = '/usr/lib/sendmail';

$recipient = 'orders@corejava.com';

# Now send mail to $recipient

print "Content-type: text/plain\n\n";
if (open (MAIL, "|$mailprog $recipient"))
{
```

```
      while (<STDIN>)
      {   print MAIL;
      }
      close (MAIL);

      print "OK\n"

}
else
{
    print "ERROR\n"
}
```

Finally, Example 13-7 is the complete applet that runs on the client's computer. When you hit the Send button, the address and order information are made into one long string and sent to the CGI script, using the POST method.

Example 13-7: MailOrderTest.java

```
import java.awt.*;
import java.applet.*;
import java.util.*;
import java.net.*;
import java.io.*;
import corejava.*;

public class MailOrderTest extends Applet
{   public void init()
    {   Panel p = new Panel();
        p.setLayout(new FlowLayout());
        name = new Choice();
        try
        {   URL url = new URL(getDocumentBase(), "prices.dat");
            prices.load(url.openStream());
        } catch(Exception e) { showStatus("Error " + e); }

        Enumeration e = prices.propertyNames();
        while (e.hasMoreElements())
            name.addItem(((String)e.nextElement()).replace('+',
                ' '));
        quantity = new IntTextField(1, 0, 100, 4);
        p.add(name);
        p.add(quantity);
        p.add(new Button("Add"));
        p.add(new Button("Done"));
        p.add(new Button("Send"));
        Panel p2 = new Panel();
```

```
      p2.setLayout(new GridLayout(2, 1));
      p2.add(addressDialog());
      p2.add(p);

      add("North", p2);
      add("Center", canvas = new PurchaseOrderCanvas());
      canvas.resize(250, 150);
      canvas.redraw(a);
   }

   private Panel addressDialog()
   {  Panel p = new Panel();
      GridBagLayout gbl = new GridBagLayout();
      p.setLayout(gbl);

      GridBagConstraints gbc = new GridBagConstraints();
      gbc.fill = GridBagConstraints.BOTH;
      gbc.weightx = 100;
      gbc.weighty = 100;
      add(p, new Label("Name"), gbl, gbc, 0, 0, 1, 1);
      add(p, nameField, gbl, gbc, 1, 0, 3, 1);
      add(p, new Label("Street"), gbl, gbc, 0, 1, 1, 1);
      add(p, streetField, gbl, gbc, 1, 1, 3, 1);
      add(p, new Label("City"), gbl, gbc, 0, 2, 1, 1);
      add(p, cityField, gbl, gbc, 1, 2, 3, 1);
      add(p, new Label("State"), gbl, gbc, 0, 3, 1, 1);
      add(p, stateField, gbl, gbc, 1, 3, 1, 1);
      add(p, new Label("Zip"), gbl, gbc, 2, 3, 1, 1);
      add(p, zipField, gbl, gbc, 3, 3, 1, 1);

      return p;
   }

   private void add(Container p, Component c,
      GridBagLayout gbl, GridBagConstraints gbc,
      int x, int y, int w, int h)
   {  gbc.gridx = x;
      gbc.gridy = y;
      gbc.gridwidth = w;
      gbc.gridheight = h;
      gbl.setConstraints(c, gbc);
      p.add(c);
   }

   public boolean action(Event evt, Object arg)
   {  if (arg.equals("Add"))
      {  if (quantity.isValid())
         {  String itemName = name.getSelectedItem();
            a.addElement(new Item(itemName,
               quantity.getValue(),
```

```
                Format.atof((String)
                    prices.get(itemName.replace(' ', '+'))))));
        }
    }
    else if (arg.equals("Done"))
    {  a.addElement(new Item("State Tax", 1, 0.00));
        a.addElement(new Item("Shipping", 1, 5.00));
        a.trimToSize();
    }
    else if (arg.equals("Send"))
    {  int i;
        String data;
        data = nameField.getText() + "\n"
            + streetField.getText() + "\n"
            + cityField.getText() + " "
            + stateField.getText() + " "
            + zipField.getText() + "\n\n";
        for (i = 0; i < a.size(); i++)
            data += a.elementAt(i).toString() + "\n";
        mailOrder(data);
        a = new Vector();
    }
    else return super.action(evt, arg);
    canvas.redraw(a);
    return true;
}

public void mailOrder(String sdata)
{  String home = "corejava.com";
    String script = "/cgi-bin/mailto.pl";
    int port = 80;
    Socket s = null;
    String rdata = "";

    try
    {  s = new Socket(home, port);

        DataOutputStream os
            = new DataOutputStream(s.getOutputStream());
        DataInputStream is
            = new DataInputStream(s.getInputStream());

        os.writeBytes("POST " + script
            + " HTTP/1.0\r\n"
            + "Content-type: application/octet-stream\r\n"
            + "Content-length: "
            + sdata.length() + "\r\n\r\n");
        os.writeBytes(sdata);

        String line;
```

```
            while ((line = is.readLine()) != null)
                rdata += line + "\n";
            showStatus(rdata);
            is.close();
            os.close();
         }
         catch (Exception e)
         {   showStatus("Error " + e);
             if (s != null)
                try
                {   s.close(); }
                catch (IOException ex) {}
         }
      }
   }

   private Vector a = new Vector();
   private Choice name;
   private IntTextField quantity;
   private PurchaseOrderCanvas canvas;
   private Properties prices = new Properties();
   private TextField nameField = new TextField();
   private TextField streetField = new TextField();
   private TextField cityField = new TextField();
   private TextField stateField = new TextField();
   private TextField zipField = new TextField();
}

class Item
{   Item(String n, int q, double u)
    {   name = n;
        quantity = q;
        unitPrice = u;
    }

    public String toString()
    {   return new Format("%-20s").form(name)
            + new Format("%6d").form(quantity)
            + new Format("%8.2f").form(unitPrice);
    }

    private String name;
    private int quantity;
    private double unitPrice;
}

class PurchaseOrderCanvas extends Canvas
{   public void redraw(Vector new_a)
    {   a = new_a;
        repaint();
    }
```

```
public void paint(Graphics g)
{  Font f = new Font("Courier", Font.PLAIN, 12);
   g.setFont(f);
   FontMetrics fm = g.getFontMetrics(f);
   int height = fm.getHeight();
   int x = 0;
   int y = 0;
   int i = 0;
   y += height;
   g.drawString("Your Order: ", x, y);
   for (i = 0; i < a.size(); i++)
   {  y += height;
      g.drawString(a.elementAt(i).toString(), x, y);
   }
}

   private Vector a;
}
```

Harvesting Information from the Web

The last example showed you how to read data that accompanies an applet stored on a server. In this section, we want to show you how to read and process data that is available anywhere on the Internet. The Internet contains a wealth of information both interesting and not: it is the lack of guidance through this mass of information that is the major complaint of most Web users. One major promise of Java is that it may help to bring order to this chaos: you can use Java to retrieve information and present it to the user in an appealing format.

There are many possible uses. Here are few that come to mind:

- An applet can look at all the Web pages the user has specified as interesting and find which have recently changed.

- An applet can visit the Web pages of all scheduled airlines to find out which is running a special.

- Applets can gather and display recent stock quotes, monetary exchange rates and other financial information.

- Applets can search FAQs, press releases, articles, and so on, and return text that contains certain keywords.

Much of the information on the Net is in HTML format, the *lingua franca* of the World Wide Web. While HTML is not difficult to parse, it is tedious enough that we will develop an applet that fetches information in plain ASCII text, instead. This allows us to focus on the networking mechanisms instead of on HTML parsing.

583

The *gopher* service presents plain text information. If you grew up in the days of the World Wide Web, you may never have seen gopher. It looks much plainer than the Web. There are no fonts. Everything is either a directory of links (Figure 13-11), plain text, (Figure 13-12), or a solitary picture.

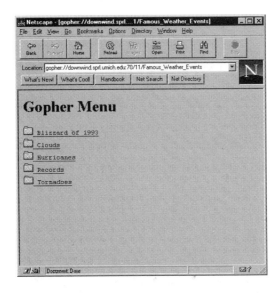

Figure 13-11: Directory of links using the gopher service

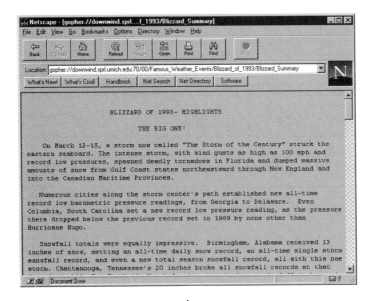

Figure 13-12: Text screen using the gopher service

Nowadays, gopher is no longer fashionable. But it is still a good workhorse for information storage, and many information providers still support it. For example, the University of Michigan has a gopher site for weather reports at

```
gopher://downwind.sprl.umich.edu.
```

Go to the subdirectory:

```
Weather_Text/U.S._City_Forecasts.
```

Then select a state subdirectory, then a city subdirectory. You will get an up-to-date weather report like that shown in Figure 13-13.

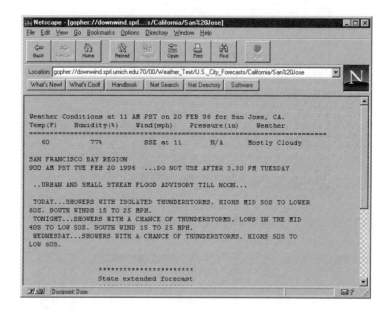

Figure 13-13: The weather forecast with gopher

We will build an applet that wraps a friendlier user interface around this information. The list box on the left contains the list of all states. You double-click on a state. Then the applet shows a list of cities in the list box on the right. When you double-click on a city, the text window in Figure 13-14 fills with the weather report.

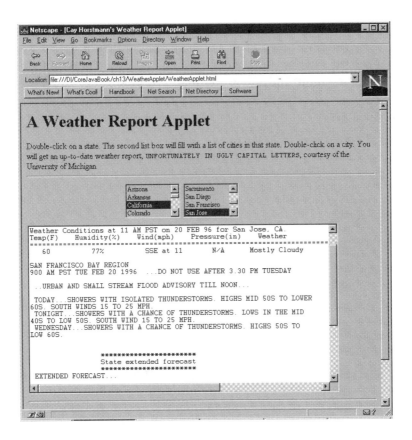

Figure 13-14: The weather report applet

Connecting to a Gopher Site

The next step to get our applet running is to connect to the University of Michigan gopher site. Unfortunately, the obvious method does not work. If you try

```
URL url = new URL("gopher://downwind.sprl.umich.edu");
```

you will get a `MalformedURLException`. Actually, there is nothing malformed about this URL. The 1.0 release of Java does not implement the gopher protocol (the Sun programmers probably just ran out of time). Gopher is an easy protocol, and we will implement it manually, which will be a good learning experience, anyway.

By convention, the gopher service uses port number 70. When a client connects to the gopher port, it simply sends the desired path of the directory. The server sends back the contents of that directory, which is either another directory or a text file.

Try it out: use telnet to connect to port 70 of a host running the gopher service such as `downwind.sprl.umich.edu`. Then type `/`. You will get a listing of the root directory. Then the server disconnects automatically. You need to reconnect to get more information. The http server that serves Web pages works the same way. The browser can retrieve one piece of information; then it must reconnect to get more data.

We can easily program this in Java.

```
Socket s = new Socket("downwind.sprl.umich.edu", 70);
PrintStream out = new PrintStream(s.getOutputStream());
DataInputStream in = new DataInputStream(s.getInputStream());
out.println("/");
String rdata = "";
String line;
while ((line = in.readLine()) != null)
   rdata += line + "\n";
```

Here is a sample listing of the gopher directory.

```
0Information           0/info.txt      turkey.acme.com     70
1Software              1/software      turkey.acme.com     70
8Stock_information                     scrooge.acme.com    3000
1Movies                1/movie_text    turkey.acme.com     70
```

The listing has a special structure. There are four columns: one for the title, one for the file, one for the host address, and one for the port number. Lines starting with 0 denote links to text files. Lines starting with 1 denote links to other directories. Lines starting with 8 denote links to other gopher sites.

In our weather applet, we use the following strategy: when the user clicks on a state, say California, we connect to the gopher site and request the directory

```
/Weather_Text/U.S._City_Forecasts/California
```

That directory contains subdirectories for the cities in California for which a weather report is available. The applet reads that file through the stream obtained from the socket. It parses the directory information by stripping off the 1 denoting a directory. Then it fills a list box with the values that it obtained.

```
String query = "/Weather_Text/U.S._City_Forecasts" + "/" +
   state;
out.println(query);
String line;
while ((line = in.readLine()) != null)
{ int i = line.indexOf("0/", 1); // start of second column
   if (i >= 0)
   {  String t = line.substring(1, i).trim();
      city.addItem(t); // add to list box
   }
}
```

Finally, when the user of the applet clicks on the city, we connect again to the server, append the name of the city, and ask for a path such as

```
/Weather_Text/U.S._City_Forecasts/California/San Jose
```

We read and display the resulting text file, which is our weather report.

```
String query = "/Weather_Text/U.S._City_Forecasts" + "/" +
    state + "/" + city;
out.println(query);
String line;
while ((line = in.readLine()) != null)
{  weather.appendText(line + "\n");
}
```

`java.net.URL`

- `URL(String spec) throws MalformedURLException`

  creates a URL object from an unparsed absolute URL string.

  Parameters: `spec`   the URL String to parse

- `String getHost()`

  returns the host name (for instance, `"java.sun.com"`).

- `String getFile()`

  gets the name of the file to be requested (for instance, `"new.html"`).

- `int getPort()`

  gets the port number. Returns –1 if the port is not set.

- `String getProtocol()`

  gets the protocol name (for instance, `"http"`).

- `InputStream openStream() throws IOException`

  opens an input stream.

Applet Security

When running the weather report applet locally, with AppletViewer, it works as described. However, if you put the applet on your Web page and have others try to read it using Netscape, it will not work. When they click on a state, the city list box never fills up. This is a security restriction in Netscape. You can test this phenomenon locally on your machine. When you load the applet into Netscape with the File|Open File command, it works. When you make a bookmark to it, quit Netscape, restart Netscape, and load the applet through the bookmark, then it will not work. Bookmarks store file URLs like this:

```
file:///C|/CoreJavaBook/ch13/WeatherApplet/WeatherApplet.html
```

Netscape applies the same security rules to file URLs and URLs on the Internet.

Unless the applet is loaded locally, Netscape will allow your applet only to read and write data on the host that serves the applet. It will let your applet connect only to sockets on the computer from which the applet came.

At first this restriction seems to make no sense. If you try, you will find that you can use Netscape to browse the gopher URL. (Netscape has no problem with gopher; it is only the Java library that cannot handle the protocol.) So why does Netscape deny the applet what the ambient browser can see? To understand the rationale, it helps to first visualize the three hosts involved shown in Figure 13-15:

- the originating host—your computer that delivers the Web page and Java applet to clients,

- the local host—the user's machine that runs your applet, and

- the third party data repository that your applet would like to see.

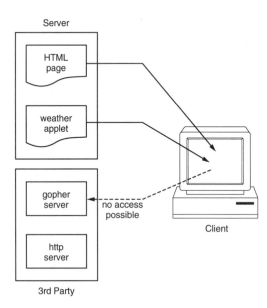

Figure 13-15: Applet security disallows connection to 3rd party

The Netscape security rule says that the applet can only read and write data on the originating host. Certainly it makes sense that the applet cannot write to the local host. If it could, it might be able to plant viruses or alter important files. After all, the applet starts running immediately when the user stumbles upon our Web page, and the user must be protected from damage by malicious or incompetent applets.

It also makes sense that the applet cannot read from the local host. Otherwise, it might browse the files on the local computer for sensitive information, such as credit card numbers, open a socket connection to the applet host, and write the information back. You might open a great-looking Web page, interact with an applet that does something fun or useful, and be completely unaware of what that applet does in other threads. Netscape denies your applet all access to the files on your computer.

DILBERT reprinted by permission of United Feature Syndicate, Inc.

But why can't the applet read other files from the Web? Isn't the Web a wealth of publicly available information, made available for everyone to read? If you browse the Web from home, through a service provider, this is indeed the situation. But it is quite different when you do your Web surfing in your office (searching only for work-relevant information, of course). Many companies have their computer sitting behind a firewall.

A firewall is a computer that filters traffic going into and out of the corporate network. This computer will deny attempts to access services with less than stellar security histories. For example, there are known security holes in protocols such as anonymous ftp. The firewall might simply disallow anonymous ftp requests, or shunt them off to an isolated ftp server. It might also deny a request to access the mail port on all machines except the mail server. Depending on the security philosophy, the firewall (shown in Figure 13-16) can also apply filtering rules to the traffic between the corporate network and the Internet, but that is much more difficult.

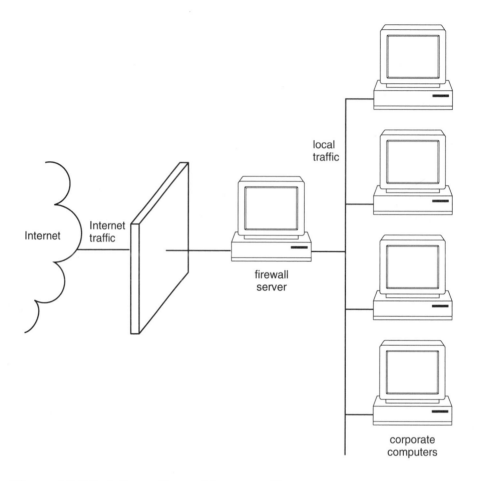

Figure 13-16: A firewall provides security

(If you are interested in this topic, turn to the book by William R. Cheswick and Steven M. Bellovin, *Firewalls and Internet Security* [Addison-Wesley, 1994].)

Having a firewall allows a company to use the Web to distribute internal information that is of interest to employees but should not be accessible outside the company. The company simply sets up a Web server, tells the address only to its employees, and programs the firewall to deny any access requests to that server from the outside. The employees can then browse the internal information with the same Web tools they already know and use.

If an employee visits your Web page, the applet is downloaded into the computer behind the firewall and starts running there. If it were able to read all the Web pages that the ambient browser can read, it would have access to the corporate information. Then it could open a connection to the host from which it came and send all that private information back. That is obviously insecure.

Since Netscape has no idea which Web pages are public and which are confidential, it disallows access to all of them.

That is too bad—you simply cannot write an applet that goes out on the Web, grabs information, processes and formats it, and presents it to the applet user. For example, our weather report applet does not want to write any information back to its host. Why doesn't Netscape let the applet strike a deal? If the applet promises not to write anywhere, it ought to be able to read from everywhere. That way, it would just be a harvester and processor, showing an ephemeral result on the user's screen.

The trouble is that Netscape cannot distinguish *read* from *write* requests. When you ask to open a stream on a URL, this is obviously a read request. Well, maybe not. The URL might be of the form

```
http://www.rogue.com/cgi-bin/cracker.pl?Garys+password+is+Sicily
```

Here the culprit is the CGI mechanism. It is designed to take arbitrary arguments and process them. The script that handles the CGI request can, and often does, store the request data. It is easy to hide information in a CGI query text. (This is called a *covert channel* in security circles.)

So, should Netscape disallow all CGI queries and only allow access to plain Web pages? The solution is not that simple. Netscape has no way of knowing that the server to which it connects on port 80 (the http port) is actually a standard http server. It might be just a shell that saves all requests to a file and returns an HTML page: "Sorry, the information you requested is not available." Then the applet could transmit information by pretending to read from the URL

```
http://www.rogue.com/Garys/password/is/Sicily
```

Since Netscape cannot distinguish read from write requests, it must disallow them both.

To summarize: Applets run on the computer browsing your Web page, but they can only access files and sockets on the computer serving the Web page.

Proxy Servers

How, then, can you distribute an applet that harvests information for your users? You could make a Web page that shows the applet in action with fake data, stored on your server. (This is exactly the approach that Sun takes with their stock ticker sample applet.) You could then provide a button with which the user downloads the applet. Users would need to load it as a local applet into Netscape, or run it from the applet viewer.

That approach will probably greatly limit the attractiveness of your applet. Many people will be too lazy or nervous to download and install the applet locally if they did not first get to use it a few times with real data on your Web page.

Fortunately, there is a way to feed the applet real data. You need to install a proxy server on your HTML server. That proxy server is a service, usually installed as a CGI script, that grabs requested information from the Web and sends it to whoever requested it. For example, if you request the URL

```
gopher://downwind.sprl.umich.edu/Weather_Text/U.S._City
    _Forecasts/California/San Jose
```

from the proxy server, you get the weather report page back through the output channel of the CGI request.

There must exist scripts for this purpose, but we could not find one, so we wrote our own in Java. The idea of the script is simple: it tests whether or not the script is a gopher script. If so, it handles it manually. Otherwise, the script uses the standard Java mechanism to open a URL. It opens the stream, reads the information line by line, and sends it to standard output.

NOTE: The compiled Java application needs to be installed in the `cgi-bin` directory on the Web server. That requires the permission of the system administrator, of course. (If your system administrator does not trust Java or know how to deal with it, try using the Perl script, with the same functionality that we explain in the sidebar.)

Example 13-8 lists the full code.

Example 13-8: ProxySvr.java

```java
import java.io.*;
import java.net.*;
import corejava.*;

public class ProxySvr
{  public static String urlDecode(String in)
   {  StringBuffer out = new StringBuffer(in.length());
      int i = 0;

      while (i < in.length())
      {  char ch = in.charAt(i);
         i++;
         if (ch == '+') ch = ' ';
         else if (ch == '%')
         {  ch = (char)(Format.atoi("0x"
               + in.substring(i, i + 2)));
            i++;
         }
```

```
            out.append(ch);
      }
      return new String(out);
   }

   public static void main(String[] args)
   {   try
      {   String urlname = urlDecode(args[0]);
         DataInputStream is = null;
         try
         {   URL url = new URL(urlname);
            is = new DataInputStream(url.openStream());
         }
         catch (MalformedURLException e)
         {   // 1.0 release doesn't know Gopher
            int pos = urlname.indexOf("://");

            String protocol = urlname.substring(0, pos);
            if (!protocol.equals("gopher")) throw e;
            pos += 3;
            int pos2 = urlname.indexOf("/", pos);
            if (pos2 < 0) throw e;
            String host = urlname.substring(pos, pos2);
            String file = urlname.substring(pos2);

            Socket t = new Socket(host, 70);
            PrintStream os
               = new PrintStream(t.getOutputStream());

            is = new DataInputStream(t.getInputStream());
            os.print(file + "\r\n");
         }

         System.out.print("Content-type: text/html\n\n");
         boolean more = true;
         while (more)
         {   String str = is.readLine();
            if (str == null) more = false;
            else System.out.println(str);
         }
      }
      catch(Exception e) { System.out.println("Error" + e); }
   }
}
```

Most of the code in the `ProxySvr` class should be straightforward. (See Figure 13-17.) The `urlDecode` method does the following:

1. changes the + signs to spaces

2. strips out the % sign and formats the digits following it in the correct form.

The `main` method assumes that the first argument is the name of the URL. It decodes it by a call to the `urlDecode` method. Then it tries to open the URL and get a data stream. If we get the `MalformedURLException`, we find out if we are using the gopher protocol by searching for the text before the '//'. If we don't detect the string `'gopher'` we rethrow the exception. Otherwise, we open a new socket for the gopher site and collect the needed information.

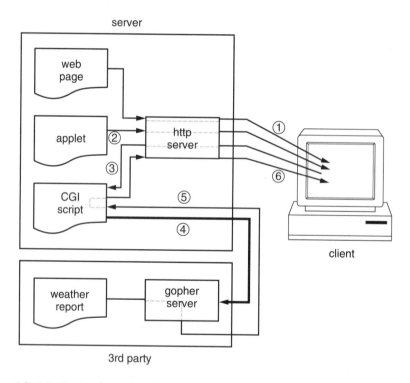

Figure 13-17: Data flow in the weather report applet

In our specific case, the `WeatherApplet` requests the information from the proxy server on its local host, which goes out to the University of Michigan, gets the data and feeds it back.

This looks like a lot of trouble, but we have avoided any security risk. Now the applet can access all data that is publicly available from our host, but none of the private data behind the firewall.

Instead, the monkey is on *our* back. By installing the `proxysvr` script on our `cgi-bin` directory, other users at our site could write applets that allow the downloading of our confidential files. Mercifully, in the case of our computer science department server, that was not a problem.

Note that your applet cannot use our proxy server—it can only access services on its host. If you want to write applications like this one, you need to install this script, or a similar mechanism, on your host.

Does it make sense to have the server merely grab the information and reflect it to the applet? In this case, it does, but in general, it might make sense for the server to cache it, thus improving performance when there are multiple requests, or even to preprocess the information.

In our case, caching was not useful because weather reports change frequently. And we had a difficult enough time installing a simple reflector on the server's `cgi-bin` directory. Had the script done some real processing, it would have taken longer to have it audited against security risks.

Comparing Java, C, and Perl for CGI Scripts

CGI scripts can be written in any language that can read from standard input and write to standard output. We first wrote the proxy server script in C because we did not realize that Perl can connect to sockets and because Java is not installed in the http server we used.

The Perl and C codes are listed in Examples 13-9 and 13-10. As you can see, the C code is much longer than the corresponding Java code. Even the most elementary operations (for example, reading a line of input) must be programmed in gory detail in C. Most of the code is completely routine. We modified a sample program from W. Richard Stevens's, *Unix Network Programming* (Prentice-Hall, 1990). It wasn't difficult to write the program, only tedious.

The Perl code is much shorter, but, as you can see by glancing at it, is completely unreadable to the uninitiated, with its charming variable names like `$!` and `$|`. Consider, for example, the statement

```
$url =~ s/%([a-fA-F0-9][a-fA-F0-9])/pack("C", hex($1))/eg;
```

Comparing Java, C, and Perl for CGI Scripts (continued)

This means "replace all strings of the form '% followed by two hex digits' by the corresponding hex value." (No, we didn't come up with that ourselves. We copied it from another script.) The remainder of the program is a modification of an example from Larry Wall's and Randal L. Schwarz's, *Programming Perl* (O'Reilly & Assoc., 1991). We don't pretend to understand the details, but it works.

Neither C nor Perl can automatically handle URLs. Both programs split the URL into service, host, and file. They handle only gopher and http at the standard port numbers, 70 and 80. They open the connection and send the name of the requested file (gopher) or GET followed by the file name (http). Then they grab the output, a line at a time, and send it to standard output.

As a result of this experiment, we can heartily recommend Java as a great language for writing CGI scripts. The network programming interface and string handling beats the daylights out of C, and the Java code is more readable and more easily maintained than the equivalent Perl code.

Example 13-9: proxysvr.c

```c
#include <netdb.h>
#include <sys/types.h>
#include <sys/socket.h>
#include <netinet/in.h>
#include <arpa/inet.h>
#include <stdio.h>
#include <string.h>
#include <stdlib.h>

#define MAXLINE 512
#define MAXNAME 128
#define HTTP 80
#define GOPHER 70

unsigned writen(fd, vptr, n)
int fd;
char* vptr;
unsigned n;
{   unsigned nleft;
    unsigned nwritten;
    char* ptr;

    ptr = (char*)vptr;
    nleft = n;
    while (nleft > 0)
```

```
    {   if ((nwritten = write(fd, ptr, nleft)) <= 0)
            return nwritten;
        nleft -= nwritten;
        ptr += nwritten;
    }
    return n - nleft;
}

unsigned readline(fd, vptr, maxlen)
int fd;
char* vptr;
int maxlen;
{   unsigned n;
    unsigned rc;
    char* ptr;
    char c;

    ptr = vptr;
    for (n = 1; n < maxlen; n++)
    {   if ((rc = read(fd, &c, 1)) == 1)
        {   *ptr++ = c;
            if (c == '\n')
            {   *ptr = 0;
                return n;
            }
        }
        else if (rc == 0)
        {   if (n == 1) return 0;
            else
            {   *ptr = 0;
                return n;
            }
        }
        else
            return -1;
    }
    *ptr = 0;
    return n;
}

void error(msg)
char* msg;
{   fputs(msg, stderr);
    fputc('\n', stderr);
    exit(1);
}
```

```
void url_decode(in, out, outlen)
char* in;
char* out;
int outlen;
{   int i = 0;
    int j = 0;
    while (in[i] != '\0' && j < outlen - 1)
    {   if (in[i] == '+') out[j] = ' ';
        else if (in[i] == '%')
        {   int ch;
            sscanf(in + i + 1, "%x", &ch);
            out[j] = ch;
            i += 2;
        }
        else out[j] = in[i];
        i++;
        j++;
    }
    out[j] = 0;
}

int main(argc, argv)
int argc;
char** argv;
{   int sockfd;
    struct sockaddr_in serv_addr;
    int i;
    int n;
    char* name;
    struct hostent* hostptr;
    char url[MAXLINE + 1];
    char sendline[MAXLINE + 1];
    char recvline[MAXLINE + 1];
    char server_name[MAXNAME];
    char file_name[MAXLINE];
    char service_name[MAXNAME];
    int port;
    int service = 0;
    char* p;
    char* q;

    url_decode(argv[1], url, sizeof(url));

    p = strstr(url, "://");
    if (p == NULL)
        error("Sorry--can only recognize service://server/file");
    strncpy(service_name, url, p - url);
    service_name[p - url] = 0;
```

```
if (strcmp(service_name, "http") == 0)
   service = HTTP;
else if (strcmp(service_name, "gopher") == 0)
   service = GOPHER;
else
   error("Sorry--can only recognize http and gopher");
p += 3;
q = strchr(p, '/');
if (q == NULL)
   error("Sorry--can only recognize service://server/file");
strncpy(server_name, p, q - p);
server_name[q - p] = '\0';
strncpy(file_name, q, sizeof(file_name) - 1);
file_name[sizeof(file_name) - 1] = '\0';
port = service;

if ((sockfd = socket(PF_INET, SOCK_STREAM, 0)) < 0)
   error("Can't open stream socket");

bzero((char*)&serv_addr, sizeof(serv_addr));
serv_addr.sin_family = AF_INET;
hostptr = gethostbyname(server_name);
if (hostptr == 0) error("Can't find host");
name = inet_ntoa(*(struct in_addr*)*hostptr->h_addr_list);
serv_addr.sin_addr.s_addr = inet_addr(name);
serv_addr.sin_port = htons(port);

if (connect(sockfd, (struct sockaddr*)&serv_addr,
   sizeof(serv_addr)) < 0)
   error("Can't connect to server");

sendline[sizeof(sendline) - 1] = 0;
if (service == GOPHER)
   strncpy(sendline, file_name, sizeof(sendline) - 1);
else if (service == HTTP)
{  strcpy(sendline, "GET ");
   strncat(sendline, file_name, sizeof(sendline) - 1
      - strlen(sendline));
}
strncat(sendline, "\r\n", sizeof(sendline) - 1
   - strlen(sendline));

n = strlen(sendline);
if (writen(sockfd, sendline, n) != n)
   error("Write error on socket");

fputs("Content-type: text/html\n\n", stdout);
```

```
        do
        {   n = readline(sockfd, recvline, MAXLINE);
            if (n < 0)
                error("Read error on socket");
            else if (n > 0)
            {   recvline[n] = 0;
                fputs(recvline, stdout);
            }
        } while (n > 0);

        return 0;
}
```

Example 13-10: proxysvr.pl

```perl
($url) = @ARGV;

$url =~ tr/+/ /;
$url =~ s/%([a-fA-F0-9][a-fA-F0-9])/pack("C", hex($1))/eg;

$pos = index($url, "://");

if ($pos < 0)
{   die "Sorry--can only recognize service://server/file";
}

$service_name = substr($url, 0, $pos);

if ($service_name eq "http")
{   $port = 80;
}
elsif ($service_name eq "gopher")
{   $port = 70;
}
else
{   die "Sorry--can only recognize http and gopher";
}

$pos += 3;
$pos2 = index($url, "/", $pos);
if ($pos2 < 0)
{   die "Sorry--can only recognize service://server/file";
}

$server_name = substr($url, $pos, $pos2 - $pos);
$file_name = substr($url, $pos2);
$AF_INET = 2;
$SOCK_STREAM =1;
```

```
$sockaddr = 'S n a4 x8';

($name, $aliases, $proto) = getprotobyname ('tcp');
($name,$aliases,$type,$len,$thataddr)
    = gethostbyname($server_name);
$that = pack($sockaddr, $AF_INET, $port, $thataddr);

if (!socket (S, $AF_INET, $SOCK_STREAM, $proto))
{  die $!;
}

if (!connect (S, $that))
{  die $!;
}

select(S); $|=1; select(STDOUT);

if ($service_name eq "http")
{  $command = "GET ".$file_name;
}
elsif ($service_name eq "gopher")
{   $command = $file_name;
}

print S $command."\r\n";

print "Content-type: text/html\n\n";
while (<S>)
{  print;
}
```

NOTE: The current interface between client- and server-side computing is still quite immature. Just as Sun is working on a seamless database connectivity interface, it and other vendors are working to make the interaction between applets and their host more standardized and convenient. When this happens, information-harvesting applets will become ubiquitous. They will perform computation, formatting, and presentation locally, and interact with servers that perform data-retrieval and caching.

CHAPTER

14

- Structured Query Language

- Installing JDBC

- Basic JDBC Programming Concepts

- Populating a Database

- Executing Queries

- Metadata

Database Connectivity: JDBC

I n the summer of 1996, Sun released the first version of the Java
Database Connectivity (JDBC) kit. This package lets Java programmers
connect to a database, query it or update it using the industry standard query
language. We think this is one of the most important developments in Java programming. It is not just that databases are among the most common use of
hardware and software today. There are a lot of products pursuing this market
and so it is reasonable to ask why do we think Java is so special for this market?
The reason Java and JDBC have an essential advantage over other database programming environments is that programs developed with this technology are
platform-independent and vendor-independent.

The same Java database program can run on a PC, a workstation or a Java-powered terminal ("network computer"). You can move your data from one database to another, for example, from Microsoft SQL Server to Oracle, and the same
program can still read your data. This is in sharp contrast to the database programming typically done on personal computers today. It is all too common
that one writes database applications in a proprietary database language, using
a database management system that is available only from a single vendor. The
result is that you can run the resulting application only on one or two platforms.
We believe that *because of its universality* Java and JDBC will eventually replace
proprietary database languages such as Borland's PAL or the various incompatible BASIC derivatives used by vendors such as Powersoft, Oracle and Microsoft
for accessing databases.

Having said this, we still must caution the reader that, as we write this chapter,
there are no tools for database programming with Java. There are no form
designers, query builders, report generators, and there certainly are no database

controls like the ones you find in Visual Basic or Delphi. Clearly, this will soon change. A large number of vendors are at work building these tools, and we expect them to become widely available in 1997.

Here is what we will do in this chapter:

- Explain some of the ideas behind JDBC—the "Java database connectivity API."

- Give you enough details and examples so that you can get started in actually using JDBC.

The first part of this chapter gives you an overview of how JDBC is put together. The last part gives you example code that illustrates the major JDBC features.

NOTE: Over the years, many technologies were invented to make database access more efficient and failsafe. Standard databases support indexes, triggers, stored procedures and transaction management. JDBC supports all these features, but we do not discuss them in this chapter. One could write an entire book on advanced database programming in Java, and undoubtedly (many) such books will be written. The material in this chapter will give you enough information to deal with a departmental database effectively in Java and to make it easy to go further with the JDBC if you want to. However, since there are no books available yet on the JDBC, for more information on the advanced features, you must turn to the JDBC documentation that is available at http://java.sun.com/jdbc/jdbc.html.

The Design of JDBC

The people at JavaSoft were aware of the potential Java showed for working with databases from the start. They began working on extending Java to deal with SQL access to databases roughly as soon as the JDK went into beta testing. (They started working in November of 1995.) What they first hoped to do was to extend Java so that it could talk to any random database using only "pure" Java. It didn't take them very long to realize that this is an impossible task: there are simply too many databases out there, utilizing too many protocols. Moreover, while database vendors were all in favor of JavasSoft providing a standard network protocol for database access, they were only in favor of it if JavaSoft decided to use *their* network protocol.

What all the database vendors and tools vendors *did* agree on was that it would be very useful if JavaSoft provided a purely Java API for SQL access *along* with a device manager to allow third party drivers to connect to specific databases. Database vendors in turn could provide their own drivers to plug into the driver manager. There would then be a simple mechanism for registering third party drivers with the device manager. The point being that all they needed to do was follow the requirements laid out in the device manager API.

After a fairly long period of public discussion, the API for database access became the JDBC API and the rules for writing device drives were encapsulated in the JDBC driver API. (The JDBC driver API is of interest only to database vendors and database tool providers, we don't cover it here.)

This follows the very successful model of Microsoft's ODBC which provided a C-programming language interface to *structured query language* (SQL) which is the standard for accessing relational databases. Both the JDBC and ODBC in turn are based on the X/Open SQL call level interface specification. In the end, the idea behind the JDBC is the same as with ODBC: programs written using the JDBC API would talk to the JDBC driver manager which in turn would use the drivers that were plugged into it at that moment to talk to the actual database.

NOTE: For a list of drivers currently available check out:
`http://splash.javasoft.com/jdbc/jdbc.drivers.html`

More precisely the JDBC consists of two layers. The top layer is the JDBC API. This API communicates with the JDBC manager driver API, sending it the various SQL statements. The manager should (transparently to the programmer) communicate with the various third part drivers that actually connect to the database and return the information from the query or perform the action specified by the query.

NOTE: The JDBC specification will actually allow you to pass any string to the underlying driver. The driver in turn can pass this string on to the database. This allows you to use specialized versions of SQL that may be supported by the driver and its associated database.

All this means the Java/JDBC layer is all that most programmers will ever have to deal with. Figure 14-1 illustrates what happens.

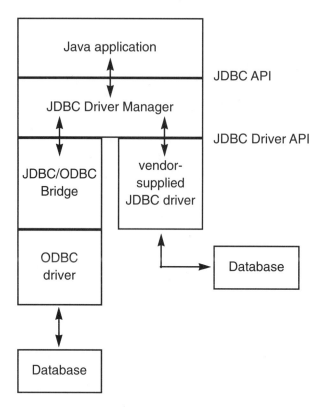

Figure 14-1: JDBC to Database communication path

In summary, the ultimate goal of the JDBC is to make it possible for:

- Programmers to write applications in Java to access any database using standard SQL statements—or even specialized extensions of SQL—while still following Java language conventions. (JavaSoft insists that all JDBC drivers support at least the entry level version of SQL 92 .)

- Database vendors and database tool vendors to supply the low level drivers. This lets them optimize their drivers for their specific situation.

NOTE: If you are curious as to why JavaSoft just didn't adopt the ODBC model, their response, as given at the JavaOne Conference in May 1996, was:

- ODBC is hard to learn.

- ODBC has a few commands with lots of complex options. The Java style is to have simple and intuitive methods, but to have lots of them.

- ODBC relies on the multiple use of `void*` pointers and other C features that are not natural in Java.

- It was felt to be too hard to map ODBC to Java because of the frequent use of multiple pointers and pointer indirection.

Typical Uses of the JDBC

Just as one can use Java for both applications and applets, one can use the JDBC enhanced version of Java in both applications and applets. When used in an applet, all the normal security restrictions apply. In particular the JDBC continues to assume that all Java applets are untrusted.

In particular, applets that use JDBC would only be able to open a database connection from the server from which they are downloaded. They can make neither explicit nor implicit use of local information. Although the JDBC extensions of the Java security model allows one to download a JDBC driver and register it with JDBC device manager on the server, that driver can only be used for connections from the same server as the applet came from. That means, the Web server and the database server must be the same machine, which is not a typical setup. Of course, the Web server can have a proxy service that routes database traffic to another machine. When signed Java applets become possible this restriction could be loosened. To summarize: You can use JDBC with applets, but you must manage the server carefully.

Applications on the other hand have complete freedom. They can give the application total access to files and remote servers. We envision that JDBC applications will be very common.

Finally, there is a third possible use for the JDBC enhanced version of Java. This is somewhat speculative and we do not give any examples of this here. But the thinking at JavaSoft is this will be an important area in the future and so we want to briefly mention it. The idea is sometimes referred to as the "three tier model." This means a Java application (or applet) calls on a middleware layer that in turn accesses the data. This would work best with RMI (see Chapter 15) or an object request broker for the communication between the client and the middle layer, and JDBC between the middle tier and a back-end database. Especially through the use of better compilation techniques (just-in-time compilers and native compilers), Java is becoming fast enough that it can be used to write the middleware layer.

Structured Query Language

JDBC is an interface to SQL,which is the interface to essentially all modern relational databases. Desktop databases usually have a graphical user interface that lets users manipulate the data directly, but server-based databases are accessed purely through SQL. Most desktop databases have an SQL interface as well, but it often does not support the full range of ANSI SQL92 features, the current standard for SQL.

The JDBC package can be thought of as nothing more than an application programming interface (API) for communicating SQL statements to databases. We will give a short introduction to SQL in this section. If you have never seen SQL before, you may not find this material sufficient. If so, you should turn to one of the many books on the topic. (One online book service lists 123 books on SQL—ranging from the expected "SQL for Dummies" to one titled (we kid you not) "SQL for Smarties".) We recommend James Martin and Joe Leben, Client/Server Databases, Prentice-Hall, or the venerable and opinionated book C.J. Date, A Guide to the SQL Standard, Addison-Wesley.

A modern relational database can be thought of as a bunch of named tables with rows and columns that can be joined on certain common columns. The rows contain the actual data (these are usually called *records*). The column headers is in each table correspond to the field names.

Figure 14-2 shows a sample table that contains a set of books on HTML that is adopted from a very useful, essentially complete, list of HTML books maintained by Cye H. Waldman at `http://wwwiz.com/books/`.

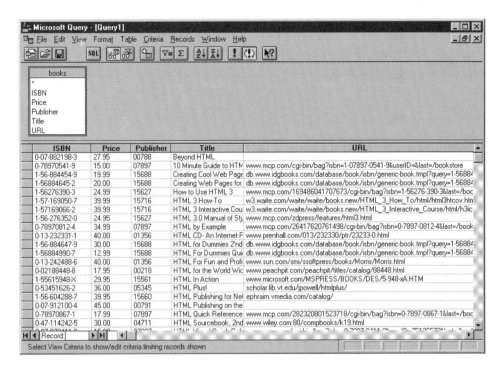

Figure 14-2: Sample table containing the HTML books

Figure 14-3 shows the result of linking this table with a table of publishers. Both the book table and the publisher table contain a numerical code for the publisher. The publisher table contains the publisher's name and web page URL. When we link both tables on the publisher code, we obtain a *query result*. Each row in the result contains the information about a book, together with the publisher name and web page URL. Note that the publisher names and URLs are duplicated across several rows since we have several rows with the same publisher.

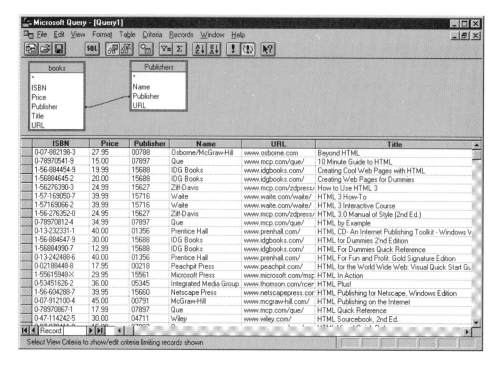

Figure 14-3: Two tables linked together

The benefit of using a relational database and the linking strategy for queries is to avoid unnecessary duplication of data in the database tables. For example, a native database design might have had columns for the publisher name and URL right in the book table. But then the database itself, and not just the query result, would have many duplicates of these entries. If a publisher's web address changed, *all* entries would need to be updated. Clearly this is somewhat error-prone. In the relational model, we distribute data into multiple tables such that no information is ever unnecessarily duplicated. For example, each publisher URL is only contained once in the publisher table. If the information needs to be combined, then the tables are joined.

In this example we used the Microsoft Query tool to inspect and link the tables. Microsoft Query is a part of Microsoft Office, so if you have Office, you already have a copy. Many other vendors have similar tools. Microsoft Query is a graphical tool that lets us express queries in a simple form by connecting column names and filling information into forms. Such tools are often called *query by example* (QBE) tools. In contrast, a query that uses SQL is written out in text, using the SQL syntax. For example:

```
SELECT Books.ISBN, Books.Price, Books.Title,
   Books.Publisher_Id,    Publishers.Name, Publishers.URL
FROM Books, Publishers
WHERE Books.Publisher_Id = Publishers.Publisher_Id
```

This is a complex query. In the remainder of this section, we will learn how to write such queries. If you are already familiar with SQL, just skip this section.

By convention, SQL keywords are written in all caps, although this is not necessary.

The `SELECT` operation is quite flexible. You can simply select all elements in the Books table with the following query:

```
SELECT * FROM Books
```

The FROM statement is required in every SQL SELECT statement. The FROM clause tells the database which tables to examine to find the data.

You can choose the columns that you want.

```
SELECT ISBN, Price, Title,
FROM Books
```

You can restrict the rows in the answer with the WHERE clause.

```
SELECT ISBN, Price, Title,
FROM Books
WHERE Price <= 29.95
```

Be careful with the "equals" comparison. SQL uses = and <>, not == or != for equality testing as in Java.

The WHERE clause can also use pattern matching using the LIKE operator. The "wildcard" characters are not the usual * and ? however. Use a % for zero or more characters and an underscore for a single character. For example:

```
SELECT ISBN, Price, Title,
FROM Books
WHERE Title NOT LIKE '%HTML%'
```

Note that strings are enclosed in single quotes, not double quotes. A single quote inside a string is denoted as a pair of single quotes. For example,

```
SELECT Title,
FROM Books
WHERE Books.Title LIKE '%''%'
```

reports all titles that contain a single quote.

You can select data from multiple tables.

```
SELECT * FROM Books, Publishers
```

Without a `WHERE` clause, this query is not very interesting. It lists *all combinations* of rows from both tables. In our case, where Books has 37 rows and

Publishers has 18 rows, the result is a table with 37 × 18 entries and lots of duplications. We really want to constrain the query to say that we are only interested in *matching* books with their publishers.

```
SELECT * FROM Books, Publishers
WHERE Books.Publisher_Id = Publishers.Publisher_Id
```

This query result has 37 rows, one for each book, since each book has a publisher in the Publisher table.

Whenever you have multiple tables in a query, you may have the same column name occur in two different places. That happened in our example. There is a publisher code column called `Publisher_Id` in both the Books and the Publishers table. To resolve ambiguities, you must prefix each column name with the name of the table to which it belongs, such as `Books.Publisher_Id`.

Now you have seen all SQL constructs that were used in the query at the beginning of this section:

```
SELECT Books.ISBN, Books.Price, Books.Title,
   Books.Publisher_Id,   Publishers.Name, Publishers.URL
FROM Books, Publishers
WHERE Books.Publisher_Id = Publishers.Publisher_Id
```

SQL can be used to change the data inside a database as well, by using so-called *action queries* (i.e., queries that move or change data). For example, suppose you want to reduce the current price of all books by $5.00 that do not have HTML 3 in their title.

```
UPDATE Books
SET Price = Price - 5.00
WHERE Title NOT LIKE '%HTML 3%'
```

Similarly, you can change several fields at the same time by separating the SET clauses with commas. There are many other SQL keywords you can use in an action query. Probably the most important besides UPDATE is DELETE, which allows the query to delete those records that satisfy certain criteria. Finally, SQL comes with built-in functions for taking averages, finding maximums and minimums in a column, and a lot more. Consult a book on SQL for more information.

Of course, before you can query and modify data, you must have a place to store data and you must have the data. There are two SQL statements you need for this purpose. The CREATE TABLE command makes a new table. You specify the name and data type for each column. Table 14-1 shows the most common SQL data types. For example,

```
CREATE TABLE Books
(Title CHAR(60),
 ISBN CHAR(13),
 Publisher_Id CHAR(5),
 URL CHAR(80),
 Price DECIMAL(6,2)
)
```

Table 14-1: SQL Data Types

Data Types	Description
INTEGER or INT	typically a 32-bit integer
SMALLINT	typically a 16-bit integer
NUMERIC(m,n)	fixed-point decimal number with m total
DECIMAL(m,n)	digits and n digits after the decimal
or DEC(m,n)	point
FLOAT(n)	a floating point number with n binary digits of precision
REAL	typically a 32-bit floating point number
DOUBLE	typically a 64-bit floating point number
CHARACTER(n)	fixed-length string of length n
or CHAR(n)	
VARCHAR(n)	variable-length strings of maximum length n
DATE	calendar date, implementation-dependent
TIME	time of day, implementation-dependent
TIMESTAMP	date and time of day, implementation-dependent

Again, there are many clauses you can add to the CREATE TABLE command that we are not discussing in this book for dealing with database information, such as keys and constraints.

Typically, to insert values into a table, you use the INSERT statement:

```
INSERT INTO Books
VALUES ('Beyond HTML', '0-07-882198-3', '00788', '', 27.95)
```

You need a separate INSERT statement for every row being inserted in the table unless you embed a SELECT statement inside an INSERT statement. (Consult an SQL book for examples of how to do this.)

Installing JDBC

If you install the software from the CD-ROM, you will already have the JDBC package installed. You can also obtain the newest JDBC version from Sun and combine it with your existing Java installation. Be sure that the version numbers are compatible, and carefully follow the installation directions.

NOTE: As of this writing, JDBC only works with Solaris for Sparc processors and Windows 95/NT. Solaris X86 and Macintosh versions are expected to be available at a later date.

Of course, you need a database program that is compatible with JDBC. You will also need to create a database for your experimental use. We assume you will call this database COREJAVA. Create a new database, or have your database administrator create one with the appropriate permissions. You need to be able to create, update and drop tables.

Some database vendors already have JDBC drivers, so you may be able to install one following your vendor's directions. For those databases that do not have a JDBC driver, you need to go a different route. Since ODBC drivers exist for most databases, JavaSoft decided to write (with the help of Intersolv) a JDBC to ODBC bridge. To make a connection between such a database and Java, you need to install the database's ODBC driver and the JDBC to ODBC bridge.

The JDBC to ODBC bridge has the advantage of letting people use the JDBC immediately. It has the disadvantage of requiring yet another layer between the database and the JDBC, although in most cases performance will be acceptable. Most major vendors have announced plans to come out with native drivers that plug directly into the JDBC driver manager that will give you access the most popular databases. We suggest you contact your database vendor to find out if (more likely when) a native JDBC driver will be available for your database. But for experimentation and in many cases, the bridge works just fine. All examples in this chapter were developed with the bridge and Microsoft SQL server running on NT Workstation 4.0.

If your database doesn't have direct JDBC support, you need to install the ODBC driver for your database. Directions for this vary widely, and you need to consult your database administrator or, if all else fails, the vendor documentation.

NOTE: Some databases support SQL through a proprietary mechanism, not JDBC. For example, Borland has a BDE engine and Microsoft a Jet engine that give somewhat better performance than ODBC for local databases. These mechanisms are not compatible with Java. If you are looking in vain for ODBC drivers, you may not have installed or purchased the correct driver.

You then need to make your experimental database into an ODBC data source. In Windows, use the ODBC control in the control panel. Click on Add. You will see a list of available ODBC drivers. Click on the one that contains your new database. Fill out the resulting dialog box with the name of the database and the location of the server. When you are done, you should see your database listed as a data source. If you have Microsoft Query, you can test your configuration using it. Start the Query program and make a new query. You will see a list of all data sources. If you see COREJAVA, then your setup is correct. Of course, there are no tables in the database yet. We will see how to use Java to create tables in the next section.

Finally, you need to install the JDBC to ODBC bridge. This is a standard component of the JDBC package. Under Windows, simply look for a file JdbcOdbc.dll and put the file into a directory that is on the command search path. We recommend putting it into \java\bin.

If you have never installed a client/server database before, you may find that setting up the database, the ODBC driver and the ODBC to JDBC bridge is somewhat complex, and that it can be difficult to diagnose the cause for failure. It may be best to seek expert help if your setup is not working correctly. When working with Microsoft SQL Sever, we found it to be a real life-saver to have a book on server and database administration such as Arthur Knowles, Microsoft BackOffice Administrator Survival Guide, Sams Publications, 1996. The same is undoubtedly true on other platforms as well.

Basic JDBC Programming Concepts

Programming with the JDBC classes is, by design, not very different then programming with the usual Java classes: you build objects from the JDBC core classes extending them by inheritance if need be. This section takes you through the details.

Database URLs

When connecting to a database, you must specify the data source, and you may need to specify additional parameters. For example, network protocol drivers may need a port and ODBC drivers may need various attributes.

As one might expect, JDBC uses a syntax similar to ordinary net URLs to describe data sources. Here is an example of the syntax you need:

```
jdbc:odbc:corejava
```

This would access an ODBC data source named `corejava` using the JDBC-ODBC bridge. The general syntax is:

```
jdbc:subprotocol name:other stuff
```

where a subprotocol is the specific driver used by JDBC to connect to the database.

> NOTE: JavaSoft has said that it will act as a temporary registry for JDBC sub-protocol names. To reserve a sub protocol name, send a message to jdbc@wombat.eng.sun.com.

The format for the `other_stuff` parameter depends on the subprotocol used. JavaSoft recommends that if you are using a network address as part of the `other_stuff` parameter, you use the standard URL naming convention of `//hostname:port/other`. For example:

```
jdbc:odbc://whitehouse.gov:5000/Cat;PWD=Hillary
```

would connect to Cat database on port 5000 of whitehouse.gov using the ODBC attribute value of PWD set to "Hillary".

Making the Connection

The `DriverManager` is the class responsible for loading database drivers and creating a new database connection. For practical programming, you need not be particularly interested in the details of driver management. You can just open a database connection with the following code:

```
String url = "jdbc:odbc:corejava";
String user = "Cay";
String password = "wombat";
Connection con = DriverManager.getConnection(url,
    user, password);
```

The JDBC manager will try to find a driver than can use the protocol specified in the database URL . It does this by iterating through the available drivers that are currently registered with the device manager.

The connection object you get via a call to `getConnection` in turn lets you use JDBC drives to manage SQL queries. You can execute queries and action statements, commit or roll back transactions.

Executing Queries

To make a query, you first create a `Statement` object. The `Connection` object that you obtained from the call to `DriverManager.getConnection` can create statement objects.

```
Statement stmt = con.createStatement();
```

You can then execute a query, simply by using the `executeQuery` object of the `Statement` class and supplying the SQL command for the query as a string. Note that you can use the same `Statement` object for multiple unrelated queries.

Of course, you are interested in the result of the query. The `executeQuery` object returns an object of type `ResultSet` that you use to walk through the result a row at a time.

```
ResultSet rs = stmt.executeQuery("SELECT * FROM Books")
```

The basic loop for analyzing a result set looks like this:

```
while (rs.next())
{   look at a row of the result set
}
```

When inspecting an individual row, you will want to know the contents of each column. There is a large number of accessor methods that give you this information.

```
string isbn = rs.getString(1);
float price = rs.getDouble("Price");
```

There are accessors for every Java *type*, such as `getString` and `getDouble`. Each accessor has two forms, one that takes a numeric argument and one that takes a string argument. When you supply a numeric argument, you refer to the column with that number. For example, `rs.getString(1)` returns the value of the first column in the current row. (Unlike array indexes, database column numbers start at 1.) When you supply a string argument, you refer to the column in the result set with that name. For example, `rs.getDouble("Price")` returns the value of the column with name `Price`. Using the numeric argument is a bit more efficient, but the string arguments make the code easier to read and maintain.

Java will make reasonable type conversions when the type of the `get` method doesn't match the type of the column. For example, the call `rs.getString("Price")` yields the price as a string.

NOTE: SQL data types and Java data types are not exactly the same. See Table 14-2 for a listing of the basic SQL datatypes and their Java equivalents.

Table 14-2: SQL Data Types and their corresponding Java types

Data type	Java data type
INTEGER or INT	int
SMALLINT	short
NUMERIC(m,n), DECIMAL(m,n) or DEC(m,n)	java.sql.Numeric
FLOAT(n)	double
REAL	float
DOUBLE	double
CHARACTER(n) or CHAR(n)	String
VARCHAR(n)	String
DATE	java.sql.Date
TIME	java.sql.Time
TIMESTAMP	java.sql.Timestamp

 java.sql.DriverManager

• static Connection getConnection(String url, String user,String password)

establishes a connection to the given database and return a Connection object.

Parameters: url   the URL for the database

                    user   the database logon ID

                    password the database logon password

`java.sql.Connection`

- `Statement createStatement()`

  creates a statement object that can be used to execute SQL queries and updates without parameters.

- `void close()`

  immediately closes the current connection.

`interface java.sql.Statement`

- `ResultSet executeQuery(String sql)`

  executes the SQL statement given in the string and returns a `ResultSet` to view the query result.

  Parameters: `sql`   the SQL query

- `int executeUpdate(String sql)`

  executes the SQL INSERT, UPDATE or DELETE statement specified by the string. Also used to execute DDL (Data Definition Language) statements. Returns the number of records affected.

  Parameters: `sql`   the SQL statement

- `void cancel()`

  cancels a JDBC statement that is being executed by another thread.

`java.sql.ResultSet`

- `boolean next()`

  makes the current row in the result set move forward by one. Returns false after the last row. Note that you must call this method to advance to the first row.

- `XXX getXXX(int columnNumber)`

- `XXX getXXX(String columnName)`
  (`XXX` is a type such as `int`, `double`, `String`, `Date`, `etc.`)

  returns the value of the column with column index c or with column name s, converted to the specified type. Not all type conversions are legal. See the JDBC documentation for details.

- `int findColumn(String columnName)`

  gives you the column index associated to a column name.

- `void close()`

  immediately closes the current result set.

SQLException

Most JDBC methods throw this exception, and you must be prepared to catch it. The following methods give more information about the exceptions.

- `String getSQLState()`

  gets the SQLState formatted using the XOPEN standard.

- `int getErrorCode()`

  gets the vendor specific exception code.

- `SQLException getNextException()`

  gets the exception chained to this one. It may contain more information about the error.

Populating a Database

We now want to write our first real JDBC program. Of course, it would be nice if we could execute some of the fancy queries that we discussed earlier. Unfortunately, we have a problem: right now, there is no data in the database. And you won't find a database file on the CD-ROM that you can simply copy onto your hard disk for the database program to read. The reason is that there is simply no database file format that lets you interchange SQL relational databases from one vendor to another. SQL does not have anything to do with files. It is a language to issue queries and updates to a database. How the database executes these statements most efficiently, and what file formats it uses towards that goal, is entirely up to the *implementation* of the database. Database vendors try very hard to come up with clever strategies for query optimization and data storage, and different vendors have arrived at different mechanisms. Thus, while SQL statements are portable, the underlying data representation is not.

To get around this we provide you with a small set of data in a series of text files. The first program we give will read such a text file and create a table whose column headings match the first line of the text file and whose column types match the second line. The remaining lines of the input file are the data and we insert them into the table. Of course, we use SQL statements and JDBC to create the table and insert the data.

At the end of this section you can see the code for the program that reads a text file and populates a database table. Even if you are not interested in looking at the implementation, you must run this program if you want to execute the more interesting examples in the next two sections. Run the program as follows:

```
java MakeDB Books.txt
java MakeDB Authors.txt
java MakeDB Publishers.txt
java MakeDB BooksAuthors.txt
```

The following steps provide an overview of the program.

1. Connect to the database.

2. If there is no command line, then ask for the input file.

3. Extract the table name from the file by removing the extension of the input file (e.g., Books.txt is stored in the table Books).

4. Read in the column names, using the `readLine` method that reads a line and splits it into an array of tokens. This is done using the `StringTokenizer` class that you saw in Chapter 11.

5. Read in the column types.

6. Use the `createTable` method to make a string command of the form:

   ```
   CREATE TABLE Name ( Column1 Type1, Column2 Type2, ... )
   ```

7. Pass this string to the `executeUpdate` method:

   ```
   stmt.executeUpdate(command);
   ```

   Here we use `executeUpdate`, not `executeQuery`, because this statement has no result. (It is a DDL SQL statement.)

8. For each line in the input file, execute an `INSERT` statement using the `insertInto` method. The only complication is that strings must be surrounded by single quotes, and that single quotes inside strings must be duplicated.

9. After all elements have been inserted, run a `SELECT * FROM Name` query using the `showTable` method to show the result. This shows that the data has been successfully inserted.

Example 14-1 provides the code for this.

Example 14-1: MakeDB.java

```java
import java.net.*;
import java.sql.*;
import java.io.*;
import java.util.*;

class MakeDB
{  public static void main (String args[])
   {  try
      {  Class.forName("jdbc.odbc.JdbcOdbcDriver"); // force
            //loading of driver
         String url = "jdbc:odbc:corejava";
         String user = "sa";
         String password = "";
         Connection con = DriverManager.getConnection(url,
            user, password);
         Statement stmt = con.createStatement();

         String fileName = "";
         if (args.length > 0)
            fileName = args[0];
         else
         {  System.out.println("Enter filename: ");
            fileName = new
               DataInputStream(System.in).readLine();
         }

         int i = 0;
         while (i < fileName.length() &&
            (Character.isLowerCase(fileName.charAt(i)) ||
            Character.isUpperCase(fileName.charAt(i))))
            i++;
         String tableName = fileName.substring(0, i);

         DataInputStream in = new DataInputStream(new
            FileInputStream(fileName));
         String[] columnNames = readLine(in);
         String[] columnTypes = readLine(in);

         createTable(stmt, tableName, columnNames,
            columnTypes);

         boolean done = false;
         while (!done)
         {  String[] values = readLine(in);
```

```
            if (values.length == 0) done = true;
            else insertInto(stmt, tableName, columnTypes,
               values);
         }

         showTable(stmt, tableName, columnNames.length);
         stmt.close();
         con.close();
      }
   catch (SQLException ex)
   {  System.out.println ("SQLException:");
      while (ex != null)
      {  System.out.println ("SQLState: " +
            ex.getSQLState());
         System.out.println ("Message:   " +
            ex.getMessage());
         System.out.println ("Vendor:    " +
            ex.getErrorCode());
         ex = ex.getNextException();
         System.out.println ("");
       }
   }
   catch (java.lang.Exception ex)
   {  System.out.println("Exception: " + ex);
      ex.printStackTrace ();
   }
}

private static String[] readLine(DataInput in) throws
    IOException
{  String line = in.readLine();
   Vector result = new Vector();
   if (line != null)
   {  StringTokenizer t = new StringTokenizer(line, "|");
      while (t.hasMoreTokens())
         result.addElement(t.nextToken().trim());
   }
   String[] retval = new String[result.size()];
   result.copyInto(retval);
   return retval;
}

private static void createTable(Statement stmt, String
    tableName, String[] columnNames, String[] columnTypes)
    throws SQLException
{  String command = "CREATE TABLE " + tableName + "(\n";
   String primary = "";
   for (int i = 0; i < columnNames.length; i++)
```

```
        {   if (i > 0) command += ",\n";
            String columnName = columnNames[i];
            if (columnName.charAt(0) == '*')
            {   if (primary.length() > 0) primary += ", ";
                columnName = columnName.substring(1,
                    columnName.length());
                primary += columnName;
            }
            command += columnName + " " + columnTypes[i];
        }
        if (primary.length() > 0) command += "\nPRIMARY KEY
            (" + primary + ")";
        command += ")\n";
        stmt.executeUpdate(command);
    }

    private static void insertInto(Statement stmt, String
        tableName, String[] columnTypes, String[] values) throws
        SQLException
    {   String command = "INSERT INTO " + tableName + "
            VALUES (";
        for (int i = 0; i < columnTypes.length; i++)
        {   if (i > 0) command += ", ";
            String columnType = columnTypes[i].toUpperCase();
            String value = "";
            if (i < values.length) value = values[i];
             if (columnType.startsWith("CHAR") ||
                columnType.startsWith("VARCHAR"))
            {   int from = 0;
                int to = 0;
                command += "'";
                while ((to = value.indexOf('\'', from)) >= 0)
                {   command += value.substring(from, to) + "''";
                    from = to + 1;
                }
                command += value.substring(from) + "'";
            }
            else command += value;
        }
        command += ")";
        stmt.executeUpdate(command);
    }

    private static void showTable(Statement stmt, String
        tableName, int numCols) throws SQLException
    {   String query = "SELECT * FROM " + tableName;
        ResultSet rs = stmt.executeQuery(query);
        while (rs.next())
```

```
    {  for (int i = 1; i <= numCols; i++)
       {  if (i > 1) System.out.print("|");
          System.out.print(rs.getString(i));
       }
       System.out.println("");
    }
    rs.close();
  }
}
```

Executing Queries

In this section, we will write a program that executes queries against the book database. For this program to work, you must have populated the `corejava` database with tables as described in the preceding section. Figure 14-4 shows the query application.

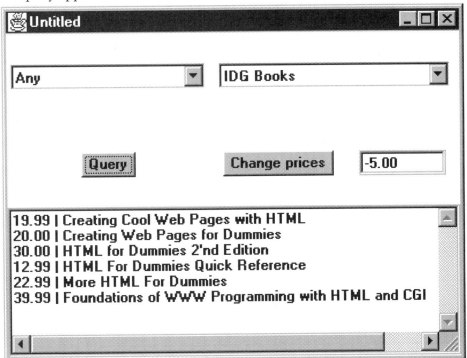

Figure 14-4: The QueryDB application

You can select the author and the publisher, or leave either of them as "Any." Click on Query and all books matching your selection will be displayed in the text box.

You can also change the data in the database. Select a publisher and type in an amount into the textbox next to the "Change prices" button. When you click the button, all prices of that publisher are adjusted by the amount you entered, and the text area contains a message indicating how many records were changed. However, to minimize unintended changes to the database, you can't change all prices at once. The author field is ignored when you change prices. After a price change, you may want to run a query to verify the new prices.

In this program, we use one new feature, *prepared statements*. Consider the query for all books by a particular publisher, independent of the author. The SQL query is

```
SELECT Books.Price, Books.Title
FROM Books, Publishers
WHERE Books.Publisher_Id = Publishers.Publisher_Id
AND Publishers.Name = the name from the list box
```

Rather than building a separate query command every time the user launches such a query, we can *prepare* a query with a host variable and use it many times, each time filling in a different string for the variable. That gives us a performance benefit. Whenever the database executes a query, it first computes a strategy of how to execute the query efficiently. By preparing the query and reusing it, that planning step is done only once. (The reason you do not *always* want to prepare a query is that the optimal strategy may change as your data changes. You have to balance the expense of optimization versus the expense of querying your data less efficiently.)

Each host variable in a prepared query is indicated with a ?. If there is more than one variable, then you must keep track of the positions of the ? when setting the values. For example, our prepared query becomes

```
String publisherQuery =
   "SELECT Books.Price, Books.Title " +
   "FROM Books, Publishers " +
   "WHERE Books.Publisher_Id = Publishers.Publisher_Id " +
   "AND Publishers.Name = ?";
PreparedStatement publisherQueryStmt
   = con.prepareStatement(publisherQuery);
```

Before executing the prepared statement, we must bind the host variables to actual values. This is done with a `set` method. As with the `ResultSet get` methods, there are different `set` methods for the various types. Here we want to set a string.

```
publisherQueryStmt.setString(1, publisher);
```

The first argument is the host variable that we want to set. The position 1 denotes the first ?. The second argument is the value that we want to assign to the host variable.

If you reuse a prepared query that you have already executed, and the query has more than one host variable, all host variables stay bound as you set them unless you change them with a `set` method. That means, you only need to call `set` on those host variables that change from one query to the next.

Once all variables have been bound to values, you can execute the query.

```
ResultSet rs = publisherQueryStmt.executeQuery();
```

You process the result set in the usual way. Here we add the information to the text area result.

```
result.setText("");
while (rs.next())
    result.appendText(rs.getString(1) + " | " +
        rs.getString(2) + "\n");
rs.close();
```

There are a total of four prepared queries in this program, one each for the cases shown in Table 14-3.

Table 14-3: Selected queries

Author	Publisher
any	any
any	specified
specified	any
specified	specified

The price update feature is implemented as a simple UPDATE statement. For variety, we did not choose to make a prepared statement in this case. Note that we call `executeUpdate`, not `executeQuery` since the UPDATE statement does not return a result set and we don't need one. The return value of `executeUpdate` is the count of changed rows. We display the count in the text area.

```
String updateStatement = "UPDATE Books ...";
int r = stmt.executeUpdate(updateStatement);
result.setText(r + " records updated");
```

The following steps help provide an overview of the program.

1. Arrange the components in the frame, using a grid bag layout (see Chapter 7).

2. Populate the author and publisher text boxes by running two queries that return all author and publisher names in the database.

3. When the user selects "Query", find which of the four query types needs to be executed. If this is the first time this query type is executed, then the prepared statement variable is `null`, and the prepared statement is constructed. Then the values are bound to the query and the query is executed.

The queries involving authors are more complex. Because a book can have multiple authors, the BooksAuthors table gives the correspondence between authors and books. For example, the book with ISBN number 1-56-604288-7 has two authors with codes HARR and KIDD. The BooksAuthors table has the rows

```
1-56-604288-7 | HARR | 1
1-56-604288-7 | KIDD | 2
```

to indicate this fact. The third column lists the order of the authors. (We can't just use the position of the records in the table. There is no fixed row ordering in a relational table.) Thus, the query has to snake (join) itself from the Books table to the BooksAuthors table, then to the Authors table to compare the author name with the one selected by the user.

```
SELECT Books.Price, Books.Title
FROM Books, Publishers, BooksAuthors, Authors
WHERE Books.Publisher_Id = Publishers.Publisher_Id
AND Publishers.Name = ?
AND Books.ISBN = BooksAuthors.ISBN
AND BooksAuthors.Author = Authors.Author
AND Authors.Name = ?
```

4. The results of the query are displayed in the results text box.

5. When the user selects Change price, then the update query is constructed and executed. The query is quite complex because the WHERE clause of the UPDATE statement needs the publisher *code* and we only know the publisher *name*. This problem is solved with a nested subquery:

```
UPDATE Books
SET Price = Price + price change
WHERE Books.Publisher_Id =
    (SELECT Publisher_Id
    FROM Publishers
    WHERE Name = publisher name)
```

NOTE: Nested subqueries are explained in most books on SQL, the book by Martin and Leben mentioned earlier for example.

6. We initialize the connection and statement objects in the constructor. We hang on to them for the life of the program. Right before the program exits, we call the `dispose` method and Java closes these objects.

```
class QueryDB extends Frame
{  QueryDB()
   {  con = DriverManager.getConnection(url, user,
         password);
      stmt = con.createStatement();
         . . .
   }
      . . .
   void dispose()
   {  stmt.close();
      con.close();
   }
      . . .
   Connection con;
   Statement stmt;
}
```

Example 14-2 is the complete program code.

Example 14-2: QueryDB.java

```
import java.net.*;
import java.sql.*;
import java.awt.*;
import java.util.*;

public class QueryDB extends Frame
{  public QueryDB()
   {  GridBagLayout gbl = new GridBagLayout();
      setLayout(gbl);
      GridBagConstraints gbc = new GridBagConstraints();
      authors = new Choice();
      authors.addItem("Any");
      publishers = new Choice();
      publishers.addItem("Any");
      result = new TextArea(4, 50);
      result.setEditable(false);
      priceChange = new TextField(8);
      priceChange.setText("-5.00");

      try
      {  Class.forName("jdbc.odbc.JdbcOdbcDriver"); // force
            //loading of driver
         String url = "jdbc:odbc:corejava";
         String user = "sa";
         String password = "";
         con = DriverManager.getConnection(url, user,
            password);
         stmt = con.createStatement();
```

```
        String query = "SELECT Name FROM Authors";
        ResultSet rs = stmt.executeQuery(query);
        while (rs.next())
            authors.addItem(rs.getString(1));

        query = "SELECT Name FROM Publishers";
        rs = stmt.executeQuery(query);
        while (rs.next())
            publishers.addItem(rs.getString(1));
    }
    catch(Exception e)
    {   result.setText("Error " + e);
    }

    gbc.fill = GridBagConstraints.NONE;
    gbc.weightx = 100;
    gbc.weighty = 100;
    add(this, authors, gbl, gbc, 0, 0, 2, 1);
    add(this, publishers, gbl, gbc, 2, 0, 2, 1);
    gbc.fill = GridBagConstraints.NONE;
    add(this, new Button("Query"), gbl, gbc, 0, 1, 1, 1);
    add(this, new Button("Change prices"), gbl, gbc, 2, 1,
        1, 1);
    add(this, priceChange, gbl, gbc, 3, 1, 1, 1);
    gbc.fill = GridBagConstraints.BOTH;
    add(this, result, gbl, gbc, 0, 2, 4, 1);
}

private void add(Container p, Component c,
    GridBagLayout gbl, GridBagConstraints gbc,
    int x, int y, int w, int h)
{   gbc.gridx = x;
    gbc.gridy = y;
    gbc.gridwidth = w;
    gbc.gridheight = h;
    gbl.setConstraints(c, gbc);
    p.add(c);
}

public boolean action(Event evt, Object arg)
{   if (arg.equals("Query"))
    {   ResultSet rs = null;
        try
        {   String author = authors.getSelectedItem();
            String publisher = publishers.getSelectedItem();
            if (!author.equals("Any") &&
                !publisher.equals("Any"))
            {   if (authorPublisherQueryStmt == null)
```

```
     {  String authorPublisherQuery =
            "SELECT Books.Price, Books.Title " +
            "FROM Books, BooksAuthors, Authors,
              Publishers " +
            "WHERE Authors.Author =
              BooksAuthors.Author AND " +
            "BooksAuthors.ISBN = Books.ISBN AND " +
            "Books.Publisher_Id = Publishers.Publisher_Id
              AND " +
            "Authors.Name = ? AND " +
            "Publishers.Name = ?";
         authorPublisherQueryStmt =
            con.prepareStatement(authorPublisherQuery);
     }
     authorPublisherQueryStmt.setString(1, author);
     authorPublisherQueryStmt.setString(2, publisher);
     rs = authorPublisherQueryStmt.executeQuery();
}
else if (!author.equals("Any") &&
   publisher.equals("Any"))
{  if (authorQueryStmt == null)
   {  String authorQuery =
         "SELECT Books.Price, Books.Title " +
         "FROM Books, BooksAuthors, Authors " +
         "WHERE Authors.Author_Id = BooksAuthors.Author_Id
            AND " +
         "BooksAuthors.ISBN = Books.ISBN AND " +
         "Authors.Name = ?";
      authorQueryStmt =
         con.prepareStatement(authorQuery);
   }
   authorQueryStmt.setString(1, author);
   rs = authorQueryStmt.executeQuery();
}
else if (author.equals("Any") &&
   !publisher.equals("Any"))
{  if (publisherQueryStmt == null)
   {  String publisherQuery =
         "SELECT Books.Price, Books.Title " +
         "FROM Books, Publishers " +
         "WHERE Books.Publisher_Id =
            Publishers.Publisher_Id AND " +
         "Publishers.Name = ?";
      publisherQueryStmt =
         con.prepareStatement(publisherQuery);
   }
   publisherQueryStmt.setString(1, publisher);
   rs = publisherQueryStmt.executeQuery();
```

```
            }
            else
            {   if (allQueryStmt == null)
                {   String allQuery =
                        "SELECT Books.Price, Books.Title FROM
                            Books";
                    allQueryStmt =
                        con.prepareStatement(allQuery);
                }
                rs = allQueryStmt.executeQuery();
            }

            result.setText("");
            while (rs.next())
                result.appendText(rs.getString(1) + " | " +
                    rs.getString(2) + "\n");
            rs.close();
        }
        catch(Exception e)
        {   result.setText("Error " + e);
        }
        return true;
    }
    else if (arg.equals("Change prices"))
    {   String publisher = publishers.getSelectedItem();
        if (publisher.equals("Any"))
            result.setText
                ("I am sorry. I am afraid I cannot do that.");
        else
            try
            {   String updateStatement =
                    "UPDATE Books " +
                    "SET Price = Price + " +
                        priceChange.getText() +
                    "WHERE Books.Publisher = " +
                    "(SELECT Publisher_Id FROM Publishers WHERE
                        Name = '" +
                    publisher + "')";
                int r = stmt.executeUpdate(updateStatement);
                result.setText(r + " records updated.");
            }
            catch(Exception e)
            {   result.setText("Error " + e);
            }
        return true;
    }
    else return false;
}
```

```java
public boolean handleEvent(Event evt)
{  if (evt.id == Event.WINDOW_DESTROY)
   {  System.exit(0);
   }
   return super.handleEvent(evt);
}

public void dispose()
{  try
   {  stmt.close();
      con.close();
   }
   catch(SQLException e) {}
}

public static void main (String args[])
{  Frame f = new QueryDB();
   f.resize(400, 300);
   f.show();
}

private Choice authors;
private Choice publishers;
private TextField priceChange;
private TextArea result;
private Connection con;
private Statement stmt;
private PreparedStatement authorQueryStmt;
private PreparedStatement authorPublisherQueryStmt;
private PreparedStatement publisherQueryStmt;
private PreparedStatement allQueryStmt;
}
```

`java.sql.Connection`

* `PreparedStatement prepareStatement(String sql)`

  the string `sql` contains a SQL statement that may contain one or more ?
  parameter placeholders. The method returns a `PreparedStatement` object
  containing the pre-compiled statement.

`java.sql.PreparedStatement`

* `void setXXX(int n, XXX x)`
  (`XXX` is a type such as `int`, `double`, `String`, `Date`, etc.)

  sets the value of the nth parameter to x.

- `void clearParameters()`

  clears all current parameters in the prepared statement.

- `ResultSet executeQuery()`

  executes a prepared SQL query and returns a ResultSet object.

- `int executeUpdate()`

  executes the prepared SQL INSERT, UPDATE or DELETE statement represented by the `PreparedStatement` object. Returns the number of rows affected or O for DDL statements.

Metadata

In the last two sections, you saw how to populate, query and update database tables. However, JDBC can give you additional information about the *structure* of a database and its tables. For example you can get a list of the tables in a particular database or the column names and types of a table. This information is not useful when implementing a particular database. After all, if you design the tables, you know the tables and their structure. It is, however, extremely useful for programmers who write tools that work with any database.

In this section, we will show you how to write such a simple tool. This tool lets you browse all tables in a database.

The choice box on top displays all tables in the database. Select one of them, and the center of the frame is filled with the field names of that table and the values of the first record, as shown in Figure 14-5. Click "Next" to scroll through the records in the table.

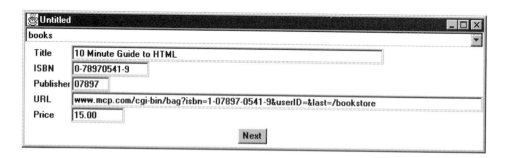

Figure 14-5: The ViewDB application

We fully expect tool vendors to develop much more sophisticated versions of programs like this one. For example, it then clearly would be possible to let the user edit the values or add new ones, and then update the database. We developed this program mostly to show you how such tools can be built.

In SQL, data that describe the database or one of its part is called *metadata* (to distinguish it from the actual data that is stored in the database). JDBC reports to us two kinds of metadata, about a database and about a result set.

To find out more about the database, you need to request an object of type `DatabaseMetaData` from the database connection.

```
DatabaseMetaData md = con.getMetaData();
```

Databases are complex, and the SQL standard leaves plenty of room for variability. There are well over a hundred methods in the `DatabaseMetaData` class to inquire about the database, including calls with exotic names such as

```
md.supportsCatalogsInPrivilegeDefinitions()
```

and

```
md.nullPlusNonNullIsNull()
```

Clearly, these are geared towards advanced users with special needs, in particular those who need to write highly portable code. In this section, we will study only one method that lets you list all tables in a database, and we won't even look at all *its* options. The call

```
String[] types = { "TABLE" };
ResultSet rs = md.getTables("", null, "%", types)
```

returns a result set that contains information of all tables in the database. (See the API note for other parameters to this method.)

Each row in the result set contains information about the table. We only care about the third entry, the name of the table. (Again, see the API note for the other columns.) Thus, `rs.getString(3)` is the table name. Here is the code that populates the choice box.

```
while (rs.next())
    tableNames.addItem(rs.getString(3));
rs.close();
```

The more interesting metadata are reported about result sets. Whenever you have a result set from a query, you can inquire about the number of columns and each column's name, type and field width.

We will make use of this information to make a label for each name and a text field of sufficient size for each value.

```
ResultSet rs = stmt.executeQuery("SELECT * FROM " + tableName);
ResultSetMetaData rsmd = rs.getMetaData();
for (int i = 1; i <= rsmd.getColumnCount(); i++)
{  String columnName = rsmd.getColumnLabel(i);
   int columnWidth = rsmd.getColumnDisplaySize(i);
   Label l = new Label(columnName);
   TextField tf = new TextField(columnWidth);
   . . .
}
```

The following steps provide a brief overview of the program.

1. Have the border layout put the table name choice component on the top, the table values in the center and the Next button in the bottom.

2. Connect to the database. Get the table names and fill them into the choice component.

3. When the user selects a table, make a query to see all its values. Get the metadata. Throw out the old components from the center panel. Create a grid bag layout of labels and text boxes. Store the text boxes in a vector. Call the pack method to have the window resize itself to exactly hold the newly added components. Then call showNextRow to show the first row.

4. The showNextRow method is called to show the first record, and also whenever the Next button is clicked. It gets the next row from the table and fills the column values into the text boxes. When at the end of the table, the result set is closed.

Example 14-3 is the program:

Example 14-3: ViewDB.java

```
import java.net.*;
import java.sql.*;
import java.awt.*;
import java.util.*;
public class ViewDB extends Frame
{  public ViewDB()
   {  tableNames = new Choice();
      dataPanel = new Panel();
      add("Center", dataPanel);
      Panel p = new Panel();
      p.add(new Button("Next"));
      add("South", p);

      fields = new Vector();

      try
```

```
   { Class.forName("jdbc.odbc.JdbcOdbcDriver"); // force
         loading of driver
      String url = "jdbc:odbc:corejava";
      String user = "sa";
      String password = "";
      con = DriverManager.getConnection(url, user,
         password);
      stmt = con.createStatement();

      md = con.getMetaData();
      String[] types = { "TABLE" };
      ResultSet mrs = md.getTables(null, "%", "%", types);

      while (mrs.next())
         tableNames.addItem(mrs.getString(3));
       mrs.close();
   }
   catch(Exception e)
   { System.out.println("Error " + e);
   }

   add("North", tableNames);
}

private void add(Container p, Component c,
   GridBagLayout gbl, GridBagConstraints gbc,
   int x, int y, int w, int h)
{  gbc.gridx = x;
   gbc.gridy = y;
   gbc.gridwidth = w;
   gbc.gridheight = h;
   gbl.setConstraints(c, gbc);
   p.add(c);
}

public boolean action(Event evt, Object arg)
{  if (evt.target.equals(tableNames))
   {  remove(dataPanel);
      dataPanel = new Panel();
      fields.removeAllElements();
      GridBagLayout gbl = new GridBagLayout();
      dataPanel.setLayout(gbl);
      GridBagConstraints gbc = new GridBagConstraints();
      gbc.fill = GridBagConstraints.NONE;
      gbc.anchor = GridBagConstraints.WEST;
      gbc.weightx = 100;
      gbc.weighty = 100;
```

```
        try
        {   String tableName = (String)arg;
            if (rs != null) rs.close();
            rs = stmt.executeQuery("SELECT * FROM " +
                tableName);
            ResultSetMetaData rsmd = rs.getMetaData();
            for (int i = 1; i <= rsmd.getColumnCount(); i++)
            {   String columnName = rsmd.getColumnLabel(i);
                int columnWidth = rsmd.getColumnDisplaySize(i);
                TextField tb = new TextField(columnWidth);
                fields.addElement(tb);
                add(dataPanel, new Label(columnName), gbl,
                    gbc, z 0, i - 1, 1, 1);
                add(dataPanel, tb, gbl, gbc, 1, i - 1, 1, 1);
            }
        }
        catch(Exception e)
        {   System.out.println("Error " + e);
        }
        add("Center", dataPanel);
        layout();
        pack();

        showNextRow();
        return true;
    }
    else if (arg.equals("Next"))
    {   showNextRow();
        return true;
    }
    else return false;
}

public void showNextRow()
{   if (rs == null) return;
    {   try
        {   if (rs.next())
            {   for (int i = 1; i <= fields.size(); i++)
                {   String field = rs.getString(i);
                    TextField tb =
                        (TextField)fields.elementAt(i - 1);
                    tb.setText(field);
                }
            }
            else
            {   rs.close();
                rs = null;
            }
```

```
          }
          catch(Exception e)
          {   System.out.println("Error " + e);
          }
      }
   }

   public boolean handleEvent(Event evt)
   {   if (evt.id == Event.WINDOW_DESTROY)
      {   System.exit(0);
      }
      return super.handleEvent(evt);
   }

   public static void main (String args[])
   {   Frame f = new ViewDB();
      f.resize(400, 300);
      f.show();
   }

   private Panel dataPanel;
   private Choice tableNames;
   private Vector fields;

   private Connection con;
   private Statement stmt;
   private DatabaseMetaData md;
   private ResultSet rs;
}
```

`java.sql.Connection`

• `DatabaseMetaData getMetaData()`

   returns the metadata for the connection as a `DataBaseMetaData` object.

`java.sql.DatabaseMetaData`

• `ResultSet getTables(String catalog, String schemaPattern, String tableNamePattern, String types[])`

   get a description of all tables in a catalog that match the schema and table name patterns and the type criteria. (A *schema* describes a group of related tables and access permissions. A *catalog* describes a related group of schemas. These concepts are important for structuring large databases.)

Parameters: catalog

schema Pattern

table Name Pattern

types []

The `catalog` and `schema` parameters can be " " to retrieve those tables without a catalog or schema, or `null` to return tables regardless of catalog or schema.

The `types` array contains the names of the table types to include. Typical types are "TABLE", "VIEW", "SYSTEM TABLE", "GLOBAL TEMPORARY", "LOCAL TEMPORARY", "ALIAS", "SYNONYM". If `types` is `null`, tables of all types are returned.

The result set has five columns, all of which are of type `String`, as shown in Table 14-4.

Table 14-4: Five columns of the result set

1	TABLE_CAT	table catalog (may be `null`)
2	TABLE_SCHEM	table schema (may be `null`)
3	TABLE_NAME	table name
4	TABLE_TYPE	table type
5	REMARKS	comment on the table

 `java.sql.ResultSet`

- `resultSetMetaData getMetaData()`

  gives you the metadata associated with the current `ResultSet` columns

 `interface java.sql.ResultSetMetaData`

- `int getColumnCount()`

  returns the number of columns in the current `ResultSet` object.

- `int getColumnDisplaySize(int column)`

  tells you what the usual maximum width of the column specified by the index parameter.

  Parameters: column   the column number

- `String getColumnLabel(int column)`

  gives you the suggested title for the column.

  Parameters: `column`   the column number

- `String getColumnName(int column)`

  gives the column name associated to the column index specified.

  Parameters: `column`   the column number

CHAPTER
15

- Remote Method Invocations
- Setting Up RMI
- Parameter Passing in Remote Methods
- Using RMI with Applets

Remote Objects

Periodically, the programming community starts thinking of "objects everywhere" as the solution to all its problems. The idea is to have a happy family of collaborating objects that communicate through a network. Like most bandwagons in programming, this plan contains a fair amount of hype that can obscure the utility of the concept. The purpose of this chapter is to

- Explain situations where distributed objects can be useful and where they are not.
- Show you how to use remote objects and the associated *remote method invocation* (RMI) for communicating between two machines running Java.

This chapter also covers the alpha2 version of the RMI interface. The CD-ROM contains the alpha2 library. The interface is changed for the beta version of RMI. We point out the relevant changes. You will need to adjust the code if you work with a more recent version of RMI.

NOTE: Remote objects and RMI are one of the two ways that JavaSoft proposes to let Java work with distributed objects. The other method is the Java-IDL interface. IDL (interface definition language) is designed to communicate between Java and objects created by other languages such as C++, via *object request brokers* (usually ones that satisfy CORBA standard). For more on the Java-IDL interface, see http://splash.javasoft.com/JavaIDL/pages/index.html.

Introduction to Remote Objects: The Roles of Client and Server

Suppose you want to collect information locally on a client computer and send the information across the Net to a server. For example, a user on a local machine may fill out an information request form. The form gets sent to the vendor's server, and the server sends back product information that the client can view, as shown in Figure 15-1.

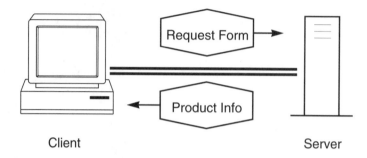

Client　　　　　　　　　　　　　　　　Server

Figure 15-1: Transmitting objects between client and server

You have seen two ways of doing this:

- Use a socket connection to send byte streams between the customer and the vendor computers.

- Use JDBC to make database queries and updates.

Both methods are useful in certain situations. For example, a socket connection is great if you just need to send raw data across the Net. JDBC is useful if the information that you are sending fits into the relational database's table model. But suppose your aren't in one of these two situations?

In a Java program, it is natural to implement the request form and the product information as objects. Using RMI, they can be transported as objects between the client and the server.

In contrast, if a program uses raw byte streams, there is a significant coding hassle: the programmer has to come up with appropriate ways of coding the data and the transmission protocols for sending the data. Of course, when connecting to a database with JDBC, all the details of communication protocols have been taken care of. But relational databases are not very effective for storing information that doesn't fit into a "rows-and-columns" database structure. In particular, they are not very good at storing collections of objects of different types, such as a mixture of employees, managers, contractors, and other types that may not be known yet. And, as you have seen, these kinds of heterogeneous object collections are very important in object-oriented programming.

How Java implements remote objects falls in between these two extremes. A transport layer handles the data encoding and the transmission and call protocols, so the programmer is not concerned with managing streams of bytes. You can use objects of any type and are not limited to the rigid structure of a database.

There is another major benefit of remote objects. Not only can you transport objects across a network, but you can invoke method calls on objects that sit on another computer *without* having to move those objects to the machine making the method call. Such method calls are called *remote method invocations*. For example, the client seeking product information can query a `Warehouse` object on the server. It calls a remote method `find` which has one parameter: the request form object. The `find` method returns an object to the client: the product information object. (See Figure 15-2.)

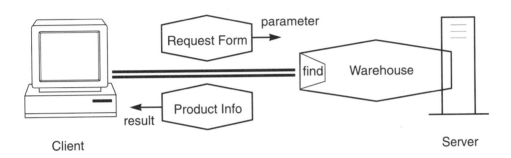

Figure 15-2: Invoking a remote method on a server object

The Java designers wanted to make it very obvious that the object executing the remote method call resides on different computers. We will see the details in the coming sections.

Remote Method Invocations

The central concept in the Java remote object implementation is a *remote method invocation* or RMI. Code on the client computer invokes a method on an object on the server. It is important to realize that the client/server terminology applies to a single method call only. The computer that runs the Java code that calls the remote method is the client for *that* call, and the computer hosting the object that processes the call is the server for *that* call. It is entirely possible that the roles are reversed somewhere down the road. The server of a previous call can itself become the client when it invokes a remote method on an object residing on another computer.

Stubs and Skeletons

When client code wants to invoke a remote method on a remote object, it actually calls a regular Java method that is encapsulated in a surrogate object called a *stub*. The stub resides on the client, not on the server. The stub takes the para-meters used in the remote method and packages them up as a block of bytes. This packaging uses a device-independent encoding for each parameter. For example, numbers are always sent in big-endian format. Strings and objects are a little trickier: they must be encoded in a way that uses no object references since object references point to memory locations on the client. These memory locations will not make sense on the server. The process of encoding the para-meters into a format that is suitable for transporting them across the Net is called *parameter marshalling*. Java uses the object serialization mechanism described in Chapter 11 for parameter marshalling. The stub method on the client builds an information block that consists of:

- An identifier of the remote object to be used;
- An operation number, describing the method to be called;
- The marshalled parameters.

It then sends this information to the server. On the server side, there is a *skeleton* object which makes sense out of the information contained in the packet and passes that information to the actual object executing the remote method. Specifically, the skeleton performs five actions for every remote method call:

- It unmarshals the parameters;
- It calls the desired method on the real remote object that lies on the server;
- It captures the return value or exception of the call on the server;
- It marshals that value;
- It sends a package consisting of the value in the marshalled form back to the stub on the client.

The stub unmarshals the return value or exception from the server. This becomes the return value of the remote method call. Or, if the remote method threw an exception, the stub rethrows it in the process space of the caller. Figure 15-3 shows the information flow of a remote method invocation.

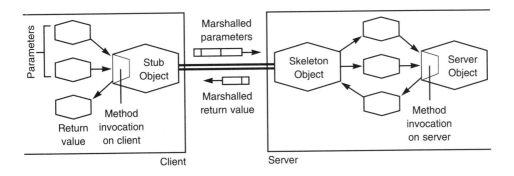

Figure 15-3: Stub and skeleton objects

This is obviously a complex process, but the good news is that it is completely automatic and, to a large extent, transparent for the Java programmer. Moreover, the designers of the Java remote object architecture tried hard to give remote objects the same "look and feel" as local objects. Nevertheless, there are important differences between local and remote objects, as we will see in this chapter.

Remote objects are garbage collected automatically, just like local objects are. However, the current distributed collector uses reference counting and cannot detect cycles of unreferenced objects. Cycles must be explicitly broken by the programmer.

The syntax for a remote method call is the same as for a local call. If `centralWarehouse` is a stub object for a central warehouse object on a remote (currently the client) machine and `getQuantity` is the method you want to invoke remotely, then a typical call looks like this:

```
centralWarehouse.getQuantity("SuperSucker 100 Vacuum Cleaner");
```

The client code always uses object variables whose type is an *interface* to access remote objects. For example, associated to this call would be an interface:

```
interface Warehouse
{  public int getQuantity(String); throws java.rmi.RemoteException
   . . .
}
```

and an object declaration for a variable that will implement the interface:

```
Warehouse centralWarehouse;
```

Of course, interfaces are abstract entities that only spell out what methods can be called along with their signatures. Variables whose type is an interface must always be bound to an actual object of some type. in the case of remote objects this is a *stub class*. The client program does not actually know the type of those objects. The stub classes and the associated objects are created automatically.

While the Java designers did a good job hiding many of the details of remote method invocation from the Java programmer, there are still a number of techniques and caveats that must be mastered. That will be the topic of the rest of this chapter.

Dynamic Class Loading

When you pass a remote object to another Java program, either as a parameter or return value of a remote method, then that program must be able to deal with the associated stub object. That is, it must have the Java code for the stub class. The stub methods don't do a lot of interesting work. They just marshal and unmarshal the parameters and then connect this information with the server. Of course, they do all this work transparently to the programmer.

Furthermore, the classes for parameters, return values and exception objects may need to be loaded as well. This can be more complex than one might think. For example, a remote method may be declared with a certain return type that is known to the client, but actually return an object of a derived class that is not known to the client. The class loader will then load that derived class.

While unglamorous, the stub classes must be available to the running client program. One obvious way for this to happen is if these classes are available on the local file system. If they aren't, then Java is quite willing to load them from another place. It does this by a process similar to what is used when running applets in a browser.

With an applet, a browser loads the applet class and checks the byte codes for validity. The loading of the applet class from a remote location is the job of a *class loader*. The applet class loader is quite restrictive. It will only load classes from the same machine that served the web page containing the applet. The stub class loader can be configured to permit more. For example, you can allow it to search for stub code on other network locations. This is particularly useful for distributed Java programs where a number of processors that are cooperating to perform a difficult computation will all want to fetch the same stubs from a central location.

The class loader determines where the classes may be loaded from. The *security manager* determines what these classes can do when they run. You have seen in Chapters 8 and 13 that the applet security manager won't let classes read and write local files or make socket connection to third parties. The stub security manager is even more restrictive than the applet security manager. Since it only governs the behavior of stub code, the stub security manager prevents all activities except those that stubs must be able to carry out. This is a safety mechanism that protects the program from viruses in stub code. For specialized applications, Java programmers can substitute their own class loaders and security managers, but those provided by the RMI system suffice for normal usage.

Setting Up RMI

Running even the simplest remote object example requires quite a bit more setup than running a standalone Java program or applet. You must run Java programs on both the server and client computers. The necessary object information must be separated into client-side interfaces and server-side implementations. There is also a special query mechanism that allows the client to locate objects on the server.

To get started with the actual coding, we want to walk you through each of these requirements using a simple example. In our first example, we will generate a couple of objects of a type `Product` on the server computer. The client computer will run a Java program that locates and queries these objects.

NOTE: You can try out this example on a single computer or on a pair of networked computers. The code is set up to run on a single computer. If you want to run the server code remotely, you need to set the URL of the server in the client code and recompile. We indicate where you need to make these changes.

You also need to distribute the class files between the client and the server. The server program classes, together with the interface, stub and skeleton classes, must be on the server. The client program, together with the interface and stub classes, must be on the client.

Even if you run this code on a single computer, you must have network services available. In particular be sure that you have TCP/IP running. If your computer doesn't have a network card, you can use the dialup networking feature under Windows 95 to set up a TCP/IP connection. (Consult the Windows 95 documentation to see how to do this.)

Interfaces and Implementations

The client program needs to manipulate server objects, but it doesn't actually have copies of them. The objects themselves reside on the server. The client must still know what it can do with those objects. Their capabilities are expressed in an *interface* that is shared between the client and server, and so resides simultaneously on both machines.

```
interface Product // shared by client and server
   extends Remote
{  public String getDescription() throws RemoteException
}
```

Just as in this example, *all* interfaces for remote objects must extend the `Remote` interface defined in the `java.rmi` package. All the methods in those interfaces must also declare that they will throw a `RemoteException`. The reason is that remote method calls are inherently less reliable than local calls—it is always possible that a remote call fails. The server or the network connection may be temporarily unavailable, or there may be a network problem. The client code must be prepared to deal with this. For these reasons, Java forces the programmer to catch the `RemoteException` with *every* remote method call, and to specify the appropriate action to take when the call does not succeed.

The client accesses the server object through a stub that implements this interface.

```
Product p = ...; // see below how the client gets a stub
                 // reference to a remote object
String d = p.getDescription();
System.out.println(d);
```

In the next section, we will see ways the client can obtain such a reference to a remote object.

On the server side, you must implement the class that actually carries out the methods advertised in the remote interface.

```
class ProductImpl // server
   extends UnicastRemoteServer
   implements Product
{  public ProductImpl(String d) throws RemoteException
      { descr = d; }
   public String getDescription()
   {  return "I am a " + descr + ". Buy me!";
   }
   private String descr;
}
```

This class has a single method, `getDescription`, that can be called from the remote client. It is a server class, since it extends `UnicastRemoteServer` which is a concrete Java class that makes objects remotely accessible.

> NOTE: When using RMI, there is a somewhat bewildering inflation of classes. In this chapter, we use a uniform naming convention for all of our examples that, hopefully, makes it easier to recognize the purpose of each class. (See Table 15-1.) You can avoid the "server" classes by putting the server methods into the `main` functions of the "implementation" classes.

Table 15-1

no suffix (e.g. `Product`)	a remote interface
`Impl` suffix (e.g. `ProductImpl`)	a server class implementing that interface
`Server` suffix (e.g. `ProductServer`)	a server program that creates server objects
`Client` suffix (e.g. `ProductClient`)	a client program that calls remote methods
`_Stub` suffix (e.g. `ProductImpl_Stub`)	a stub class that is automatically generated by the `rmic` program
`_Skel` suffix (e.g. `ProductImpl_Skel`)	a skeleton class that is automatically generated by the `rmic` program

Actually, all server classes must extend the class `RemoteServer` from the `java.rmi.server` package. But this is an abstract class that only defines the basic mechanisms for the communication between server objects and their remote stubs. The `UnicastRemoteServer` class that comes with RMI extends the `RemoteServer` abstract class and is concrete—so it can be used without writing any code. It is the "path of least resistance" for a server class to derive from `UnicastRemoteServer`, and all server classes in this chapter will do so. Figure 15-4 shows the inheritance relationship between these classes.

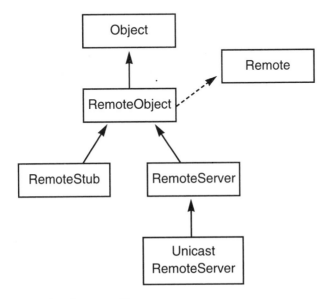

Figure 15-4: Inheritance diagram

A `UnicastRemoteServer` object resides on a server. It must be alive when a service is requested, and reachable through the TCP/IP protocol. This is the class that we will be extending for all the server classes in this book and is the only server class available in the current version of the RMI package. Sun or third party vendors may, in the future, design other classes for use by servers for RMI. For example, Sun is already talking about a `MulticastRemoteServer` class for objects that are replicated over multiple servers. Other possibilities are for objects that are activated on demand or ones that can use other communications protocols, such as UDP.

> NOTE: Sun has announced their intention to change the names of several classes used in RMI. This chance will likely be effective with the beta release. We use the names of the alpha2 release in this chapter, which is also the version on the CD-ROM. If you use a newer version of the RMI package, then you need to change the names. Here are the changes:
>
> | alpha2 | beta |
> |---|---|
> | UnicastRemoteServer | UnicastRemoteObject |
> | StubSecurityManager | RMISecurityManager |
> | StubClassLoader | RMIClassLoader |
>
> The `RMISecurityManager` class will be in the `java.rmi` package, not in `java.rmi.server`.

Creating Server Objects

For a client to access a remote object that exists on the server, there must be a mechanism to obtain a remote reference that can access the remote object.

There are a number of methods for the client code to gain access to a server object. The most common one is to call a remote method whose return value is a server object. When a server object is returned to the client as a method result, the RMI mechanism automatically sends back a remote reference, not the actual object. There is, however, a chicken-and-egg problem here. The *first* server object needs to be located some other way. That object typically has plenty of methods to return other objects. The Sun RMI library provides a
bootstrap registry service for this purpose.

The server registers objects with the bootstrap registry service, and the client retrieves stubs to those objects. A server object is registered by giving the bootstrap registry service a reference to the object and a *name*. The name is a string that is (hopefully) unique.

```
// server
ProductImpl p1 = new ProductImpl("Blackwell Toaster");
Naming.bind("toaster", p1);
```

The client code gets a stub to access that server object by specifying the server name and the object name in a URL-style format:

```
// client
String url = "";
    // change to rmi://www.yourserver.com/
    // if server runs remotely on www.yourserver.com
Product c1 = (Product)Naming.lookup(url + "toaster");
```

> NOTE: Because it is notoriously difficult to keep names unique in a global registry, you should not use this as the general method for locating objects on the server. Instead, there should be relatively few *named* server objects registered with the bootstrap service. In our example, we temporarily violate this rule and register relatively trivial objects. The reason is that we need to show you the mechanics for registering and locating objects.

However, we aren't quite ready to register any objects yet. Because the bootstrap registry service must be available, it also must stay active for the duration. Under Windows 95 or NT, you can do this by executing the statement:

```
start java java.rmi.registry.RegistryImpl
```

at a DOS prompt or from the Run dialog box. (The `start` command is a Windows command that starts a program in a new window.)

Under Unix, use:

```
java java.rmi.registry.RegistryImpl &
```

> Note: This process will be simpler in the beta version of RMI. You just run the `rmiregistry` program supplied with the JDK.

> TIP: You must see the desired class path **before** starting the registry service. Otherwise, the registry won't find the stub classes.

Next, you need to generate skeletons and stubs for the `ProductImpl` class. Recall that skeletons and stubs are on the server-level and client-level classes and that these are used by the RMI mechanism in order to marshal (encode and send) the parameters and marshal the results of method calls across the network. The Java programmer never uses these classes directly. Moreover, they need *not* be written by hand. The `rmic` tool generates them automatically as in the following example.

```
rmic ProductImpl
```

This call to the rmic tool generates two class files named, `ProductImpl_Skel.class` and `ProductImpl_Stub.class`. If your class is in a package, you must call `rmic` with the full package name.

NOTE: Remember to first compile the Java source file with `javac` before running `rmic`. If you are generating stubs and skeletons for a class in a package, you must give `rmic` the full package name.

All server and client programs that use RMI need to install a security manager to control the code of any skeletons and stubs that are dynamically loaded off a network location. Java provides such a security manager, the `StubSecurityManager`. We install it with the instruction

```
System.setSecurityManager(new StubSecurityManager());
```

NOTE: In this case, we do not actually need dynamic class loading. All the classes are available in the local file system. Nevertheless, Java insists that a security manager is in place. For applets, there is already a security manager that makes sure that the applet code does not do any harm. When dealing with applications, there is no default security manager, so we always need to set a security manager when using RMI.

Here is a complete program that registers two `Product` objects under the names `toaster` and `microwave`.

Example 15-1: ProductServer.java

```
import java.rmi.*;
import java.rmi.server.*;

public class ProductServer
{  public static void main(String args[])
   {  System.setSecurityManager(new StubSecurityManager());

      try
      {  ProductImpl p1
             = new ProductImpl("Blackwell Toaster");
         ProductImpl p2
             = new ProductImpl("ZapXpress Microwave Oven");

         Naming.rebind("toaster", p1);
         Naming.rebind("microwave", p2);
      }
      catch(Exception e)
      {  System.out.println("Error: " + e);
      }
   }
}
```

Once you compile this program, you need to run it as a separate process. Under Windows, use the command:

```
start java ProductServer
```

Under Unix, use the command

```
java ProductServer &
```

> If you run the server program as
>
> ```
>   java ProductServer
> ```
>
> then the program will never exit normally. This seems strange—after all, the program just creates two objects and registers them. Actually, the `main` function does exit immediately after registration as you would expect. But, when you create an object of a class that extends `UnicastRemoteServer`, Java starts a separate thread that keeps the program alive indefinitely. Thus, the program stays around in order to allow clients to connect to it.

TIP: The JDK contains a command `javaw` that starts the Java interpreter as a separate Windows process and keeps it running. Older versions of the documentation recommend that you use `javaw`, not `start java`, to run a Java session in the background in Windows for RMI. That is not a good idea, for two reasons. Windows has no tool to kill a `javaw` background process—it does not show up in the task list. It turns out that you need to kill and restart the bootstrap registry service when you change the stub of a registered class. To kill a process that you started with the `start` command, all you have to do is click on the window and hit Ctrl+C.

There is another important reason. When a server process is run using `javaw`, messages that are sent to the output or error streams are discarded. In particular they *are not* displayed anywhere. If you want to see output or error messages, use `start` instead. Then error messages show up on the console. And trust us, you will want to see these messages. There are lots of things that can go wrong when you experiment with RMI. The most common error is probably that you forget to run `rmic`. Then the server complains about missing stubs. If you use `javaw`, you won't see that error message and you'll scratch your head wondering why the client can't find the server objects.

Before writing the client program, let's verify that we succeeded in registering the remote objects. The `Naming` class has a method `list` that returns a list of all currently registered names. Here is a simple program that lists the names in the registry.

Example 15-2: ShowBindings.java

```java
import java.rmi.*;
import java.rmi.server.*;

public class ShowBindings
```

```
{  public static void main(String[] args)
   {  System.setSecurityManager(new StubSecurityManager());
      try
      {  String[] bindings = Naming.list("");
         for (int i = 0; i < bindings.length; i++)
            System.out.println(bindings[i]);
      }
      catch(Exception e)
      {  System.out.println("Error: " + e);
      }
   }
}
```

In our case, its output is

```
rmi:/toaster
rmi:/microwave
```

The Client Side

Now we can write the client program that asks each newly registered product objects to print its description.

Example 15-3: ProductClient.java

```
import java.rmi.*;
import java.rmi.server.*;

public class ProductClient
{  public static void main(String[] args)
   {  System.setSecurityManager(new StubSecurityManager());
      String url = "";
         // change to "rmi://www.yourserver.com/"
         // when server runs on remote machine
         // www.yourserver.com
      try
      {  Product c1 = (Product)Naming.lookup(url + "toaster");
         Product c2 = (Product)Naming.lookup(url +
            "microwave");
         System.out.println(c1.getDescription());
         System.out.println(c2.getDescription());
      }
      catch(Exception e)
      {  System.out.println("Error " + e);
      }
      System.exit(0);  // not necessary for beta
   }
}
```

You run this program on the client, in the usual way:

```
java ProductClient.
```

It simply prints

```
I am a Blackwell Toaster. Buy me!
I am a ZapXpress Microwave Oven. Buy me!
```

This doesn't sound all that impressive, but consider what goes on behind the scenes when Java executes the call to the `getDescription` method. The client program has a reference to a stub object that it obtained from the `lookup` method. It calls the `getDescription` method which sends a network message to the skeleton object on the server side. The skeleton object invokes the `getDescription` method on the `ProductImpl` object located on the server. That method computes a string. The string is returned to the skeleton, sent across the network, received by the stub and returned as the result. See Figure 15-5.

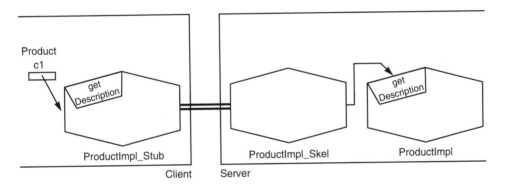

Figure 15-5: Calling a remote method

Summary

Here is a summary of the steps you need to take to get remote method invocation working:

1. Place the interface class extending `Remote` on the server and the client;

2. Place the implementation class extending `RemoteObject` on the server;

3. Generate stubs and skeletons on the server by running `rmic`. Copy the stubs to the client;

4. Start the bootstrap registry service on the server;

5. Start a program that creates and registers objects of the implementation class on the server;

6. Run a program that looks up server objects and invokes remote methods on the client.

java.rmi.server.Naming

*   `static Remote lookup(String url)`

    Returns the remote object for the URL. Throws the `NotBound` exception if the name is not currently bound.

*   `static void bind(String name, Remote obj)`

    Binds `name` to the remote object `obj`. Throws the `AlreadyBoundException` if the object is already bound.

*   `static void unbind(String name)`

    Unbinds the name. Throws the `NotBound` exception if the name is not currently bound.

*   `static void rebind(String name, Remote obj)`

    Binds `name` to the remote object `obj`. Replaces any existing binding.

*   `static String[] list(String url)`

    Returns an array of strings of the URLs in the registry located at the given URL. The array contains a snapshot of the names present in the registry.

Parameter Passing in Remote Methods

You often want to pass parameters to remote objects. This section explains some of the techniques for doing so—along with some of the pitfalls.

Passing Non-Remote Objects

When Java passes a remote object from the server to the client, the client receives a stub. Using the stub, it can manipulate the server object by invoking remote methods. The object, however, stays on the server. It is also possible to pass and return *any* objects via a remote method call, not just those that implement the `Remote` interface. For example, the `getDescription` method of the preceding section returned a `String` object. That string was created on the server and had to be transported to the client. Since `String` does not implement the `Remote` interface, the client cannot return a string stub object. Instead, the client gets a *copy* of the string. Then, after the call, the client has its own `String` object to work. This means that there is no need for any further connection to any object on the server to deal with that string.

Whenever an object that is not a remote object needs to be transported from one Java virtual machine to another, the Java virtual machine makes a copy and sends that copy across the network connection. This is very different from parameter passing in a local method. When you pass objects into a local method, or return them as method results, only object *references* are passed. However, object references are memory addresses of objects in the local Java virtual machine. This information is meaningless to a different Java virtual machine.

It is not difficult to imagine how a copy of a string can be transported across a network. Java can also make copies of objects that instantiate more general classes using the serialization mechanism described in Chapter 11. Currently, all classes are serializable by default. In Java 1.1, only those classes that implement the `serializable` interface are serializable by default. However, this means that Java will *not* be able to copy the information in classes for which the programmer has explicitly restricted copying or those classes where the Java language itself prohibits serialization. (See Chapter 11 for how to restrict serialization.)

The following program shows the copying of parameters and return values in action. This program is a simple application that lets you shop for a gift. The user runs a program on the client that gathers information about the gift recipient, in this case, age, sex, and hobbies (see Figure 15-6).

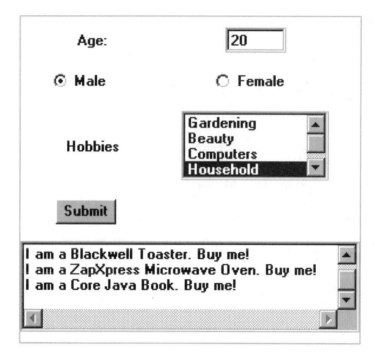

Figure 15-6: Obtaining product suggestions from the server

An object of type `Customer` is then sent to the server. Since `Customer` is not a remote object, a copy of the object is made on the server. The server program sends back a vector of products. The vector contains those products that match the customer profile, and it always contains that one item that will delight anyone, namely a copy of the book *Core Java*. Again, `Vector` is not a remote class, so the vector is copied from the server back to its client. As described in Chapter 11, the serialization mechanism makes copies of all objects that are referenced inside a copied object. In our case, it makes a copy of all vector entries as well. We added an extra complexity: The entries are actually remote `Product` objects. Thus, the recipient gets a copy of the vector, filled with stub objects to the products on the server (see Figure 15-7).

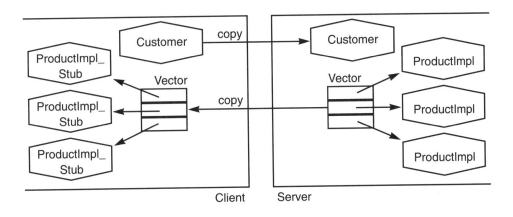

Figure 15-7: Copying local parameter and result objects

To summarize, remote objects are passed across the network as stubs. Non-remote objects are copied. All of this is automatic and requires no programmer intervention.

Whenever a remote method is called, the stub makes a package that contains copies of all parameter values and sends it to the server, using the object serialization mechanism to marshal the parameters. The server skeleton unmarshals them. Naturally, the process can be quite slow—especially when the parameter objects are large.

Let us now look at the complete program. First, we have the interfaces for the product and warehouse services.

Example 15-4: Product.java

```
import java.rmi.*;

public interface Product
    extends Remote
{   String getDescription()
        throws RemoteException;

    static final int MALE = 1;
    static final int FEMALE = 2;
    static final int BOTH = MALE + FEMALE;
}
```

Example 15-5: Warehouse.java

```
import java.rmi.*;
import java.util.*;

public interface Warehouse
    extends Remote
{   public Vector find(Customer c)
        throws RemoteException;
}
```

Example 15-6 shows the implementation for the product service. Products store a description, an age range, the buyer's appropriate sex (male, female or both), and the matching hobby. Note that this class implements the getDescription method advertised in the Product interface, and it also implements another method, match, which is not a part of that interface. The match method is an example of a *local method*, a method that can only be called from the local program, not remotely. Since the match method is local, it need not be prepared to throw a RemoteException.

Example 15-6: ProductImpl.java

```
import java.rmi.*;
import java.rmi.server.*;

public class ProductImpl
    extends UnicastRemoteServer
    implements Product
{   public ProductImpl(String n, int s, int age1, int age2,
        String h)
        throws RemoteException
    {   name = n;
        ageLow = age1;
        ageHigh = age2;
        sex = s;
        hobby = h;
    }

    public boolean match(Customer c) // local method
    {   if (c.getAge() < ageLow || c.getAge() > ageHigh)
            return false;
        if (!c.hasHobby(hobby)) return false;
        if ((sex & c.getSex()) == 0) return false;
        return true;
    }
}
```

```
    public String getDescription()
       throws RemoteException
    {  return "I am a " + name + ". Buy me!";
    }

    private String name;
    private int ageLow;
    private int ageHigh;
    private int sex;
    private String hobby;
}
```

Example 15-7 shows the implementation for the warehouse service. Like the
ProductImpl class, the WarehouseImpl class too has remote and local
methods. The add method is local. It is used by the server to add products to
the warehouse. The find method is remote. It is used to find items in the
warehouse.

To show you that the Customer object is actually copied, the find method of
the WarehouseImpl class actually clears the customer object it receives. When
the remote method returns, the WarehouseClient displays the customer
object that it sent to the server. As you will see, that object has not changed. The
server only cleared *its copy*. In this case, the clear operation serves no useful
purpose. It only demonstrates that local objects are copied when they are passed
as parameters.

Example 15-7: WarehouseImpl.java

```
import java.rmi.*;
import java.util.*;
import java.rmi.server.*;


public class WarehouseImpl
    extends UnicastRemoteServer
    implements Warehouse
{  public WarehouseImpl()
       throws RemoteException
    {  products = new Vector();
    }

    public synchronized void add(ProductImpl p) // local method
    {  products.addElement(p);
    }
```

```
public synchronized Vector find(Customer c)
    throws RemoteException
{  Vector result = new Vector();
    for (int i = 0; i < products.size(); i++)
    {  ProductImpl p = (ProductImpl)products.elementAt(i);
        if (p.match(c)) result.addElement(p);
    }
    result.addElement(new ProductImpl("Core Java Book",
        0, 200, Product.BOTH, ""));
    c.reset();
    return result;
}

private Vector products;
}
```

In general, the methods of server classes such as `ProductImpl` and `WarehouseImpl` should be `synchronized`. Then it is possible for multiple client stubs to make simultaneous calls to a server object, even if some of the methods change the state of the server. See Chapter 12 for more details on synchronized methods. In Example 15-7, we synchronize the methods of the `WarehouseImpl` class because it is conceivable that the local `add` and the remote `find` methods are called simultaneously. We don't synchronize the methods of the `ProductImpl` class because the product server objects don't change their state.

Example 15-8 shows the server program that creates a warehouse object and registers it with the bootstrap registry service.

Example 15-8: WarehouseServer.java

```
import java.rmi.*;
import java.rmi.server.*;

public class WarehouseServer
{  public static void main(String args[])
    {  System.setSecurityManager(new StubSecurityManager());
        try
        {  WarehouseImpl w = new WarehouseImpl();
            fillWarehouse(w);
            Naming.rebind("central_warehouse", w);
        }
        catch(Exception e)
        {  System.out.println("Error: " + e);
        }
    }
```

```
public static void fillWarehouse(WarehouseImpl w)
    throws RemoteException
{   w.add(new ProductImpl("Blackwell Toaster", Product.BOTH,
        18, 200, "Household"));
    w.add(new ProductImpl("ZapXpress Microwave Oven",
        Product.BOTH,
        18, 200, "Household"));
    w.add(new ProductImpl("Jimbo After Shave", Product.MALE,
        18, 200, "Beauty"));
    w.add(new ProductImpl("Handy Hand Grenade", Product.MALE,
        20, 60, "Gardening"));
    w.add(new ProductImpl("DirtDigger Steam Shovel",
        Product.MALE,
        20, 60, "Gardening"));
    w.add(new ProductImpl("U238 Weed Killer", Product.BOTH,
        20, 200, "Gardening"));
    w.add(new ProductImpl("Van Hope Cosmetic Set",
        Product.FEMALE,
        15, 45, "Beauty"));
    w.add(new ProductImpl("Persistent Java Fragrance",
        Product.FEMALE,
        15, 45, "Beauty"));
    w.add(new ProductImpl("Rabid Rodent Computer Mouse",
        Product.BOTH,
        6, 40, "Computers"));
    w.add(new ProductImpl("Learn Bad Java Habits in 21 Days
        Book", Product.BOTH,
        20, 200, "Computers"));
    w.add(new ProductImpl("My first Espresso Maker",
        Product.FEMALE,
        6, 10, "Household"));
    w.add(new ProductImpl("JavaJungle Eau de Cologne",
        Product.FEMALE,
        20, 200, "Beauty"));
    w.add(new ProductImpl("Fast/Wide SCSI Coffee Maker",
        Product.MALE,
        20, 50, "Computers"));
    w.add(new ProductImpl("ClueLess Network Computer",
        Product.BOTH,
        6, 200, "Computers"));
    }
}
```

> NOTE: Remember that you must start the registry and the server program and keep both running (with `start java` or `java &`) before you start the client.

Example 15-9 shows the code for the client. When the user clicks the Submit button, a new customer object is generated and passed to the remote `find` method. Then the customer record is displayed in the text area (to prove that the `clear` call in the server did not affect it). Finally, the product descriptions of the returned products in the vector are added to the text area. Note that each `getDescription` call is again a remote method invocation.

Example 15-9: WarehouseClient.java

```java
import java.awt.*;
import java.rmi.*;
import java.rmi.server.*;
import java.util.*;
import corejava.*;

public class WarehouseClient extends Frame
{   public WarehouseClient()
    {   GridBagLayout gbl = new GridBagLayout();
        setLayout(gbl);

        GridBagConstraints gbc = new GridBagConstraints();
        gbc.fill = GridBagConstraints.NONE;
        gbc.weightx = 100;
        gbc.weighty = 100;
        add(this, new Label("Age:"), gbl, gbc, 0, 0, 1, 1);
        add(this, age = new IntTextField(0, 0, 200, 4), gbl,
            gbc, 1, 0, 1, 1);
        CheckboxGroup cbg = new CheckboxGroup();
        add(this, male = new Checkbox("Male", cbg, true), gbl,
            gbc, 0, 1, 1, 1);
         add(this, female = new Checkbox("Female", cbg, true),
             gbl, gbc, 1, 1, 1, 1);
        add(this, new Label("Hobbies"), gbl, gbc, 0, 2, 1, 1);
        hobbies = new List(4, true);
        hobbies.addItem("Gardening");
        hobbies.addItem("Beauty");
        hobbies.addItem("Computers");
        hobbies.addItem("Household");
        hobbies.addItem("Sports");
        add(this, hobbies, gbl, gbc, 1, 2, 1, 1);
        add(this, new Button("Submit"), gbl, gbc, 0, 3, 1, 1);
        result = new TextArea(4, 40);
        result.setEditable(false);
```

```
        add(this, result, gbl, gbc, 0, 4, 2, 1);

        System.setSecurityManager(new StubSecurityManager());
        String url = "";
            // change to "rmi://www.yourserver.com/"
            // when server runs on remote machine
            // www.yourserver.com
        try
        {   centralWarehouse =
            (Warehouse)Naming.lookup("central_warehouse");
        }
        catch(Exception e)
        {   System.out.println("Error: Can't connect to
            warehouse. " + e);
        }
    }

    private void add(Container p, Component c,
        GridBagLayout gbl, GridBagConstraints gbc,
        int x, int y, int w, int h)
    {   gbc.gridx = x;
        gbc.gridy = y;
        gbc.gridwidth = w;
        gbc.gridheight = h;
        gbl.setConstraints(c, gbc);
        p.add(c);
    }

    public boolean action(Event evt, Object arg)
    {   if (arg.equals("Submit"))
        {   if (age.isValid())
            {   Customer c = new Customer(age.getValue(),
                    (male.getState() ? Product.MALE : 0)
                    + (female.getState() ? Product.FEMALE : 0),
                    hobbies.getSelectedItems());
                String t = c + "\n";
                try
                {   Vector result = centralWarehouse.find(c);
                    for (int i = 0; i < result.size(); i++)
                    {   Product p = (Product)result.elementAt(i);
                        t += p.getDescription() + "\n";
                    }
                }
                catch(Exception e)
                {   t = "Error: " + e;
                }
                result.setText(t);
            }
```

```
            return true;
        }
        else return false;
    }

    public boolean handleEvent(Event evt)
    {   if (evt.id == Event.WINDOW_DESTROY) System.exit(0);
        return super.handleEvent(evt);
    }

    public static void main(String[] args)
    {   Frame f = new WarehouseClient();
        f.resize(300, 300);
        f.show();
    }

    private Warehouse centralWarehouse;
    private IntTextField age;
    private Checkbox male;
    private Checkbox female;
    private List hobbies;
    private TextArea result;
}
```

Passing Remote Objects

Passing remote objects from the server to the client is simple. The client receives a stub object, then saves it in an object variable whose type is the same as the remote interface. It can now access the actual object on the server through this variable. The client can copy this variable in its own local machine—all those copies are simply references to the same stub.

It is important to note that only the *remote interfaces* can be accessed through the stub. A remote interface is any interface extending Remote. All local methods are inaccessible through the stub. A local method is any method that is not defined in a remote interface. Local methods can only run on the virtual machine containing the actual object.

Stubs are generated only from classes that implement a remote interface, and only the methods specified in the interfaces are provided in the stub classes. If a derived class doesn't implement a remote interface but a base class does, and an object of the derived class is passed to a remote method, only the base class methods are accessible. To understand this better, consider the following example. We derive a class BookImpl from ProductImpl:

```
class BookImpl extends ProductImpl
{  public BookImpl(String title, String theISBN,
       int sex, int age1, int age2, String hobby)
   {  super(title + " Book", sex, age1, age2, hobby);
      ISBN = theISBN;
   }
   public String getStockCode() { return ISBN; }
   String ISBN;
}
```

Now suppose we pass a book object to a remote method, either as a parameter or as a return value. The recipient obtains a stub object. But that stub is not a book stub. Instead, it is a stub to the base class `ProductImpl` since only that class implements a remote interface (see Figure 15-8).

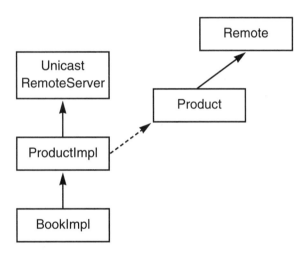

Figure 15-8: Inheritance diagram

A remote class can implement multiple interfaces. For example, the `BookImpl` class can implement a second interface in addition to `Product`. Here we define a remote interface `StockUnit` and have the `BookImpl` class implement it.

```
interface StockUnit extends Remote
{  public String getStockCode() throws RemoteException;
}

class BookImpl extends ProductImpl implements StockUnit
{  public BookImpl(String title, String theISBN,
       int sex, int age1, int age2, String hobby)
```

```
      throws RemoteException
{   super(title + " Book", sex, age1, age2, hobby);
      ISBN = theISBN;
}
public String getStockCode() throws RemoteException
{ return ISBN; }

      private String ISBN;
}
```

Figure 15-9 shows the inheritance diagram.

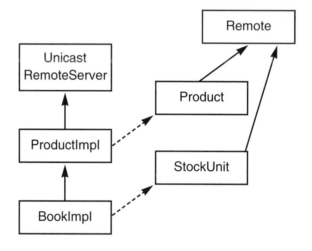

Figure 15-9: Inheritance diagram

NOTE: There is a limitation in the alpha2 version of `rmic`. It does not yet pick up inherited interfaces. As a workaround, until this is fixed, repeat the interface of the base class:

```
class BookImpl extends ProductImpl
    implements StockUnit
    ,Product // workaround
```

This will be fixed in the beta version.

Now, when Java passes a book object to a remote method, the recipient obtains a stub that has access to the remote methods in both the `Product` and the `StockUnit` class. In fact, you can use the `instanceof` operator to find out whether a particular remote object implements an interface.

Here is a typical situation. Suppose you receive a remote object through a variable of type `Product`.

```
Vector result = centralWarehouse.find(c);
for (int i = 0; i < result.size(); i++)
{  Product p = (Product)result.elementAt(i);
    . . .

}
```

Now the remote object may or may not be a book. We'd like to use `instanceof` to find out whether it is or not. But we can't test

```
if (p instanceof BookImpl) // wrong
{  BookImpl b = (BookImpl)p;
    . . .

}
```

The object p refers to a stub object, and `BookImpl` is the class of the server object. We could cast the stub object to a `BookImpl_Stub`.

```
if (p instanceof BookImpl_Stub)
{  BookImpl_Stub b = (BookImpl_Stub)p; // not useful
    . . .

}
```

But that would not do us much good. The stubs are generated mechanically by the `rmic` program for internal use by the RMI mechanism, and clients should not have to think about them. Instead, we cast to the second interface:

```
if (p instanceof StockUnit)
{  StockUnit s = (StockUnit)p;
    String c = s.getStockCode();

    . . .

}
```

This code tests whether the stub object to which p refers implements the `StockUnit` interface. If so, it calls the `getStockCode` remote method of that interface.

To summarize: If an object that belongs to a class which implements a remote interface is passed to a remote method, the remote method receives a stub object. You can cast that stub object to any of the remote interfaces which the implementation class implements. You can call all remote methods defined in those interfaces but you cannot call any local methods through the stub.

Using Remote Objects in Hash Tables

As we saw in Chapter 9, objects that are inserted in a hash table need to override the `equals` and `hashCode` methods. Both methods are necessary to find an object in a hash table. First, the hash code is computed to find the appropriate bucket. Then each object in that bucket is compared with the object to be matched, using the `equals` method.

However, there is a problem when trying to do this for remote objects. To find out if two remote objects have the same contents, the call to `equals` would need to contact the servers containing the objects and compare their contents. And that call could fail. But the `equals` method in the class `Object` is not declared to throw a `RemoteException`, whereas all methods in a remote interface must throw that exception. Since a subclass method cannot throw more exceptions than the superclass method that it replaces, you cannot define an `equals` method in a remote interface. The same holds for `hashCode`.

Instead, you must rely on the redefinitions of the `equals` and `hashCode` methods in the `RemoteObject` class that is the base class for all stub and server objects. These methods do not look at the object contents, just at the location of the server objects. Two stubs that refer to the same server object are found to be equal by the `equals` method. Two stubs that refer to different server objects are never equal, even if those objects have identical contents. Similarly, the hash code is only computed from the object identifier. Stubs that refer to different server objects will likely have different hash codes, even if the server objects have identical contents.

This limitation only refers to stubs. You can redefine `equals` or `hashCode` for the server object classes. Those methods are called when inserting server objects in a hash table on the server. But they are never called when comparing or hashing stubs.

To clarify the difference between client and server behavior, look at the inheritance diagram in Figure 15-10.

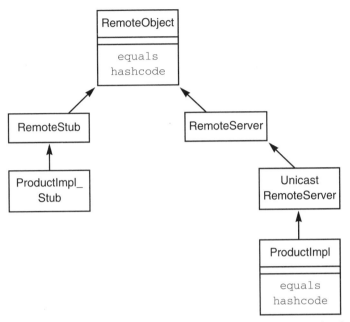

Figure 15-10: Inheritance of `equals` and `hashcode` methods

The `RemoteObject` class is the base for *both* stub and server classes. On the stub side, you cannot override the `equals` and `hashCode` methods since the stubs are mechanically generated. On the server side, you can override the methods for the implementation classes, but they are only used locally on the server. If you do override these methods, implementation and stub objects are no longer considered identical.

The situation is the same for the `clone` method. Stubs don't define `clone` and, therefore, cannot be cloned. Implementation classes on the server are free to override `clone`, but that method is a local method and can only be used in server code. Actually, this behavior will be improved in the beta version. The `UnicastRemoteObject` class will define `clone` to make and export a clone of the original implemetation object.

To summarize: You can use stub objects in hash tables, but you must remember that equality testing and hashing does not take the contents of the remote objects into account.

Inappropriate Remote Parameters

Suppose we enhance our shopping application by having the application show a picture of each gift. Why not simply add a remote method

```
void paint(Graphics g) throws RemoteException
```

to the `Product` interface? Unfortunately, this code cannot work, and it is important to understand why. The `Graphics` class does not implement remote interfaces. Therefore, objects of type `Graphics` are passed by copy. Actually, `Graphics` is an abstract class. The `Graphics` objects that are obtained as parameters of the `paint` method or return values of the `getGraphics` method of the `Component` class actually belong to some subclass that implements a graphics context on a particular platform. Those objects, in turn, need to interact with the native graphics code. They store pointers to memory blocks that are needed by the native graphics methods. Java has no pointers, so they are stored as integers in the graphics object and are cast back to pointers in the native methods.

Therefore, it makes no sense to copy a graphics object. First of all, the target machine may be a different platform. For example, if the client runs Windows and the server runs X11, then the server does not have the native methods available to render Windows graphics. But even if the server and the client have the same graphics system, the pointer values would not be valid on the server.

NOTE: For that reason, the `Graphics` class should refuse to have itself serialized. At the time of this writing, the `Graphics` class can be serialized, but that will change in a future version of Java that fully integrates serialization and RMI support.

Instead, if the server wants to send an image to the client, it has to come up with some other mechanism for transporting the data across the network. As it turns out, this is actually difficult to do for images. The `Image` class is just as device-dependent as the `Graphics` class. We could send the image data as a sequence of bytes in JPEG format, but there is no method in the AWT package to turn a block of JPEG data into an image. (Currently, this can be done only by using unpublished classes in the `sun.awt.image` package.) In the next section, we will show how to solve this problem in a more mundane way, by sending a URL to the client and using a method of the `Applet` class that can read an image from a URL.

Using RMI with Applets

There are a number of special concerns when running RMI with applets. Applets have their own security manager since they run inside a browser. Thus, we do not use the `StubSecurityManager` on the client side.

We must take care where to place the stub and server files. Consider a browser that opens a Web page with an `APPLET` tag. The browser loads the class file referenced in that tag and all other class files as they are needed during execution. The class files are loaded from the same host that contains the Web page. Because of applet security restrictions, the applet can make network connections only to its originating host. Therefore, the server objects must reside on the same host as the Web page as well. That is, the same host must store:

- the Web page
- the applet code
- the stub code
- the skeletons and server objects
- the bootstrap registry

Here is a sample applet that further extends our shopping program. Just like the preceding application, the applet gets the customer information and then recommends matching purchases. When the user clicks on one of the suggestions, the applet displays an image of the item. As we mentioned previously, it is not possible to send an image object from the server to the client because image objects are stored in a format that depends on the local graphics system. Instead, the server simply sends the client a string with the image file name, and we use the getImage method of the Applet class to obtain the image (see Figure 15-11).

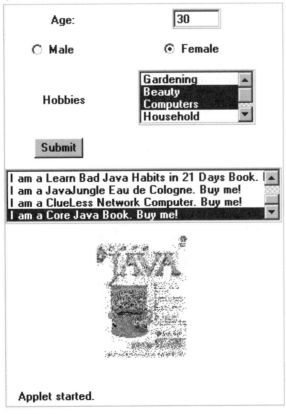

Figure 15-11: The warehouse applet

Here is how you must distribute the code for this kind of situation:

`java.rmi.registry.RegistryImpl`: anywhere on host (This must be running before applet starts.)

`WarehouseServer`: anywhere on host (This must be running before the applet starts.)

`WarehouseImpl`, skeletons. (Can be anywhere on the host as long as the `WarehouseServer` can find it.)

`WarehouseApplet` (directory referenced in APPLET tag)

Stubs (This must be in the same directory as WarehouseApplet.)

Do not try this code with a browser that does not support the RMI features of Java 1.1. The code will not work, and may even crash browsers that are not ready for RMI applets. The applet works fine with the JDK appletviewer.

Here is the code for the applet. Note that the applet does not install a security manager, and that it looks for the bootstrap registry on the same host that contains the applet.

Example 15-10: WarehouseApplet.java

```
import java.awt.*;
import java.applet.*;
import java.rmi.*;
import java.rmi.server.*;
import java.util.*;
import corejava.*;

public class WarehouseApplet extends Applet
{  public void init()
   {  GridBagLayout gbl = new GridBagLayout();
      setLayout(gbl);

      GridBagConstraints gbc = new GridBagConstraints();
      gbc.fill = GridBagConstraints.NONE;
      gbc.weightx = 100;
      gbc.weighty = 100;
      add(this, new Label("Age:"), gbl, gbc, 0, 0, 1, 1);
      add(this, age = new IntTextField(0, 0, 200, 4), gbl,
         gbc, 1, 0, 1, 1);
      CheckboxGroup cbg = new CheckboxGroup();
      add(this, male = new Checkbox("Male", cbg, true), gbl,
         gbc, 0, 1, 1, 1);
```

```
        add(this, female = new Checkbox("Female", cbg, true),
            gbl, gbc, 1, 1, 1, 1);
        add(this, new Label("Hobbies"), gbl, gbc, 0, 2, 1, 1);
        hobbies = new List(4, true);
        hobbies.addItem("Gardening");
        hobbies.addItem("Beauty");
        hobbies.addItem("Computers");
        hobbies.addItem("Household");
        hobbies.addItem("Sports");
        add(this, hobbies, gbl, gbc, 1, 2, 1, 1);
        add(this, new Button("Submit"), gbl, gbc, 0, 3, 1, 1);
        descriptions = new List(4, false);
        gbc.fill = GridBagConstraints.HORIZONTAL;
        add(this, descriptions, gbl, gbc, 0, 4, 2, 1);
        gbc.fill = GridBagConstraints.NONE;
        canvas = new Canvas();
        canvas.resize(100, 150);
        add(this, canvas, gbl, gbc, 0, 5, 2, 1);

        String url = getCodeBase().getHost();
        if (!url.equals("")) url = "rmi:" + url + "//";
        try
        {   centralWarehouse = (Warehouse)Naming.lookup(url +
            "central_warehouse");
        }
        catch(Exception e)
        {   showStatus("Error: Can't connect to warehouse. " + e);
        }
    }

    private void add(Container p, Component c,
        GridBagLayout gbl, GridBagConstraints gbc,
        int x, int y, int w, int h)
    {   gbc.gridx = x;
        gbc.gridy = y;
        gbc.gridwidth = w;
        gbc.gridheight = h;
        gbl.setConstraints(c, gbc);
        p.add(c);
    }

    public boolean action(Event evt, Object arg)
    {   if (arg.equals("Submit"))
        {   if (age.isValid())
            {   Customer c = new Customer(age.getValue(),
                    (male.getState() ? Product.MALE : 0)
                    + (female.getState() ? Product.FEMALE : 0),
                    hobbies.getSelectedItems());
```

```
         try
         {  products = centralWarehouse.find(c);
            descriptions.clear();
            for (int i = 0; i < products.size(); i++)
            {  Product p = (Product)products.elementAt(i);
               descriptions.addItem(p.getDescription());
            }
         }
         catch(Exception e)
         {  System.out.println("Error: " + e);
         }
      }
      return true;
   }
   else return false;
}

public boolean handleEvent(Event evt)
{  if (evt.id == Event.WINDOW_DESTROY) System.exit(0);
   else if (evt.id == Event.LIST_SELECT && evt.target ==
      descriptions)
   {  int index = descriptions.getSelectedIndex();
      if (index < 0) return true;
      try
      {  Product p = (Product)products.elementAt(index);
         productImage = getImage(getCodeBase(),
            p.getImageFile());
         repaint();
      }
      catch(Exception e)
      {  System.out.println("Error: " + e);
      }
      return true;
   }
   return super.handleEvent(evt);
}

public void paint(Graphics g)
{  if (productImage == null) return;
   Graphics cg = canvas.getGraphics();
   cg.drawImage(productImage, 0, 0, this);
   cg.dispose();
}

private Warehouse centralWarehouse;
private IntTextField age;
private Checkbox male;
private Checkbox female;
```

```
      private List hobbies;
      private List descriptions;
      private Vector products;
      private Canvas canvas;
      private Image productImage;
  }
```

The `Product` interface has an additional method to get the name of the image file, as illustrated in Examples 15-11 and 15-12.

Example 15-11: Product.java

```
import java.rmi.*;
import java.awt.*;

public interface Product
    extends Remote
{   String getDescription()
        throws RemoteException;
    String getImageFile()
        throws RemoteException;

    static final int MALE = 1;
    static final int FEMALE = 2;
    static final int BOTH = MALE + FEMALE;
}
```

Example 15-12: ProductImpl.java

```
import java.rmi.*;
import java.rmi.server.*;
import java.awt.*;

public class ProductImpl
    extends UnicastRemoteServer
    implements Product
{   public ProductImpl(String n, int s, int age1, int age2,
        String h, String i)
        throws RemoteException
    {   name = n;
        ageLow = age1;
        ageHigh = age2;
        sex = s;
        hobby = h;
        imageFile = i;
    }
```

```java
public boolean match(Customer c) // local method
{  if (c.getAge() < ageLow || c.getAge() > ageHigh)
      return false;
   if (!c.hasHobby(hobby)) return false;
   if ((sex & c.getSex()) == 0) return false;
   return true;
}

public String getDescription() throws RemoteException
{  return "I am a " + name + ". Buy me!";
}

public String getImageFile() throws RemoteException
{  return imageFile;
}

private String name;
private int ageLow;
private int ageHigh;
private int sex;
private String hobby;
private String imageFile;
}
```

The server sets the file names when it populates the database.

Example 15-13: WarehouseServer.java

```java
import java.rmi.*;
import java.rmi.server.*;

public class WarehouseServer
{  public static void main(String args[])
   {  System.setSecurityManager(new StubSecurityManager());
      try
      {  WarehouseImpl w = new WarehouseImpl();
         fillWarehouse(w);
         Naming.rebind("central_warehouse", w);
      }
      catch(Exception e)
      {  System.out.println("Error: " + e);
      }
   }

   public static void fillWarehouse(WarehouseImpl w)
      throws RemoteException
   {  w.add(new ProductImpl("Blackwell Toaster", Product.BOTH,
```

```
            18, 200, "Household", "toaster.jpg"));
        w.add(new ProductImpl("Jimbo After Shave", Product.MALE,
            18, 200, "Beauty", "shave.jpg"));
        w.add(new ProductImpl("U238 Weed Killer", Product.BOTH,
            20, 200, "Gardening", "weed.jpg"));
        w.add(new ProductImpl("Rabid Rodent Computer Mouse",
            Product.BOTH,
            6, 40, "Computers", "rodent.jpg"));
        w.add(new ProductImpl("Learn Bad Java Habits in 21 Days
            Book", Product.BOTH,
            20, 200, "Computers", "book.jpg"));
        w.add(new ProductImpl("JavaJungle Eau de Cologne",
            Product.FEMALE,
            20, 200, "Beauty", "cologne.jpg"));
        w.add(new ProductImpl("Fast/Wide SCSI Coffee Maker",
            Product.MALE,
            20, 50, "Computers", "coffee.jpg"));
        w.add(new ProductImpl("ClueLess Network Computer",
            Product.BOTH,
            6, 200, "Computers", "computer.jpg"));
        w.add(new ProductImpl("Digging Dinosaur", Product.BOTH,
            6, 200, "Gardening", "dino.jpg"));
        w.add(new ProductImpl("Fantastic Fan", Product.BOTH,
            6, 200, "Household", "fan.jpg"));
        w.add(new ProductImpl("Japanese Cat", Product.BOTH,
            6, 200, "Gardening", "cat.jpg"));
        w.add(new ProductImpl("Ms. Frizzle Curling Iron",
            Product.FEMALE,
            6, 200, "Beauty", "curl.jpg"));
    }
}
```

CHAPTER
16

Native Methods

As you have seen, Java code has a number of advantages over code written in languages like C or C++—even when used for applications running on a specific platform. In this situation of course, it is not the portability that matters but the knowledge that you are more likely to produce bug free code using Java. Portability is simply a bonus that you may take advantage of down the line. Nevertheless, there are situations where a Java programmer will want to write (or use) code written in another language and then call this code from Java. (Such code is usually called *native* code.) There are three obvious reasons why you may want to do this.

1. Substantial amounts of code exist which has been tested extensively in that language. Porting the code to Java would be time consuming, and the resulting code would need to be debugged again.

2. An application requires access to system features or devices and using Java would be cumbersome, at best, or impossible, at worst.

3. Maximizing the speed of the code is absolutely essential. The task may be time critical or it may be code that is used so often that optimizing it has a big payoff. (Of course, with just in time compilation (JIT), this is less likely to occur. Intensive computations coded in Java are, after processing by a JIT, not *that* much slower than compiled C code.)

In these three situations, it *might* make sense to call the code from Java.

To make this possible, Java has a way of calling code that is already compiled. By the way, the language used doesn't have to be C or C++; you could use code compiled with a FORTRAN compiler if you have access to a Java-to-FORTRAN binding.

Of course, because of Java's security restrictions, once you start using native code you are restricted to applications rather than applets. In particular, the library that you are calling will probably have to lie on the client machine. You cannot expect to download C libraries from the Net and then run them on the client machine.

Use native methods and you lose portability. This is because even when distributing your program as an application, you must supply a separate native method library for every platform that you wish to support. This means you must also educate your users on how to install these libraries! Also, while a user may trust that applets can neither damage data nor steal confidential information, he or she may not want to extend the same trust to Java code that uses native method libraries. For that reason, many potential users will be reluctant to use Java programs that require native code. Independent of the security issue, native libraries are unlikely to be as safe as Java code, especially if they are written in a language like C or C++ that offer no protection against overwriting memory through invalid pointer usage. It is easy to write native methods that corrupt the Java virtual machine, compromise its security, or trash the operating system.

Thus, we suggest using native code only as a last resort. If you must gain access to a device such as the printer or serial port in a Java program, then you may need to write native code. If you need to access an existing body of code, why not consider native methods as a stopgap measure and eventually port the code to Java? If you are concerned about efficiency, benchmark a Java implementation. In most cases, the speed of Java using a JIT will be sufficient. (Just-in-time compilers and other emerging compiler technologies will soon exist on all platforms that Java has been ported to. They already exist under Windows and Solaris.) A talk at the 1996 Java One Conference showed this very clearly. The implementers of the cryptography library at Sun Microsystems reported that a pure Java implementation of their cryptographic functions was more than adequate. It was true that they were not as fast as a C implementation would have been, but it turned out not to matter. The Java implementation was far faster than the network I/O. And *this* turns out to be the real bottleneck.

In summary, there is no point in sacrificing portability for a meaningless speed improvement; don't go native until you determine that you have no other choice.

Finally, we will use C as our language for native methods in this chapter. This is because C is probably the language most often used for Java native methods. In particular, you'll see how to make the correspondence between Java and C data types, feature names and function calls. (This is usually called the C *binding*.)

NOTE: The binding between Java and C code that we describe in this chapter works with the 1.02 release of Java . There is absolutely no guarantee that the same binding will stay unchanged in future releases of Java from Sun Microsystems. In addition, other vendors are free to choose different implementations for their virtual machines, and at least one vendor (Microsoft) has announced its intention to do so. Finally, bindings for other programming languages such as C++, FORTRAN or Ada will likely differ considerably from the C binding described in this chapter.

Calling a C Function from Java

Let's start with a very simple situation: we will write a native method that prints the message "Hello, Native World," using the `printf` function of the C language rather than using the `System.out.print` method of Java. Of course, there is no advantage to doing this, but this is a good test case to start with. You can then use it to check that your own C compiler works as expected, before you try implementing more ambitious native methods.

First, declare a native method in a class. The `native` keyword alerts the Java compiler that the method will be defined externally. Of course, native methods contain no Java code. The method header must immediately be followed by a terminating semicolon. Thus, native method declarations look similar to abstract method declarations.

```
class HelloNative
{  public native static void greeting();
   . . .

}
```

In this particular example, we declare the native method as `static`. Native methods can be both static and non-static. We made this because we do not yet want to deal with parameter passing, not even implicit parameters.

Next, write a corresponding C function. That function must be named *exactly* the way the Java run time system expects. You must follow these rules.

1. Use the full Java method name, such as `HelloNative.greeting`. If the `HelloNative` class is in a package, say corejava, then use `coreJava.HelloNativegreeting`.

2. Replace every period with an underscore. If the class name contains characters that are not ASCII letters or digits, that is, `'_'`, `'$'` or Unicode characters with code > `'\U007F'`, replace them with _0*xxxx* where *xxxx* is the sequence of four hexadecimal digits of the character's Unicode value. For example, the Java name `corejava.HelloNative.greeting` is mapped to the C name `corejava_HelloNative_greeting`.

NOTE: The parameters of the method are not used to form the C name. Thus, it is not possible to overload native methods that are implemented in C. This means you cannot use two native methods with the same name but different parameter types in the same class. At some later point, Java may have a binding to a language such as C++, which supports name overloading to remove this limitation.

In our example, we do not actually want to put the `HelloNative` class into the `corejava` package. Therefore, we just need to write a C function called `HelloNative_greeting`.

```
void HelloNative_greeting(HHelloNative* unused)
{  printf("Hello, Native World!\n");
}
```

The `HHelloNative*` parameter of the function is `NULL` for static methods. Had `greeting` not been a static function, then this would have been the implicit argument of the method.

Next, we need to compile the Java code, compile the C++ code and do a bit of general magic to put the two together. Here are the steps.

1. Compile the Java file

    ```
    javac HelloNative.java
    ```

2. Invoke the `javah` utility twice to produce Java headers and stubs. The javah.exe file may be found in the \java\bin directory. (What javah does is create a bunch of files that give the definitions of the native methods and the basic Java types.)

    ```
    javah HelloNative
    javah -stubs HelloNative
    ```

    The first invocation of `javah` creates a header file `HelloNative.h`, and the second source file `HelloNative.c`.

3. Create a file `HelloNative_impl.c`. In that file, `#include` the file `HelloNative.h` and also supply the implementations of the native methods. (Actually, you can give the implementation file any name you like, except you shouldn't call it `HelloNative.c`. The `javah` utility uses that name for the stub file.)

4. Compile both the stub file and the implementation file. Create a DLL that contains both compiled files. (Follow the instructions in your C++ compiler for creating a DLL.)

5. Add code to the class that uses the native methods that ensure the library is loaded prior to the first use of the class. This is achieved by using a static initialization block as in the following example:

```
class HelloNative
{   public native static void greeting();
    static
    {   System.loadLibrary("HelloNative");
    }
    . . .
}
```

NOTE: Before running `javah` to generate the headers and the stubs, you must first compile the Java file into byte codes. (It is probably best to use javac for this rather than some third part byte code compiler.) The `javah` program looks at the compiled class file not the Java source file. Furthermore, under Windows, you also must unzip the classes.zip file in the \java\lib directory. If you don't do this, javah won't be able to find the Java library classes. (Just use the WinZip utility that we supply on the CD-ROM and place the unzipped files into the \java\lib subdirectory.)

Do not edit the C file created by `javah -stubs`. Whenever you change the Java file and change the declaration of the native methods, you need to run `javah` again. Then the header and stub files are overwritten. In particular, do *not* place the implementation of the native methods into the file `classname.c`.

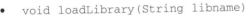

`java.lang.System`

- `void loadLibrary(String libname)`

  loads the library with the given name. The library is located in the library search path. The exact method for locating the library is operating-system dependent. Under DOS/Windows, first the current directory, then the directories on the PATH are searched.

- `void load(String filename)`

  loads the library with the given file name. If the library is not found, then Java throws an `UnsatisfiedLinkError`.

C++ NOTE: You can use C++ to implement native methods. However, you must then declare the functions that are called from Java as `extern "C"`. For example,

```
extern "C" {
#include "HelloNative.h"
}

extern "C" void HelloNative_greeting(HHelloNative* unused)
{ printf("Hello, Native World!");
}
```

Example 16-1 shows the Java program that calls the native `greeting` method.

Example 16-1: HelloNative.java

```
class HelloNative
{   public static native void greeting();
    static
    {   System.loadLibrary("HelloNative");
    }
}
```

Example 16-2 show the c program implementing the method:

Example 16-2: HelloNative_impl.c

```
#include "HelloNative.h"

void HelloNative_greeting(HHelloNative* unused)
{   printf("Hello Native World!\n");
}
```

Example 16-3 shows the header file that is generated by `javah`.

Example 16-3: HelloNative.h

```
#include <StubPreamble.h>

/* Stubs for class HelloNative */
/* SYMBOL: "HelloNative/greeting()V", Java_HelloNative_greet-
ing_stub */
__declspec(dllexport) stack_item
*Java_HelloNative_greeting_stub(stack_item *_P_,struct execenv
*_EE_) {
```

```
    extern void HelloNative_greeting(void *);
    (void) HelloNative_greeting(NULL);
    return _P_;
}
```

TIP: It is worth looking inside the header file since it contains the prototypes of the C functions that you need to implement.

Example 16-4 shows the stub file that is generated by `javah -stubs`.

Example 16-4: HelloNative.c

```
#include <native.h>
/* Header for class HelloNative */

#ifndef _Included_HelloNative
#define _Included_HelloNative

typedef struct ClassHelloNative {
    char PAD;     /* ANSI C requires structures to have a
                    least one member */
} ClassHelloNative;
HandleTo(HelloNative);

#ifdef __cplusplus
extern "C" {
#endif
__declspec(dllexport) void HelloNative_greeting(struct
HHelloNative *);
#ifdef __cplusplus
}
#endif
#endif
```

Note that the stub file contains nothing of interest to the programmer. It is just some intermediate glue between the Java runtime system and the C functions that you implemented.

O.K., assuming you have followed all the steps given above, you are now ready to run the HelloNativeTest application from Java. If you do run this Java program, the message "Hello, Native World!" should appear in a DOS window.

Of course, this is not particularly impressive by itself. However, remember that the message will be generated by the C `printf` command and not by any Java code. We, therefore, have succeeded in bridging the gap between Java and C.

Numeric Parameters and Return Values

When passing numbers between C and Java code, it is important to understand which C types correspond to which Java types. C does have data types called `int` and `long`, but their implementation is dependent on the underlying platform. On some platforms, `int` are 16-bit quantities and on others they are 32-bit quantities. In Java, of course, an `int` is *always* a 32-bit integer.

Here is the correspondence between Java and C types:

Java	C
boolean	long (false = 0, true = 1)
byte	long
char	long (the Unicode value)
short	long
int	long
long	int64_t
float	float
double	double

Because in C, a `long` is always at least a 32-bit quantity, all integer types in Java are simply mapped to `long`, except for `long` itself. In Java, `long` denotes a 64-bit quantity, but on many C compilers, both `int` and `long` use 32 bit. Use the special type `int64_t` to hold a 64-bit integer.

Here is a simple example, a native method that prints a floating-point number with a certain field width and precision, using the C function `printf`. Recall that Java has no provision for formatted printing of floating-point numbers. For this book, we reimplemented the functionality of `printf` in the `corejava.Format` class. Another way to implement the same functionality is to call the `printf` function in a native method. Of course, there is a disadvantage of that approach—the native code needs to be compiled for every target platform.

Here is a first version of a class `Printf` that prints a floating-point number.

```
class Printf1
{   public native static int printDouble(int width, int
        precision, double x);
}
```

When implementing the method in C, we must change all `int` parameters to `long`.

```
long Printf1_printDouble(HPrintf1* unused, long width,
        long precision, double x)
{   char fmt[30];
    long ret;
    sprintf(fmt, "%%%d.%df", width, precision);
    ret = printf(fmt, x);
    return ret;
}
```

The function simply assembles a format string `"%w.pf"` in the variable `fmt`, then calls `printf`. It then returns the number of characters it printed.

Example 16-5: Printf1Test.java

```
class Printf1Test
{   public static void main(String[] args)
    {   int x = Printf1.printDouble(8, 4, 3.14);
        Printf1.printDouble(8, 4, (double)x);
    }
}
```

Example 16-6: Printf1.java

```
class Printf1
{   public static native int printDouble(int width, int
        precision, double x);
    static
    {   System.loadLibrary("Printf1");
    }
}
```

Example 16-7: Printf1_impl.c

```c
#include "Printf1.h"

long Printf1_printDouble(HPrintf1* unused, long width,
    long precision, double x)
{   char fmt[30];
    long ret;
    sprintf(fmt, "%%%d.%df", width, precision);
    ret = printf(fmt, x);
    return ret;
}
```

String Parameters

Next, consider how to transfer strings into and out of native methods. Strings in Java and C are quite different. Java strings are sequences of 16-bit Unicode characters; C strings are null-terminated strings of 8-bit characters.

A native method with a `String` parameter in its Java declaration actually receives a pointer to a structure of type `Hjava_lang_String`. A method with Java return value of type `String` must return a pointer to a `Hjava_lang_String` structure. The header file javaString.h contains several helper functions to convert between Java strings, or, to be precise, `Hjava_lang_String` structures, and C strings. Here are the most common functions and some of their uses.

Accessing Java strings from C code

- `int javaStringLength(Hjava_lang_String* str)`

  returns the number of (Unicode) characters in the string

The next three functions are not Unicode-aware. They simply use the less significant byte when converting a Unicode character to a C character.

- `char* allocCString(Hjava_lang_String* str)`

  this returns a pointer to a block of memory into which a copy of `str` was placed. This also supplies a null terminator. The memory for the string is obtained from `malloc`, and you must call `free` when you are done using the string.

- `char* makeCString(Hjava_lang_String* str)`

  this returns a pointer to a block of memory into which a copy of `str` was placed. This also supplies a null terminator. The memory used for the string will eventually be garbage collected by the Java garbage collector. In the usual Sun implementations, the garbage collector actually scans the memory of native methods when marking the memory blocks that are in use by a Java program. However, other implementations of the Java Virtual Machine may not. For that reason, it is a good idea to use `allocCString` instead and free the memory manually.

- `char* javaString2CString(Hjava_lang_String* str, char buffer[], int buffer_length)`

  this places a copy of up to `buffer_length - 1` characters from `str` into `buffer`. It also supplies a null terminator. This function is useful if you know an upper bound on the length of the Java string. The buffer can then be allocated on the runtime stack and need not be freed explicitly. The function returns buffer as a convenience.

To make a new Java string out of a C string, use

- `Hjava_lang_String* makeJavaString(char* str, int len)`

  this function returns a pointer to a Java string handle, constructed from the first `len` characters in `str`. The value `len` must not include the null terminator of the string. Do not free the handle—it will be deallocated by the Java garbage collector.

Finally, there is a function that turns a Java string into an array of values of type `unicode`, a 16-bit number type (such as `unsigned short`) defined in the header native.h.

- `unicode* javaString2unicode(Hjava_lang_String* str, unicode buffer, int n)`

  this function places a copy of n Unicode characters from `str` into `buffer`. It *does not* supply a null terminator. The Java string must have at least n characters available, or the function will copy garbage into the buffer. The function returns `buffer` as a convenience.

There is no function to convert a Unicode string to a Java string.

Let us put these functions to work to write a Java equivalent of the C function `sprintf`. We would like to call the function as follows:

```
class Printf2Test
{   public static void main(String[] args)
    {   double price = 44.95;
        double tax = 7.75;
        double amountDue = price * (1 + tax / 100);
        String s = Printf2.sprintDouble("Amount due = %8.2f",
            amountDue);
        System.out.println(s);
    }
}
```

Note that we cannot write an overloaded `sprintf` native method that can take both integer and floating-point arguments.

Here is the class with the native `sprintfDouble` method.

```
class Printf2
{  public static native String sprintDouble(String format,
      double x);
   static
   {  System.loadLibrary("Printf2");
   }
}
```

Therefore, the C function that formats a floating-point number has the prototype

```
Hjava_lang_String* Printf2_sprintfDouble(HPrintf2* unused,
   Hjava_lang_String* format, double x)
```

Here is the code for the C implementation:

```
#include <string.h>
#include <stdlib.h>
#include <float.h>
#include <javaString.h>
#include "Printf2.h"

char* find_format(char format[])
{  char* p = strchr(format, '%');
   char* q;
   size_t n;
   while (p != NULL && *(p + 1) == '%') /* skip %% */
      p = strchr(p + 2, '%');
   if (p == NULL) return NULL;
   /* now check that % is unique */
   p++;
   q = strchr(p, '%');
   while (q != NULL && *(q + 1) == '%') /* skip %% */
      q = strchr(q + 2, '%');
   if (q != NULL) return NULL; /* % not unique */
   q = p + strspn(p, " -0+#"); /* skip past flags */
   q += strspn(q, "0123456789"); /* skip past field width */
   if (*q == '.') { q++; q += strspn(q, "0123456789"); }
      /* skip past precision */
   if (strchr("eEfFgG", *q) == NULL) return NULL;
      /* not a floating point format */
   return p;
}
```

```
Hjava_lang_String* Printf2_sprintDouble(HPrintf2* unused,
    Hjava_lang_String* hformat, double x)
{  char* format = allocCString(hformat);
   char* fmt = find_format(format);
   Hjava_lang_String* hret;
   if (fmt == NULL)
      hret = makeJavaString(format, strlen(format));
   else
   {  char* ret;
      int width = atoi(fmt);
      if (width == 0) width = DBL_DIG + 10;
      ret = (char*)malloc(strlen(format) + width);
      sprintf(ret, format, x);
      hret = makeJavaString(ret, strlen(ret));
      free(ret);
   }
   free(format);
   return hret;
}
```

In this function, we chose to keep the error handling very simple. If the format code to print a floating point number is not of the form $%w.pc$, where c is one of the characters e, E, f, g or G, then we simply don't format the number. We will see later how we can have the native method throw an exception instead.

Object Parameters

All native methods that we saw so far were static methods with number and string parameters. Next, let us consider native methods that operate on objects. For every class type, there are two types that you need to manipulate in a C program, the *handle type* and the *class type*. For example, if you have a class Employee, there is a handle type HEmployee and a class type ClassEmployee.

Here is the C structure that javah generates for the Employee class from Chapter 4.

```
typedef struct ClassEmployee {
    struct Hjava_lang_String *name;
    double salary;
    struct Hcorejava_Day *hireDay;
} ClassEmployee;
```

As you can see, the numeric fields are left intact, and references to classes are replaced by pointers to handles.

All object parameters and return values are pointers to handles. To actually access the data fields, you need to convert the handle pointers to class type pointers—the unhand macro achieves that. Here is an example of what we would do if we write the `raiseSalary` method as a native method.

```
void Employee_raiseSalary(HEmployee* hobj, double by)
{  ClassEmployee cobj = unhand(hobj);
   cobj->salary *= 1 + by / 100;
}
```

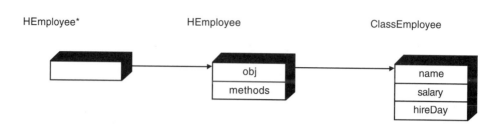

Figure 16-1: The relationship between handle and class objects

Figure 16-1 shows the relationship between handle and class objects. Actually, you should take that picture with a grain of salt. While it reflects the data layout in the virtual machine used by Sun, other implementations of the Java virtual machine are free to choose a different scheme. For example, the Microsoft implementation dispenses with the double indirection. Their implementation still has the unhand macro, defined as a do-nothing operation.

In our next program, we will do something useful—we show how to create a printout of a graph. Recall the sketch program from Chapter 6 that lets the user draw spiral shapes on the screen. Suppose the user wants to save a masterpiece sketch for posterity. At this point, there is no provision for *printing* graphics in Java. (This will change in a future version of Java. Printing will be added to an enhanced version of the `Graphics` class.) In fact, because printing is highly system-dependent, it must be implemented with native methods. For example, under Windows and the Macintosh, there is operating system support for printing graphics on a wide variety of printers, but under Unix there is not. Instead, most Unix applications assume that the printer understands the PostScript printer control language and produce PostScript code.

We will just define the most rudimentary interface for printing graphics. Our printer class will only be able to print lines.

```
class Printer
{   public native void startPrint();
    public native void endPrint();
    public native void printLine(Point from, Point to);
    private int handle;
}
```

We enhance the scribble application to call `startPrint` at the beginning of the program, `printLine` whenever a new line is added, and `endPrint` when the user quits the program. This is shown in Example 16-8.

Example 16-8: PrintSketch.java

```java
import java.awt.*;

public class PrintSketch extends Frame
{   public PrintSketch()
    {   setTitle("PrintSketch");
        printer.startPrint();
    }

    public boolean handleEvent(Event evt)
    {   if (evt.id == Event.WINDOW_DESTROY)
        {   printer.endPrint();
            System.exit(0);
        }
        return super.handleEvent(evt);
    }

    public boolean keyDown(Event evt, int key)
    {   int d = ((evt.modifiers & Event.SHIFT_MASK) == 0) ?
        1 : 5;
        if (key == Event.LEFT) add(-d, 0);
        else if (key == Event.RIGHT) add(d, 0);
        else if (key == Event.UP) add(0, -d);
        else if (key == Event.DOWN) add(0, d);
        else return false;
        return true;
    }

    public void update(Graphics g)
    {   paint(g);
        requestFocus();
    }
```

```
public void paint(Graphics g)
{   g.drawLine(start.x, start.y, end.x, end.y);
    start.x = end.x;
    start.y = end.y;
}

public void add(int dx, int dy)
{   end.x += dx;
    end.y += dy;
    printer.printLine(start, end);
    repaint();
}

public static void main(String[] args)
{   Frame f = new PrintSketch();
    f.resize(300, 200);
    f.show();
}

private Point start = new Point(0, 0);
private Point end = new Point(0, 0);
private Printer printer = new Printer();
}
```

Now let us implement the printing functionality for Windows using the C language. Most of the details of printing are technical and only of interest if you are a Windows programmer. What is important to us is how to access Java objects. Look at the `startPrint` function. In Java, it has one implicit parameter and no explicit parameters. In C, the implicit parameter is turned into an explicit parameter.

```
void Printer_startPrint(HPrinter* hobj)
```

The `startPrint` function does some Windows magic, and there is only one line of interest to us. A Windows data structure, the so-called printer device context, is opened and we must remember it in successive calls to methods of the `Printer` object. For that reason, the `Printer` class defines a data field `handle`. Here is how we store the device context in the handle field.

```
void Printer_startPrint(HPrinter* hobj)
{   ClassPrinter* cobj = unhand(hobj);
    HDC hdc;
    . . .
    hdc = CreateDC(. . .);
    cobj->handle = (long)hdc;
}
```

Similarly, when printing a line, we must be able to access the device context of the printer and the coordinates of the points.

```
void Printer_printLine(HPrinter* hobj, Hjava_awt_Point* hfrom,
    Hjava_awt_Point* hto)
{   ClassPrinter* cobj = unhand(hobj);
    if (hfrom == NULL || hto == NULL) return;
    Classjava_awt_Point* cfrom = unhand(hfrom);
    Classjava_awt_Point* cto = unhand(hto);
    HDC hdc = (HDC)cfrom->handle;
    . . .
    LineTo(hdc, cto->x, cto->y);
}
```

Before applying unhand to a data field or explicit parameter, check if the `Hclass` pointer is NULL. That indicates a null reference. However, in a non-static method, the pointer to the implicit parameter is never NULL.

The `Printer_printLine` method needs to access data fields of the `java.awt.Point` class. As a programmer, you want to know what the data fields are called. And, of course, the compiler needs to have a structure definition for the point class as well. You use `javah` to obtain that information. To do this, run

```
javah java.awt.Point
```

to obtain the file `java_awt_Point.h`

```
#include <native.h>
/* Header for class java_awt_Point */

#ifndef _Included_java_awt_Point
#define _Included_java_awt_Point

typedef struct Classjava_awt_Point {
    long x;
    long y;
} Classjava_awt_Point;
HandleTo(java_awt_Point);

#ifdef __cplusplus
extern "C" {
#endif
#ifdef __cplusplus
}
#endif
#endif
```

As you can see, the coordinates of a point can be accessed as `cpoint->x` and `cpoint->y`. Include the `java_awt_Point.h` into the `Printer_impl.c` program.

If you don't like to have a separate file for every class, you can tell `javah` to put several structure definitions into one class. Here is an example.

```
javah -o Printer_impl.h java.awt.Point java.awt.Font
```

Here is the implementation file for the methods of the `Printer` class. (We won't show the automatically generated header and stub files.)

```c
#include <windows.h>
#include "Printer.h"
#include "java_awt_Point.h"

void Printer_startPrint(HPrinter* hobj)
{   DOCINFO di = { sizeof(DOCINFO), "Sketch", NULL };
    PRINTER_INFO_5 pinfo5[3];
    HDC hdc;
    DWORD dwNeeded, dwReturned;
    ClassPrinter* cobj = unhand(hobj);

    if (EnumPrinters(PRINTER_ENUM_DEFAULT, NULL, 5,
        (LPBYTE) pinfo5, sizeof(pinfo5), &dwNeeded,
        &dwReturned))
    {   hdc = CreateDC(NULL, pinfo5[0].pPrinterName,
        NULL, NULL);
        cobj->handle = (long)hdc;
    }
    else
    {   cobj->handle = 0;
        return;
    }
    if (StartDoc(hdc, &di) <= 0
        || StartPage(hdc) <= 0)
    {   DeleteDC(hdc);
            cobj->handle = 0;
            return;
    }
    SetMapMode(hdc, MM_ISOTROPIC);
    SetViewportExtEx(hdc, GetDeviceCaps(hdc, HORZRES),
        GetDeviceCaps(hdc, VERTRES), NULL);
}

void Printer_printLine(HPrinter* hobj, Hjava_awt_Point* hfrom,
Hjava_awt_Point* hto)
{   ClassPrinter* cobj = unhand(hobj);
    Classjava_awt_Point* cfrom = unhand(hfrom);
```

```
        Classjava_awt_Point* cto = unhand(hto);
        HDC hdc = (HDC)cobj->handle;
        if (!hdc) return;
        MoveToEx(hdc, cfrom->x, cfrom->y, NULL);
        LineTo(hdc, cto->x, cto->y);
    }

    void Printer_endPrint(HPrinter* hobj)
    {   ClassPrinter* cobj = unhand(hobj);
        HDC hdc = (HDC)cobj->handle;
        if (!hdc) return;
        EndPage(hdc);
        EndDoc(hdc);
        DeleteDC(hdc);
        cobj->handle = 0;
    }
```

Windows programmers will note that this code is not the most robust way of implementing printing. We don't let the user choose a printer, and we don't handle printer errors. The point of this example is simply to show how to access a highly system-dependent activity, such as printing, by using native methods. Furthermore, you saw how to access the contents of objects that are passed as parameters.

Calling Java Methods

Non-static Methods

Of course, Java functions can call C functions—that is what native methods are for. Can we go the other way and call Java code from C? Why would we want to do this anyway? The answer is that it often happens that a native method needs to request a service from an object that was passed to it.

As an example of this, let's enhance the `Printf` class and add a member function that works similar to the C function `fprintf`. That is, it should be able to print a string on an arbitrary PrintStream object.

```
    class Printf3
    {   public native static void fprintDouble(PrintStream ps,
            String s, double x);
            . . .
    }
```

We first assemble the string to be printed into a `String` object s, as in the `sprintDouble` method that we already implemented. Then we want to call `ps.print(s)` from the C function that implements the native method.

You can call any Java method from C using the function call

```
execute_java_dynamic_method(EE(), handle_pointer, method_name,
    method_signature, explicit parameters)
```

The first argument is `EE()`, the default *execution environment*. In our case, the second argument is simply the `HPrintStream*` handle that we obtained as a parameter to the native method. The third argument is the method name, `"print"`. As you saw in Chapter 11, the `PrintStream` class has at least nine different methods, all called `print`. The fourth parameter of the function is a string describing the parameters and return value of the specific function that you want to use. For example, we want to use `void print(java.lang.String)`. Unfortunately, we must now "mangle" the parameter types, following a set of rules that we will describe later in this section. In our case, the mangled name is `"(Ljava/lang/string;)V"`. Finally, we supply all parameters that the function needs. These are either handle pointers or numbers.

Note that we don't need to know anything about the internals of the `java.io.PrintStream` class. Hence, a type declaration

```
typedef struct Hjava_io_PrintStream Hjava_io_PrintStream;
```

suffices—we need not generate and include the file java_io_PrintStream.h.

Here is the entire sprintDouble function.

```
#include <string.h>
#include <stdlib.h>
#include <float.h>
#include <javaString.h>
#include "Printf3.h"
typedef struct Hjava_io_PrintStream Hjava_io_PrintStream;

char* find_format(char format[])
{   char* p = strchr(format, '%');
    char* q;
    size_t n;
    while (p != NULL && *(p + 1) == '%') /* skip %% */
        p = strchr(p + 2, '%');
    if (p == NULL) return NULL;
    /* now check that % is unique */
    p++;
    q = strchr(p, '%');
    while (q != NULL && *(q + 1) == '%') /* skip %% */
        q = strchr(q + 2, '%');
    if (q != NULL) return NULL; /* % not unique */
```

```
    q = p + strspn(p, " -0+#"); /* skip past flags */
    q += strspn(q, "0123456789"); /* skip past field width */
    if (*q == '.') { q++; q += strspn(q, "0123456789"); }
        /* skip past precision */
    if (strchr("eEfFgG", *q) == NULL) return NULL;
        /* not a floating point format */
    return p;
}

void Printf3_fprintDouble(HPrintf3* unused,
Hjava_io_PrintStream* ps,
    Hjava_lang_String* hformat, double x)
{   char* format = allocCString(hformat);
    char* buffer;
    int width;
    char* fmt = find_format(format);
    if (fmt == NULL) return;
    width = atoi(fmt);
    if (width == 0) width = DBL_DIG + 10;
    buffer = (char*)malloc(strlen(format) + width);
    sprintf(buffer, format, x);
    execute_java_dynamic_method(EE(), (Hjava_lang_Object*)ps,
        "print",
        "(Ljava/lang/String;)V", makeJavaString(buffer,
        strlen(buffer)));
    free(buffer);
    free(format);
}
```

> When passing numbers to a Java method, remember that you must use `long` for all of Java's integer types except Java's `long` type itself. Because the `execute_java_dynamic_method` function uses the "variable arguments" feature of C, it does not perform any type conversion for you.

The return value of `execute_java_dynamic_method` is always a `long`. You must cast it to either an integer or a handle pointer. If the native method returned a Java `long` or `double` value, and on your platform the C type `long` is only a 32-bit value, you are out of luck. Of course, if the Java method had return type `void`, you can simply ignore the return value of `execute_java_dynamic_method`.

Signatures

To call an arbitrary Java method, you need to learn the rules for "mangling" the names of method signatures. (A method signature describes the parameters and return type of the method.) Here is the encoding scheme:

B	byte
C	char
D	double
F	float
I	int
J	long
L*classname*;	a class type
S	short
V	void
Z	boolean

For the complete signature, you list the parameter types inside a pair of parentheses and then list the return type. For example, a method receiving two integers and returning an integer is encoded as

```
(II)I
```

The print method that we used in the preceding example has a mangled signature of

```
(Ljava/lang/String;)V
```

That is, the method receives a string and returns `void`.

Note that the semicolon at the end of the L expression is the terminator of the type expression, not a separator between parameters. Also note that in this encoding scheme only, you must use / instead of . to separate the package and class names.

To describe an array type, use a [. For example, an array of strings is

```
[Ljava/lang/String;
```

A `double[]` is mangled into

```
[[D
```

> NOTE: There is no rational reason why programmers are forced to use this mangling scheme for describing signatures. The designers of Java could have just as easily written a function that reads Java style signatures such as `void(int,java.lang.String)` and encodes them into whatever internal representation they prefer. Then again, using the mangled signatures lets you partake in the mystique of programming close to the virtual machine.

Static Methods

When calling a non-static method (such as `PrintStream.print(String)`), the Java runtime system locates the appropriate method by looking at the type of the implicit argument (an object of type `PrintStream` in our example), the name of the function and the signature. You can also call static Java methods from C, but the procedure is slightly different since there is no implicit argument to help locate the Java function you want to call. Instead, you need to obtain the `Class` object that describes the class of the static method. (See Chapter 5 for a description of the `Class` class.)

Use the `FindClass` function for this purpose. For example,

```
ClassClass* systemClass;
. . .
systemClass = FindClass(EE(), "java/lang/System", TRUE);
```

The first argument of the `FindClass` function describes the execution environment which is obtained from the `EE` function. The second argument is the name of the class. The third argument is `TRUE` if the classes should be *resolved*, that is, if the class loader should load the class and the classes that it requires into the virtual machine. This is what we need to do whenever we use `FindClass` to call a static method.

Once the class object has been found, we can call

```
execute_java_static_method(EE(), class_object, method_name,
    method_signature, parameters)
```

Here is an example of a static method call to the `getProperty` method of the `System` class.

```
ClassClass* systemClass
    = FindClass(EE(), "java/lang/System", TRUE);
char classPathKey[] = "java.class.path";
Hjava_lang_String* hclassPathKey
    = makeJavaString(classPathKey, strlen(classPathKey));
Hjava_lang_String* hclassPath
    = (Hjava_lang_String*)execute_java_static_method(EE(),
        systemClass, "getProperty",
        "(Ljava/lang/String;)Ljava/lang/String;",
        hclassPathKey);
```

You cannot access *static data members* of a class. They are not translated into C variables, nor is there any other mechanism for accessing or modifying them. If you need access to static data members, you must write a Java method to provide access and call the Java method from C. For example, if you want to have access to the stream `System.out`, you need to implement a Java method that returns that stream object.

Constructors

A native method can create a new Java object by invoking its constructor. This is achieved by calling

```
execute_java_constructor(EE(), class_name, class_object,
    constructor_signature, construction parameters)
```

When calling `execute_java_constructor`, you specify either the class name or the class object. The other parameter must be `NULL`!

For example, here is how a native method can create a `FileOutputStream` object:

```
char* fileName;
Hjava_lang_String* hfileName;
Hjava_io_FileOutputStream* hstream;
. . .
hfileName = makeJavaString(fileName, strlen(fileName));
hstream =(Hjava_io_FileOutputStream*)execute_java_constructor
    (EE(), "java/io/FileOutputStream", NULL,
    "(Ljava/lang/String;)", hfileName);
```

Note that the signature string of a constructors don't have a return value. To call the default constructor, you simply use " () " as the signature:

```
hemployee = (HEmployee*)execute_java_constructor(EE(),
    "Employee", NULL, "()");
```

We will see an example of a constructor call in the code of the next section.

Executing Java methods from C code

- ```
  long execute_java_dynamic_method(ExecEnv*, HObject*, char
  method_name[], char method_signature[], ...)
  ```

  calls the specified non-static method of the given object. The explicit parameters must be passed after the method signature. The return value must be cast to the appropriate method return type.

- ```
  long execute_java_static_method(ExecEnv*, ClassClass*, char
  method_name[], char method_signature[], ...)
  ```

  calls the specified static method of the given class. The explicit parameters must be passed after the method signature. The return value must be cast to the appropriate method return type.

- ```
  HObject* execute_java_constructor(ExecEnv*, char class_name[],
  ClassClass* class_object, char constructor_signature[], ...)
  ```

  calls the specified constructor of the given class. Either the class name or the class object must be NULL. The explicit parameters must be passed after the method signature. The return value must be cast to the appropriate method return type.

- ```
  ClassClass* FindClass(ExecEnv*, char class_name[], bool_t
  resolve)
  ```

  finds the class object belonging to the class with the given name. The resolve parameter determines if a class needs to load all classes that it references. It should be set to true.

Arrays

A Java array is accessible as a C structure to a native methods. The exact definition of the structure depends on the type of the Java array.

Java type	C type
boolean[]	typedef struct { long* body; } ArrayOfInt;
byte[]	typedef struct { char* body; } ArrayOfByte;
char[]	typedef struct { unicode* body; } ArrayOfChar;
int[]	typedef struct { long* body; } ArrayOfInt;
short[]	typedef struct { short* body; } ArrayOfShort;
long[]	typedef struct { int64_t* body; } ArrayOfLong;
float[]	typedef struct { float* body; } ArrayOfFloat;
double[]	typedef struct { double* body; } ArrayOfDouble;
Object[]	typedef struct { HObject* body; } ArrayOfObject;

The actual array elements are allocated by Java and are accessed through the `body` pointer.

Note that there are subtle differences between the mappings for the simple Java types and the mappings for arrays. (Remember, Java arrays are objects.) For example, a `short` is mapped to a `long`, but `short[]` is mapped to a structure containing a `short*` pointer that points to an array of `short` value. The rationale is that it doesn't matter if you waste some space for a single value, but arrays need to be efficient.

The `obj_length` macro returns the number of elements that can be stored in an array.

Native methods receive handles to the array types. Just as for class types, you use the `unhand` macro to obtain a pointer to the actual structure. Here is an example, a native static method that gives every employee in an `Employee[]` array a raise.

```
void Employee_raise_salaries(HEmployee* unused,
   HArrayOfObject* hstaff, double by)
{  ArrayOfObject* staff = unhand(hstaff);
   int length = obj_length(staff);
   int i;
   for (i = 0; i < length; i++)
   {  HEmployee* he = (HEmployee*)staff->body[i];
      ClassEmployee* ce = unhand(he);
      ce->salary *= 1 + by / 100;
   }
}
```

Note that all arrays of objects of any class are mapped to the same class, `ArrayOfObject`. To access an array element, you need to cast between the `HObject*` pointer and the pointer to the handle for the class of your array elements.

To create an array, use the `ArrayAlloc` function. It has two parameters, the type of the array and the size of the array. The type is one of the values shown in Table 16-1.

Table 16-1: Various types associated with ArrayAlloc

Java type	ArrayAlloc type parameter
boolean[]	T_BOOLEAN
byte[]	T_BYTE
char[]	T_CHAR
int[]	T_INT
short[]	T_SHORT
long[]	T_LONG
float[]	T_FLOAT
double[]	T_DOUBLE
Object[]	T_CLASS

When an array of *objects* is created, the array has one additional element at the end. You must store a class object into the slot that represents the type of the actual objects that can be inserted into the array. For example, here is how you create an array of 100 employees.

```
HArrayOfObject* hstaff
    = (HArrayOfObject*)ArrayAlloc(T_CLASS, 100);
ArrayOfObject* staff = unhand(hstaff);
staff->body[100] = (HObject*)FindClass(EE(), "Employee", TRUE);
```

There is a reason for this. As we discussed in Chapter 5, it is legal to store objects of type Employee and of any derived class in an Employee[] array. Whenever an element is stored in an array, the virtual machine checks that the type of the element equals the class object in the extra slot of the array. If not, Java throws an ArrayStoreException. If you store elements into an array in a native method, you are responsible for ensuring the integrity of the array.

The extra element that specifies the array type is only present with arrays of objects. All arrays of numbers have distinct types and do not use a type identifier.

Creating Java Arrays in C code

- `Handle* ArrayAlloc(int type, int size)`

    creates an array of `size` elements. type is one of `T_BOOLEAN`, `T_BYTE`, `T_CHAR`, `T_INT`, `T_SHORT`, `T_LONG`, `T_FLOAT`, `T_DOUBLE`, `T_CLASS`. In the case of `T_CLASS`, one additional element is allocated that must be filled with the `ClassClass*` pointer describing the type of the array elements. The memory of the array is garbage collected by Java.

Error Handling

Native methods are a significant security risk for Java programs. The C runtime system has no protection against array bounds errors, indirection through bad pointers, and so on. It is particularly important that programmers of native methods handle all error conditions to preserve the integrity of the Java system.

In particular, when your native method diagnoses a problem that it cannot handle, then it must signal the problem to the Java virtual machine. In Java code, you would naturally throw an exception in this case. However, C has no exceptions. Instead, you call the `SignalError` function to create an exception object. When the native method exits, Java will throw that exception. The call syntax is

```
SignalError(EE(), exception_class_name, construction_argument)
```

For example, here is how you would throw an IO exception:

```
SignalError(EE(), "java/io/IOException", "File not found");
```

You don't have to supply a description string. If the last parameter is `NULL`, Java constructs the exception object with its default constructor. For example,

```
SignalError(EE(), "java/lang/OutOfMemoryException", NULL);
```

 C++ NOTE: If you implement native methods in C++, you cannot currently throw a Java exception object in your C++ code. In a C++ binding, it would be possible to implement a translation between C++ and Java exceptions—unfortunately, this is not currently implemented. You need to use `SignalError` to throw a Java exception and make sure that your native methods throw no C++ exceptions.

Here is the `fprintDouble` native method, implemented with the paranoia that is appropriate for a native method. Here are the exceptions that we throw:

- a `NullPointerException` if the format string is `NULL`

- an `IllegalArgumentException` if the format string doesn't contain a % specifier that is appropriate for printing a `double`

In addition, the `makeJavaString` can signal an `OutOfMemoryException` if it can't allocate the string to be printed. In that case, it returns a `NULL` pointer and we exit the function. Since `makeJavaString` already called `SignalError`, we should not call it again.

Finally, after every call to the Java method `PrintStream.print`, we call `exceptionOccurred` to find out if an exception occurred during the call to the Java code. In that case, we return immediately. The exception will then be propagated to the caller of the native method.

```c
#include <string.h>
#include <stdlib.h>
#include <float.h>
#include <javaString.h>
#include "Printf4.h"
typedef struct Hjava_io_PrintStream Hjava_io_PrintStream;

char* find_format(char format[])
{   char* p = strchr(format, '%');
    char* q;
    size_t n;
    while (p != NULL && *(p + 1) == '%') /* skip %% */
        p = strchr(p + 2, '%');
    if (p == NULL) return NULL;
    /* now check that % is unique */
    p++;
    q = strchr(p, '%');
    while (q != NULL && *(q + 1) == '%') /* skip %% */
        q = strchr(q + 2, '%');
    if (q != NULL) return NULL; /* % not unique */
    q = p + strspn(p, " -0+#"); /* skip past flags */
    q += strspn(q, "0123456789"); /* skip past field width */
    if (*q == '.') { q++; q += strspn(q, "0123456789"); }
        /* skip past precision */
    if (strchr("eEfFgG", *q) == NULL) return NULL;
        /* not a floating point format */
    return p;
}

void Printf4_fprintDouble(HPrintf4* unused,
    Hjava_io_PrintStream* ps,
    Hjava_lang_String* hformat, double x)
{   char* format;
    char* fmt;
    char* buffer;
    int width;
    int i;
    if (hformat == NULL)
    {   SignalError(EE(), "java/lang/NullPointerException", NULL);
        return;
    }
```

```
        format = allocCString(hformat);
        fmt = find_format(format);
        if (fmt == NULL)
        {  SignalError(EE(), "java/lang/IllegalArgumentException",
              NULL);
           free(format);
           return;
        }
        width = atoi(fmt);
        if (width == 0) width = DBL_DIG + 10;
        buffer = (char*)malloc(strlen(format) + width);
        sprintf(buffer, format, x);
        for (i = 0; buffer[i] != 0 && !exceptionOccurred(EE());
              i++)
           execute_java_dynamic_method(EE(), (Hjava_lang_Object*)ps,
              "print",
              "(C)V", buffer[i]);
        free(buffer);
        free(format);
}
```

Error handling in C code

- `void SignalError(ExecEnv*, char classname[], char description[])`

  this prepares an exception to throw upon exiting from the native code. Java will throw the exception of the given name. The exception will be constructed using the default constructor if `description` is `NULL`, or from the description string otherwise.

- `bool_t exceptionOccurred(ExecEnv*)`

  this checks whether an exception has occurred, typically in the execution of a Java method.

A Complete Example: Big Numbers

In this section, we want to describe a full working example that covers everything we discussed in this chapter: strings, arrays, objects, constructor calls and error handling. We will put a Java wrapper around a C library for big number arithmetic. These big numbers are integers with an arbitrary number of digits, typically many hundreds of bits. One of the authors wrote the C code several years ago for cryptographic applications. The code may not be the most elegant code, but it has one great advantage: it works and illustrates all the techniques you will probably ever need. It would actually not be difficult to convert the code to Java.

NOTE: The `java.sql.Numeric` class that is part of JDBC contains an arbitrary precision arithmetic package written entirely in Java.

Here is the C code for the big number arithmetic. The only complex function is the division. The details of the code are not important. Just note that it looks just like typical production code—poorly commented and patched together until it works. Our goal is to provide a Java wrapper around this C code.

```c
#include <stdlib.h>
#include <string.h>
#include <ctype.h>

#define MAX(A, B) ((A) > (B) ? (A) : (B))

typedef unsigned short Uint16_t;
typedef unsigned int Uint32_t;

void add(const Uint16_t acoeff[], int asize,
    const Uint16_t bcoeff[], int bsize,
    Uint16_t ccoeff[], int csize)
{   int i;
    Uint32_t carry = 0;
    for (i = 0; (i < asize || i < bsize) && i < csize; i++)
    {   Uint32_t sum = (i < asize ? (Uint32_t)acoeff[i] : 0) +
            (i < bsize ? (Uint32_t)bcoeff[i] : 0) + carry;
        ccoeff[i] = (Uint16_t) sum;
        carry = sum >> 8 * sizeof(Uint16_t);
    }
    if (i < csize) ccoeff[i] = (Uint16_t)carry;
    for (i++; i < csize; i++) ccoeff[i] = 0;
}

void sub(const Uint16_t acoeff[], int asize,
    const Uint16_t bcoeff[], int bsize,
    Uint16_t ccoeff[], int csize)
{   int i;
    Uint32_t borrow = 0;
    for (i = 0; (i < asize || i < bsize) && i < csize; i++)
    {   Uint32_t diff = (i < asize ? (Uint32_t)acoeff[i] : 0) -
            (i < bsize ? (Uint32_t)bcoeff[i] : 0) + borrow;
        ccoeff[i] = (Uint16_t) diff;
        borrow = diff >> 8 * sizeof(Uint16_t);
        if (diff & (1 << (8 * sizeof(Uint32_t) - 1))) borrow |=
            (~0) << 8 * sizeof(Uint16_t);
    }
    while (i < csize) ccoeff[i++] = borrow;
}
```

```
int cmp(const Uint16_t acoeff[], int asize,
   const Uint16_t bcoeff[], int bsize)
{  int i;
   for (i = MAX(asize, bsize) - 1; i >= 0; i-)
   {  if (i >= bsize && acoeff[i] != 0) return 1;
      else if (i >= asize && bcoeff[i] !=0) return -1;
      else if (i < asize && i < bsize && acoeff[i] !=
         bcoeff[i])
         return (int)acoeff[i] - (int)bcoeff[i];
   }
   return 0;
}

void mul(const Uint16_t acoeff[], int asize,
   const Uint16_t bcoeff[], int bsize,
   Uint16_t ccoeff[], int csize)
{  int i;
   memset(ccoeff, 0, csize * sizeof(Uint16_t));
   for (i = 0; i < asize; i++)
   {  Uint32_t adigit = acoeff[i];
      if (adigit)
      {  Uint32_t carry = 0;
         int j;
         for (j = 0; j < bsize; j++)
         {  Uint32_t sum = adigit * (Uint32_t)bcoeff[j]
               + (Uint32_t)ccoeff[i + j] + carry;
            if (i + j < csize) ccoeff[i + j] = (Uint16_t)
               sum;
            carry = sum >> (8 * sizeof(Uint16_t));
         }
         if (i + j < csize) ccoeff[i + j] = (Uint16_t)carry;
      }
   }
}

void divmod(const Uint16_t acoeff[], int asize,
   const Uint16_t bcoeff[], int bsize,
   Uint16_t qcoeff[], int qsize,
   Uint16_t rcoeff[], int rsize)
{  int tsize = asize;
   Uint16_t* tcoeff = (Uint16_t*)malloc(tsize *
      sizeof(Uint16_t));
   int ttop;
   Uint32_t ttopval;
   int btop;
   Uint32_t btopval;
   memcpy(tcoeff, acoeff, asize * sizeof(Uint16_t));
   memset(qcoeff, 0, qsize * sizeof(Uint16_t));
```

```
btop = bsize - 1;
while (btop >= 0 && bcoeff[btop] == 0) btop—; /* top
   non-zero position */
if (btop < 0) { /* Divide by 0 */ return; }
btopval = (Uint32_t)bcoeff[btop]  << 8 * sizeof(Uint16_t);
if (btop > 0) btopval += bcoeff[btop - 1];
ttop = tsize - 1;
while (cmp(tcoeff, ttop + 1, bcoeff, bsize) >= 0) /* t >=
   b */
{  Uint32_t quot;
   int shift;
   while (ttop >= 0 && tcoeff[ttop] == 0) ttop—; /* top
      non-zero position */
   ttopval = (Uint32_t)tcoeff[ttop] << 8 *
      sizeof(Uint16_t);
   if (ttop > 0) ttopval += tcoeff[ttop - 1];
   quot = ttopval/(btopval+1);
   shift = 0;
   if (quot == 0)
   {  if (ttop == btop) quot = 1;   /* we know t >= b */
      else
      {  quot = ttopval/(bcoeff[btop]+1);
         shift = 1;
      }
   }
   if (quot != 0)
   {  Uint32_t borrow = 0;
      int i;

      if (ttop - btop - shift < qsize)
      {  Uint32_t qd = qcoeff[ttop - btop - shift] + quot;
         Uint32_t carry = qd >> 8 * sizeof(Uint16_t);
         qcoeff[ttop - btop - shift] = (Uint16_t)qd;
         i = ttop - btop - shift + 1;
         while (i < qsize && carry)
         {  qd = qcoeff[i] + carry;
            qcoeff[i] = (Uint16_t)qd;
            carry = qd >> 8 * sizeof(Uint16_t);
            i++;
         }
      }
      /* now we are computing t = t - quot * B^(ttop -
         btop - shift) * b */
      for (i = 0; i <= btop; i++)
      {  Uint32_t s1 = tcoeff[i + ttop - btop - shift];
         Uint32_t s2 = quot *
         (Uint32_t)bcoeff[i] + borrow;
         Uint16_t diff = (Uint16_t)(s1 - s2);
```

```
                          if (s1 < s2)
                          {   borrow = ((s2 - s1) >> 8 * sizeof(Uint16_t));
                              if (diff != 0) borrow++;
                          }
                          else
                          borrow = 0;
                          tcoeff[i + ttop - btop - shift] = diff;
                     }
                     if (shift && borrow)
                     tcoeff[ttop] -= borrow;
                }
          }

          if (rsize <= tsize)
             memcpy(rcoeff, tcoeff, rsize * sizeof(Uint16_t));
          else
          {   memcpy(rcoeff, tcoeff, tsize * sizeof(Uint16_t));
              memset(rcoeff + tsize, 0, (rsize - tsize) *
                 sizeof(Uint16_t));
          }

          free(tcoeff);
     }

     void toString(Uint16_t* acoeff, int asize, char* s, int ssize)
     {   Uint16_t* tcoeff;
         Uint16_t* qcoeff;
         int tsize = asize;
         Uint16_t ten = 10;
         Uint16_t r;
         int i = 0;
         if (asize == 0) { if (ssize >= 2) strcpy(s, "0");
             return; }

         tcoeff = (Uint16_t*)malloc(sizeof(Uint16_t) * asize);
         memcpy(tcoeff, acoeff, asize * sizeof(Uint16_t));
         qcoeff = (Uint16_t*)calloc(sizeof(Uint16_t), asize);

             /* write the reverse string */
         while (tsize > 0)
         {   divmod(tcoeff, tsize, &ten, 1, qcoeff, asize, &r, 1);
             if (i < ssize - 1) s[i++] = r + '0';
             while (tsize > 0 && tcoeff[tsize - 1] == 0)
             tsize--;
             memcpy(tcoeff, qcoeff, tsize * sizeof(Uint16_t));
         }
             /* strip off leading zeroes */
         while (i > 1 && s[i - 1] == '0') i--;
         if (ssize > 0)
```

```
    {      s[i] = 0;
        strrev(s);
    }
    free(tcoeff);
    free(qcoeff);
}

void fromString(Uint16_t* acoeff, int asize, char* s)
{   Uint16_t ten = 10;
    int rsize = strlen(s) / 4 + 1;
    Uint16_t* rcoeff = (Uint16_t*)calloc(sizeof(Uint16_t),
        rsize);
    int tsize = rsize;
    Uint16_t* tcoeff = (Uint16_t*)calloc(sizeof(Uint16_t),
        tsize);
    int i = 0;
    while (isdigit(s[i]))
    {   Uint16_t digit;
        mul(rcoeff, rsize, &ten, 1, tcoeff, tsize);
        digit = s[i] -'0';
        add(tcoeff, tsize, &digit, 1, rcoeff, rsize);
        i++;
    }
    if (asize <= rsize)
        memcpy(acoeff, rcoeff, asize * sizeof(Uint16_t));
    else
    {   memcpy(acoeff, rcoeff, rsize * sizeof(Uint16_t));
        memset(acoeff + rsize, 0, (asize - rsize) *
        sizeof(Uint16_t));
    }

    free(rcoeff);
    free(tcoeff);
}
```

A big number is represented as an array of short integers. We can construct a Bignum from a single integer, or from a string that contains digits. Note that constructors can't be native. Thus, the constructors are implemented in Java and then need to call a native method. The arithmetic functions and toString are native methods.

```
class Bignum
{   public Bignum()
    {   coeff = null;
    }

    public Bignum(int n)
    {   if (n <= 0) coeff = null;
        else if (n == (short)n)
        {   coeff = new short[1];
            coeff[0] = (short)n;
        }
        else
        {   coeff = new short[2];
            coeff[0] = (short)n;
            coeff[1] = (short)(n >> 16);
        }
    }

    public Bignum(String s)
    {   Bignum b = fromString(s);
        coeff = b.coeff;
    }

    public native static Bignum fromString(String s);
    public native String toString();
    public native Bignum add(Bignum b);
    public native Bignum sub(Bignum b);
    public native Bignum mul(Bignum b);
    public native Bignum div(Bignum b);
    public native Bignum mod(Bignum b);
    public native int cmp(Bignum b);

    static
    {   System.load("Bignum.dll");
    }

    private short[] coeff;
}
```

Now we need to implement the native methods. Each of them:

- Peels away the Java layer

- Exposes the C array of characters or `short` values

- Calls the C code library

- And, finally, converts the result back to a Java object.

(The only errors that we report are null references and memory exhaustion.)

```
#include <stdlib.h>
#include <string.h>
#include <ctype.h>

#include "Bignum.h"
#include "Bignum_lib.h"


#define MAX(A, B) ((A) > (B) ? (A) : (B))

static int bignum_size(HBignum* hb)
{   ClassBignum* cb = unhand(hb);
    HArrayOfShort* ha = cb->coeff;
    if (ha == NULL) return 0;
    return obj_length(ha);
}

static Uint16_t* bignum_coeff(HBignum* hb)
{   ClassBignum* cb = unhand(hb);
    HArrayOfShort* ha = cb->coeff;
    ClassArrayOfShort* ca;
    if (ha == NULL) return 0;
    ca = unhand(ha);
    return (Uint16_t*)ca->body;
}

HBignum* make_bignum(Uint16_t coeff[], int size)
{   int rsize;
    int i;
    HArrayOfShort* hr;
    HBignum* hretval;
    ClassBignum* cretval;
    for (rsize = size - 1; rsize >= 0 && coeff[rsize] == 0;
        rsize--)
        ;
    rsize++;
    if (rsize == 0)
        hr = NULL;
    else
    {   Uint16_t* rcoeff;
    hr = (HArrayOfShort*)ArrayAlloc(T_SHORT, rsize);
        rcoeff = (Uint16_t*)unhand(hr)->body;
        for (i = 0; i < rsize; i++) rcoeff[i] = coeff[i];
    }
    hretval = (HBignum*)execute_java_constructor(EE(), "Bignum",
        NULL, "()");
    cretval = unhand(hretval);
    cretval->coeff = hr;
```

```
      return hretval;
   }

   HBignum* Bignum_fromString(struct HBignum *unused, struct
      Hjava_lang_String *js)
   {  char* cs = allocCString(js);
      int rsize = strlen(cs) / 4 + 1;
      Uint16_t* rcoeff = (Uint16_t*)calloc(sizeof(Uint16_t),
         rsize);
      HBignum* retval;
      fromString(rcoeff, rsize, cs);
      retval = make_bignum(rcoeff, rsize);
      free(rcoeff);
      free(cs);
      return retval;
   }

   Hjava_lang_String* Bignum_toString(struct HBignum *a)
   {  char* s;
      Hjava_lang_String* retval;
      int asize = bignum_size(a);
      int ssize = 5 * asize + 2;
      s = malloc(ssize);
      toString(bignum_coeff(a), asize, s, ssize);
      retval = makeJavaString(s, strlen(s));
      free(s);
      return retval;
   }

   struct HBignum *Bignum_add(struct HBignum *a, struct HBignum
      *b)
   {  int asize = bignum_size(a);
      int bsize = bignum_size(b);
      int csize = MAX(asize, bsize) + 1;
      Uint16_t* acoeff = bignum_coeff(a);
      Uint16_t* bcoeff = bignum_coeff(b);
      Uint16_t* ccoeff = (Uint16_t*)calloc(sizeof(Uint16_t),
         csize);

      HBignum* retval;
      add(acoeff, asize, bcoeff, bsize, ccoeff, csize);
      retval = make_bignum(ccoeff, csize);
      free(ccoeff);
      return retval;
   }

   struct HBignum *Bignum_sub(struct HBignum *a,struct HBignum *b)
   {  int asize = bignum_size(a);
```

```
    int bsize = bignum_size(b);
    int csize = MAX(asize, bsize) + 1;
    Uint16_t* acoeff = bignum_coeff(a);
    Uint16_t* bcoeff = bignum_coeff(b);
    Uint16_t* ccoeff = (Uint16_t*)calloc(sizeof(Uint16_t),
        csize);

    HBignum* retval;
    sub(acoeff, asize, bcoeff, bsize, ccoeff, csize);
    retval = make_bignum(ccoeff, csize);
    free(ccoeff);
    return retval;
}

struct HBignum *Bignum_mul(struct HBignum *a,struct HBignum *b)
{   int asize = bignum_size(a);
    int bsize = bignum_size(b);
    int csize = asize + bsize + 1;
    Uint16_t* acoeff = bignum_coeff(a);
    Uint16_t* bcoeff = bignum_coeff(b);
    Uint16_t* ccoeff = (Uint16_t*)calloc(sizeof(Uint16_t),
        csize);

    HBignum* retval;
    mul(acoeff, asize, bcoeff, bsize, ccoeff, csize);
    retval = make_bignum(ccoeff, csize);
    free(ccoeff);
    return retval;
}

struct HBignum *Bignum_div(struct HBignum *a,struct HBignum *b)
{   int asize = bignum_size(a);
    int bsize = bignum_size(b);
    int qsize = MAX(asize - bsize + 1, 1);
    int rsize = bsize;
    Uint16_t* acoeff = bignum_coeff(a);
    Uint16_t* bcoeff = bignum_coeff(b);
    Uint16_t* qcoeff = (Uint16_t*)calloc(sizeof(Uint16_t),
        qsize);
    Uint16_t* rcoeff = (Uint16_t*)calloc(sizeof(Uint16_t),
        rsize);
    HBignum* retval;
    divmod(acoeff, asize, bcoeff, bsize, qcoeff, qsize, rcoeff,
        rsize);
    retval = make_bignum(qcoeff, qsize);
    free(qcoeff);
    free(rcoeff);
    return retval;
}
```

```
struct HBignum *Bignum_mod(struct HBignum *a,struct HBignum *b)
{  int asize = bignum_size(a);
   int bsize = bignum_size(b);
   int qsize = MAX(asize - bsize + 1, 1);
   int rsize = bsize;
   Uint16_t* acoeff = bignum_coeff(a);
   Uint16_t* bcoeff = bignum_coeff(b);
   Uint16_t* qcoeff = (Uint16_t*)calloc(sizeof(Uint16_t),
      qsize);
   Uint16_t* rcoeff = (Uint16_t*)calloc(sizeof(Uint16_t),
      rsize);
   HBignum* retval;
   divmod(acoeff, asize, bcoeff, bsize, qcoeff, qsize, rcoeff,
      rsize);
   retval = make_bignum(rcoeff, rsize);
   free(qcoeff);
   free(rcoeff);
   return retval;
}


long Bignum_cmp(struct HBignum *a,struct HBignum *b)
{  int asize = bignum_size(a);
   int bsize = bignum_size(b);
   Uint16_t* acoeff = bignum_coeff(a);
   Uint16_t* bcoeff = bignum_coeff(b);

   return cmp(acoeff, asize, bcoeff, bsize);
}
```

Finally, here is a test function for the library. There are two computations. First, we compute $100! = 1 \cdot 2 \cdot 3 \cdot \ldots \cdot 100$. Then we encrypt and decrypt a number using the RSA encryption scheme. Here n is the modulus, a product of two primes, e is the public encryption key and d is the private decryption key. To encrypt a number x, we raise it to the eth power modulo n. To decrypt, we raise it to the dth power modulo n. Amazingly enough, we get the original number back. It would be easy to implement an RSA encryption package, but we did not do that due to patent and export restrictions. This is shown in Example 16-9.

Example 16-9: BignumTest.java

```
class BignumTest
{  public static Bignum factorial(Bignum n)
   {  Bignum one = new Bignum(1);
      Bignum product = one;
      while (n.cmp(new Bignum(1)) > 0)
      {  product = product.mul(n);
         n = n.sub(one);
```

```
        }
        return product;
    }

    public static Bignum npow(Bignum a, Bignum b, Bignum n)
    {   Bignum zero = new Bignum(0);
        Bignum one = new Bignum(1);
        Bignum two = new Bignum(2);
        Bignum r = one;
        while (b.cmp(zero) > 0)
        {   if (b.mod(two).cmp(one) == 0) // b1 is odd
            {
                b = b.sub(one);
                r = r.mul(a).mod(n);
            }
            else
            {   b = b.div(two);
                a = a.mul(a).mod(n);
            }
        }
        return r;
    }

    public static void main(String[] args)
    {   System.out.println("100! = " + factorial(new
        Bignum(100)));

        Bignum x = new
Bignum("123456789012345678901234567890123456789012345678901234567890123456789012345678901234567890123456789012345678901234567890");
        Bignum n = new
Bignum("57046542440058195389946057059597737196610706009782269919235436259180889408425692976070001614001921421445064237310930158282688666559259549536059321309952733");
        Bignum d = new
Bignum("346164904667803359648692567975924353943166808761304288384033526142967493007676541369132663537182856586969606179779341311642315050505421376771130358335723");
        Bignum e = new Bignum("1333333333333333333331");

        Bignum y = npow(x, e, n);
        System.out.println("Encrypted data = " + y);
        x = npow(y, d, n);
        System.out.println("Decrypted data = " + x);
    }
}
```

CHAPTER 17

- JAR Files (Java Archive Files)

- Reflection

- Java IDL

- Security

- Object-Oriented Databases

Survey of Future Directions for Java

We hope to give you some perspective in this chapter on where we think Java is going. However, we are not employees of Sun nor have we signed any non-disclosure agreements. What we say here is based solely on public information. In particular, we have used information from talks given at the Java One conference that dealt with future directions along with what has been posted to the Net by JavaSoft.

TIP: Adobe Acrobat files for slides from the Java One conference may be found at:

    `http://www.javasoft.com/java.sun.com/javaone/sess.pres.html`

Cassettes containing tape recordings of the talks are available by calling "Convention Cassettes Unlimited" at 1-800-776-5454. The key URLs where Sun posts new information about Java are:

    `http://java.sun.com/products/JDK/1.1/designspecs/index.html`

and

    `http://java.sun.com/products/apiOverview.html`

Introduction

As we indicated in Chapter 1, when you think about changing the core language, the need for compatibility with existing code will always rear its ugly head. No one wants to change the code in the thousands of applets containing nervous text and dancing teeth that are out there. This means any changes in the base language are constrained by this overriding requirement. It is no surprise then that JavaSoft has made it clear that they will do their best to maintain compatibility with existing code.

A good example of the kind of change that *can* be made is the Object Serialization mechanism discussed in Chapter 11. This was added onto the existing stream mechanism; there were no underlying changes in the actual object model. Similarly, adding (as has been announced) object wrapper classes for Bytes, Shorts and even Voids isn't going to break any existing code. Similarly, Solaris platforms will get the ability to use either the Java 'Green' thread package or native Solaris threads. More speculatively, making the `Switch` statement capable of selecting on a richer set of situations would not break any existing code as long as the necessity for a break statement remains. (This one hasn't been announced; it is just a suggestion.)

Of course, there are changes that don't technically break any existing Java code but may give you more work. As an example of this, JavaSoft has announced that they intend to come out with a new standard for writing Java native methods. The idea is to make all native method libraries compatible on a specific platform. We suspect this will have the effect of requiring that all native code be re-compiled, new headers be generated and so on—although the actual Java code may not change.

Speculative Additions to the Language

The two most commonly requested new language features seem to be method references (normally called method pointers) and a mechanism for templates. At his talk at Java One, James Gosling suggested that they are seriously considering adding these features—some time down the road. For example, the keyword `generic` that would obviously be the one used for templates is already reserved.

However, he was also fairly cautious as to when this would happen. These kinds of features (especially templates) greatly add to the complexity of the underlying language and thus could violate the "simplicity" buzzword discussed in Chapter 1. We don't think these two features will be in Java 1.1. However, if we have to guess, we expect method pointers to be added before templates. This is because method pointers are inherently less complicated than templates and they make callbacks so much easier to handle than the cumbersome methods needed in the current version of Java.

Ultimately, we think the problem is that somewhere at JavaSoft, some very smart people are thinking: "If we add templates, are we falling too fast down the slippery slope of having Java converge on C++ in complexity?" We tend to agree. When you start adding the features to Java that go a long way toward giving you the power of C++, you will inevitably create a Java that is nearly as complex as C++.

New Libraries

While the basic Java language is going to stabilize pretty soon, there is explosive activity in *libraries*. Not only are existing libraries such as AWT being revamped, but there are a multitude of new proposed libraries, reaching all the way from commerce to multimedia. The idea is of course that there should be exactly one standard way of moving money out of your wallet and playing a video for you in return.

JAR Files (Java Archive Files)

If there has been one request made uniformly by Java developers, it has been for "zip class loaders." These would let you package all the information in your applet in a single file. The idea is that the user could then get your applet via a single HTTP request. The reason why this is important is that usually each class, image or audio file that is part of an applet must be requested via a separate HTTP request. This can take anywhere from a second or two to a *long* time to finish depending on the site and the state of your connection. (A few experimental zip loaders have actually been written to do this but none have received official support. For example, Netscape 3.0 has some support for actual zip format and Microsoft Internet Explorer has support for its cab format.) The JAR (Java ARchive) format is JavaSoft's implementation of this feature.

The JAR format is designed to be platform-independent. It will allow you to combine all the files (class files, images and sounds) you need into one single file. It will also allow compression to further reduce load times. The format will not be compatible with the ordinary Zip format but should be fairly easy to implement. Moreover, since they intend to write all the tools in Java, JAR will be available on any platform that has a Java virtual machine. They have also announced that JAR will be compatible with digital signing of applets. (See below for more on digital signatures.)

In our opinion, this is a nice addition to the infrastructure behind the language. It has no downside and lots of potential gain. (Although why they have to make yet another archive format is a bit beyond us.) We expect this feature to make it into Java 1.1.

Internationalization Issues

Since Java supports Unicode by design, one would think this is easy. However, it doesn't seem to be. For example, Java doesn't currently support the display of Unicode characters in the AWT and there is currently only minimal support for localized date/times/number display.

Another problem comes when converting GUI applications—even if you confine yourself to the currently supported character set. Since there is no notion of resource files in Java, the localized GUI interface must be manually re-coded for things like captions or images.

We expect them to add most everything one would want in the next version of Java *except* for an easy way to localize GUI-based programs. These changes will continue to need to be hand-coded. Java Beans (see below) may help here.

The AWT

Anyone who has worked with the AWT for any length of time knows that it is

- buggy (especially on X11, Windows and Mac);

- clumsy in many of the features that do work;

- lacking in features that one really needs (like printing).

The question is how to fix it—without breaking all the existing code. For example, JavaSoft has said they will be using a new event model in the next version of the AWT. This "delegation-based event model" will be constructed along the lines of the callback mechanism you saw in Chapter 5. In particular, it looks like the new event model will work something like this. The key notions will now be that of the *source* and the *listener*. Events will be encapsulated in a new `java.util.EventObject` hierarchy. Objects that should be capable of "listening" (responding) to an event will implement an interface called `java.util.EventListener`. The methods in the interface will correspond to the events. Event sources on the other hand will define listener event registrations by having methods that accept parameters implementing specific `EventListener` interfaces. How all this will interact with existing code is beyond us but, as we said, we expect existing code to continue to work in the same fashion it already does.

What else? JavaSoft has said they will be rewriting the peer part of the AWT for Windows 95 from scratch. But, more importantly they will be including:

- APIs for printing (we assume there will be a printer context that works essentially identically to the current graphics contents);

- A clipboard that allows cut/copy/paste between Java applications and the host windowing system. It will be a real challenge to develop a clipboard mechanism that actually works with both text and graphics on Windows, the Mac and X11/Motif;

- Custom cursors;

- Popup menu capability.

NOTE: At Java One, JavaSoft announced an alliance with Adobe to come out with what is in effect a "display/printer Postcript lite" called Bravo. We expect portions of the results of this alliance to be incorporated in the 1.1 version of the AWT but for the full version we will probably have to wait for Java 2.0.

Reflection

In the first edition of this book, we implemented a serialization mechanism manually. The programmer using that mechanism had to write code for every class to explicitly load and save its data fields. There was no way for a class to automatically enumerate all of its data members. A class knew its name, its superclass and nothing else about itself. Now there is an object serialization mechanism, but it wasn't implemented in Java. It is tightly linked to the virtual machine.

This will change in Java 1.1. Classes will be able to find out a lot about themselves, hence the term "reflection". The API defines four new classes, `Field`, `Method`, `Constructor`, and `Array`. They add methods to the `Class` class. For example, the call `x.getClass().getMethods()` returns an array of `Method` objects that describe all public methods of the class to which x belongs. Of course, there are security provisions to ensure that private properties of a class are only revealed to authorized code.

What can you do with this kind of information? As an application programmer, you will not usually want to write code that queries object capabilities at run-time. After all, compile-time type checking is a great security feature. This API is really for tool builders. Object inspectors, such as the property sheets in a GUI builder, need to be able to find out the relevant parts of the public interface of a component. Debuggers, browsers and object services such as serialization need to know the data representation of objects.

Inner Classes

It will be possible to define classes that are nested inside other classes. As in C++, the scope of the inner class is hidden inside the enclosing class. However, unlike nested classes in C++, an object of an inner class in Java must be created by an object in an enclosing class. It has access to all data fields in that object. Classes can even be defined inside methods, and the methods of such a class can access the local variables of the enclosing method. Anonymous inner classes can be created on the fly. For example, you can make a new object of an anonymous class extending Thread, whose run method has access to the local variables of the method creating it as well as the data fields of the implicit argument of that method. Inner classes provide a more convenient mechanism for writing callback functions that have access to instance and local variables.

Java IDL

IDL (which stands for *interface definition language*) is a complementary technology to RMI (see Chapter 15). IDL is an accepted standard defined and maintained by the Object Management Group (usually abbreviated OMG). Their web site is at www.omg.org.

As you have already seen, RMI lets you move objects and invoke methods back and forth between two machines running Java. The IDL is language-neutral and designed to work across platforms and languages. For example, you can send Java objects to code written in C++ or Smalltalk, and that code can invoke your Java methods. IDL defines a way of mapping specifications of objects defined across languages. IDLs depend on what are usually called *object request brokers* or ORBs to do the translations between the different platforms. Java's implementation of IDL follows the CORBA standard (common object request broker) that is supported by the more than 600 companies that make up the OMG. The actual ORB that works with IDL is something you usually need to buy (although JavaSoft has made one available for testing IDL with Java called DOOR).

Although an IDL ORB is potentially complicated for the tool vendor to implement (because of the problem of mapping one language's objects to another), in practice, using IDL is similar to using RMI. Of course, because IDL is language-neutral, there is no support for Java-specific features like distributed garbage collection. Thus, you would use RMI for Java-to-Java communication and IDL for Java-to-C++ communication.

Java Server API and Servlets

The idea is to develop a Java-powered server that is extendable via Java objects. (JavaSoft's prototype is currently called Jeeves—check out: www.javasoft.com/jeeves). Having a Java server would make it platform-independent, but this API can do more. In particular, this API would enable you to write Java objects ('servlets') that extend the power of any server that was written using these APIs. The advantage to this approach is that you can extend your server via objects that could be loaded on demand, at run time, in response to a specific request by a client. Servlets could completely replace CGI scripts, for example, or make it easy to provide new proxy servers for filtering and traffic control.

NOTE: If one is on an Intranet behind a firewall, the servlet could be uploaded from the client. (Hence the name 'servlet' to correspond to 'applet'.)

The advantage of a servlet over a CGI script is clear—CGI scripts can do many insecure things, and system administrators are naturally extremely cautious about installing untested scripts. Servlets can be configured to only "play in a sandbox," just as applets do.

Security

The trouble with applets is that the security restrictions are getting tighter and tighter, while what you can use them for is becoming less and less significant. Every time the Princeton group comes out with another hole, the noose tightens. (For example, inter-applet communications is now restricted by Netscape 3.0.)

This security blanket is sometimes described as "being stuck in a sandbox" and for applets (especially behind an intranet firewall) we need a way to break out of the sandbox. The Java Security API will provide the framework for things such as secure signatures for applets. Then, if you trust the person or organization who wrote the applet, you could let it do more to your system and thereby break out of the sandbox. This API will also allow you to plug in the encryption algorithm (DES, RSA…) of your choice. There will also be facilities for exchanging keys.

NOTE: JavaSoft has not announced whether they will use the depository approach to signatures or the "web of trust" approach. They have indicated that they are actually leaning towards a combination of the two.

At Java One in May, James Gosling indicated that this API was essentially complete. He said that the primary problem with getting it out the door was the various security restrictions on encryption technology imposed by the U.S. government. We assume that this is the reason why the first release of the Java security API will not be a complete one.

Java Commerce API

This API is designed to facilitate commerce on the Internet. It will not only support secure credit card transaction and home banking; it will also support what the people at JavaSoft are calling *microtransactions*. A microtransaction is the way applet writers hope to get rich. The idea is that if you download a signed

- The applet can request payment before it runs;

- It will support both a parking meter "spend down" and taxi meter "spend up" model for transactions.

Thus, if you decide to run such an applet, it could reduce your stock of "digital cash" by even a fraction of a cent. It will do this by debiting an account stored securely on your machine or on a third party server.

The current design of the Commerce API consists of three layers:

- a merchant layer for 'shopping carts' content along with a mechanism for identifying and charging the user;

- a cassette layer that will contain the various payment protocols;

- a wallet layer that is the user interface, security and database issues.

The wallet layer is designed to be the on-line equivalent of your physical wallet. Early demos of Java Commerce in fact show it is based on a GUI interface that even resembles a wallet.

A Java wallet can be filled with various *cassettes*. These cassettes can be dynamically added or removed in a secure way from a specific wallet. Each cassette will probably be a single JAR file that is signed digitally. The cassette will be object-based and encapsulate the user's identity along with the other things the cassette can do. For example, you could have both payment cassettes and cassettes for securely uploading personal data.

Java Management API

This API is designed for tool vendors of network administration software. That software helps network administrators manage their network, pinpoint trouble spots and tune performance. Sun has signed up a long list of industry partners, including AutoTrol, Bay Networks, BGS, BMC, Central Design Systems, Cisco Systems, Computer Associates, CompuWare, LandMark Technologies, Legato Systems, Novell, OpenVision, Platinum Technologies, Tivoli Systems, and 3Com, to ensure that these network component vendors agree on a common interface for gathering network management information. The advantage of using Java for network management is that networks tend to be multi-platform. It remains to be seen whether this effort will become significant—there are already well-established solutions for network management today.

Java Media API

The Java Media APIs are quite large. They range from the Bravo 2-D imaging model developed jointly with Adobe that would allow the equivalent of PostScript to be used for both displays and printing to a Java-based connection to VRML via a 3-D imaging model that JavaSoft is developing together with

SGI. These APIs will include the needed additions to Java in order to make it possible to take full advantage of multimedia. There are five different libraries proposed.

Java 2D is what is usually called the Bravo API. It is being developed with Adobe. It will probably include facilities for vector graphics, line art, fancier device-independent fonts, and better manipulation of images via transformations such as rotation and scaling, along with a richer color model that will allow overlays and transparencies.

Java Media Framework will have a new media player object that you can use to deal with a larger class of audio files in the Sun AU format. There will also be facilities for video playback with a richer clock model to allow synchronization of various events. (This is needed for processes such as MIDI playback and voice synthesis.)

Java Share provides for sharing of applications among multiple users. This will let you write shared whiteboard applets more easily.

Java Animation will let you animate 2D objects following the sprite model. For example, sprite collision detection would be built in. It will make use of the Java Media Framework API in order to deal with synchronization, composition and timing and use the 2D API for the richest possible display.

Java Telephony lets you integrate your telephone system into the Internet. You'll be able to save on long distance phone calls, perform sophisticated tele-conferencing and encrypt your conversations.

Java 3D is based on work with Silicon Graphics. This API will provide an abstract, interactive imaging model for behavior and control of 3D objects. It should be able to interface with VRML as well.

Java Beans API

We believe that Java Beans may be the key to the success of Java on the desktop. It is sometimes hard for OOP programmers to accept that *Visual Basic is the single most successful case of object reuse in the programming universe.* Java Beans is designed to bring the same idea that made Visual Basic so successful—reusable components—to Java.

Visual Basic programmers will immediately be comfortable with this notion. You work in a graphical development environment. You add components that have been developed by third parties, choosing from generic ones (a calendar) to specialized ones (a controller for a scientific instruments). Components expose properties for customization that you can set. For example, you can choose the font of the calendar or the sampling rate of the instrument. Each component typically has dozens of properties that suffice to control most of its behavior. You then write a few lines of glue code and you have a nice fancy GUI-based program in hours or days that would have taken weeks to create in C++, or, we hate to admit, in Java 1.0.

For those who have never seen Visual Basic or Delphi in action, here are two examples of potential Java Beans at work.

Suppose you want your user to enter a date. Wouldn't it be nice if you could have them click on an icon that pops up to a calendar from which they would choose the date? And if the calendar would show weekends and holidays in gray? You'd never write that from scratch, because it is just too much trouble. Someone did, though, and in Visual Basic, you can drop it in with a mouse drag. You deserve the same functionality in Java.

For a more serious example, consider the contortions we had to go through in the JDBC chapter to display the information in a specific database table on the fly. Compare this to how it is done in Visual Basic or Delphi:

- put a database control on your page;

- tell it the name of the database via a *property setting at design time or via code that sets a property at run time*;

- tell it the name of the table or the query you want it to display also via a property setting at design time or run time.

The control then fetches the data, resizes itself automatically based on the data it receives (adding scroll bars if necessary), and finally displays the data. All this can be done at design time or run time and takes at most 5 lines of code for the run-time version. (Oh yes, there are data-aware list boxes that could fetch the names of the tables for you with one line of code as well.)

Although the details are necessarily complicated (taking more than 70 pages at present) in the end Java Beans is nothing more than a *platform-independent* API for the Visual Basic/Delphi component model. (These two platforms are currently tied to Windows.)

NOTE: Microsoft is obviously pushing their ActiveX model to be used everywhere Java Beans hopes to go. As Microsoft's J++ product shows, it is very easy to build a bridge between ActiveX and Java, using Java's notion of an interface. It will probably come down to a race. Will Microsoft have a platform-independent version of ActiveX before Java Beans achieves critical mass? Your guess is as good as ours.

Object-Oriented Databases

JDBC is designed for dealing with relational databases, those for which a group of tables is the right model. There are also *object databases* which use an object-oriented model for the database. JavaSoft has announced plans for a Java *object-relational mapping* that would let object databases be used with JDBC. The URL to look for more details is www.odmg.org.

Appendix I
Java Keywords

Keyword	Meaning	See Chapter
abstract	an abstract class or method	5
boolean	the Boolean type	3
break	break out of a `switch` or loop	3
byte	the 8-bit integer type	3
case	a case of a `switch`	3
catch	the clause of a `try` block catching an exception	10
char	the Unicode character type	3
class	defines a class type	4
const	not used	
continue	continue at the end of a loop	
default	the default clause of a `switch`	3
do	the top of a `do`/`while` loop	3
double	the double precision floating number type	3
else	the `else` clause of an `if` statement	3
extends	defines the parent class of a class	4
final	a constant, or a class or method that cannot be overridden	5
finally	the part of a `try` block that is always executed	10
float	the single-precision floating point type	3
for	a loop type	3
future	not used	
generic	not used	
goto	not used	3
if	a conditional statmement	3
implements	defines the interface(s) that a class implements	5
import	import a package	4
inner	not used	

instanceof	test if an object is an instance of a class	5
int	the 32-bit integer type	3
interface	an abstract type with methods that a class can implement	3
long	the 64-bit long integer type	3
native	a method implemented by the host system	
new	allocates a new object or array	3
null	a null reference	3
operator	not used	
outer	not used	
package	a package of classes	4
private	a feature that is accessible only by methods of this class	4
protected	a feature that is accessible only by methods of this class, its children, and other classes in the same package	5
public	a feature that is accessible by methods of all classes	4
rest	not used	
return	return from a method	3
short	the 16-bit integer type	3
static	a feature that is unique to its class, not to objects of its class	3
super	the superclass object or constructor	4
switch	a selection statement	3
synchronized	a method that is atomic to a thread	12
this	the implicit argument of a method, or a constructor of this class	4
throw	throw an exception	10
throws	the exceptions that a method can throw	10
transient	used to mark data that should not be persistent	16
try	a block of code that traps exceptions	10
var	not used	
void	denotes a method that returns no value	3
volatile	not used	
while	a loop	3

Appendix II
The `javadoc` Utility

The `javadoc` utility parses source files for classes, methods and `/** . . . */` comments. It produces an HTML file in the same format as the API documentation. (In fact, they are basically the `javadoc` output of the Java source files.)

If you add comments that start with the special delimiter `/**` to your source code, you too can produce professional looking documentation easily. This is a very nice scheme because it lets you keep your code and documentation in one place. Traditional documentation efforts suffered from the problem that the code and comments diverged over time. But since the comments are in the same file as the source code, it is an easy matter to update both and run `javadoc` again.

We used the `/**` comments and `javadoc` on the files in our corejava package. Point your Web browser to `\CoreJavaBook\corejava\api\tree.html`, and you will see the corejava documentation in a format that looks startlingly familiar.

How to Insert Comments

The `javadoc` utility extracts information for every

    package

    public class

    public interface

    public or protected method

    public or protected instance variable

    public or protected constant

You can (and should) supply a comment for each of these features.

Each comment is placed immediately *above* the feature it describes. A comment starts with a `/**` and ends with a `*/`. Each separate line of the comment must start with an `*`. Like all comments, they are ignored by the Java compiler.

A comment is freeform text with optional HTML markups, followed by *tags*. A tag starts with an `@` and extends to the end of the line. In the freeform text, you can use HTML modifiers such as `<i>...</i>` for italics, `<tt>...</tt>` for a monospaced "typewriter" font, `<b>...</b>` bold for bold, and even `<img ...>` to include an image. You should, however, stay away from heading `<h1>` or rules `<hr>` since they interfere with the formatting of the document.

The following tags are supported:

```
@see class
@see class#method
```

These tags add a hyperlink to the class or method.

```
@version text
```

This tag makes a "version" entry. Can be used only with classes and interfaces.

```
@author name
```

This tag makes an "author" entry. There may be multiple author tags, but they must all be together. Can be used only with classes and interfaces.

```
@param variable description
```

This tag adds an entry to the "Parameters" section of the current method. The description can span multiple lines and use HTML tags. All @param tags for one method must be kept together. Can be used only with methods.

```
@return description
```

This tag adds a "Returns" section to the current method. The description can span multiple lines and use HTML tags. Can be used only with methods.

```
@throws class description
```

This tag adds an entry to the "Throws" section of the current method. A hyperlink is automatically created. The description can span multiple lines and use HTML tags. All @throws tags for one method must be kept together. Can be used only with methods.

Here is an example of a class comment:

```
/**
 * A class for formatting numbers that follows <tt>printf</tt>
 * conventions. Also implements C-like <tt>atoi</tt> and
 * <tt>atof</tt> functions
 * @version 1.01 15 Feb 1996
 * @author Cay Horstmann
 */
```

Here is an example of a method comment:

```
/**
 * Formats a double into a string (like <tt>sprintf</tt> in C)
 * @param x the number to format
 * @return the formatted string
 * @throws IllegalArgumentException if bad argument
 */
```

How to Extract Comments

Here `docDirectory` is the name of the directory you want the HTML files to go to. Follow these steps:

1. Move to the directory that contains the source files you want to document. If you have nested packages to document, such as `COM.horstmann.corejava`, you must be in the directory that contains the subdirectory COM.

2. Run the command

   ```
   javadoc -d docDirectory nameOfPackage
   ```

   for a single package. Or run

   ```
   javadoc -d docDirectory nameOfPackage1 nameOfPackage2...
   ```

   to document multiple packages.

Note that the HTML files expect GIF files in a subdirectory named `images`. You can just copy the GIF files from \java\api\images.

Appendix III
Macintosh Specific Issues
By Kamal Abdali

What this appendix tries to do is give you some tips on getting the code in this book to run on a Macintosh. We can make no guarantees. For one thing, traditionally, versions of the JDK come out a bit later for the Macintosh than for Solaris or Wintel platforms. For example. we can't supply you with versions of JDBC and RMI for the Macintosh, since none are available as we write this. Moreover, the JDK for the Macintosh have had a tendency when they first come out to be buggier than the corresponding ones for Solaris or Wintel platforms and to have operating system dependencies (i.e., to work on System 7.5 but not on 7.53 or vice versa) as well.

Excluding RMI and JDBC (for which our only suggestion is to check out `java.sun.com` to see when versions of them will be released), the most serious problems that the Mac JDK user encounters in running examples in this book are:

- Specifying the CLASSPATH

- Providing "console" inputs.

In particular, the intuitive and obvious ways of doing these things often don't work. After trying various kind of MacOS gymnastics, we have chosen to give here one set of procedures that work and are fairly simple to carry out in practice.

NOTE: If you are using a commercial environment such as Café, Code Warrior, or Roaster, contact the vendor for information on how to work with command line and console inputs.

Getting Started

Since there is no concept of a "command line" on the Mac, the JDK operation is different under the MacOS than under Windows or Solaris. Some applications running on the Mac do have nice, intuitive interfaces to specify command line arguments, input-output redirection, and the console windows. But the current version of the JDK has a different, less convenient interface. (It also does not consistently follow the usual Mac conventions regarding cursor shapes, preference specification, and menu highlighting … to name a few other problem areas.)

The JDK does not have a built-in editor, so you need to prepare your Java program files using an external editor. The JDK does "interface" with certain editors in the following sense: When the JDK detects an error while compiling a program, the Java compiler lists the error messages and then displays the erroneous program lines in a window. The window also has two buttons: one to launch an editor and display the program, so you can edit it, and another to resubmit the edited program to the compiler.

The editors that are supported in this way by the JDK are not user-specifiable; they come from a fixed lists. Some of the supported editors are the ones built into commercial Java development environments (Café, Code Warrior, and Roaster). But, of course, if you have one of these, it is unlikely that you would be using the JDK directly. Two other editors that are supported are SimpleText and BBEdit. The former comes bundled with the MacOS. It is simple to use, but is fairly limited in capability. For example, it can open only one window at a time and is restricted to files of maximum length 32K bytes. The latter has a freeware version, called BBEdit Lite. It is more powerful than SimpleText. BBEdit can open several windows simultanously and has quite sophisticated search/replace operations.) We recommend it. To download BBEdit Lite, visit `http://www.barebones.com/freeware.html`.

NOTE: To deal with the CLASSPATH the way we suggest here, you'll also need the ResEdit application.

Installing the MacJDK

First copy the JDK102.SEA from the CD-ROM to your hard disk, and then double click on the copy. The Mac will open up an installer window. Clicking on the "Easy Install" button will install the software in a folder called "JDK 1.0.2" on your hard disk. (You can click on the "Select Folder" button to place the JDK in some other location. But we assume you have chosen the default installation.) The installer will also create a folder called "JavaSoft Folder" inside the Extensions folder of your System Folder, and a folder called "MacJava Preferences" inside the Preferences folder of your System Folder.

Installing the Core Java Code

Copy COREJAVA.SEA to your hard disk, and double click on the copy. Files from this self-extracting archive will be placed in a folder called "COREJAVA" on your hard disk.

Installing CoreJava Classes

Open the "COREJAVA" folder, then the "CoreJavaBook" folder inside it. You'll see inside of it a folder called "corejava". This folder contains the classes that are used by some of the programs in this book via a call to import corejava.*.

1. Click once on corejava to select it.

2. Then go to the File menu, and select Make Alias (or press Cmd-M).

This will create an alias with the name "corejava alias." Move "corejava alias" to the desktop for the moment, and close the open folders CoreJavaBook and COREJAVA to reduce the clutter on your desktop. Next:

1. Open the "JavaSoft Folder" which is inside the Extensions folder of the System Folder.

2. Move "corejava alias" from the desktop to the folder called "Class Files" inside the "JavaSoft Folder."

3. Then rename "corejava alias" to just "corejava."

Again close the folders you just opened. The next step is to modify the JDK applications using the ResEdit. These applications are:

1. "Java Compiler" inside "JDK 1.0.2" (in your hard disk folder).

2. "Applet Viewer" inside "Applets" inside "JDK 1.0.2"

3. "Java Runner" inside "Standalone Apps" inside "JDK 1.0.2"

> Caution: To make sure you can revert back to the original applications if you mess up, we recommend making a backup copy of these first.

To do this, do the following with each of the three in turn. Click once on the application icon to select it, then select Duplicate from the File menu (or press Cmd-D). You will be creating new files called "Java Compiler copy", and so on. These are your backups while you modify the originals. In case of a problem (all too common when using ResEdit), just throw away the originals to the Trash, change the names back ("Java Compiler copy" to Java Compiler", and so on), and start all over again.

Here are the steps needed to modify the applications.

1. Launch ResEdit.

2. Choose Open from the File menu, and navigate the File Open dialog to "Java Compiler". ResEdit will open a window showing the resources in this application.

3. Double click on the STR (*not* STR#) icon. A window listing STR resources will open.

4. Double click on the line with the name "Compiler Classpath".

5. In the window that opens, there is an entry labeled "The String". Append the following to it

    ```
    :/$INSTALLATION_CLAS
    ```

   (Remember to type a single S in CLAS.)

6. Figures 1 & 2 show the ResEdit windows before and after the change. From the File menu, choose Save. Now close all the windows. You have now modified the Java Compiler application to deal correeectly with classpaths.

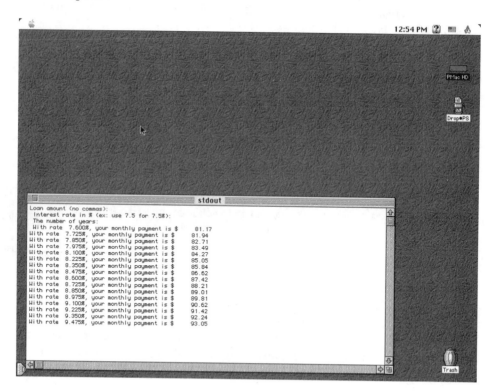

Figure A3-1

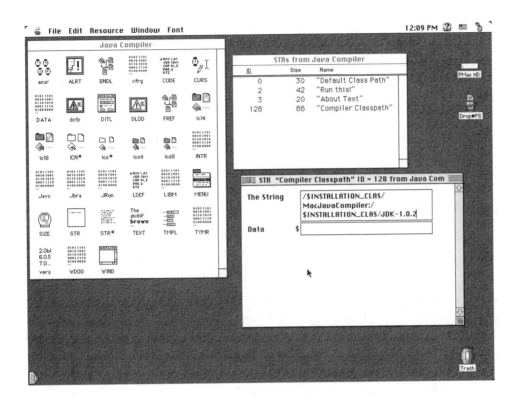

Figure A3-2

Do the same for the Applet Viewer and Java Runner. The name of the string resource in Step 4 is "AppletViewer Classpath" for the Applet Viewer, and "Default Classpath" for Java Runner.

Compiling Java Programs

To start the compiler, just double click on "Java Compiler". The default editor that the compiler launches is SimpleText. If you want to use a different editor (e.g., BBEdit), then go to the File menu and select "Properties..." (or press Cmd-,). The Compiler Properties menu opens up. Press on the dropdown menu showing the currently chosen editor, and select the one you like from the list.

To compile a program, go to the File menu and select "Compile File..." (or press Cmd-O), and navigate through the dialog box to the Java file you want to compile. The compiler will write the compiled (class) file in the same directory where the Java file was. If there are errors, the compiler will open a window and list the error messages in it. If you click on an error message, the compiler will automatically launch the currently selected editor, display the Java source program in it, and will scroll so that the erroneous line of code is in view. (Or, you can launch the editor yourself by clicking on the Edit button in the compiler message window.)

To quit the Java Compiler, close the "javac" window, or choose Quit from the File menu (or press Cmd-Q). If you quit, any changes you made in Compiler Properties are gone, and you have to make them again when you relaunch the compiler. You can also leave the compiler running (the javac window will show the compiler state as "idle" when it's not actually compiling anything), and then come back to it again when you want to compile another file.

Running Standalone Applications. Console Input-Output

To run standalone applications (not applets), launch the Java Runner application. It opens a file dialog box through which you have to navigate to the class file you want to run. The JDK does not implement a console in a traditional way. For standard output, what it does is open a window, and display all program output there as one might expect. But for standard input, what it does is *prompt the user for one input line at a time by opening a one line text window.*

When the Java program starts, the Java Runner opens this window and asks for "command line arguments". Type the arguments you want (i.e., what should be args[] in main, then click on OK. If you don't want to provide any command line arguments, then you can just click on OK.

Whenever the program needs an input, the Java Runner opens a one line text window, and then asks for:

```
Command line for stdin
```

Type what you want to enter and then click on OK (or press the Enter key). As long as the input is incomplete (for example, if several lines of input are needed), the Runner keeps opening the window again. When finished with the input, click on Cancel (or press the Escape key).

Figure 3 shows the MortgageLoop program from Chapter 3. To display the prompts produced by the program more clearly, we have added line feed characters "\n" to the end of prompt strings. This program needs three inputs: loan amount, interest rate, and loan period. Figures 4 & 5 show you some input windows that the Runner brings up. For each input, you first type the input data, and click on OK the first time, then just click on Cancel the next time. By the way, the cursor in the input window has the globe shape, conventionally used on the Mac to indicate that a computation is going on. This is misleading because there is nothing to wait for. Ignore this shape, and go ahead with your typing.

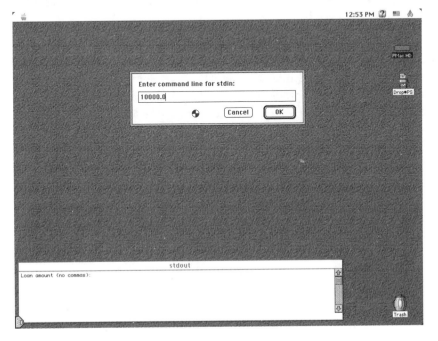

```
 File  Edit  Text  Search  Extensions  Windows                    1:06 PM
                              MortgageLoop.java
     Last Saved: 8/23/96 1.06.13 PM

 * BY LICENSEE AS A RESULT OF USING, MODIFYING OR DISTRIBUTING
 * THIS SOFTWARE OR ITS DERIVATIVES.
 */

/**
 * @version 1.00 07 Feb 1996
 * @author Gary Cornell
 */

import corejava.*;

public class MortgageLoop
{  public static void main(String[] args)
   {  double principal;
      double yearlyInterest;
      int years;

      //principal = Console.readDouble
         //("Loan amount (no commas):");
      //yearlyInterest = Console.readDouble
         //("Interest rate in % (ex: use 7.5 for 7.5%):") / 100;
      //years = Console.readInt
         //("The number of years:");
      principal = Console.readDouble("Loan amount (no commas):\n");
      yearlyInterest = Console.readDouble("Interest rate in % (ex: use 7.5 for 7.5%):\n") / 100;
      years = Console.readInt("The number of years:\n");

      double y;
      for (y = yearlyInterest - 0.01;
         y <= yearlyInterest + 0.01; y += 0.00125)
      {  double monthlyInterest = y / 12;
         double payment = principal * monthlyInterest
            / (1 - (Math.pow(1/(1 + monthlyInterest),
               years * 12)));
         Format.print(System.out,
            "With rate %6.3f", 100 * y);
         Format.print(System.out,
            "%%, your monthly payment is $%10.2f\n", payment);
      }
   }
}
```

Figure A3-3

Figure A3-4

Figure A3-5

After the program terminates, you can examine the output window. When you're done, you can close this window. This does not terminate the Runner, although you can't run another application using the same Runner invocation. To end the Runner session, go to to Apple menu, select the submenu Java Runtime..., then select Quit (or press Cmd-Q). Sometimes when you want to do this, the entire menu bar, including the Apple menu, appears deselected. Don't worry, it just looks that way but it really is active.

Running Applets

To run applets, launch the applet viewer application. It opens a file dialog box from which you can navigate to the HTML file that corresponds to the applet. Applets run rather smoothly, essentially as discussed in Chapter 8 of this book.

Index

SUNSOFT PRESS

Prentice Hall PTR is pleased to publish SunSoft Press books. This year's SunSoft catalog has unprecedented breadth and depth, covering not only the inner workings of Sun operating systems, but also guides to multiprocessing, internationalization of software, networking, and other topics important to anyone working with these technologies.

These and other Prentice Hall PTR books are available at your local Magnet Store. To locate the store nearest you fax (201) 236-7123 or visit our web site at:

http://www.prenhall.com

ALL ABOUT ADMINISTERING NIS+, Second Edition

Rick Ramsey

Updated and revised for Solaris™ 2.3, this book is ideal for network administrators who want to know more about NIS+: its capabilities, requirements, how it works, and how to get the most out of it. Includes planning guidelines for both new installations and for transitions from NIS; detailed descriptions of the structure of NIS+ objects and security; and setup instructions for both standard NIS+ comands and NIS+ shell scripts. Presents modular, fully-tested, step-by-step instructions and many illustrations, examples, and tips.

1995, 480 pp., Paper, 0-13-309576-2 (30957-5)

AUTOMATING SOLARIS INSTALLATIONS

Paul Anthony Kasper and Alan L. McClellan

If you want to minimize the time you spend installing the Solaris environment on SPARC™ or x86 systems, this book is for you! It describes how to set up "hands-off" Solaris installations for hundreds of SPARC or x86 systems. It explains in detail how to configure your site so that when you install Solaris, you simply boot a system and walk away—the software installs automatically! Topics covered include setting up network booting, enabling automatic system configuration, setting up custom JumpStart files, booting and installing, debugging and trouble-shooting. A diskette containing working shell scripts that automate pre- and post-installation tasks is provided.

1995, 320 pp., Paper, 0-13-312505-X (31250-4) Book/Disk

CONFIGURATION AND CAPACITY PLANNING FOR SOLARIS SERVERS

Brian L. Wong

Written for MIS staff, this book provides information on planning and configuring Solaris servers for use in NFS™, DBMS, and timesharing environments. The material concentrates on applied computer architecture, case studies and experimentally-based, real-world results rather than on queueing models.

1996, 300 pp., Paper. 0-13-349952-9 (34995-1)

THE UNIX BOOK OF GAMES

Janice Winsor

A collection of classic games with complete rules and illustrated tips and hints. Includes commentary by the programmers who created each game. Includes complete source code and binaries for SCO and Linux.

1997, 256 pp., Paper, 0-13-490079-0 (49007-8) Book/CD-ROM

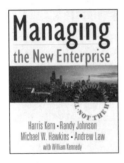

MANAGING THE NEW ENTERPRISE:
The Proof, Not The Hype

Harris Kern, Randy Johnson, Andrew Law, and Michael Hawkins with William Kennedy

In this follow-up to the best selling *Rightsizing the New Enterprise*, the authors discuss how to build and manage a heterogeneous client/ server environment. *Managing the New Enterprise* describes in detail the key technology support infrastructures, including networking, data centers, and system administration, as well as how Information Technology must change in order to manage the New Enterprise. This is an indispensable reference for anyone within Information Technology who is facing the challenges of building and managing client/server computing.

1996, 240 pp., Cloth, 0-13-231184-4 (23118-3)

PC HARDWARE CONFIGURATION GUIDE:
For DOS and Solaris

Ron Ledesma

This book eliminates trial-and-error methodology by presenting a simple, structured approach to PC hardware configuration. The author's time-tested approach is to configure your system in stages, verify and test at each stage, and troubleshoot and fix problems before going on to the next stage. Covers both standalone and networked machines. Discusses how to determine x86 hardware configuration requirements, how to configure hardware components (MCA, ISA, and EISA), partitioning hard disks for DOS and UNIX, and installing DOS and/or UNIX (Solaris x86). Includes configuration instructions, checklists, worksheets, diagrams of popular SCSI host bus, network, and video adapters, and basic installation troubleshooting.

1995, 352 pp., Paper, 0-13-124678-X (12467-7)

NEW!

NETWORKING THE NEW ENTERPRISE:
The Proof, Not The Hype

Harris Kern and Randy Johnson

The final volume in the New Enterprise Trilogy, this book focuses on planning network projects, developing architectures, and implementations of expanding distributed computing and client server technologies. A must for any business in today's growing marketplace.

Networking the New Enterprise includes in-depth ideas for developing network architectures; including, key methods, and strategies for network management, security and design; details on implementing Network Management Systems; Methods for enhancing, securing and optimizing Networks.

1997, 350 pages, paper, 0-13-263427-9 (26342-6)

INTERACTIVE UNIX OPERATING SYSTEM:
A Guide for System Administrators

Marty C. Stewart

Written for first-time system administrators and end users, this practical guide describes the common system administration menus and commands of the INTERACTIVE UNIX System V/386 Release 3.2, Version 4.0 and SVR 3.2 UNIX in general. Loaded with step-by-step instructions and examples, it discusses how to install and configure the INTERACTIVE UNIX system, including the hardware requirements. It describes the unique CUI menu interface, basic OS commands, administration of new user accounts, configuration of customized kernels, and working with the INTERACTIVE UNIX system as an end user.

1996, 320 pp., Paper, 0-13-161613-7 (16161-2)

MULTIPROCESSOR SYSTEM ARCHITECTURES:
A Technical Survey of Multiprocessor / Multithreaded Systems Using SPARC, Multi-level Bus Architectures and Solaris (SunOS)
Ben Catanzaro

Written for engineers seeking to understand the problems and solutions of multi-processor system design, this hands-on guide is the first comprehensive description of the elements involved in the design and development of Sun's multiprocessor systems. Topics covered include SPARC processor design and its implementations, an introduction to multilevel bus architectures including MBus and XBus/XDBus, an overview of the Solaris/SunOS™ multithreaded architecture and programming, and an MBus Interface Specification and Design Guide. This book can serve as a reference text for design engineers as well as a hands-on design guide to MP systems for hardware/software engineers.

1994, 528 pp., Paper, 0-13-089137-1 (08913-6)

PANIC! UNIX System Crash Dump Analysis
Chris Drake and Kimberley Brown

PANIC! is the first book to discuss in detail UNIX system panics, crashes and hangs, their causes, what to do when they occur, how to collect information about them, how to analyze that information, and how to get the problem resolved. *PANIC!* presents this highly technical and intricate subject in a friendly, easy style which even the novice UNIX system administrator will find readable, educational and enjoyable. It is written for systems and network administrators and technical support engineers who are responsible for maintaining and supporting UNIX computer systems and networks. Includes a CD-ROM containing several useful analysis tools, such as adb macros and C tags output from the source trees of two different UNIX systems.

1995, 496 pp., Paper, 0-13-149386-8 (14938-5) Book/CD-ROM

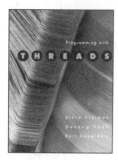

PROGRAMMING WITH THREADS
Steve Kleiman, Devang Shah, and Bart Smaalders

Written by senior threads engineers at Sun Microsystems, Inc., this book is the definitive guide to programming with threads. It is intended for both novice and more sophisticated threads programmers, and for developers multithreading existing programs as well as for those writing new multithreaded programs. The book provides structured techniques for mastering the complexity of threads programming with an emphasis on performance issues. Included are detailed examples using the new POSIX threads (Pthreads) standard interfaces. The book also covers the other UNIX threads interface defined by UNIX International.

1996, 250 pp., Paper, 0-13-172389-8 (17238-9)

RIGHTSIZING THE NEW ENTERPRISE:
The Proof, Not The Hype
Harris Kern and Randy Johnson

A detailed account of how Sun Micro-systems implemented its rightsizing strategy going from a mainframe data center to a heterogeneous client/server distributed environment. This book covers the key infrastructures of an IT organization (the network, data center, and system administration), the rightsizing/management tools, and the training/resource issues involved in transitioning from mainframe to UNIX support. The facts contained in this book provide you with the PROOF that 'rightsizing' can be done.and has been done.

1995, 352 pp., Cloth, 0-13-490384-6 (49038-3)

RIGHTSIZING FOR CORPORATE SURVIVAL:
An IS Manager's Guide
Robert Massoudi, Astrid Julienne, Bob Millradt, and Reed Hornberger

This book provides IS managers with "hands-on" guidance for developing a rightsizing strategy and plan. Based upon research conducted through customer visits with multinational corporations, it details the experiences and insights gained by IS professionals that have implemented systems in distributed, client-server environments. Topics covered include:

- Why rightsize?
- What business results can rightsizing produce?
- Key technologies critical to rightsizing
- Good starting points for rightsizing
- What is the process to rightsize an information system?
- Cost considerations and return on investment (ROI) analysis

- How to manage the transition

Throughout the book, case studies and "lessons learned" reinforce the discussion and document best practices associated with rightsizing.

1995, 272 pp., Paper,
0-13-123126-X (12312-5)

READ ME FIRST!
A Style Guide for the Computer Industry

Sun Technical Publications

A comprehensive look at documenting computer products, from style pointers to legal guidelines, from working with an editor to building a publications department—in both hard copy and electronic copy with an on line viewer, FrameMaker templates for instant page design, and a detailed guide to establishing a documentation department and its processes. Based on an internationally award-winning Sun Microsystems style guide (Award of Excellence in the STC International Technical Publications Competition, 1994)

1996, 300 pp., Paper,
0-13-455347-0 (45534-6)
Book/CD-ROM

SOLARIS IMPLEMENTATION:
A Guide for System Administrators

George Becker, Mary E. S. Morris and Kathy Slattery

Written by three expert Sun system administrators, this book discusses real world, day-to-day Solaris 2 system administration for both new installations and for those migrating an installed Solaris 1 base. It presents tested procedures to help system administrators to improve and customize their networks by eliminating trial-and-error methodologies. Also includes advice for managing heterogeneous Solaris environments and provides autoinstall sample scripts and disk partitioning schemes (with recommended sizes) used at Sun.

1995, 368 pp., Paper,
0-13-353350-6 (35335-9)

CREATING WORLD WIDE WEB SOFTWARE:
SOLARIS, Second Edtion

Bill Tuthill and David Smallberg

Written for software developers and business managers interested in creating global applications for the Solaris environment (SPARC and x86), this second edition expands on the first edition and has updated information on international markets, standards organizations, and writing international documents. New topics in the second edition include CDE/Motif, NEO (formerly project DOE)/ OpenStep, Universal codesets, global internet applications, code examples, and success stories.

1996, 250 pp., Paper,
0-13-494493-3 (49449-2)

SOLARIS PORTING GUIDE,
Second Edition

SunSoft Developer Engineering

Ideal for application programmers and software developers, the *Solaris Porting Guide, Second Edition*, provides a comprehensive technical overview of the Solaris 2.x operating environment and its related migration strategy. The second edition is current through Solaris 2.4 (both the SPARC and x86 platforms) and provides all the information necessary to migrate from Solaris 1 (SunOS 4.x) to Solaris 2 (SunOS 5.x). Other additions include a discussion of emerging technologies such as the Common Desktop Environment (CDE), hints for application performance tuning, and extensive pointers to further information, including Internet sources.

1995, 752 pp., Paper,
0-13-443672-5 (44367-1)

SUN PERFORMANCE AND TUNING:
SPARC and Solaris

Adrian Cockcroft

An indispensable reference for anyone working with Sun workstations running the Solaris environment, this book provides detailed performance and configuration information on all SPARC machines and peripherals, as well as on all operating system releases from SunOS 4.1 through Solaris 2.4. It includes hard-to-find tuning information and offers insights that cannot be found elsewhere. This book is written for developers who want to design for performance and for system administrators who have a system running applications on which they want to improve performance.

1995, 288 pp., Paper,
0-13-149642-5 (14964-1)

THREADS PRIMER:

A Guide to Solaris Multithreaded Programming

Bil Lewis and Daniel J. Berg

Written for developers interested in MT programming, this primer overviews the concepts involved in multithreaded development. Based on the Solaris multithreaded architecture, the primer delivers threading concepts that can be applied to almost any multithreaded platform. The book covers the design and implementation of multithreaded programs as well as the business and technical benefits of threads. Both the Solaris and the POSIX threads API are used as the interface needed to develop applications. Extensive examples highlight the use of threads in real-world applications. This book is a must read for developers interested in MT technology!

1996, 352 pp., Paper, 0-13-443698-9 (44369-7)

WABI 2: Opening Windows

Scott Fordin and Susan Nolin

Wabi™ 2 is here and now you can run Microsoft and Windows 3.1 applications on UNIX-based computers! Written for both users and system administrators of Wabi software, this book covers everything you wanted to know about Wabi 2, including: Wabi technical history, how Wabi works, UNIX for Microsoft Windows users, Microsoft Windows for UNIX users, X Window terminology and interface objects, additional sources of information on Wabi, sample settings in which Wabi is used, and common questions asked by users.

1996, 400 pp., Paper, 0-13-461617-0 (46161-6)

NEW!

VERILOG HDL:

A Guide to Digital Design and Synthesis

Samir Palnitkar

Everything you always wanted to know about Verilog HDL, from fundamentals such as gate, RTL and behavioral modeling to advanced concepts such as timing simulation, switch level modeling, PLI and logic synthesis. This book approaches Verilog HDL from a practical design perspective rather than from a language standpoint. Includes over 300 illustrations, examples, and exercises, and a Verilog Internet reference resource list. Learning objectives and summaries are provided for each chapter. The CD-ROM contains a verilog simulator with a graphical user interface and the source code for the examples in the book. This book is of value to new and experienced Verilog HDL users, both in industry and at universities (logic design courses).

1996, 400 pp., Cloth, 0-13-451675-3 (45167-4) Book/CD-ROM

TOOLTALK AND OPEN PROTOCOLS:

Interapplication Communication

Astrid M. Julienne and Brian Holtz

This book discusses how to design, write, and implement open protocols and includes examples using the ToolTalk™ messaging service. Both procedural and object-oriented protocols are covered in detail. While the ToolTalk service is used as a point of reference throughout, the information provided conforms to the standardization efforts currently in progress for inter-application communication. A valuable resource for the developer writing applications for both the common desktop environment (CDE) and SunSoft's Project DOE system (now known as NEO™).

1994, 384 pp., Paper, 0-13-031055-7 (03105-4)

WEB PAGE DESIGN:

A Different Multimedia

Mary E. S. Morris and Randy J. Hinrichs

Everything you always wanted to know about practical Web page design from the best-selling author of *HTML for Fun and Profit*. Written for Web page authors, this hands on guide covers the key aspects of designing a successful web site including cognitive design, content design, audience consideration, interactivity, organization, navigational pathways, and graphical elements. Includes designing for VRML and Java sites as well as designing with templates, style sheets, and Netscape Frames. Also contains many examples of successful Web pages, including 16 color plates.

1996, 200 pp., Paper, 0-13-239880-X (23988-9)

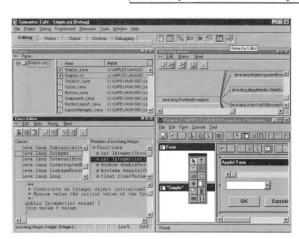

State Sales/Use Tax

In the following states, add sales/use tax: CO-3%; GA, LA, NY-4%; VA-4.5%; KS-4.9%; AZ, IA, IN, MA, MD, OH, SC, WI-5%; CT, FL, ME, MI, NC, NJ, PA, TN-6%; CA, IL, TX-6.25%; MN, WA-6.5%;DC-5.75%.

Please add local tax for AZ, CA, FL, GA, MO, NY, OH, SC, TN, TX, WA, WI.

Order Information:

- Please allow 2-4 weeks for processing your order.
- Please attach the order form with your payment.
- No P.O. boxes and no C.O.D.s accepted.
- Order form good in the U.S. only.
- If you are tax exempt, please include exemption certificate or letter with tax-exempt number.
- Resellers not eligible.
- Offer not valid with any other promotion.
- One copy per product, per order.

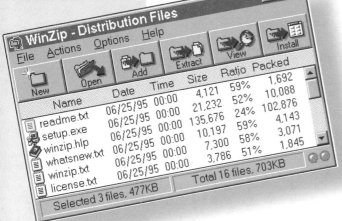

IMPORTANT—READ CAREFULLY BEFORE OPENING SEALED CD-ROM

This CD-ROM contains the Java Development Kit and sample code from Core Java, as well as other copyrighted software.

SUN MICROSYSTEMS LICENSE AGREEMENT

This is a legal agreement between the purchaser of this book/CD-ROM package ("You") and Sun Microsystems, Inc. By opening the sealed CD-ROM you are agreeing to be bound by the terms of this agreement. If you do not agree to the terms of this agreement, promptly return the unopened book/CD-ROM package to the place you obtained it for a full refund.

SOFTWARE LICENSE FOR SAMPLE CODE

1. Grant of License. Sun Microsystems grants to you ("Licensee") a non-exclusive, non-transferable license to use the software programs (sample code) included on the CD-ROM without fee. The software is in "use" on a computer when it is loaded into the temporary memory (i.e. RAM) or installed into the permanent memory (e.g. hard disk, CD-ROM, or other storage device). You may network the software or otherwise use it on more than one computer or computer terminal at the same time.

2. Copyright. The CD-ROM is copyrighted by Sun Microsystems, Inc. and is protected by United States copyright laws and international treaty provisions. Therefore, you must treat the CD-ROM like any other copyrighted material. Individual software programs on the CD-ROM are copyrighted by their respective owners and may require separate licensing. The Java Development Kit is copyrighted by Sun Microsystems, Inc. and is covered by a separate license agreement provided on the CD-ROM and reprinted below.

3. Core Java Sample Code. Sun Microsystems, Inc. grants you a royalty-free right to reproduce and distribute the sample code or applets provided that you: (a) distribute the sample code or applets only in conjunction with and as a part of your software application; (b) do not use Sun Microsystems, Inc. or its authors' names, logos, or trademarks to market your software product; and (c) agree to indemnify, hold harmless and defend Sun Microsystems, Inc. and its authors and suppliers from and against any claims or lawsuits, including attorneys fees, that arise or result from the use or distribution of your software product.

DISCLAIMER OF WARRANTY

The SOFTWARE (including instructions for its use) is provided "AS IS" WITHOUT WARRANTY OF ANY KIND. SUN MICROSYSTEMS and any distributor of the SOFTWARE FURTHER DISCLAIM ALL IMPLIED WARRANTIES INCLUDING WITHOUT LIMITATION ANY IMPLIED WARRANTIES OF MERCHANTABILITY OR OF FITNESS FOR A PARTICULAR PURPOSE. THE ENTIRE RISK ARISING OUT OF THE USE OR PERFORMANCE OF THE SOFTWARE OR DOCUMENTATION REMAINS WITH YOU.

IN NO EVENT SHALL SUN MICROSYSTEMS, ITS AUTHORS, OR ANY ONE ELSE INVOLVED IN THE CREATION, PRODUCTION, OR DELIVERY OF THE SOFTWARE BE LIABLE FOR ANY DAMAGES WHATSOEVER (INCLUDING, WITHOUT LIMITATION, DAMAGES FOR LOSS OF BUSINESS PROFITS, BUSINESS INTERRUPTION, LOSS OF BUSINESS INFORMATION, OR OTHER PECUNIARY LOSS) ARISING OUT OF THE USE OF OR INABILITY TO USE THE SOFTWARE OR DOCUMENTATION, EVEN IF SUN MICROSYSTEMS HAS BEEN ADVISED OF THE POSSIBILITY OF SUCH DAMAGES, BECAUSE SOME STATES/COUNTRIES DO NOT ALLOW THE EXCLUSION OF LIMITATION OF LIABILITY FOR CONSEQUENTIAL OR INCIDENTAL DAMAGES, THE ABOVE LIMITATION MAY NOT APPLY TO YOU.

U.S. GOVERNMENT RESTRICTED RIGHTS

The SOFTWARE and documentation are provided with RESTRICTED RIGHTS. Use, duplication, or disclosure is subject to restrictions as set forth in subparagraph (c)(1)(ii) of The Rights in Technical Data and Computer Software clause at DFARS 252.227-7013 or subparagraphs (c)(1) and (2) of the Commercial Computer Software—Restricted Rights 48 CFR 52.227-19.

Java Development Kit, Version 1.0.2, Binary Code License

This binary code license ("License") contains rights and restrictions associated with use of the accompanying software and documentation ("Software"). Read the License carefully before installing Software. By installing Software, you agree to the terms and conditions of this License.

1. Limited License Grant. Sun grants to you ("Licensee") a non-exclusive, non-transferable limited license to use Software without fee. Licensee may re-distribute complete and unmodified Software to third parties provided that this License conspicuously appear with all copies of the Software and that Licensee does not charge a fee for such re-distribution of Software.

2. Java Platform Interface. In the event that Licensee creates any Java-related API and distributes such API to others for applet or application development. Licensee must promptly publish an accurate specification for such API for free use by all developers of Java-based software. Licensee may not modify the Java Platform Interface ("JPI," identified as classes contained within the "java" package or any subpackages of the "java" package), by creating additional classes within the JPI or otherwise causing the addition to or modification of the classes in the JPI.

3. Restrictions. Software is confidential copyrighted information of Sun and title to all copies is retained by Sun and/or its licensors. Licensee shall not modify, decompile, disassemble, decrypt, extract, or otherwise reverse engineer Software. Software may not be leased, assigned, or sublicensed, in whole or in part. Software is not designed or intended for use in on-line control of aircraft, air traffic, aircraft navigation or aircraft communications; or in the design, construction, operation or maintenance of any nuclear facility. Licensee warrants that it will not use or redistribute the Software for such purposes.

4. Trademarks and Logos. Licensee acknowledges that Sun owns the Java trademark and all Java-related trademarks, logos, and icons including the Coffee Cup and Duke ("Java Marks") and agrees to: (i) comply with the Java Trademark Guidelines at http://java.com/trademarks.html; (ii) not do anything harmful to or inconsistent with Sun's rights in the Java Marks; and (iii) assist Sun in protecting those rights, including assigning to Sun any rights acquired by Licensee in any Java Mark.

5. Disclaimer of Warranty. Software is provided "AS IS," without a warranty of any kind. ALL EXPRESS OR IMPLIED REPRESENTATIONS AND WARRANTIES, INCLUDING ANY IMPLIED WARRANTY OF MERCHANTABILITY, FITNESS FOR A PARTICULAR PURPOSE OR NON-INFRINGEMENT, ARE HEREBY EXCLUDED.

6. Limitation of Liability. SUN AND ITS LICENSORS SHALL NOT BE LIABLE FOR ANY DAMAGES SUFFERED BY LICENSEE OR ANY THIRD PARTY AS A RESULT OF USING OR DISTRIBUTING SOFTWARE. IN NO EVENT WILL SUN OR ITS LICENSORS BE LIABLE FOR ANY LOST REVENUE, PROFIT OR DATA, OR FOR DIRECT, INDIRECT, SPECIAL, CONSEQUENTIAL, INCIDENTAL OR PUNITIVE DAMAGES, HOWEVER CAUSED AND REGARDLESS OF THE THEORY OF LIABILITY, ARISING OUT OF THE USE OF OR INABILITY TO USE SOFTWARE, EVEN IF SUN HAS BEEN ADVISED OF THE POSSIBILITY OF SUCH DAMAGES.

7. Termination. Licensee may terminate this License at any time by destroying all copies of Software. This License will terminate immediately without notice from Sun if Licensee fails to comply with any provisions of this License. Upon such termination, Licensee must destroy all copies of Software.

8. Export Regulations. Software, including technical data, is subject to U.S. export control laws, including the U.S. Export Administration Act and its associated regulations, and may be subject to export or import regulations in other countries. Licensee agrees to comply strictly with all such regulations and acknowledges that it has the responsibility to obtain licenses to export, re-export, or import Software. Software may not be downloaded, or otherwise exported or re-exported (i) into, or to a national or resident of, Cuba, Iraq, Iran, North Korea, Libya, Sudan, Syria or any country to which the U.S. has embargoed goods; or (ii) to anyone on the U.S. Treasury Department's list of Specially Designated Nations or the U.S. Commerce Department's Table of Denial Orders.

9. Restricted Rights. Use, duplication or disclosure by the United States government is subject to the restrictions as set forth in the Rights in Technical Data and Computer Software Clauses in DFARS 252.227-7013(c) (1) (ii) and FAR 52.227-19(c) (2) as applicable.

10. Governing Law. Any action related to this License will be governed by California law and controlling U.S. federal law. No choice of law rules of any jurisdiction will apply.

11. Severability. If any of the above provisions are held to be in violation of applicable law, void, or unenforceable in any jurisdiction, then such provisions are herewith waived to the extent necessary for the License to be otherwise enforceable in such jurisdiction. However, if in Sun's opinion deletion of any provisions of the License by operation of this paragraph unreasonably compromises the rights or increase the liabilities of Sun or its licensors, Sun reserves the right to terminate the License and refund the fee paid by License, if any, as Licensee's sole and exclusive remedy.

LICENSE AGREEMENT AND LIMITED WARRANTY

Read before opening CD package!

This CD-ROM is a standard ISO-9660 disc. Software on this CD-ROM requires Windows 95, Windows NT, Solaris 2.x or Macintosh (System 7.5).

Windows 3.1 IS NOT SUPPORTED